Pearson New International Edition

Public School Law
Teachers' and Students' Rights
McCarthy Cambron-McCabe E. Eckes
Seventh Edition

Pearson Education Limited
Edinburgh Gate
Harlow
Essex CM20 2JE
England and Associated Companies throughout the world

Visit us on the World Wide Web at: www.pearsoned.co.uk

ISBN 10: 1-292-04181-1
ISBN 13: 978-1-292-04181-0

British Library Cataloguing-in-Publication Data
A catalogue record for this book is available from the British Library

ARP Impression 98
Printed in Great Britain by Ashford Colour Press Ltd

Table of Contents

School Attendance and Instructional Issues

MyEdLeadershipLab™

Visit the MyEdLeadershipLab™ site for *Public School Law: Teachers' and Students' Rights*, Seventh Edition, to enhance your understanding of chapter concepts. You'll have the opportunity to practice your skills through video- and case-based Assignments and Activities as well as Building Leadership Skills units, and to prepare for your certification exam with Practice for Certification quizzes.

Although U.S. citizens have no federal constitutional right to a public education, each state constitution places a duty on its legislature to provide for free public schooling, thus creating a state entitlement (property right) for all children to be educated at public expense.[1] State interests in guaranteeing the general welfare have collided with individual interests in exercising constitutional and statutory rights, resulting in substantial litigation. This chapter focuses on legal mandates pertaining to various requirements and rights associated with school attendance and the instructional program.

COMPULSORY SCHOOL ATTENDANCE

Presently, all fifty states compel children between specified ages, usually six to sixteen, to be educated. The legal basis for compulsory education is grounded in the common law doctrine of *parens patriae*, which allows the state, in its guardian role, to enact reasonable laws for the welfare of its citizens or the state. Parents can face criminal prosecution or civil suits for failing to meet their legal obligations under compulsory school attendance laws; furthermore, their children can be expelled for excessive truancy or judicially

[1]*See* Goss v. Lopez, 419 U.S. 565 (1975).

ordered to return to school.[2] In some instances, truant children have been made wards of juvenile courts, with probation officers supervising their school attendance.[3]

State laws generally recognize certain exceptions to compulsory attendance mandates. A common exemption is for married students; some states release married students from required school attendance because they have assumed adult responsibilities. Statutes often include other exceptions, such as students serving temporarily as pages for the state legislature and children who have reached age fourteen and have obtained lawful employment certificates. In addition to statutory exceptions from compulsory attendance mandates, the Supreme Court has granted an exemption on First Amendment religious grounds to Amish children who have successfully completed the eighth grade.[4] Most other attempts to keep children out of school on sectarian or other grounds have not been successful.[5]

States generally do not compel school attendance beyond age sixteen, but a number of states encourage students to stay in school by conditioning a driver's license on school attendance for students under age eighteen.[6] In an illustrative case, the West Virginia high court upheld such a state law as sufficiently related to the legitimate goals of keeping teenagers in school and reducing automobile accidents among children who have not exhibited responsibility.[7] The federal Dropout Prevention Act of 2002, which is part of the No Child Left Behind (NCLB) Act, also encourages school districts to enact measures to keep high school students in school.[8]

Alternatives to Traditional Public Schooling

States can mandate that children be educated, but it was settled in 1925 that private school attendance can satisfy such requirements. In *Pierce v. Society of Sisters*, the United States Supreme Court invalidated an Oregon statute requiring children between eight

[2]*See, e.g.*, *In re* N.H., 155 S.W.3d 820 (Mo. Ct. App. 2005); State *ex rel.* Estes v. Egnor, 443 S.E.2d 193 (W. Va. 1994). *But see In re* Gloria H., 979 A.2d 710 (Md. 2009) (stating that the school must provide proof beyond a reasonable doubt that the student was not attending school; once the student is in the custody of the school, the parent cannot be held responsible for the student skipping class); Missouri v. Self, 155 S.W.3d 756 (Mo. Ct. App. 2005) (holding that state officials failed to show that a mother purposefully caused her pregnant child to be truant).

[3]*See, e.g.*, G.N. v. Indiana, 833 N.E.2d 1071 (Ind. Ct. App. 2005) (holding that the state need only show that absences occurred in finding a student delinquent; the student has the burden of showing that the absences were excused or based on good reasons); *see also In re* Marbella P., 221 P.3d 38 (Ariz. Ct. App. 2009) (finding that a minor on probation can be required to attend school until the age of majority). *But see* Rivera v. Lebanon Sch. Dist., 825 F. Supp. 2d 561 (M.D. Pa. 2011) (denying school district's request to dismiss parents' equal protection and due process challenges to the imposition of fines for their children's truancy); *In re* Interest of Kevin K., 742 N.W.2d 767 (Neb. 2007) (holding that juvenile court's jurisdiction over a truant student ended because the student turned sixteen, and his mother authorized the discontinuance of his enrollment).

[4]Wisconsin v. Yoder, 406 U.S. 205 (1972).

[5]*See, e.g.*, Johnson v. Charles City Cmty. Schs., 368 N.W.2d 74 (Iowa 1985) (refusing to exempt fundamentalist Baptist children from compulsory education); Johnson v. Prince William Cnty. Sch. Bd., 404 S.E.2d 209 (Va. 1991) (upholding school board's denial of parents' application for a religious exemption from the compulsory school attendance law because the parents failed to establish that their request was based on bona fide religious beliefs).

[6]*See* Kristin Timberman, *Kentucky's No Pass-No-Drive Statute: Flawed or Flawless*, 38 J. L. & Educ. 205–10 (2009).

[7]Means v. Sidiropolis, 401 S.E.2d 447 (W. Va. 1990) (holding, however, that before a license is revoked, a school dropout must be provided a hearing with appropriate school officials to ascertain if the circumstances for dropping out are beyond the individual's control). School personnel must be certain that they do not violate students' privacy or equal protection rights in releasing information about individuals who do not meet such prerequisites to obtaining their licenses.

[8]20 U.S.C. §§ 6551–61 (2012).

and sixteen years old to attend public schools. The Court declared that "the fundamental theory of liberty upon which all governments in this Union repose excludes any general power of the state to standardize its children by forcing them to accept instruction from public teachers only."[9] In essence, parents do not have the right to determine *whether* their children are educated, but they do have some control over *where* such education takes place. If a child's parents are divorced, the parent with sole legal custody controls educational decisions,[10] but if custody is shared, educational decisions cannot be made unilaterally by one parent.[11]

Interest in alternatives to traditional public schools has increased significantly in recent years. And despite states' legal authority to regulate alternatives to public education, there has been a trend since the 1980s to ease personnel and curriculum requirements and instead to monitor the quality of private education by subjecting students to state-prescribed tests. Private schools may have to adhere to specific standards to receive state accreditation or to have their students compete interscholastically, but enrollment in *nonaccredited* private programs generally can satisfy compulsory school attendance.

Strategies are being adopted in some states to increase parental choice in terms of voucher plans and tax credit programs that allow state aid to flow to religious schools because of parents' decisions.[12] In addition, more than four-fifths of the states and the District of Columbia have charter school laws that relax some state requirements for public schools that are chartered by various entities to implement innovative educational programs.[13] Also, compulsory education laws in most states have been interpreted as permitting home education programs that meet state standards.[14] Developments pertaining to charter schools and home education are briefly reviewed below.

[9]268 U.S. 510, 535 (1925); *see also* Troxel v. Granville, 530 U.S. 57, 66 (2000) (recognizing extensive precedent leaving little doubt "that the Due Process Clause of the Fourteenth Amendment protects the fundamental right of parents to make decisions concerning the care, custody, and control of their children" in holding that a state's overbroad child visitation law as applied to grandparent visitations violated a mother's fundamental right to direct the upbringing of her child).

[10]*See* Elk Grove Unified Sch. Dist. v. Newdow, 542 U.S. 1 (2004) (holding that the noncustodial parent did not have standing to bring suit on behalf of his daughter to contest her saying "under God" in the Pledge of Allegiance); Fuentes v. Bd. of Educ., 569 F.3d 46 (2d Cir. 2009) (recognizing that under New York law, the parent with exclusive custody has sole authority to make education decisions; a noncustodial parent did not have a right to participate in such decisions about his son with disabilities); *see also infra* text accompanying note 165.

[11]*See, e.g.*, Crowley v. McKinney, 400 F.3d 965 (7th Cir. 2005) (recognizing the noncustodial parent's rights to review his children's educational records but not to micromanage the school's educational program); Pierron v. Pierron, 782 N.W.2d 480 (Mich. 2010) (finding that moving a child to a school district farther from the noncustodial father's residence did not affect the custodial arrangement, but remanding to determine if the move was in the child's best interests); Staub v. Staub, 960 A.2d 848 (Pa. Super. Ct. 2008) (holding that when divorcing parents disagreed about the continuance of home schooling, the best interests of the child should be considered; where children had been excelling in the home school environment, it should continue).

[12]Intentionally left blank so that the remaining footnotes in the chapter can remain numbered as is.

[13]Jaclyn Zubrzycki, *Charters: Good, Bad, Old, and New*, EDUC. WK., Mar. 7, 2012, at 57.

[14]*See, e.g.*, Gatchel v. Gatchel, 824 N.E.2d 576 (Ohio Ct. App. 2005); Tex. Educ. Agency v. Leeper, 893 S.W.2d 432 (Tex. 1994); *see also* Jonathan L. v. Super. Ct., 81 Cal. Rptr. 3d 571 (Ct. App. 2008) (finding that home schooling was a permissible practice under California law but that the right to home school was not universal, because the state has an interest in protecting children's safety); Iowa v. Trucke, 410 N.W.2d 242 (Iowa 1987) (recognizing that unclear language in the compulsory attendance law precluded conviction of home-educating parents).

CHARTER SCHOOLS. Charter schools are public schools with reduced regulations from both state agencies and local school boards to provide flexibility for instructional experimentation. More than 500 new charter schools were created in the 2011–2012 school year, representing the largest annual growth since the first charter school was established in Minnesota two decades ago.[15] As of May 2012, forty-one states had authorized 5,600 charter schools that enrolled more than two million students.[16] States vary as to what entities, such as school districts, mayors, and universities, can charter schools, and they differ regarding the number of charter schools allowed. Additionally, states reflect a range as to who may submit charter applications and what state regulations apply to charter schools. Increasingly, charter management organizations are managing networks of charter schools that reflect particular philosophies and instructional approaches.

A body of law is starting to emerge asserting the rights of charter schools or contesting specific charter school practices.[17] For example, a Colorado court held that a state law allowing state-run charter schools was permissible, because it did not require school districts to design or pay for instruction.[18] A California appellate court also rejected a claim that requiring public schools to share facilities with charter schools would abridge local school board authority.[19] However, a Florida court found that the state law empowering a state commission to authorize charter schools was facially unconstitutional, because it infringed on local schools' ability to "operate, control, and supervise all free public schools within the school district."[20] Additionally, a North Carolina appeals court ruled that states can fund charter schools differently from traditional public schools in terms of support for school facilities.[21]

Cyber schools characterized by instruction delivered over the Internet and hybrid models (combining online and face-to-face instruction) are relatively new forms of charter schools.[22] Unique legal challenges have accompanied the rise of this type of charter school, focusing mainly on funding issues. For example, in Pennsylvania, the home school district must reimburse the cyber-charter school that its students attend, but the manner and amount of reimbursement has been legally disputed.[23] Given the advances in technology and popularity of online courses, legal challenges pertaining to residency and funding issues in cyber-charter schools are likely to increase.

HOME EDUCATION. Estimates indicate that the number of children being educated at home increased from about 15,000 children nationwide in the mid-1970s to more than

[15]*Number of Students in Charters Rises*, EDUC. WK., Dec. 14, 2011, at 4.

[16]Sean Cavanagh, *State, Local Officials Wrangle Over Charter School Primacy*, EDUC. WK., May 23, 2012, at 1, 21.

[17]Kevin P. Brady, Regina R. Umpstead & Suzanne E. Eckes, *Unchartered Territory: The Current Legal Landscape of Public Cyber Charter Schools*, 2010 BYU EDUC. & L.J. 191–25 (2010).

[18]Boulder Valley Sch. Dist. RE-2 v. Colo. State Bd. of Educ., 217 P.3d 918 (Colo. App. 2009) (finding also that the intent of the legislature was to provide uniform regulation of charter schools; if a school district could meet certain quality requirements, it could apply to be the exclusive provider of charters within its boundaries).

[19]Cal. Sch. Bds. Ass'n v. State, 119 Cal. Rptr. 3d 596 (Ct. App. 2010).

[20]Duval Cnty. Sch. Bd. v. Bd. of Educ., 998 So. 2d 641, 643 (Fla. Dist. Ct. App. 2008).

[21]Sugar Creek Charter Sch., Inc. v. North Carolina, 712 S.E.2d 730 (N.C. Ct. App. 2011).

[22]*See* Ian Quillen, *Variety of Models Fuel Hybrid Charter Growth*. EDUC. WK., Mar. 7, 2012, at S10; Brady, Umpstead & Eckes, *supra* note 17.

[23]*See, e.g.*, Slippery Rock Area Sch. Dist. v. Pa. Cyber Charter Sch., 31 A.3d 657 (Pa. 2011) (finding that the public school district was not obligated to fund a cyber-charter school's program for a four-year-old student; the district had exercised its discretion in *not* providing services for this age group).

two million students in 2010.[24] Parents educating their children at home can be charged with violating compulsory education laws for failing to report their children's course of study, texts, and instructors to the local school district.[25] In 2008, the Third Circuit rejected parents' claim that the home education law's requirement of a minimum amount of time and days of instruction in specific courses placed a substantial burden on the exercise of their religion.[26]

Not until the early 1990s did all states authorize home education, and since then, the majority of states have reduced restrictions on home education; no state has strengthened such regulations.[27] Ten states have no requirements for home education, and another fifteen have very weak requirements in that parents simply must notify school authorities that they are educating their children at home.[28] And only half of the states require students educated at home to be subjected to a state-supervised form of assessment to ensure that students are mastering basic skills.[29]

Some legal disputes have focused on the rights of children with disabilities if their parents elect to educate them at home or in private schools. The Establishment Clause does not bar states from furnishing services for children with disabilities in private schools. However, this does not necessarily mean that education agencies must provide the services on private school premises or in the children's homes so long as appropriate programs are made available elsewhere for children with disabilities.[30]

Another controversial issue is whether private school students and those who are home schooled are entitled to take selected courses and participate in extracurricular activities in public schools. A few states by law authorize such participation, but statutes in most states are silent on this issue.[31] In the absence of a state law, the Tenth Circuit upheld an Oklahoma school district's prohibition on part-time enrollment except for

[24]Brian Ray, Nat'l Home Educ. Research Inst., *2.04 Million Homeschool Students in the United States in 2010* (Jan. 3, 2011), http://www.nheri.org/HomeschoolPopulationReport2010.pdf. Accurate estimates are difficult to obtain, because some parents may not report that their children are being educated at home. Many parents select home education for religious reasons, but others have concerns about public school safety or academic rigor or want to use a nonstandard approach in educating their children (unschooling).

[25]*See, e.g.*, Battles v. Anne Arundel Cnty. Bd. of Educ., 95 F.3d 41 (4th Cir. 1996) (unpublished table decision; full text available at 1996 WL 482689); Hartfield v. E. Grand Rapids Pub. Schs., 960 F. Supp. 1259 (W.D. Mich. 1997).

[26]Combs v. Homer Ctr. Sch. Dist., 540 F.3d 231 (3d Cir. 2008) (upholding state law's reporting and review requirements for home-schooled children but remanding the question of whether the law violated the state's Religious Freedom Protection Act due to lack of subject matter jurisdiction); *see also In re* Rebekah T., 654 N.W.2d 744 (Neb. Ct. App. 2002) (holding that the state may require home schools to maintain a sequential program of instruction in language arts, mathematics, science, social studies, and health; parents had neglected their children by failing to provide proper home instruction).

[27]*See* Ray, *supra* note 24.

[28]Home School Legal Defense Ass'n (2012), http://www.hslda.org/laws.

[29]*See* Murphy v. Arkansas, 852 F.2d 1039 (8th Cir. 1988) (upholding a test requirement for home-schooled students and rejecting parents' assertion that Arkansas Home School Act impaired privacy, free exercise, and equal protection rights by treating home education differently from private schools); Null v. Bd. of Educ., 815 F. Supp. 937 (S.D. W. Va. 1993) (rejecting parents' challenge to the state law making children ineligible for home schooling if they score poorly on standardized tests and do not improve after home remediation).

[30]*See, e.g.*, Hooks v. Clark Cnty. Sch. Dist., 228 F.3d 1036 (9th Cir. 2000); Forstrom v. Byrne, 775 A.2d 65 (N.J. Super. Ct. App. Div. 2001).

[31]*See* Joshua Roberts, *Dispelling the Rational Basis for Homeschooler Exclusion from High School Interscholastic Athletics*, 38 J. L. & Educ. 195–203 (2009). Increasingly, home education programs are drawing on parent co-ops and online providers as well as university and school district teachers. *See* Sarah Sparks, *"Hybrid" Home-Teaching Options Grow in Popularity*, Educ. Wk., Aug. 8, 2012, at 16.

fifth-year seniors and special education students.[32] The school district justified its policy because it could not receive state aid for part-time students, and the court found no burden on the religious liberties or parental rights of families who educate their children at home. An Indiana appeals court also vacated the Indiana State Board of Education's order for a school district to enroll two home-schooled students on a part-time basis, reasoning that state law authorized local districts to deny such part-time enrollment.[33]

High school activities associations in most states govern interscholastic competition for students attending qualifying public and private schools, and some associations prohibit interscholastic participation of home-schooled pupils. One justification is to ensure that home schoolers cannot avoid academic eligibility requirements that public and private school students must satisfy. Several courts have ruled that home-schooled students do not have an equal protection right to participate in interscholastic sports or other extracurricular activities because such participation is a privilege rather than a right.[34]

With increasing interest in private schools and home-education programs, controversies seem likely to continue over dual enrollment, the provision of special services, and participation in public school extracurricular activities. The legal status of specific arrangements will depend on judicial interpretations of applicable state statutes and administrative regulations.

Health Requirements

State agencies have the power not only to mandate school attendance but also to require that students be in good health to protect the well-being of others. In an early case, the Supreme Court rejected a federal constitutional challenge to a Texas law authorizing local school officials to condition public and private school attendance on vaccination against communicable diseases.[35] Numerous lower courts have upheld mandatory immunization, even when challenged on religious grounds, declaring that a pending epidemic is not necessary to justify such health requirements.[36] Parents have been convicted for indirectly violating compulsory attendance laws by refusing to have their children vaccinated as a prerequisite to school admission.

Statutes in most states provide for an exemption from required immunization for members of religious sects whose teachings oppose the practice.[37] Several courts have broadly interpreted such provisions as not requiring official church doctrine to prohibit

[32]Swanson v. Guthrie Indep. Sch. Dist., 135 F.3d 694 (10th Cir. 1998).

[33]Ind. State Bd. of Educ. v. Brownsburg Cmty. Sch. Corp., 865 N.E.2d 660 (Ind. Ct. App. 2007); *see also* Hassberger v. Bd. of Educ., No. 00 C 7873, 2003 U.S. Dist. LEXIS 20477 (N.D. Ill. Nov. 13, 2003) (upholding school district's denial of a request for a private school student to enroll in a public school algebra course).

[34]*See, e.g.*, Pelletier v. Me. Principals' Ass'n, 261 F. Supp. 2d 10 (D. Me. 2003); Jones v. W. Va. State Bd. of Educ., 622 S.E.2d 289 (W. Va. 2005); *see also* Angstadt v. Midd-West Sch. Dist., 182 F. Supp. 2d 435 (M.D. Pa. 2002) (holding that cyber-schooled student had no property right to participate in the school district's interscholastic basketball program). However, some states, such as Tennessee and Virginia, are considering policies to allow home-schooled students to participate in interscholastic sports.

[35]Zucht v. King, 260 U.S. 174 (1922).

[36]*See, e.g.*, Workman v. Mingo Cnty. Sch., 419 F. App'x 348 (4th Cir. 2011), *cert. denied*, 132 S. Ct. 590 (2011); Boone v. Boozman, 217 F. Supp. 2d 938 (E.D. Ark. 2002).

[37]*See, e.g.*, Turner v. Liverpool Cent. Sch. Bd., 186 F. Supp. 2d 187 (N.D.N.Y. 2002); Fla. Dep't of Health v. Curry, 722 So. 2d 874 (Fla. Dist. Ct. App. 1998). West Virginia and Mississippi do not allow such religious exemptions from immunization. *See* Nat'l Sch. Bds. Ass'n, *West Virginia Court Stays Ruling on State Mandatory Vaccination Law for Children Attending School,* LEGAL CLIPS (Oct. 2, 2012), http://legalclips.nsba.org/?p=16541.

vaccination or individuals to be church members to qualify for the religious exemption.[38] However, courts have denied parental attempts to use statutory religious exemptions for opposition to immunization based on fear of health risks[39] or beliefs that immunization is contrary to the "genetic blueprint"[40] or "chiropractic ethics."[41] The Supreme Court of Mississippi even questioned the rationale for religious exemptions from mandatory immunization, noting that such an exemption discriminated against parents opposed to immunization for nonreligious reasons and defeated the purpose of an immunization requirement, which is to protect all students from exposure to communicable diseases.[42] Most other courts have reasoned that states are empowered to enact religious exemptions but are not obligated to do so.

Although it is well established that school attendance can be conditioned on immunization against communicable diseases, states cannot abdicate their responsibility to educate children with such diseases. For example, courts have held that children infected with acquired immune deficiency syndrome (AIDS) are protected by federal statutes barring discrimination against individuals with disabilities and have ruled that public schools must enroll children with AIDS upon certification by health officials that they pose minimal danger of infecting others.[43] Children can be denied enrollment in the regular school program if their presence poses a genuine health threat, but it is generally assumed that an alternative educational program (e.g., home instruction by computer) must be provided.

Some controversies have focused on children taking medications at school. Many school districts require medications to be kept in the school office and to be dispensed by designated personnel. Policies must be explicit regarding exceptions to such regulations. In a California case, a student with severe asthma died before he could get assistance at the school office, and his mother was unaware that an exception to the medications policy would have allowed him to carry his inhaler at school. The mother was awarded damages for the school district's negligence in not informing parents of the policy exception.[44] A related issue pertains to disruptive children who need medication to keep their behavior under control. Several states have enacted laws preventing schools from forcing parents to medicate their children as a condition of attending school, and federal

[38] *See, e.g.*, McCarthy v. Boozman, 212 F. Supp. 2d 945 (W.D. Ark. 2002); Berg v. Glen Cove City Sch. Dist., 853 F. Supp. 651 (E.D.N.Y. 1994); *see also In re* LePage, 18 P.3d 1177 (Wyo. 2001) (holding that the religious exemption was self-executing upon a written objection; the department of health could not require additional explanation as to why the requested exemption was based on the parents' faith). *But see* Caviezel v. Great Neck Pub. Schs., 814 F. Supp. 2d 209 (E.D.N.Y. 2011) (holding that parents failed to produce evidence of a valid religious objection to vaccination under state law); Caviezel v. Great Neck Pub. Schs., 739 F. Supp. 2d 273 (E.D.N.Y. 2010) (rejecting parents' claim that the vaccination requirement violated their federal constitutional rights as well).

[39] *See, e.g.*, *Workman*, 419 F. App'x 348; Farina v. Bd. of Educ., 116 F. Supp. 2d 503 (S.D.N.Y. 2000).

[40] Mason v. Gen. Brown Cent. Sch. Dist., 851 F.2d 47, 49 (2d Cir. 1988).

[41] *See* Hanzel v. Arter, 625 F. Supp. 1259 (S.D. Ohio 1985) (rejecting additional claims that the immunization requirement also impaired constitutional privacy and due process rights).

[42] Brown v. Stone, 378 So. 2d 218 (Miss. 1979).

[43] *See, e.g.*, Doe v. Dolton Elementary Sch. Dist. No. 148, 694 F. Supp. 440 (N.D. Ill. 1988); Thomas v. Atascadero Unified Sch. Dist., 662 F. Supp. 376 (C.D. Cal. 1987); *see also* Martinez v. Sch. Bd., 861 F.2d 1502, 1506 (11th Cir. 1988), *on remand*, 711 F. Supp. 1066 (M.D. Fla. 1989) (finding the "remote theoretical possibility" of transmitting AIDS from a child's tears, saliva, and urine did not support segregation of the child with AIDS in a separate cubicle).

[44] Gonzalez v. Hanford Elementary Sch. Dist., Nos. F033659, F034555, 2002 Cal. App. LEXIS 1341 (Ct. App. May 22, 2002).

legislation to this effect was incorporated in the 2004 reauthorization of the Individuals with Disabilities Education Act.[45]

The recent national concern about improving childhood health and well-being has prompted consideration of state and federal measures to strengthen requirements regarding physical activity for public school students and to curtail the availability of unhealthy snacks in schools. The federal Healthy, Hunger-Free Kids Act, signed into law in 2010, includes improved nutritional standards and the first noninflationary increase for school lunches in more than thirty years.[46] School districts also increasingly are creating nut-free zones in schools because of students with severe allergic reactions to peanuts and other types of nuts.[47]

To address childhood obesity, a number of school districts are requiring students to have their body composition monitored. In 2011, more than two-fifths of the states required tracking body mass of students, whereas only four states did so in 2005.[48] Several states also are considering an increase in the number of minutes of physical activity that students are required to participate in during the school day. A California appeals court in 2010 ruled that a student had a legitimate cause of action to enforce the state law requirement that elementary schools comply with the minimum 200 minutes of physical activity every ten school days.[49]

Some school boards, particularly in urban areas, have addressed various student health issues by establishing school-based clinics that offer services from immunization to disease diagnosis and treatment. There are close to 2,000 school-based health centers nationally.[50] The most controversial aspect of the school clinics has been their involvement in prescribing and dispensing forms of birth control. Several courts have upheld the authority of school boards to place condom machines in high school restrooms and allow students to request condoms from school nurses, reasoning that such programs are within the boards' statutory powers to promote health services that prevent disease.[51]

[45]*See* 20 U.S.C. § 1412, 25(A) (2012); *see also* Children's Mental Health Act of 2003, 405 Ill. Comp. Stat. 49/1–49/15 (2012).

[46]*See* Nat'l Sch. Bds. Ass'n, *President Obama Signs Federal School Lunch Bill into Law*, Legal Clips (Dec. 16, 2010), http://legalclips.nsba.org/?p=3582.

[47]*See* Nat'l Sch. Bds. Ass'n, *Massachusetts School District Implements Policy Making Its Schools Nut Free Zones*, Legal Clips (Sept. 7, 2010), http://legalclips.nsba.org/?p=1985. *But see* Pace v. Maryland, 38 A.2d 418 (Md. 2012) (finding no duty under the National School Lunch Act to ensure that schools have an effective program to identify students with food allergies).

[48]*See* Trust for America's Health, *F as in Fat: How Obesity Threatens America's Future 2011* (July 2011), http://www.healthyamericans.org/report/88/.

[49]Doe v. Albany Unified Sch. Dist., 118 Cal. Rptr.3d 507 (Ct. App. 2010), *review denied*, No. S189670, 2011 Cal. LEXIS 2622 (Cal. Mar. 16, 2011).

[50]J. Strolin-Goltzman, *The Relationship Between School-Based Health Centers and the Learning Environment*, 80 J. Sch. Health 153–59 (Mar. 2010); *see also* Nat'l Assembly on School-Based Health Care, *School-Based Health Centers: National Census School Year 2007–2008*, http://www.nasbhc.org/atf/cf/%7Bcd9949f2-2761-42fb-bc7a-cee165c701d9%7D/NASBHC%202007-08%20CENSUS%20REPORT%20FINAL.PDF.

[51]*See, e.g.*, Parents United for Better Schs. v. Sch. Dist., 148 F.3d 260 (3d Cir. 1998); Curtis v. Sch. Comm., 652 N.E.2d 580 (Mass. 1995). *But see* Alfonso v. Fernandez, 606 N.Y.S.2d 259 (App. Div. 1993) (striking down a school district's program of distributing condoms without parental consent as violating parents' constitutional right to direct the upbringing of their children and their statutory right to give consent before health services are provided to their children).

RESIDENCY REQUIREMENTS

In general, courts have ruled that public schools are obligated to educate school-age children who are residents, meaning they live in the district with their parents or legal guardian, are emancipated minors, or are adult students who live independently from their parents. In an important 1982 decision, *Plyler v. Doe*, the Supreme Court held that school districts could not deny a free public education to resident children whose parents had entered the country illegally.[52] Recognizing the individual's significant interest in receiving an education, the Court reasoned that classifications affecting access to education must be substantially related to an important governmental objective to satisfy the Equal Protection Clause. The Court found that Texas's asserted interest in deterring aliens from entering the country illegally was not important enough to deny students an opportunity to be educated. Subsequently, the Ninth Circuit enjoined implementation of several sections of a 1994 California law denying free education and health care services to aliens residing in the state illegally (including the denial of free public education to children of illegal aliens).[53]

Despite these decisions, states continue to consider and enact provisions that place obligations on schools to identify illegal immigrants and to notify state authorities regarding undocumented students. Although these laws do not specifically bar the education of such students at public expense, which Texas was not allowed to do in *Plyler*, the required identification of undocumented students is viewed as a deterrent for these children to enroll in public schools. In 2012, the Eleventh Circuit blocked implementation of such a provision in the Alabama law as violating the equal protection rights of the affected children.[54] A few months earlier the Supreme Court had struck down several parts of the Arizona immigration law as intruding on the federal government's responsibilities to regulate immigration, but it upheld the provision allowing police officers to verify the immigration status of those arrested.[55] The Arizona law does not have a student identification provision, and whether states can require public schools to identify undocumented students has not yet been addressed by the Supreme Court. However, it is clear that such children cannot be denied a public education.

Homeless children being sheltered in a school district also are entitled to an education at public expense.[56] In 1987, Congress passed the Stewart B. McKinney Education for Homeless Children Act, later renamed the McKinney-Vento Homeless Assistance Act, providing federal aid for the education of homeless children, including transportation to school.[57] The most recent reauthorization of this law in the No Child Left Behind Act of 2001 strengthened protections for homeless children, requiring each state's plan to

[52]457 U.S. 202 (1982). Students temporarily in the district because their parents are assigned to federal installations for a short period of time are also considered bona fide residents. *See, e.g.*, United States v. Onslow Cnty. Bd. of Educ., 728 F.2d 628 (4th Cir. 1984).

[53]Gregorio T. v. Wilson, 59 F.3d 1002 (9th Cir. 1995). The litigation was ended through a court-approved mediation signed on July 29, 1999.

[54]*See* Hispanic Interest Coalition v. Governor of Ala., 691 F.3d 1236 (11th Cir. 2012); United States v. Alabama, 691 F.3d 1269 (11th Cir. 2012).

[55]Arizona v. United States, 132 S. Ct. 2492 (2012).

[56]*See, e.g.*, Orozco *ex rel.* Arroyo v. Sobol, 703 F. Supp. 1113 (S.D.N.Y. 1989).

[57]42 U.S.C. §§ 11431–11435 (2012).

include a description of how services for the homeless will be coordinated and integrated with other educational services.[58]

In contrast to the judiciary's position that school boards must provide free public schooling for resident students, courts generally have not required public schools to admit *nonresident* students tuition free.[59] The Supreme Court upheld a Texas requirement allowing local school boards to deny tuition-free schooling to any unemancipated minor who lives apart from a parent or legal guardian for the primary purpose of attending public school.[60] The Court ruled that the requirement advanced the substantial state interest of assuring high-quality public education for residents, which it defined as those living in a school district with the intent to remain.

Other courts similarly have upheld residency requirements, reasoning that tuition can be charged if students legally reside outside the school district, even though they may live in the district with someone other than their legal guardians.[61] When students move to another school district, they do not have a right to continue attending their former public school tuition free, although often they are allowed to complete the term in their former school.[62] Several cases involving residency disputes have involved student athletes, and courts consistently have rejected efforts to establish limited guardianships to enable students to attend a particular school for athletic reasons.

Children who are wards of the state and live in state facilities are usually considered residents of the school district where the facility is located, despite their parents living elsewhere.[63] But students who are not wards of the state are the responsibility of their resident districts even though they are living in a childcare facility located in another school district.[64] Children with disabilities who have court-appointed guardians are entitled to an appropriate education where their guardians reside or from the district initiating their placement in a group facility.[65]

Minnesota was the first state to enact an interdistrict open enrollment plan, allowing students to apply for transfers to any public school district within the state. Transfer

[58]20 U.S.C. § 6312(b)(1)(E) (2012). Among its mandates, the McKinney-Vento Act requires schools to identify students who fit a broad definition of homeless and to provide them transportation to school. For a discussion of legal protections for children in or awaiting foster care, see Jesse Hahnel & Caroline Van Zile, *The Other Achievement Gap: Court-Dependent Youth and Educational Advocacy,* 41 J. L. & Educ. 435–81 (2012).

[59]*See, e.g.*, Joshua W. v. Unified Sch. Dist. 259, 211 F.3d 1278 (10th Cir. 2000); Behm v. Wilmington Area Sch. Dist., 996 A.2d 60 (Pa. Commw. Ct. 2010); *see also* Student Doe 1 v. Lower Merion Sch. Dist., 665 F.3d 524 (3d Cir. 2011) (finding a school board's redistricting plan rationally related to the goal of equalizing enrollments in the district's two high schools and based on nondiscriminatory factors rather than race), *cert. denied*, 132 S. Ct. 2773 (2012).

[60]Martinez v. Bynum, 461 U.S. 321 (1983).

[61]*See, e.g., Joshua W.*, 211 F.3d 1278; Hallissey v. Sch. Admin. Dist. No. 77, 755 A.2d 1068 (Me. 2000); Graham v. Mock, 545 S.E.2d 263 (N.C. Ct. App. 2001).

[62]*See, e.g.*, Daniels v. Morris, 746 F.2d 271 (5th Cir. 1984).

[63]*See, e.g.*, Steven M. v. Gilhool, 700 F. Supp. 261 (E.D. Pa. 1988) (holding that the school district housing a state facility is responsible for the education of the residents but that tuition can be charged for children who are legal wards of another state).

[64]*See, e.g.*, Bd. of Educ. v. Greek Archdiocese Inst., 962 N.E.2d 247 (N.Y. 2012).

[65]*See, e.g.*, Manchester Sch. Dist. v. Crisman, 306 F.3d 1 (1st Cir. 2002) (holding that fiscal responsibility is determined by state law, and under New Hampshire law, the school district where the child resided prior to placement in a children's home was the sending district and thus responsible for the costs, regardless of the child's legal residency); Catlin v. Sobol, 93 F.3d 1112 (2d Cir. 1996) (interpreting New York law as assigning financial liability to the district where the parent resided; a child living in a group home since infancy while receiving parental support was not entitled to free schooling in the district of the home's location).

requests are subject to certain restrictions, such as space limitations, and participation by local districts is optional under some plans. The majority of states now allow for some type of open enrollment within districts and/or across district boundaries. Assessing a claim under an open enrollment plan, a Wisconsin appeals court found no rational basis for a school district's assertion that lack of space caused it to deny a nonresident student's transfer request when it had admitted three other nonresident students; the rejection of one student while admitting others was arbitrary and unreasonable.[66] In the absence of authorized open enrollment plans, students do not have a right to attend school outside their resident district or even outside their attendance zone within the district.[67]

In some situations, however, courts have found that there are legitimate reasons for children to live apart from their parents, such as health concerns or the need to provide a more suitable home environment.[68] The Eighth Circuit invalidated an Arkansas school district's residency requirement as (1) abridging equal protection rights by discriminating against students living apart from their parents with no control over the situation and (2) violating due process guarantees by creating an irrebuttable presumption that a student not residing with a parent or guardian is not living in the school district with the intent to remain.[69] A New Jersey appeals court ruled that a Korean student living with relatives in New Jersey was entitled to free public schooling under the hardship exception to the residency requirement because his parents in Korea could not care for him.[70]

Courts typically have rejected parental claims that restricting school enrollment to an allegedly inadequate resident school district is detrimental to their children's welfare and impairs protected rights,[71] but such assertions may be more successful in the future. Under the federal NCLB Act, students assigned to schools that have not met annual progress goals for two consecutive years must be offered other education options with transportation provided.[72] A number of states have enacted similar accountability legislation that includes technical assistance and sanctions for schools and districts that are not meeting state academic standards and provides educational choices for students attending failing public schools. Moreover, several states have enacted, and many others are considering, "parent trigger" laws to allow parents who are dissatisfied with the way a school is being run to turn it into a charter school, replace the staff, or even shut it down, if a majority of the school's

[66]McMorrow v. Benson, 617 N.W.2d 247 (Wis. Ct. App. 2000).

[67]*See* Mullen v. Thompson, 31 F. App'x 77 (3d Cir. 2002) (rejecting the assertion that students who attended Pittsburgh public schools slated to be closed had any constitutional interest in attending schools of their choice).

[68]*See, e.g.*, Major v. Nederland Indep. Sch. Dist., 772 F. Supp. 944 (E.D. Tex. 1991) (holding that a student whose negative relationship with her mother and stepfather precipitated a move to live with another family must be allowed to attend school without charge in the new district as the move was not for educational reasons); Joel R. v. Bd. of Educ., 686 N.E.2d 650 (Ill. App. Ct. 1997) (holding that a student must be admitted to the public school where he resided with his aunt even though his parents lived in Mexico).

[69]Horton v. Marshall Pub. Schs., 769 F.2d 1323 (8th Cir. 1985) (noting that family circumstances can necessitate students living with relatives who are not their parents or legal guardians). Also, school districts have been required to educate students where they mistakenly enrolled nonresidents. *See, e.g.*, Cohen v. Wauconda Cmty. Unit Sch. Dist. No. 118, 779 F. Supp. 88 (N.D. Ill. 1991); Burdick v. Indep. Sch. Dist. No. 52, 702 P.2d 48 (Okla. 1985).

[70]P.B.K. v. Bd. of Educ., 778 A.2d 1124 (N.J. Super. Ct. App. Div. 2001).

[71]*See* Ramsdell v. N. River Sch. Dist. No. 200, 704 P.2d 606, 609 (Wash. 1985) (holding that denial of parents' request for their children to transfer from an allegedly inadequate school district did not abridge their children's state constitutional right to an "ample education").

[72]20 U.S.C. § 6316(b) (2012).

families agree.[73] These measures may negate some of the traditional discretion enjoyed by school districts in establishing residency requirements for students.

SCHOOL FEES

Public schools face mounting financial pressures due to escalating costs of facilities, personnel, supplies, insurance, and various services. Furthermore, intergovernmental competition for tax dollars is increasing while citizens continue to press for tax relief.[74] Thus, it is not surprising that school officials are attempting to transfer some of the fiscal burden for public school services and materials to students and their parents. Although the law is clear that public schools cannot charge *tuition* as a prerequisite to school attendance, various *user fees* have been imposed for transportation, books, and course materials in states where courts have interpreted the respective state constitutions to allow them.

Transportation

Several courts have distinguished transportation charges from tuition charges, concluding that transportation is not an essential part of students' entitlement to free public schooling.[75] Courts have upheld policies allowing school districts to differentiate between private and public school students in providing transportation,[76] to impose geographic limitations on bus services and fees charged,[77] to deny transportation to an independent state-chartered school in the district,[78] and to charge for summer school transportation.[79]

In its only decision involving public school user fees, the Supreme Court in 1988 upheld a North Dakota statute permitting selected school districts to charge a transportation fee, not to exceed the school district's estimated cost of providing the service.[80] When the school district in question implemented door-to-door bus service, it assessed a fee for approximately 11 percent of the costs, with the remainder supported by state and local tax revenues. Rejecting a parental challenge, the Supreme Court concluded that the law served the legitimate purpose of encouraging school districts to provide bus services. Noting that the state is not obligated to provide school transportation services at all, the Court held that such services need not be free.

[73] *Hopes and Fears for Parent Trigger Laws*, N.Y. TIMES (Mar. 18, 2012), http://www.nytimes.com/roomfordebate/2012/03/18/hopes-and-fears-for-parent-trigger-laws.

[74] *See* Zuni Pub. Sch. Dist. No. 89 v. Dep't of Educ., 550 U.S. 81, 90 (2007) (upholding the U.S. Department of Education's findings that New Mexico's local aid program qualified as a program that "equalized expenditures" so the state could offset federal impact aid to individual districts by reducing state aid to those districts).

[75] *See, e.g.*, Kadrmas v. Dickinson Pub. Schs., 487 U.S. 450 (1988); Salazar v. Eastin, 890 P.2d 43 (Cal. 1995).

[76] *See, e.g.*, Pucket v. Hot Springs Sch. Dist., 526 F.3d 1151 (8th Cir. 2008) (finding that parents of sectarian school students did not have standing to challenge the public school district's denial of transportation to their children during the period prior to enactment of a new state law authorizing such services); Manbeck v. Katonah-Lewisboro Sch. Dist., 435 F. Supp. 2d 273 (S.D.N.Y. 2006), *aff'd mem.*, 264 F. App'x 61 (2d Cir. 2008) (upholding school district's denial of transportation to a private school for a kindergarten student who was not of public school age); C.E. v. Bd. of Educ., 970 N.E.2d 1287 (Ill. App. Ct. 2012) (holding that public school district was not required to provide transportation for private school students when public schools were not in session).

[77] *See, e.g.*, Sch. Dist. v. Hutchinson, 508 N.W.2d 832 (Neb. 1993).

[78] *See* Racine Charter One v. Racine Unified Sch. Dist., 424 F.3d 677 (7th Cir. 2005) (finding that the charter school functioned as an independent school district surrounded by the public school district; state law does not require schools to transport students to other districts).

[79] *See, e.g.*, Crim v. McWhorter, 252 S.E.2d 421 (Ga. 1979).

[80] *See Kadrmas*, 487 U.S. 450 (noting that school districts have the discretion to waive any fee for families financially unable to pay, and benefits such as diplomas and grades are not to be affected by nonpayment of fees).

In general, it appears that as long as school officials have a rational basis for their decisions, reasonable school transportation fees can be imposed. State law, however, can be interpreted as requiring transportation to be provided free for all students.[81] States do not have the same discretion regarding transportation for children with disabilities. Under federal and state laws, transportation is a related service that must be provided free if necessary for a child with disabilities to participate in the educational program.

Textbooks, Courses, and Materials

The imposition of fees for the use of public school textbooks has been contested with mixed results. Because the Supreme Court has not invalidated textbook fees under federal equal protection guarantees,[82] the legality of such fees rests on interpretations of state law. Public schools in four-fifths of the states loan textbooks to students without charge, and courts in several states, such as Idaho, Michigan, North Dakota, and West Virginia, have interpreted state constitutional provisions as precluding textbook fees.[83] However, courts in some states, such as Arizona, Colorado, Illinois, Indiana, and Wisconsin, have interpreted their constitutional provisions as permitting rental fees for public school textbooks.[84] While authorizing textbook fees, an Indiana federal district court ruled that the state student disciplinary code and federal equal protection guarantees precluded school boards from suspending students for their parents' failure to pay the rental fees.[85] Where textbook fees have been condoned, waivers generally have been available for students who cannot pay the assessed amount. Given the number of school districts using or considering electronic textbooks, issues regarding access to equipment to read the books and imposition of technology fees in connection with such books will likely generate legal disputes.

In addition to fees for textbooks, fees for courses and supplies also have been challenged, generating a range of judicial opinions. The Supreme Court of Missouri held that the practice of charging course fees as a prerequisite to enrollment in classes for academic credit impaired students' rights to free public schooling.[86] The Indiana Supreme Court more recently ruled that a mandatory $20 fee for all students was in effect a charge for attending school in violation of the state constitution.[87] The high courts of Montana and New Mexico

[81]The Indiana Attorney General issued an advisory opinion in 2010 that charging public school students a fee to ride a bus to public school violates the state constitutional guarantee of a free public education. *See* Nat'l Sch. Bds. Ass'n, *Indiana Attorney General Tells School Districts Charging Bus Fees Is Unconstitutional*, Legal Clips (July 13, 2010), http://legalclips.nsba.org/?p=951.

[82]*See* Johnson v. N.Y. State Educ. Dep't, 449 F.2d 871 (2d Cir. 1971), *vacated and remanded*, 409 U.S. 75 (1972) (*per curiam*).

[83]*See* Paulson v. Minidoka Cnty. Sch. Dist. No. 331, 463 P.2d 935 (Idaho 1970); Bond v. Pub. Schs., 178 N.W.2d 484 (Mich. 1970); Cardiff v. Bismarck Pub. Sch. Dist., 263 N.W.2d 105 (N.D. 1978); Randolph Cnty. Bd. of Educ. v. Adams, 467 S.E.2d 150 (W. Va. 1995).

[84]*See* Carpio v. Tucson High Sch. Dist. No. 1, 524 P.2d 948 (Ariz. 1974); Marshall v. Sch. Dist. RE No. 3, 553 P.2d 784 (Colo. 1976); Hamer v. Bd. of Educ., 265 N.E.2d 616 (Ill. 1970); Chandler v. S. Bend Cmty. Sch. Corp., 312 N.E.2d 915 (Ind. Ct. App. 1974). Some states, such as Hawaii, allow fees to be charged only for damaged books, and others, such as Rhode Island, allow a security deposit to be charged.

[85]Carder v. Mich. City Sch. Corp., 552 F. Supp. 869 (N.D. Ind. 1982).

[86]Concerned Parents v. Caruthersville Sch. Dist. No. 18, 548 S.W.2d 554 (Mo. 1977).

[87]Nagy v. Evansville-Vanderburgh Sch. Corp., 844 N.E.2d 481 (Ind. 2006) (invalidating the universal fee for all students, but recognizing that user fees for participating in extracurricular activities would be allowed), *on remand*, 870 N.E.2d 12 (Ind. Ct. App. 2007) (holding that parents who were prevailing parties could receive attorneys' fees).

interpreted their state constitutions as prohibiting fees for required courses, but allowing reasonable fees for elective courses.[88] In contrast, the supreme courts of Illinois, Ohio, and North Carolina have concluded that their state constitutions permit public schools to charge instructional supply fees for *any* courses.[89] In some cases, the concept of charging parents for materials and other supplies has received judicial endorsement, but the manner of fee collection (e.g., inadequate waiver provisions) has been invalidated.[90]

Currently, school districts in many states solicit fees from students for various consumable materials. The legality of such practices varies across states and depends primarily on the state judiciary's assessment of state constitutional provisions. Another issue receiving some attention is the imposition of fees for participation in extracurricular activities.

THE SCHOOL CURRICULUM

The public school curriculum is controlled primarily by states and local school boards. The federal government, however, influences the curriculum through funds it provides for particular initiatives. For example, under the No Child Left Behind Act, states can apply for federal aid to strengthen reading instruction in the early grades.[91] Unlike the federal government, state legislatures exercise broad authority to impose curriculum mandates. State legislation regarding the public school curriculum has become increasingly explicit, and some laws as well as local school board policies have been challenged as violating individuals' protected rights. Building on state standards, a national initiative was launched in 2010 to develop common core state standards, which are designed to provide a clear understanding of what students nationally are expected to learn at each grade level and to reflect the knowledge and skills that individuals need for success in college and careers.[92] This section focuses on legal developments involving curriculum requirements and restrictions and instructional censorship.

Requirements and Restrictions

Courts have repeatedly recognized that the state retains the power to determine the public school curriculum so long as federal constitutional guarantees are respected. A few state constitutions include specific curriculum mandates, but, more typically, the legislature is given responsibility for curricular determinations. States vary as to the specificity of legislative directives, but most states mandate instruction pertaining to the Federal

[88]Granger v. Cascade Cnty. Sch. Dist. No. 1, 499 P.2d 780 (Mont. 1972); Norton v. Bd. of Educ., 553 P.2d 1277 (N.M. 1976). Fees for drivers' education have generated conflicting rulings. *Compare* Cal. Ass'n for Safety Educ. v. Brown, 36 Cal. Rptr. 2d 404 (Ct. App. 1994) (charging fees for drivers' education violates the free school guarantee of the state constitution) *with* Sherman v. Twp. High Sch. Dist. 214, 937 N.E.2d 286 (Ill. App. Ct. 2010) (upholding drivers' education fee as not violating the Illinois Constitution), *review denied*, 943 N.E.2d 1109 (Ill. 2011).

[89]*See* Beck v. Bd. of Educ., 344 N.E.2d 440 (Ill. 1976); Sneed v. Greensboro City Bd. of Educ., 264 S.E.2d 106 (N.C. 1980); Massie v. Gahanna-Jefferson Pub. Schs., 669 N.E.2d 839 (Ohio 1996).

[90]*See, e.g.*, Sodus Cent. Sch. v. Rhine, 406 N.Y.S.2d 175 (App. Div. 1978); *Sneed*, 264 S.E.2d at 114; Lorenc v. Call, 789 P.2d 46 (Utah Ct. App. 1990).

[91]20 U.S.C. § 6362 (2012).

[92]The District of Columbia and forty-six states have adopted these standards in language arts, and forty-five states have adopted them in mathematics. *See* Andrew Ujifusa, *New Tests Put States on Spot*, EDUC. WK., June 8, 2012, at 1, 24; Council for Chief State Sch. Officers & Nat'l Governors Ass'n, *Common Core State Standards Initiative* (2012), http://www.corestandards.org.

Constitution; American history; English; mathematics; and health, drug, character, and physical education. As noted above, states increasingly are specifying what subjects will be taught in which grades, and many states have detailed legislation pertaining to vocational education, bilingual education, and special services for children with disabilities.[93] With almost universal adoption of the common core state standards, curricular uniformity across states is likely to increase.

State laws usually stipulate that local school boards must offer the state-mandated minimum curriculum, which they may supplement unless there is a statutory prohibition. In about half of the states, local school boards (and, in some instances, school-based councils) are empowered to adopt courses of study, but often they must secure approval from the state board of education. And in some states, charter schools are given considerable curricular flexibility.

Despite states' substantial discretion in curricular matters, some legislative attempts to impose curriculum restrictions have run afoul of federal constitutional rights. The first curriculum case to reach the Supreme Court involved a 1923 challenge to a Nebraska law that prohibited instruction in a foreign language to any public or private school students who had not successfully completed the eighth grade.[94] The state high court had upheld the dismissal of a private school teacher for teaching reading in German to elementary school students. In striking down the statute, the Supreme Court reasoned that the teacher's right to teach, the parents' right to engage him to instruct their children, and the children's right to acquire useful knowledge were protected liberties under the Due Process Clause of the Fourteenth Amendment.

The Supreme Court on occasion has ruled that other curriculum decisions, such as barring instruction pertaining to evolution, violate constitutional rights.[95] If constitutional rights are not implicated, however, courts will uphold decisions of state and local education agencies in curricular matters. For example, many school districts have implemented community service requirements as part of the mandatory high school curriculum, and federal appellate courts have rejected allegations that such requirements represent involuntary servitude prohibited by the Thirteenth Amendment, forced expression of altruistic values in violation of the First Amendment, or impairments of parents' Fourteenth Amendment rights to direct the upbringing of their children.[96] Also, the Supreme Court in 2011 declined to review a decision in which the First Circuit held that revisions in the state's curriculum guide constituted government speech related to the school curriculum so did not implicate the First Amendment. Turkish groups unsuccessfully challenged politically motivated changes in the guide that addresses teaching about genocide and human rights.[97]

[93]Reflecting the discretion of state legislatures, in 2011, California adopted a law requiring all grade levels to address historical contributions of people with disabilities and lesbian, gay, bisexual, and transgender individuals. CAL. EDUC. CODE § 51204.5 (West 2012). The same year, Arizona adopted a law banning the teaching of ethnic studies courses that promote the overthrow of the U.S. government, foster resentment toward a race or class of people, are designed for a certain ethnicity, or advocate ethnic solidarity. ARIZ. REV. STAT. §§ 15–112 (2012).

[94]Meyer v. Nebraska, 262 U.S. 390 (1923).

[95]*See* Epperson v. Arkansas, 393 U.S. 97 (1968) (holding that the First Amendment precludes states from barring public school instruction about evolution simply because it conflicts with certain religious views).

[96]*See, e.g.*, Herndon v. Chapel Hill-Carrboro City Bd. of Educ., 89 F.3d 174 (4th Cir. 1996); Immediato v. Rye Neck Sch. Dist., 73 F.3d 454 (2d Cir. 1996).

[97]Griswold v. Driscoll, 616 F.3d 53 (1st Cir. 2010), *cert. denied*, 131 S. Ct. 1006 (2011).

Courts defer to school authorities not only in determining courses of study but also in establishing standards for pupil performance and imposing other instructional requirements. For example, school districts can establish prerequisites and admission criteria for particular courses so long as such criteria are not arbitrary and do not disadvantage certain groups of students. The Fifth Circuit recognized that, absent a state law or other authoritative source entitling students to a particular course of study, students have no property right to be admitted to any class that is offered in the public school.[98]

In addition to having authority over the content of the public school curriculum, states also have the power to specify textbooks and to regulate the method by which such books are obtained and distributed. In most states, textbooks are prescribed by the state board of education or a textbook commission. Typically, the state board of education or a textbook commission adopts a list of acceptable books, and local school boards then adopt specific texts for their course offerings. However, in some states, such as Colorado, local boards are delegated almost complete authority to make textbook selections.[99] Courts will not interfere with textbook decisions unless established procedures are not followed or overtly biased materials are adopted.

Censorship of Instructional Materials

Attempts to remove books from classrooms and libraries and to tailor curricular offerings and methodologies to particular religious and philosophical values have led to substantial litigation. Few aspects of the public school program remain untouched by censorship activities. Although most people agree that schools transmit values, little consensus exists regarding *which* values should be transmitted or *who* should make this determination.

PARENTAL CHALLENGES. Some challenges to public school materials and programs emanate from civil rights and consumer groups contesting materials that allegedly promote racism, sexism, or bad health habits for students. But most of the challenges come from conservative parent groups, alleging that the use of instructional activities and materials considered immoral and anti-Christian impairs parents' rights to control their children's course of study in public schools.[100] Courts have endorsed requests for specific children to be excused from selected course offerings (e.g., sex education) that offend their religious beliefs, so long as the exemptions do not impede the students' academic progress or the management of the school. Challenges to the courses themselves, however, have not found a receptive judicial forum. The discussion here focuses primarily on censorship of library and classroom materials.

To date, courts have not allowed mere parental disapproval of instructional materials to dictate the public school curriculum. In an early West Virginia case, parents alleged

[98]Arundar v. DeKalb Cnty. Sch. Dist., 620 F.2d 493 (5th Cir. 1980).

[99]*See* Colo. Const. art. IX, § 16 (2012).

[100]Some well-established conservative groups that are active in this debate are the American Coalition for Traditional Values, the Christian Coalition, Citizens for Excellence in Education, Concerned Women for America, the Eagle Forum, and Focus on the Family. In addition to these conservative citizen organizations, a new type of advocacy group is having a significant impact on education, including the instructional program. These organizations (e.g., Education Reform Now, Stand for Children, Students First, and Democrats for Education Reform) focus on raising standards for teacher evaluation (based in part on evidence of student learning), implementing higher standards for students, and increasing educational options for families. Some of these groups claim to be nonpartisan, and supporters versus critics view them quite differently on the liberal-conservative continuum. *See* Stephen Sawchuk, *Advocacy Groups Target Local Politics*, Educ. Wk., May 23, 2012, at 1, 13.

that the adopted English curriculum materials were godless, communistic, and profane. National attention was aroused as the protests evolved into school boycotts, a coal miners' strike, shootings, a courthouse bombing, and even public prayer calling for the death of school board members. The Fourth Circuit upheld the board's authority to determine curricular materials and rejected the parents' contention that the use of the books posed an infringement of constitutionally protected rights,[101] but a reconstituted school board eventually eliminated the series.

In subsequent cases, federal circuit courts similarly have been unsympathetic to claims that reading series or individual novels used in public schools conflict with Christian doctrine and advance an antitheistic creed, finding the challenged materials to be religiously neutral and related to legitimate educational objectives.[102] According to the American Library Association, the most challenged book in 2010 was *And Tango Makes Three* (a children's book about two male penguins who raised a baby); in 2011, the novel *ttyl* (following three high school girls through their instant messages) topped the list of challenged books.[103] The Harry Potter books received the most challenges overall during the past decade.

While many challenges have religious overtones, some simply assert parents' rights to determine their children's education. The Supreme Court declined to review a case in which the First Circuit denied parents' claim that the school district was liable for subjecting their children to a mandatory AIDS-awareness assembly that featured a streetwise, comedic approach to the topic. The appeals court observed that "if all parents had a fundamental constitutional right to dictate individually what the schools teach their children, the schools would be forced to cater a curriculum for each student whose parents had genuine moral disagreements with the school's choice of subject matter."[104] The Ninth Circuit subsequently held that the Oregon law restructuring public schools to impose a rigorous academic program and student assessments, develop alternative learning environments, and create early childhood programs with an emphasis on work-related learning experiences did not abridge speech rights or "freedom of mind."[105] The court reasoned that nothing in the law compelled students to adopt state-approved views. The same court dismissed African American parents' complaint that their daughter suffered psychological injuries from being required to read two literary works that contained repeated use of the word "nigger."[106]

[101]Williams v. Bd. of Educ., 530 F.2d 972 (4th Cir. 1975); *see also* Skipworth v. Bd. of Educ., 874 P.2d 487 (Colo. App. 1994) (rejecting parental claim that public schools must teach morality).

[102]*See, e.g.*, Monteiro v. Tempe Union High Sch. Dist., 158 F.3d 1022 (9th Cir. 1998) (*The Adventures of Huckleberry Finn* and *A Rose for Emily*); Fleischfresser v. Dirs. of Sch. Dist. 200, 15 F.3d 680 (7th Cir. 1994) (*Impressions* reading series); Smith v. Sch. Comm'rs of Mobile Cnty., 827 F.2d 684 (11th Cir. 1987) (*Homemaking Skills for Everyday Living*).

[103]Molly Driscoll, *10 Most Challenged Books on the American Library Association's 2011 List*, Christian Science Monitor (Apr. 9, 2012), http://www.csmonitor.com/Books/chapter-and-verse/2012/0409/10-most-challenged-books-on-the-American-Library-Association-s-2011-list.

[104]Brown v. Hot, Sexy & Safer Prods., 68 F.3d 525, 534 (1st Cir. 1995); *see also* Parker v. Hurley, 514 F.3d 87 (1st Cir. 2008) (finding that the school district's refusal to exempt young students from instruction recognizing differences in sexual orientation did not abridge their parents' First Amendment rights to exercise religious beliefs or their Fourteenth Amendment substantive due process rights); Mooney v. Garcia, 143 Cal. Rptr. 3d 195 (Ct. App. 2012) (rejecting parental request to be on the school board agenda to object to a student-sponsored "Rainbow Day" observance at an individual school).

[105]Tennison v. Paulus, 144 F.3d 1285, 1287 (9th Cir. 1998).

[106]*Monteiro*, 158 F.3d 1022 (remanding the case for further proceedings regarding allegations that school personnel failed to respond to complaints of a racially hostile environment in violation of Title VI of the Civil Rights Act of 1964).

Sometimes school districts have *not* prevailed, if shown that they acted arbitrarily or in violation of parents' or students' protected rights. For example, a Maryland federal district court enjoined implementation of a school district's pilot sex education program, reasoning that additional investigation was needed to determine if the materials on "sexual variation" constitute viewpoint discrimination by presenting only the perspective that homosexuality is natural and a morally correct lifestyle. The curriculum subsequently was revised and approved by the school board with the directive that teachers must convey that sexual orientation is an innate characteristic.[107]

CENSORSHIP BY POLICY MAKERS. Whereas courts have not been receptive to challenges to school boards' curricular decisions simply because some materials or course content offend the sensibilities of specific students or parents, the legal issues are more complicated when policy makers (e.g., legislators, school board members) support the censorship activity. Bills calling for instructional censorship have been introduced in Congress and numerous state legislatures, and policies have been proposed at the school board level to eliminate "objectionable" materials from public school classrooms and libraries.[108]

The Supreme Court has recognized the broad discretion of school boards to make decisions that reflect the "legitimate and substantial community interest in promoting respect for authority and traditional values be they social, moral, or political."[109] Thus, the judiciary has been reluctant to interfere with school boards' prerogatives in selecting and eliminating instructional materials. The Second Circuit on two occasions upheld a school board's right to remove vulgar or obscene books from public school libraries, noting that a book does not acquire tenure and can be removed by the same authority that made the initial selection.[110] Similarly, the Seventh Circuit endorsed an Indiana federal district court's conclusion that "it is legitimate for school officials . . . to prohibit the use of texts, remove library books, and delete courses from the curriculum as a part of the effort to shape students into good citizens,"[111] unless the board flagrantly abuses its broad discretion to make curricular decisions.

More recently, the Eleventh Circuit eliminated a preliminary injunction that had stopped the school board's effort in Miami-Dade to remove from elementary school libraries the book *Vamos a Cuba!* along with twenty-three other books in a series about life in other countries. The appellate court concluded that removal was constitutionally sound because evidence showed that the books were removed for factual inaccuracies and not because of impermissible viewpoint discrimination.[112]

[107]Citizens for a Responsible Curriculum v. Montgomery Cnty. Pub. Schs., No. AW 05 1194, 2005 U.S. Dist. LEXIS 8130, at *3 (S.D. Md. May 5, 2005); Citizens for a Responsible Curriculum v. Montgomery Cnty. Pub. Schs., No. 284980 (Md. Ct. Spec. App. Jan. 31, 2008).

[108]*See, e.g.*, Nampa Classical Acad. v. Goesling, 447 F. App'x 776 (9th Cir. 2011) (denying a charter school's claim that the Idaho Attorney General's ban on the use of religious documents in public schools abridged the Free Speech, Establishment, and Equal Protection Clauses), *cert. denied*, 132 S. Ct. 1795 (2012).

[109]Bd. of Educ., Island Trees Union Free Sch. Dist. No. 26 v. Pico, 457 U.S. 853, 864 (1982); *see also* Bethel Sch. Dist. No. 403 v. Fraser, 478 U.S. 675, 684 (1986).

[110]Bicknell v. Vergennes Union High Sch. Bd. of Dirs., 638 F.2d 438 (2d Cir. 1980); Presidents Council, Dist. 25 v. Cmty. Sch. Bd. No. 25, 457 F.2d 289 (2d Cir. 1972).

[111]Zykan v. Warsaw Cmty. Sch. Corp., 631 F.2d 1300, 1303 (7th Cir. 1980); *see also* Seyfried v. Walton, 668 F.2d 214 (3d Cir. 1981) (holding that the high school drama club's performances were a part of the school program and therefore the school board could prohibit performance of the musical *Pippin* because of its explicit sexual scenes).

[112]ACLU v. Miami-Dade Cnty. Sch. Bd., 557 F.3d 1177 (11th Cir. 2009).

Although the judiciary has generally upheld school boards' authority in determining curricular offerings, the censorship of specific library books and materials has been invalidated under the First Amendment if motivated by a desire to suppress particular viewpoints or controversial ideas. For example, the Fifth Circuit held that there were material issues of fact regarding whether a Louisiana school board intended to suppress ideas in removing from public school libraries all copies of *Voodoo & Hoodoo*, which traces the development of African tribal religion and its evolution in African American communities in the United States.[113] Likewise, the Eighth Circuit struck down a Minnesota school board's attempt to ban certain films from school because of their ideological content.[114] And an Arkansas federal district court struck down a school district's policy requiring parental permission for students to check out certain library books dealing with witchcraft and the occult. The court found insufficient justification for the policy that stigmatized certain materials and abridged students' First Amendment rights to have access to the materials without parental permission.[115]

Despite substantial activity in lower courts, the Supreme Court has rendered only one decision involving censorship in public schools. This case, *Board of Education, Island Trees Union Free School District No. 26 v. Pico*,[116] unfortunately did not provide significant clarification regarding the scope of school boards' authority to restrict student access to particular materials. In fact, seven of the nine Supreme Court Justices wrote separate opinions, conveying a range of viewpoints about the governing legal principles. At issue in *Pico* was the school board's removal of certain books from junior high and high school libraries and the literature curriculum, notwithstanding the contrary recommendation of a committee appointed to review the books.

The Supreme Court narrowly affirmed the appellate court's remand of the case for a trial because of irregularities in the removal procedures and unresolved factual questions regarding the school board's motivation. But even the three Justices who contended that students have a right to receive information recognized the broad authority of school boards to remove materials that are vulgar or educationally unsuitable. The *Pico* plurality also emphasized that the controversy involved *library* books, which are not required reading for students, noting that school boards "might well defend their claim of absolute discretion in matters of *curriculum* by reliance upon their duty to inculcate community values."[117]

Further strengthening the broad discretion of school authorities in curriculum-related censorship was the 1988 Supreme Court decision involving students' free speech rights, *Hazelwood School District v. Kuhlmeier*.[118] The Court's conclusion that expression appearing to represent the school can be restricted for educational reasons has been cited

[113]Campbell v. St. Tammany Parish Sch. Bd., 64 F.3d 184 (5th Cir. 1995) (noting that the board's failure to consider recommendations of two committees and its vote to remove the book, even though many board members had viewed only excerpts supplied by the Christian Coalition, suggested unconstitutional motivation).

[114]Pratt v. Indep. Sch. Dist., 670 F.2d 771 (8th Cir. 1982) (noting that the board was inconsistent in retaining the book in the school library but banning two films based on the book).

[115]Counts v. Cedarville Sch. Dist., 295 F. Supp. 2d 996 (W.D. Ark. 2003).

[116]457 U.S. 853 (1982).

[117]*Id.* at 869 (emphasis added). Following the Supreme Court's *Pico* decision, the school board voted to return the controversial books to the school libraries, thus averting the need for a trial regarding the board's motivation for the original censorship.

[118]484 U.S. 260 (1988).

by courts in upholding states' and school boards' censorship decisions.[119] For example, the Fifth Circuit denied a claim by two students and the author of a textbook that the state's rejection of a book from the Texas State Board of Education's approved list of texts implicated the First Amendment. The court reasoned that the selection of curricular materials is government speech, not a forum for expression, and that the state board has wide discretion in making such decisions.[120] Also, the Eleventh Circuit upheld a Florida school board's decision to ban a humanities textbook because it included Aristophanes's *Lysistrata* and Chaucer's *The Miller's Tale*, which board members considered vulgar and immoral. While not addressing the wisdom of the board basing its decision on fundamentalist religious views, the court nonetheless relied on *Hazelwood* in deferring to the board's broad discretion in curricular matters.[121]

Specific issues may change, but controversies surrounding the selection of materials for the public school library and curriculum will likely persist, reflecting the "inherent tension" between the school board's two essential functions of "exposing young minds to the clash of ideologies in the free marketplace of ideas" and instilling basic community values in our youth.[122] School boards would be wise to establish procedures for reviewing objections to course content and library materials, and to do so *before* a controversy arises. Criteria for the acquisition and elimination of instructional materials should be clearly articulated and educationally defensible. Once a process is in place to evaluate complaints relating to the instructional program, school boards should follow it carefully, as courts show little sympathy when a school board ignores its own established procedures.

ELECTRONIC CENSORSHIP. Some recent censorship activity has focused on the electronic frontier. It was estimated in 2011 that approximately 95 percent of American teenagers went online, and 74 percent owned computers.[123] In addition to issues addressed regarding students' postings on the Internet, concerns are being raised about adults transmitting sexually explicit and other harmful material to minors electronically. A number of states have enacted laws or are considering measures that would prohibit sending obscene materials over the Internet. Also, the federal government has enacted several measures to restrict minors' access to harmful Internet materials,[124] but only one of these measures has survived judicial scrutiny. The Children's Internet Protection Act (CIPA) received Supreme Court endorsement in 2003.[125] This law requires libraries and school districts that receive technology funds to implement technology protection measures that safeguard students from access to harmful content and to monitor student Internet use.[126] The Supreme Court reasoned that unlike the federal provisions that

[119]*See, e.g.*, Borger v. Bisciglia, 888 F. Supp. 97 (E.D. Wis. 1995) (upholding school district's ban on showing R-rated films as related to legitimate pedagogical concerns).

[120]Chiras v. Miller, 432 F.3d 606 (5th Cir. 2005).

[121]Virgil v. Sch. Bd., 862 F.2d 1517 (11th Cir. 1989).

[122]Seyfried v. Walton, 668 F.2d 214, 219 (3d Cir. 1981) (Rosenn, J., concurring).

[123]*See* Pew Internet & American Life Project, *Demographics of Teen Internet Users* (July 2011), http://www.pewinternet.org/Trend-Data-%28Teens%29/Whos-Online.aspx.

[124]*See* Ashcroft v. ACLU, 535 U.S. 564 (2002), *on remand*, 322 F.3d 240 (3d Cir. 2003), *aff'd and remanded*, 542 U.S. 656 (2004), *on remand*, 478 F. Supp. 2d 775 (E.D. Pa. 2007), *aff'd*, 534 F.3d 181 (3d Cir. 2008) (permanently enjoining the enforcement of the Child Online Protection Act as vague and overbroad in violation of the First and Fifth Amendments); Reno v. ACLU, 521 U.S. 844 (1997) (striking down the Communications Decency Act as unconstitutionally vague and overinclusiive).

[125]United States v. Am. Library Ass'n, 539 U.S. 194 (2003).

[126]20 U.S.C. § 9134(f) (2012); 47 U.S.C. § 254(h)(5) (2012).

were invalidated as abridging the First Amendment, CIPA places a condition on the use of federal funds. The Court concluded that this condition poses a small burden for library patrons, and the law does not penalize those posting materials on the Internet.[127]

In implementing the required Internet safety plans, most school districts are relying on filtering software and thus delegating to private companies the decisions concerning what materials are appropriate for their students. There are some fears that measures such as CIPA will have a chilling effect on schools using computer networks to enhance instructional experiences for students.[128] For example, a Missouri federal district court in 2012 enjoined a school district's use of filtering software that blocked websites with resources directed toward lesbian, gay, bisexual, and transgender youth, reasoning that the publishers of the websites and students would likely prevail in their First Amendment claim.[129] The competing government and individual interests affected by legislative restrictions on information distributed electronically will undoubtedly generate additional litigation.

STUDENT PROFICIENCY TESTING

Student testing has increased dramatically in the past decade and shows no signs of dissipating. Acknowledging the state's authority to establish academic standards, including mandatory examinations, the judiciary traditionally has been reluctant to interfere with assessments of pupil performance. The Supreme Court has distinguished academic determinations from disciplinary actions, noting that the former "judgment is by its nature more subjective and evaluative than the typical factual questions presented in the average disciplinary decision."[130] Emphasizing that academic performance is properly assessed by professional educators who have expertise in this area, the judiciary has rejected challenges to teachers' grading practices unless they constitute extreme and outrageous conduct.

Courts have recognized that assurance of an educated citizenry is an appropriate government goal and that the establishment of minimum performance standards to give value to a high school diploma is a rational means to attain that goal. Four decades ago, only four states had enacted student proficiency testing legislation. Now all states have laws or administrative regulations pertaining to statewide performance testing programs, and the majority of states condition receipt of a high school diploma on passage of a test. Moreover, a national test to assess mastery of the common core state standards is expected to be administered in almost all states in the near future.[131]

Although other forms of performance assessment, such as portfolios, have received attention, machine-scorable tests continue to be used and are strongly supported by the

[127] *Id.* For information on state laws pertaining to Internet filtering requirements, see Pew Internet & American Life Project, *supra* note 123.

[128] *See* Martha McCarthy, *The Continuing Saga of Internet Censorship: The Child Online Protection Act*, 2005 BYU Educ. & L. J. 83–101 (2005).

[129] Parents, Families, & Friends v. Camdenton R-III Sch. Dist., No. 2:11-CV-04212, 2012 WL 510977 (W.D. Mo. Feb. 15, 2012).

[130] Bd. of Curators v. Horowitz, 435 U.S. 78, 89–90 (1978).

[131] *See* Catherine Gewertz, *SAT Future: Alignment to Standards,* Educ. Wk., May 23, 2012, at 1, 18; Council for Chief State Sch. Officers & Nat'l Governors Ass'n, *Common Core State Standards Initiative, supra* note 92.

federal government.[132] Under the NCLB Act, tests are used to assess whether schools have made appropriate annual progress, and variations across states in the rigor of the mandatory exams and the selection of passing scores have been controversial.[133] High-stakes assessments not only shape the instructional program, but also states increasingly are evaluating educators' performance based on their students' test scores. Not surprisingly, claims are being made that teachers are limiting classroom activities to material covered on the tests and/or unfairly coaching students for the exams.[134] For example, substantial publicity surrounded the 2011 test-score tampering controversy in Atlanta that implicated numerous school administrators.[135]

The state's authority to evaluate student performance has not been questioned, but implementation of specific assessment programs has been legally challenged as impairing students' rights to fair and nondiscriminatory treatment. In a case still widely cited as establishing the legal standards, *Debra P. v. Turlington*, the Fifth Circuit in 1981 recognized that by making schooling mandatory, Florida created a property interest—a valid expectation that students would receive diplomas if they passed required courses. This property right necessitates sufficient notice of conditions attached to high school graduation and an opportunity to satisfy the standards before a diploma can be withheld. The court found that thirteen months was insufficient notice of the test requirement and further concluded that the state may have administered a fundamentally unfair test covering material that had not been taught in Florida schools. The appeals court also enjoined the state from using the test as a diploma prerequisite for four years to provide time for the vestiges of prior school segregation to be removed and to ensure that all minority students subjected to the requirement started first grade under desegregated conditions.[136] However, the court held that continued use of the test to determine remediation needs was constitutionally permissible, noting that the disproportionate placement of minority students in remedial programs per se without evidence of intentional discrimination does not abridge the Equal Protection Clause.

On remand, the district court ruled that the injunction should be lifted, and the appeals court affirmed this decision in 1984.[137] By presenting substantial evidence, including curriculum guides and survey data, the state convinced the judiciary that the test

[132]20 U.S.C. § 6301 (2012). Among professional associations issuing statements with concerns about high-stakes testing programs and decisions based primarily on test results are the American Educational Research Association, American Evaluation Association, National Council for Teachers of English, National Council for Teachers of Mathematics, International Reading Association, National Council for the Social Studies, and National Education Association.

[133]*See* Sharon L. Nichols & David C. Berliner, Collateral Damage: How High-Stakes Testing Corrupts America's Schools (Cambridge, MA: Harvard Education Press, 2007). Although President Obama has approved waivers from some of the NCLB Act's requirements for more than three-fifths of the states and has suggested revisions for the law, as of December 2012, the law had not been reauthorized. *See* U.S. Dep't of Educ., *A Blueprint for Reform: The Reauthorization of the Elementary and Secondary Education Act* (Mar. 13, 2010), http://www2.ed.gov/policy/elsec/leg/blueprint/index.html.

[134]*See, e.g.*, Buck v. Lowndes Cnty. Sch. Dist., 761 So. 2d 144 (Miss. 2000) (upholding nonrenewal of teachers' contracts for noncompliance with testing procedures that resulted in a reduction in the district's accreditation level).

[135]*See* Jeneba Ghatt, *Atlanta's Cheating Ways: School Officials Changed Test Scores*, Wash. Times (July 7, 2011), http://communities.washingtontimes.com/neighborhood/politics-raising-children/2011/jul/7/.

[136]Debra P. v. Turlington, 644 F.2d 397, 407 (5th Cir. 1981).

[137]Debra P. v. Turlington, 564 F. Supp. 177 (M.D. Fla. 1983), *aff'd*, 730 F.2d 1405 (11th Cir. 1984). It should be noted that the Fifth Circuit was divided into the Fifth and Eleventh Circuits while this case was in progress.

was instructionally valid in that it covered material taught to Florida students. Also, data showed significant improvement among African American students during the six years the test had been administered, which convinced the court that the testing program could help remedy the effects of past discrimination.

Other courts have reiterated the principles established in *Debra P.* and have reasoned that despite evidence of higher minority failure rates, such testing and remediation programs are effectively addressing the effects of past discrimination.[138] The Supreme Court declined to review a decision in which the lower courts rejected a challenge to a Louisiana school district's policy that conditioned promotion at the fourth and eighth grades on test passage, finding no property or liberty interest in grade promotion.[139] Yet courts have not clarified whether similar notice and due process protections required for tests used as a condition of receiving a diploma also must accompany tests used as a prerequisite to grade promotion. Most high-stakes testing programs include provisions for students who fail proficiency examinations to receive remediation and retake the tests.

Several school districts have unsuccessfully asserted that they have been provided inadequate resources for their schools to make adequate yearly progress in terms of test results under the NCLB Act. The courts have rejected the contention that the federal government must provide 100 percent of the funds necessary to devise and administer tests and train teachers before it can expect schools to comply with federal requirements.[140]

Most testing controversies have focused on statewide exams and usually on their use as a diploma sanction, but other test requirements also have generated some legal controversies. For example, the judiciary has upheld school district requirements that all students transferring from nonaccredited schools must take proficiency tests at their own expense.[141] In a Kentucky case, the Sixth Circuit ruled that requiring a high school student to pass equivalency exams to gain public school credit for a religious home study program did not violate rights to freely exercise religious beliefs or to equal protection of the laws.[142] Local school districts also can impose test requirements beyond those mandated by the state.[143] The Eleventh Circuit upheld a school district's ability grouping plan, under which middle school students are tracked based primarily on test scores and performance recommendations of former teachers.[144]

[138]*See, e.g.*, GI Forum v. Tex. Educ. Agency, 87 F. Supp. 2d 667 (W.D. Tex. 2000); Anderson v. Banks, 540 F. Supp. 761 (S.D. Ga. 1982); Bd. of Educ. v. Ambach, 457 N.E.2d 775 (N.Y. 1983).

[139]Parents Against Testing Before Teaching v. Orleans Parish Sch. Bd., 273 F.3d 1107 (5th Cir. 2001). Other courts have upheld the practice of conditioning grade promotion on test scores. *See, e.g.*, Bester v. Tuscaloosa City Bd. of Educ., 722 F.2d 1514 (11th Cir. 1984); Sandlin v. Johnson, 643 F.2d 1027 (4th Cir. 1981).

[140]*See* Connecticut v. Duncan, 612 F.3d 107 (2d Cir. 2010) (dismissing without prejudice Connecticut's claim that NCLB's testing requirements violated the Unfunded Mandates Provision of the Act, because the issue was not ripe for resolution), *cert. denied*, 131 S. Ct. 1471 (2011); Sch. Dist. v. Sec'y of U.S. Dep't of Educ., 584 F.3d 253 (6th Cir. 2009) (vacating en banc the panel's decision that school districts and education associations had standing to challenge compliance with the NCLB Act; granting the Department of Education's motion to dismiss the school district's complaint), *cert. denied*, 130 S. Ct. 3385 (2010). The Supreme Court's recent decision in *National Federation of Independent Business v. Sebelius*, 132 S. Ct. 2566 (2012) (holding in part that states cannot be threatened with loss of Medicaid funding if they refuse to expand Medicaid coverage) may encourage challenges to education spending laws, such as the NCLB Act.

[141]*See* Hubbard v. Buffalo Indep. Sch. Dist., 20 F. Supp. 2d 1012 (W.D. Tex. 1998).

[142]Vandiver v. Hardin Cnty. Bd. of Educ., 925 F.2d 927 (6th Cir. 1991).

[143]*See* Triplett v. Livingston Cnty. Bd. of Educ., 967 S.W.2d 25 (Ky. Ct. App. 1997).

[144]Holton v. Thomasville Sch. Dist., 490 F.3d 1257 (11th Cir. 2007) (noting that the placement of low-income African American students disproportionately in lower tracks does not by itself substantiate a constitutional violation).

As stakes continue to increase based on test scores, the procedures and scales for scoring the exams seem likely to come under additional scrutiny.[145] Also, the administration of proficiency tests to children with limited mastery of English and to children with disabilities remains controversial. After school districts and others challenged California's failure to make appropriate testing accommodations under the NCLB Act for students who were English Language Learners (ELLs),[146] the parties reached a settlement under which the U.S. Department of Education changed its classification of schools needing improvement to allow more accommodations for ELL students.

Courts in general have ruled that the state does not have to alter its academic standards for students with disabilities; these students can be denied grade promotion or a diploma if they do not meet the specified standards.[147] Such children, however, cannot be denied the *opportunity* to satisfy requirements (including tests) for promotion or a diploma. A child with mental disabilities may be given the option of not taking a proficiency examination if the team charged with planning the individualized education program (IEP) concludes that there is little likelihood of the child mastering the material covered on the test. Children excused from the test requirement usually are awarded certificates of school attendance instead of diplomas.

The Seventh Circuit suggested that children with disabilities may need earlier notice of a proficiency test requirement than other students to ensure an adequate opportunity for the material on the test to be incorporated into their IEPs.[148] However, an Indiana appeals court subsequently ruled that diplomas for children with disabilities can be conditioned on test passage with three years' notice of the requirement.[149] In upholding the statewide testing requirement, the court also noted that there were ample opportunities to receive remediation and retake the exam and that the plaintiff student's IEP sufficiently covered material on the test.

Students with disabilities are entitled to special accommodations in the administration of examinations to ensure that their knowledge, rather than their disability, is being assessed, but the nature of the required accommodations remains controversial. In the Indiana case cited above, the court rejected accommodations that would jeopardize the validity of the graduation test, such as reading to the student a test measuring reading comprehension, even though such accommodations were part of the student's IEP.[150] A California federal court conversely held that students with disabilities were entitled to

[145]*See* Russo v. NCS Pearson, 462 F. Supp. 2d 981 (D. Minn. 2006) (denying most requested relief but allowing negligence claims to proceed in connection with the allegation that uncorrected inflated scores on the SAT gave some students a competitive advantage over other students); *infra* text accompanying note 162.

[146]Coachella Valley Unified Sch. Dist. v. California, 98 Cal. Rptr. 3d 9 (Ct. App. 2009) (denying a writ of mandamus and declaratory relief where the State Board of Education did not abuse its discretion in developing a testing system); *see also* U.S. Dep't of Educ., *Assessment and Accountability for Recently Arrived and Former Limited English Proficient (LEP) Students*, Non-Regulatory Guidance (May 2007). Under the NCLB Act, once a student has attended school in the United States for three years, with some exceptions, the student must be tested in English.

[147]*See, e.g.*, Brookhart v. Ill. State Bd. of Educ., 697 F.2d 179 (7th Cir. 1983); Anderson v. Banks, 540 F. Supp. 761 (S.D. Ga. 1982); Bd. of Educ. v. Ambach, 457 N.E.2d 775 (N.Y. 1983).

[148]*Brookhart*, 697 F.2d at 187.

[149]Rene v. Reed, 751 N.E.2d 736 (Ind. Ct. App. 2001).

[150]*Id.* The Office for Civil Rights in the U.S. Department of Education has also reasoned that states can deny use of reading devices to accommodate children with disabilities on graduation exams, even though their IEPs allow use of such devices. *See* Ala. Dep't of Educ., 29 IDELR 249 (1998).

all accommodations in their IEPs when taking the state's graduation test, but the Ninth Circuit found parts of the order overbroad and not ready for judicial resolution because the claim rested on future harm that may or may not occur.[151] The NCLB regulations allow states to use alternative assessments for students with the most severe cognitive disabilities based on modified academic standards; such alternative assessments may be less rigorous, but they must assess the same content.[152]

Specific proficiency testing programs will likely generate additional litigation on constitutional and statutory grounds. Educators can take steps to defeat legal challenges by ensuring that (1) students have the opportunity to be adequately prepared for the tests, (2) students are advised upon entrance into high school of test requirements as a prerequisite to graduation, (3) tests are not intentionally discriminatory and do not perpetuate the effects of past school segregation, (4) students who fail are provided remedial opportunities and the chance to retake the examinations, and (5) children with disabilities and English language deficiencies receive appropriate accommodations.

EDUCATIONAL MALPRACTICE/INSTRUCTIONAL NEGLIGENCE

A topic that has prompted some litigation since the mid-1970s is instructional negligence, commonly referred to as *educational malpractice*. Initial suits focused on whether students have a right to attain a predetermined level of achievement in return for state-mandated school attendance; parents asserted a right to expect their children to be functionally literate upon high school graduation. More recent cases have involved allegations that school authorities have breached their duty to diagnose students' deficiencies and place them in appropriate instructional programs. This section includes an overview of claims in which parents have sought damages from school districts for instructional negligence.

In the first educational malpractice suit to receive substantial attention, a California student in the mid-1970s asserted that the school district was negligent in teaching, promoting, and graduating him from high school with the ability to read at only the fifth-grade level.[153] He also claimed that his performance and progress had been misrepresented to his parents, who testified that they were unaware of his deficiencies until he was tested by a private agency after high school graduation. Concluding that the school district was not negligent, a California appeals court reasoned that the complexities of the teaching/learning process made it impossible to place the entire burden on the school to ensure that *all* students attain a specified reading level before high school graduation.

Other courts also have denied instructional malpractice claims, indicating a reluctance to interfere with professional judgments in such educational policy decisions. For example, state courts have denied damages claims for allegations that school districts disregarded a school psychologist's report and erroneously instructed a student for twelve years in special education classes,[154] breached the duty to evaluate and develop

[151]Smiley v. Cal. Dep't of Educ., 53 F. App'x 474 (9th Cir. 2002) (dissolving the parts of the lower court's injunction pertaining to required test waivers and alternative assessments for children with disabilities).
[152]34 C.F.R. § 200.1(d) (2012).
[153]Peter W. v. S.F. Unified Sch. Dist.,131 Cal. Rptr. 854 (Dist. Ct. App. 1976).
[154]*See* Hoffman v. Bd. of Educ., 410 N.Y.S.2d 99 (App. Div. 1978), *rev'd*, 400 N.E.2d 317 (N.Y. 1979); *see also* Donohue v. Copiague Union Free Schs., 391 N.E.2d 1352 (N.Y. 1979) (dismissing an educational malpractice suit brought by a learning-disabled high school graduate who claimed that because of the school district's negligence, he was unable to complete job applications and cope with the problems of everyday life).

an individualized program for a student with a learning disability,[155] failed to provide remedial instruction for a student,[156] misclassified a student with dyslexia,[157] and failed to provide students with a quality education resulting in alleged intellectual and emotional harm and diminished future opportunities.[158]

Although educational malpractice claims have not yet been successful, some courts have recognized limited circumstances under which plaintiffs possibly could recover damages in an instructional tort action. For example, the Maryland Supreme Court rejected parents' instructional malpractice claim for unintentional negligent acts in evaluating a child's learning disabilities and inappropriately instructing the child, but held that parents might secure damages if they could meet the formidable burden of proving that the defendants intentionally engaged in acts that injured a child placed in their educational care.[159] The Third Circuit, though not awarding monetary damages, ruled that a student with severe disabilities who had not progressed over the past decade was entitled to compensatory services from a New Jersey school district, because school authorities should have known that the child's individualized education program was inadequate.[160] And the California Supreme Court recognized that charter schools and their chartering school districts might be liable for failure to deliver promised instructional services, equipment, and supplies as required by law.[161] Also, a Minnesota federal court declined to dismiss a negligence suit against the College Entrance Examination Board and a national test-scoring service for injuries resulting from incorrectly scoring and reporting SAT scores for some students.[162]

The increasing specificity of legislation pertaining to student proficiency standards and special education placements may strengthen the grounds for tort suits involving *placement negligence*. Also, state and federal legislation making school districts accountable for ensuring student mastery of curriculum standards may increase school districts' potential liability. Even though it seems unlikely in the near future that public schools will be held responsible for a specified quantum of student achievement, it is conceivable that schools will be legally accountable for diagnosing pupils' needs and placing them in appropriate instructional programs.

INSTRUCTIONAL PRIVACY RIGHTS

The protection of students' privacy rights has become an increasingly volatile issue in political forums. The Supreme Court has recognized that the U.S. Constitution protects a zone of personal privacy.[163] Thus, there must be a compelling justification for governmental action that impairs privacy rights, including the right to have personal information

[155]Suriano v. Hyde Park Cent. Sch. Dist., 611 N.Y.S.2d 20 (App. Div. 1994).

[156]Myers v. Medford Lakes Bd. of Educ., 489 A.2d 1240 (N.J. Super. Ct. App. Div. 1985).

[157]D.S.W. v. Fairbanks N. Star Borough Sch. Dist., 628 P.2d 554 (Alaska 1981); *see also* Johnson v. Clark, 418 N.W.2d 466 (Mich. Ct. App. 1987) (ruling that a student who was reading on a fourth-grade level at graduation could not recover damages for the school's failure to assess him annually).

[158]Denver Parents Ass'n v. Denver Bd. of Educ., 10 P.3d 662 (Colo. App. 2000); *see also* Waugh v. Morgan Stanley, 966 N.E.2d 540 (Ill. App. Ct. 2012) (finding educational malpractice claim that a pilot was improperly trained not to be cognizable in Illinois).

[159]Hunter v. Bd. of Educ., 439 A.2d 582 (Md. 1982).

[160]M.C. v. Cent. Reg'l Sch. Dist., 81 F.3d 389 (3d Cir. 1996).

[161]Wells v. One2One Learning Found., 141 P.3d 225 (Cal. 2006).

[162]Russo v. NCS Pearson, 462 F. Supp. 2d 981 (D. Minn. 2006).

[163]*See* Griswold v. Connecticut, 381 U.S. 479 (1965).

kept confidential. A Texas federal district court held in 2011 that a student had a substantive due process right to challenge school authorities' disclosure of her sexual orientation to her mother. The court reasoned that the school's action was not taken to protect the student, but to retaliate for alleged rumors the student had started about the high school softball coach.[164] The same year, a parent was unsuccessful in asserting that she had a constitutional right to obtain information about her children from their school.[165] Because her ex-husband had primary physical custody of the children, the Eighth Circuit ruled that the mother had no valid constitutional claim to the requested information.

State and federal laws additionally place dual duties on the government—to protect the public's right to be informed about government activities and to protect the personal privacy of individuals. Often there is a tension between these two legitimate government interests. Laws also have been enacted to protect students from mandatory participation in research projects and instructional activities designed to reveal personal information in sensitive areas. This section provides an overview of legal developments pertaining to students' privacy rights in instructional matters.

Student Records

Due to widespread dissatisfaction with educators' efforts to ameliorate abuses associated with student record-keeping practices, Congress enacted the Family Educational Rights and Privacy Act (FERPA) in 1974.[166] This law stipulates that federal funds may be withdrawn from any education agency or institution that (1) fails to provide parents access to their child's education records or (2) disseminates such information (with some exceptions) to third parties without parental permission. Upon reaching the age of majority, students may exercise the rights guaranteed to their parents before they turned eighteen.[167] FERPA was amended in 1992 to allow the release of records for purposes of law enforcement, which includes school districts' security units, and again in 1998 to specify that records related to discipline for crimes of violence or sex crimes were excluded from FERPA protection.[168] In 2009, the Department of Education issued changes in FERPA rules stipulating that FERPA can apply to alumni records as well as those of current students, and in 2011, the definition of education programs was broadened to cover any programs primarily involved in the provision of education, including early childhood, elementary and secondary, postsecondary, special education, job training, career and technical, and adult education.[169]

[164]Wyatt v. Kilgore Indep. Sch. Dist., No. 6:10-cv-674, 2011 WL 6016467 (E.D. Tex. Nov. 30, 2011).

[165]Schmidt v. Des Moines Pub. Schs., 655 F.3d 811 (8th Cir. 2011).

[166]20 U.S.C. § 1232g (2012); 34 C.F.R. §§ 99.1–99.67 (2012). Parents are not entitled to *free* copies of their children's records, but they do have a right to have them interpreted.

[167]The Family Policy Compliance Office was created to investigate alleged FERPA violations. 20 U.S.C. § 1232g(g). This office reviews complaints and responses from accused agencies and submits written findings with steps the agency must take to comply. 34 C.F.R. §§ 99.65(a)(2), 99.66(b), 99.66(c)(1). For a discussion of FERPA protections, see Student Press Law Ctr., *FERPA and Access to Public Records* (2011), http://www.splc.org/pdf/ferpa_wp.pdf.

[168]*See* 34 C.F.R. § 99.8; U.S. Dep't of Educ., *Addressing Emergencies on Campus* (June 2011), http://www2.ed.gov/policy/gen/guid/fpco/pdf/emergency-guidance.pdf; *see also* Commonwealth v. Buccella, 751 N.E.2d 373 (Mass. 2001) (holding that a school district did not violate a student's privacy rights when it shared samples of the student's school work with police to compare his handwriting with graffiti on school property in connection with criminal charges).

[169]*See* 34 C.F.R. §§ 99.3, 99.35; *see also* Souffrance v. Doe, 968 N.E.2d 477 (Ohio 2012) (holding that FERPA precluded releasing records with the identities of students who had used particular school computer terminals during specific times; although the individuals no longer were students, they were students when the records were created and originally maintained).

After reviewing a student's permanent file, the parent or eligible student can request amendments to any information thought to be inaccurate, misleading, or in violation of the student's protected rights. If school authorities decide that an amendment is not warranted, the parent or eligible student must be advised of the right to a hearing and of the right to place in the file a personal statement specifying objections to the hearing officer's decision. Education officials should assume that a parent is entitled to exercise rights under FERPA unless state law or a court order bars a parent's access to his or her child's records under specific circumstances. Joint custodial parents must be given equal access to education information about their child.

Individuals can file a complaint with the U.S. Department of Education if they believe a school district exhibits a custom or practice of violating FERPA provisions. The remedy for FERPA violations is the withdrawal of federal funds, and the Department of Education has enforcement authority. Some school districts have been advised to remedy their practices to conform to FERPA, but to date, no district has lost federal funds for noncompliance.[170]

The Department of Education functioned without direction from the Supreme Court until 2002 when the Court rendered two FERPA decisions. In *Gonzaga University v. Doe*, the Court held that FERPA's nondisclosure provisions do not create privately enforceable rights; Congress must create such rights in unambiguous terms.[171] Resolving the conflict among lower courts, the Supreme Court further ruled that since FERPA contains no rights-creating language, the law cannot be enforced through individual lawsuits for damages based on the deprivation of federal rights.[172] The Court reiterated that FERPA has an aggregate rather than individual focus, and the remedy for violations is the denial of federal funds to schools that exhibit a policy or practice of noncompliance. School personnel were relieved that the Court did not authorize private suits for damages to enforce FERPA, as such a ruling would have provided a significant incentive for parents to challenge student record-keeping practices in court.

In the second 2002 Supreme Court ruling, *Owasso Independent School District v. Falvo*, the Court reversed the Tenth Circuit's conclusion that peer grading practices violate FERPA.[173] The Supreme Court concluded that peer graders are not "maintaining" student records under FERPA, and even though students may call out the scores in class, they are not "acting for" the educational institution.[174] There may be educational reasons for not having students grade each others' work, but given the *Falvo* ruling, there is no legal barrier under FERPA.

Under FERPA, education records are files, documents, and other materials that contain information identifying a student and are maintained by the education agency.[175]

[170]Only 150 notices of violations were issued to school districts from the enactment of FERPA through 2011. *See* Student Press Law Ctr., *supra* note 167.

[171]536 U.S. 273 (2002) (overturning an award of damages to a student for an alleged FERPA violation in connection with a private university's release to the state education department an unsubstantiated allegation of sexual misconduct, which resulted in the student being denied an affidavit of good moral character required to become a public school teacher).

[172]*Id.* at 285; *see* Civil Rights Act of 1871, § 1 (codified at 42 U.S.C. § 1983 (2012)).

[173]233 F.3d 1203 (10th Cir. 2000), *rev'd and remanded*, 534 U.S. 426 (2002), *on remand*, 288 F.3d 1236 (10th Cir. 2002) (granting summary judgment in favor of defendant school district and administrators).

[174]*Falvo*, 534 U.S. at 433. Although peers can call out scores, students' grades cannot be posted or disseminated in any manner that allows individual students to be identified (e.g., by name or listed in alphabetical order).

[175]20 U.S.C. § 1232g(a)(4)(A). According to the Student Press Law Ctr., *supra* note 167, a document must not simply mention a student, but the information must be *about* the student to be protected by FERPA.

In 2009, the Department of Education broadened the definition of education records, specifying that schools can deny requests for records even with identifiable information removed if the records could be linked to a particular student by someone in the school community with inside knowledge.[176] Once the identifying information is removed (redacted), it ceases to be an education record and may then be subject to disclosure under state open records or freedom of information laws.[177]

The Tenth Circuit held that school personnel could advise parents of harassment and assault victims regarding how the school dealt with the perpetrator; disclosures to parents of victims and to witnesses of the playground assaults did not comprise an education record that would implicate FERPA.[178] Also, a Kentucky appeals court ruled that a special education teacher could view videotapes of students in her classroom for the purpose of evaluating her performance and improving her classroom management if established on remand that she had a legitimate educational interest in the material sought.[179] Since the teacher was in the classroom when the tapes were recorded, there was no student confidentiality issue.

A student's records can be released to school employees authorized to review such information and to officials of a school where the student is transferring if the parents or eligible student are notified or if the sending institution has given prior notice that it routinely transfers such records. Students' records must be disclosed if subpoenaed by a grand jury or law enforcement agency, and schools may disclose information pursuant to other court orders or subpoenas if a reasonable effort is made to notify the parent or eligible student.[180] The Sixth Circuit ruled that records related to substitute teachers' use of corporal punishment must be disclosed in a suit challenging the use of this disciplinary technique because FERPA does not prevent discovery of such records.[181]

Identifiable information also can be disclosed to appropriate authorities or to advocacy groups if necessary to protect the health or safety of the student or others.[182] For example, the Seventh Circuit ruled that the Wisconsin Department of Public Instruction must provide names of students in connection with a state-designated advocacy agency's investigation of alleged abuse or neglect without first obtaining parental consent because the need to investigate suspected abuse or neglect can outweigh privacy interests.[183]

Personal notes pertaining to pupil progress that are kept by educators and shared only with substitute teachers are not considered education records that must be made available to parents. For example, a California federal district court concluded that e-mail

[176]34 C.F.R. § 99.3.

[177]Student Press Law Ctr., *supra* note 167.

[178]Jensen v. Reeves, 3 F. App'x 905 (10th Cir. 2001); *see also* Lindeman v. Kelso Sch. Dist. No. 458, 172 P.3d 329 (Wash. 2007) (holding that a videotape recorded on the school bus for safety reasons was not a record maintained for students, so it did not qualify as exempt from public disclosure under state law).

[179]Medley v. Bd. of Educ., 168 S.W.3d 398 (Ky. Ct. App. 2004).

[180]20 U.S.C. § 1232g(b)(1)(J)(i) & (ii); 20 U.S.C. § 1232g(b)(2)(B).

[181]Ellis v. Cleveland Mun. Sch. Dist., 455 F.3d 690 (6th Cir. 2006); *see also* People v. Owens, 727 N.Y.S.2d 266 (Sup. Ct. 2001) (finding no FERPA violation in prosecution based in part on records subpoenaed from educational institutions).

[182]*See, e.g.*, Disability Law Ctr. of Alaska v. Anchorage Sch. Dist., 581 F.3d 936 (9th Cir. 2009) (holding that advocacy organization could have access to personally identifiable information about students with disabilities as part of its investigation of alleged violations of the Developmental Disabilities Assistance and Bill of Rights Act); Doe v. Woodford Cnty. Bd. of Educ., 213 F.3d 921 (6th Cir. 2000) (upholding disclosure to coach of information that student was a hemophiliac and carrier of hepatitis B); 34 C.F.R. § 99.36.

[183]Disability Rights Wis., Inc. v. Wis. Dep't of Pub. Instruction, 463 F.3d 719 (7th Cir. 2006).

messages about students stored on individual teachers' computers were not education records because they were not maintained by the school.[184] Private notes, however, become education records and are subject to legal specifications once they are shared, even among educators who have a legitimate need for access to such information.

Under FERPA, certain public directory information, such as students' names, addresses, dates and places of birth, major fields of study, e-mail addresses, pictures, and degrees and awards received can be released without parental consent.[185] Any educational agency releasing such data must give public notice of the specific categories it has designated as "directory" and must allow a reasonable period of time for parents to inform the agency that any or all of this information on their child should not be released without their prior consent. Directory data about a student cannot be released if accompanied by other personally identifiable information unless it is among the specified exceptions to the general rule against nonconsensual disclosure.

Students' privacy rights do not preclude federal and state authorities from having access to data needed to audit and evaluate the effectiveness of publicly supported education programs.[186] These data usually must be collected in a way that prevents the disclosure of personally identifiable information. However, FERPA was amended in 2001 in accordance with the provisions of the USA PATRIOT (Uniting and Strengthening America by Providing Appropriate Tools Required to Intercept and Obstruct Terrorism) Act[187] to give institutions permission to disclose, without parental or student consent, personally identifiable information to representatives of the U.S. Attorney General based on an order from a court of competent jurisdiction in connection with investigations of terrorism crimes.[188] A provision of the No Child Left Behind Act also requires public secondary schools to provide military recruiters with access to personal contact information for every student, although parents can request that their children's records be withheld.[189]

Composite information on pupil achievement and discipline can be released to the public so long as individual students are not personally identified.[190] Disciplinary information (number of occurrences and when they occurred without identifiable data) *must*

[184]S.A. v. Tulare Cnty. Office of Educ., No. CV F 08-1215 LJO GSA, 2009 WL 3216322 (Sept. 24, 2009); *see also* Easton Area Sch. Dist. v. Baxter, 35 A.3d 1259 (Pa. Commw. Ct. 2012) (holding that personal e-mails of board members and the superintendent that did not document a transaction or school district activity were not records subject to disclosure under the state's right-to-know law; but FERPA does not shield disclosure of the records of district transactions or activities so long as personally identifiable information is redacted); Hill v. Fairfax Cnty. Sch. Bd., 727 S.E.2d 75 (Va. 2012) (ruling that e-mail exchanges between board members did not constitute a meeting under the state's Freedom of Information Act).

[185]For a complete list of directory items, see 34 C.F.R. § 99.3. In 2011, the Department of Education clarified that students may be allowed to wear badges or other types of identification at school without abridging FERPA if the IDs cannot be used to access education records without a password or PIN.

[186]34 C.F.R. §§ 99.31(a)(6), 99.31(a)(3), 99.35.

[187]18 U.S.C. § 2332b(g)(5)(B) (2012); *see also* Electronic Communications Privacy Act of 1986, 18 U.S.C. § 2510 (2012), designed primarily to prevent unauthorized government access to private electronic communications.

[188]20 U.S.C. § 1232g(j) (2012). Schools are required to record such disclosures in students' permanent files.

[189]20 U.S.C. § 1232h(c)(4)(a)(i) (2012); *see also* Rumsfeld v. Forum for Academic & Institutional Rights, 547 U.S. 47 (2006) (finding no First Amendment violation by conditioning federal aid to law schools on allowing military recruiters access to law school campuses and students).

[190]*See, e.g.*, Laplante v. Stewart, 470 So. 2d 1018 (La. Ct. App. 1985) (finding that the public had the right to examine the rankings of schools participating in a school effectiveness study conducted by the state department of education). *But see* Fish v. Dallas Indep. Sch. Dist., 170 S.W.3d 226 (Tex. App. 2005) (rejecting open-records request for longitudinal student performance data on the Iowa Test of Basic Skills because the requested information could be traced to students in violation of FERPA).

be released to the media under some state open-records laws,[191] But personally identifiable data cannot be released under FERPA,[192] and state law may be more restrictive. For example, a Florida appeals court ruled that discipline forms and surveillance videotapes about incidents on school buses could not be disclosed to a television station even with personally identifying information redacted, because Florida law goes further than FERPA in preventing the release of such information.[193]

FERPA cannot be used by parents to assert a right to review faculty evaluations used to determine which students will be given academic honors, such as membership in the National Honor Society.[194] Also, students cannot rely on FERPA to challenge teachers' grading procedures, other than whether grades were accurately calculated and recorded.[195] The Fourth Circuit ruled that FERPA does not entitle students to see an answer key to exams to check the accuracy of their grades, because the key is not part of students' education records.[196]

Other federal laws provide additional protections regarding the confidentiality and accessibility of student records.[197] Many states also have enacted legislation addressing the maintenance and disclosure of student records. Both state and federal privacy laws recognize certain exceptions to "access and disclosure" provisions, such as a teacher's daily notes, discussed previously.

Since Congress, state legislatures, and the judiciary have indicated a continuing interest in safeguarding students' privacy rights in connection with school records, school boards would be wise to reassess their policies to ensure they are adhering to federal and state laws.[198] School personnel should use some restraint, however, before purging information from student files. Pertinent material that is necessary to provide continuity in a student's instructional program *should* be included in a permanent record and be available for use by authorized personnel. It is unfortunate that school personnel, fearing federal sanctions under FERPA, have deleted useful information—along with material that should be removed—from student records. The mere fact that information in a student's file is negative does not imply that the material is inappropriate. Public school officials have a *duty* to record and communicate true, factual information about students to schools where they are transferring, including institutions of higher learning.

[191]*See e.g.*, Hardin Cnty. Schs. v. Foster, 40 S.W.3d 865 (Ky. 2001); Bd. of Trs. v. Cut Bank Pioneer Press, 160 P.3d 482 (Mont. 2007)

[192]*See, e.g.*, United States v. Miami Univ., 294 F. 3d 797 (6th Cir. 2002); Press-Citizen Co. v. Univ. of Iowa, 817 N.W.2d 480 (Iowa 2012); State *ex rel.* ESPN v. Ohio State Univ., 970 N.E.2d 939 (Ohio 2012).

[193]WFTV v. Sch. Bd., 874 So. 2d 48 (Fla. Dist. Ct. App. 2004); *see also* K.L. v. Evesham Twp. Bd. of Educ., 32 A.3d 1136 (N.J. Super. Ct. App. Div. 2011) (holding that notes prepared by school personnel concerning bullying incidents would not have to be released to the public under the state's open-records law; confidentiality concerns were overriding).

[194]*See, e.g.*, Moore v. Hyche, 761 F. Supp. 112 (N.D. Ala. 1991); Price v. Young, 580 F. Supp. 1 (E.D. Ark. 1983); Becky v. Butte-Silver Bow Sch. Dist. 1, 906 P.2d 193 (Mont. 1995).

[195]*See, e.g.*, Tarka v. Cunningham, 917 F.2d 890 (5th Cir. 1990); *see also* Hurd v. Hansen, 230 F. App'x 692 (9th Cir. 2007) (finding no violation of a student's due process and equal protection rights in a teacher's award of a "C" grade to the student).

[196]Lewin v. Cooke, 28 F. App'x 186 (4th Cir. 2002).

[197]*See, e.g.*, Individuals with Disabilities Education Act, 20 U.S.C. § 1415(b)(1) (2012) (protecting the right of parents to examine all school records maintained on their children with disabilities); Children's Online Privacy Protection Act, 15 U.S.C. § 6501 (2012) (requiring operators of websites that collect or maintain personal information about the website visitors to obtain parental consent before such information is collected on children under age thirteen).

[198]*See* L.S. v. Mt. Olive Bd. of Educ., 765 F. Supp. 2d 648 (D.N.J. 2011) (finding a school social worker and special education instructor liable for violating a high school student's federal and state privacy rights by intentionally disclosing to classmates his confidential psychiatric evaluation that was not properly redacted).

Pupil Protection and Parental Rights Laws

Congress and state legislatures have enacted laws to protect family privacy in connection with school research activities and treatment programs. Under federal law, human subjects are protected in research projects supported by federal grants and contracts in any private or public institution or agency.[199] Informed consent must be obtained before placing subjects at risk of being exposed to physical, psychological, or social injury as a result of participating in research, development, or related activities. All education agencies are required to establish review committees to ensure that the rights and welfare of all subjects are adequately protected.

In 1974, two amendments to the General Education Provisions Act required, among other things, that all instructional materials in federally assisted research or experimentation projects (designed to explore new or unproven teaching methods or techniques) be made available for inspection by parents of participating students. The amendments also stipulated that children could not be required to participate in such research or experimentation projects if their parents objected in writing. In 1978, Congress enacted the Hatch Amendment, which retained the protection of parents' rights to examine instructional materials in experimental programs and further required parental consent before students could participate in federally supported programs involving psychiatric or psychological examination, testing, or treatment designed to reveal information in specified sensitive areas pertaining to personal beliefs, behaviors, and family relationships.[200]

Several amendments have extended federal privacy protections for students and their families. Parents must be allowed to review in advance all instructional materials in programs administered by the Department of Education, and federally assisted education programs cannot require students, without prior written parental consent, to be subjected to surveys or evaluations administered by the Department of Education that reveal sensitive information about students or their families.[201] The department is charged with reviewing complaints under this law; if an educational institution is found to be in violation and does not comply within a reasonable period, federal funds can be withheld.

Parents have not been successful in using these provisions to require parental consent for a student to be seen by a school counselor,[202] to challenge use of certain questions in the statewide student assessment program,[203] or to negate surveying elementary students about their attitudes and behaviors so long as the data are reported only in the aggregate.[204] The Ninth Circuit held that parents do not have a freestanding fundamental right, or a right encompassed by any other fundamental right, to prevent the school from providing elementary school students with important information pertaining

[199]42 U.S.C. § 289 (2012); 45 C.F.R. §§ 46.101–46.124 (2012).

[200]20 U.S.C. § 1232h(2) (2012); 34 C.F.R. §§ 75.740, 76.740, 98.4 (2012).

[201]The sensitive areas specified in the most recent amendment are political affiliations; mental or psychological problems of students or families; sexual behavior and attitudes; illegal, antisocial, self-incriminating, and demeaning behavior; critical appraisals of individuals with whom respondents have close family relationships; legally recognized, privileged relationships; religious practices, affiliations, or beliefs of the student or parents; or income (other than that required to determine eligibility for financial assistance programs). Parents must be notified at least annually of their rights under this law. 20 U.S.C. § 1232h.

[202]Newkirk v. E. Lansing Pub. Schs., No. 91-CV563, 1993 U.S. Dist. LEXIS 13194 (W.D. Mich. Aug. 19, 1993), *aff'd mem.*, 57 F.3d 1070 (6th Cir. 1995).

[203]Triplett v. Livingston Cnty. Bd. of Educ., 967 S.W.2d 25 (Ky. Ct. App. 1997).

[204]C.N. v. Ridgewood Bd. of Educ., 430 F.3d 159 (3d Cir. 2005).

to psychological barriers to learning.[205] Proclaiming that "schools cannot be expected to accommodate the personal, moral or religious concerns of every parent,"[206] the court found the school's psychological survey to be a reasonable way to advance legitimate state interests.

There is concern among educators that the federal pupil protection requirements and similar provisions being considered or enacted by many states that allow parents to seek alternative assignments for instruction they find offensive will cause certain instructional activities to be dropped. Although these measures are couched in terms of protecting students' privacy rights by granting them *exemptions* from particular instructional activities, if a substantial number of exemptions are requested, the instructional activity may be eliminated from the curriculum.

Conclusion

The state and its agents enjoy considerable latitude in regulating various aspects of public education, but any requirements that restrict students' activities must be reasonable and necessary to carry out legitimate educational objectives. When students' or parents' protected rights are impaired, school authorities must be able to substantiate that there is an overriding public interest to be served. Based on an analysis of court cases and legislation pertaining to general requirements and rights associated with school attendance and the instructional program, the following generalizations seem warranted:

1. The state can compel children between specified ages to attend school.[207]
2. Students can satisfy compulsory attendance mandates by attending private schools and, in most states, by receiving equivalent instruction (e.g., home tutoring) that is comparable to the public school program.
3. Most states authorize the creation of a limited number of charter schools designed to encourage innovation; some state regulations are waived for these public charter schools.
4. School officials can require immunization against diseases as a condition of school attendance and can allow religious exemptions to such requirements.
5. Students cannot be excluded from public school because of particular health conditions, unless school attendance would endanger the health of others.
6. Public school districts must provide an education for resident children (even those whose parents entered the country illegally and homeless children sheltered in the districts), but children who live apart from their parents or guardians for educational purposes are not entitled to tuition-free schooling.
7. Fees can be charged for public school transportation so long as the fees are rationally related to legitimate state objectives and are not prohibited by state law.
8. Fees can be charged for the use of public school textbooks and for supplies associated with courses unless such fees are prohibited by state constitutional or statutory provisions.
9. The state and its agencies have the authority to determine public school course offerings and instructional materials, and such curricular determinations will be upheld by courts unless clearly arbitrary or in violation of constitutional or statutory rights.

[205]Fields v. Palmdale Sch. Dist., 427 F.3d 1197, 1206 (9th Cir. 2005) (citing Brown v. Hot, Sexy & Safer Prods., 68 F.3d 525, 533–34 (1st Cir. 1995)).
[206]*Fields*, 427 F.3d at 1206.
[207]The notable exception to compulsory attendance pertains to Amish children who have successfully completed eighth grade. *See* Wisconsin v. Yoder, 406 U.S. 205 (1972).

10. School boards can eliminate instructional materials considered educationally unsuitable if objective procedures are followed in making such determinations.
11. Public schools are required by federal law to implement measures to shield students from access to harmful Internet content on school computers.
12. Courts defer to school authorities in assessing student performance, in the absence of evidence of arbitrary or discriminatory academic decisions.
13. Proficiency examinations can be used to determine pupil remedial needs and as a prerequisite to high school graduation if students are given sufficient notice prior to implementation of the test requirements and are provided adequate preparation for the examinations.
14. Public schools do not owe students a duty to ensure that a specified level of achievement is attained.
15. Parents and eighteen-year-old students must be granted access to the student's school records and an opportunity to contest the contents.
16. Individuals do not have a private right to bring suits for damages under the Family Educational Rights and Privacy Act; the remedy for violations is the withdrawal of federal aid from the noncomplying agency.
17. School personnel must ensure the accuracy of information contained in student records and maintain the confidentiality of such records.
18. Under FERPA, education records are files, documents, and other materials that contain information identifying a student and are maintained by the education agency; educators' personal notes about students (shared only with substitute teachers) are not considered education records.
19. FERPA allows certain directory information, such as students' names, addresses, pictures, and degrees, to be released without parental consent so long as parents have the opportunity to request that specific information be withheld.
20. Parents have the right to inspect materials used in federally funded experimental projects or surveys; students have a right to be excused from participation in such programs or activities involving psychiatric or psychological testing or treatment designed to reveal information in specified sensitive areas pertaining to personal beliefs, behaviors, and family relationships.

MyEdLeadershipLab™

Go to Topic 2: *State and Local Laws Affecting Public Schools* and Topic 8: *Instructional Issues* on the MyEdLeadershipLab™ site (www.myedleadershiplab.com) for *Public School Law: Teachers' and Students' Rights*, Seventh Edition, where you can

- Find learning outcomes for *State and Local Laws Affecting Public Schools* and *Instructional Issues* along with the national standards that connect to these outcomes.
- Complete Assignments and Activities that can help you more deeply understand the chapter content.
- Apply and practice your understanding of the core skills identified in the chapter with the Building Leadership Skills unit.
- Prepare yourself for professional certification with a Practice for Certification quiz.

Students' Rights in Noninstructional Matters

MyEdLeadershipLab™

Visit the MyEdLeadershipLab™ site for *Public School Law: Teachers' and Students' Rights*, Seventh Edition, to enhance your understanding of chapter concepts. You'll have the opportunity to practice your skills through video- and case-based Assignments and Activities as well as Building Leadership Skills units, and to prepare for your certification exam with Practice for Certification quizzes.

Students continue to test the limits of their personal freedoms in public schools, frequently colliding with educators' efforts to maintain an appropriate school environment. When controversies cannot be resolved locally, courts often are called on to address the legal issues involved. For example, what types of student expression are constitutionally protected? Does it matter if the expression is initiated electronically from students' homes? Under what circumstances must student-initiated groups be allowed to meet in public schools? What restrictions can be placed on student appearance? What conditions can be attached to participation in school-related activities? This chapter addresses these and other questions regarding students' rights in connection with selected noninstructional issues with an emphasis on First Amendment freedoms of speech and press and closely related association rights.

FREEDOM OF SPEECH AND PRESS

The First Amendment, as applied to the states through the Fourteenth Amendment, restricts governmental interference with citizens' free expression rights. The government, including public school boards, must have a compelling justification to curtail citizens' expression. The First Amendment also shields the individual's right to remain silent when confronted with an illegitimate government demand for expression, such as mandatory participation in saluting the American flag in public schools.[1] In short, the First Amendment protects decisions regarding what to say and what not to say, with no constitutional distinction between compelled speech and compelled silence.

In our nation, free expression rights are perhaps the most preciously guarded individual liberties and often are relied on to protect unpopular viewpoints. For example, the United States Supreme Court has used the First Amendment to protect political protesters' right to burn the American flag[2] and the Ku Klux Klan's right to place a cross on public property.[3] But free speech guarantees apply only to conduct that constitutes expression. Where conduct is meant to communicate an idea that is likely to be understood by the intended audience, it is considered expression for First Amendment purposes.[4]

Even if specific conduct qualifies as expression, it is not assured constitutional protection; the judiciary has recognized that defamatory,[5] obscene,[6] and inflammatory[7] communications are outside the protective arm of the First Amendment. In addition, as discussed below, lewd and vulgar comments and expression that promote illegal activity for minors are not protected in the public school context.[8] Also, commercial expression, although constitutionally protected, has not been afforded the same level of First Amendment protection as has speech intended to convey a particular point of view. The Supreme Court has recognized that governmental restrictions on commercial speech that has economic motives do not have to be the least restrictive means to achieve the desired end; rather, there only needs to be a reasonable "fit" between the restrictions and the governmental goal.[9]

[1]*See* W. Va. State Bd. of Educ. v. Barnette, 319 U.S. 624 (1943).

[2]Texas v. Johnson, 491 U.S. 397 (1989). Despite their fundamental significance, free expression rights can be restricted. As Justice Holmes noted about a century ago, freedom of speech does not allow an individual to yell "fire" in a crowded theater when there is no fire. Schenck v. United States, 249 U.S. 47, 52 (1919).

[3]Capitol Square Review & Advisory Bd. v. Pinette, 515 U.S. 753 (1995). *But see* Virginia v. Black, 538 U.S. 343 (2003) (upholding a statutory prohibition on cross burning with the intent to intimidate).

[4]For a discussion of these requirements, see *Johnson*, 491 U.S. at 404; United States v. O'Brien, 391 U.S. 367, 376 (1968). In the school context, *see, e.g., Jarman v. Williams*, 753 F.2d 76 (8th Cir. 1985) (holding that social and recreational dancing in public schools is not expression that enjoys First Amendment protection).

[5]Intentionally left blank so that the remaining footnotes in the chapter can remain numbered as is.

[6]The judiciary has held that individuals cannot claim a First Amendment right to voice or publish obscenities, although there is not a bright-line rule regarding what expression falls in this category. *See* Miller v. California, 413 U.S. 15, 24 (1973) (identifying the following test to distinguish obscene material from constitutionally protected material: "(1) whether 'the average person, applying contemporary community standards' would find that the work, taken as a whole, appeals to the prurient interests; (2) whether the work depicts or describes, in a patently offensive way, sexual conduct specifically defined by the applicable state law; and (3) whether the work, taken as a whole, lacks serious literary, artistic, political, or scientific value"). The Supreme Court has recognized the government's authority to adjust the definition of obscenity as applied to minors. *See, e.g.*, Ginsberg v. New York, 390 U.S. 629 (1968) (upholding a state law prohibiting the sale to minors of magazines depicting female nudity).

[7]Courts have differentiated fighting words and other expression that agitates, threatens, or incites an immediate breach of peace from speech that conveys ideas and stimulates discussion. *See* Gooding v. Wilson, 405 U.S. 518, 524 (1972). There is a growing body of litigation pertaining to student expression considered inflammatory or threatening. *See infra* text accompanying notes 39–51.

[8]*See* Bethel Sch. Dist. No. 403 v. Fraser, 478 U.S. 675 (1986); *infra* text accompanying note 17; Morse v. Frederick, 551 U.S. 393 (2007); *infra* text accompanying note 21.

[9]Bd. of Trs. v. Fox, 492 U.S. 469 (1989). Courts generally have upheld regulations prohibiting sales and fund-raising activities in public schools as justified to preserve schools for their educational function and to prevent commercial exploitation of students.

Where protected expression is at issue, an assessment of the type of forum the government has created for expressive activities has been important in determining whether the expression can be restricted. The Supreme Court has recognized that public places, such as streets and parks, are traditional public forums for assembly and communication where content-based restrictions cannot be imposed unless justified by a compelling government interest.[10] In contrast, expression can be confined to the governmental purpose of the property in a nonpublic forum, such as a public school. Content-based restrictions are permissible in a nonpublic forum to ensure that expression is compatible with the intended governmental purpose, provided that regulations are reasonable and do not entail viewpoint discrimination.[11]

The government can create a limited public forum for expression on public property that otherwise would be considered a nonpublic forum and reserved for its governmental function. For example, a student activities program held after school might be established as a limited forum for student expression. A limited forum can be restricted to a certain class of speakers (e.g., students) and/or to specific categories of expression (e.g., noncommercial speech).[12] Otherwise, expression in a limited forum is subject to the same protections that govern a traditional public forum.

Legal Principles

This section reviews the four Supreme Court decisions that have established the legal principles governing student expression rights in public schools. Application of these principles is addressed in subsequent sections.

In 1969, the Supreme Court rendered its landmark decision, *Tinker v. Des Moines Independent School District*, the Magna Carta of students' expression rights.[13] In *Tinker*, three students were suspended from school for wearing black armbands to protest the Vietnam War. Hearing about the planned silent protest, the school principals met and devised a policy forbidding the wearing of armbands at school. School officials did not attempt to prohibit the wearing of all symbols, but instead prohibited one form of expression. Concluding that the students were punished for expression that was not accompanied by any disorder or disturbance, the Supreme Court ruled that "undifferentiated fear or apprehension of disturbance is not enough to overcome the right to freedom of expression."[14] Furthermore, the Court declared that school officials must have "more than a mere desire to avoid the discomfort and unpleasantness that always accompany an unpopular viewpoint" in order to justify curtailment of student expression.[15]

[10]Cornelius v. NAACP Legal Def. & Educ. Fund, 473 U.S. 788 (1985); Perry Educ. Ass'n v. Perry Local Educators' Ass'n, 460 U.S. 37 (1983).

[11]*Cornelius*, 473 U.S. at 800. Some speech in public schools, such as that related to the curriculum, is considered government speech that is not subject to First Amendment analysis. *See* Nelda Cambron-McCabe, *When Government Speaks: An Examination of the Evolving Government Speech Doctrine*, 274 EDUC. L. REP. 753–73 (2012).

[12]*See* R.O. *ex rel.* Ochshorn v. Ithaca City Sch. Dist., 645 F.3d 533, 539 (2d Cir. 2011) (noting that in a limited forum, school authorities can restrict speech in a viewpoint-neutral manner that is reasonable in light of the forum's purpose), *cert. denied*, 132 S. Ct. 422 (2011); *infra* text accompanying note 33.

[13]393 U.S. 503 (1969).

[14]*Id.* at 508.

[15]*Id.* at 509.

In *Tinker*, the Supreme Court echoed statements made in an earlier federal appellate ruling: a student may express opinions on controversial issues in the classroom, cafeteria, playing field, or any other place, so long as the exercise of such rights does not "materially and substantially interfere with the requirements of appropriate discipline in the operation of the school" or collide with the rights of others.[16] The Supreme Court emphasized that educators have the authority and duty to maintain discipline in schools, but they must consider students' constitutional rights as they exert control.

The Supreme Court did not render another student expression case until 1986. In a significant decision, *Bethel School District No. 403 v. Fraser*, the Supreme Court granted school authorities considerable latitude in censoring lewd, vulgar, and indecent student expression. Overturning the lower courts, the Supreme Court upheld disciplinary action against a student for using a sexual metaphor in a nomination speech during a student government assembly.[17] Concluding that the sexual innuendos were offensive to both teachers and students, the majority held that the school's legitimate interest in protecting the captive student audience from exposure to lewd and vulgar speech justified the disciplinary action.

The Court in *Fraser* reiterated that speech protected by the First Amendment for adults is not necessarily protected for children, reasoning that in the public school context, the sensibilities of fellow students must be considered. The majority recognized that an important objective of public schools is the inculcation of fundamental values of civility and that the school board has the authority to determine what manner of speech is appropriate in classes or assemblies.[18] The majority further rejected the contention that the student had no way of knowing that his expression would evoke disciplinary action; the school rule barring obscene and disruptive expression and teachers' admonitions that his planned speech was inappropriate provided adequate warning of the consequences of the expression.

Only two years after *Fraser*, the Court rendered a seminal decision further limiting, but not overturning, the reach of *Tinker*. In *Hazelwood School District v. Kuhlmeier*, the Court held that school authorities can censor student expression in school publications and other school-related activities so long as the censorship decisions are based on legitimate pedagogical concerns.[19] At issue in *Hazelwood* was a high school principal's deletion of two pages from the school newspaper because of the content of articles on divorce and teenage pregnancy and fears that individuals could be identified in the articles.

Rejecting the assertion that the school newspaper had been established as a public forum for student expression, the Court declared that only with school authorities' clear

[16] *Id.* (quoting Burnside v. Byars, 363 F.2d 744, 749 (5th Cir. 1966)). Debate surrounds whether the two prongs of this standard are independent guarantees or linked in that evidence of a disruption is required for the expression to collide with others' rights. *See* Martha McCarthy, *Curtailing Student Expression: Is a Link to a Disruption Required?* 38 J. Law & Educ. 607–21 (2009).

[17] 478 U.S. 675 (1986). Throughout his speech, Fraser employed a sexual metaphor to refer to the candidate, using such phrases as "he's firm in his pants, . . . his character is firm," "a man who takes his point and pounds it in," "he doesn't attack things in spurts—he drives hard, pushing and pushing until finally—he succeeds," and "a man who will go to the very end—even the climax, for each and every one of you." *Id.* at 687 (Brennan, J., concurring). Fraser was suspended for two days and disqualified as a candidate for commencement speaker. However, he did eventually deliver a commencement speech, so his claim that the disqualification violated due process rights was not reviewed by the appellate court.

[18] *Id.* at 683. As addressed subsequently, application of *Fraser* by lower courts has not been consistent. Especially ambiguous is whether *Fraser* applies to electronic expression. *See infra* text accompanying notes 85–97 for a discussion of litigation involving student Internet expression.

[19] 484 U.S. 260 (1988), *on remand*, 840 F.2d 596 (8th Cir. 1988).

intent do school activities become a public forum.[20] The Court drew a distinction between a public school's *toleration* of private student expression, which is constitutionally required under some circumstances, and its *promotion* of student speech that represents the school. Reasoning that student expression appearing to bear the school's imprimatur can be censored, the Court acknowledged school authorities' broad discretion to ensure that such expression occurring in school publications and all school-sponsored activities (including extracurricular) is consistent with educational objectives. The Court's expansive interpretation of what constitutes school-sponsored expression has narrowed the circumstances under which students can prevail in First Amendment claims.

Almost two more decades passed before the Supreme Court rendered its fourth decision pertaining to public school student expression rights. In 2007, the Court in *Morse v. Frederick* held that given the special circumstances in public schools, students can be disciplined for expression reasonably viewed as promoting or celebrating illegal drug use; incitement to lawless conduct is not required.[21] *Morse* focused on a banner containing the phrase, "BONG HITS 4 JESUS," which Joseph Frederick and some friends unfurled across the street from their school as the Olympic torch relay passed by. The Supreme Court reasoned that the students were under the school's control when they were allowed to cross the street and watch the torch relay because it was a school-authorized event supervised by school personnel. Although Frederick had not yet been on school grounds when he joined his friends across the street, the Court declined to apply legal standards used to assess students' off-campus behavior.

Reversing the Ninth Circuit's conclusion that the school could not "punish and censor non-disruptive, off-campus speech by students during school-authorized activities because the speech promotes a social message contrary to the one favored by the school,"[22] the divided Supreme Court upheld disciplinary action against the student for displaying the banner.[23] The majority emphasized the importance of deterring drug use by students and concluded that Frederick's action violated the school board's policy of prohibiting expression advocating the use of illegal substances. The Court declared that its earlier *Fraser* decision stands for the proposition that considerations beyond the *Tinker* disruption standard are appropriate in assessing student expression in public schools.[24] However, a majority of the Justices declined to extend school authorities' discretion to the point that they can curtail any student expression they find "plainly offensive" or at odds with the school's "educational mission."[25] All Justices agreed that students can be disciplined for promoting the use of illegal drugs, but they differed regarding whether the banner at issue actually did so.[26]

[20]*Id.*, 484 U.S. at 267.

[21]551 U.S. 393 (2007); *see* Brandenburg v. Ohio, 395 U.S. 444, 449 (1969) (distinguishing "mere advocacy" that is protected expression from unprotected incitement to lawless behavior).

[22]Frederick v. Morse, 439 F.3d 1114, 1118 (9th Cir. 2006).

[23]*Morse*, 551 U.S. 393.

[24]*Id.*; *see* Tinker v. Des Moines Indep. Sch. Dist., 393 U.S. 503 (1969); *supra* text accompanying note 13. All of the Justices agreed that the principal should not be held liable for violating clearly established law, and Justice Breyer thought the decision should have focused only on this issue. *See Morse,* 551 U.S. at 425–33 (Breyer, J., concurring in part and dissenting in part).

[25]*See Morse*, 551 U.S. at 423. Justices Alito and Kennedy emphasized that this decision is restricted to the promotion of illegal drug use and does not extend to censorship of expression on social or political issues that may be viewed as inconsistent with the school's mission. *Id.* at 422 (Alito, J., joined by Kennedy, J., concurring).

[26]*See id.* at 393 (majority opinion); *id.* at 433 (Stevens, J., joined by Ginsberg & Souter, JJ., dissenting) (arguing that the banner was a nonsensical effort for the student to get on television and promoted nothing).

Students' Rights in Noninstructional Matters

Lower courts have rendered a range of decisions in applying these legal principles articulated by the Supreme Court. Some of these rulings are reviewed below in connection with school-sponsored expression; threats and other inflammatory expression; prior restraints versus punishment after the fact; anti-harassment and anti-bullying provisions; electronic expression; and time, place, and manner restrictions. For a display of the questions that must be answered in assessing student expression rights, see Figure 1.

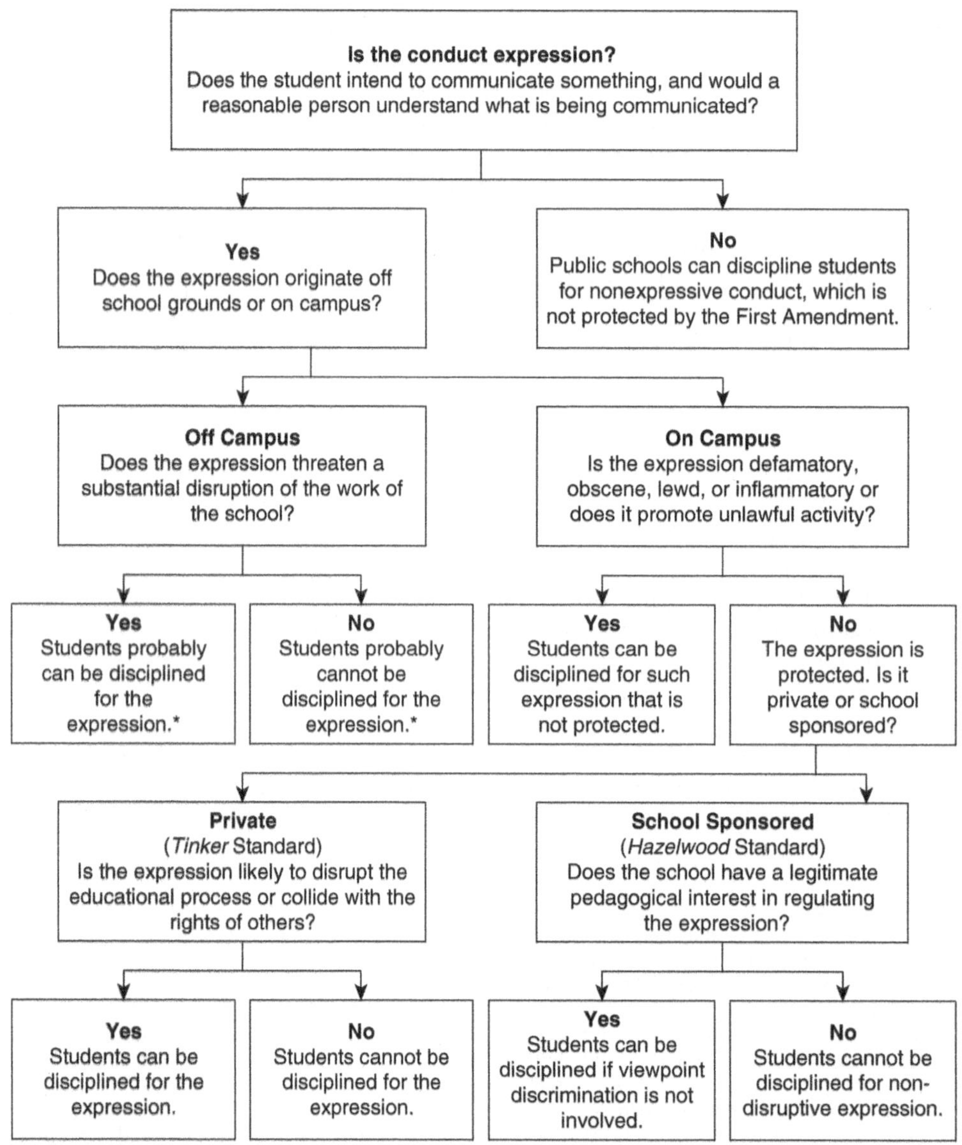

FIGURE 1 Assessing Student Expression Rights

School-Sponsored Expression

During the 1970s and early 1980s, many courts broadly interpreted the circumstances under which limited forums for student expression were created in public schools. School-sponsored newspapers often were considered such a forum, and accordingly, courts held that articles on controversial subjects such as the Vietnam War, abortion, and birth control could not be barred from these publications.[27] Courts placed the burden on school authorities to justify prior administrative review of the content of both school-sponsored and nonsponsored literature.

However, since *Hazelwood*, expression appearing to bear the school's imprimatur can be censored for pedagogical reasons. The *Tinker* standard applies *only* to protected *private* expression, and some lower courts have broadly interpreted student expression that might be perceived as representing the school.[28] Relying on *Hazelwood*, the Sixth Circuit held that a student could be disqualified from running for student council president because his candidacy speech at a school-sponsored assembly was discourteous. Recognizing that "the universe of legitimate pedagogical concerns is by no means confined to the academic" and includes teaching values such as courtesy and respect for authority, the court emphasized that "limitations on speech . . . unconstitutional outside the schoolhouse are not necessarily unconstitutional within it."[29] Also echoing the *Hazelwood* rationale, the Ninth Circuit rejected Planned Parenthood's claim that a school district's denial of its request to advertise in school newspapers, yearbooks, and programs for athletic events violated free speech rights, concluding that the district could bar advertisements inconsistent with its educational mission.[30]

Similarly reflecting the broad discretion granted to school authorities, the Fourth Circuit upheld a high school principal's decision to bar the school's use of the Johnny Reb symbol following complaints that it offended African American students.[31] The Eighth Circuit also relied on *Hazelwood* in upholding a principal's decision to disqualify a student council candidate who handed out condoms with stickers bearing his campaign slogan, noting that *Hazelwood* grants school authorities considerable discretion to control student expression in school-sponsored activities.[32] More recently, the Second Circuit

[27]*See, e.g.*, Gambino v. Fairfax Cnty. Sch. Bd., 564 F.2d 157 (4th Cir. 1977) (holding that a school-sponsored newspaper was established as a forum for student expression).

[28]In response to *Hazelwood*, a number of state legislatures considered and several enacted laws granting student editors of school-sponsored papers specific rights in determining the content of their publications. As of 2012, ten states (Arkansas, California, Colorado, Illinois, Iowa, Kansas, Oregon, Massachusetts, Pennsylvania, and Washington) had laws or state board of education regulations in this regard. *See* Student Press Law Ctr., *State Legislation* (Mar. 2012), http://www.splc.org/knowyourrights/statelegislation.asp. State laws can be more protective of student expression rights, but they cannot drop below constitutional minimums. Some federal courts have applied *Hazelwood* to curricular speech in state-supported institutions of higher education. *See, e.g.*, Ward v. Polite, 667 F.3d 727, 741 (6th Cir. 2012). As with legislative responses to *Hazelwood* at the high school level, states can give student editors of publications in state-supported postsecondary institutions substantial statutory protection. *See* Illinois Public Forum law, 110 ILL. COMP. STAT. 13/10 (2012).

[29]Poling v. Murphy, 872 F.2d 757, 761 (6th Cir. 1989) (acknowledging that decisions regarding whether specific comments are rude are "best left to the locally elected school board, not to a distant, life-tenured judiciary").

[30]Planned Parenthood v. Clark Cnty. Sch. Dist., 887 F.2d 935, 942 (9th Cir. 1989), *rehearing en banc*, 941 F.2d 817 (9th Cir. 1991).

[31]Crosby v. Holsinger, 852 F.2d 801 (4th Cir. 1988) (noting also that the one-day delay in posting students' notices of the upcoming board meeting constituted a minimal impairment of expression rights).

[32]Henerey v. City of St. Charles Sch. Dist., 200 F.3d 1128 (8th Cir. 1999); *see also* Fister v. Minn. New Country Sch., 149 F.3d 1187 (8th Cir. 1998) (upholding the suspension and ultimate expulsion of a student for defying school personnel and repeatedly reposting a letter on the divider around her workspace; the letter offended two classmates and severely affected their schoolwork).

applied *Hazelwood* in ruling that school authorities were justified in prohibiting students from running a lewd, sexually explicit cartoon in the school-sponsored paper, as the decision was reasonably related to legitimate pedagogical concerns. Even though students wrote the paper's content, its operation was supervised by the faculty advisor so the paper was not considered a limited forum for student expression.[33]

Courts have reasoned that the school has the right to disassociate itself from controversial expression that conflicts with its mission and have considered school-sponsored activities to include student newspapers supported by the public school, extracurricular activities sponsored by the school, school assemblies, and classroom activities. The key consideration is whether the expression is viewed as bearing the school's imprimatur; only under such circumstances is *Hazelwood*'s broad deference to school authorities triggered.

Ironically, since *Hazelwood*, student expression in underground (not school-sponsored) student papers distributed at school enjoys greater constitutional protection than does expression in school-sponsored publications. The former is considered private expression governed by the *Tinker* principle, whereas the latter represents the school and is subject to censorship under *Hazelwood*. Most courts have treated the distribution of religious literature by secondary students like the distribution of other material that is not sponsored by the school.[34]

There are limits, however, on school authorities' wide latitude to censor student expression that bears the public school's imprimatur.[35] For example, blatant viewpoint discrimination in a nonpublic forum abridges the First Amendment.[36] And even if viewpoint discrimination is not involved, censorship actions in a nonpublic forum still must be based on legitimate pedagogical concerns. A Michigan federal district court found no legitimate pedagogical reason to remove from the school newspaper a student's article on a pending lawsuit alleging that school bus diesel fumes constituted a neighborhood nuisance.[37]

Furthermore, a school-sponsored publication might be considered a forum for student expression under certain circumstances. In a Massachusetts case, school authorities had given students editorial control of school publications, so independent decisions of the students could not be attributed to school officials. In this situation, the student editors of the school newspaper and yearbook rejected advertisements from a parent who was a

[33]R.O. *ex rel.* Ochshorn v. Ithaca City Sch. Dist., 645 F.3d 533 (2d Cir. 2011) (holding also that school authorities could bar distribution on campus of an independent student publication with the same cartoon, which was considered lewd and vulgar and thus not protected), *cert. denied*, 132 S. Ct. 422 (2011).

[34]Of course, proselytizing materials in *school-sponsored* publications would be barred by the Establishment Clause.

[35]*See* Bd. of Regents v. Southworth, 529 U.S. 217 (2000) (upholding a university's mandatory student activities fees used to facilitate the free and open exchange of ideas among students so long as the institution operated in a viewpoint-neutral manner, but striking down the use of a student referendum to determine what clubs would be subsidized, because the referendum disenfranchised minority viewpoints); *see also* Collegians for a Constructive Tomorrow v. Regents of Univ. of Wis. Sys., 820 F. Supp. 2d 932 (W.D. Wis. 2011) (rejecting conservative student organization's claim that it was discriminatorily denied student services funding).

[36]*See, e.g.*, Searcey v. Harris, 888 F.2d 1314 (11th Cir. 1989) (placing the burden on school authorities to justify viewpoint discrimination against a peace activist group that was not allowed to display its literature on school premises or participate in career day when military recruiters were allowed such access); San Diego Comm. against Registration & the Draft v. Governing Bd., 790 F.2d 1471 (9th Cir. 1986) (finding a violation of students' First Amendment rights because the school board failed to produce a compelling justification for excluding an anti-draft organization's advertisement from the school newspaper, while allowing military recruitment advertisements).

[37]Dean v. Utica Cmty. Schs., 345 F. Supp. 2d 799 (E.D. Mich. 2004) (ruling that the censorship was based on the superintendent's disagreement with the views expressed about the lawsuit against the school district).

leading opponent of the district's condom distribution policy. The First Circuit concluded that school officials, who had recommended that the students publish the ads, could not be held liable for the students' decisions, because the student editors were not state actors.[38]

Threats and Other Inflammatory Expression

The U.S. Supreme Court has not addressed the application of the First Amendment to alleged threats made by students toward classmates or school personnel, but there is a growing body of lower court litigation. For example, the Ninth Circuit upheld suspension of a student for threatening to shoot a counselor, despite conflicting testimony regarding what was actually said.[39] The appeals court emphasized that threats of physical violence are not shielded by the First Amendment.

In determining if a true threat has been made, courts consider a number of factors, such as (1) reactions of the recipient and other listeners, (2) whether the maker of the alleged threat had made similar statements to the victim in the past, (3) if the utterance was conditional and communicated directly to the victim, and (4) whether the victim had reason to believe that the speaker would engage in violence.[40] In an illustrative case, the Fifth Circuit held that a student's notebook, outlining a pseudo-Nazi group's plan to commit a "Columbine shooting," constituted a "terroristic threat" that was not protected by the First Amendment.[41] The Eleventh Circuit similarly ruled that a student's story about shooting her math teacher was a threat of violence; her suspension was justified because she shared the story with another student.[42] Citing *Morse*, the court reasoned that disciplining students for threats of violence is even more important than curtailing their promotion of illegal drug use.[43]

Also finding a threat, the Eighth Circuit reversed the lower court and upheld expulsion of a student for writing a letter indicating he was going to rape and murder his former girlfriend. The court was convinced that the writer intended to communicate the threat, because he shared the letter with a friend whom he assumed would give it to his former girlfriend.[44] In 2011, the same court found a true threat in a student's online instant message sent from home to a classmate in which he mentioned getting a gun and shooting other students at school.[45] The serious statements were communicated to a third party, and combined with the speaker's admitted depression and access to weapons, the appeals court reasoned that school authorities did not need to wait until the threat was carried out before taking action. Thus, the student's immediate placement in juvenile detention[46] and his subsequent expulsion for the remainder of the school year were found to be appropriate responses to the true threat.

[38]Yeo v. Town of Lexington, 131 F.3d 241 (1st Cir. 1997).

[39]Lovell v. Poway Unified Sch. Dist., 90 F.3d 367 (9th Cir. 1996).

[40]United States v. Dinwiddie, 76 F.3d 913 (8th Cir. 1996).

[41]Ponce v. Socorro Indep. Sch. Dist., 508 F.3d 765, 767 (5th Cir. 2007) (relying on *Morse v. Frederick*, 551 U.S. 393 (2007), in reasoning that evidence of a disruption is not required when there is a threat of special danger to the safety of students); *see also* Jones v. Arkansas, 64 S.W.3d 728 (Ark. 2002) (holding that a student-composed rap song did not entail fighting words but was a true threat, as it contained an unconditional threat to the life of a classmate and was delivered to the targeted student who perceived it as unequivocally threatening).

[42]Boim v. Fulton Cnty. Sch. Dist., 494 F.3d 978 (11th Cir. 2007).

[43]*Id.* at 984 (citing *Morse*, 551 U.S. 393).

[44]Doe v. Pulaski Cnty. Special Sch. Dist., 306 F.3d 616 (8th Cir. 2002).

[45]D.J.M. v. Hannibal Pub. Sch. Dist. # 60, 647 F.3d 754 (8th Cir. 2011).

[46]School authorities notified the police, who placed the student in juvenile detention.

Utterances can be considered inflammatory and thus unprotected, even if *not* found to be true threats or fighting words. The Ninth Circuit ruled that a student could be subject to emergency expulsion, with a hearing occurring afterward, for writing a poem about someone who committed multiple murders in the past and decided to kill himself for fear of murdering others.[47] The poem was not considered a true threat or to contain fighting words. The Wisconsin Supreme Court similarly held that school authorities had more than enough reason to suspend a student for his creative writing assignment, describing a student removed from class for being disruptive (as the writer had been) who returned the next day to behead his teacher, even though the court found no true threat that would justify prosecution of the student for disorderly conduct.[48] The Fifth Circuit also found no true threat in a student's drawing—featuring violence, obscenities, and racial epithets—that the student's brother brought on campus two years later. Nonetheless, the court held that the principal, who suspended the artist, was entitled to qualified immunity because of the unsettled nature of the law in this regard.[49]

The Second Circuit in 2011 ruled in favor of school authorities who detained a middle school student to determine if he posed a danger to himself or others and reported his parents to Child and Family Services for possible neglect in connection with an essay he wrote that included illegal acts, violence, and his own suicide. The court reasoned that school authorities did not violate the student's expression rights or his parents' substantive due process rights by taking precautionary actions.[50] The following year, the same court ruled that school authorities reasonably could forecast a disruption from an elementary school student's picture expressing a desire to blow up the school and its teachers.[51] Upholding the student's six-day suspension, the appeals court reasoned that the student's actual intent and capacity to carry out the threat were irrelevant. Courts generally seem more inclined to uphold school disciplinary action, in contrast to criminal prosecution, for students' alleged threats or other inflammatory expression.

Prior Restraints versus Punishment After the Fact

When determined that protected private expression is at issue, courts then are faced with the difficult task of assessing whether restrictions are justified. Under the *Tinker* principle,

[47]LaVine v. Blaine Sch. Dist., 257 F.3d 981 (9th Cir. 2001) (holding, however, that the placement of negative notations in the student's file, after he was readmitted to school and the concern about harm had subsided, went beyond the school district's documentation needs); *see also* Cuesta v. Sch. Bd., 285 F.3d 962 (11th Cir. 2002) (upholding a principal's compliance with the school's zero tolerance policy by reporting to the police a student's distribution of a threatening pamphlet).

[48]*In re* Douglas D., 626 N.W.2d 725 (Wis. 2001); *see also* S.G. v. Sayreville Bd. of Educ., 333 F.3d 417 (3d Cir. 2003) (upholding suspension of a kindergarten student for saying, "I'm going to shoot you," during a game at recess, which violated the school's prohibition on speech threatening violence and the use of firearms); Wynar v. Douglas Cnty. Sch. Dist., No. 3:09-cv-0626-LRH-VPC, 2011 WL 3512534 (D. Nev. Aug. 10, 2011) (upholding student's ninety-day expulsion for sending instant messages with assertions that he would do bodily harm toward other students; school personnel could reasonably expect a substantial disruption).

[49]Porter v. Ascension Parish Sch. Bd., 393 F.3d 608 (5th Cir. 2004); *see also* Shoemaker v. Arkansas, 38 S.W.3d 350 (Ark. 2001) (finding a state law unconstitutionally vague that criminalized student conduct or expression abusing or insulting a teacher; a student could not be charged with a misdemeanor for calling her teacher "a bitch" because this utterance did not entail fighting words); New Hampshire v. McCooey, 802 A.2d 1216 (N.H. 2002) (overturning a disorderly conduct conviction of a student who said he might "shoot up the school" if a teacher did not give him a hug; finding no evidence that the expression caused a school disruption to justify the conviction).

[50]Cox v. Warwick Valley Cent. Sch. Dist., 654 F.3d 267 (2d Cir. 2011) (noting that the student had a history of misbehavior and was on probation and under a behavior contract when the essay was written).

[51]Cuff v. Valley Cent. Sch. Dist., 677 F.3d 109 (2d Cir. 2012).

private expression can be curtailed if it is likely to disrupt the educational process or intrude on the rights of others. For example, bans on wearing buttons at school have been upheld where linked to an interference with the educational process.[52]

The law clearly allows students to be punished after the fact if they cause a disruption, but school authorities have a greater burden of justification when they impose prior restraints on such expression. The Supreme Court has recognized that "a free society prefers to punish the few who abuse rights of speech after they break the law [rather] than to throttle them and all others beforehand."[53] The imposition of prior restraints on student speech must bear a substantial relationship to an important government interest, and any regulation must contain narrow, objective, and unambiguous criteria for determining what material is prohibited and procedures that allow a speedy determination of whether materials meet those criteria. Recognizing that the Constitution requires a high degree of specificity when imposing restraints on private expression, the Ninth Circuit held that school authorities in a Washington school district could not suspend students for distributing a student paper produced off campus and could not subject the paper's content to prior review. Because "prior restraints are permissible in only the rarest of circumstances," the Ninth Circuit considered the policy subjecting *all* nonschool publications to prior review for the purpose of censorship to be overbroad.[54]

The burden is on school authorities to justify policies requiring administrative approval of unofficial (underground) student publications, but such prior review is not unconstitutional per se.[55] Of course, courts are more inclined to support disciplinary action and confiscation of materials *after* the expression has occurred, if it is considered unprotected (i.e., comments that are libelous, inflammatory, vulgar, or promote illegal activity), threatens a disruption of the educational process, interferes with the rights of others, or represents the school. For example, students can be disciplined after the fact for expression advocating the destruction of school property in publications they distribute at school. The Seventh Circuit recognized that a "reason to believe" or "reasonable forecast" standard can be applied to punish a student for such expression, even though the anticipated destruction of school property never materializes.[56] In this case, a student was expelled for one year for publishing and distributing at school an article in an underground paper that contained information about how to disable the school's computer system. More recently, the Second Circuit upheld school authorities in sending a student home for allegedly making a racial slur and in denying the student's request to return to school to explain his version of events to classmates, given the significant threat of a disruption. In light of the racial tensions created by the situation and concern for the student's safety, his expulsion for the remainder of the school year was considered reasonable.[57]

[52]*See, e.g.*, Guzick v. Drebus, 431 F.2d 594 (6th Cir. 1970); Blackwell v. Issaquena Cnty. Bd. of Educ., 363 F.2d 749 (5th Cir. 1966).

[53]Se. Promotions v. Conrad, 420 U.S. 546, 559 (1975).

[54]Burch v. Barker, 861 F.2d 1149, 1155 (9th Cir. 1988).

[55]*See, e.g.*, Muller v. Jefferson Lighthouse Sch., 98 F.3d 1530 (7th Cir. 1996) (upholding school district policy requiring copies of nonschool student literature to be given to the principal at least one day before distribution and allowing censorship of material that encourages disruption or illegal acts or is libelous, obscene, or insulting).

[56]Boucher v. Sch. Bd., 134 F.3d 821, 828 (7th Cir. 1997).

[57]DeFabio v. E. Hampton Union Free Sch. Dist., 623 F.3d 71 (2d. Cir. 2010), *cert. denied*, 131 S. Ct. 1578 (2011).

Sometimes state law has a bearing on whether students can be disciplined after the fact for their expression. States can be more protective of students' expression rights, but they cannot drop below federal constitutional minimums. To illustrate, the Supreme Court declined to review a California appeals court's decision that a school district violated a student's expression rights when it refused to publish his caustic editorial about immigration. The appeals court held that the expression was not prohibited under the state law that bars student speech inciting others and creating a clear and present danger of disrupting the schools. The court concluded that speech communicating ideas, "even in a provocative manner, may not be prohibited merely because of the disruption it may cause due to reactions by the speech's audience."[58] Noting that the article was politically charged because it suggested that individuals who do not speak English are illegal immigrants and likely to turn to crime, the court did not find the speech so inflammatory that it would incite a disturbance, even though opponents of the expression might cause a disruption.

Courts have condoned disciplinary action against students who have engaged in walkouts, boycotts, sit-ins, or other protests involving conduct that blocks hallways, damages property, causes students to miss class, or interferes with essential school activities in other ways.[59] The Sixth Circuit held that a petition circulated by four football players denouncing the head coach justified their dismissal from the varsity football team. The court reasoned that the petition disrupted the team, and athletes are subject to greater restrictions than are applied to the general student body.[60] The Ninth Circuit also ruled that student athletes could be disciplined for protesting actions of the coach by refusing to board the team bus and to play in a basketball game, which substantially disrupted a school activity.[61] However, this court departed from the Sixth Circuit in finding that the students' petition requesting that the coach resign because of derogatory remarks he made toward players was protected speech. Thus, the Ninth Circuit remanded the case for a determination of whether the students were impermissibly removed from the basketball team in retaliation for their petition. In an earlier Ninth Circuit case, the appeals court overturned the suspension of students for wearing buttons containing the word "scab" in connection with a teachers' strike.[62] Recognizing that such expression is governed by *Tinker*, the court held that students could not be disciplined for nondisruptive, private expression that was merely critical of school personnel or policies. However, the court acknowledged that vulgar, lewd, obscene, or plainly offensive buttons could be banned *even if* considered private expression.

Anti-Harassment and Anti-Bullying Policies

A number of school districts have adopted policies prohibiting expression that constitutes verbal or physical harassment based on race, religion, color, national origin, sex, sexual orientation, disability, or other personal characteristics. Also, forty-nine states and

[58]Smith v. Novato Unified Sch. Dist., 59 Cal. Rptr. 3d 508, 519 (Ct. App. 2007); *see infra* text accompanying note 84 for a discussion of the "hecklers' veto."

[59]*See, e.g.*, Corales v. Bennett, 567 F.3d 554 (9th Cir. 2009); Madrid v. Anthony, 510 F. Supp. 2d 425 (S.D. Tex. 2007).

[60]Lowery v. Euverard, 497 F.3d 584 (6th Cir. 2007).

[61]Pinard v. Clatskanie Sch. Dist. 6J, 467 F.3d 755 (9th Cir. 2006).

[62]Chandler v. McMinnville Sch. Dist., 978 F.2d 524 (9th Cir. 1992).

the District of Columbia have anti-bullying provisions that often share similar language with anti-harassment policies.[63] In some of these provisions, the terms "harassment" and "bullying" are used interchangeably, even though "harassment" is associated with specific legal liability under federal civil rights laws that do not apply to bullying.[64]

The public school policies prohibiting bullying and harassment traditionally have not appeared vulnerable to First Amendment challenges, whereas "hate speech" policies have been struck down in municipalities and public higher education.[65] Public schools have been considered a special environment in terms of government restrictions on private expression,[66] because of their purpose in educating America's youth and inculcating basic values, such as civility and respect for others with different backgrounds and beliefs.[67]

A growing body of cases interpreting anti-harassment provisions has focused on students displaying Confederate flags, and some courts have upheld restrictions on such displays. In a typical case, the Sixth Circuit Court of Appeals in 2010 upheld a student's suspension for wearing clothing depicting the Confederate flag in violation of the school's dress code. The court held that school officials reasonably could forecast a substantial disruption from such displays but noted that such a link to a disruption was not required to curtail displays that convey racial hostility.[68] The same court previously upheld a school district's ban on students displaying the Confederate flag, again finding the potential for

[63]Three-fourths of the anti-bullying laws specifically prohibit cyberbullying. New Jersey's Anti-Bullying Bill of Rights, enacted in 2011, is among the most comprehensive laws in prohibiting bullying, harassment, or intimidation that disrupts the school or interferes with the rights of others. Under the law, each school district must have an anti-bullying specialist, and complaints must be investigated within ten days. Schools get a grade on how they handle such complaints, and school principals can be disciplined for failure to comply with this law. N.J. STAT. ANN. § 18A:37-13 (West 2012). The law is being contested because it does not provide funds for its costly implementation, *N.J. Anti-Bullying Plan Falls Short for Schools*, EDUC. WK., July 18, 2012, at 4.

[64]According to an initiative sponsored by the federal government, peer bullying is a major concern nationally because victims can become depressed, fearful of being at school, and can contemplate suicide. *See* U.S. Dep't of Health & Human Servs., *Who Is at Risk?* (Feb. 2012), http://www.StopBullying.gov; *see also* Bully Police USA (Jan. 2012), http://www.bullypolice.org/; Cyberbullying Research Ctr. (Feb. 2012), http://www.cyberbullying.us/. For a discussion of the different legal meanings of "harassment" and "bullying," see Martha McCarthy, *Student Electronic Expression: Unanswered Questions Persist*, 277 EDUC. L. REP. 1–19 (2012). A coalition of religious and educational organizations issued a pamphlet in 2012 to assist school personnel in balancing free expression and school safety concerns. Am. Jewish Comm., *Harassment, Bullying and Free Expression: Guidelines for Free and Safe Public Schools* (Washington, D.C., 2012).

[65]*Compare* R.A.V. v. City of St. Paul, 505 U.S. 377 (1992) (invalidating under the First Amendment a St. Paul ordinance barring expression that could arouse anger or resentment on the basis of race, color, creed, religion, or gender) *with* West v. Derby Unified Sch. Dist., 206 F.3d 1358 (10th Cir. 2000); *see infra* text accompanying note 70.

[66]School districts' anti-discrimination provisions that conflict with organizations' expression rights also have been controversial. After the Supreme Court upheld the Boy Scouts' constitutional rights to bar homosexuals from being troop leaders, *Boy Scouts v. Dale*, 530 U.S. 640 (2000), some school districts attempted to deny after-school access to the Boy Scouts to comply with their anti-discrimination policies. *See, e.g.*, Boy Scouts v. Till, 136 F. Supp. 2d 1295 (S.D. Fla. 2001) (finding unconstitutional viewpoint discrimination in the school board's prohibition on the Boy Scouts using school facilities when other groups were allowed access).

[67]*See, e.g.*, Bethel Sch. Dist. No. 403 v. Fraser, 478 U.S. 675 (1986); *supra* text accompanying note 17; Wildman v. Marshalltown Sch. Dist., 249 F.3d 768 (8th Cir. 2001) (finding no impairment of speech rights in requiring a student to apologize to the varsity basketball coach and teammates for distributing a letter criticizing the coach).

[68]Defoe v. Spiva, 625 F.3d 324 (6th Cir. 2010), *rehearing denied en banc*, 674 F.3d 505 (6th Cir. 2011), *cert. denied*, 132 U.S. 399 (2011); *see also* B.W.A. v. Farmington R-7 Sch. Dist., 554 F.3d 734 (8th Cir. 2009). (upholding school district's ban on clothing depicting the Confederate flag); A.M. *ex rel.* McAllum v. Cash, 585 F.3d 214 (5th Cir. 2009) (holding that school district's policy barring Confederate flag displays on school grounds did not violate free expression or equal protection rights and was not unconstitutionally vague).

a school disturbance but acknowledging that school authorities could ban this symbol *without* having to forecast a school disruption.[69] The Tenth Circuit also upheld disciplinary action against a Kansas middle school student for drawing a Confederate flag during math class in violation of the school district's anti-harassment policy.[70] The student had been disciplined numerous times during the school year and had been accused of using racial slurs. The court was persuaded that the school district had reason to believe that the display of the Confederate flag might cause a disruption and interfere with the rights of others, as the school district had already experienced some racial incidents related to the Confederate flag.

Also, the Eleventh Circuit applied a "flexible reasonableness standard" drawn from *Fraser*, instead of *Tinker*'s disruption standard, to assess a student's display of a small Confederate flag to a group of friends during an outdoor lunch break.[71] Holding that school authorities were not liable for disciplining the student for the display that intruded on the school's legitimate function of inculcating manners and habits of civility, the court observed: "Racist and other hateful views can be expressed in a public forum. But an elementary school under its custodial responsibilities may restrict such speech that could crush a child's sense of self-worth."[72] The same court found that a school's unwritten policy banning the display of Confederate flags could be justified because there had been race-based fights in the school, and the flag can be viewed as an offensive symbol of racism.[73]

A few courts, however, have struck down such restrictions on Confederate flag displays. These courts have reasoned that students should prevail in the absence of a link to disruption[74] or if the policies were applied inconsistently. For example, the Sixth Circuit found no evidence that a shirt with the image of a country singer on the front and the Confederate flag on the back, worn to express Southern heritage, would cause a disruption. The court furthermore questioned whether there may have been viewpoint discrimination in applying the school's prohibition on emblems with racial implications.[75]

Several cases have focused on the conflict between expressing religious views and promoting civil expression; these cases are particularly sensitive because they pit free speech and free exercise guarantees against the school's authority to instill basic values, including respect for others. The Third Circuit struck down a Pennsylvania school district's anti-harassment policy challenged by plaintiffs who feared reprisals for voicing their religious views about moral issues, including the harmful effects of homosexuality.[76] The

[69]Barr v. Lafon, 538 F.3d 554 (6th Cir. 2008).

[70]*West*, 206 F.3d 1358; *see also* Governor Wentworth Reg'l Sch. Dist. v. Hendrickson, 421 F. Supp. 2d 410 (D.N.H. 2006) (upholding suspension of a gay student for wearing an arm patch with a swastika and the international "no" symbol superimposed over it, given the friction between gay students and students identifying themselves as "rednecks" and the administrators' need to promote safety), *vacated as moot*, 201 F. App'x 7 (1st Cir. 2007).

[71]Denno v. Sch. Bd., 218 F.3d 1267, 1272 (11th Cir. 2000).

[72]*Id.* at 1273.

[73]Scott v. Sch. Bd., 324 F.3d 1246 (11th Cir. 2003).

[74]*See, e.g.*, Bragg v. Swanson, 371 F. Supp. 2d 814 (S.D. W. Va. 2005) (overturning disciplinary action against a student for wearing a T-shirt displaying the Confederate flag in observance of his Southern heritage and finding the policy prohibiting displays of the Rebel flag within the category of racist symbols to be overbroad).

[75]Castorina *ex rel.* Rewt v. Madison Cnty. Sch. Bd., 246 F.3d 536 (6th Cir. 2001); *infra* text accompanying note 131.

[76]Saxe v. State Coll. Area Sch. Dist., 240 F.3d 200 (3d Cir. 2001); *see also* Flaherty v. Keystone Oaks Sch. Dist., 247 F. Supp. 2d 698 (W.D. Pa. 2003) (finding that student handbook policies did not adequately define "abusive," "offensive," "harassment," and "inappropriate," so disciplinary action against a student for postings on a website message board could not be based on the vague and overbroad policy).

court reviewed existing anti-discrimination laws to refute the district court's conclusion that the policy simply curtailed expression already prohibited under such federal and state laws. The court found no evidence that the policy was necessary to advance the recognized compelling government interests in maintaining an orderly school and protecting the rights of others. Concluding that the policy was unconstitutionally overbroad, the court reasoned that the policy went beyond expression that could be curtailed under the *Tinker* disruption standard.

Yet most other anti-harassment or anti-bullying policies have not been struck down, even if the students have prevailed in their free speech claims. For example, a year after the Third Circuit decision discussed above, the same court upheld a school district's anti-harassment policy enacted to respond to incidents of race-based conflicts and narrowly designed to reduce racially divisive expression. Although finding that the policy as applied violated the students' expression rights in this case, the court voiced approval of the school's anti-harassment provision.[77]

The Ninth Circuit found the second prong of the *Tinker* standard to be controlling when it ruled that a student wearing a T-shirt degrading homosexuality "'collides with the rights of other students' in the most fundamental way."[78] The court reasoned that the school is allowed to prohibit such expression, regardless of the adoption of a valid anti-harassment policy, so long as it can show that the restriction is necessary to prevent the violation of other students' rights *or* a substantial disruption of school activities. The court disagreed with the suggestion that injurious slurs interfering with the rights of others cannot be barred unless they *also* are disruptive, reasoning that the two *Tinker* prongs are independent restrictions.[79]

But other courts have applied the *Tinker* disruption standard in ruling that students have a right to express their religious views that denounce homosexuality.[80] The Seventh Circuit found a T-shirt with "Be Happy, Not Gay" to be much less offensive than the expression in the Ninth Circuit case above and not linked to a substantial disruption.[81] Thus, the court ruled that school authorities could not bar students from wearing the shirt because "people in our society do not have a legal right to prevent criticism of their beliefs or for that matter their way of life."[82] Reasoning that in the absence of fighting words, there is no "generalized 'hurt feelings'" defense to a high school's impairment of students'

[77]Sypniewski v. Warren Hills Reg'l Bd. of Educ., 307 F.3d 243 (3d Cir. 2002) (upholding the policy but ordering the phrase banning speech that "creates ill will" to be eliminated as it reached some protected expression). *See infra* text accompanying note 128 for a discussion of the application of the policy. Also upholding school anti-harassment policies while ruling in favor of student plaintiffs, see *Laysbock v. Hermitage School District*, 650 F.3d 205 (3d Cir. 2011); *infra* text accompanying note 88; Zamecnik v. Sch. Dist. # 204, 636 F.3d 874 (7th Cir. 2011); *infra* text accompanying note 81.

[78]Harper v. Poway Unified Sch. Dist., 445 F.3d 1166, 1178 (9th Cir. 2006) (quoting Tinker v. Des Moines Indep. Sch. Dist., 393 U.S. 503, 508 (1969)), *cert. granted, judgment vacated, and case remanded to dismiss as moot*, 549 U.S. 1262 (2007).

[79]*Harper*, 445 F.3d at 1180; *see also* Kowalski v. Berkeley Cnty. Schs., 652 F.3d 565 (4th Cir. 2011), *cert. denied*, 132 S. Ct. 1095 (2012); *infra* text accompanying note 93.

[80]*See, e.g.*, Nixon v. N. Local Sch. Dist., 383 F. Supp. 2d 965, 971–74 (S.D. Ohio 2005) (rejecting school administrators' assertion that a shirt denigrating homosexuality, Islam, and abortion was "plainly offensive" under *Fraser*; applying *Tinker* instead and finding no disruption or evidence that the expression interfered with the rights of others).

[81]Zamecnik v. Sch. Dist. #204, 636 F.3d 874, 877 (7th Cir. 2011) (citing Nuxoll *ex rel.* Nuxoll v. Ind. Prairie Sch. Dist. No. 204, 523 F.3d 668, 676 (7th Cir. 2008)).

[82]*Zamecnik*, 636 F.3d at 876.

free expression rights,[83] the court recognized that the expression could not be curtailed based on the "hecklers' veto.[84] Otherwise, those opposing the expression could always stifle speakers simply by mounting a riot. Yet the court did not enjoin enforcement of the school's rule that prohibited students from making derogatory comments referring to race, ethnicity, religion, gender, sexual orientation, or disability. Since the Supreme Court has not rendered an opinion in these sensitive cases, the collision of religious views and anti-harassment policies seems destined to remain controversial.

Electronic Expression

The most volatile current disputes involve Internet expression, particularly pertaining to social networks. These cases are particularly troublesome because students often prepare and disseminate the materials from their homes, but their expression is immediately available to the entire school population and beyond. Although the judiciary has not spoken with a single voice on the First Amendment issues raised in these cases, most courts have applied the *Tinker* disruption standard in assessing Internet expression.[85] With the increasing use of cellular phones and the amount of material posted on Facebook, MySpace, and other social networking sites, legal activity in this arena is bound to increase. A 2011 report indicated that teens on average sent more than 100 text messages per day.[86] And concerns over students sending sexually explicit or suggestive messages electronically are resulting in legislative responses to curtail such "sexting."[87]

Students have prevailed in several challenges to disciplinary actions for the creation of web pages or postings on social networks that have originated from their homes. For example, the full Third Circuit in 2011 rendered decisions favoring students' expression rights in two cases that had generated conflicting decisions by different Third Circuit panels.[88] At issue were mock MySpace profiles of the school principals that were vulgar and linked the principals to drugs, alcohol, sexual abuse, and other degrading activities. Finding no disruption of the educational process, the appeals court required off-campus

[83]*Id.* at 877.

[84]*Id.* at 879; *see* Brown v. Louisiana, 383 U.S. 131 (1966) (reversing convictions under Louisiana's breach of peace statute of five African American citizens who refused to leave a segregated public library; any disorder was caused by critics of the passive demonstrators and could not be the basis for penalizing the nonviolent protestors).

[85]393 U.S. 503, 508 (1969); *supra* text accompanying note 13.

[86]Digital Media Learning Central, *An Analytical Take on Youth, Social Networking, and the Web 2.0: A Few Moments with Amanda Lenhart*, http://dmlcentral.net/newsletter/05/2012/analytical-take-youth-social-networking-and-web-20-few-moments-amanda-lenhart.

[87]The National Conference of State Legislatures (NCSL) reported in 2011 that twenty-one states had introduced legislation on sexting, with fourteen requiring youth offenders to register as sex offenders. *See* NCSL, *2011 Legislation Related to "Sexting": 2011 Year-End Summary* (Jan. 23, 2012), http://www.ncsl.org/default.aspx?tabid=22127. *But see* T.V. v. Smith-Green Cmty. Sch. Corp., 807 F. Supp. 2d 767 (N.D. Ind. 2011) (invalidating suspension from extracurricular activities of students who took sexually suggestive pictures of themselves at a slumber party and posted them on the Internet; reasoning that the photos did not constitute child pornography under state law or pose a threat of a school disruption).

[88]Layshock v. Hermitage Sch. Dist., 650 F.3d 205 (3d Cir. 2011), *cert. denied sub nom.* J.S. *ex rel.* Snyder v. Blue Mountain Sch. Dist., 132 S. Ct 1097 (2012); *J.S. ex. rel.* Snyder v. Blue Mountain Sch. Dist., 650 F.3d 915 (3d. 915 (3d Cir. 2011), *cert. denied*, 132 S. Ct. 1097 (2012); *see also* R.S. v. Minnewaska Area Sch. Dist., No. 2149, 2012 WL 3870868 (D. Minn. Sept. 6, 2012) (finding a valid claim that school officials violated a middle school student's free speech rights by disciplining her for Facebook posts critical of a school employee and whoever alerted authorities; school personnel also implicated her Fourth Amendment rights by searching her Facebook posts against her will).

expression to be linked to a school disruption to justify disciplinary action. The court cited an earlier Second Circuit decision in which the appeals court struck down disciplinary action against students for off-campus distribution of a satirical magazine with some vulgar language because an adverse impact on the school was lacking.[89] The Third Circuit reasoned that school districts cannot punish students for expression that originates outside school and does not create a substantial disruption of the school environment.[90] However, the school policies requiring students to express their ideas in a respectful manner and to refrain from verbal abuse were not found to be overbroad.

Not all courts have agreed with the Third Circuit's stand that a link to a disruption is required for students' off-campus Internet expression to be curtailed. The Second Circuit ruled in favor of school authorities who prevented a student from running for senior class secretary because of a vulgar blog entry she posted from home that urged others to complain to the school administrators about a change in scheduling an event, Jamfest, an annual battle of the bands concert.[91] The court found that school officials reasonably could conclude that the expression might disrupt student government functions. Also at issue were T-shirts supporting her freedom of speech that students planned to wear to the school assembly where candidates for the class offices were to give their speeches. Acknowledging that the shirts might be protected under *Tinker* if not linked to a disruption, the court held that the school defendants were entitled to qualified immunity on this claim as well because the rights at issue were not clearly established.

The same court in an earlier case also supported a semester expulsion of a student for displaying in his instant messaging buddy icon a drawing of a pistol firing at a person's head with the caption "Kill Mr. VenderMolen," his English teacher. The court found the icon, although displayed outside of school, violated school rules and disrupted school operations.[92]

[89]Thomas v. Bd. of Educ., 607 F.2d 1043 (2d Cir. 1979). In 2011, the Second Circuit, which rendered *Thomas,* distinguished the off-campus distribution of print material at issue in *Thomas* from electronic expression initiated from home that reaches a broad school audience with one click. Doninger v. Niehoff, 642 F.3d 334, 346–47 (2d Cir. 2011), *cert. denied*, 132 S. Ct. 499 (2011); *infra* text accompanying note 91.

[90]*Layshock*, 650 F.3d 205; *J.S. ex rel. Synder*, 650 F.3d 915; *see also* J.C. v. Beverly Hills Unified Sch. Dist., 711 F. Supp. 2d 1094 (C.D. Cal. 2010) (finding a violation of a student's free speech rights in disciplinary action imposed for posting a YouTube video that was disparaging toward a classmate because there was not a sufficient link to a school disruption); Mahaffey v. Aldrich, 236 F. Supp. 2d 779 (E.D. Mich. 2002) (finding an insufficient connection between the disruption of any school activity and a student's website called "Satan's Web Page," that contained likes and dislikes, including a list of people he wished would die); Emmett v. Kent Sch. Dist. No. 415, 92 F. Supp. 2d 1088 (W.D. Wash. 2000) (invalidating a student's suspension for creating a website on which he posted mock obituaries of students and allowed visitors to the site to vote on who would "die" next).

[91]*Doninger*, 642 F.3d 334; *see also* Bell v. Itawamba Cnty. Sch. Bd., 859 F. Supp. 2d 834 (N.D. Miss. 2012) (upholding disciplinary action against a student for the Internet posting of a vulgar rap song that accused two school coaches of improper contact with female students). *But see* TC v. Valley Cent. Sch. Dist., 777 F. Supp. 2d 577 (S.D.N.Y. 2011) (finding a violation of free speech rights, in addition to racial discrimination, in the suspension of a student who possessed a rap song with offensive lyrics because there was no evidence that the lyrics created a distraction).

[92]Wisniewski v. Bd. of Educ., 494 F.3d 34 (2d Cir. 2007); *see also* O.Z. v. Bd. of Trustees, No. CV 08-5671 ODW (AJWx), 2008 U.S. Dist. LEXIS 110409 (C.D. Cal. Sept. 9, 2008) (upholding disciplinary transfer of a student who created and posted a video during spring break that dramatized her teacher's murder); Requa v. Kent Sch. Dist. No. 415, 492 F. Supp. 2d 1272 (W.D. Wash. 2007) (denying a preliminary injunction to a student who was suspended for posting on YouTube a video he had secretly filmed of one of his teachers bending over with a classmate standing behind her making pelvic thrusts in her direction); J.S. v. Bethlehem Area Sch. Dist., 807 A.2d 847 (Pa. 2002) (upholding a student's expulsion for creating a website on his home computer that contained derogatory comments about teachers and administrators and a graphic depiction of the algebra teacher's death because the off-campus activities substantially disrupted the school).

In 2011, the Fourth Circuit upheld West Virginia school authorities in suspending a student for creating a website primarily used to ridicule a classmate with accusations that she was a slut with herpes.[93] The disciplined student alleged that the suspension violated her free speech rights because the expression was private speech initiated from her home. But the court sided with the school administrators who reasoned that the student had created a "hate website" in violation of the school's policy forbidding "harassment, bullying, and intimidation."[94] The court concluded that the student's website "materially and substantially interferes with the requirements of appropriate discipline in the operation of the school and collides with the rights of others," seeming to rely on both prongs of the *Tinker* standard.[95] The court emphasized that conduct does not have to physically originate in the school building or during the school day to affect the learning environment and the rights of others.[96]

In these cases, the key determinant of disciplinary action appears to be whether the material created off campus has a direct and detrimental impact on the school. But since the Supreme Court has refused to review these decisions, and federal appellate courts have rendered a range of opinions, school personnel have insufficient guidance as to the application of the First Amendment to electronic expression that originates off school grounds. Given students' preference to communicate electronically and the growing popularity of social networking sites, texting, and blogs, Supreme Court clarification of the First Amendment standard is sorely needed.

The National School Boards Association (NSBA), joined by several other professional education organizations, has argued that the Internet has blurred the line between off-campus and in-school expression. The NSBA has contended that if the expression pertains to members of the school community, it should be considered in-school speech and subject to sanctions, regardless of its origin.[97] In the absence of a Supreme Court ruling, the only consolation for school authorities is that they likely can claim immunity for disciplining students for their electronic expression because the law on this topic is far from clearly established.

Time, Place, and Manner Regulations

Although private expression enjoys greater constitutional protection than does school-sponsored expression, the judiciary consistently has upheld reasonable policies regulating the time, place, and manner of private expression. For example, students can be

[93]Kowalski v. Berkeley Cnty. Schs., 652 F.3d 565 (4th Cir. 2011), *cert. denied*, 132 S. Ct. 1095 (2012). The student originally was suspended for ten days, which was reduced to five days, and she received a ninety-day social suspension from school-related activities.

[94]652 F.3d at 574.

[95]*Id.* at 572 (quoting Tinker v. Des Moines Indep. Sch. Dist., 393 U.S. 503, 513 (1969)). The Fourth Circuit reasoned that expression interfering with another's rights creates the necessary disruption to trigger *Tinker*'s exclusion from constitutional protection.

[96]Kowalski also claimed that she did not receive an adequate opportunity to be heard, but the court concluded that notice of the charges and an opportunity to refute them were sufficient for a short-term suspension. *See also* S.J.W. *ex rel.* Wilson v. Lee's Summit R-7 Sch. Dist., 696 F.3d 771 (8th Cir. 2012) (holding that students suspended for creating a racist and sexist website and blog were not entitled to a preliminary injunction lifting their suspensions).

[97]Nat'l Sch. Bds. Ass'n, amicus brief in support of petition for certiorari in *Blue Mountain School District v. Snyder*, No. 11-502 (2011). If the Supreme Court would consider student electronic expression to be "in school" so long as it targets the school community, this would resolve the debate over whether *Fraser*'s exclusion of lewd and vulgar expression from constitutional protection applies to Internet expression.

prohibited from voicing political and ideological views and distributing literature during instructional time. Additionally, school authorities can ban literature distribution near the doors of classrooms while class is in session, near building exits during fire drills, and on stairways when classes are changing to ensure that the distribution of student publications does not impinge upon other school activities. The Fifth Circuit reasoned that student literature distribution could be prohibited in the cafeteria to maintain order and discipline because ample other opportunities were available for students to distribute their materials at school.[98]

Time, place, and manner regulations, however, must be reasonable, content neutral, and uniformly applied to expressive activities. Also, they cannot restrict more speech than necessary to ensure nondisruptive distribution of materials. School officials must provide students with specific guidelines regarding when and where they can express their ideas and distribute materials.[99] Moreover, literature distribution cannot be relegated to remote times or places either inside or outside the school building, and regulations must not inhibit any person's right to accept or reject literature that is distributed in accordance with the rules. Policies governing demonstrations should convey to students that they have the right to gather, distribute petitions, and express their ideas under nondisruptive circumstances. If regulations do not precisely inform demonstrators of behavior that is prohibited, the judiciary may conclude that punishment cannot be imposed.

STUDENT-INITIATED CLUBS

Free expression and related association rights have arisen in connection with the formation and recognition of student clubs. Freedom of association is not specifically included among First Amendment protections, but the Supreme Court has held that associational rights are "implicit in the freedoms of speech, assembly, and petition."[100] Public school pupils have not prevailed in asserting that free expression and association rights shield student-initiated social organizations or secret societies with exclusive membership usually determined by a vote of the clubs' members.[101]

In contrast, prohibitions on student-initiated organizations with *open* membership are vulnerable to First Amendment challenge. Even before Congress enacted the Equal Access Act (EAA), it was generally accepted that public school access policies for student meetings must be content neutral and cannot disadvantage selected groups. The EAA, enacted in 1984, stipulates that if federally assisted secondary schools provide a limited open forum for noncurricular student groups to meet during noninstructional time, access cannot be denied based on the religious, political, philosophical, or other content of the groups' meetings.[102] The EAA was championed by the Religious Right, but its protection encompasses far more than student-initiated religious expression.

The Supreme Court in 1990 rejected an Establishment Clause challenge to the EAA in *Board of Education of the Westside Community Schools v. Mergens*.[103] The Court held

[98]Morgan v. Plano Indep. Sch. Dist., 589 F.3d 740 (5th Cir. 2009), *cert. denied*, 130 S. Ct. 3503 (2010).
[99]*See id.*
[100]Healy v. James, 408 U.S. 169, 181 (1972).
[101]*See* Passel v. Ft. Worth Indep. Sch. Dist., 453 S.W.2d 888 (Tex. App. 1970); Robinson v. Sacramento Unified Sch. Dist., 53 Cal. Rptr. 781 (Ct. App. 1966).
[102]20 U.S.C. § 4071 (2012).

that if a federally assisted secondary school allows even one noncurricular group to use school facilities during noninstructional time, the EAA guarantees equal access for other noncurricular student groups. Of course, meetings that threaten a disruption can be barred. Moreover, school authorities can decline to establish a limited forum for student-initiated meetings and thus confine school access to student organizations that are an extension of the curriculum, such as drama groups, language clubs, and athletic teams.

Controversies have surfaced over what constitutes a curriculum-related group, since the EAA is triggered only if noncurriculum student groups are allowed school access during noninstructional time. Many of these cases have focused on the Gay-Straight Alliance (GSA). For example, after the Salt Lake City School Board implemented a policy denying school access to all noncurriculum student groups, it rejected the GSA's petition to hold meetings in a public high school. The GSA then asserted that it was related to the curriculum and should be treated like other curriculum-related groups. The federal district court ultimately enjoined school authorities from denying access to the student club designed to address issues related to the school's history and sociology courses, even though the club's major focus was on the rights of lesbian, gay, bisexual, and transgender (LGBT) persons.[104] Also, a California federal district court ruled that a school board had established a limited forum by allowing some noncurriculum student groups to meet during noninstructional time and thus could not discriminate against the GSA. The board claimed that the club was not protected under the EAA because it was related to the sex education curriculum, but the court held that the board cannot foreclose access to its limited forum "merely by labeling a group curriculum-related."[105]

The Eighth Circuit addressed a Minnesota school district's distinction between *curricular* student groups that were allowed to use the public address system and other forms of communication and *noncurricular* groups that could not use such communication avenues or participate in fundraising activities or field trips.[106] Concluding that some groups identified as curricular, such as cheerleading and synchronized swimming, were not related to material regularly taught in the curriculum, the court enjoined the district from treating the club, Straights and Gays for Equality, differently from other student groups. More recently, a New York federal district court recognized a sufficient EAA claim where the school district did not give equal access and benefits to the student GSA, such as not recognizing the GSA with other student groups on the district's web page.[107] Even if agreed that a secondary

[103]496 U.S. 226 (1990) (rejecting the contention that only noncurricular *advocacy* groups are protected under the EAA).

[104]E. High Sch. Prism Club v. Seidel, 95 F. Supp. 2d 1239 (D. Utah 2000).

[105]Colin v. Orange Unified Sch. Dist., 83 F. Supp. 2d 1135, 1146 (C.D. Cal. 2000).

[106]Straights & Gays for Equality (SAGE) v. Osseo Area Schs., 471 F.3d 908 (8th Cir. 2006); *see also* Gay-Straight Alliance v. Sch. Bd., 483 F. Supp. 2d 1224 (S.D. Fla. 2007) (enjoining the school district from prohibiting GSA meetings based on the substantial likelihood that the GSA would prevail in establishing that it was not a "sex-based club," to which student access can be restricted until age eighteen under state law; also finding no conflict between the club's purpose and the school's abstinence-based policy).

[107]Pratt v. Indian River Cent. Sch. Dist., 803 F. Supp. 2d 135 (N.D.N.Y. 2011). This case involved other claims on various grounds pertaining to differential treatment of a student and his sister based on sexual orientation. *But see* Caudillo v. Lubbock Indep. Sch. Dist., 311 F. Supp. 2d 550 (N.D. Tex. 2004) (upholding school authorities in denying the Gay and Proud Youth Group's request to hold meetings and post flyers at school because some of the group's materials were inappropriate for minors and did not promote the district's abstinence policy).

school has *not* established a limited forum, it still cannot exert viewpoint discrimination against particular curriculum-related groups.[108]

STUDENT APPEARANCE

Fads and fashions in hairstyles and clothing have regularly evoked litigation as educators have attempted to exert some control over pupil appearance. Courts have been called upon to weigh students' interests in selecting their hairstyle and attire against school authorities' interests in preventing disruptions and promoting school objectives.

Hairstyle

Considerable judicial activity in the 1970s focused on school regulations governing the length of male students' hair. The Supreme Court, however, refused to hear appeals of these cases, and federal circuit courts reached different conclusions in determining the legality of policies governing student hairstyle. The First, Fourth, Seventh, and Eighth Circuits declared that hairstyle regulations impaired students' First Amendment freedom of symbolic expression, the Fourteenth Amendment right to personal liberty, or the right to privacy included in the Ninth Amendment's unenumerated rights.[109] In contrast, the Third, Fifth, Sixth, Ninth, and Tenth Circuits upheld grooming policies pertaining to pupil hairstyle, finding no constitutional rights at stake.[110]

If school officials have offered health or safety reasons for grooming regulations, such as requiring hair nets, shower caps, and other hair restraints intended to protect students from injury or to promote sanitation, the policies typically have been upheld. Furthermore, restrictions on male students' hairstyles at vocational schools have been upheld to create a positive image for potential employers visiting the school for recruitment purposes. Special grooming regulations have been endorsed as conditions of participation in extracurricular activities for legitimate health or safety reasons and, in some instances, to enhance the school's image.[111] Of course, students can be disciplined for hairstyles that cause a disruption, such as hair groomed or dyed in a manner that distracts classmates from educational activities.

It appears that different hair length and hairstyle restrictions can be applied to male and female students to reflect community norms or to deter gang activity. In two cases, the Texas Supreme Court rejected claims that restrictions applied only to the length of

[108]Intentionally left blank so that the remaining footnotes in the chapter can remain numbered as is.

[109]*See* Massie v. Henry, 455 F.2d 779 (4th Cir. 1972); Bishop v. Colaw, 450 F.2d 1069 (8th Cir. 1971); Richards v. Thurston, 424 F.2d 1281 (1st Cir. 1970); Breen v. Kahl, 419 F.2d 1034 (7th Cir. 1969).

[110]*See* Zeller v. Donegal Sch. Dist., 517 F.2d 600 (3d Cir. 1975), *overruling* Stull v. Sch. Bd. of W. Beaver Jr.-Sr. High Sch., 459 F.2d 339 (3d Cir. 1972); King v. Saddleback Jr. Coll. Dist., 445 F.2d 932 (9th Cir. 1971); Freeman v. Flake, 448 F.2d 258 (10th Cir. 1971); Jackson v. Dorrier, 424 F.2d 213 (6th Cir. 1970); Ferrell v. Dallas Indep. Sch. Dist., 392 F.2d 697 (5th Cir. 1968).

[111]*See, e.g.*, Davenport v. Randolph Cnty. Bd. of Educ., 730 F.2d 1395 (11th Cir. 1984) (finding neither arbitrary nor unreasonable a coach's requirement that student athletes, as representatives of the school, must be clean-shaven); Menora v. Ill. High Sch. Ass'n, 683 F.2d 1030 (7th Cir. 1982) (holding that Jewish basketball players had no First Amendment right to wear yarmulkes fastened by bobby pins in violation of the state high school association rule forbidding players from wearing hats or other headgear during games for safety reasons); Long v. Zopp, 476 F.2d 180 (4th Cir. 1973) (recognizing that legitimate health and safety concerns might justify a restriction on hair length during football season, but finding no justification for denying a letter to a student who violated such a restriction after football season ended).

male students' hair constituted sex discrimination, refusing to use the state constitution to micromanage public schools.[112] Also, a Louisiana federal district court upheld a school rule forbidding only male students from wearing braids as justified to promote unity and deter gang activity.[113]

But hairstyle regulations cannot be arbitrary or devoid of an educational rationale. For example, a Texas federal district court ruled that school officials failed to show a valid justification to impair Native American students' protected expression right to wear long hair that posed no disruption.[114] More recently, the Fifth Circuit relied on a Texas law protecting religious liberties in ruling that a school district violated a Native American student's rights to express his religious beliefs by requiring him to wear one long braid tucked in his shirt or a bun on top of his head instead of wearing his two long braids in plain view.[115]

Attire

Although public school students' hair length has subsided as a major subject of litigation, other appearance fads have become controversial as students have asserted a First Amendment right to express themselves through their attire at school. Some courts have distinguished attire restrictions from hair regulations because clothes, unlike hair length, can be changed after school. Even in situations where students' rights to govern their appearance have been recognized, the judiciary has upheld restrictions on attire that is immodest, disruptive, unsanitary, or promotes illegal behavior.

If school authorities can link particular attire to gang activities or other school violence, restrictions likely will be upheld. For example, a Nebraska federal district court in 2012 supported school authorities in suspending students for wearing bracelets and T-shirts with the phrase, "Julius RIP" (rest in peace) in remembrance of their friend who had been shot at his apartment complex allegedly for gang-related reasons.[116] The court agreed with school authorities that the attire could be banned in the interest of safety because it might trigger violence at the school. Two years earlier, a West Virginia federal district court upheld a student's suspension for writing a slogan on his hands about freeing a classmate who was accused of shooting a police officer. The court agreed with school officials' prediction that the expression would contribute to gang-related disturbances.[117]

Several recent controversies have focused on students wearing cancer awareness bracelets with the message, "I love Boobies (Keep a Breast)." Some school authorities have argued that the bracelets are vulgar and can be barred under *Fraser*. However, a Pennsylvania federal district court found no evidence that these bracelets were linked to a disruption and did not consider the word "boobies" to be vulgar in this context, so it granted a preliminary injunction against the school district's ban on wearing the bracelets.[118]

[112]Bd. of Trs. v. Toungate, 958 S.W.2d 365 (Tex. 1997); Barber v. Colo. Indep. Sch. Dist., 901 S.W.2d 447 (Tex. 1995); *infra* text accompanying note 121.

[113]Fenceroy v. Morehouse Parish Sch. Bd., No. 05-0480, 2006 U.S. Dist. LEXIS 949 (W.D. La. Jan. 6, 2006). *But see* McMillen v. Itawamba Cnty. Sch. Dist., 702 F. Supp. 2d 699 (N.D. Miss. 2010) (upholding a female student's right to wear a tuxedo to the prom and to bring her girlfriend as her date).

[114]Ala. & Coushatta Tribes v. Trs., 817 F. Supp. 1319 (E.D. Tex. 1993), *remanded*, 20 F.3d 469 (5th Cir. 1994).

[115]A.A. v. Needville Indep. Sch. Dist., 611 F.3d 248 (5th Cir. 2010).

[116]Kuhr v. Millard Pub. Sch. Dist., No. 8:09CV363, 2012 U.S. Dist. LEXIS 56189 (D. Neb. Apr. 23, 2012).

[117]Brown v. Cabell Cnty. Bd. of Educ., 714 F. Supp. 2d 587 (S.D. W. Va. 2010).

[118]B.H. v. Easton Area Sch. Dist., 827 F. Supp. 2d 392 (E.D. Pa. Apr. 12, 2011).

DRESS CODES. Under the principle established in *Fraser*, lewd and vulgar expression is outside the protective arm of the First Amendment. Thus, indecent attire can be curtailed regardless of whether the attire would meet the *Tinker* test of threatening a disruption. For example, an Idaho federal district court held that a school could prevent a student from wearing a T-shirt that depicted three high school administrators drunk on school grounds, noting that the student had no free expression right to portray administrators in a fashion that would undermine their authority and compromise the school's efforts to educate students about the harmful effects of alcohol.[119] A Georgia federal district court also upheld the suspension of a student who wore a T-shirt with the phrases "kids have civil rights too" and "even adults lie."[120] The court ruled that wearing the shirt was the last incident in a series of disruptions justifying the student's suspension.

A few courts have upheld dress codes that prohibit male students from wearing earrings, rejecting the assertion that jewelry restrictions must be applied equally to male and female students. In an illustrative case, an Illinois federal district court found the school district's ban on male students wearing earrings rationally related to the school's legitimate objective of inhibiting the influence of gangs, as earrings were used to convey gang-related messages.[121] Also, while acknowledging the absence of a gang-related justification, an Indiana appeals court nonetheless upheld a school district's ban on male students wearing earrings in elementary schools as advancing legitimate educational objectives and community values supporting different attire standards for males and females.[122]

In a New Mexico case, the federal district court upheld a student's suspension for wearing "sagging" pants in violation of the school's dress code.[123] Rejecting the student's contention that his attire conveyed an African American cultural message, the court noted that "sagging" pants could as easily be associated with gang affiliation or simply reflect a fashion trend among adolescents. The Seventh Circuit found no First Amendment right for gifted students to wear a T-shirt they had designed that depicted in a satirical manner a physically disabled child with the word "gifties." The students wore their shirt to protest the election to select a class shirt, which they alleged was rigged because school authorities did not like their design.[124]

In one of the most expansive interpretations of *Fraser*, the Sixth Circuit upheld a school district's decision to prohibit students from wearing Marilyn Manson T-shirts. The appeals court agreed with school authorities that the shirts were offensive, promoted destructive conduct, and were counter to the school's efforts to denounce drugs and promote human dignity and democratic ideals.[125] The court held that under *Fraser*, schools

[119]Gano v. Sch. Dist. No. 411, 674 F. Supp. 796 (D. Idaho 1987); *see also* Madrid v. Anthony, 510 F. Supp. 2d 425 (S.D. Tex. 2007) (upholding a ban on students, who were mostly Hispanic, wearing T-shirts with "We Are Not Criminals" to protest pending immigration legislation; school authorities instituted the ban to curb the escalating racial tension in the school that threatened student safety).

[120]Smith v. Greene Cnty. Sch. Dist., 100 F. Supp. 2d 1354 (M.D. Ga. 2000); *see also* Broussard v. Sch. Bd., 801 F. Supp. 1526 (E.D. Va. 1992) (upholding one-day suspension of a student who refused to change her shirt printed with the words "Drugs Suck," because "suck" is offensive and vulgar to many people).

[121]Olesen v. Bd. of Educ., 676 F. Supp. 820 (N.D. Ill. 1987); *see also* Barber v. Colo. Indep. Sch. Dist., 901 S.W.2d 447 (Tex. 1995) (upholding earring as well as hair-length restrictions applied only to male students).

[122]Hines v. Caston Sch. Corp, 651 N.E.2d 330 (Ind. Ct. App. 1995).

[123]Bivens *ex rel.* Green v. Albuquerque Pub. Schs., 899 F. Supp. 556 (D.N.M. 1995), *aff'd mem.*, 131 F.3d 151 (10th Cir. 1997).

[124]Brandt v. Bd. of Educ., 480 F.3d 460 (7th Cir. 2007).

can prohibit student expression that is inconsistent with its basic educational mission even though such speech might be protected by the First Amendment outside the school environment.

Several restrictive dress codes have received judicial endorsement. The Fifth Circuit upheld a dress code prohibiting any clothing with printed words except for school logos as content neutral.[126] Also upholding a restrictive dress code as reasonable to create unity and focus attention on learning, the Sixth Circuit found no violation of a student's free expression rights, her right to wear clothes of her choice, or her father's right to control his daughter's attire.[127]

However, as with hairstyle regulations, school authorities must have an educational rationale for attire restrictions, such as enhancing learning or preventing class disruptions. The Third Circuit struck down a prohibition on wearing T-shirts with the comedian Jeff Foxworthy's "red-neck sayings," as not sufficiently linked to racial harassment or other disruptive activity.[128] A New York federal court denied a school board's request to dismiss a student's claim that her free expression rights were violated by school authorities who said she could not wear a necklace supporting the war in Iraq because it could be viewed as violating the school's policy prohibiting gang-related clothing.[129] A student also prevailed in wearing a T-shirt depicting three black silhouettes holding firearms with "NRA" and "Shooting Sports Camp" superimposed over the silhouettes. School authorities asked the student to change the shirt, contending that it conflicted with the school's mission of deterring violence. Applying *Tinker* instead of *Fraser*, the Fourth Circuit held that the student's free expression rights were overriding because the shirt was not disruptive and did not promote gun use.[130]

[125]Boroff v. Van Wert City Bd. of Educ., 220 F.3d 465 (6th Cir. 2000); *see also* Dariano v. Morgan Hill Unified Sch. Dist., 822 F. Supp. 2d 1037 (N.D. Cal. 2011) (rejecting a First Amendment challenge to a dress code that barred American flag emblems where there had been conflicts between Hispanic and Caucasian students).

[126]Palmer *ex rel.* Palmer v. Waxahachie Indep. Sch. Dist., 579 F.3d 502 (5th Cir. 2009), *cert. denied*, 130 S. Ct. 1055 (2010).

[127]Blau v. Ft. Thomas Pub. Sch. Dist., 401 F.3d 381 (6th Cir. 2005). Among other things, the code prohibited revealing or baggy clothing; tops and bottoms that do not overlap; visible body piercing (other than ears); clothing that is distressed or has holes; flip-flop sandals or high platform shoes; pants, shorts, or skirts that are not solid navy, black, khaki, or white; tops with writing on them and logos larger than the size of a quarter except for the school's logo; and tops that are not a solid color. *Id.* at 385–86; *see also* Long v. Bd. of Educ., 121 F. Supp. 2d 621 (W.D. Ky. 2000), *aff'd mem.*, 21 F. App'x 252 (6th Cir. 2001) (upholding a restrictive student dress code devised by a Kentucky school-based council that limits the colors, materials, and type of clothing allowed and bars logos, shorts, cargo pants, jeans, and other specific items; the court found legitimate safety justifications and no intent to suppress free speech).

[128]Sypniewski v. Warren Hills Reg'l Bd. of Educ., 307 F.3d 243 (3d Cir. 2002); *supra* text accompanying note 77; *see also* Stephenson v. Davenport Cmty. Sch. Dist., 110 F.3d 1303 (8th Cir. 1997) (finding a policy prohibiting gang symbols, which was challenged by a student who was forced to remove a small tattoo of a cross on her hand, to give insufficient notice to students of what is prohibited and to allow school officials unfettered discretion to decide what constitutes banned symbols).

[129]Grzywna v. Schenectady Cent. Sch. Dist., 489 F. Supp. 2d 139 (N.D.N.Y. 2006); *see also* DePinto v. Bayonne Bd. of Educ., 514 F. Supp. 2d 633 (D.N.J. 2007) (enjoining school authorities from prohibiting the wearing of buttons depicting Hitler youth to protest the school's dress code; the buttons, while in poor taste, were not disruptive, vulgar, or sexually charged).

[130]Newsom v. Albemarle Cnty. Sch. Bd., 354 F.3d 249 (4th Cir. 2003); *see also* Griggs v. Ft. Wayne Sch. Bd., 359 F. Supp. 2d 731 (N.D. Ind. 2005) (finding no legitimate pedagogical reason to ban a T-shirt with the Marine Creed and a large picture of an M16 rifle, as the shirt did not threaten violence). *But see* Douglass v. Londonderry Sch. Bd., 413 F. Supp. 2d 1 (D.N.H. 2005) (holding that student yearbook editors could refuse to run a senior portrait of a student in trap shooting attire and holding a shotgun; the student editors were not acting under color of state law, and school policy banning props from school portraits did not abridge free speech rights).

In addition, dress codes must not be discriminatorily enforced. The Sixth Circuit ordered a school district to reconsider suspensions of two students who refused to change or turn inside out T-shirts with a country singer on the front and the Confederate flag on the back.[131] School authorities asserted that the shirts violated the school's dress code prohibiting clothing or emblems that contain slogans or words depicting alcohol or tobacco or have illegal, immoral, or racist implications, but the court found no indication of racial tension in the school or that the shirt would likely lead to a disruption. There also was evidence that the dress code had been selectively enforced in a viewpoint-specific manner; students had been allowed to wear shirts celebrating Malcolm X. Thus, the court remanded the case to determine if the students' First Amendment rights had been violated.

Additionally, students cannot be disciplined for expressing their disagreement with a dress code in a nondisruptive manner. Applying *Tinker*, the Eighth Circuit ruled that students had a First Amendment right to wear black armbands to protest the district's student apparel policy. Thus, the students were entitled to injunctive relief, nominal damages, and attorneys' fees.[132]

The Second Circuit relied on *Tinker* in protecting a student's right to wear a shirt expressing political views; the shirt depicted George W. Bush negatively (i.e., calling him "Chicken Hawk in Chief" and linking him to drinking, taking drugs, and being a crook and draft dodger).[133] Reasoning that simply because the expression is in poor taste is not a sufficient reason to curtail students' expression rights, the appeals court interpreted *Fraser* narrowly, concluding that student expression would have to contain sexual innuendos or profanity to be censorable as plainly offensive under *Fraser*. Since neither was at issue, the court applied the *Tinker* disruption standard and found that the student wearing the controversial shirt was not linked to a disruption of the educational process.

STUDENT UNIFORMS. A number of attire controversies could be eliminated if public school students were required to wear uniforms, as is true in many countries. Voluntary and mandatory student uniforms increasingly are being adopted by school districts nationally, especially those in urban settings.[134] Advocates assert that student uniforms eliminate gang-related attire, reduce violence and socioeconomic distinctions, and improve school climate by placing the emphasis on academics rather than fashion fads. And the line is not always clear between restrictive dress codes and student uniforms.

The Fifth Circuit rejected challenges to uniform policies in Louisiana and Texas school districts. Recognizing that attire can communicate a message entitled to First Amendment protection, the court nonetheless reasoned that the student uniform policies are justified by substantial government interests unrelated to suppressing

[131]Castorina *ex rel.* Rewt v. Madison Cnty. Sch. Bd., 246 F.3d 536 (6th Cir. 2001). Other courts have upheld restrictions on Confederate flag displays under anti-harassment policies, finding no viewpoint discrimination; *see supra* text accompanying note 68.

[132]Lowry *ex rel.* Crow v. Watson Chapel Sch. Dist., 540 F.3d 752 (8th Cir. 2008). *But see* Hardwick v. Heyward, No. 4:06-cv-1042-TLW, 2012 WL 761249 (D.S.C. Mar. 8, 2012) (holding that a student could not protest the ban on Confederate flag displays with a shirt depicting the flag, although other nondisruptive "protest" shirts would be allowed).

[133]Guiles v. Marineau, 461 F.3d 320, 322 (2d Cir. 2006).

[134]*See* Erik Hayden, *No Uniform Solution*, Pacific Standard (Nov. 23, 2009), http://www.miller-mccune.com/culture-society/no-uniform-solution-5609/.

expression, such as improving achievement, decreasing disciplinary problems, improving safety, decreasing socioeconomic tensions, and increasing attendance. In the Louisiana case, the court rejected the parents' claim that the uniforms posed a financial burden, noting that the uniforms were inexpensive and a donation program was available for those who could not afford them.[135] In the Texas case, the court noted that parents could apply for their children to be exempt from wearing the uniform based on philosophical or religious objections or medical necessity; thus, the court found no violation of parents' religious freedom or their Fourteenth Amendment right to direct the upbringing of their children.[136]

After the New York City school board adopted a citywide uniform policy for children in elementary schools, a father brought suit claiming that if his child took advantage of the "opt-out" provision, the child would "stick out" in violation of the child's rights.[137] But the Second Circuit held that the opt-out provision adequately addressed parents' rights to direct the upbringing of their children. Courts have not been persuaded that any rights are violated because a stigma is associated with exercising the First Amendment right to be exempt from certain requirements. The Third Circuit also rejected parents' request to use the religious exemption for their children to be exempt from the school district's mandatory dress code based on their atheistic beliefs. The court reasoned that the narrow religious exemption allowed for students to exercise their religious convictions without undermining the goals of the uniform policy.[138]

Since the federal judiciary has recognized that public schools can impose restrictive dress codes and even mandate uniforms for students, perhaps this is depressing challenges to attire regulations. Nonetheless, school officials would be wise to ensure that they have a legitimate educational justification for any grooming or dress restrictions. Policies designed to protect students' health and safety, reduce violence and discipline problems, and enhance learning usually will be endorsed. Given the current student interest in tattoos, body piercing, and other fashion fads and school authorities' concerns about attire linked to gangs and violence, controversies over student appearance in public schools seem likely to persist.

EXTRACURRICULAR ACTIVITIES

School-sponsored activities that are not part of the regular academic program have generated considerable litigation. Almost every secondary school offers some extracurricular activities, and about 80 percent of high school students participate in at least one activity.

[135] Canady v. Bossier Parish Sch. Bd., 240 F.3d 437 (5th Cir. 2001); *see also* Derry v. Marion Cmty. Schs., 790 F. Supp. 2d 839 (N.D. Ind. 2008) (rejecting equal protection and due process challenges to a school district's uniform policy).

[136] Littlefield v. Forney Indep. Sch. Dist., 268 F.3d 275 (5th Cir. 2001) (upholding policy requiring students to wear specific types of shirts or blouses of particular colors with blue or khaki pants, shorts, skirts, or jumpers; specifying that clothing be made of specific materials; requiring certain types of shoes; and prohibiting any clothing suggesting gang affiliation).

[137] Lipsman v. N.Y. City Bd. of Educ., 13 F. App'x 13 (2d Cir. 2000).

[138] Wilkins v. Penns Grove-Carneys Point Reg'l Sch. Dist., 123 F. App'x 493 (3d Cir. 2005); *see also* Jacobs v. Clark Cnty. Sch. Dist., 526 F.3d 419 (9th Cir. 2008) (rejecting free speech and free exercise challenges to a viewpoint- and content-neutral uniform policy); Frudden v. Pilling, 842 F. Supp. 2d 1265 (D. Nev. 2012) (holding that uniform policy did not violate students' or parents' First Amendment rights).

In most states, a not-for-profit private organization regulates interscholastic sports and often has jurisdiction over other competitive activities among private and public schools. The Supreme Court ruled in 2001 that where such associations are extensively entwined with state school officials, they are considered state actors.[139] Thus, these private organizations are subject to constitutional restrictions on their activities and can be liable for constitutional violations.

It is clear that once a state provides public education, students cannot be denied attendance without due process of law,[140] but this state-created property right to attend school does not extend to extracurricular activities. The prevailing view is that conditions can be attached to extracurricular participation, because such participation is a privilege rather than a right.[141] Even though school authorities may not be required by the Fourteenth Amendment to provide due process when denying students extracurricular participation, a hearing for the students to defend their actions is always advisable. And if school boards have established rules for suspending or expelling students from extracurricular activities, they must abide by their adopted policies.

As noted, most states have independent associations that establish rules for interscholastic athletic competition, and courts consistently have indicated that they will not substitute their judgment for that of such associations.[142] Yet courts will invalidate regulations that are arbitrary or not rationally related to the organization's asserted goals. For example, a New York federal district court ruled that private schools stated a valid equal protection claim that the state high school athletic association's rule classifying public and private schools differently lacked a rational relationship to its goal of ensuring equitable competition.[143] Private school plaintiffs presented evidence to refute that private schools have a competitive advantage based on their success.

The remainder of this section provides a brief overview of various features of extracurricular activities that have generated legal activity.

Recruitment and Eligibility

State athletic associations place various restrictions on member public and private schools in terms of recruiting athletes. The Supreme Court ruled in 2007 that the Tennessee Secondary School Athletic Association's enforcement of its anti-recruitment rule against Brentwood Academy, a private school member, does not violate the academy's free expression rights. The Court declared that the anti-recruitment rule strikes "nowhere near

[139]Brentwood Acad. v. Tenn. Secondary Sch. Athletic Ass'n, 531 U.S. 288 (2001); *see also* Tenn. Secondary Sch. Athletic Ass'n v. Brentwood Acad., 551 U.S. 291 (2007); *infra* text accompanying note 144.

[140]*See* Goss v. Lopez, 419 U.S. 565 (1975).

[141]*See, e.g.*, Doe v. Silsbee Indep. Sch. Dist., 440 F. App'x 421 (5th Cir. 2011), *cert. denied*, 131 S. Ct. 2875 (2011) (upholding the removal of a student from the cheerleading squad for refusing to cheer for a basketball player whom she had accused of sexually assaulting her, because students have no constitutional right to participate in extracurricular activities).

[142]*See, e.g.*, Ind. High Sch. Athletic Ass'n v. Watson, 938 N.E.2d 672 (Ind. 2010).

[143]Immaculate Heart Cent. Sch. v. N.Y. State Pub. High Sch. Athletic Ass'n, 797 F. Supp. 2d 204 (N.D.N.Y. 2011) (rejecting the due process claim, however, because participation in interscholastic athletics or in a specific classification is not protected by procedural due process).

the heart of the First Amendment."[144] Recognizing that such associations do not have unlimited authority to condition membership on the relinquishment of constitutional rights, the Court held that they can impose only conditions necessary to manage an efficient and effective high school athletic league. The Court reasoned that the content-neutral restriction on high schools communicating with middle school students is necessary to protect vulnerable students from schools using undue influence to attract athletes and to foster an appropriate competitive environment. Noting that schools make voluntary decisions to join such associations, the Supreme Court reasoned that those electing to do so must abide by the association's reasonable rules.

More recently, the Supreme Court declined to review a decision in which the Sixth Circuit upheld a rule of the Kentucky High School Athletic Association that restricts the amount of merit-based financial aid students may receive and still remain eligible for interscholastic competition.[145] The rule, which was challenged by four private school students, was enacted to deter recruitment of student athletes by private schools. Under the rule, students cannot receive more than 25 percent of their tuition in merit aid, whereas they can receive up to 100 percent in need-based aid. The court reasoned that the rule may not be perfect, but it is a legitimate strategy to limit improper athletic recruitment.

Courts have allowed school authorities considerable flexibility in formulating eligibility requirements for extracurricular activities. Schools can impose conditions such as skill prerequisites for athletic teams, academic and leadership criteria for honor societies,[146] and musical proficiency for band and choral groups. Members of athletic teams and other extracurricular groups often are selected through a competitive process, and students have no inherent right to be chosen. Selection can be based on subjective judgments, and as long as fair procedures are uniformly applied without discrimination, courts will not interfere with such decisions.

One of the most obvious conditions of eligibility is that students can be required to have physical examinations and be in good physical health to participate on athletic teams. School districts want to be certain that rigorous training regimens do not put student athletes at risk because of their health conditions.[147] The Supreme Court also

[144]*Brentwood*, 551 U.S. at 296 (finding also no due process violation as appropriate procedures were followed, and even if there was a closed-door meeting, this presented a harmless infringement of due process rights); *see also* NCAA v. Lasege, 53 S.W.3d 77 (Ky. 2001) (holding that high school and collegiate athletic association rules will not be invalidated unless such associations act arbitrarily and capriciously toward student athletes). Courts also have upheld the exclusion of home-schooled students from interscholastic teams in the absence of state legislation authorizing such participation.

[145]Seger v. Ky. High Sch. Athletic Ass'n, 453 F. App'x 630 (6th Cir. 2011), *cert. denied*, 132 S. Ct. 2432 (2012).

[146]*See, e.g.*, Doninger v. Niehoff, 642 F.3d 334 (2d Cir. 2011), *cert. denied*, 132 S. Ct. 499 (2011) (upholding school authorities in barring a student from running for class office because of a vulgar blog entry that degraded school administrators); *supra* text accompanying note 91; Pfeiffer v. Marion Ctr. Area Sch. Dist., 917 F.2d 779 (3d Cir. 1990) (holding that a pregnant student could be dismissed from the National Honor Society for engaging in premarital sex in violation of the Society's standards).

[147]School districts also are adopting strategies to prevent injuries to student athletes. Given the national attention on concussion-related injuries, many school districts and some states are requiring schools to adopt concussion management plans to educate students, parents, and school personnel about concussion prevention and responses. Also, the nation's largest youth football organization, Pop Warner, has barred some common contact drills to reduce the risk of head injuries. *See, e.g.*, Nat'l Sch. Bds. Ass'n, *Youth Football Organization Adopts New Rules Aimed at Reducing Player Concussions*, Legal Clips (June 21, 2012), http://legalclips.nsba.org/?p=14941. In addition, school districts are placing restrictions on the length of practice sessions and type of attire worn in preseason football training to avoid heat-related injuries. *See, e.g.*, Elliott Francis, *Coaches Prepare for New Preseason Heat Rules in Maryland* (Aug. 8, 2012), http://wamu.org/news/morning_edition/12/08/08/coaches_prepare_for_new_preseason_heat_rules_in_maryland.

has upheld policies requiring student athletes and those participating in other extracurricular activities to submit to random urinalysis as a condition of participation.[148] The imposition of additional health restrictions on athletes with disabilities has generated litigation. Given federal and state protections of such children, school authorities would be wise to have evidence of legitimate health or safety risks before excluding specific children with disabilities from trying out for athletic teams.[149]

Courts generally approve transfer rules and residency requirements as conditions of interscholastic competition. To prevent schools, including private schools, from recruiting student athletes, most state athletic associations prohibit involvement in interscholastic competition for one year after a change in a student's school without a change in the parents' address. Several federal as well as state courts have ruled that such residency requirements applied to public and private schools are rationally related to legitimate government interests and do not place an impermissible burden on students' rights to travel or on their freedom of family association.[150] For example, the Supreme Court of Indiana reversed the courts below in upholding a student's athletic ineligibility following his transfer.[151] The court found evidence that the move was athletically, rather than economically, motivated and thus supported the high school athletic association's rule. The Supreme Court of Oklahoma also upheld application of a transfer rule that made a student ineligible to participate in interscholastic varsity sports for a year, noting that courts should defer to association requirements for eligibility so long as they are consistent and not arbitrary.[152]

Some courts, however, have ordered exceptions where a student's welfare has necessitated the move. For example, the Seventh Circuit concluded that the state athletic association acted arbitrarily and capriciously when it declared a student ineligible for athletic competition for one year after he moved from his divorced father's home to his mother's home in another district because he was not performing well in school.[153] Furthermore, if there are compelling medical reasons necessitating a student's change of residence or the change is necessitated for the student to receive special education services, courts will order exceptions to transfer restrictions. Nonetheless, most residency requirements continue to receive judicial endorsement, even though the impact of voucher and other choice plans on these regulations have not yet been sufficiently addressed.

[148]Bd. of Educ. v. Earls, 536 U.S. 822 (2002); Vernonia Sch. Dist. 47J v. Acton, 515 U.S. 646 (1995).

[149]*See, e.g.*, Doe v. Woodford Cnty. Bd. of Educ., 213 F.3d 921 (6th Cir. 2000) (upholding exclusion of a student with hemophilia and hepatitis B from athletic participation that would put him at increased risk of physical injury).

[150]*See, e.g.*, Niles v. Univ. Interscholastic League, 715 F.2d 1027 (5th Cir. 1983); *see also* Ryan v. Cal. Interscholastic Fed'n, 114 Cal. Rptr. 2d 798 (Ct. App. 2001) (upholding residency requirement for a student transferring from another country).

[151]Ind. High Sch. Athletic Ass'n v. Watson, 938 N.E.2d 672 (Ind. 2010).

[152]Morgan v. Okla. Secondary Sch. Activities Ass'n, 207 P.3d 362 (Okla. 2009).

[153]Crane v. Ind. High Sch. Athletic Ass'n, 975 F.2d 1315 (7th Cir. 1992); *see also* Crocker v. Tenn. Secondary Sch. Athletic Ass'n, 735 F. Supp. 753 (M.D. Tenn. 1990) (holding that a student with learning disabilities who transferred from a private school to a public school to receive special education could not be denied extracurricular participation for one year); Ind. High Sch. Athletic Ass'n v. Durham, 748 N.E.2d 404 (Ind. Ct. App. 2001) (finding that a student qualified for a hardship exception to the residency rule where a change in family finances caused him to transfer from a private to a public school).

Training Regulations and Other Conditions on Participation

Schools frequently condition extracurricular participation on students' attending practice sessions and games or performances, and such requirements have been judicially upheld.[154] Courts also have recognized that to foster discipline, school officials should be given latitude in establishing training and conduct standards for high school athletes. The judiciary has upheld the suspension of students from interscholastic athletic competition for violating regulations prohibiting smoking and drinking, even if the regulations apply to athletes' off-campus, off-season conduct.[155] Recognizing that team participation can be conditioned on good sportsmanship, courts have upheld school authorities in suspending students from teams for engaging in off-campus fights or hazing incidents.[156] In general, courts will not interfere with attendance requirements or training regulations simply because they appear harsh; students voluntarily subject themselves to the regulations as a condition of participation. The judiciary is reluctant to invalidate disciplinary action for rule violations unless the rules are clearly arbitrary, discriminatory, or excessive.

Courts also have upheld age restrictions on extracurricular participation to equalize competitive conditions and protect athletes.[157] Similarly, courts usually have endorsed rules limiting athletic eligibility to eight consecutive semesters or four years after completion of the eighth grade.[158] However, several courts have enjoined state athletic associations from enforcing maximum age and eight-semester requirements where the students in question had been required to repeat courses or withdraw from school for a term because of extensive illnesses.[159] Also the application of such eligibility requirements to students with disabilities has been controversial.[160]

A nationwide trend among school districts is to condition extracurricular participation on satisfactory academic performance. Several states through legislation or

[154] *See, e.g.*, Bernstein v. Menard, 728 F.2d 252 (4th Cir. 1984) (upholding a student's removal from the high school band for missing a required band trip); Keller v. Gardner Cmty. Consol. Grade Sch. Dist. 72C, 552 F. Supp. 512 (N.D. Ill. 1982) (upholding a regulation that students missing a practice session cannot play in the next game).

[155] *See, e.g.*, Ky. High Sch. Athletic Ass'n v. Edwards, 256 S.W. 3d 1 (Ky. 2008); Taylor v. Enumclaw Sch. Dist. No. 216, 133 P.3d 492 (Wash. Ct. App. 2006); *see also* Doe v. Banos, 416 F. App'x 185 (3d Cir. 2010) (upholding school district in conditioning interscholastic participation on parents agreeing to the board's anti-drug and anti-alcohol policy; school personnel did not have to accept parents' edited agreement form with the notation that it was returned "under duress").

[156] *See, e.g.*, Sala v. Warwick Valley Cent. Sch. Dist., No. 06 CV 8185 (HB), 2009 U.S. Dist. LEXIS 67353 (S.D.N.Y. July 29, 2009) (holding that a student could be denied participation on the football team because of two run-ins with police and school authorities); L.A. v. Bd. of Educ., No. 14241-11 (N.J. Office Admin. Law Dec. 1, 2011) (denying students' petition to lift suspension from championship football game resulting from involvement in off-campus brawl). *But see* G.D.M. v. Bd. of Educ., 48 A.3d 378 (N.J. Super. Ct. App. Div. 2012) (striking down school district's regulation allowing it to deny extracurricular participation based on students' illegal conduct off school grounds with no connection to school order or safety).

[157] *See, e.g.*, Ark. Activities Ass'n v. Meyer, 805 S.W.2d 58 (Ark. 1991); Mahan v. Agee, 652 P.2d 765 (Okla. 1982). *But see* Or. Sch. Activities Ass'n v. State Bd. of Educ., 260 P.3d 735 (Or. Ct. App. 2011) (dismissing appeal of state board's decision that association's age limit for athletic participation must be waved for nineteen-year-old senior who qualified under federal law as homeless during part of his high school years).

[158] *See, e.g.*, Ala. High Sch. Athletic Ass'n v. Medders, 456 So. 2d 284 (Ala. 1984); Grabow v. Mont. High Sch. Ass'n, 59 P.3d 14 (Mont. 2002).

[159] *See, e.g.*, Jordan v. Ind. High Sch. Athletic Ass'n, 813 F. Supp. 1372 (N.D. Ind. 1993), *vacated*, 16 F.3d 785 (7th Cir. 1994) (allowing student to play his senior year because his move from Illinois to Indiana, where he repeated his junior year, was not athletically motivated, and he had not been redshirted).

[160] *See, e.g.*, Washington v. Ind. High Sch. Athletic Ass'n, 181 F.3d 840 (7th Cir. 1999) (affirming preliminary injunction for learning-disabled student to receive a waiver from the eight-semester rule to accommodate his disability).

administrative rules have adopted statewide "no pass, no play" provisions, and these measures consistently have been upheld as advancing the state's legitimate interest in educational excellence.[161] In an illustrative case, the West Virginia Supreme Court endorsed academic standards for extracurricular participation, holding that the state board of education's rule, requiring students to maintain a 2.0 grade point average (GPA) to participate, was a legitimate exercise of its supervisory power. Moreover, the court upheld a county school board's regulation that went beyond the state policy by requiring students to maintain a passing grade in all classes as a prerequisite to extracurricular participation.[162] A Kentucky appeals court similarly upheld a school board's policy requiring students to maintain a 2.0 GPA in five of six subjects as a condition of participating in extracurricular activities.[163] In view of the national concern about achieving educational excellence, school boards and state legislatures are apt to place additional academic conditions on extracurricular participation. Only if academic standards are not uniformly applied are they likely to be invalidated.[164]

Other conditions have been attached to extracurricular participation as well. Some courts, for example, have upheld limitations on student participation in out-of-school athletic competition as a condition of varsity participation to protect students from overtaxing themselves and to make interscholastic athletics more competitive and fair.[165] Restrictions on the number of team members allowed to participate in championship games also have been upheld as rationally related to the legitimate state objectives of reducing costs of play-off contests and promoting fair play in championship games.[166]

Fees for Participation

Financially strapped school districts increasingly are considering the imposition of fees for extracurricular participation. Some districts are using a set fee (e.g., $30 or $50), regardless of how many activities the student participates in, with an adjustment for students on free or reduced lunch.[167] Several courts have ruled that public schools can condition extracurricular participation on the payment of such fees. For example, the Montana and Wisconsin high courts upheld the legality of charging fees for activities that are optional or elective.[168] In upholding fees for playing on interscholastic athletic teams, a Michigan appeals court recognized the availability of a confidential waiver process for students

[161]*See, e.g.*, Mont. v. Bd. of Trs., 726 P.2d 801 (Mont. 1986); Spring Branch Indep. Sch. Dist. v. Stamos, 695 S.W.2d 556 (Tex. 1985).

[162]Truby v. Broadwater, 332 S.E.2d 284 (W. Va. 1985).

[163]Thompson v. Fayette Cnty. Pub. Schs., 786 S.W.2d 879 (Ky. Ct. App. 1990).

[164]*See, e.g.*, Fontes v. Irvine Unified Sch. Dist., 30 Cal. Rptr. 2d 521 (Ct. App. 1994) (striking down a policy imposing a higher GPA for eligibility for the cheerleading squad than for interscholastic sports as not rationally related to a realistically conceivable purpose).

[165]*See, e.g.*, Burrows v. Ohio High Sch. Athletic Ass'n, 891 F.2d 122 (6th Cir. 1989) (finding prohibition of soccer squad members participating in spring independent soccer if they play fall interscholastic soccer to be rationally related to the association's legitimate interest of promoting fairness in competition); Kite v. Marshall, 661 F.2d 1027 (5th Cir. 1981) (upholding rational basis for interscholastic league's rule restricting participation by students who attended summer camps).

[166]*See, e.g.*, Fla. High Sch. Activities Ass'n v. Thomas, 434 So. 2d 306 (Fla. 1983).

[167]Demond Fernandez, *CCISD Approves New Fees for Extracurricular Activities* (Mar. 6, 2012), http://abclocal.go.com/ktrk/story?section=news/education&id=8570743.

[168]*See* Granger v. Cascade Cnty. Sch. Dist. No. 1, 499 P.2d 780 (Mont. 1972); Bd. of Educ. v. Sinclair, 222 N.W.2d 143 (Wis. 1974); *see also* Paulson v. Minidoka Cnty. Sch. Dist. No. 331, 463 P.2d 935, 938 (Idaho 1970) (finding extracurricular activities to be outside the regular academic courses that must be provided for free).

who could not afford the fees. The court noted that no student had been denied participation because of inability to pay and further declared that interscholastic athletics are not considered an integral, fundamental part of the educational program, which would necessitate providing them at no cost to students.[169]

The Indiana Supreme Court struck down a uniform $20 activities fee for all students, considering it a charge for attending public school, but the court recognized that fees could be assessed for participation in specific extracurricular activities.[170] However, individual state mandates may preclude charging students for extracurricular activities.[171] Given the fiscal constraints faced by school districts, an increasing number of school boards are likely to consider charging such fees, and the legality of these arrangements will depend on judicial interpretations of state law.

Although extracurricular activities continue to generate controversies, typically, courts have allowed school authorities discretion in attaching a variety of conditions to student participation. Educators should ensure, however, that all policies pertaining to extracurricular activities are reasonable, clearly stated, related to an educational purpose, publicized to parents and students, and applied without discrimination.

Conclusion

Noninstructional issues have generated a significant amount of school litigation. Many cases have focused on students' First Amendment freedoms of speech and press, but other constitutional rights, such as due process and equal protection guarantees, also have been asserted in challenging restrictions on students' noninstructional activities. In the late 1960s and early 1970s, the federal judiciary expanded constitutional protections afforded to students in noninstructional matters following the Supreme Court's landmark *Tinker* decision. Yet the reach of the *Tinker* standard was narrowed somewhat after the Supreme Court ruled in *Fraser* and *Hazelwood* that lewd or vulgar speech and attire are not protected by the First Amendment and that school authorities can censor student expression that appears to represent the school. The Supreme Court in *Morse* again restricted use of the disruption standard if expression can be viewed as promoting or celebrating illegal activity. *Tinker* has not been overturned, but it governs more limited circumstances than was true in the 1970s.

However, *Tinker* has been revitalized as the primary standard used in First Amendment challenges to anti-harassment and anti-bullying policies and electronic expression. Significant questions persist regarding whether school authorities can discipline students for vulgar and hurtful electronic expression that originates from their homes but can reach the entire school community instantaneously.

Students do not need to rely solely on constitutional protections because federal and state laws, most notably the Equal Access Act, also protect students' expression and association rights and afford protections in noninstructional matters. Also, state association rules govern many

[169]Attorney Gen. v. E. Jackson Pub. Schs., 372 N.W.2d 638 (Mich. Ct. App. 1985).

[170]Nagy v. Evansville-Vanderburgh Sch. Corp., 844 N.E.2d 481 (Ind. 2006).

[171]*See, e.g.*, Hartzell v. Connell, 679 P.2d 35, 44–45 (Cal. 1984) (finding that extracurricular activities are an integral part of the educational program and thus encompassed within the state constitution's guarantee of a free public education and the state administrative code's stipulation that students shall not be required to pay any fees or deposits). A 2012 settlement between the American Civil Liberties Union and the state reiterated that school districts must provide extracurricular activities free of charge, but donations can be solicited to support such activities.

aspects of extracurricular activities among member schools. Although judicial criteria applied in weighing the competing interests of students and school authorities continue to be refined, the following generalizations characterize the current posture of the courts.

1. Students do not have a First Amendment right to engage in expression that is defamatory, obscene, lewd, or inflammatory or that promotes illegal activity in public schools.
2. School boards can ban commercial solicitation on school premises, but they also have the authority to contract with companies to advertise in public schools unless there is a state prohibition.
3. Private student-initiated expression of ideological views that merely occurs at school cannot be curtailed unless a material interference with or substantial disruption of the educational process can reasonably be forecast from the expression.
4. Student expression that represents the school is subject to restrictions; school authorities have broad discretion to censor such expression, provided the decisions are based on pedagogical concerns and do not entail viewpoint discrimination.
5. Students can be disciplined for making true threats toward classmates or school personnel and for expression considered inflammatory.
6. School authorities cannot bar controversial or critical content from student literature that is not school-sponsored even though it is distributed at school; policies requiring prior administrative review of such material must specify the procedures for review and the types of material that are prohibited.
7. School districts' anti-harassment and anti-bullying provisions will likely be upheld unless they are vague or overly broad in restricting protected expression.
8. Student electronic expression can be the basis for disciplinary action if it directly disrupts the work of the school; whether such expression can be censored because it is vulgar or interferes with the rights of others has not been clarified.
9. Any regulation imposing time, place, and manner restrictions on student expression must be specific, publicized to students and parents, and applied without discrimination.
10. Under the Equal Access Act (EAA), if a federally assisted secondary school establishes a limited open forum for student-initiated clubs to meet during noninstructional time, the access policy must be content neutral; however, public schools are not required to create such a forum for noncurriculum student groups to meet.
11. Student and community groups not covered by the EAA have First Amendment expressive association and private speech protections against viewpoint discrimination in terms of public school access.
12. School authorities can restrict student hairstyles and attire that are vulgar, jeopardize health and safety, or threaten to disrupt the educational process; any restrictions must be justified for educational reasons.
13. Restrictive student dress codes and uniforms can be imposed in public schools if not designed to suppress expression and justified by legitimate educational objectives, such as reducing violence and improving achievement.
14. Students do not have an inherent right to participate in extracurricular activities.
15. Nonprofit, private associations that regulate interscholastic sports and other competitive activities among private and public schools within states are considered state actors and subject to constitutional restrictions on their actions.
16. School authorities possess considerable latitude in attaching reasonable conditions to extracurricular participation (e.g., skill criteria, attendance and training regulations, residency rules, academic standards, age restrictions, and length of eligibility requirements).

17. Restrictions can be imposed on student participation in extracurricular activities based on legitimate health and safety considerations, and student athletes can be subjected to drug testing.

18. Whether public schools can charge fees for extracurricular participation depends upon judicial interpretation of a state's constitutional and statutory provisions.

MyEdLeadershipLab™

Go to Topic 5: *Student and Family Rights* on the MyEdLeadershipLab™ site (www.myedleadershiplab.com) for *Public School Law: Teachers' and Students' Rights*, Seventh Edition, where you can

- Find learning outcomes for *Student and Family Rights* along with the national standards that connect to these outcomes.
- Complete Assignments and Activities that can help you more deeply understand the chapter content.
- Apply and practice your understanding of the core skills identified in the chapter with the Building Leadership Skills unit.
- Prepare yourself for professional certification with a Practice for Certification quiz.

Student Classifications

MyEdLeadershipLab™

Visit the MyEdLeadershipLab™ site for *Public School Law: Teachers' and Students' Rights*, Seventh Edition, to enhance your understanding of chapter concepts. You'll have the opportunity to practice your skills through video- and case-based Assignments and Activities as well as Building Leadership Skills units, and to prepare for your certification exam with Practice for Certification quizzes.

It might appear from a literal translation of the word *equality* that once a state establishes an educational system, all students must be treated in the same manner. Courts, however, have recognized that individuals are different and that equal treatment of unequals can have negative consequences. Accordingly, valid classification practices, designed to enhance the educational experiences of children by recognizing their unique needs, generally have been accepted as a legitimate prerogative of educators. While educators' authority to classify students has not been seriously contested, the bases for certain classifications and the procedures used to make distinctions among students have been the focus of substantial litigation.

This chapter explores differential treatment of students based on race, native language, ability and achievement, age, sex, and sexual orientation. It examines historical cases involving student classifications as well as more recent controversies. For example, some charter schools recently have been accused of stratifying students by race, sex, language, sexual orientation, and ability. Specifically, the increased flexibility that charter schools have to experiment within public education gives charter school leaders more power than traditional public school leaders to shape their educational communities, which has oftentimes led to charter schools that are designed to attract a specific student population. To illustrate, some charter schools have been specifically designed to serve

From Chapter 5 of *Public School Law: Teachers' and Students' Rights*, Seventh Edition. Martha M. McCarthy, Nelda H. Cambron-McCabe, Suzanne E. Eckes.

only Native American students, female students, students with disabilities, gifted students, or lesbian, gay, bisexual, and transgendered (LGBT) students. Some of these specialized charter schools have raised legal concerns that will be noted throughout this chapter.[1]

LEGAL CONTEXT

The Equal Protection Clause of the Fourteenth Amendment to the United States Constitution states in part that no state shall deny to any person within its jurisdiction equal protection of the laws. This applies to subdivisions of states, including school districts. The Equal Protection Clause requires that similarly situated individuals be treated the same.[2] As a result, equal protection claims often arise when a government law or policy creates a classification that advantages or disadvantages one group over another. When examining a government policy, courts apply three different levels of scrutiny (i.e., strict, intermediate, and rational basis scrutiny) for different classes of people and if different interests are at stake.

Identifying the appropriate standard of review requires in part a determination of whether a *suspect class* is involved.[3] To date, only alienage, race, and national origin have been identified by the Supreme Court as suspect classes.[4] Any grouping or school assignment based on these characteristics would be strictly scrutinized by courts and upheld only if it advances a compelling government interest and is narrowly tailored. Intermediate scrutiny is applied to challenged classifications based on sex.[5] This standard requires governmental actions to be substantially related to advancing significant governmental objectives. Moreover, the classification must be necessary, not merely convenient, and will not be upheld if there are reasonable, less restrictive means of reaching the same goal. Where any other classification or form of discrimination is present (e.g., disability, age, sexual orientation), courts apply rational basis scrutiny. All that is required under this level of review is that some rational basis was used in the state's decision. This is a very low threshold and is generally met with relative ease. Thus, under the Equal Protection Clause, it would be much more difficult to open a public school that serves only Latino students than it would be to open a public school that serves only gay students. The school serving only Latino students would need to demonstrate a compelling government interest in segregating students by race and that the classification serves a necessary interest. The school serving only gay students would need to show simply a legitimate governmental objective with a rational relationship between the means and the ends.

A fourth level of review is applied where the state's acts have the outward appearance of being neutral but in reality have a disproportionate adverse affect on a protected class of persons; when this occurs, the aggrieved individual must prove that the state intended to discriminate. For example, if standardized test scores provide the basis for

[1]*See, e.g.*, Suzanne Eckes, Robert Fox & Nina Buchanan, ***Legal and Policy Issues Regarding Niche Charter Schools: Race, Religion, Culture and the Law***, 5 J. SCH. CHOICE 85 (2011).

[2]*See* City of Cleburne v. Cleburne Living Ctr., 473 U.S. 432 (1985).

[3]Level of scrutiny also is determined by the presence of fundamental or quasi-fundamental rights (e.g., the right to marry). Such rights will not be reviewed in this chapter as this discussion focuses on classifications.

[4]*See* Graham v. Richardson, 403 U.S. 365 (1971) (alienage); Hunter v. Erickson, 393 U.S. 385 (1969) (race); Korematsu v. United States, 323 U.S. 214 (1944) (national origin).

[5]Miss. Univ. for Women v. Hogan, 458 U.S. 718 (1982). Intermediate scrutiny also applies in cases dealing with illegitimacy. *See* Clark v. Jeter, 486 U.S. 456 (1988).

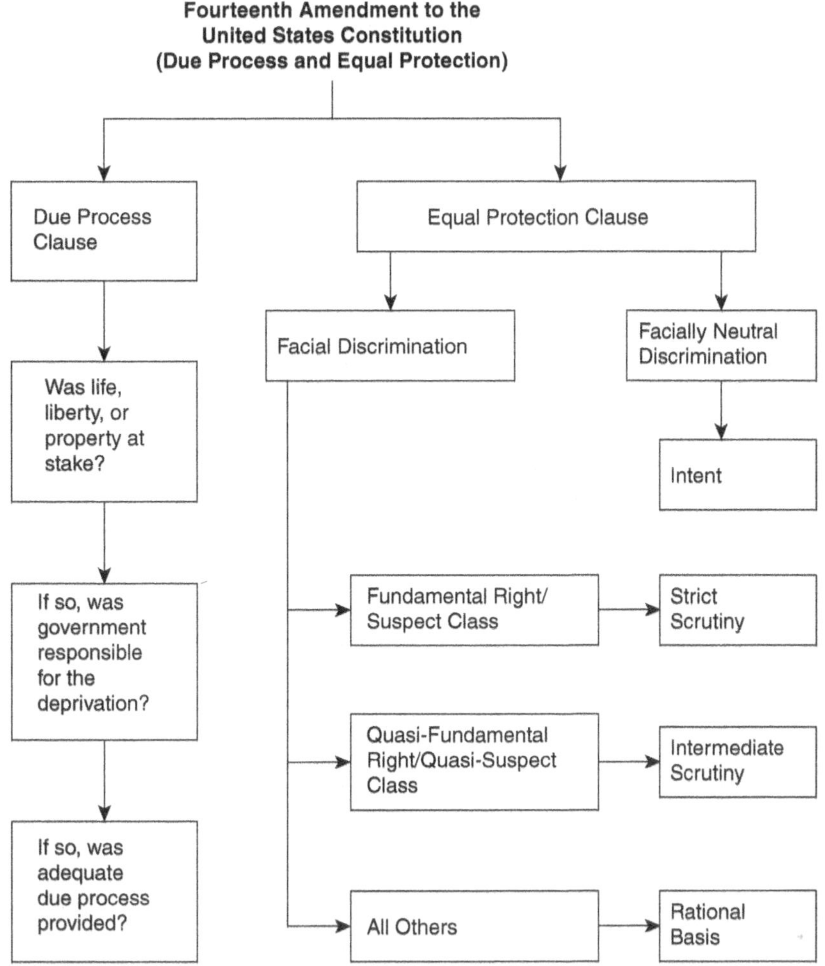

FIGURE 1 Fourteenth Amendment

assigning students to various programs (e.g., gifted, developmental) and result in disproportionate placement according to race, the students bear the burden of demonstrating that school personnel intended to discriminate in their selection and use of the tests. This standard is difficult to meet and generally results in a verdict for the state. (See Fourteenth Amendment, Figure 1.)

In addition to those constitutional protections, equal educational opportunities are guaranteed through various federal and state laws. In many instances, the statutes create new substantive rights that are more extensive than constitutional guarantees. Among the more significant federal laws discussed in this chapter are Title VI of the Civil Rights Act of 1964 (barring discrimination on the basis of race, color, or national origin by recipients of federal financial assistance), the Equal Educational Opportunities Act of 1974 (guaranteeing public school students equal educational opportunity without regard to race, color, sex, or national origin), Title IX of the Education Amendments of 1972 (prohibiting sex discrimination in institutions with federally assisted educational programs), and the Age Discrimination Act of 1975 (prohibiting federal aid recipients from discriminating based on age).

CLASSIFICATIONS BASED ON RACE

Historically, the most prevalent reason for classifying students according to race has been to establish or perpetuate racially segregated schools. Widespread racial segregation in educational institutions existed in this country from the colonial period well into the twentieth century. Even after the adoption of the Fourteenth Amendment in 1868, most schools remained segregated either by state constitution or statute, local ordinance, district policy or practice, or court interpretation, and were seldom equal. When such practices were challenged, courts generally mandated only that children be provided with access to public education. They did not require equal access to integrated schools or to equal school facilities, the provision of equal curricular or extracurricular opportunities, instruction by equally trained professionals, or instruction of equal duration (i.e., an equivalent school year or school day). Some scholars have noted that despite laws and policies to racially integrate student bodies, some school districts remain highly segregated. In addition to traditional public schools, charter schools have also been accused of racially segregating students.[6]

Most lawsuits challenging school segregation claim a violation of the Fourteenth Amendment. Because race qualifies as a suspect class, the state or local school district must demonstrate a compelling interest in its use of facially discriminatory racial classifications *and* show that its procedures are narrowly tailored if it were to use race as a basis to segregate school children, to deny equal educational opportunity, or to advantage one student over another.

Pre-*Brown* Litigation

The first published school segregation case was *Roberts v. City of Boston* in 1849, nineteen years prior to the passage of the Fourteenth Amendment.[7] In that case, the city had established separate primary schools for minority children but had staffed them with teachers receiving the same compensation and having the same qualifications as other teachers in the system. When a minority child was denied admission to the Caucasian school nearest her home due to her race, she filed unsuccessful administrative appeals. The court concluded that just because the black school was farther from her house did not mean that she had been excluded from public schools.

Perhaps the most infamous case supporting the "separate but equal" interpretation was *Plessy v. Ferguson* in 1896, in which the Supreme Court upheld racial segregation of passengers in railroad coaches as required by Louisiana law.[8] Violation of the statute

[6]Suzanne Eckes, Charter School Legislation's Impact on Diversity, in the Charter School Experiment: Expectations, Evidence and Implications (Christopher Lubienski & Peter Weitzel eds., Harvard Education Press, 2010).

[7]59 Mass. (5 Cush.) 198 (1849).

[8]163 U.S. 537 (1896); *see also* Bolling v. Sharpe, 347 U.S. 497 (1954) (invalidating school segregation in Washington, D.C., under the Fifth Amendment's Due Process Clause because the Fourteenth Amendment does not apply in that jurisdiction).

resulted in a $25 fine or imprisonment for twenty days. Such a penalty could be imposed against either the individual who attempted to occupy the coach or compartment reserved for members of another race or the officer of any railroad who failed to make the proper assignment. The only identified exemption to this requirement was a nurse who was attending a child of another race. Although "separate but equal" case law and state statutes were common 75 to 100 years before *Plessy*, it nevertheless is *Plessy* that most often is mentioned today when the standard is discussed.

However, four key higher education appeals reached the Supreme Court between 1938 and 1950 that began to question the constitutionality of separate but equal policies. These cases included claims from minority students that there were no separate but equal programs available (two cases), that the separate program was inferior, or that the education received within a previously all-Caucasian institution was unequal due to the student's separation from the rest of the student body.[9] The plaintiffs in each case prevailed.

Given the success of the higher education plaintiffs, the time appeared ripe to attack the PK–12 "separate but equal" standard directly. This occurred in 1954 when the Supreme Court combined cases from four states—Kansas, South Carolina, Virginia, and Delaware.[10] Although these cases differed regarding conditions and facts, minority children in each state sought the assistance of the courts under the Fourteenth Amendment to obtain admission to public schools on a nonsegregated basis. In the landmark decision, collectively called *Brown v. Board of Education*, Chief Justice Warren, writing for a unanimous Court, declared education to be "perhaps the most important function of state and local governments"[11] and repudiated the separate but equal doctrine, stipulating that racially segregated public schools were "inherently unequal."[12]

Because of the significant impact of this decision and the difficulty in fashioning an immediate remedy, the Supreme Court delayed an implementation decree for one year, soliciting friend-of-the-court briefs[13] regarding strategies to convert de jure segregated dual school districts into integrated unitary districts.[14] Then, in 1955 in *Brown II*, the Court concluded that the conversion from dual to unitary districts must occur "with all deliberate speed,"[15] although it gave little guidance as to what specific time frame was required or to what extent integration was mandated. As a result, states varied widely in their efforts to comply.

[9]McLaurin v. Okla. State Regents for Higher Educ., 339 U.S. 637 (1950); Sweatt v. Painter, 339 U.S. 629 (1950); Sipuel v. Bd. of Regents, 332 U.S. 631 (1948) (*per curiam*); Missouri *ex rel.* Gaines v. Canada, 305 U.S. 337 (1938).

[10]Brown v. Bd. of Educ., 98 F. Supp. 797 (D. Kan. 1951); Briggs v. Elliott, 98 F. Supp. 529 (E.D.S.C. 1951), *vacated and remanded*, 342 U.S. 350 (1952), *on remand*, 103 F. Supp. 920 (E.D.S.C. 1952); Davis v. Cnty. Sch. Bd., 103 F. Supp. 337 (E.D. Va. 1952); Gebhart v. Belton, 87 A.2d 862, *aff'd*, 91 A.2d 137 (Del. 1952).

[11]347 U.S. 483, 493 (1954) (Brown I).

[12]*Id.* at 495.

[13]Friend-of-the-court (amicus curiae) briefs are provided by nonparties to inform or perhaps persuade the court.

[14]De jure segregated schools are those where the separation of the races is required by law or the result of other action by the state or its agents. De facto segregation occurs by practice (e.g., families choosing to live in a particular neighborhood).

[15]Brown v. Bd. of Educ., 349 U.S. 294, 301 (1955) (Brown II).

De Jure Segregation in the South

Despite the *Brown* mandate to end unconstitutional segregation, during the next decade, the Supreme Court was forced to react to a number of blatant violations, such as state officials' efforts to physically block the desegregation of schools in Little Rock[16] and an attempt to avoid integration by closing public schools in one Virginia county while maintaining public schools in other counties in the state.[17] The Court also invalidated provisions in Knoxville that allowed students to transfer back to their former schools if, after rezoning, they would be assigned to a school where their race would be in the minority[18] and found unconstitutional a one-grade-per-year plan[19] that had been adopted in Fort Smith, Arkansas.[20] Such a practice was not an overt violation of *Brown* but certainly represented an effort to strain the "all deliberate speed" mandate.

Even where violations were found, however, many lower courts hesitated to require anything more than the removal of barriers to integration, given the dearth of guidance regarding compliance.[21] Then, in a trilogy of cases in 1968, the Supreme Court announced that school officials in systems that were segregated by law in 1954 had an affirmative duty to take whatever steps were necessary to convert to unitary school systems and to eliminate the effects of past discrimination.[22] Furthermore, the Court declared that desegregation remedies would be evaluated based on their effectiveness in dismantling dual school systems. Thus, the notion of state neutrality was transformed into a requirement of affirmative state action to desegregate; the mere removal of barriers to school integration was not sufficient.

In one of these 1968 cases, *Green v. County School Board*, the Court reviewed a freedom-of-choice plan adopted by a small district in Virginia. The district historically operated only two schools, both kindergarten through twelfth grade: one for African Americans, the other for Caucasians. To eliminate race-based assignments within the district, the local board had implemented a plan to allow children to attend the school of their choice. During the three-year period immediately following implementation, no Caucasian children enrolled in the historically African American school, while only a few African American children enrolled in the historically Caucasian school. The district contended that any resulting segregation was due to the choices of individuals, not to government action, and was therefore permissible; the Supreme Court disagreed. The problem with this plan was not that it was unconstitutional per se, but that it simply was not achieving school integration. As a result, the district was ordered to come forward

[16]Cooper v. Aaron, 358 U.S. 1 (1958).

[17]Griffin v. Cnty. Sch. Bd., 377 U.S. 218 (1964).

[18]Goss v. Bd. of Educ., 373 U.S. 683 (1963).

[19]A one-grade-per-year plan requires the integration of one grade each fall term until the system is unitary and all grades are integrated.

[20]Rogers v. Paul, 382 U.S. 198 (1965) (*per curiam*).

[21]*See, e.g.*, Briggs v. Elliott, 132 F. Supp. 776, 777 (E.D.S.C. 1955) (declaring that the Constitution "does not require integration" but "merely forbids discrimination").

[22]Green v. Cnty. Sch. Bd., 391 U.S. 430 (1968); Raney v. Bd. of Educ., 391 U.S. 443 (1968); Monroe v. Bd. of Comm'rs, 391 U.S. 450 (1968).

with a new plan that promised "realistically to work and to work now."[23] In addition, the Court ruled that school authorities must eliminate the racial identification of schools in terms of the *composition of the student body, faculty, and staff; transportation; extracurricular activities; and facilities.* These six elements still are used today and are referred to in the aggregate simply as the *Green* criteria.

In 1971, additional direction was provided when the Supreme Court ruled in *Swann v. Charlotte-Mecklenburg Board of Education* that the elimination of invidious racial distinctions may be sufficient in connection with transportation, support personnel, and extracurricular activities, but that more was necessary in terms of constructing facilities and making faculty and student assignments.[24] The Court endorsed the practice of assigning teachers on the basis of race until faculties were integrated and declared that new schools must be located so that the dual school system would not be perpetuated or reestablished.

Correcting racial imbalance among student populations, however, was more difficult. For the vestiges of segregation to be eliminated, the school district had to achieve racial balance in a sufficient number of schools, although every school did not have to reflect the racial composition of the school district as a whole. The presence of a small number of predominantly one-race schools in the district did not necessarily mean that it continued to practice state-imposed segregation, but the burden of proof was placed on school officials to establish that such schools were not the result of present or past discriminatory action. To achieve the desired racial balance, the Court suggested pairing or consolidating schools, altering attendance zones, and using racial quotas, but rejected the practice of assigning students to the schools nearest their homes if it failed to eliminate de jure segregation. The Court also endorsed the use of reasonable busing as a means to integrate schools yet qualified that endorsement by noting that the soundness of any transportation plan must be evaluated based on the time involved, distance traveled, and age of the students.

By applying the criteria established in *Green* and *Swann*, substantial desegregation was attained in southern states during the 1970s. Where unconstitutional segregation was found, federal courts exercised broad power in ordering remedies affecting student and staff assignments, curriculum, school construction, personnel practices, and budgetary allocations. Judicial activity was augmented by threats from the former Department of Health, Education, and Welfare to terminate federal funds to school districts not complying with Title VI of the Civil Rights Act of 1964.[25] Title VI, like the Fourteenth Amendment, requires the integration only of de jure segregated school districts.

Distinguishing between De Jure and De Facto Segregation

Since the Supreme Court carefully limited its early decisions to states and school districts with a long history of school segregation by official policy, questions remained regarding what type of evidence—other than explicit legislation requiring

[23]*Green*, 391 U.S. at 439.
[24]402 U.S. 1 (1971).
[25]42 U.S.C. §§ 2000d–2000d-7 (2012).

school segregation—was necessary to establish unconstitutional de jure segregation.[26] That is, what factors would distinguish de jure segregation from permissible de facto segregation? The answer to this question began to evolve in *Keyes v. School District No. 1, Denver*, in which the Supreme Court in 1973 held that if "no statutory dual system has ever existed, plaintiffs must prove not only that segregated schooling exists but also that it was brought about or maintained by intentional state action."[27] Some federal courts have assumed that a presumption of unlawful purpose can be established if the natural, probable, and foreseeable results of public officials' acts perpetuate segregated conditions,[28] while others have required evidence that policy makers actually harbored a desire to segregate.[29] Although courts vary in the processes they use to determine whether school districts are guilty of discriminatory intent, they often consider the impact of the disputed governmental act, the history of discriminatory official action, procedural and substantive departures from norms generally followed, and discriminatory statements made publicly or in legislative or administrative sessions. If intent is proven, courts then are responsible for fashioning appropriate remedies.[30]

School districts that either have no history of unlawful segregation or have become unitary while under court supervision will not be responsible for correcting any future racial imbalance they have not created. In 1976, the Supreme Court in *Pasadena City Board of Education v. Spangler* held that the school district, having implemented a student reassignment plan to comply with a court order, did not have an affirmative duty to revise remedial efforts annually when demographic shifts resulted in some schools becoming more than 50 percent minority.[31] The district court had made a lifetime commitment to the "no majority of any minority" rule. The Supreme Court held that although the original lower court decision was justified to correct de jure segregation, the continuation of the order exceeded the court's authority once integration goals had been achieved.

In a later case, a federal district court in San Francisco refused to extend an expired consent decree created to integrate the public schools in regard to nine racial and ethnic groups.[32] The school district had never been found guilty of de jure segregation or in noncompliance with the decree. In rejecting plaintiff's request, the court reasoned that there were no vestiges of prior de jure segregation; the district had fulfilled its responsibilities under the decree in good faith; and the prior agreement had proven to be ineffective, if not counterproductive, in achieving diversity.

[26]In the 1960s, some courts reasoned that school segregation did not warrant remedial action in school districts where segregation was not imposed by law in 1954. *See, e.g.*, Deal v. Cincinnati Bd. of Educ., 369 F.2d 55 (6th Cir. 1966).

[27]413 U.S. 189, 198 (1973).

[28]*See, e.g.*, Arthur v. Nyquist, 573 F.2d 134 (2d Cir. 1978).

[29]*See, e.g.*, Vill. of Arlington Heights v. Metro. Hous. Dev. Corp., 429 U.S. 252 (1977).

[30]*See, e.g.*, Price v. Austin Indep. Sch. Dist., 945 F.2d 1307 (5th Cir. 1991).

[31]427 U.S. 424 (1976); *see also* Holton v. City of Thomasville Sch. Dist., 425 F.3d 1325 (11th Cir. 2005) (concluding that the segregation occurring since acquiring unitary status was caused by demographic changes and not official action; although the school district could voluntarily develop a new desegregation plan, federal law did not require it, and courts were without the authority to order it).

[32]S.F. NAACP v. S.F. Unified Sch. Dist., 413 F. Supp. 2d 1051 (N.D. Cal. 2005).

Fashioning Appropriate Remedies

Because each desegregation case involves a combination of unique circumstances and violations, it is not surprising that each remedy also is unique and at times requires rezoning; the provision of thematic magnet schools; the development of new curricular offerings; the closing, reopening, renovation, or construction of schools; busing; the transfer and/or retraining of current staff; or the hiring of additional staff. Basically, the courts can require nearly anything of districts and states that would result in fulfillment of the primary objective—the integration of public schools. "All deliberate speed" in many instances has taken decades, while cost often seemed irrelevant.

REZONING AND THE CLOSING, REOPENING, OR CONSTRUCTION OF SCHOOLS. Although at times politically unpopular, the rezoning of schools often was the fastest, least expensive, and simplest way to integrate students. Because of a long history of gerrymandering boundary lines with the intent to segregate, many school boundaries during the 1950s and 1960s had little to do with geographic barriers (e.g., rivers, hills); safety issues (e.g., location of busy roads, factories); or the size, location, or dispersion of the student population. As a result, significant integration often has resulted through the simple use of good-faith redistricting and/or, in fairly narrow circumstances, the creation of new or consolidated school districts.[33]

In addition, early in the twentieth century, many school districts were able to remain or become segregated by strategically locating new schools; downsizing or closing existing buildings; or operating schools that were overenrolled, often requiring the use of mobile units or temporary classrooms. Just as these methods were used to segregate, they also have been used to integrate. Where there has been a history of de jure segregation, it is common to require adjustments in building use and to determine site selection of future schools at least in part on the impact that their locations will have on the effort to integrate.

BUSING. Contributing to the cost and controversy was the use of busing to accomplish integration when other alternatives had not succeeded. Even though busing is admittedly effective at achieving student integration, it also represents a significant expense; is inefficient in the use of student time; and is an unpopular option with many students, parents, taxpayers, and voters of all races. Consequently, several bills to limit the authority of federal courts to order the busing of students have been introduced in Congress. Foremost among these were provisions included in Title IV of the Civil Rights Act of 1964[34] and the Equal Educational Opportunities Act (EEOA) of 1974.[35] Title IV provides technical assistance in the preparation, adoption, and implementation of desegregation plans; gives direction in the operation of training institutes to improve the ability of educators to deal effectively with special education problems occasioned by desegregation; and places limitations on court-ordered busing. Furthermore, the EEOA prohibits public schools from denying equal educational opportunities to students based on their race, color, sex, or national origin; purports that the neighborhood is the appropriate basis for determining

[33]Newburg Area Council v. Bd. of Educ., 510 F.2d 1358 (6th Cir. 1974).
[34]42 U.S.C. §§ 2000c–2000c-9 (2012).
[35]20 U.S.C. § 1701 (2012).

public school assignment; and stipulates that busing may be used only in situations where the intent to segregate is established.

Moreover, state busing limitation measures have generated litigation. In 1971, the Supreme Court in *North Carolina State Board of Education v. Swann* struck down a state law forbidding the busing of students to create racially balanced schools. The Court concluded that the provision unconstitutionally restricted the discretion of local school authorities to formulate plans to eliminate dual school systems.[36] Furthermore, the Court reasoned that busing was one of the truly effective remedies to racially integrate students.

PROGRAMMATIC OPTIONS. Since the early 1980s, the federal judiciary has become less aggressive in requiring massive student reassignment plans to integrate schools. In the alternative, compensatory education programs, bilingual/bicultural programs, and counseling and career guidance services, among others, have been included in desegregation plans to help overcome the effects of prior racial isolation.[37] Most plans include magnet schools that offered theme-oriented instructional programs or an expanded curriculum in an effort to attract a racially balanced student body and to limit the use of busing.[38] Other plans provide specialized learning centers to improve remediation for underachieving pupils.[39] As with freedom of choice or transfer plans, courts will uphold the use of these program and curricular options to integrate schools, but only if they succeed in achieving the desired level of integration within a reasonable period of time.

INTERDISTRICT REMEDIES. Another controversial approach to integration has been the use of remedies that cross school district boundaries. Many city school districts experienced both real and percentage increases in minority populations due to a variety of reasons, including "white flight" and "zone jumping."[40] Integration in these areas then becomes problematic, given the presence primarily of one race. As a result, several courts have reasoned that if racial integration in a predominantly one-race district is to be achieved, adjacent districts must be involved in student transfer and busing plans.

In *Milliken v. Bradley*, the Sixth Circuit had ordered a metropolitan desegregation remedy for Detroit and fifty-three suburban school districts, reasoning that intentional school segregation implicated the entire metropolitan area. The Supreme Court disagreed in 1974, however, and held that the plaintiffs did not carry their burden of proof in substantiating purposeful discrimination on the part of the suburban districts.[41] Moreover, the Court emphasized that a remedy must not be broader in scope than warranted by the constitutional violation. Since intentional school segregation was proven only in the Detroit system, the case was remanded for the formulation of a remedy within that district.

[36]402 U.S. 43 (1971). *But see* Crawford v. Bd. of Educ., 458 U.S. 527 (1982) (upholding a state constitutional amendment in California that permitted busing only when de jure segregation was present).

[37]*See, e.g.*, Keyes v. Sch. Dist. No. 1, 895 F.2d 659 (10th Cir. 1990).

[38]*See, e.g.*, Bradley v. Pinellas Cnty. Sch. Bd., 165 F.R.D. 676 (M.D. Fla. 1994).

[39]Tasby v. Black Coal. to Maximize Educ., 771 F.2d 849 (5th Cir. 1985).

[40]Zone jumping occurs when a student transfers from the assigned attendance zone to an adjacent zone. *See, e.g.*, Elston v. Talladega Cnty. Bd. of Educ., 997 F.2d 1394 (11th Cir. 1993).

[41]418 U.S. 717 (1974) (Milliken I).

Three years later, in *Milliken II*, the Court articulated a three-part framework to guide district courts in the exercise of their authority. This framework requires that the nature and scope of the desegregation remedy:

- be determined by the nature and scope of the constitutional violation;
- be remedial so as to restore the victims of discriminatory conduct to the position they would have occupied in the absence of such conduct; and
- take into account the interests of state and local authorities in managing their own affairs.[42]

Accordingly, an interdistrict remedy may include only those districts that were involved in de jure segregation; courts are not authorized to include districts that were not segregated or were segregated only due to de facto circumstances.[43]

In a 1995 decision involving interdistrict remedies, *Missouri v. Jenkins*, the Supreme Court evaluated Kansas City's lengthy history of desegregation orders.[44] The district court reasoned that the expenditures related to teacher salaries and a variety of programs were needed if educational opportunities were to be improved to the degree necessary to attract nonminority students (i.e., those either residing outside the district or attending private schools) to the Kansas City public schools.

Disagreeing with the lower court, the Supreme Court noted that racial imbalance within a school district, without additional evidence supporting a Fourteenth Amendment violation, did not infringe the Constitution and that the lower court's plan to attract nonresident nonminority students represented an interdistrict remedy and was therefore inappropriate for the court to have ordered. Furthermore, the district court's order requiring the continued funding of the costly educational programs clearly exceeded its authority.

The district court attempted to justify its decision by noting that student achievement levels still were at or below national norms and that students had not yet reached their maximum potential. The Supreme Court admonished that instead of a "maximum potential" standard, the court should have determined whether the lower achievement of minority students was attributable to prior de jure segregation and, if so, whether it had been remedied to the extent practicable. Once this had been accomplished, control of the schools was ordered to be returned to state and local school officials. The Court also held that federal courts may order school districts to impose tax increases to fund desegregation remedies but that courts may not impose such increases directly.[45] However, if the school district is unable to further increase its taxes due to existing state laws, the courts have the limited authority to override such provisions as they apply to a de jure district.

In addition, courts at times have held states responsible for all or part of desegregation costs, depending on the extent to which the state was found culpable in causing or perpetuating the segregation.[46] Such was the case in Michigan in 1977 when the Supreme

[42]Milliken v. Bradley, 433 U.S. 267, 280–81 (1977) (Milliken II).

[43]*See, e.g.*, Edgerson v. Clinton, 86 F.3d 833 (8th Cir. 1996); Lauderdale Cnty. Sch. Dist. v. Enter. Consol. Sch. Dist., 24 F.3d 671 (5th Cir. 1994).

[44]515 U.S. 70 (1995).

[45]495 U.S. 33 (1990).

[46]*See, e.g.*, Jenkins *ex rel.* Agyei v. Missouri, 13 F.3d 1170 (8th Cir. 1994). *But see* DeKalb Cnty. Sch. Dist. v. Schrenko, 109 F.3d 680 (11th Cir. 1997) (concluding that the state need not reimburse the school district for costs associated with desegregation-related transportation, majority-to-minority transfer initiatives, and a magnet school program).

Court in *Milliken v. Bradley* ordered the state to underwrite half of the costs of remedial programs, in-service training, guidance and counseling services, and community relations programs in Detroit because of the role the state played in creating the dual system.[47]

STAFF DESEGREGATION REMEDIES. The Supreme Court has emphasized that integration of the school staff is an essential component of an effective desegregation remedy.[48] Staff integration will allow students to be exposed to faculty of their own race as well as to faculty of other races. This often is accomplished through the use of race-based faculty assignment and transfer procedures. However, having a diverse faculty in each school will not be possible if a critical mass of underrepresented faculty has not been hired for the school district as a whole. Although districts may aggressively recruit qualified minority and other faculty, racial preference in hiring will not be permitted unless remedial in nature and court-ordered. Where proof of prior discrimination exists, courts then are responsible for preparing a narrowly tailored plan to correct the constitutional violation. To accomplish this task, courts will compare the racial composition of the faculty with that of the qualified relevant labor market—rather than with that of the surrounding community or the student body—in determining the targeted number, percent, or ratio. It is important to note that neither societal discrimination, racial imbalance, nor the desire for role models or diversity will justify imposing racial quotas in employment.

The racial balance of a school faculty also can be affected when it is necessary to downsize the staff. This can occur when either fewer schools are used (e.g., when two de jure districts are combined and fewer schools of larger size are operated) or fewer students are educated (e.g., when students move from the district or enroll in private schools). Although there may be exceptional circumstances where preference in hiring is permitted, that is not the case when determining whom to lay off. As a result, the diversity gained through the use of goals, court-ordered quotas, or affirmative action may be lost during a reduction-in-force (RIF) as the consideration of race in identifying the persons to be released is not permitted. The Supreme Court in *Wygant v. Jackson Board of Education* struck down a school district's negotiated agreement that gave preferential protection to minority teachers from layoffs to maintain the percentage of minority teachers employed prior to a RIF.[49] The Court concluded that the practice violated the Fourteenth Amendment and reasoned that the justification for the contested staff reduction policy—the need for minority role models—failed to qualify as a compelling interest and that the preferential layoff procedures were not narrowly tailored. Although *Wygant* did not involve a school district engaged in court-ordered integration, there is no reason to believe that the use of racial preferences would be permitted in such districts. Race-based relief may perhaps help remedy one constitutional violation, but it would create another.

Achieving Unitary Status

Federal courts have found numerous school systems guilty of having engaged in de jure segregation and have fashioned a variety of remedies. Some orders required only a few

[47]433 U.S. 267 (1977) (Milliken II).

[48]*See, e.g.*, Swann v. Charlotte-Mecklenburg Bd. of Educ., 402 U.S. 1, 19 (1971); United States v. Montgomery Cnty. Bd. of Educ., 395 U.S. 225, 232 (1969); *see also* Lee v. Lee Cnty. Bd. of Educ., No. 70-T-845-E, 2002 U.S. Dist. LEXIS 10277 (M.D. Ala. May 29, 2002) (declaring the district unitary except for faculty assignments to two schools).

[49]476 U.S. 267 (1986).

years to demonstrate compliance, while others continue to exist today, even though the original decisions may have been rendered in the 1950s, 1960s, or 1970s. Such lengthy supervision has usurped the traditional roles of trained and licensed school administrators, elected school boards, and state legislatures regarding funding, facilities, personnel, and curriculum. Although federal judges generally lack the knowledge and expertise to properly administer schools or to make curricular or instructional decisions, on occasion they assumed control of these matters and then retained it for decades, even when compliance seemingly had occurred. With key decisions in 1991 and 1992, however, the Supreme Court provided complying districts with a means to an end.

In *Board of Education v. Dowell*, the school district had been operating since 1972 under a court-ordered plan that entailed substantial student busing to achieve integration. Five years after the initial decision, the federal district court ruled that the board had complied with the order in good faith and was entitled to pursue its legitimate policies without further court supervision. At that time, judicial monitoring was removed, but the 1972 decree was not dissolved. Later, after demographic changes led to greater burdens on minority students in continuing the student busing program, the school board in 1984 adopted a neighborhood school assignment policy for kindergarten through grade four. The new plan was challenged because it would result in about half of the elementary schools becoming 90 percent minority or 90 percent Caucasian. The lower court upheld the plan, but the Tenth Circuit reversed. The appeals court reasoned that the district's circumstances had not changed enough to justify modifying the 1972 decree.[50] The court conjectured that compliance alone could not be the basis for dissolving an injunction and concluded that the school board failed to meet its burden of proof.

On further appeal, the Supreme Court held that the appellate court's standard for dissolving the original decree was too stringent and emphasized that federal supervision of local school systems was intended only as a temporary measure to remedy past discrimination. The Court reasoned that the intent of a desegregation plan is met upon finding—as the district court had done—that the school system was operating in compliance with the Equal Protection Clause and was not likely to return to its former ways. Furthermore, the Court concluded that the federal judiciary should terminate supervision of school districts where school boards have complied with desegregation mandates in good faith and have eliminated vestiges of past discrimination "to the extent practicable."[51]

Then, in 1992 the Supreme Court clarified several related issues in a Georgia case, *Freeman v. Pitts*. In *Freeman*, the Court purported that a district court must relinquish its supervision and control over those aspects of a school system in which there has been compliance with a desegregation decree even if other aspects of the decree have not been met. Through this approach, the Court sought to restore to state and local authorities control over public schools at the earliest possible date and noted that "[p]artial relinquishment of judicial control . . . can be an important and significant step in fulfilling the district court's duty to return the operations and control of schools to local authorities."[52]

[50]890 F.2d 1483 (10th Cir. 1989).
[51]Bd. of Educ. v. Dowell, 498 U.S. 237, 249–50 (1991).
[52]503 U.S. 467, 489 (1992).

To guide the lower courts in determining whether supervision should be removed, the Court identified three questions:

- Has there been full and satisfactory compliance with the decree in those aspects of the system where supervision is to be withdrawn?
- Is the retention of judicial control necessary or practicable to achieve compliance with the decree in other facets of the school system?
- Has the district demonstrated a good faith commitment to the court's entire decree and relevant provisions of federal law?

With this guidance, numerous districts have been able to show that they have achieved a unitary operation. In 2001, the Seventh Circuit released an Illinois school district from an extensive lower court order requiring the expenditure of over $238 million. The schools were found to be desegregated, and although advanced elective courses enrolled proportionately more majority than minority students, there was no proof that such imbalance was caused by discrimination, past or present.[53] Similarly, the Eleventh Circuit supported the position that Hillsborough County, Florida, schools were unitary notwithstanding the current demographic imbalance that the court reasoned could not be assumed to be due to prior de jure segregation.[54] After noting the district's involvement in desegregation since 1956, the Eighth Circuit also released the Little Rock School District from further court supervision in 2009.[55] The court reasoned that the district had substantially complied with each of the requirements set forth in the desegregation agreement. In a subsequent case involving the Little Rock metropolitan area, the Eighth Circuit ruled that one school district had achieved unitary status, but a second district in the case had not.[56] Unitary status also was recognized in a number of additional cases, including those from Duval County, Florida; Charlotte-Mecklenburg, North Carolina; Muscogee County, Georgia; Russell County, Alabama; Auburn, Alabama; and Shelby County, Tennessee.[57]

Postunitary Transfer and School Assignment

Litigation will not end simply because the school district has achieved unitary status and has initially been relieved of judicial control and supervision. Any decision that may even potentially result in racial imbalance, whether de jure or de facto, is likely to be challenged. Accordingly, the placement of a new school or the creation of a new school district will foreseeably be scrutinized,[58] as will policies regarding school transfer, initial

[53]People Who Care v. Rockford Bd. of Educ., 246 F.3d 1073 (7th Cir. 2001).

[54]Manning v. Sch. Bd., 244 F.3d 927 (11th Cir. 2001).

[55]Little Rock Sch. Dist. v. N. Little Rock, 461 F.3d 746 (8th Cir. 2009).

[56]Little Rock Sch. Dist. v. Ark., 664 F.3d 738 (8th Cir. 2011) (finding second district in the case had not achieved unitary status because there was noncompliance with student assignment reporting, discipline, advanced placement, employment, staff, and special education).

[57]Robinson v. Shelby Cnty. Bd. of Educ., 566 F.3d 642 (6th 2009); NAACP, Jacksonville Branch v. Duval Cnty. Sch., 273 F.3d 960 (11th Cir. 2001); Belk v. Charlotte-Mecklenburg Bd. of Educ., 269 F.3d 305 (4th Cir. 2001); Lockett v. Bd. of Educ., 111 F.3d 839 (11th Cir. 1997); Lee v. Russell Cnty. Bd. of Educ., No. 70-T-848-E, 2002 U.S. Dist. LEXIS 4075 (M.D. Ala. Feb. 25, 2002); Lee v. Auburn City Bd. of Educ., No. 70-T-851-E, 2002 U.S. Dist. LEXIS 2527 (M.D. Ala. Feb. 14, 2002). *But see* Fisher v. Tucson Unified Sch. Dist., 652 F.3d 1131 (9th Cir. 2011); Jenkins v. Missouri, 216 F.3d 720 (8th Cir. 2000); Liddell v. Special Sch. Louis Cnty., 149 F.3d 862 (8th Cir. 1998); Brown v. Bd. of Educ., 978 F.2d 585 (10th Cir. 1992), *vacated and remanded*, 503 U.S. 978 (1992).

[58]*See, e.g.*, Anderson v. Canton Mun. Separate Sch. Dist., 232 F.3d 450 (5th Cir. 2000); Valley v. United States, 173 F.3d 944 (5th Cir. 1999).

school assignment, open enrollment, or charter schools. However, a transfer policy that results in only an insignificant change in minority-majority enrollment within the district will not typically justify reasserting judicial supervision.[59]

Furthermore, students have challenged school district policies that were designed and administered to maintain the racial balance accomplished through years of court supervision, integrate de facto segregated communities, or achieve the goal of a diverse student body. In such instances, students generally were permitted to enroll in schools where their race was a minority or otherwise underrepresented, but not vice versa. Given the use of race, numerous cases have been filed, with courts rendering mixed opinions.[60] Guidance for lower courts began to emerge in 2003 when the Supreme Court, in *Grutter v. Bollinger*,[61] permitted a law school to consider race as one of several factors in determining the composition of its first-year class. In denying the plaintiff's race-based Fourteenth Amendment claim, the Court majority identified a compelling interest (i.e., the benefits derived from a diverse student body) and reasoned that the school's admission procedures were sufficiently narrowly tailored not to adversely affect the rights of rejected Caucasian applicants.[62]

With *Grutter* as justification, if not incentive, school districts[63] once again are considering race in making placement decisions, but this time with the motive to integrate rather than segregate. Nonetheless, numerous questions remain concerning the legality of such practices. A partial answer was provided in a 2007 Supreme Court decision, *Parents Involved in Community Schools v. Seattle School District No. 1*. The plurality opinion identified an Equal Protection Clause violation where both the Seattle, Washington, and Jefferson County, Kentucky, school districts considered race to determine school assignment once residence and availability of space were considered.[64] Seattle had never been found guilty of de jure segregation or been subjected to court-ordered desegregation, while Jefferson County had its court order dissolved in 2000 after it had eliminated the vestiges of prior segregation to the greatest extent practicable.

The Court reasoned that each district's diversity plan relied on race in a nonindividualized, mechanical way even though other means were available to address integration goals of the de facto segregated communities. The plans were neither race neutral nor narrowly tailored. Moreover, they were not designed to result in the achievement of

[59]United States v. Texas, 457 F.3d 472 (5th Cir. 2006).

[60]*Compare* Eisenberg v. Montgomery Cnty. Pub. Schs., 197 F.3d 123 (4th Cir. 1999) (concluding that a race-based transfer plan used to determine enrollment in a magnet school with an enriched curriculum violated the Fourteenth Amendment even if diversity qualified as a compelling state interest, as the action of the board was not narrowly tailored) *with* Brewer v. W. Irondequoit Cent. Sch. Dist., 212 F.3d 738 (2d Cir. 2000) (concluding that plaintiff had not demonstrated a likelihood of success as the state had a compelling interest in its use of racial classifications to reduce racial isolation and de facto segregation).

[61]539 U.S. 306 (2003). Since *Grutter*, Michigan voters amended the state constitution to prohibit the consideration of race in making admissions decisions. MICH. CONST. art. I, § 26. However, the state ban was overturned as unconstitutional by the Sixth Circuit in 2012. *See* Coal. to Defend Affirmative Action v. Regents of the Univ. of Mich., No. 08-1387, 2012 U.S. App. LEXIS 23433 (6th Cir. Nov. 15, 2012).

[62]The U.S. Supreme Court has agreed to hear another case involving affirmative action in higher education. *See* Fisher v. Univ. of Texas, No. 11-345 (argued Oct. 10, 2012).

[63]At the university level since *Grutter*, see also *Smith v. University of Washington*, 392 F.3d 367 (9th Cir. 2004) (upholding the consideration of race and ethnicity as factors in the university's admissions program).

[64]551 U.S. 701 (2007) (aggregating claims from *Parents Involved in Cmty. Sch. v. Seattle Sch. Dist., No. 1*, 426 F.3d 1162 (9th Cir. 2005) and *McFarland v. Jefferson Cnty. Pub. Schs.*, 416 F.3d 513 (6th Cir. 2005)).

broad-based student diversity, but rather were created to address the racial balancing of whites and nonwhites in Seattle and blacks and "others" in Jefferson County.

Although both of these race-based programs were disallowed, only four Justices appeared to foreclose the use of race in making placement decisions where there has been no proven history of race discrimination. The fifth member of the plurality opinion and the Justices in the minority were willing to consider a school district's use of race in making student assignments even in de facto segregated school districts, assuming such practices address a compelling interest (i.e., diversity) and are narrowly tailored. Accordingly, expect to see continued growth in the number of cases regarding student assignment as school districts go beyond complying with court-ordered desegregation plans and attempt to identify narrowly tailored means to achieve diversity.[65] Guidelines issued in December 2011 by the U.S. Department of Justice and the U.S. Department of Education provide assistance to both public K–12 schools and universities when developing student assignment plans that consider race.[66] The guidelines offer examples of what is permissible when school districts are trying to achieve a higher level of student body diversity.

Race as a Factor in Admission to Private Schools

When private schools use race as a factor to determine admission, only Title VI and 42 U.S.C. § 1981 at the federal level will apply, in addition to any related state laws or local ordinances. Title VI forbids race discrimination but applies only to those schools that receive federal financial assistance. On the other hand, § 1981 prohibits both race and ethnicity discrimination in entering into and fulfilling contracts and requires compliance of all public and private schools, regardless of whether they qualify as recipients of federal aid. The seminal case applying this law to a private education setting is *Runyon v. McCrary*, in which the Supreme Court held that § 1981 was violated when private school administrators rejected all applicants to their school who were not Caucasian.[67] The Court concluded that the practice violated the right to contract due to race and purported that its ruling violated neither parents' privacy rights nor their freedom of association.

Notwithstanding, the Ninth Circuit in 2006 found no § 1981 violation where a private school in Hawaii founded by the descendants of King Kamehameha I denied admission to an applicant because he was not of Hawaiian ancestry. In fact, only one non-Hawaiian had previously been admitted, given the highly unusual situation that year where the pool of Hawaiian applicants was one less than the number of available openings.[68] Students were required to pay a modest tuition, thus establishing a contract. In rendering its decision permitting continued use of race in making admission decisions and distinguishing the present case from *Runyon*, the court reasoned that:

- the preference was remedial in nature in that it was targeted to assist native Hawaiian students who were performing less well academically than all other classes of students;

[65] *See, e.g.*, Lewis v. Ascension Parish Sch. Bd., 662 F.3d 343 (5th Cir. 2011) (finding that school district's plan to maintain unitary status by considering race in student assignment was impermissible); *see also* Doe v. Lower Merion Sch. Dist., 665 F.3d 524 (3d Cir. 2011) (finding school district did not select students based on racial classifications).

[66] U.S. Dep't of Justice & U.S. Dep't of Educ., *Guidance on the Voluntary Use of Race to Achieve Diversity and Avoid Racial Isolation in Elementary and Secondary Schools* (2011), http://www.justice.gov/crt/about/edu/documents/guidanceelem.pdf.

[67] 427 U.S. 160 (1976).

[68] Doe v. Kamehameha Schs., 470 F.3d 827 (9th Cir. 2006).

- non-Hawaiian applicants did not have their rights unnecessarily trammeled or face an absolute bar to their advancement—other schools were available that provided adequate education for non-Hawaiians; and
- the preference was limited—first, when the number of openings exceeds the number of Hawaiian applicants, non-Hawaiians will be admitted; second, the preference will last only long enough to remedy the current educational effects of past, private, and government-sponsored discrimination as well as existing social and economic deprivation.

The next decade should continue to provide ample case law dealing with strategies designed to remedy past discrimination and to promote racial diversity in schools.

Race Discrimination and Matriculated Students

Although there are a number of laws that prohibit race discrimination in educational settings, there is no doubt that discrimination continues, although it is likely to be more subtle and therefore more difficult to prove than in prior years. Such discrimination has been alleged in such areas as the assignment to ability-based courses or programs (e.g., gifted, advanced, developmental);[69] athletic eligibility;[70] racial profiling;[71] academic dismissal from special programs;[72] sexual harassment and molestation;[73] the creation of a hostile environment;[74] and the like. More recent controversies have focused on the overrepresentation of minority students in school disciplinary matters, but little litigation has been generated in this area.[75]

Claims of racial discrimination also have been at issue in cases involving school mascots. In these cases, courts have addressed school mascots that are considered offensive to Native Americans. In one case, Native American students and their mother contended that the school district's use of the Indian logo as a mascot was racially discriminatory. The Wisconsin Appellate Court did not find the logo to be discriminatory because it did not depict a negative stereotype.[76] The court further reasoned that the logo did not depict any particular tribe. Likewise, an Illinois appellate court did not find Chief Illiniwek, the mascot and official symbol at the University of Illinois, to be discriminatory under state law.[77] The plaintiffs had alleged that Chief Illiniwek's performances at basketball games were demeaning to Native Americans. Given these controversies, it is not surprising that

[69] *See, e.g.*, Hobson v. Hansen, 269 F. Supp. 401 (D.D.C. 1967), *aff'd sub nom.* Smuck v. Hobson, 408 F.2d 175 (D.C. Cir. 1969).

[70] *See, e.g.*, Allen-Sherrod v. Henry Cnty. Sch. Dist., 248 F. App'x 145 (11th Cir. 2007).

[71] *See, e.g.*, Carthans v. Jenkins, No. 04 C 4528, 2005 U.S. Dist. LEXIS 23294 (N.D. Ill. Oct. 6, 2005).

[72] *See, e.g.*, Brewer v. Bd. of Trs. of Univ. of Ill., 479 F.3d 908 (7th Cir. 2007) (finding no discrimination and identifying no comparable student of another race who had ever been retained with a grade point average lower than plaintiff's who did not have extraordinarily compelling circumstances).

[73] Doe v. Smith, 470 F.3d 331 (7th Cir. 2006).

[74] Qualls v. Cunningham, 183 F. App'x 564 (7th Cir. 2006) (finding no support for the claim that school officials had created a racially hostile environment that caused plaintiff to receive poor grades and ultimately resulted in his academic dismissal).

[75] *See* Russ Skiba, Suzanne Eckes & Kevin Brown, *African American Disproportionality in School Discipline: The Divide Between Best Evidence and Legal Remedy*, 54 N.Y.L. Sch. L. Rev. 1071 (2010) (finding that students of color are disproportionately represented in school discipline matters, but few recent cases involve this issue).

[76] Munson v. State Superintendent of Pub. Instruction, 577 N.W.2d 387 (Wisc. Ct. App. 1998) (unpublished).

[77] Ill. Native Am. Bar Ass'n v. Univ. of Ill., 368 Ill. App.3d 321 (App. Ct. 2006); *see also* Dupuis v. Bd. of Trs., 128 P.3d 1010 (Mont. 2006) (determining that plaintiff failed to exhaust administrative remedies in a case involving a Native American school mascot).

the Oregon State Board of Education recently decided to ban Native American themed mascots in schools.[78]

Even though there are only a limited number of cases reported with regard to racial discrimination involving matriculated students, it is still prudent for school officials to establish a written policy prohibiting race and other forms of impermissible discrimination, inform educators and staff of their individual responsibilities, promptly and thoroughly investigate claims of impropriety, conduct fair and impartial hearings, and determine an appropriate response (e.g., suspension of a student, termination of an employee) for those who have engaged in discriminatory behavior.

CLASSIFICATIONS BASED ON NATIVE LANGUAGE

Among the numerous identifiable "classes" of students in American schools are "linguistic minorities," some of whom have been denied an adequate education due to the failure of the school district to address their language differences through appropriate instruction. Although programs that are designed to meet the educational needs of linguistic minorities are largely financed through state and local funds, the federal government provides modest funding for research regarding how students learn a second language, how to train instructors, and the effectiveness of alternative teaching methodologies and programs.[79] The Office of English Language Acquisition administers the grant programs, provides leadership and technical assistance, coordinates services, promotes best practice, and assesses outcomes. Through efforts such as these, many students today are provided with bilingual and English language instruction that allows them to benefit from the public school curriculum. However, when access to school is denied or when language differences are not removed,[80] students often turn to federal courts for protection. The rights of linguistic minorities are protected by the Fourteenth Amendment,[81] Title VI of the Civil Rights Act of 1964, and the Equal Educational Opportunities Act of 1974 (EEOA).

Title VI stipulates that "[n]o person in the United States shall, on the ground of race, color, or national origin, be excluded from participation in, be denied the benefits of, or be subjected to discrimination under any program or activity receiving [f]ederal financial assistance from the Department of Education."[82] Moreover, this statute requires compliance throughout a school district if *any* activity is supported by federal funds (e.g., special education). Discrimination against linguistic minorities is considered a form of national origin discrimination and is therefore prohibited by Title VI. However, a school district policy that treats students with limited English proficiency differently than other

[78]Kim Murphy, *Home of the Braves No More: Oregon Bans Native American Mascots,* L.A. TIMES (May 18, 2012), http://articles.latimes.com/2012/may/18/nation/la-na-nn-native-mascots-20120518.

[79]20 U.S.C. §§ 3420, 3423d, 6931, 6932 (2012).

[80]Most bilingual and ESL programs are intended to eliminate foreign language barriers. As a result, there have been times when students speaking minority English dialects or American Sign Language have been denied specialized language services. *See, e.g.*, Kielbus v. N.Y. City Bd. of Educ., 140 F. Supp. 2d 284 (E.D.N.Y. 2001) (sign language); Martin Luther King Junior Elementary Sch. Children v. Ann Arbor Sch. Dist. Bd., 473 F. Supp. 1371 (E.D. Mich. 1979) (black English).

[81]*Strict scrutiny* is applied when the acts are facially discriminatory; *intent* is required when the acts are facially neutral (e.g., when tests administered only in English are used to determine enrollment in gifted programs).

[82]42 U.S.C. § 2000d (2012). Regulations may be found at 34 C.F.R. § 100 (2012).

students does not necessarily "facially discriminate based on national origin."[83] In addition, the Equal Educational Opportunities Act (EEOA) of 1974 requires public school systems to develop appropriate programs for limited English proficient (LEP) students.[84] The Act mandates in part that "[n]o state shall deny equal educational opportunity to an individual on account of his or her race, color, sex, or national origin, by . . . the failure by an educational agency to take appropriate action to overcome language barriers that impede equal participation by its students in its instructional program."[85]

In the first U.S. Supreme Court decision involving the rights of LEP students, *Lau v. Nichols*, Chinese children asserted that the San Francisco public schools failed to provide for the needs of non-English-speaking students. The Supreme Court agreed with the students and held that the lack of sufficient remedial English instruction violated Title VI. The Court reasoned that equality of treatment was not realized merely by providing students with the same facilities, textbooks, teachers, and curriculum, and that requiring children to acquire English skills on their own before they could hope to make any progress in school made "a mockery of public education."[86] The Court emphasized that "basic English skills are at the very core of what these public schools teach," and, therefore, "students who do not understand English are effectively foreclosed from any meaningful education."[87]

Lower courts have also addressed important issues involving the rights of English language learners (ELL). The Colorado federal district court, in assessing compliance of the Denver public schools, concluded that the law does not require a full bilingual education program for every LEP student but does place a duty on the district to take action to eliminate barriers that prevent LEP children from participating in the educational program. Good faith effort is inadequate. What is required, according to the court, is an effort that "will be reasonably effective in producing intended results."[88] Such an effort was not found in the Denver public schools. Although a transitional bilingual program was selected by district personnel, it was not being implemented effectively, primarily due to poor teacher training, selection, and assignment. Accordingly, an EEOA violation was found. Likewise, the Seventh Circuit, in examining Illinois's compliance, argued that "appropriate action" under the law certainly means more than "no action."[89] Once again, the court found that the selection of transitional bilingual education was appropriate, but that it had not been effectively implemented. The court identified both an EEOA violation and a violation of Title VI regulations.

In contrast, a California school district's Spanish bilingual program and three forms of English as a Second Language were judicially endorsed. District teachers were found to be proficient, qualified, and experienced; native-language academic support was available for thirty-eight languages in all subjects; and a cultural enrichment program was operating for kindergarten through grade three. Plaintiffs claimed a violation of the EEOA and Title VI and requested instruction in the students' native tongue. The court disagreed

[83]Mumid v. Abraham Lincoln High Sch., 618 F.3d 789, 795 (8th Cir. 2010) (holding in favor of the school district in a case involving immigrant students who were ELL and treated differently than other students in the district).
[84]20 U.S.C. § 1701 (2012).
[85]20 U.S.C. § 1703(f) (2012).
[86]Lau v. Nichols, 414 U.S. 563, 566 (1974).
[87]*Id.*
[88]Keyes v. Sch. Dist. No. 1, 576 F. Supp. 1503, 1520 (D. Colo. 1983).
[89]Gomez v. Ill. State Bd. of Educ., 811 F.2d 1030, 1043 (7th Cir. 1987).

and found that the program was based on sound theory, implemented consistent with that theory, and produced satisfactory results (i.e., LEP students were learning at rates equal to or higher than their English-speaking counterparts).[90]

California has generated a significant amount of case law involving the instruction of non- and limited-English-speaking students. Many suits have attacked Proposition 227, which requires that all children in public schools be taught English through "sheltered English immersion" (SEI).[91] This approach requires the use of specially designed materials and procedures where "nearly all" classroom instruction is in English. In most instances, the law requires school districts to abandon their use of bilingual education. Notwithstanding the prior use of bilingual programming, immigrant children within the state had experienced a high dropout rate and were low in English literacy. Only those children who already possess good English language skills or those for whom an alternate course of study would be better suited may be excused from the SEI initiative. Even then, twenty or more exempted students per grade level are required before an alternative program such as bilingual education needs to be provided.

To ensure that the SEI approach is used, the state legislature included a *parental enforcement provision* in the law, which gives parents the right to sue to receive SEI instruction as well as for actual damages and attorneys' fees. Any educator who willfully and repeatedly refuses to teach "overwhelmingly" in English may be held personally liable. The state teachers' association attacked this provision as being unconstitutionally vague. But the Ninth Circuit found terms such as "nearly all" and "overwhelmingly" to be no more vague than other descriptive terms used in the writing of statutes and reasoned that such language was likely to chill only a negligible amount of non-English speech, if any.[92]

In *Horne v. Flores*, the Supreme Court provided further guidance in this area when it held that states and local educational authorities have wide latitude in determining which programs and techniques they will implement to meet their obligations under the Equal Educational Opportunity Act.[93] The state of Arizona was ultimately given relief from a decree related to an ELL program. The Court looked beyond funding for ELL instruction and determined that obligations under the original decree had been satisfied in other ways.

Another type of national origin/language discrimination was alleged in Kansas where the principal and several teachers prohibited students from speaking Spanish while on school grounds.[94] Following his suspension for speaking Spanish, a student claimed Fourteenth Amendment, Section 1983, and Title VI violations. The court dismissed the Fourteenth Amendment and § 1983 claims against the school district, as the district could not be vicariously liable under respondeat superior because the principal and teachers were not final decision makers—such authority was held by the school board and could not be delegated. Similar claims against individual defendants also were dismissed, as the educators were entitled to qualified immunity. Moreover, the plaintiff failed to establish that there was a clearly established right to speak a foreign language while at a public

[90]Teresa P. v. Berkeley Unified Sch. Dist., 724 F. Supp. 698 (N.D. Cal. 1989).

[91]Other states have passed similar ballot initiatives. For example, Arizona passed Proposition 203 in 2000 (ARIZ. REV. STAT. ANN. § 15-751(5) (2012)), and Massachusetts passed Question 2 in 2002 (MASS. GEN. LAWS ch. 386, § 1 (2002) (amending ch. 71A).

[92]Cal. Teachers Ass'n v. State Bd. of Educ., 271 F.3d 1141 (9th Cir. 2001).

[93]557 U.S. 433 (2009).

[94]Rubio v. Turner Unified Sch. Dist. No. 202, 453 F. Supp. 2d 1295 (D. Kan. 2006).

school. In spite of the above, the court refused to dismiss the plaintiff's Title VI claim, given the disparate impact the practice had on Hispanic students.

In light of the significant growth of Hispanic and other populations immigrating to the United States, expect more litigation in this area. One related topic that has received recent attention involves changes in state immigration laws that may have an impact on student classifications with regard to language, race, or national origin. Since Arizona passed the Support Our Law Enforcement and Safe Neighborhoods Act,[95] at least five other states have passed similar laws (i.e., Alabama, Georgia, South Carolina, Utah, and Indiana). Alabama's law required schools to determine the immigration status of their students. However, in 2012, the Eleventh Circuit blocked implementation of the provision as violating the equal protection rights of the affected children.[96] Some of the other laws have pending litigation, and it is likely that legal challenges to state laws targeting immigrants will continue.

CLASSIFICATIONS BASED ON ABILITY OR ACHIEVEMENT

Courts have generally upheld decisions related to grade placement, denial of promotion, and assignment to instructional groups. Ability grouping purportedly permits more effective and efficient teaching by allowing teachers to concentrate their efforts on students with similar needs. Grouping according to ability or achievement is permissible, although there have been challenges concerning the use of standardized intelligence and achievement tests for determining pupil placements in regular classes and special education programs. These suits have alleged that such tests are racially and culturally biased and that their use to classify or track pupils results in erroneous placements that stigmatize children. Other challenges have arisen regarding the rights of gifted and talented students to an appropriate education.

Tracking Schemes

In the most widely publicized case pertaining to ability grouping, *Hobson v. Hansen*, the use of standardized intelligence test scores to place elementary and secondary students in various ability tracks in Washington, D.C., was attacked as unconstitutional.[97] Plaintiffs contended that some children were incorrectly assigned to lower tracks and had very little chance of advancing to higher ones because of the limited curriculum and lack of remedial instruction. The federal district court examined the test scores used to track students, analyzed the accuracy of the test measurements, and concluded that mistakes often resulted from placing pupils on this basis. For the first time, a federal court evaluated testing methods and held that they discriminated against minority children. In prohibiting the continued use of such test scores, the court emphasized that it was not abolishing the use of tracking systems per se and reasoned that "[w]hat is at issue here is not whether defendants are entitled to provide different kinds of students with different kinds of

[95]Ariz. Rev. Stat. § 11-1051 (2012).
[96]*See* United States v. Alabama, 691 F.3d 1269 (11th Cir. 2012).
[97]269 F. Supp. 401 (D.D.C. 1967), *aff'd sub nom.* Smuck v. Hobson, 408 F.2d 175 (D.C. Cir. 1969). Because ability grouping based on various forms of assessment (usually testing) is facially neutral, the appropriate Fourteenth Amendment standard is *intent.* Meeting this standard of review has been difficult, particularly when cases do not also involve de jure segregation.

education."[98] The court noted that classifications reasonably related to educational purposes are constitutionally permissible unless they result in discrimination against identifiable groups of children.

The Fifth Circuit agreed with this latter point in its evaluation of a tracking scheme in Jackson, Mississippi.[99] Although the court had previously struck down the plan given its impact on integration efforts, it later noted that "as a general rule, school systems are free to employ ability grouping, even when such a policy has a segregative effect, so long . . . as such a practice is genuinely motivated by educational concerns and not discriminatory motives."[100]

Based on evidence indicating that ability grouping provided better educational opportunities for African American students, the Eleventh Circuit upheld grouping practices in several Georgia school districts even though they had not achieved desegregated status.[101] Ability grouping allowed resources to be targeted toward low-achieving students and resulted in both gains on statewide tests and the reassignment of many students to higher-level achievement groups. The court further noted that, unlike students in earlier cases, these students had not attended inferior segregated schools. School systems undergoing desegregation may be subjected to closer judicial review when implementing ability grouping, but such plans will be prohibited only if found to be a ploy to resegregate or discriminate.[102]

When children are evaluated and provided with appropriate programs or grouped by ability, it is essential that all testing instruments be reliable, valid, and unbiased to the extent practical and possible. Although a few courts have found some tests to include specific questions that are racially biased[103] or administered in discriminatory ways (e.g., not in the student's native language or other mode of communication), such cases occur far less often today. Test developers have made extensive efforts to improve the reliability and validity of their instruments and to remove known forms of cultural, ethnic, and racial bias. As a result, it is unlikely that a nationally normed and marketed test used to measure ability or aptitude will be found racially biased. Nonetheless, prudent educators should take every precaution to ensure that accurate assessments are employed, only qualified personnel are hired, tests are administered in a nondiscriminatory manner, multiple criteria are used in determining an appropriate track or placement, and test results are used in good faith. Care also should be taken to ensure that teachers do not discriminate against students assigned to lower tracks or develop stereotypes about their abilities or potential.[104]

Gifted and Talented Students

Often overlooked when identifying unique needs and providing appropriate programs are those students labeled as "gifted" or "talented." Included within these populations are

[98]*Hobson*, 269 F. Supp. at 511.

[99]Singleton v. Jackson Mun. Separate Sch. Dist., 419 F.2d 1211 (5th Cir. 1969).

[100]Castaneda v. Pickard, 648 F.2d 989, 996 (5th Cir. 1981).

[101]Ga. State Conference of Branches of NAACP v. Georgia, 775 F.2d 1403 (11th Cir. 1985).

[102]*See, e.g.*, Bester v. Tuscaloosa City Bd. of Educ., 722 F.2d 1514 (11th Cir. 1984); *see also* Holton v. City of Thomasville Sch. Dist., 425 F.3d 1325 (11th Cir. 2005) (remanding with instructions to assess whether the tracking scheme employed by the school district is based on the present results of past segregation or is designed to remedy such results through better educational opportunities).

[103]*See* Larry P. v. Riles, 495 F. Supp. 926 (N.D. Cal. 1979), *aff'd*, 793 F.2d 969 (9th Cir. 1984).

[104]*See, e.g.*, United States v. City of Yonkers, 197 F.3d 41 (2d Cir. 1999).

students who give evidence of high performance capability in areas such as intellectual, creative, artistic, or leadership capacity or in specific academic fields. Over the years, the federal government has provided only minimal aid for gifted education, and there is no federal statute specifying substantive rights for the gifted, as there is for children with disabilities.

Given a limited federal role, rights for gifted and talented students are based overwhelmingly on state law or local school board policy. These laws vary greatly by state. Pennsylvania, one of the leading states in mandating programs for the gifted, includes gifted and talented students under its designation of "exceptional children" who "deviate from the average in physical, mental, emotional or social characteristics to such an extent that they require special educational facilities or services."[105] The Pennsylvania Supreme Court interpreted this law as placing a mandatory obligation on school districts to establish individualized programs for gifted students beyond the general enrichment program.[106] However, the court qualified its interpretation of state statute by observing that the law does not require "exclusive individual programs outside or beyond the district's existing, regular, and special education curricular offerings"[107] and does not impose a duty to maximize a child's potential.

A similar case was filed in California, where the parents of an "extremely" gifted child under the age of sixteen sued the state to require it to pay for their child's post-secondary college education.[108] The parents argued that the state was responsible for providing children with a free public education and that a program should be tailored to meet his special needs, as is done for students with disabilities. A California appeals court disagreed and identified no federal or state law that obligated the state to pay for the college education of its children, even if within compulsory school age.

Parental demands for individualized programming designed to meet their child's special needs also emanated from parents in Connecticut. A gifted student claimed to have the right to individualized education under state statute, given that gifted children were included within the state definition of exceptional children (i.e., those who do not progress effectively in a regular school program without special education). The local school board refused to provide the program, and the student filed suit. The Supreme Court of Connecticut disagreed with the student's claim and held that he was not entitled to special education, that the state never intended to extend such a right, and that special education must be provided only for students with disabilities. No equal protection violation was proven because the state's action of serving individuals with disabilities, but not the gifted, met rational basis scrutiny.[109]

Along these same lines, New York law stipulates that school districts *should* develop programs to assist gifted students in achieving their full potential. However, an appellate court found that the use of the word "should" indicated that the development of gifted programs was optional, not mandatory.[110] Consequently, the court held that a district was

[105]24 Pa. Stat. Ann. § 13-1371(1) (2012).

[106]Centennial Sch. Dist. v. Commonwealth Dep't of Educ., 539 A.2d 785 (Pa. 1988).

[107]*Id.* at 791; *see also* Saucon Valley Sch. Dist. v. Robert O., 785 A.2d 1069 (Pa. Commw. Ct. 2001) (determining that a hearing panel exceeded its authority when it ordered that a gifted student should be placed in the graduating class before his own, given that the district had failed to provide him with accelerated and enriched programming).

[108]Levi v. O'Connell, 50 Cal. Rptr. 3d 691 (App. Ct. 2006).

[109]Broadley v. Bd. of Educ., 639 A.2d 502 (Conn. 1994).

[110]Bennett v. City Sch. Dist., 497 N.Y.S.2d 72 (App. Div. 1985).

permitted to serve only a portion of the students identified as gifted and to select those students through a lottery system. Although use of a lottery may seem illogical, it provides an equal opportunity for each qualified youth to participate and does not illegally discriminate. Likewise, charter schools in most states that have a gifted and talented focus must remain open to all students. When such schools are oversubscribed, they need to implement a lottery.[111]

The procedures used to select students who are to participate in gifted programs continue to be challenged. Criteria such as intelligence, test scores, grade point average, and teacher evaluations are used in the selection process. Although under certain circumstances age may be a permissible criterion for admission (see discussion below), race will seldom be permitted unless court ordered.[112]

CLASSIFICATIONS BASED ON AGE

Age is one of the factors most commonly used to classify individuals, not only in schools but also in society. For example, a specified age is used as a prerequisite to obtaining a driver's license, buying alcoholic beverages, viewing certain movies, and receiving federal benefits. The two primary federal grounds used by students when they claim age-based violations are the Fourteenth Amendment[113] and the Age Discrimination Act of 1975,[114] which applies to recipients of federal financial assistance. The Age Discrimination Act is seldom used today, and when a violation is claimed, it generally is directed toward a college or university (e.g., a claim that age was used as a basis to deny admission[115]) rather than toward PK–12 schools. The few cases that have been filed against elementary and secondary schools tend to concentrate in the areas of early school admission or eligibility for advanced programs[116] or other services.[117] It is important to note that before filing an Age Discrimination Act case in court, the plaintiff must first file a charge with the Equal Employment Opportunities Commission (EEOC).[118]

Ranges vary, but within most states, students must attend school between the ages of six and sixteen. Students below or above state-established age limits have neither a state property right nor a federal constitutional right to public school attendance.

[111]*See, e.g.*, Cent. Dauphin Sch. Dist. v. Founding Coalition of the Infinity Charter Sch., 847 A.2d 195 (Pa. 2004) (holding that charter school could recruit gifted students but needed to remain open to anyone).

[112]Rosenfeld v. Montgomery Cnty. Pub. Schs., 25 F. App'x 123 (4th Cir. 2001) (affirming dismissal of case as the plaintiff eventually was admitted to the gifted program; the court acknowledged, however, that if different, less stringent selection criteria had been used for minority students, the plaintiff would have had a basis for seeking damages).

[113]Under the Fourteenth Amendment, rational basis scrutiny is required in age cases in which the policy or practice is facially discriminatory, and intent must be shown where the act is facially neutral.

[114]42 U.S.C. §§ 6101–6107 (2012).

[115]*See, e.g.*, Harris v. Members of the Bd. of Governors, No. 10-11384, 2011 U.S. Dist. LEXIS 96010 (E.D. Mich. Aug. 26, 2011) (denying motion for partial summary judgment to fifty-four-year-old who claimed age discrimination when he was denied admission to a graduate program).

[116]*See, e.g.*, Long v. Fulton Cnty. Sch. Dist., No. 1:10-cv-3033, 2011 U.S. Dist. LEXIS 85700 (N.D. Ga. Aug. 4, 2011) (allowing age discrimination claim to proceed by five-year-old gifted student who was denied placement in a first-grade classroom).

[117]D.A. v. Houston Indep. Sch. Dist., 716 F. Supp. 2d 603 (S.D. Tex. 2009) (granting school district's motion for summary judgment for a claim involving the Age Discrimination Act because school district was not required to test pre-kindergarten students for special education services).

[118]Cureton v. Montgomery Cnty. Bd. of Educ., No. AW-09-334, 2009 U.S. Dist. LEXIS 107596 (D. Md. Nov. 18, 2009).

Nevertheless, parents have challenged state and local decisions denying admission or services. In a Texas case, a policy was challenged that excluded children under the age of six as of September 1 of the current year from admission to the first grade.[119] The plaintiff had completed kindergarten in a private accredited school and had scored well on a standardized test but was two months too young to qualify for admission. The district had uniformly adhered to the state statute and local policy, refusing all requests for early admission. Noting this uniform application, the Texas Court of Appeals upheld the school district's action.

Similar decisions have been reached by other courts in denying students admission to kindergarten and other programs.[120] Rationales used to justify the consideration of age include the state's right to limit the benefit of public education and related curricular and extracurricular opportunities to children between specific ages, the administrative need to project enrollment, the costs of assessing learning readiness, the difficulty of meeting a wide range of individual needs, and the desire for children to develop emotionally, socially, and physiologically prior to admission.

CLASSIFICATIONS BASED ON SEX[121]

Classifications and discriminatory treatment based on sex in public education are as old as public education itself, as the first public schools and colleges primarily served males only. When women were eventually allowed to enroll, programs were typically segregated and inferior. Over the years, sex equality in public schools has improved, but at times classifications based on sex have limited both academic as well as extracurricular activities for females. Aggrieved parties often turn to federal courts to vindicate their rights. In most cases, plaintiffs allege a violation of either the Fourteenth Amendment[122] or Title IX of the Education Amendments of 1972.[123] Under Title IX, educational recipients of federal financial assistance are prohibited from discriminating, excluding, or denying benefits because of sex.[124]

In addition, Title IX has been interpreted to prohibit retaliation against both students and staff who themselves are not the target of intentional discrimination but are adversely treated due to their advocacy roles. The Supreme Court addressed this issue in 2005 in *Jackson v. Birmingham Board of Education*, where a teacher/coach was removed from his coaching position, allegedly due to his complaints about the treatment of the girls' basketball team (i.e., not receiving equal funding, equal access to equipment and

[119]Wright v. Ector Cnty. Indep. Sch. Dist., 867 S.W.2d 863 (Tex. App. 1993); *see also* Morrison v. Chi. Bd. of Educ., 544 N.E.2d 1099 (Ill. App. Ct. 1989) (holding that local board had discretion whether to assess a child to determine readiness to attend kindergarten).

[120]*See, e.g.*, Zweifel v. Joint Dist. No. 1, Belleville, 251 N.W.2d 822 (Wis. 1977); O'Leary v. Wisecup, 364 A.2d 770 (Pa. Commw. Ct. 1976).

[121]"Sex" generally refers to having male or female reproductive systems, whereas "gender" typically refers to social identity related to one's sex.

[122]Under the Fourteenth Amendment, *intermediate scrutiny* is applied in sex-based cases where facial discrimination exists, while *intent* is used where facially neutral practices result in alleged discrimination.

[123]20 U.S.C. § 1681 (2012).

[124]If aid is received by any program or activity within the school system, compliance must be demonstrated district-wide. Also, although Title IX does not include a specific statute of limitations, courts have elected to borrow the relevant limitations period for personal injury. *See, e.g.*, Stanley v. Trs. of Cal. State Univ., 433 F.3d 1129 (9th Cir. 2006) (identifying the appropriate limitations period to be one year).

facilities, and so forth).[125] The Court reasoned that discriminatory treatment against advocates was impliedly prohibited by Title IX and remanded the case for a determination of whether the coach's advocacy was in fact the motivating factor in his removal.

Interscholastic Sports

Sex discrimination litigation involving interscholastic sports has focused on two primary themes: the integration of single-sex teams and the unequal treatment of males and females. Although courts will issue injunctions to correct discriminatory conduct where it is found, they will not award monetary damages unless the school receives actual notice of the violation and then is shown to be deliberately indifferent to the claim.[126] It is important to note that although most athletic associations that regulate interscholastic competition are private corporations, the Supreme Court has found that they are entwined with their respective state governments and therefore are involved in state action.[127] As a result, some of the cases discussed below include challenges to both school districts and athletic associations.

SINGLE-SEX TEAMS. One of the more controversial issues involving high school athletics is the participation of males and females together in contact sports (e.g., wrestling, rugby, ice hockey, football, basketball, and other sports that involve physical contact). Title IX explicitly permits separation of students by sex within contact sports. However, individual school districts can determine whether to allow coeducational participation in contact sports in their efforts to provide equal athletic opportunities for males and females.[128] Where integration is either permitted or required in a contact sport, each athlete must receive a fair, nondiscriminatory opportunity to participate. The Ninth Circuit denied summary judgment to a university in a case involving female wrestlers who were removed from the coed wrestling team after they were unable to defeat males in their weight class.[129] The court reasoned that once females were permitted to join the wrestling team, which was considered a contact sport, the university did not have discretion to discriminate against them.

A Fourteenth Amendment claim was proffered in a case heard by a federal district court in New York, when it reviewed a female student's request to try out for the junior varsity football squad.[130] The school district was unable to show that its policy of prohibiting mixed competition served an important governmental objective, as is required under intermediate scrutiny. In rejecting the district's assertion that its policy was necessary to ensure the health and safety of female students, the court noted that no female student was given the opportunity to show that she was as fit, or more fit, than the weakest male member of the team.

[125] 544 U.S. 167 (2005); *see also* Burch v. Regents of the Univ. of Cal., 433 F. Supp. 2d 1110 (E.D. Cal. 2006) (denying summary judgment where a nonrenewed coach advocated for the rights of female wrestlers and claimed retaliation).

[126] Grandson v. Univ., 272 F.3d 568 (8th Cir. 2001).

[127] Brentwood Acad. v. Tenn. Secondary Sch. Athletic Ass'n, 531 U.S. 288 (2001).

[128] Elborough v. Evansville Cmty. Sch. Dist., 636 F. Supp. 2d 812 (W.D. Wis. 2009).

[129] Mansourian v. Regents of the Univ. of Cal., 594 F.3d 1095 (9th Cir. 2010).

[130] Lantz v. Ambach, 620 F. Supp. 663 (S.D.N.Y. 1985); *see also* Adams v. Baker, 919 F. Supp. 1496 (D. Kan. 1996) (upholding female student's right under the Fourteenth Amendment to participate in wrestling).

A Wisconsin federal district court similarly ruled that female students have the constitutional right to compete for positions on traditionally male contact teams, declaring that once a state provides interscholastic competition, such opportunities must be provided to all students on equal terms.[131] The court reasoned that the objective of preventing injury to female athletes was not sufficient to justify the prohibition of coeducational teams in contact sports. If school officials were reluctant to permit sex-integrated play, they had other options available—interscholastic competition in contact sports could be eliminated for all students or separate and equal teams for females could be established. But if comparable sex-segregated programs were provided, female athletes could not assert the right to try out for the male team simply because of its higher level of competition.

In a 1999 case from North Carolina, a female kicker made the football team but was later dropped; she also was given only limited opportunities to participate or to condition. The Fourth Circuit concluded that where integration is permitted, it may not be accompanied by sex discrimination; the court then remanded for a determination of whether the restrictions placed on the kicker were sex based.[132]

In addition to the controversies regarding coeducational participation in contact sports, there have been numerous challenges to policies denying integration of males and females in noncontact sports. Females filed the majority of these suits and prevailed in nearly every instance.[133] Title IX regulations explicitly require recipient districts to allow coeducational participation in those sports that are available only to one sex, presuming that athletic opportunities for that sex have been historically limited. Thus, females tend to succeed in their claims, whereas males tend to fail.[134] As a rule, school districts have been able to show an important governmental interest (e.g., redressing disparate athletic opportunities for females) in support of their decisions to exclude males from participating on teams traditionally reserved for females, while males have had difficulty supporting the claim that their athletic opportunities have been historically limited.

FEWER SPORTS OPPORTUNITIES FOR FEMALES. Although athletic opportunities for females have significantly increased since passage of Title IX in 1972, equal opportunity has not been achieved within all school districts. The Office for Civil Rights' Policy Interpretation requires that for schools to be in compliance they should (1) provide interscholastic sports opportunities for both sexes in terms of numbers of participants that are substantially proportionate to the respective enrollments of male and female students, (2) show a history of expanding sports programs for the underrepresented sex, or (3) provide enough opportunities to match the sports interests and abilities of the underrepresented sex.[135] Given such financial constraints, equality of athletic opportunities for males and females often has been achieved either by reducing the number of sports traditionally available for males,[136] or by lowering the number of participants on boys' teams

[131]Leffel v. Wis. Interscholastic Athletic Ass'n, 444 F. Supp. 1117 (E.D. Wis. 1978).

[132]Mercer v. Duke Univ., 190 F.3d 643 (4th Cir. 1999).

[133]*See, e.g.*, Croteau v. Fair, 686 F. Supp. 552 (E.D. Va. 1988); Israel v. W. Va. Secondary Sch. Activities Comm'n, 388 S.E.2d 480 (W. Va. 1989).

[134]*See, e.g.*, Williams v. Sch. Dist., 998 F.2d 168 (3d Cir. 1993); B.C. v. Bd. of Educ., Cumberland Reg'l Sch. Dist., 531 A.2d 1059 (N.J. Super. Ct. App. Div. 1987).

[135]U.S. Dep't of Educ. Office for Civil Rights' 1979 Policy Interpretation, 44 Fed. Reg. 71,413 (Dec. 11, 1979).

[136]*See, e.g.*, Chalenor v. Univ. of N.D., 291 F.3d 1042 (8th Cir. 2002); Boulahanis v. Bd. of Regents, 198 F.3d 633 (7th Cir. 1999); Miami Univ. Wrestling Club v. Miami Univ., 195 F. Supp. 2d 1010 (S.D. Ohio 2001).

(e.g., football) to provide generally equal opportunities for males and females.[137] Also, efforts have been made to disguise the existing inequity (e.g., double counting participants in women's indoor and outdoor track, but not double counting men in fall/spring events such as track, golf, and tennis) to avoid taking corrective action.

At times, female athletes have expressed an insufficient interest in a given sport to have it approved by the state athletic association. In a Kentucky case, high school athletes claimed a Title IX violation when the state athletic association refused to approve females' interscholastic fast-pitch softball. The association's decision was based on its policy of not sanctioning a sport unless at least 25 percent of its member institutions demonstrated an interest in participation. Since only 17 percent indicated an interest, approval was denied. In the original hearing on this controversy, the Sixth Circuit had held that the 25 percent requirement did not violate the Equal Protection Clause, as the facially neutral policy was not proven to entail intentional discrimination.[138] The case then was remanded and later appealed. The court again found no Title IX violation and further concluded that grouping sports by sex did not violate federal law. Moreover, the court resolved that the plaintiffs did not qualify for attorneys' fees because they did not prevail.[139] Plaintiffs had argued that since fast-pitch softball had become now available in the state, they ultimately were the winning party. The court noted, however, that such relief was not court ordered, and plaintiffs could not show that they were responsible for the change in state law directing the association to offer the requested sport.

The U.S. Department of Education issued a "Dear Colleague" letter in 2008 to provide further guidance to schools regarding how athletic opportunities are counted for Title IX compliance.[140] The letter outlines factors that may be considered in determining whether an institution has complied with Title IX. It stresses that the Office for Civil Rights will evaluate each institution on a case-by-case basis to allow flexibility in offering sports that align with the specific interests of the student body. Despite attempts to further explain the law, litigation in both PK–12 and higher education will likely continue as schools attempt to achieve greater sex equity.[141]

MODIFIED SPORTS AND SEPARATE SEASONS FOR FEMALES. Among the equity claims initiated by female athletes are those contesting the use of sex-based modifications in sports. Although federal courts historically have permitted different rules for males and females (e.g., split-court rules for women's basketball[142]), differential treatment of male and female athletes cannot be justified by unfounded and unsupported perceptions about either sex regarding strength, endurance, or ability.

[137]Neal v. Bd. of Trs., 198 F.3d 763 (9th Cir. 1999).

[138]Horner v. Ky. High Sch. Athletic Ass'n, 43 F.3d 265 (6th Cir. 1994).

[139]Horner v. Ky. High Sch. Athletic Ass'n, 206 F.3d 685 (6th Cir. 2000); *see also* Kelley v. Bd. of Trs., 35 F.3d 265 (7th Cir. 1994) (permitting the termination of men's swimming while retaining women's swimming).

[140]U.S. Dep't. of Educ., *Dear Colleague Letter: Athletic Activities Counted for Title IX Compliance* (Sept. 17, 2008), http://www2.ed.gov/about/offices/list/ocr/letters/colleague-20080917.pdf.

[141]*See, e.g.*, Equity in Athletics, Inc. v. Dep't of Educ., 639 F.3d 91 (4th Cir. 2011) (finding nonprofit organization failed to show that the three-part test violated the Equal Protection Clause); Pederson v. La. State Univ., 213 F.3d 858 (5th Cir. 2000) (concluding that university had violated Title IX by failing to accommodate the interests and abilities of female athletes); Cohen v. Brown Univ., 101 F.3d 155 (1st Cir. 1996) (rejecting university's claim that female students were less interested in sports).

[142]*Compare* Cape v. Tenn. Secondary Sch. Athletic Ass'n, 563 F.2d 793 (6th Cir. 1977) (permitting the use of split-court rules as they reflected physical differences between males and females) *with* Dodson v. Ark. Activities Ass'n, 468 F. Supp. 394 (E.D. Ark. 1979) (invalidating the use of separate basketball rules for males and females).

Also, maintaining separate playing seasons for female and male teams has been challenged as a violation of the equal protection clauses of both federal and state constitutions. In some instances, separate seasons have been upheld due to a lack of adequate facilities and general comparability of programs;[143] in other instances, separate seasons have been found to violate equal protection rights. This was the case in Michigan where the Sixth Circuit upheld a lower court ruling concluding that the difficulty in finding facilities, coaches, and officials did not justify the use of separate seasons for males and females where the girls bore the burden of off-season participation.[144] The court opined that if single-sex seasons were in fact necessary, the burden must be shared. For example, the junior varsity teams of both sexes could be placed into the disadvantageous season; as a result, the varsity teams then could compete during the preferred time period. This plan would result in the same utilization of facilities and staff, yet the advantages and disadvantages of off-season play would be equally divided between the sexes.

School districts also need to ensure that the scheduling of the games during the season is not inequitable. In one case, the parents of two female basketball players alleged such a disparity in that the boys were scheduled 95 percent of the time in a prime time slot, whereas the girls were scheduled only 53 percent of the time in a prime time slot. Holding in favor of the female players, the Seventh Circuit vacated the federal district court's entry of summary judgment in favor of the school district and remanded the case for further review.[145] Similarly, female athletes claimed that their high school athletic program maintained disparities between the boys' and girls' athletic programs with regard to locker rooms, equipment, travel, coaching facilities, scheduling of games, and funding. The students also argued that the school district did not offer female students equal athletic participation opportunities, even though there was an interest in additional offerings. A California federal district court granted female students' motion for summary judgment in part, holding that the school district permitted significant gender-based disparities, failed to demonstrate a history and continuing practice of expanding opportunities for female athletes, and did not fully and effectively accommodate female interest and abilities.[146]

Academic Programs

Allegations of sex bias in public schools have not been confined to athletic programs. Differential treatment of males and females in academic courses and schools also has generated litigation.[147] Because the "separate but equal" principle has been applied in cases alleging a Fourteenth Amendment violation, public school officials are required to show an exceedingly persuasive justification for classifications based on sex that are used to segregate the sexes or exclude either males or females from academic programs.

SINGLE-SEX SCHOOLS AND CLASSROOMS. The Third Circuit held that the operation of two historically sex-segregated public high schools (one for males, the other for females) in which enrollment is voluntary and educational offerings are essentially equal,

[143] *See, e.g.*, Ridgeway v. Mont. High Sch. Ass'n, 749 F. Supp. 1544 (D. Mont. 1990).
[144] Cmtys. for Equity v. Mich. High Sch. Athletic Ass'n, 459 F.3d 676 (6th Cir. 2006).
[145] Parker v. Franklin Cnty. Cmty. Sch. Corp., 667 F.3d 910 (7th Cir. 2012).
[146] Ollier v. Sweetwater Union High Sch. Dist., 604 F. Supp. 2d 1264 (S.D. Cal. 2009).
[147] Gossett v. Oklahoma, 245 F.3d 1172 (10th Cir. 2001).

is permissible under the Equal Protection Clause, Title IX, and the Equal Educational Opportunities Act of 1974.[148] Noting that Philadelphia's sex-segregated college preparatory schools offered functionally equivalent programs, the court concluded that the separation of the sexes was justified because youth might study more effectively in sex-segregated high schools. The court emphasized that the female plaintiff was not compelled to attend the sex-segregated academic school; she had the option of enrolling in a coeducational school within her attendance zone. Furthermore, the court stated that her petition to attend the male academic high school was based on personal preference rather than on an objective evaluation of the offerings available in the two schools. Subsequently, an equally divided United States Supreme Court affirmed this decision without delivering an opinion. Interestingly, in another case that involved the same Philadelphia school as the *Vorchheimer* case, three female students were denied admission at the all-male Philadelphia high school.[149] In this case, a common pleas court in Pennsylvania did not find the public school for the girls and the public school for the boys to be substantially similar. Some of the alleged inequities between the two schools included a "Bachelor of Arts" degree instead of a typical high school diploma, smaller class sizes, a larger building, and more books and computers at the boys' school. As a result of some of the inequities, the court held that the female students must be admitted to the all-male school.

Detroit school officials did not prevail in their attempt to segregate inner-city, African American male students to address more effectively these students' unique educational needs. Three African American male academies (preschool to fifth grade, sixth to eighth grade, and high school) were proposed. The three-year experimental academies were designed to offer an Afrocentric curriculum, emphasize male responsibility, provide mentors, offer Saturday classes and extended classroom hours, and provide individual counseling. No comparable program existed for females, although school authorities indicated that one would be forthcoming. The district court issued a preliminary injunction prohibiting the board from opening the academies, given the likelihood that the practice violated the Equal Protection Clause. Additionally, the court reasoned that failing to provide the injunction could result in irreparable injury to the female students and cause great disruption if the schools were allowed to open and then were forced to close.[150] The court noted that the district failed to show a substantial justification for its actions, as is required under the Fourteenth Amendment for facially discriminatory acts involving sex.

In a higher education case with PK–12 implications, the Supreme Court in 1982 struck down a nursing school's admission policy that restricted admission in degree programs to females without providing comparable opportunities for males.[151] The Court found no evidence that women had ever been denied opportunities in the field of nursing that would justify remedial action by the state. In applying intermediate scrutiny, the Court concluded that the university failed its burden of showing that the facially discriminatory sex classification served an important governmental objective, or that its discriminatory means were substantially related to the achievement of those objectives.

[148]Vorchheimer v. Sch. Dist., 532 F.2d 880 (3d Cir. 1976), *aff'd by equally divided court*, 430 U.S. 703 (1977).
[149]Newberg v. Bd. of Pub. Educ., 26 Pa. D. & C.3d 682 (Ct. C.P. Phila. Cnty. 1983).
[150]Garrett v. Bd. of Educ., 775 F. Supp. 1004 (E.D. Mich. 1991).
[151]Miss. Univ. for Women v. Hogan, 458 U.S. 718 (1982).

Similarly, the U.S. Supreme Court addressed male-only admissions policies in *United States v. Virginia*. Reversing the lower courts, the Court held that the state had violated the Fourteenth Amendment by its failure to provide equal opportunities for women in the area of military training when they were denied admission at the Virginia Military Institute.[152] A new program at a private, women-only institution would never be able to approach the success, quality, and prestige associated with that provided at VMI. Also, the Court refuted the reasons given by VMI for its refusal to admit women. The exclusion of women from VMI failed to further the institution's purported purpose of providing diversity in higher education. VMI's distinctive teaching methods and techniques could be used unchanged in many instances or slightly modified in the instruction of women, and privacy issues were resolvable.[153]

In 2006, the U.S. Department of Education issued new regulations that permit school districts to offer voluntary public single-sex classrooms and schools.[154] These regulations were a result of language included in the No Child Left Behind Act of 2001, which encourages school districts to experiment with public single-sex education programs.[155] Under Title IX regulations, coeducational schools must offer equal educational opportunities to both sexes, and enrollment in a single-sex class should be completely voluntary. Specifically, public single-sex schools are permitted, but a substantially coeducational school or single-sex school for students of the other sex must be available. Also, one of two objectives must be satisfied before implementing a single-sex educational program. The program must (1) improve the educational achievement of a recipient's students through an established policy to provide diverse educational opportunities or (2) meet the particular, identified educational needs of a recipient's students.[156] As a result of these amendments, many school districts have begun to experiment with single-sex educational programs. For example, while only three single-sex public education programs existed in the United States in 1995,[157] there are now roughly 500 schools that offer some single-sex classes in 40 states[158] and 90 single-sex public schools nationally.[159]

Recent litigation involves the amended Title IX regulations as well as the Equal Protection Clause in combination with other claims arising out of state law. In these legal challenges, the female students generally argue that school officials have failed to demonstrate an "exceedingly persuasive" justification for creating single-sex educational programs.[160] The outcomes of these cases have been mixed.

[152]518 U.S. 515 (1996).

[153]*See* Faulkner v. Jones, 51 F.3d 440 (4th Cir. 1995) (admitting a female applicant to an all-male cadet corps as the state was unable to show a substantial justification for the discrimination as is required under the Fourteenth Amendment; and reasoning that establishing a comparable parallel all-female cadet corps would not address the female student's interest in a timely manner).

[154]Title IX Regulations, 34 C.F.R. § 106.34 (2012).

[155]No Child Left Behind Act § 5131(a)(23)-c (2012).

[156]Title IX Regulations (2006), 34 C.F.R. §106.34(b)(1)(i)(A) & (B) (2012).

[157]Diane Schemo, *Change in Federal Rules Backs Single-Sex Public Education*, N.Y. Times, Oct. 25, 2006, at A1.

[158]Tamar Lewin, *Single-Sex Education is Assailed in Report*, N.Y. Times, Sept., 23, 2011, at A19.

[159]Meagan Patterson & Erin Pahlke, *Student Characteristics Associated with Girls' Success in a Single-Sex School*, 65 Sex Roles 737 (2010).

[160]*See, e.g.*, Doe v. Vermilion Parish Sch. Bd., 421 Fed. App'x 366 (5th Cir. 2011) (denying school district's motion to dismiss because students provided sufficient evidence that single-sex program may be harmful). *But see* A.N.A. v. Breckinridge Cnty. Bd. of Educ., 833 F. Supp. 2d 673 (W.D. Ky. 2011) (finding that female students did not suffer an injury when school district offered optional single-sex classes).

Sexual Harassment of Students

Title IX and the Equal Protection Clause of the Fourteenth Amendment also have been applied in sex-based claims of sexual harassment and abuse of students. Under the Equal Protection Clause, students have the right to be free from harassment on an equal basis with all other students, while Title IX prohibits discrimination on the basis of sex. Historically, charges of sexual harassment against school districts generally were dismissed.[161] But in 1992, the Supreme Court heard the appeal of a case in which a female student alleged that a coach initiated sexual conversations, engaged in inappropriate touching, and had coercive intercourse with her on school grounds on several occasions. In this case, *Franklin v. Gwinnett County Public Schools*, the Court held that Title IX prohibited the sexual harassment of students and that damages could be awarded where appropriate.[162] Since *Gwinnett*, numerous other cases with mixed results have been filed by current and former students alleging hostile environment,[163] student-to-student harassment,[164] sexual involvement and abuse of students by school staff,[165] off-campus harassment that resulted in an on-campus hostile environment,[166] harassment by a student teacher,[167] and same-sex harassment.[168] With *Gwinnett* as a starting point, two similar but slightly different standards have evolved: one for employee-to-student harassment and the other for student-to-student harassment.

EMPLOYEE-TO-STUDENT HARASSMENT. In 1998, the Supreme Court provided further guidance in *Gebser v. Lago Vista Independent School District* regarding the liability of school districts when students are harassed by school employees.[169] In this case, a high school student and a teacher were involved in a relationship that had not been reported to the administration until the couple was discovered having sex and the teacher was arrested. The district then terminated the teacher's employment, and the parents sued under Title IX. On appeal, the Supreme Court held that to be liable, the district had to have *actual notice* of the harassment. The Court reasoned that allowing recovery of damages based on either respondeat superior or constructive notice (i.e., notice that is inferred or implied) would be inconsistent with the objective of the Act, as liability would attach even though the district had no actual knowledge of the conduct or an opportunity to take action to end the harassment.[170] Accordingly, for there to be an award of damages,

[161] *See, e.g.*, D.R. v. Middle Bucks Area Vocational Technical Sch., 972 F.2d 1364 (3d Cir. 1992); J.O. v. Alton Cmty. Unit Sch. Dist. 11, 909 F.2d 267 (7th Cir. 1990).

[162] 503 U.S. 60 (1992).

[163] *See, e.g.*, Jennings v. Univ. of N.C., 444 F.3d 255 (4th Cir. 2006).

[164] *See, e.g.*, Estate of Brown v. Ogletree, No. 11-cv-1491, 2012 U.S. Dist. LEXIS 21968 (S.D. Tex. Feb. 21, 2012); Price v. Scranton, 11-0095, 2012 U.S. Dist. LEXIS 1651 (M.D. Pa. Jan. 6, 2012).

[165] *See, e.g.*, Blue v. District of Columbia, 850 F. Supp. 2d 16 (D.D.C. 2012).

[166] *See, e.g.*, Patricia H. v. Berkeley Unified Sch. Dist., 830 F. Supp. 1288 (N.D. Cal. 1993).

[167] *See, e.g.*, Oona R.-S. v. Santa Rosa City Schs., 890 F. Supp. 1452 (N.D. Cal. 1995).

[168] *See, e.g.*, Shrum v. Kluck, 249 F.3d 773 (8th Cir. 2001); Martin v. Swartz Cmty. Schs., 419 F. Supp. 2d 967 (E.D. Mich. 2006).

[169] 524 U.S. 274 (1998).

[170] *See* Henderson v. Walled Lake Consol. Schs., 469 F.3d 479 (6th Cir. 2006) (observing that even if administrators had notice that a female soccer player was involved in a relationship with her coach, such awareness did not establish notice that the plaintiff, another member of the team, had been exposed to a hostile environment); Baynard v. Malone, 268 F.3d 228 (4th Cir. 2001) (noting that actual notice may be established where an appropriate person is notified that a teacher is abusing a student; the identity of the particular child is unnecessary).

an official who has the authority to address the alleged discrimination must have *actual knowledge* of the inappropriate conduct and then fail to ameliorate the problem. Moreover, the failure to respond must amount to *deliberate indifference* to the discrimination. In the instant case, the plaintiff did not argue that actual notice had been provided, and the district's failure to promulgate a related policy and grievance procedure failed to qualify as deliberate indifference.

In subsequent litigation, courts have assessed who is an "appropriate official" with authority to act, what constitutes "actual knowledge," and what substantiates "deliberate indifference." *Gebser* did not identify which individuals in the school district must have knowledge.[171] Without deciding whether a principal possesses this authority, several courts have assumed for the purpose of analyzing claims that principals have the power to remedy abuse.[172] To illustrate, the Eleventh Circuit concluded that a principal's knowledge of the harassment was sufficient and that he was an appropriate person because of his authority to take corrective measures.[173]

Questions also have arisen concerning notice of sexual harassment or abuse. Evidence indicating a potential or theoretical risk has not been equated with actual knowledge. The Third Circuit warned that "a 'possibility' cannot be equated with a 'known act.'"[174] The Eighth Circuit noted that the principal was unaware of the high school basketball coach having a sexual relationship with a student. Although the coach had sent inappropriate text messages to several female players, the court did not find the messages to have provided the principal with actual notice of the specific relationship. Further, when the victim's mother asked the principal if something was going on between her daughter and the coach, the court observed that the parent's question did not constitute actual notice.[175] The Eleventh Circuit, however, reasoned that a principal's knowledge of a teacher's alleged touching and propositions to students provided sufficient notice to principal.[176] The Fourth Circuit also found that a principal had actual knowledge that one of the teachers at the school presented a risk to students. In this case, the principal failed to respond after both a student and a librarian informed him that the teacher had sexually molested a student. In a similar case, a New York federal district court found that a principal had notice of a teacher's sexual harassment of a student when the student's mother reported the teacher's inappropriate sexual comments, touching, and innuendoes.[177]

[171]*See* Warren v. Reading Sch. Dist., 278 F.3d 163 (3d. Cir. 2002) (remanding for a determination of who may qualify as an "appropriate person" to receive actual notice under the *Gebser* standard; a criminally prosecuted male teacher was fired due to his sexual involvement with male students).

[172]Davis v. Dekalb Cnty. Sch. Dist., 233 F.3d 1367 (11th Cir. 2000); Doe v. Dallas Indep. Sch. Dist., 220 F.3d 380 (5th Cir. 2000); Flores v. Saulpaugh, 115 F. Supp. 319 (N.D.N.Y. 2000).

[173]Doe v. Sch. Bd., 604 F.3d 1248 (11th Cir. 2010).

[174]Bostic v. Smyrna Sch. Dist., 418 F.3d 355, 361 (3d Cir. 2005). *But see* Jane Doe v. Green, 298 F. Supp. 2d 1025, 1034 (D. Nev. 2004) (stating "a complaint of harassment need not be undisputed or uncorroborated before it can be considered to fairly alert the school district of the potential for sexual harassment").

[175]Doe v. Flaherty, 623 F.3d 577 (8th Cir. 2010); *see also* N.R. Doe v. St. Francis Sch. Dist., No. 12-1039, 2012 U.S. App. LEXIS 18954 (7th Cir. Sept. 10, 2012) (finding that staff suspicions of an inappropriate relationship between a teacher and student did not qualify as actual knowledge, even when communicated to the principal); Blue v. District of Columbia, 850 F. Supp. 2d 16 (D.D.C. 2012) (finding that appropriate person lacked knowledge of student's sexual relationship with teacher).

[176]Doe v. Sch. Bd. of Broward Cnty., 604 F.3d 1248 (11th Cir. 2010).

[177]*Flores*, 115 F. Supp. 319.

A few courts have addressed whether other school officials have the power to respond to abuse. For example, the Eighth Circuit stated that "we do not hold that guidance counselors and school teachers are never 'appropriate persons' for the purposes of finding a school district liable for discrimination under Title IX," but in this particular case, they had not been vested with sufficient authority to address the harassment.[178] It should also be noted that school districts that "shuffle" abusive teachers to other districts might also generate legal challenges.[179]

To counter claims of deliberate indifference, school officials must show that they took action on complaints. For example, a principal was not found to be deliberately indifferent because he contacted his superior and took corrective measures by asking the counselor to interview the student, the accused teacher, and other possible witnesses.[180] Although these actions may have appeared insufficient and did not prevent the teacher from sexually molesting students, the court found the relevant fact to be that the principal did not act with deliberate indifference.

Also of relevance in hostile environment cases where school personnel are allegedly involved is the fact that, at least for younger children, the behavior does not have to be "unwelcome," as it does in Title VII (Civil Rights Act of 1964) employment cases.[181] The Seventh Circuit reviewed a case where a twenty-one-year-old male kitchen worker had a consensual sexual relationship with a thirteen-year-old middle school female.[182] The court noted that under Indiana criminal law, a person under the age of sixteen cannot consent to sexual intercourse and that children may not even understand that they are being harassed. To rule that only behavior that is not unwelcome is actionable would permit violators to take advantage of young, impressionable youth who voluntarily participate in requested conduct. Moreover, if welcomeness were an issue properly before the court, the children bringing the suits would be subject to intense scrutiny regarding their degree of fault.

STUDENT-TO-STUDENT HARASSMENT. Educators must be in control of the school environment, including student conduct, and eliminate known dangers and harassment. Not all harassment will be known, however, and not all behavior that is offensive will be so severe as to violate Title IX. Also, for student-to-student harassment to be actionable, the behavior must be unwelcome. Further clarification regarding liability associated with student-to-student harassment was provided in 1999 when the Supreme Court in *Davis v. Monroe County Board of Education*[183] proposed a two-part test: (1) whether the board acted with deliberate indifference to known acts of harassment[184] and (2) whether the harassment was so severe, pervasive, and objectively offensive that it effectively barred the victim's access to an educational opportunity or benefit.[185] The Court remanded the case

[178]Plamp v. Mitchell Sch. Dist. No. 172, 565 F.3d 450, 459 (8th Cir. 2009).

[179]*See, e.g.*, Doe-2 v. McLean Cnty. Unit Dist. No. 5, 593 F.3d 507, 517 (7th Cir. 2010); Shrum v. Kluck, 249 F.3d 773 (8th Cir. 2001).

[180]Davis v. Dekalb Cnty. Sch. Dist., 233 F.3d 1367 (11th Cir. 2000).

[181]J.F.K. v. Troup Cnty. Sch. Dist., 678 F.3d 1254 (11th Cir. 2012).

[182]Mary M. v. N. Lawrence Cmty. Sch. Corp., 131 F.3d 1220 (7th Cir. 1997).

[183]526 U.S. 629 (1999).

[184]*See* Long v. Murray Cnty. Sch. Dist., No. 4:10-CV-00015, 2012 U.S. Dist. LEXIS 86155 (N.D. Ga. May 21, 2012) (concluding that administrators were not deliberately indifferent toward harassment because they had disciplined the harassers and took steps to prevent harm).

[185]*See* Bruneau v. S. Kortright Cent. Sch. Dist., 163 F.3d 749 (2d Cir. 1998) (affirming lower court's determination that offensive behavior of male students against a female student did not qualify as harassment or adversely affect her education).

to determine whether these standards were met. The plaintiff's daughter had allegedly been subjected to unwelcome sexual touching and rubbing as well as sexual talk. On one occasion, the violating student put a doorstop in his pants and acted in a sexually suggestive manner toward the plaintiff. Ultimately, the youth was charged with and pled guilty to sexual battery for his misconduct. The victim and her mother notified several teachers, the coach, and the principal of these incidences. No disciplinary action was ever taken other than to threaten the violating student with possible sanctions.

Since the *Davis* decision, courts have addressed several cases involving peer harassment under Title IX. In these cases, plaintiffs sometimes have a difficult time proving that school officials had actual knowledge of the harassment or acted with deliberate indifference. For example, when a cheerleader claimed that she had been harassed by another cheerleader, the school official was not found to have acted with deliberate indifference because he took the action that was required under the school's harassment policy.[186] Specifically, the principal created a formal report outlining the investigation and actions taken to prevent further harassment. He removed the alleged perpetrator from the plaintiff's sixth period class and took other efforts to keep the two students apart.

Likewise, when school officials acted to protect a student by separating him from the harassing students, the court observed that the district was not unreasonable in responding to the harassment.[187] As noted, plaintiffs also need to demonstrate that they were denied educational benefits as a result of the harassment. In a Sixth Circuit case, although a mother outlined that the harassment her daughter experienced at school was pervasive, she failed to explain how the incidents deprived her daughter access to educational opportunities and benefits.[188] Some plaintiffs have struggled to demonstrate that the harassment is sufficiently severe or pervasive.[189] Interestingly, courts have found that "pervasiveness" may be established under Title IX by a one-time sexual assault.[190] Thus, if the conduct is quite egregious, it does not have to be repeated to abridge Title IX.

Neither Eleventh Amendment immunity[191] nor the claim that the violator was engaged in First Amendment protected free speech may be used as defenses to Title IX actions.[192] As a result, damages awards[193] are available from educational institutions receiving federal funds, although not from those persons who were directly responsible for the harassment.[194] "Individuals" are not "recipients" and cannot, therefore, be held

[186]Sanches v. Carrolton-Farmers Branch Indep. Sch. Dist, 647 F.3d 156 (5th Cir. 2011).

[187]Levarge v. Preston Bd. of Educ., 552 F. Supp. 2d 248 (D. Conn. 2008).

[188]Pahssen v. Merrill Cmty. Sch. Dist., 668 F.3d 356 (6th Cir. 2012), *cert. denied*, No. 12-8, 2012 U.S. LEXIS 6437 (Oct. 1, 2012).

[189]McSweeney v. Bayport Bluepoint Cent. Sch. Dist., No. 08-cv-4603, 2012 U.S. Dist. LEXIS 39557 (E.D.N.Y. Mar. 20, 2012) (holding that incidents involving a book being dropped on a finger and other threats were not severe or pervasive, nor were they based on sex or gender); *see also* Wolfe v. Fayetteville, 648 F.3d 860 (8th Cir. 2011) (holding that name-calling does not amount to sex-based harassment under Title IX unless motivated by hostility toward a person's sex); L.W. v. Toms River Reg'l Schs. Bd. of Educ., 915 A.2d 535, 547 (N.J. 2007) (finding harassment must be more than "school yard insults" or "classroom taunts").

[190]Doe T.Z. v. City of N.Y., 634 F. Supp. 2d 263 (E.D. N.Y. 2009); S.S. v. Alexander, 177 P.3d 724 (Wash. Ct. App. 2008).

[191]*See, e.g.*, Franks v. Ky. Sch. for the Deaf, 142 F.3d 360 (6th Cir. 1998).

[192]*See, e.g.*, Cohen v. San Bernardino Valley Coll., 883 F. Supp. 1407 (C.D. Cal. 1995), *aff'd in part, rev'd in part, remanded*, 92 F.3d 968 (9th Cir. 1996).

[193]*See, e.g.*, Doe v. E. Haven Bd. of Educ., 200 F. App'x 46 (2d Cir. 2006) (affirming award of $100,000 to a victim of student-to-student harassment; finding officials deliberately indifferent to the harassment, taunting, and name-calling following plaintiff's rape). However, it is unlikely that punitive awards are available under Title IX. *See* Schultzen v. Woodbury Cent. Cmty. Sch. Dist., 187 F. Supp. 2d 1099 (N.D. Iowa 2002).

[194]*See, e.g.*, Hartley v. Parnell, 193 F.3d 1263 (11th Cir. 1999); Floyd v. Waiters, 133 F.3d 786 (11th Cir. 1998).

liable under this particular law.[195] Also, plaintiffs can allege that they are entitled to damages under § 1983 for a violation of their federal constitutional or statutory claims.[196] Of course, violators can be sued directly under state tort law for sexual battery or intentional infliction of emotional distress,[197] and criminal charges may be filed against perpetrators where force is used or minors are involved. It is important to note that in 2011, the U.S. Department of Education issued additional guidance related to the harassment of students.[198] The Department explained that in addition to prohibiting harassment based on sex, Title IX also prohibits gender-based harassment, including hostility based on sex or sex stereotyping and harassing conduct that is not sexual in nature.

Also, the Department of Education's Revised Sexual Harassment Guidance states that "sexual harassment directed at gay or lesbian students that is sufficiently serious to limit or deny a student's ability to participate in or benefit from the school's program constitutes sexual harassment prohibited by Title IX under the circumstances of this guidance."[199] In recent years, several cases have been filed under Title IX that have addressed same-sex or gender-based harassment or harassment based on perceived sexual orientation.[200] The students have generally been successful in demonstrating that these claims are covered by Title IX.

The high volume of sexual harassment litigation will likely continue. Even when administrators deal with claims of sexual harassment in timely and effective ways, parents still may file suit. They will be understandably angry that their child has been subjected to inappropriate behavior and will be looking for someone to blame, if not pay.

Marriage and Pregnancy

Legal principles governing the rights of married and pregnant students have changed dramatically since 1960. The evolution of the law in this area is indicative of the judicial commitment to protect students from unjustified classifications that limit educational opportunities. When public school students are discriminated against because they are married, both the Fourteenth Amendment and Title IX may be violated. Strict scrutiny is used

[195]*Floyd*, 133 F.3d 786.

[196]*See, e.g.*, Fitzgerald v. Barnstable Sch. Comm., 555 U.S. 246 (2009).

[197]*See, e.g.*, Johnson v. Elk Lake Sch. Dist., 283 F.3d 138 (3d Cir. 2002).

[198]U.S. Dep't. of Educ. *Dear Colleague Letter* (Apr. 4, 2011), http://www2.ed.gov/about/offices/list/ocr/letters/colleague-201104.html. (This letter is a supplement to the Office for Civil Rights OCR's *Revised Sexual Harassment Guidance* issued in 2001.)

[199]Office for Civil Rights, Dep't of Educ., *Revised Sexual Harassment Guidance: Harassment of Students by School Employees, Other Students, or Third Parties* (Jan. 2001), http://www2.ed.gov/about/offices/list/ocr/docs/shguide.pdf.

[200]Patterson v. Hudson Area Schs., 551 F.3d 438 (6th Cir. 2009) (finding issues of fact remained regarding whether school district was deliberately indifferent in responding to harassment of student who was perceived to be gay); Dawn L. v. Greater Johnstown Sch. Dist., 586 F. Supp. 2d 332 (W.D. Pa. 2008) (finding same sex sexual harassment had occurred in violation of Title IX); Martin v. Swartz Cmty. Schs., 419 F. Supp. 2d 967 (E.D. Mich. 2006) (denying school district's motion for summary judgment involving a gay student's Title IX claim of peer harassment); Riccio v. New Haven Bd. of Educ., 467 F. Supp. 2d 218 (D. Conn. 2006) (finding issues of fact about whether sexual orientation harassment amounts to gender-based discrimination under Title IX); Theno v. Tonganoxis Unified Sch. Dist., 377 F. Supp. 2d 952 (D. Kan. 2005) (ruling that name-calling, such as "fag," "queer," "flamer" over four-year period could constitute sexual harassment under Title IX's theory of gender stereotyping); *But see* Tyrrell v. Seaford Union Free Sch. Dist., 792 F. Supp. 2d 601 (E.D.N.Y. 2011) (holding that student failed to demonstrate that alleged harassment based on website postings of her engaged in sexual activity with another female student were related to gender).

in evaluating claims under the Equal Protection Clause, because marriage qualifies as an implied fundamental right.[201] Accordingly, states will have to show a compelling interest in their differential treatment of married students to satisfy the Constitution.

Title IX regulations explicitly prohibit a recipient from applying "any rule concerning a student's actual or potential parental, family, or marital status which treats students differently on the basis of sex."[202] Discrimination based on pregnancy, childbirth, false pregnancy, termination of pregnancy, or recovery therefrom is prohibited. Moreover, student privacy is protected by state and federal privacy laws, including the Fourth Amendment. In an illustrative case, a federal district court held that requiring a student to take a pregnancy test administered in a coercive environment constitutes an unreasonable search and seizure.[203]

Where separate programs for pregnant students are available, the student may volunteer to participate but may not be automatically enrolled or coerced. However, the school district may require the student to obtain a physician's statement attesting that she is physically and emotionally able to continue in general education, assuming that students with other physical or emotional conditions also are required to provide such documentation. If programs are provided separately, they must be comparable to those offered to nonpregnant students.

In Massachusetts, a federal district court held that school authorities could not exclude a pregnant, unmarried student from regular high school classes.[204] School officials had proposed that the pregnant student be allowed to use all school facilities, attend school functions, participate in senior activities, and receive assistance from teachers in continuing her studies. The district stipulated, however, that she was not to attend school during regular school hours. Since there was no evidence of any educational or medical reason for this special treatment, the court held that the pregnant student had a constitutional right to attend classes with other pupils. Other cases have addressed pregnant students being barred from National Honor Society membership,[205] school personnel coercing students to take a pregnancy test,[206] and parental notification policies with regard to pregnant students.[207]

Conclusion

A basic purpose of public education is to prepare students for postsecondary life, regardless of their innate characteristics. Accordingly, courts and legislatures have become increasingly assertive in guaranteeing that students have the chance to realize their capabilities while in school. Arbitrary classification practices that disadvantage certain groups are not tolerated. Conversely, valid

[201]Loving v. Virginia, 388 U.S. 1, 12 (1967).

[202]34 C.F.R. § 106.40 (2012).

[203]Villanueva v. San Marcos Consol. Indep. Sch. Dist., No. A-05-CA-455 LY, 2006 U.S. Dist. LEXIS 68280 (W.D. Tex. Sept. 7, 2006).

[204]Ordway v. Hargraves, 323 F. Supp. 1155 (D. Mass. 1971).

[205]Chipman v. Grant Cnty. Sch. Dist., 30 F. Supp. 2d 975 (E.D. KY. 1998) (issuing an injunction requiring that two pregnant students, who met the National Honor Society requirements, be invited to join the group).

[206]*Villanueva*, 2006 U.S. Dist. LEXIS at 68280 (granting student's motion for summary judgment because school district may have violated student's constitutional rights by coercing her to take pregnancy test).

[207]Port Washington Teachers' Ass'n v. Bd. of Educ., 361 F. Supp. 2d 69 (E.D.N.Y. 2005) (reasoning that the school has an obligation to inform parents about a student's pregnancy for health and safety reasons).

classifications, applied in the best interests of students, are generally supported. In exercising professional judgment pertaining to the classification of students, educators should be cognizant of the following generalizations drawn from judicial and legislative mandates.

1. School segregation resulting from state laws or other intentional state action (e.g., gerrymandering school attendance zones) violates the Equal Protection Clause of the Fourteenth Amendment.
2. Where a school district has not achieved unitary status, school officials have an affirmative duty to eliminate the vestiges of past intentional discrimination; under such a duty, official action (or inaction) is assessed in terms of its effect on reducing segregation.
3. Segregatory effect alone does not establish unconstitutional intent; however, the consequences of official actions can be considered in substantiating discriminatory motive.
4. The scope of a desegregation remedy cannot exceed the scope of the constitutional violation.
5. States can, but are not obligated to, go beyond the requirements of the Fourteenth Amendment in remedying school segregation; such additional state mandates can subsequently be repealed without violating the United States Constitution.
6. Interdistrict desegregation remedies cannot be judicially imposed unless there is evidence of intentional discrimination with substantial effect across district lines.
7. School districts cannot plead "lack of funds" as a defense for failing to remedy unconstitutional school segregation; a state can be required to share the costs of remedial plans if it played a role in creating or maintaining the segregated system.
8. Courts can set aside state limitations on local taxing authorities and can order school boards to raise sufficient funds to support remedial plans, but courts cannot directly impose tax increases.
9. Judicial supervision can be terminated, in whole or in part, where school districts have complied with desegregation mandates in good faith and have eliminated the vestiges of past discrimination as far as practicable.
10. In determining whether a school district has eliminated the vestiges of school segregation, courts assess racial equality in student, faculty, and staff assignments; transportation; extracurricular activities; and facilities.
11. Once a school district has eliminated the vestiges of its prior discriminatory conduct to the court's satisfaction, future acts must represent purposeful discrimination to violate the Fourteenth Amendment; school districts are not obligated to continue remedies after unitary status is attained and resegregation occurs through no fault of school officials.
12. Many state laws require that charter schools conduct a lottery if the school is oversubscribed, and charter school leaders may not limit admissions to students of a certain race, language, or ability level.
13. The use of race in determining school or program assignment to achieve diversity in student bodies will not be permitted unless shown to be narrowly tailored.
14. Children who are English deficient are entitled to compensatory instruction designed to overcome English language barriers.
15. Students can be classified by age, but such classifications must be substantiated as necessary to advance legitimate educational objectives.
16. Ability-tracking schemes are permissible, but pupil assignments should be based on multiple criteria.
17. Although school districts may operate segregated schools and classes for males and females, they must provide a substantially coeducational school or single-sex school.
18. Criteria for admission to selective public programs or schools must be the same for males and females.
19. If a school district establishes an interscholastic athletic program, opportunities must

be made available to male and female athletes on an equal basis (i.e., mixed-sex teams or comparable sex-segregated teams).

20. Sexual harassment of students, by either employees or other students, can result in liability against the school district when an official with the authority to correct the situation has received actual notice of the harassment and has failed to correct it or shown deliberate indifference toward the victim; additionally, peer harassment must be severe, pervasive, and objectively offensive for liability to be assessed.

21. Students cannot be disadvantaged based on marital status or pregnancy.

MyEdLeadershipLab™

Go to Topic 4: *Security, Liability, and School Safety* on the MyEdLeadershipLab™ site (www.myedleadershiplab.com) for *Public School Law: Teachers' and Students' Rights*, Seventh Edition, where you can

- Find learning outcomes for *Security, Liability, and School Safety* along with the national standards that connect to these outcomes.
- Complete Assignments and Activities that can help you more deeply understand the chapter content.
- Apply and practice your understanding of the core skills identified in the chapter with the Building Leadership Skills unit.
- Prepare yourself for professional certification with a Practice for Certification quiz.

Student Discipline

From Chapter 7 of *Public School Law: Teachers' and Students' Rights*, Seventh Edition. Martha M. McCarthy, Nelda H. Cambron-McCabe, Suzanne E. Eckes.

Student Discipline

MyEdLeadershipLab™

Visit the MyEdLeadershipLab™ site for *Public School Law: Teachers' and Students' Rights*, Seventh Edition, to enhance your understanding of chapter concepts. You'll have the opportunity to practice your skills through video- and case-based Assignments and Activities as well as Building Leadership Skills units, and to prepare for your certification exam with Practice for Certification quizzes.

Student misconduct continues to be one of the most persistent and troublesome problems confronting educators. Public concern has focused on school disciplinary problems, particularly those involving use of illicit drugs, alcohol abuse,[1] and violence. In response, schools have directed more efforts toward prevention strategies, including not only stringent security measures but also modification of the curricula to strengthen students' social skills. Also, more attention has been directed toward the training of teachers and administrators to monitor the school climate. Some states and local school districts have enacted restrictive laws or policies that call for zero tolerance of weapons, drugs, and violence on campus. The efficacy of legislating tougher approaches

[1]In March 2007, the U.S. Surgeon General's Office issued its first "call to action" to stop underage drinking, which poses a significant threat to the health and safety of the nation's youth. Kenneth Moritsugu (acting Surgeon General), "Foreword from the Acting Surgeon General," *The Surgeon General's Call to Action to Prevent and Reduce Underage Drinking* (Mar. 6, 2007), http://www.surgeongeneral.gov/topics/underagedrinking/moritsugu.html. A national survey reported 9.7 million underage drinkers aged twelve to twenty (25.1 percent of the age group) in 2011; 6.1 million were binge drinkers (15.8 percent) and 1.7 million were heavy drinkers (4.4 percent). Substance Abuse and Mental Health Services Administration, *Results from the 2011 National Survey on Drug Use and Health: National Findings* (Rockville, MD: U.S. Dep't of Health and Human Services, 2012).

to create safe schools, however, has evoked volatile debates.[2] This chapter does not address the merits of these measures; rather, it examines the range of strategies employed by educators to maintain a safe and secure learning environment from a legal perspective. The analyses focus on the development of conduct regulations, the imposition of sanctions for noncompliance, and the procedures required in the administration of student punishments.

The law clearly authorizes the state and its agencies to establish and enforce reasonable conduct codes to protect the rights and safety of students and to ensure that school environments are conducive to learning. Historically, courts exercised limited review of student disciplinary regulations, and pupils seldom were successful in challenging policies governing their behavior. Courts were reluctant to interfere with the judgment of school officials because public education was considered to be a privilege bestowed by the state.

A quantum leap occurred from this early judicial posture to the active protection of students' rights in the late 1960s and early 1970s,[3] but judicial developments have not eroded educators' rights or their responsibilities.[4] The Seventh Circuit noted that the United States Supreme Court "has repeatedly emphasized the need for affirming the comprehensive authority of the states and of school officials, consistent with fundamental constitutional safeguards, to prescribe and control conduct in the schools."[5] Reasonable disciplinary regulations, even those impairing students' protected liberties, have been upheld if justified by a legitimate educational interest.

Educators have not only the authority but also the duty to maintain discipline in public schools. Although rules made at any level (e.g., classroom, building, school board) cannot conflict with higher authorities (e.g., constitutional and statutory provisions), building administrators and teachers retain substantial latitude in establishing and enforcing conduct codes that are necessary for instructional activities to take place. In the subsequent sections of this chapter, educators' prerogatives and students' rights are explored in connection with conduct regulations, expulsions and suspensions, corporal punishment, academic sanctions, and search and seizure.

CONDUCT REGULATIONS

School boards are granted considerable latitude in establishing and interpreting their own disciplinary rules and regulations.[6] The Supreme Court has held that the interpretation of a school regulation resides with the body that adopted it and is charged with its enforcement.[7] Disciplinary policies, however, have been struck down if unconstitutionally vague. Policies prohibiting improper conduct and behavior inimical to the best interests of the school have been invalidated because they have not specified the precise nature of

[2]Daniel Losen, *Discipline Policies, Successful Schools, and Racial Justice* (Boulder: National Policy Center, 2011); Catherine Kim, Daniel Losen & Daniel Hewitt, The School-to-Prison Pipeline (New York: NYU Press, 2010).

[3]*See, e.g.*, Tinker v. Des Moines Indep. Sch. Dist., 393 U.S. 503 (1969).

[4]*See* Hazelwood Sch. Dist. v. Kuhlmeier, 484 U.S. 260 (1988); Bethel Sch. Dist. No. 403 v. Fraser, 478 U.S. 675 (1986).

[5]Boucher v. Sch. Bd., 134 F.3d 821, 827 (7th Cir. 1998).

[6]*See* Price v. N.Y.C. Bd. of Educ., 837 N.Y.S.2d 507 (App. Div. 2008) (holding that a ban on possession of cell phones had a rational basis).

[7]*See* Bd. of Educ. v. McCluskey, 458 U.S. 966 (1982); Wood v. Strickland, 420 U.S. 308 (1975).

the impermissible conduct.[8] Although policies should be precise, courts have recognized that disciplinary regulations do not have to satisfy the stringent criteria or level of specificity required in criminal statutes.[9] The Eighth Circuit noted that the determining factor is whether a regulation's wording is precise enough to notify an individual that specific behavior is clearly unacceptable.[10]

In addition to reviewing the validity of the conduct regulation on which a specific punishment is based, courts evaluate the nature and extent of the penalty imposed in relation to the gravity of the offense. Courts also consider the age, sex, mental condition, and past behavior of the student in deciding whether a given punishment is appropriate. The judiciary has sanctioned punishments such as the denial of privileges, suspension, expulsion, corporal punishment, and detention after school. Any of these punishments, however, could be considered unreasonable under a specific set of circumstances. Consequently, courts study each unique factual situation; they do not evaluate the validity of student punishments in the abstract.

Litigation challenging disciplinary practices often has focused on the procedures followed in administering punishments rather than on the substance of disciplinary rules or the nature of the sanctions imposed. Implicit in all judicial declarations regarding school discipline is the notion that severe penalties require more formal procedures, whereas minor punishments necessitate only minimal due process. Nonetheless, any disciplinary action should be accompanied by some procedure to ensure the rudiments of fundamental fairness and to prevent mistakes in the disciplinary process. The Fifth Circuit noted: "The quantum and quality of procedural due process to be afforded a student varies with the seriousness of the punishment to be imposed."[11]

The judiciary has recognized that punishment for student conduct off school grounds must be supported by evidence that the behavior has a detrimental impact on other pupils, teachers, or school activities.[12] In an early case, the Connecticut Supreme Court held that school officials could regulate student conduct outside of school hours and off school property if such conduct affected the management of the school.[13] This has become a much more contentious area with students' increased use of the Internet at home. Personal websites and the use of social networks such as MySpace and Facebook

[8]*See* Monroe Cnty. Bd. of Educ. v. K.B., 62 So. 3d 513 (Ala. Civ. App. 2010) (concluding that school's policy prohibiting *use* of alcohol at school or a school function did not encompass consumption prior to a school function; policy was found to be unconstitutionally vague); Killion v. Franklin Reg'l Sch. Dist., 136 F. Supp. 2d 446, 459 (W.D. Pa. 2001) (finding school district's retaliatory policy against verbal or other abuse of teachers unconstitutionally vague—"devoid of any detail"). *But see* Esfeller v. O'Keefe, 391 F. App'x 337, 342 (5th Cir. 2010) (ruling that student code prohibiting "extreme, outrageous or persistent acts, or communications that are intended or reasonably likely to harass, intimidate, harm, or humiliate another" was not facially overbroad); *In re* D.H., 663 S.E.2d 139, 140 (Ga. 2008) (ruling that state statute making it unlawful for anyone to "disrupt or interfere with the operation of any public school" was not vague; court found that the ordinary meaning of these words gave fair notice).

[9]*See* Bethel Sch. Dist. No. 403 v. Fraser, 478 U.S. 675 (1986).

[10]Woodis v. Westark Cmty. Coll., 160 F.3d 435 (8th Cir. 1998).

[11]Pervis v. LaMarque Indep. Dist., 466 F.2d 1054, 1057 (5th Cir. 1972).

[12]*See* A.B.E. v. Sch. Bd. of Brevard Cnty., 33 So. 3d 795 (Fla. Dist. Ct. App. 2010) (holding that insufficient evidence supported expulsion of a student who had two sips of alcohol at her home before coming to school since she did not appear to be impaired, nor was she disrupting the learning environment).

[13]O'Rourke v. Walker, 102 Conn. 130 (1925); *see also* Collins v. Prince William Cnty. Sch. Bd., 142 F. App'x 144 (4th Cir. 2005) (upholding student's expulsion for making and using explosive devices off campus; incident created substantial disruption in school operations with media and other attention).

raise difficult First Amendment issues for school officials attempting to discipline students for off-campus conduct.[14] The Third Circuit in two cases held that students could not be punished for MySpace parodies of their principals that were created at their homes and did not create a substantial and material disruption of the school environment.[15] The Third Circuit cautioned: "It would be an unseemly and dangerous precedent to allow the state, in the guise of school authorities, to reach into a child's home and control his/her actions there to the same extent that it can control that child when he/she participates in school sponsored activities."[16]

In assessing off-campus disciplinary actions, courts look for a detrimental impact on the school environment. Accordingly, courts have upheld sanctions imposed on students for engaging in assault or criminal acts off school grounds;[17] compiling a list of other students noting derogatory characteristics;[18] making threatening, racist phone calls to another student;[19] and writing a threatening letter over the summer break to a former girlfriend.[20] Courts, however, have prohibited school authorities from punishing students for misbehavior off school grounds if pupils had not been informed that such conduct would result in sanctions,[21] if the conduct could not be considered a true threat,[22] or if the misbehavior had no direct relationship to the welfare of the school.[23]

School personnel should avoid placing unnecessary constraints on student behavior. In developing disciplinary policies, all possible means of achieving the desired outcomes should be explored, and means that are least restrictive of students' personal freedoms should be selected. Once it is determined that a specific conduct regulation is necessary, the rule should be clearly written so that it is not open to multiple interpretations. Each regulation should include the rationale for enacting the rule as well as the penalties for infractions. Considerable discretion exists in determining that certain actions deserve harsher penalties (i.e., imposing a more severe punishment for the sale of drugs as opposed to the possession or use of drugs).

To ensure that students are knowledgeable of the conduct rules, it is advisable to require them to sign a form indicating that they have read the conduct regulations. With such documentation, they would be unable to plead ignorance of the rules as a defense

[14]The Cyberbullying Research Center examined twenty-two studies published in peer-reviewed journals showing the percentage of students who are victims of cyberbullying range from 5.5 percent to 72 percent, with an average of about 27 percent; the Center's researchers' most recent study in 2010 found 21 percent, http://cyberbullying.us/research.php.

[15]Layshock v. Hermitage Sch. Dist., 650 F.3d 205 (3d Cir. 2011), *cert. denied sub nom.*, Blue Mountain Sch. Dist. v. J.S. *ex rel.* Snyder, 132 S. Ct. 1097 (2012); J.S. *ex rel.* Snyder v. Blue Mountain Sch. Dist., 650 F.3d 915 (3d Cir. 2011), *cert. denied*, 132 S. Ct. 1097 (2012).

[16]*Layshock*, 650 F.3d at 216.

[17]Pollnow v. Glennon, 757 F.2d 496 (2d Cir. 1985); Nicholas v. Sch. Comm. 587 N.E.2d 211 (Mass. 1992).

[18]Donovan v. Ritchie, 68 F.3d 14 (1st Cir. 1995).

[19]E.K. v. Stamford Bd. of Educ., 557 F. Supp. 2d 272 (D. Conn. 2008).

[20]Doe v. Pulaski Cnty. Special Sch. Dist., 306 F.3d 616 (8th Cir. 2002). The junior high school student did not send the letter, but another student who read the letter communicated its content to the former girlfriend.

[21]Galveston Indep. Sch. Dist. v. Boothe, 590 S.W.2d 553 (Tex. Civ. App. 1979).

[22]Porter v. Ascension Parish Sch. Bd., 393 F.3d 608 (5th Cir. 2004).

[23]Killion v. Franklin Reg'l Sch. Dist., 136 F. Supp. 2d 446 (W.D. Pa. 2001).

for their misconduct. In general, educators would be wise to adhere to the following guidelines:[24]

- Rules must have an explicit purpose and be clearly written to accomplish that purpose.
- Any conduct regulation adopted should be necessary in order to carry out the school's educational mission; rules should not be designed merely to satisfy the preferences of school board members, administrators, or teachers.
- Rules should be publicized to students and their parents.
- Rules should be specific and clearly stated so that students know what behaviors are expected and what behaviors are prohibited.
- Student handbooks that incorporate references to specific state laws also should include the law or paraphrase the statutory language.
- Regulations should not impair constitutionally protected rights unless there is an overriding public interest, such as a threat to the safety of others.
- A rule should not be "ex post facto"; it should not be adopted to prevent a specific activity that school officials know is being planned or has already occurred.
- Regulations should be consistently enforced and uniformly applied to all students, without discrimination.
- Punishments should be appropriate to the offense, taking into consideration the child's age, sex, disability (if any), and past behavior.
- Some procedural safeguards should accompany the administration of all punishments; the formality of the procedures should be in accord with the severity of the punishment.
- Periodic review to revise and refine the student handbook should involve students and school staff members.

In designing and enforcing pupil conduct codes, it is important for school personnel to bear in mind the distinction between students' substantive and procedural rights. If a disciplinary regulation or the administration of punishment violates substantive rights (e.g., restricts protected speech), the regulation cannot be enforced nor the punishment imposed. When only procedural rights are impaired, however, the punishment eventually can be administered if determined at an appropriate hearing that the punishment is warranted.

EXPULSIONS AND SUSPENSIONS

Expulsions and suspensions are among the most widely used disciplinary measures. Courts uniformly have upheld educators' authority to use such measures as punishments, but due process is required to ensure that students are afforded fair and impartial treatment. Although states have recognized that students have a property right to an education, this right may be taken away for violations of school rules. This section focuses on disciplinary action in which students are removed from the regular instructional program.

[24] *See* Thomas Baker, *Construing the Scope of Student Conduct Codes*, 174 Educ. L. Rep. 555–88 (2003), for an extensive discussion of the development of conduct codes.

Expulsions

State laws and school board regulations are usually quite specific regarding the grounds for expulsions—that is, the removal of students from school for a lengthy period of time (usually in excess of ten days). Such grounds are not limited to occurrences during school hours and can include infractions on school property immediately before or after school or at any time the school is being used for a school-related activity. Expulsions also can result from infractions occurring en route to or from school or during school functions held off school premises. Although specific grounds vary from state to state, infractions typically considered legitimate grounds for expulsion include violence, stealing or vandalizing school or private property, causing or attempting to cause physical injury to others, possessing a weapon, possessing or using drugs or alcohol, and engaging in criminal activity or other behavior forbidden by state laws.

PROCEDURAL REQUIREMENTS. State statutes specify procedures for expulsion and length limitations. Except for the possession of weapons, a student generally cannot be expelled beyond the end of the current academic year unless the expulsion takes place near the close of the term. A teacher or administrator may initiate expulsion proceedings, but usually only the school board can expel a student. Prior to expulsion, students must be provided procedural protections guaranteed by the United States Constitution; however, school officials can remove students immediately if they pose a danger or threat to themselves or others. No duty exists to provide an educational alternative for a properly expelled student unless the school board policies or state mandates specify that alternative programs must be provided or the student is receiving special education services.[25]

Although the details of required procedures must be gleaned from state statutes and school board regulations, courts have held that students facing expulsion from public school are guaranteed at least minimum due process under the Fourteenth Amendment. Expulsion hearings do not have to conform to the judicial requirements of a trial, but it is advisable to provide the following safeguards:

- written notice of the charges; the intention to expel; the place, time, and circumstances of the hearing; and sufficient time for a defense to be prepared;[26]
- a full and fair hearing before an impartial adjudicator;[27]
- the right to legal counsel or some other adult representation;[28]
- the right to be fully apprised of the proof or evidence;[29]
- the opportunity to present witnesses or evidence;
- the opportunity to cross-examine opposing witnesses; and

[25]*See infra* text accompanying note 65; Gun-Free Schools Act, 20 U.S.C. § 7151 (2012) (allowing school officials to place students expelled for gun possession in alternative instructional programs).
[26]*See, e.g.*, Brian A. v. Stroudsburg Area Sch. Dist., 141 F. Supp. 2d 502 (M.D. Pa. 2001) (ruling that a five-day notice was adequate when the student and parent had been aware of the pending expulsion for weeks).
[27]*See, e.g.*, Christy v. McCalla, 79 So. 3d 293, 304 (La. 2011) (holding that a student was not deprived of due process when he received "full opportunity to present his version of events").
[28]Courts have recognized students' right to seek advice of legal counsel but have not held that a right exists for students' attorneys to participate in a disciplinary proceeding in the role of trial counsel.
[29]*See* E.K. v. Stamford Bd. of Educ., 557 F. Supp. 2d 272 (D. Conn. 2008) (holding hearsay evidence was admissible in an expulsion hearing).

- some type of written record demonstrating that the decision was based on the evidence presented at the hearing.[30]

Students and parents cannot claim denial of due process rights if they waive the right to a hearing[31] or choose not to involve counsel or present evidence.[32] Also, students who decline to attend a scheduled expulsion hearing waive the right to present their case.[33]

The specific procedural safeguards required, however, may vary, depending on the circumstances of a particular situation. In a Mississippi case, a student and his parents claimed that prior to an expulsion hearing, they should have been given a list of the witnesses and a summary of their testimony.[34] Recognizing that such procedural protections generally should be afforded prior to a long-term expulsion, the Fifth Circuit nonetheless held that they were not requisite in this case. The parents had been fully apprised of the charges, the facts supporting the charges, and the nature of the hearing. Consequently, the court concluded that the student suffered no material prejudice from the school board's failure to supply a list of witnesses; the witnesses provided no surprises or interference with the student's ability to present his case. In another case involving expulsion for possession of drugs, the same court found no impairment of a student's rights when he was denied an opportunity to confront and rebut witnesses who accused him of selling drugs.[35] The names of student witnesses had been withheld to prevent retaliation against them.

Similarly, the Sixth Circuit noted that it is critical to protect the anonymity of students who "blow the whistle" on classmates involved in serious offenses such as drug dealing.[36] Although the right to cross-examine witnesses did not constitute a denial of due process in this case, the court held that the student's procedural rights were violated because the superintendent disclosed evidence in the school board's closed deliberations that was not introduced during the open hearing. Given this violation, the appellate court remanded the case to determine if the student was entitled to injunctive and compensatory relief.

State laws and school board policies often provide students facing expulsion with more elaborate procedural safeguards than the constitutional protections noted earlier. Once such expulsion procedures are established, courts will require that they be followed.[37] Under Ohio law, a student's expulsion hearing two weeks after he received the notice was

[30]*See, e.g.*, Hass v. W. Shore Sch. Dist., 915 A.2d 1254 (Pa. Commw. Ct. 2007).

[31]*See* Porter v. Ascension Parish Sch. Bd., 393 F.3d 608 (5th Cir. 2004) (concluding that when a student admits his guilt, the need for a hearing to determine guilt is significantly lessened).

[32]*See, e.g.*, Stinney v. Sumter Sch. Dist. 17, 707 S.E.2d 397 (S.C. 2011).

[33]*See, e.g.*, Remer v. Burlington Area Sch. Dist., 286 F.3d 1007 (7th Cir. 2002).

[34]Keough v. Tate Cnty. Bd. of Educ., 748 F.2d 1077 (5th Cir. 1984); *see also* Covington Cnty. v. G.W., 767 So. 2d 187 (Miss. 2000) (ruling that school officials' failure to provide a list of witnesses did not violate a student's due process rights).

[35]Brewer v. Austin Indep. Sch. Dist., 779 F.2d 260 (5th Cir. 1985); *see also* Brown v. Plainfield Cmty. Consol. Dist. 202, 522 F. Supp. 2d 1068 (N.D. Ill. 2007) (ruling that a student expelled for inappropriately touching a teacher did not possess a constitutional due process right to cross-examine student witnesses in his hearing).

[36]Newsome v. Batavia Local Sch. Dist., 842 F.2d 920 (6th Cir. 1988); *see also* Scanlon v. Las Cruces Pub. Schs., 172 P.3d 185 (N.M. Ct. App. 2007) (ruling that a student's procedural due process rights were not violated when school officials did not disclose the names of student informants who reported that the student had marijuana in his car).

[37]The failure to enact required state rules or to follow them, however, would violate state law rather than the Federal Constitution; *see, e.g.*, Vann *ex rel.* Vann v. Stewart, 445 F. Supp. 2d 882 (E.D. Tenn. 2006); Rogers v. Gooding Pub. Joint Sch. Dist., 20 P.3d 16 (Idaho 2001).

found to violate a statutory requirement that hearings be held no later than five school days after notification.[38] A Washington appellate court held that a student's due process rights were violated when he was not allowed to question witnesses at his expulsion hearing;[39] Washington law specifically provides students the right to confront witnesses.

Students also have challenged expulsions as violating their substantive due process rights. In these instances, school officials have provided full procedural due process, but students allege that the government has deprived them of rights (i.e., school attendance) without reasonable justification. It is often referred to as government abuse of power that "shocks the conscience."[40] The Seventh Circuit ruled that a student's substantive due process rights were not violated when he was expelled for public indecency and possession of pornography after a fellow student jokingly took pictures of him and several classmates in the shower after a wrestling match. The court said the educators' actions in expelling the student simply did not rise to the level of a constitutional violation. The court reasoned that even though officials overreacted and used questionable judgment, their actions did not elevate the expulsion to a constitutional matter.[41] In an Ohio case, a student charged with defacing school property, threatening student lives, and creating widespread panic, claimed violation of her substantive due process rights because the school district based the expulsion on her confession, which was suppressed by a juvenile court.[42] The court held that a rational relationship existed between the school board's expulsion and the student's offenses, and the board did not violate her constitutional rights in considering the confession, which was made during her hearing,

ZERO-TOLERANCE POLICIES. The concern about school safety has led to specific federal and state laws directed at the discipline of students who bring weapons onto school campuses. Under the Gun-Free Schools Act of 1994 requirements, all states have enacted legislation requiring at least a one-year expulsion for students who bring firearms to school.[43] In expanding the scope of the law, states have added to the list of prohibitions by including weapons such as knives, explosive devices, hand chains, and other offensive weapons as well as drugs and violent acts.[44] The federal law also requires state laws to

[38]Kresser v. Sandusky Bd. of Educ., 748 N.E.2d 620 (Ohio Ct. App. 2001).

[39]Stone v. Prosser Consol. Sch. Dist. No. 116, 971 P.2d 125 (Wash. Ct. App. 1999); *see also* T.T. v. Bellevue Sch. Dist., 376 F. App'x 769 (9th Cir 2010), *on remand* No. C08-365RAJ, 2010 U.S. Dist. LEXIS 131409 (W.D. Wash. Dec. 13, 2010) (confirming a student's right under state law to confront witnesses).

[40]*See infra* text accompanying note 79.

[41]Tun v. Whitticker, 398 F.3d 899 (7th Cir. 2005).

[42]Lausin v. Bishko, 727 F. Supp. 2d 610 (N.D. Ohio 2010); *see also* Hannemann v. S. Door Cnty. Sch. Dist., 673 F.3d 746 (7th Cir. 2012) (ruling that a former student, who was subsequently banned from school property, did not have a constitutional right as a member of the general public to access school property; court concluded that the ban did not violate the former student's liberty interests).

[43]20 U.S.C. § 7151 (2012). Additionally, most states have enacted gun-free or weapons-free school zone laws restricting possession of firearms in or near schools.

[44]*See* R.H. v. State, 56 So. 3d 156 (Fla. Dist. Ct. App. 2011) (holding that a student who brought a common pocketknife to school could not be adjudicated of a crime because Florida law, unlike many other state laws, specifically exempts pocketknives from its ban on weapons); F.R. v. State, 81 So. 3d 572 (Fla. Dist. Ct. App. 2012) (determining that a folding knife with a notch grip, a locking blade mechanism, and a hilt guard was not a pocketknife exempt under Florida law).

permit the local school superintendent to modify the expulsion requirement on a case-by-case basis.[45]

Severe criticism has been directed at zero-tolerance policies when school officials fail to exercise discretion and flexibility. The American Bar Association and others have called for an end to policies that require automatic penalties without assessing the circumstances.[46] A Virginia case underscores the harsh consequences when students encounter inflexible policies. In that case, a thirteen-year-old student, attempting to save a suicidal friend's life, took the friend's binder containing a knife and placed it in his own locker. Upon hearing about the knife, the assistant principal asked him to retrieve it from his locker. Although the assistant principal felt that the student was acting in the best interest of his friend and at no time posed a threat to anyone, he was expelled from school for four months. In upholding the expulsion, the Fourth Circuit noted its harshness but found no violation of the student's due process rights. In a concurring opinion, one Justice commented: "The panic over school violence and the intent to stop it has caused school officials to jettison the common sense idea that a person's punishment should fit his crime in favor of a single harsh punishment, namely, mandatory school suspension."[47] Such harshness, however, has led policy makers and educators to rethink zero tolerance discipline measures, particularly for behavior unrelated to the possession of weapons.[48] Among the states debating new laws or policies to lessen the impact of zero tolerance are California, Colorado, Georgia, Maryland, Michigan, North Carolina, and Virginia.

Invoking mandatory expulsion policies may implicate constitutional rights if administrators fail to take into consideration the individual student's history and the circumstances surrounding the conduct. The Sixth Circuit noted that expelling a student for weapons possession when the student did not know that the weapon was in his car could not survive a due process challenge.[49] The Tenth Circuit, however, ruled that a

[45]*See* Rouleau v. Williamstown Sch. Bd., 892 A.2d 223 (Vt. 2005) (ruling that superintendent's modification of the expulsion requirement because of a student's limited involvement in bringing a pellet gun to campus did not prevent the board from barring the student's participation in cocurricular and other school functions for the remainder of the year).

[46]Report to the ABA House of Delegates, Feb. 19, 2001, American Bar Association, Chicago, IL; *see also* Peter Follenweider, *Zero Tolerance: A Proper Definition*, 44 J. Marshall L. Rev. 1107 (2011); American Psychological Association Zero Tolerance Task Force, *Are Zero Tolerance Policies Effective in the Schools?*, 63 Am. Psychologist 852–62 (Dec. 2008) (finding zero tolerance has not been an effective means of improving school safety or climate).

[47]Ratner v. Loudoun Cnty. Pub. Schs., 16 F. App'x 140, 143 (4th Cir. 2001). *See Virginia Student's Expulsion Renews Debate Over Zero Tolerance Policies,* Legal Clips, Feb. 3, 2011, http://legalclips.nsba.org/?p=4572, (reporting a school board's expulsion of a student under its rule against violent criminal conduct when the student used a plastic pipe to blow plastic pellets at other students during lunch). Under the zero-tolerance discipline policy, the student was expelled for the possession and use of a weapon. The school board's decision was upheld by a state court judge, and the state supreme court and U.S. Supreme Court denied review. Mikel v. Sch. Bd. of Spotsylvania Cnty., No. 11-1276, 2012 U.S. LEXIS 4675 (U.S. June 25, 2012); *see also* Vann *ex rel.* Vann v. Stewart, 445 F. Supp. 2d 882 (E.D. Tenn. 2006) (holding that a one-year expulsion for the possession of a pocketknife bore a rational relationship to a student's offense; school officials were not required to consider modifying the punishment); S. Gibson Sch. Bd. v. Sollman, 768 N.E.2d 437 (Ind. 2002) (ruling that the judiciary's role is to determine whether a school board acted arbitrarily or capriciously and not to assess the harshness of zero-tolerance policies).

[48]Donna St. George, *More Schools Rethinking Zero Tolerance-Discipline Stand*, Wash. Post (June 1, 2011), http://www.washingtonpost.com/local/education/more-schools-are-rethinking-zero-tolerance/2011/05/26/AGSIKmGH_story.html.

[49]Seal v. Morgan, 229 F.3d 567 (6th Cir. 2000); *see also* Colvin v. Lowndes Cnty., Miss. Sch. Dist., 114 F. Supp. 2d 504 (N.D. Miss. 1999) (holding that expulsion under the school board's zero-tolerance policy violated due process rights where the school board did not consider facts and circumstances of the student's case).

one-year removal from school did not violate a student's substantive due process rights when the student "should have known" that a weapon was in his car; the court said the student did not "unknowingly" bring the weapon to school because it was visible in the front console to anyone standing outside the car.[50] In general, courts have been reluctant to impose the *knowing possession* standard that would require the determination of a student's intent.[51]

Suspensions

Suspensions are frequently used to punish students for violating school rules and standards of behavior when the infractions are not of sufficient magnitude to warrant expulsion. Suspensions include the short-term denial of school attendance as well as the denial of participation in regular courses and activities (in-school suspension). Most legal controversies have focused on out-of-school suspensions, but it is advisable to apply the same legal principles to any disciplinary action that separates the student from the regular instructional program even for a short period of time.

PROCEDURAL REQUIREMENTS. Historically, state laws and judicial decisions differed widely in identifying and interpreting procedural safeguards for suspensions. In 1975, however, the Supreme Court clarified the constitutional rights of students faced with short-term suspensions. The Court majority in *Goss v. Lopez* held that minimum due process must be provided before a student is suspended for even a brief period of time.[52] Recognizing that a student's state-created property right to an education is protected by the Fourteenth Amendment, the Court ruled that such a right cannot be impaired unless the student is afforded notice of the charges and an opportunity to refute them. The Supreme Court also emphasized that suspensions implicate students' constitutionally protected liberty interests because of the potentially damaging effects that the disciplinary process can have on a student's reputation and permanent record.

The *Goss* majority strongly suggested that the holding applied to all short-term suspensions, including those of only one class period. Consequently, many school boards have instituted policies that require informal procedures for every brief suspension and more formal procedures for longer suspensions. In the absence of greater specificity in state statutes or administrative regulations, students have a constitutional right to the following protections prior to suspension:

- oral or written notification of the nature of the violation and the intended punishment;
- an opportunity to refute the charges before an objective decision maker (such a discussion may immediately follow the alleged rule infraction); and
- an explanation of the evidence on which the disciplinarian is relying.

[50]Butler v. Rio Rancho Pub. Sch. Bd. of Educ., 341 F.3d 1197, 1201 (10th Cir. 2003).

[51]*See In re* B.N.S., 641 S.E.2d 411 (N.C. Ct. App. 2007) (noting that North Carolina's weapons law does not require a showing of criminal intent; mere possession of a pocketknife justified adjudication of the student as delinquent under North Carolina law); Bundick v. Bay City Indep. Sch. Dist., 140 F. Supp. 2d 735, 740 (S.D. Tex. 2001) (holding that knowledge "can be imputed from the fact of possession").

[52]419 U.S. 565 (1975). Individuals posing a danger or threat may be removed immediately with notice and a hearing following as soon as possible.

The requirement of an impartial decision maker does not infer that an administrator or teacher who is familiar with the facts cannot serve in this capacity. The decision maker simply must judge the situation fairly and on the basis of valid evidence.

The Supreme Court's *Goss* decision established the rudimentary procedural requirements for short-term suspensions, but students continue to seek expansion of their procedural rights. The Supreme Court specifically noted that such formal procedures as the right to secure counsel, to confront and cross-examine witnesses, and to call witnesses are not constitutionally required. The Court reiterated this stance in a later case by noting that a two-day suspension "does not rise to the level of a penal sanction calling for the full panoply of procedural due process protections applicable to a criminal prosecution."[53] Decisions by lower state and federal courts indicate a reluctance to impose these additional requirements unless mandated by state law. In a Maine case, a student claimed a violation of procedural due process because the school administrator denied him permission to leave during questioning and failed to advise him of his right to remain silent or to have his parents present during the interrogation.[54] The court rejected all claims, noting that there was no legal authority to substantiate any of the asserted rights. The court reasoned that to rule otherwise would, in fact, contradict the informal procedures outlined in *Goss* allowing for immediate questioning and disciplinary action. Also relying on *Goss*, the Third Circuit ruled that the suspension of a five-year-old kindergartener for telling his friends, "I'm going to shoot you" while playing a game of cops and robbers, satisfied required informal procedures even though the parents contended that they should have been present to help him understand the process.[55]

Although the Supreme Court in *Goss* recognized the possibility of "unusual situations" that would require more formal procedures than those outlined, little guidance was given as to what these circumstances might be. The only suggestion offered in *Goss* was that a disciplinarian should adopt more extensive procedures in instances involving factual disputes "and arguments about cause and effect."[56] Courts have declined to expand on this brief listing. The Sixth Circuit rejected a student's contention that drug charges constituted such an "unusual situation" because of the stigmatizing effect on his

[53]Bethel Sch. Dist. No. 403 v. Fraser, 478 U.S. 675, 686 (1986); *see, e.g.*, Smith v. Seligman Unified Sch. Dist. 40, 664 F. Supp. 2d 1070 (D. Ariz. 2009); D.L. v. Pioneer Sch. Corp., 958 N.E.2d 1151 (Ind. Ct. App. 2011).

[54]Boynton v. Casey, 543 F. Supp. 995 (D. Me. 1982). The "right to remain silent" also has been advanced in other cases, with students arguing that school disciplinary proceedings should be governed by the Supreme Court's principle established in *Miranda v. Arizona*, 384 U.S. 436 (1966) (holding that persons subjected to custodial interrogation must be advised of their right to remain silent, that any statement made may be used against them, and that they have the right to legal counsel). Courts have readily dismissed these claims, finding that discussions with school administrators are noncustodial. Clearly, in the *Miranda* decision, the Supreme Court was interpreting an individual's Fifth Amendment right against self-incrimination when first subjected to police questioning in connection with criminal charges; *see, e.g.*, State v. Schloegel, 769 N.W.2d 130 (Wis. Ct. App. 2009). *But see* J.D.B. v. North Carolina, 131 S. Ct. 2394 (2011) (holding that a child's age is relevant in determining whether he has been taken into custody for police interrogation and was aware of his rights; a thirteen-year-old was questioned at school by police without being informed of his right to remain silent); *In re* T.A.G., 663 S.E.2d 392 (Ga. 2008) (affirming trial court's suppression of a student's statements when he was interviewed by an assistant principal and an armed police officer); *In re* R.H., 791 A.2d 331 (Pa. 2002) (holding that school police officers were required to give a student *Miranda* warnings prior to interrogation, since they exercised the same powers as municipal police, and the interrogation led to charges by the police, not punishment by school officials).

[55]S.G. *ex rel.* A.G. v. Sayreville Bd. of Educ., 333 F.3d 417 (3d Cir. 2003). *But see In re* Andre M., 88 P.3d 552 (Ariz. 2004) (finding that a sixteen-year-old student's rights were violated when police interrogated him at school and refused to permit his parent to be present).

[56]Goss v. Lopez, 419 U.S. 565, 583–84 (1975).

reputation. The court did not believe that an eighth-grade student suspended for ten days for possessing a substance that resembled an illegal drug was "forever faced with a tarnished reputation and restricted employment opportunities."[57] Similarly, more extensive procedures were found unnecessary when a student was barred from interscholastic athletics and other activities in addition to a ten-day suspension.[58]

Students also have asserted that suspensions involving loss of course credit or occurring during exam periods require greater due process than outlined in *Goss*. The Fifth Circuit, however, did not find persuasive the argument that the loss incurred for a ten-day suspension during final examinations required more than a mere give-and-take discussion between the principal and the student. In refusing to require more formal proceedings, the court noted that *Goss* makes no distinction as to when a short-term suspension occurs, and a contrary ruling would "significantly undermine, if not nullify, its definitive holding."[59] Similarly, the Seventh Circuit rejected a student's claim that additional procedures were required because a suspension occurred at the end of the school year and precluded the student from taking his final exams and graduating.[60]

Courts have continued to resist attempts to elaborate or formalize the minimal due process requirements outlined in *Goss* for short-term suspensions. As the Supreme Court noted: "Further formalizing the suspension process and escalating its formality and adversary nature may not only make it too costly as a regular discipline tool but also destroy its effectiveness as part of the teaching process."[61]

IN-SCHOOL SUSPENSIONS. In-school suspensions may be equivalent to out-of-school suspensions, thereby necessitating minimum due process procedures. A Mississippi federal district court noted that whether procedural due process is required depends on the extent to which the student is deprived of instruction or the opportunity to learn.[62] The physical presence of a student at school does not conclusively relieve school officials of their duty to provide due process for disciplinary measures that exclude a student from the learning process. A Tennessee federal district court found that a student's placement in a classroom "time-out box" did not require due process because he continued to work on class assignments and could hear and see the teacher from the confined area.[63] The court emphasized that teachers must be free to administer minor forms of classroom discipline such as time-out, denial of privileges, and special assignments. Similarly, the Sixth Circuit held that a one-day suspension in which a student completed school work and was considered in attendance did not implicate a property interest in educational benefits or a liberty interest in reputation; it was simply too de minimis.[64]

[57]Paredes v. Curtis, 864 F.2d 426, 429 (6th Cir. 1988).

[58]Palmer v. Merluzzi, 868 F.2d 90 (3d Cir. 1989); *see also* Donovan v. Ritchie, 68 F.3d 14 (1st Cir. 1995) (ruling that a bar to interscholastic athletics and other activities in addition to a ten-day suspension did not necessitate the provision of more formal procedures); Mather v. Loveland City Sch. Dist., 908 N.E.2d 1039 (Ohio Ct. App. 2009) (interpreting an Ohio law, OHIO REV. CODE § 3313.66(E), as providing a student the right to appeal an expulsion or suspension from curricular activities but not extracurricular ones).

[59]Keough v. Tate Cnty. Bd. of Educ., 748 F.2d 1077, 1081 (5th Cir. 1984).

[60]Lamb v. Panhandle Cmty. Unit Sch. Dist., 826 F.2d 526 (7th Cir. 1987).

[61]*Goss*, 419 U.S. at 583.

[62]Cole v. Newton Special Mun. Separate Sch. Dist., 676 F. Supp. 749 (S.D. Miss. 1987), *aff'd*, 853 F.2d 924 (5th Cir. 1988).

[63]Dickens v. Johnson Cnty. Bd. of Educ., 661 F. Supp. 155 (E.D. Tenn. 1987).

[64]Laney v. Farley, 501 F.3d 577 (6th Cir. 2007).

DISCIPLINARY TRANSFERS TO ALTERNATIVE EDUCATIONAL PLACEMENTS. Closely related to suspensions are *involuntary transfers* of students to alternative educational placements for disciplinary reasons. Such transfers generally do not involve denial of public education, but they might implicate protected liberty or property interests. Legal challenges to the use of disciplinary transfers have addressed primarily the adequacy of the procedures followed. Recognizing that students do not have an inherent right to attend a given school, some courts nonetheless have held that pupils facing involuntary reassignment are entitled to minimum due process if such transfers are occasioned by misbehavior[65] or if required by school board policy.[66]

A Pennsylvania federal district court ruled that "lateral transfers" for disciplinary reasons affected personal liberty and property interests of sufficient magnitude to require procedural due process. Even though such transfers involved comparable schools, the court reasoned that a disciplinary transfer carried with it a stigma and thus implicated a protected liberty right. Noting that a transfer of a student "during a school year from a familiar school to a strange and possibly more distant school would be a terrifying experience for many children of normal sensibilities," the court concluded that such transfers were more drastic punishments than suspensions, and thus necessitated due process.[67] As to the nature of the procedures required, the court held that the student and parents must be given notice of the proposed transfer and that a prompt informal hearing before the school principal must be provided. The court stipulated that if parents were still dissatisfied with the arrangement after the informal meeting, they had the right to contest the transfer recommendation at a more formal hearing.

The Fifth Circuit, however, declined to find a federally protected property or liberty interest when a student arrested for aggravated assault was reassigned to an alternative education program under a Texas statute. According to the court, the student was not denied, even temporarily, a public education. In dismissing the case, the court did note that to ensure fairness, the state and local school districts should provide students and parents an opportunity to explain why a disciplinary transfer may not be warranted; however, failure to do so does not impair constitutional rights.[68]

Under state law, North Carolina local school boards must establish at least one alternative educational program, and students facing long-term suspensions or expulsions are to be provided learning alternatives when feasible and appropriate. A North Carolina student, who was subjected to a long-term suspension without the offer of an alternative education assignment, challenged the denial as a violation of her state constitutional right to a sound basic education. The Supreme Court of North Carolina ruled that a student

[65]*See, e.g.*, McCall v. Bossier Parish Sch. Bd., 785 So. 2d 57 (La. Ct. App. 2001). *But see* Martinez v. Sch. Dist. No. 60, 852 P.2d 1275 (Colo. Ct. App. 1992) (rejecting students' argument that a disciplinary transfer for ninety days required a hearing because education was not interrupted).

[66]Rone v. Winston-Salem/Forsyth Cnty. Bd. of Educ., 701 S.E.2d 284 (N.C. Ct. App. 2010).

[67]Everett v. Marcase, 426 F. Supp. 397, 400 (E.D. Pa. 1977).

[68]Nevares v. San Marcos Consol. Indep. Sch. Dist., No. 96-50420, 1997 U.S. App. LEXIS 14955 (5th Cir. April 11, 1997); *see also* Swindle v. Livingston Parish Sch., 655 F.3d 386 (5th Cir. 2011) (ruling that an expelled student had a right under Louisiana law to continued public alternative education; she could not be deprived of it without procedural due process); Harris v. Pontotoc Cnty. Sch. Dist., 635 F.3d 685 (5th Cir. 2011) (finding that minimum due process requirements had been met for a short suspension and noting that an assignment to an alternative school does not involve a denial of education requiring procedural protection); Anderson v. Hillsborough Cnty. Sch. Bd., 390 F. App'x 902 (11th Cir. 2010) (finding that the due process provided was sufficient for an alternative placement).

who violated lawful school rules did not have a constitutional right to an alternative education but did have a constitutional right to know the reasons for denial since state law provided for alternative educational programs. The court did not find "the requirement that school administrators articulate an important or significant reason for denying educational services" to be unduly burdensome.[69]

ANTI-BULLYING LAWS. Numerous studies document the pervasiveness of bullying behavior and its detrimental impact on students' learning and mental health. All states except Montana have enacted anti-bullying legislation because of concerns about connections between school violence and bullying. Like the mandate under the federal zero-tolerance law, these state laws, which may reside in the education, criminal, and/or juvenile justice codes, require local school districts to include an anti-bullying policy in their discipline codes.[70] Most state laws provide a broad definition of what constitutes bullying behavior. The laws refer to intentional, aggressive behavior, repeated over time, that imposes harm on others. Typically, proscribed behavior includes name-calling, teasing, intimidation, ridicule, humiliation, physical acts, and taunts.[71] The scope of the laws specifies behavior occurring not only on school property but also at school-sponsored events and on school buses and at bus stops, as well as off-campus conduct. For example, Massachusetts's law prohibits bullying at any location unrelated to the school "if the bullying creates a hostile environment at school for the victim, infringes on the rights of the victim at school, or materially and substantially disrupts the education process or the orderly operation of a school." [72] Thirty-six states specifically include cyberbullying that inflicts fear and harm.

Although a few state laws identify the specific penalties for bullying behavior, most states mandate that school districts develop a bullying policy that delineates the penalties and the measures that will be taken to prevent bullying. Oregon law is typical, requiring that policies include consequences for bullying behavior, but it also goes further by specifying that remedial measures should be taken with the students who bully.[73] Georgia law does not address initial consequences but specifies student assignment to an alternative school after three bullying offenses.[74]

School personnel have always had the authority to discipline students for bullying. The new laws, however, formalize the responsibility for disrupting and deterring such behavior. Since the anti-bullying state laws are relatively new, case law is quite limited in interpreting students' rights and school districts' liability.[75] Nonetheless, in developing and

[69]King v. Beaufort Cnty. Bd. of Educ., 704 S.E.2d 259, 265 (N.C. 2010).

[70]For an analysis of state bullying laws adopted through April 2011, see Victoria Stuart-Cassel, Ariana Bell & Fred Springer, *Analysis of State Bullying Laws and Policies* (Washington: U.S. Dep't of Education, Dec. 6, 2011), http://www.ed.gov/news/press-releases/us-education-department-releases-analysis-state-bullying-laws-and-policies.

[71]*See, e.g.*, IND. CODE ANN. § 20-33-8-0.2 (2012) (defining bullying as "overt, repeated acts or gestures, including (1) verbal or written communications transmitted; (2) physical acts committed; or (3) any other behaviors committed by a student or group of students against another student with the intent to harass, ridicule, humiliate, intimidate, or harm the other student").

[72]MASS. GEN. LAWS, ch. 71 § 370 (2012).

[73]OR. REV. STAT. § 339.356(1) (2012).

[74]GA. CODE ANN. § 20-2-751.4(b)(2) (2012).

[75]In addition to state laws, victims of bullying may rely on federal civil rights laws if they are in a protected class (i.e., race, sex, national origin, or religion) or seek a remedy for negligence against the aggressor and the school district under state tort law.

administering anti-bullying policies, school officials must take into consideration students' procedural due process rights. Policies imposing short-term suspensions must comply at least with the minimum requirements of *Goss*;[76] more extensive disciplinary measures for bullying behavior will necessitate formal hearings.

Fundamental fairness requires at least minimal due process procedures when students are denied school attendance or removed from the regular instructional program. Severity of the separation dictates the amount of process due under the United States Constitution and state laws. Permanent expulsion from school triggers the most extensive process, whereas minor infractions may involve a brief give-and-take between school officials and students. Simply providing students the opportunity to be heard can preserve trust in the school system.

CORPORAL PUNISHMENT

Although some states permit educators to administer corporal punishment, increasingly, states are banning the practice either by law or state regulation. In 1971, only one state prohibited corporal punishment; today, thirty-two proscribe its use.[77] Generally, where state law permits corporal punishment, courts have upheld its reasonable administration and have placed the burden on the aggrieved students to prove otherwise. In evaluating the reasonableness of a teacher's actions in a given situation, courts have assessed the child's age, maturity, and past behavior; the nature of the offense; the instrument used; any evidence of lasting harm to the child; and the motivation of the person inflicting the punishment. This section provides an overview of the constitutional and state law issues raised in the administration of corporal punishment.

Constitutional Issues

In 1977, the Supreme Court addressed the constitutionality of corporal punishment that resulted in the severe injury of two students. The Court held in *Ingraham v. Wright* that the use of corporal punishment in public schools does not violate either the Eighth Amendment's prohibition against the government's infliction of cruel and unusual punishment or the Fourteenth Amendment's procedural due process guarantees.[78] While recognizing that corporal punishment implicates students' constitutionally protected liberty interests, the Court emphasized that state remedies are available, such as assault and battery suits under tort laws, if students are excessively or arbitrarily punished by school personnel. In essence, the Court majority concluded that state courts under provisions of state laws should handle cases dealing with corporal punishment. The majority distinguished corporal punishment from a suspension by noting that the denial of school attendance

[76]*See supra* text accompanying notes 52–55.

[77]Most recently, New Mexico (2011) and Ohio (2009) enacted laws to abolish corporal punishment. *See Global Initiative to End All Corporal Punishment of Children* (2012), http://www.endcorporalpunishment.org/pages/frame.html, for the status of corporal punishment laws in each state and country in the world. The American Academy of Pediatrics has recommended that corporal punishment be abolished in all states because of its detrimental effect on students' self-image and achievement as well as possible contribution to disruptive and violent behavior. American Academy of Pediatrics, *Corporal Punishment in Schools*, 106 PEDIATRICS 343 (Aug. 2000); reaffirming 2000 statement, 118 PEDIATRICS 1266 (Sept. 2006).

[78]430 U.S. 651 (1977).

is a more severe penalty that deprives students of a property right and thus necessitates procedural safeguards. Furthermore, the majority reasoned that the purpose of corporal punishment would be diluted if elaborate procedures had to be followed prior to its use.

The Supreme Court's ruling in *Ingraham*, however, does not foreclose a successful constitutional challenge to the use of *unreasonable* corporal punishment. Most federal appellate courts have held that students' substantive due process right to be free of brutal and egregious threats to bodily security might be impaired by the use of shockingly, excessive corporal punishment.[79] For example, the Fourth Circuit concluded that although *Ingraham* bars federal litigation on procedural due process issues, excessive or cruel corporal punishment may violate students' substantive due process rights, which protect individuals from arbitrary and unreasonable governmental action. According to the appellate court, the standard for determining if such a violation has occurred is "whether the force applied caused injury so severe, was so disproportionate to the need presented, and was so inspired by malice or sadism rather than a merely careless or unwise excess of zeal that it amounted to a brutal and inhumane abuse of official power literally shocking to the conscience."[80] Clearly, student challenges to the *reasonable use* of ordinary corporal punishment are precluded by this standard.

Substantive due process claims generally are evaluated by examining the need for administering corporal punishment, the relationship between the need and the amount of punishment administered, whether force was applied to maintain or restore discipline or used maliciously with the intent of causing harm, and the extent of a student's injury.[81] The Fifth and Seventh Circuits, disagreeing with the stance of the majority of the appellate courts, concluded that constitutional claims cannot be raised if states prohibit unreasonable student discipline and provide adequate postpunishment civil or criminal remedies for abuse.[82]

Courts allowing substantive due process claims have found the threshold for recovery for the violation of a student's rights to be high. Minor pain, embarrassment, and hurt feelings do not rise to this level; actions must literally be "shocking to the conscience."[83] Disciplinary actions that have not risen to this level include requiring a ten-year-old boy to clean out a stopped-up toilet with his bare hands,[84] physically and forcefully restraining

[79]*See, e.g.*, Johnson v. Newburgh Enlarged Sch. Dist., 239 F.3d 246 (2d Cir. 2001); Neal v. Fulton Cnty. Bd. of Educ., 229 F.3d 1069 (11th Cir. 2000); P.B. v. Koch, 96 F.3d 1298 (9th Cir. 1996); Metzger v. Osbeck, 841 F.2d 518 (3d Cir. 1988).

[80]Hall v. Tawney, 621 F.2d 607, 613 (4th Cir. 1980).

[81]Some courts, however, have moved away from substantive due process for analyzing claims of excessive force in § 1983 actions. The Ninth Circuit noted that the specific constitutional provisions of the Fourth Amendment "provide more guidance to judicial decision makers than the more open-ended concept of substantive due process," Doe *ex rel.* Doe v. Haw. Dep't of Educ., 334 F.3d 906, 908 (9th Cir. 2003); *see also* Preschooler II v. Clark Cnty. Sch. Bd. of Trs., 479 F.3d 1175 (9th Cir. 2007) (finding that a teacher's excessive physical force in disciplining a seriously disabled four-year-old child was not reasonable under the Fourth Amendment). *But see* Flores v. Sch. Bd. of DeSoto Parish, 116 F. App'x 504 (5th Cir. 2004) (ruling that permitting excessive force claims to be considered under the Fourth Amendment would undermine the court's [Fifth Circuit] prohibition against substantive due process claims where state law remedies exist).

[82]Moore v. Willis Indep. Sch. Dist., 233 F.3d 871 (5th Cir. 2000); Wallace v. Batavia Sch. Dist. 101, 68 F.3d 1010 (7th Cir. 1995).

[83]*See* Davis v. Carter, 555 F.3d 979 (11th Cir. 2009) (finding that a coach's deliberate indifference to a football player who suffered from dehydration and exhaustion was insufficient to establish a constitutional violation; coach's actions did not involve corporal punishment, nor did the coach act in a malicious way with the intent to injure the student).

a student in multiple incidents,[85] and shoving a student's head into a trash can.[86] In contrast, substantive due process rights were implicated where a nine-year-old girl was paddled with a split paddle while she was held upside down by another teacher, resulting in severe bruises, cuts, and permanent scarring.[87] Similarly, other conscience-shocking behavior involved a coach knocking a student's eye out of the socket with a metal weight lock[88] and a teacher physically restraining a student until he lost consciousness and fell to the floor, suffering significant injuries.[89] The Fourth Circuit found that a student's substantive due process rights were implicated when a wrestling coach "initiated and encouraged" wrestling team members to repeatedly beat the student.[90]

State Law

Although the Supreme Court has ruled that the United States Constitution does not prohibit corporal punishment in public schools, its use may conflict with state law, school board policy, or local administrative regulations. As noted, the majority of states now prohibit corporal punishment, and others have established procedures or conditions for its use. Teachers can be disciplined or discharged for violating these state and local provisions regulating corporal punishment. Courts have upheld dismissals based on insubordination for failure to comply with reasonable school board requirements in administering corporal punishment. Teachers also have been dismissed under the statutory grounds of "cruelty" for improper use of physical force with students. In Illinois, a tenured teacher was dismissed on this ground for using a cattle prod in punishing students.[91] Other disciplinary measures also may be taken against teachers. A Nebraska teacher who "tapped" a student on the head was suspended without pay for thirty days under a state law that prohibits the use of corporal punishment.[92]

Beyond statutory or board restrictions, other legal means exist to challenge the use of unreasonable corporal punishment in public schools. Teachers can be charged with criminal assault and battery, which might result in fines and imprisonment. Civil assault and battery suits for monetary damages also can be initiated against school personnel.[93]

[84]Harris v. Robinson, 273 F.3d 927 (10th Cir. 2001).

[85]T.W. v. Sch. Bd. of Seminole Cnty., 610 F.3d 588 (11th Cir. 2010).

[86]Monroe v. Ben Hill Cnty. Sch. System, 377 F. App'x 913 (11th Cir. 2010).

[87]Garcia v. Miera, 817 F.2d 650 (10th Cir. 1987).

[88]Neal v. Fulton Cnty. Bd. of Educ., 229 F.3d 1069 (11th Cir. 2000).

[89]Metzger v. Osbeck, 841 F.2d 518 (3d Cir. 1988); *see also* Ellis *ex rel.* Pendergrass v. Cleveland Mun. Sch. Dist., 455 F.3d 690 (6th Cir. 2006) (concluding that a substitute teacher slamming an elementary student's head into a chalkboard, throwing her to the floor, and choking her violated the student's substantive due process rights).

[90]Meeker v. Edmundson, 415 F.3d 317 (4th Cir. 2005). A few years later in another case the Fourth Circuit concluded: "We have little difficulty finding that a reasonable teacher would know that maliciously restraining a child in her chair for hours at a time interferes with that child's constitutional liberty interest." H.H. v. Moffett, 335 F. App'x 306, 314 (4th Cir. 2009).

[91]Rolando v. Sch. Dirs. 358 N.E.2d 945 (Ill. App. Ct. 1976).

[92]Daily v. Bd. of Educ., 588 N.W.2d 813 (Neb. 1999).

[93]*Ex parte* Monroe Cnty. Bd. of Educ. v. Monroe Cnty. Bd. of Educ., 48 So. 3d 621 (Ala. 2010) (ruling that a teacher was not entitled to state-agent immunity in a tort suit because she did not follow the school board's policy for administering corporal punishment).

When corporal punishment is allowed, educators should use caution in administering it, since improper administration can result in dismissal, monetary damages, and even imprisonment. Corporal punishment should never be administered with malice, and the use of excessive force should be avoided. Teachers would be wise to keep a record of incidents involving corporal punishment and to adhere to minimum procedural safeguards, such as notifying students of behavior that will result in a paddling, asking another staff member to witness the act, and providing parents on request written reasons for the punishment. Moreover, teachers should become familiar with relevant state laws and school board policies before attempting to use corporal punishment in their classrooms.

ACADEMIC SANCTIONS

It is indisputable that school authorities have the right to use academic sanctions for poor academic performance. Consistently, courts have been reluctant to substitute their own judgment for that of educators in assessing students' academic accomplishments. Failing grades, denial of credit, academic probation, retention, and expulsion from particular programs have been upheld as legitimate means of dealing with poor academic performance. Courts usually have granted broad discretionary powers to school personnel in establishing academic standards, but there has been less agreement regarding the use of grade reductions or academic sanctions as punishments for student absences and misbehavior. More complex legal issues are raised when academic penalties are imposed for nonacademic reasons.

Absences

Excessive student absenteeism continues to be a concern and has led many school boards to impose academic sanctions for absences. These practices have generated legal challenges related to students' substantive due process rights. To meet the due process requirements, however, the sanction must be reasonable—that is, rationally related to a valid educational purpose. Since students must attend class to benefit from the educational program, most courts have found that academic penalties for absenteeism serve a valid educational goal.

In an illustrative case, an Illinois student claimed that a school regulation stipulating that grades would be lowered one letter grade per class for an unexcused absence impaired protected rights.[94] In defending the rule, school officials asserted that it was the most appropriate punishment for the serious problem of truancy. They argued that students could not perform satisfactorily in their class work if they were absent, since grades reflected class participation in addition to other standards of performance. The appeals court was not persuaded by the student's argument that grades should reflect only scholastic achievement, and therefore concluded that the regulation was reasonable.

The Supreme Court of Connecticut upheld a school-wide policy that provided for a five-point reduction in course grades for each unapproved absence and that denied course credit for such absences in excess of twenty-four. The court drew a sharp distinction between academic and disciplinary sanctions, noting that the school board's policy was academic, rather than disciplinary, in intent and effect. Specifically, the court found

[94]Knight v. Bd. of Educ., 348 N.E.2d 299 (Ill. App. Ct. 1976).

that a board's determination that grades should reflect more than examinations and papers "constitutes an academic judgment about academic requirements."[95] The Supreme Court of Missouri drew a similar distinction between academic and disciplinary sanctions but concluded that a school district's policy providing for loss of credit for previously earned academic work was punishment for unsatisfactory attendance rather than deductions for academic performance. Therefore, the court ruled that the student was entitled to a due process hearing prior to imposition of the penalty.[96]

Some courts have upheld even those policies that do not differentiate between excused and unexcused absences in imposing academic penalties, noting that students are missing instructional and learning time regardless of why they are absent. For example, the Supreme Court of Arkansas upheld a board policy that disallowed course credit and permitted expulsion of students who accumulated more than twelve absences per semester.[97] The court, in refusing to substitute its judgment for the school board's, concluded that under state law, this action was within the board's power to make reasonable rules and regulations for the administration of the schools. A Michigan appellate court upheld a school board's authority to require students with more than three days of excused absences to attend after-school study sessions or have their letter grades reduced.[98]

Given the serious truancy problem confronting many school districts, it seems likely that school officials will continue to consider the imposition of academic sanctions. The legality of such policies will depend primarily on judicial interpretation of applicable state law.

Misconduct

Academic sanctions imposed for student misconduct also have been challenged. It is generally accepted that students can be denied credit for work missed while suspended from school. In fact, if students could make up such work without penalty, a suspension might be viewed as a vacation rather than a punishment. More controversy has surrounded policies that impose an additional grade reduction for suspension days, and courts have not agreed regarding the legality of this practice.

For example, a Pennsylvania court found grade reductions for suspensions to be beyond a school board's authority.[99] In the court's opinion, it was a clear misrepresentation of students' scholastic achievement; the penalty went beyond the five-day suspension and downgraded achievement for a full grading period. The Mississippi Supreme Court, relying on a state law mandating the maintenance of alternative schools for suspended students, concluded that students attending these schools are not absent from school.[100] Under this law, a school board cannot count suspension days as unexcused for grading purposes unless the student fails to attend the alternative school. In contrast, the Supreme Court of Indiana upheld the denial of course credit for a high school junior expelled three

[95]Campbell v. Bd. of Educ., 475 A.2d 289, 294 (Conn. 1984).

[96]State v. McHenry, 915 S.W.2d 325 (Mo. 1995).

[97]Williams v. Bd. of Educ., 626 S.W.2d 361 (Ark. 1982).

[98]Slocum v. Holton Bd. of Educ., 429 N.W.2d 607 (Mich. Ct. App. 1988).

[99]Katzman v. Cumberland Valley Sch. Dist., 479 A.2d 671 (Pa. Commw. Ct. 1984); *see also In re* Angela, 340 S.E.2d 544 (S.C. 1986) (ruling that under state law, suspension absences could not be counted as unexcused for determining delinquency).

[100]Bd. of Trs. v. T.H., 681 So. 2d 110 (Miss. 1996).

days before the end of a semester after the discovery of a small amount of marijuana in his truck. The court noted that although state law did not mandate loss of credit, the board could impose such a penalty.[101]

Generally, courts have ruled that academic course credit or high school diplomas cannot be withheld solely for disciplinary reasons. A Pennsylvania court held that a student who completed all coursework and final exams while expulsion proceedings were pending could not be denied a diploma because state law specifies that a diploma must be issued once all requirements are met.[102]

Courts have issued conflicting decisions regarding the legality of denying a student the right to participate in graduation ceremonies as a disciplinary measure. The Arkansas Supreme Court held that a student suspended at the end of the semester could be denied participation in the graduation ceremony.[103] A Pennsylvania appellate court reversed a trial court order permitting a student to participate in the graduation ceremony after he was suspended for violating the district's alcohol policy.[104] The appeals court found no arbitrary, capricious, or prejudicial actions on the part of the school board to justify judicial interference with the school's decision. Similarly, a Texas federal district court denied a preliminary injunction to prevent a school district from prohibiting a student's participation in the graduation ceremony and the deliverance of the valedictorian address, finding that no property right existed in attending the ceremony or delivering the address.[105]

Although the use of academic sanctions for student misconduct and truancy is prevalent, students will likely continue to challenge such practices. To ensure fairness, any regulation stipulating that grades will be lowered for nonacademic reasons should be reasonable, related to absences from class, and serve a legitimate school purpose. Furthermore, students must be informed of these rules through the school's official student handbook or similar means.

SEARCH AND SEIZURE

The majority of search and seizure cases in public schools involve the confiscation of either illegal drugs or weapons. Students have asserted that warrantless searches conducted by school officials impair their rights under the Fourth Amendment of the Constitution. Through an extensive line of decisions, the Supreme Court has affirmed that the basic purpose of the Fourth Amendment is to "safeguard the privacy and security of individuals against arbitrary invasions by governmental officials."[106] This amendment protects individuals against unreasonable searches by requiring state agents to obtain a warrant based on probable cause prior to conducting a search. Under the *probable cause standard*, a governmental official must have reasonable grounds of suspicion, supported by sufficient evidence, to cause a cautious person to believe that the suspected individual is guilty of the alleged offense and that the search will produce evidence of the crime committed. Governmental officials

[101]S. Gibson Sch. Bd. v. Sollman, 768 N.E.2d 437 (Ind. 2002).

[102]Ream v. Centennial Sch. Dist., 765 A.2d 1195 (Pa. Commw. Ct. 2001); 24 PA. STAT. ANN. § 16-1613 (2012).

[103]Walters v. Dobbins, 370 S.W.3d 209 (Ark. 2010).

[104]Flynn-Scarcella v. Pocono Mountain Sch. Dist., 745 A.2d 117 (Pa. Commw. Ct. 2000).

[105]Khan v. Fort Bend Indep. Sch. Dist., 561 F. Supp. 2d 760 (S.D. Tex. 2008).

[106]Camara v. Mun. Ct. of S.F., 387 U.S. 523, 528 (1967).

violating Fourth Amendment rights may be subject to criminal or civil liability, but the most important remedy for the aggrieved individual is the exclusionary rule.[107] This rule renders evidence of an illegal search inadmissible in criminal prosecutions.[108] Also, under the "fruit of the poisonous tree" doctrine, additional evidence obtained later, resulting from the events set in motion by the illegal search, may be excluded.

Since Fourth Amendment protections apply only to searches conducted by agents of the state, a fundamental issue in education cases was whether school authorities function as private individuals or as state agents. In 1985, the Supreme Court in *New Jersey v. T.L.O.* held that the amendment's prohibition of unreasonable searches applied to school authorities.[109] The Court concluded that school officials are state agents, and all governmental actions—not merely those of law enforcement officers—come within the constraints of the Fourth Amendment.

Although finding the Fourth Amendment applicable, the Court in *T.L.O.* concluded that educators' substantial interest in maintaining discipline required "easing" the warrant and probable cause requirements imposed on police officers. The Court reasoned that "requiring a teacher to obtain a warrant before searching a child suspected of an infraction of school rules (or of the criminal law) would unduly interfere with the maintenance of the swift and informal disciplinary procedures needed in the schools."[110] In modifying the level of suspicion required to conduct a search, the Court found the public interest was best served in the school setting with a standard less than probable cause. Accordingly, the Court held that the legality of a search should depend "simply on the reasonableness, under all the circumstances, of the search."[111]

The Court in *T.L.O.* advanced two tests for determining reasonableness. First, is the search justified at its inception? That is, are there "reasonable grounds for suspecting that the search will turn up evidence that the student has violated or is violating either the law or the rules of the school?"[112] Second, is the scope of the search reasonable? In the Court's words, are "the measures adopted reasonably related to the objectives of the search and not excessively intrusive in light of the age and sex of the student and the nature of the infraction?"[113]

The "reasonableness" standard allows courts substantial latitude in interpreting Fourth Amendment rights. Among the factors courts have considered in assessing reasonable grounds for a search are the child's age, history, and record in the school; prevalence and seriousness of the problem in the school to which the search is directed; exigency to make the search without delay and further investigation; probative value and reliability of the information used as a justification for the search; school officials' experience with the student and with the type of problem to which the search is directed; and the type of search. Clearly, reasonable suspicion requires more than a hunch, good intentions, or good faith. The Supreme Court, in upholding an exception to the warrant requirement

[107]*See* Mapp v. Ohio, 367 U.S. 643 (1961).

[108]Evidence seized by a private person, however, is admissible since the exclusionary rule does not apply.

[109]469 U.S. 325 (1985).

[110]*Id.* at 340. *See In re* M.A.D., 233 P.3d 437 (Or. 2010) (holding that under the state constitution, probable cause was not required to search when a school official had credible information that a student possessed drugs and attempted to sell them earlier in the day).

[111]*T.L.O.*, 469 U.S. at 341.

[112]*Id.* at 342.

[113]*Id.*

for a "stop and frisk" search for weapons by police officers, concluded that to justify the intrusion, the police officer must be able to point to *specific and articulable facts.*[114] In recognizing an exception for school searches, it appears that, at a minimum, the judiciary will require searches of students to be supported by objective facts.[115]

Informants often play an important role in establishing the "specific and articulable facts" necessary to justify a search. Reliability of informants can be assumed unless school officials have reason to doubt the motives of the reporting student, teacher, parent, citizen, or anonymous caller.[116] The amount of detail given by an informant adds to the veracity of the report—that is, identifying a student by name, what the student is wearing, and the specific contraband and where it is located will help support a decision to search.[117] Additionally, even with limited information, the level of danger presented by an informant's tip may require an immediate response.

A further requirement of reasonableness is individualized suspicion. The Supreme Court in *T.L.O.* did not address individualized suspicion, but the Court did state that "exceptions to the requirement of individualized suspicion are generally appropriate only where the privacy interests implicated by a search are minimal and where 'other safeguards' are available 'to assure that the individual's reasonable expectation of privacy is not subject to the discretion of the official in the field.'"[118] In the absence of exigency requiring an immediate search, courts have been reluctant to support personal searches lacking individualized suspicion.

In assessing the constitutionality of searches in public schools, two questions are central: (1) what constitutes a search? (2) what types of searches are reasonable? What constitutes a search must be appraised in the context of the Supreme Court's statement that "the Fourth Amendment protects people, not places. What a person knowingly exposes to the public, even in his own home or office, is not a subject of Fourth Amendment protection. But what he seeks to preserve as private, even in an area accessible to the public, may be constitutionally protected."[119] According to the Court's rulings, essential considerations in determining whether an action is a search are an individual's reasonable expectation of privacy (reasonable in the sense that society is prepared to recognize the privacy)[120] and the extent of governmental intrusion.[121]

The reasonableness of a specific type of search must be evaluated in terms of all of the circumstances surrounding the search.[122] This would include variables such as who initiated the search, who conducted the search, need for the search, purpose of the

[114]Terry v. Ohio, 392 U.S. 1, 21 (1968).

[115]*See, e.g.*, Cornfield v. Consol. High Sch. Dist., 991 F.2d 1316 (7th Cir. 1993).

[116]*See* People v. Perreault, 781 N.W.2d 796 (Mich. 2010) (holding that an anonymous tip providing names of students, grade levels, vehicle types, and drugs being sold established reasonable suspicion to search student's vehicle); *In re* L.A., 21 P.3d 952 (Kan. 2001) (finding that a student's tip to the Crime Stoppers organizer established reasonable suspicion). The Supreme Court in *T.L.O.* noted that because the expectation of privacy is diminished in school settings, officials do not have to show the reliability level required of police officers. For a discussion of the higher standards for law enforcement, see *Florida v. J.L.*, 529 U.S. 266 (2000).

[117]*See, e.g.*, Wofford v. Evans, 390 F.3d 318 (4th Cir. 2004).

[118]*T.L.O.*, 469 U.S. at 342 n.8.

[119]Katz v. United States, 389 U.S. 347, 351–52 (1967).

[120]*Id.* at 361 (Harlan, J., concurring).

[121]United States v. Chadwick, 433 U.S. 1, 7 (1977).

[122]Terry v. Ohio, 392 U.S. 1, 9 (1968).

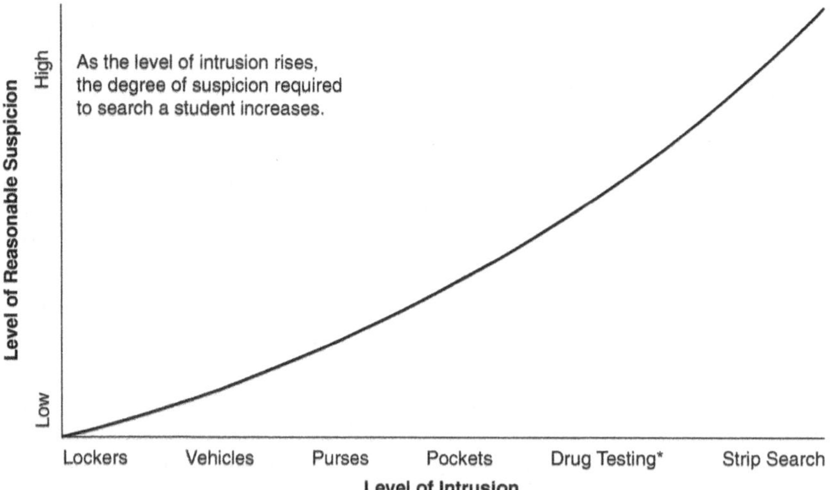

FIGURE 1 Degree of Suspicion Required to Conduct Student Searches
*Under school district drug-testing policies, athletes and students participating in extracurricular activities can be subjected to drug tests without individualized suspicion.

search, information or factors prompting the search, what or who was searched, and use of the evidence.

An individual may waive entitlement to Fourth Amendment protection by consenting to a search or volunteering requested evidence. The consent, however, is valid only if voluntarily given in the absence of coercion. Serious questions arise as to whether a student's consent is actually voluntary. Did the student have a free choice? Was the student aware of his or her Fourth Amendment rights? The very nature of the school setting diminishes the presumption of consent. Students are accustomed to receiving and following orders of school officials; refusal to obey a request is considered insubordination. A threat to call a student's parents and the police if he or she does not cooperate can further substantiate a coercive atmosphere. The Sixth Circuit stated that there is "a presumption against the waiver of constitutional rights," placing the burden on school officials to show that students knowingly and intelligently waived their Fourth Amendment rights.[123] Although some courts have found student consent valid, the inherent pitfalls of pursuing such a search in the absence of reasonable suspicion must be duly considered.

In the following sections, various types of school searches are examined as to reasonableness. As can be seen in Figure 1, the degree of suspicion required to search rises as the invasiveness of the search increases.

Lockers

In concluding that students have some legitimate expectation of privacy in their lockers, the Mississippi high court relied on the United States Supreme Court's statement that "schoolchildren may find it necessary to carry with them a variety of legitimate, noncontraband items, and there is no reason to conclude that they have necessarily waived all rights to privacy in such items merely by bringing them onto school grounds."[124] Courts,

[123]Tarter v. Raybuck, 742 F.2d 977, 980 (6th Cir. 1984).
[124]*In re* S.C., 583 So. 2d 188 (Miss. 1991) (quoting New Jersey v. T.L.O., 469 U.S. 325, 339 (1985)).

however, have singled out school lockers as generating a lower expectation of privacy, frequently distinguishing locker searches on the basis that a locker is school property, and students do not retain exclusive possession, particularly when they have signed a form acknowledging that the locker is school property and subject to inspection. Under the view of joint control, school officials have been allowed to inspect lockers or even to consent to searches by law-enforcement officers.[125]

An early Kansas case illustrates the general judicial view toward locker searches. The Supreme Court of Kansas held that the right of inspection is inherent in the authority granted to school officials to manage schools.[126] The court maintained that it is a proper function of school personnel to inspect the lockers under their control and to prevent the use of lockers in illicit ways or for illegal purposes. The Tenth Circuit also concluded that "school authorities have, on behalf of the public, an interest in these lockers and a duty to police the school, particularly where possible serious violations of the criminal laws exist."[127] An important point in both cases, however, is that school officials retained a list of the combinations and had occasionally inspected the lockers. These points have been emphasized in other cases to support the nonexclusive nature of lockers.[128]

Applying the *T.L.O.* standard for reasonableness, a Texas appellate court concluded that a student informant's tip indicating another student was "high" on drugs justified the search of a student and his locker.[129] Similarly, a California appellate court reasoned that an anonymous parent informant reporting that a student had been seen at an evening school event with a gun substantiated reasonable suspicion to inspect the student's locker several days later.[130] The court commented that the locker search represented minimal intrusion in the context of the threat firearms pose to the safety of all students. The Massachusetts high court also concluded that a student eyewitness to an attempted sale of marijuana provided not only reasonable suspicion but also probable cause to search the suspected student's locker.[131]

Most student conduct codes and some state laws specify guidelines for locker searches. These codes or laws may establish that reasonable suspicion is required prior to conducting a search. In a Pennsylvania case, the state supreme court relied on the *T.L.O.* decision and the student code in establishing a legitimate expectation of privacy in lockers. The code specified: "Prior to a locker search a student shall be notified and given an opportunity to be present. However, where school authorities have a *reasonable suspicion* a locker contains materials that pose a threat to the health, welfare, and safety of students in the school, students' lockers may be searched without prior

[125]*But see infra* text accompanying notes 197–205 for cases addressing the involvement of law enforcement personnel.

[126]State v. Stein, 456 P.2d 1, 2 (Kan. 1969).

[127]Zamora v. Pomeroy, 639 F.2d 662, 670 (10th Cir. 1981).

[128]*See, e.g., In re* Patrick Y., 746 A.2d 405 (Md. 2000); Commonwealth v. Cass, 709 A.2d 350 (Pa. 1998); *In re* Isiah B., 500 N.W.2d 637 (Wis. 1993); *see also In re* S.C., 583 So. 2d 188 (holding that the existence of a master key did not lower the expectation of privacy, but that a policy of regularly inspecting the students' lockers might have that effect).

[129]*In re* S.M.C., 338 S.W.3d 161 (Tex. Ct. App. 2011); *see also In re* Juvenile, 931 A.2d 1229 (N.H. 2007) (finding student reports to a teacher that the accused juvenile possessed a "large pot pipe" justified an assistant principal's search of the juvenile's locker).

[130]*In re* Joseph G., 38 Cal. Rptr. 2d 902 (Ct. App. 1995).

[131]Commonwealth v. Snyder, 597 N.E.2d 1363 (Mass. 1992).

warning."[132] Although the court held that students possessed a reasonable expectation of privacy in their lockers, it was minimal. In balancing students' privacy interests and school officials' concerns, the court found the school-wide blanket search reasonable based on the heightened awareness of drug activity that permeated the entire school and the compelling concern about drug use.

Due to incidents of school violence in recent years, some states have enacted broad laws eliminating any presumption of privacy in school lockers. For example, a Michigan law states: "A pupil who uses a locker that is the property of a school district . . . is presumed to have no expectation of privacy in that locker or that locker's content."[133] Furthermore, school officials can search the lockers at any time and can request the assistance of the local law enforcement agency.

Search of Personal Possessions: Purses, Book Bags, and Other Property

Students have a greater expectation of privacy in their personal property or effects than in their school lockers. In the Supreme Court's *T.L.O.* decision, a teacher had reported that a student was smoking in the restroom. Upon questioning by the assistant principal, the student denied smoking and, in fact, denied that she even smoked. The assistant principal then opened the student's purse, seeking evidence to substantiate that she did smoke. In the process of removing a package of cigarettes, he spotted rolling papers and subsequently found marijuana and other evidence implicating her in drug dealing. Using the "reasonable suspicion" test, the Supreme Court found that the search in *T.L.O.* was reasonable. The school official had a basis for suspecting that the student had cigarettes in her purse. Although possession was not a violation of a school rule, it was not irrelevant; discovery of cigarettes provided evidence to corroborate that she had been smoking and challenged her credibility. No direct evidence existed that the student's purse contained cigarettes, but, based on a teacher's report that the student had been smoking, it was logical to suspect that she might have cigarettes in her purse. Characterizing this as a "commonsense" conclusion, the Court noted that "the requirement of reasonable suspicion is not a requirement of absolute certainty: 'sufficient probability, not certainty, is the touchstone of reasonableness under the Fourth Amendment.'"[134]

Other courts have noted that searches of students' personal possessions—such as wallets, purses, and book bags—do violate students' subjective expectations of privacy and, as such, require individualized suspicion that a violation of a law or school rule has occurred. The Eighth Circuit found that a Little Rock school district policy permitting school officials to conduct full-scale, random, periodic inspections of students' book bags and other personal possessions without any individualized suspicion constituted a major

[132] *Cass*, 709 A.2d at 353 (emphasis added); *see also Snyder*, 597 N.E.2d 1363 (finding expectation of privacy of lockers based on the student handbook). *But see In re* Patrick Y., 746 A.2d 405 (holding that a local policy specifying probable cause to search lockers did not establish a reasonable expectation of privacy because state law provided that lockers were school property and could be searched without even reasonable suspicion).

[133] MICH. COMP. LAWS § 380.1306 (2012); *see also* OHIO REV. CODE § 3313.20 (2012) (specifying that a locker can be searched when reasonable suspicion exists that it contains evidence of the violation of a school rule or the law, or can be subject to random search if the board of education posts notice in a conspicuous place in each school building to that affect).

[134] New Jersey v. T.L.O., 469 U.S. 325, 346 (1985).

invasion of students' expectation of privacy.[135] The court held that school officials could not argue that under the policy students waived their privacy rights when they brought their possessions onto school property. In a Louisiana case, a high school student was caught smoking cigarettes in the restroom. As part of the search, the student was required to remove his shoes, thereby revealing narcotics. A state appellate court affirmed a lower court's ruling suppressing the evidence because the search of the shoes was "excessive and unwarranted;" it would not be possible to conceal cigarettes in shoes and still smoke them.[136] No reasonable grounds existed to search the shoes.

On the other hand, the New York high court concluded that a security officer's investigation of a student's book bag was reasonable based on hearing an unusual metallic thud when the student tossed the bag on a metal shelf. Following the sound, the security officer ran his fingers over the outside of the book bag and detected the outline of a gun. The court noted that the sound alone was insufficient to justify searching the bag, but the discovery of the presence of a gun-like shape established reasonable suspicion to open the bag.[137] In a California case, the court found the search of a student's pockets and backpack reasonable under the school district's established policy that all students who leave campus during the school day and return are subjected to a search.[138] Students and parents were informed of the policy, and it was deemed necessary to maintain a safe school environment.

With the prevalent use of cell phones by students, the phones have become ubiquitous in schools and thus subject to search when school officials suspect wrongdoing. Like other personal items, reasonable suspicion is needed to search a cell phone. In a Pennsylvania case, school officials seized Christopher Klump's cell phone when it fell from his pocket; his action violated the school policy against displaying or using a cell phone during the school day.[139] School officials, attempting to determine if other students were violating the policy, used Christopher's phone to call students in the phone's directory, check the messages, and hold an instant messaging conversation without identifying themselves. The court found school officials justified in taking the cell phone, however, the scope of the search was unreasonable. According to the court, the officials "had no reason to suspect at the outset that such a search would reveal that Christopher Klump himself was violating another school policy; rather, they hoped to utilize his phone as a tool to catch other students' violations."[140] A Mississippi federal district court, however, held that school officials did not violate a middle school student's rights when they opened the phone and saw personal photographs of the student. Unlike the Pennsylvania case, the court noted that the cell phone was contraband, with the student having

[135]Doe v. Little Rock Sch. Dist., 380 F.3d 349 (8th Cir. 2004). *But see* H.Y. *ex rel.* K.Y. v. Russell Cnty. Bd. of Educ., 490 F. Supp. 2d 1174 (M.D. Ala. 2007) (holding that the classroom search of students' book bags and personal possessions for missing money was justified even though individualized suspicion did not exist; school officials had an important interest in promoting order and discipline).

[136]State v. Taylor, 50 So. 3d 922, 924 (La. Ct. App. 2010), *review denied*, 57 So. 3d 333 (La. 2011).

[137]*In re* Gregory M., 627 N.E.2d 500 (N.Y. 1993).

[138]*In re* Sean, 120 Cal. Rptr. 3d 72 (Ct. App. 2010).

[139]Klump v. Nazareth Area Sch. Dist., 425 F. Supp. 2d 622 (E.D. Pa. 2006); *see also* Koch v. Adams, 361 S.W.3d 817 (Ark. 2010) (rejecting student's claim that state law did not permit school authorities to seize his cell phone; the state law specified types of penalties for violating school discipline codes but did not limit school authorities in using others, such as seizure of cell phone).

[140]*Klump*, 425 F. Supp. 2d at 640.

diminished expectations of privacy since he could not possess or use a cell phone at school.[141] Although the cell phone search was justified, expulsion of the student for a full year based on pictures containing gang symbols raised questions to be resolved by a jury.

In a Massachusetts case, the state high court assessed whether a student had a legitimate expectation of privacy in his handwriting.[142] The charges against the student grew out of several incidents of graffiti on school property containing obscenities and racial slurs, some directed toward one teacher. Because prior occurrences made the student a potential suspect, several of his homework assignments, along with two other students' papers, were analyzed to determine if they matched the graffiti. Based on a match with the student's writing, he was charged with malicious destruction of property and violation of the targeted teacher's civil rights. The court refused to suppress the handwriting analyses and samples, finding that it was reasonable for school authorities to suspect the student and that the inspection of the papers involved minimal intrusion.

A student's car, like other personal possessions, may be searched if reasonable suspicion can be established. The Supreme Court of New Jersey rejected a student's claim that a greater expectation of privacy existed for his automobile parked on school grounds, necessitating probable cause to conduct a search.[143] Noting school officials' responsibilities to maintain safety and order, the state high court held that only reasonable suspicion was required. A report from a student who appeared to be intoxicated from a pill purchased from the student as well as items found in his locker established reasonable suspicion. Similarly, reasonable suspicion was found in an Idaho case when a school official searched a student's car because he smelled tobacco smoke on him.[144] A school policy banned the possession of tobacco products on campus; individualized suspicion existed that the student was in violation of this school rule.

A Texas federal district court, however, declined to uphold a general dragnet search of a school parking lot.[145] The school's interest in the contents of the cars was viewed as minimal since students did not have access to their cars during the school day. Furthermore, the search was indiscriminate, lacking any evidence of individualized suspicion.

Personal Search of a Student

Warrantless searches of a student's person raise significant legal questions. Unlike locker searches, it cannot be asserted that there is a lower expectation of privacy. Students have a legitimate expectation of privacy in the contents of their pockets and their person. The Fifth Circuit noted that "the Fourth Amendment applies with its fullest vigor against any intrusion on the human body."[146] In personal searches, not only is it necessary to have

[141]J.W. v. Desoto Cnty. Sch. Dist., No. 2:09-cv-00155-MPM-DAS, 2010 U.S. Dist. LEXIS 116328 (N.D. Miss. Nov. 1, 2010).

[142]Commonwealth v. Buccella, 751 N.E.2d 373 (Mass. 2001).

[143]State v. Best, 987 A.2d 605 (N.J. 2010); *see also* State v. Schloegel, 769 N.W.2d 130 (Wis. Ct. App. 2009) (finding search of a vehicle reasonable when school officials were alerted that a student was in possession of drugs).

[144]State v. Voss, 267 P.3d 735 (Idaho Ct. App. 2011), *review denied*, No. 38366-2010, 2012 Idaho LEXIS 41 (Idaho Jan. 27, 2012); *see also* People v. Perreault, 781 N.W.2d 796 (Mich. 2010) (ruling that an anonymous tip established reasonable suspicion to search a student's truck when based on the totality of the circumstances).

[145]Jones v. Latexo Indep. Sch. Dist., 499 F. Supp. 223 (E.D. Tex. 1980).

[146]Horton v. Goose Creek Indep. Sch. Dist., 690 F.2d 470, 478 (5th Cir. 1982).

reasonable cause to search, but also the search itself must be reasonable. Reasonableness is assessed in terms of the specific facts and circumstances of a case.

SEARCH OF STUDENTS' CLOTHING. A New Mexico appellate court found the search of a student's pockets reasonable under the *T.L.O.* standard.[147] In this case, an assistant principal and a police officer assigned full-time to the school asked a student to empty his pockets based on his evasive behavior, smell of burnt marijuana, and a large bulge in his right pocket. When the student refused to remove his hand from his pocket, the school official felt that the incident had become a safety issue. She then asked the resource officer to search the student. The officer removed the student's hand from his right pocket and reached in and pulled out a .38 caliber handgun. The court held that the search was justified on the basis of suspicious behavior and that the scope of the search was not excessive or intrusive. Similarly, the Alabama Supreme Court found the search of two fifth-grade students for the alleged theft of nine dollars reasonable based on the fact that they had been alone in the classroom at the time the money disappeared.[148] In finding this to be a very limited search, the court concluded that it was reasonable for the teacher to suspect the two students and that a search would turn up evidence of the theft.

The Washington appellate court, however, declined to support the search of a student's pockets because he was in the school parking lot during the school day, a violation of the closed campus policy. The court emphasized that "there must be a nexus between the item sought and the infraction under investigation."[149] In the absence of other suspicious factors about the student, violation of the school's closed campus rule did not justify the automatic search that led to the discovery of marijuana.

The Minnesota federal district court concluded that school officials violated the Fourth Amendment rights of special education students when the students were subjected each day to searches of their backpacks and purses, as well as being asked to "remove their shoes and socks, turn down the waistband of their pants, empty their pockets, and (at least sometimes) to submit to a pat down."[150] In issuing a temporary restraining order, the New Mexico federal district court noted a substantial likelihood that students attending the high school prom would be successful in showing an intrusive pat-down search of all students violated the Fourth Amendment.[151] The court, however, concluded that a search of possessions, which is less intrusive, would not be unconstitutional since it served a valid purpose in ensuring a safe environment.

[147]*In re* Josue T., 989 P.2d 431 (N.M. Ct. App. 1999); *see also In re* B.A.H., 263 P.3d 1046 (Or. Ct. App. 2011) (holding under the Oregon Constitution that the search of a student's clothing was reasonable based on reliable information that he possessed illegal drugs).

[148]Wynn v. Bd. of Educ., 508 So. 2d 1170 (Ala. 1987); *see also* Bridgman v. New Trier High Sch. Dist. No. 203, 128 F.3d 1146 (7th Cir. 1997) (holding that a student's unruly behavior, bloodshot eyes, and dilated pupils established reasonable suspicion to conduct search).

[149]State v. B.A.S., 13 P.3d 244, 246 (Wash. Ct. App. 2000); *see also In re* Anthony F., 37 A.3d 429 (N.H. 2012) (ruling that the search of a student who was leaving campus and forced to return was not justified at its inception under the state constitution; the school policy specified that students would be searched if they returned after leaving an assigned area, but in this situation the student was *forced* to return).

[150]Hough v. Shakopee Pub. Schs., 608 F. Supp. 2d 1087, 1103, 1105 (D. Minn. 2009) (finding the searches to be "extraordinarily intrusive").

[151]Herrera v. Santa Fe Pub. Sch. Dist., 792 F. Supp. 2d 1174 (D.N.M. 2011).

STRIP SEARCHES. Early court decisions proclaimed the seriousness of school officials conducting strip searches of students. The Second Circuit noted that "as the intrusiveness of the search intensifies, the standard of Fourth Amendment 'reasonableness' approaches probable cause, even in the school context."[152] The Seventh Circuit, in a strongly worded statement, proclaimed in an Indiana case: "It does not require a constitutional scholar to conclude that a nude search of a thirteen-year-old child is an invasion of constitutional rights of some magnitude. More than that: it is a violation of any known principle of human decency."[153] Most courts agreed that a high level of suspicion, if not probable cause, was required to conduct a strip search of a student.

In a long awaited case, the U.S. Supreme Court in *Safford Unified School District v. Redding* in 2009 provided guidance regarding students' constitutional rights related to strip searches.[154] Based on another student's report that Savanna Redding had given her prescription-strength and over-the-counter pain medication, the assistant principal took Savanna to his office, where he unzipped her planner and showed her four white pills and one blue one. Savanna admitted that the planner belonged to her but denied that the pills were hers or that she had given them to anyone. Savanna agreed to let the assistant principal search her backpack. Finding no pills, the assistant principal asked a female administrative assistant to take Savanna to the school nurse's office. At that point, the assistant and the nurse searched Savanna's jacket, socks, and shoes and told her to remove her pants and T-shirt. Then, Savanna was told to pull her bra away from her body and shake it as well as to pull out the elastic of her underpants. No contraband was found.

The Supreme Court applied the reasonableness standard articulated in *T.L.O.*, quoting its earlier statement that a school search "will be permissible in its scope when the measures adopted are reasonably related to the objectives of the search and not excessively intrusive in light of the age and sex of the student and the nature of the infraction."[155] The Court found that sufficient evidence existed related to pill distribution to justify searching Savanna's backpack and outer clothing. The further "strip search," however, was found to be unreasonable. The Court noted that requiring Savanna to expose her breasts and pelvic area violated "societal expectations of personal privacy," thereby "requiring distinct elements of justification on the part of school authorities for going beyond a search of outer clothing and belongings."[156] In this case, the level of suspicion fell far short for the degree of intrusion. The painkillers, which violated school rules, posed only a limited threat to the school and, furthermore, no evidence pointed to Savanna hiding the pills in her underwear. Thus, the Court stated that there must be a reasonable suspicion of danger or that the search of underwear will produce evidence of wrongdoing before the "quantum leap from outer clothes and backpacks to exposure of intimate parts."[157]

In *Redding*, the Supreme Court concluded that school officials could not be held liable for the unreasonable search since the law was not well established regarding strip searches.[158] Following *Redding*, several courts, however, have denied school officials

[152]M.M. v. Anker, 607 F.2d 588, 589 (2d Cir. 1979).

[153]Doe v. Renfrow, 631 F.2d 91, 92–93 (7th Cir. 1980).

[154]557 U.S. 364 (2009).

[155]*Id.* at 370.

[156]*Id.* at 374.

[157]*Id.* at 377.

[158]On remand, however, the appellate court was asked to determine the possible liability of the school district.

qualified immunity for actions that occurred prior to the Supreme Court's ruling, noting that the law in their circuits was already "clearly established." For example, the Sixth Circuit, in a case on remand following *Redding*, ruled that school officials were not entitled to qualified immunity when they subjected about fifteen nursing students in a vocational school to a highly intrusive search for a missing credit card and some cash.[159] Students in this instance were required to unhook and shake their bras under their tops and to lower their pants halfway down their thighs. The scope of the search was found to be unreasonable—the search was to find monetary items not something that posed a threat to student safety, all students in the class were searched, and school officials did not suspect any particular student. Because the Sixth Circuit had established in an earlier case that strip searches such as this one were unconstitutional, the court denied the school officials qualified immunity.[160]

Similar to the Sixth Circuit ruling, a Georgia federal district court denied qualified immunity to a school official who required a female high school student, to remove her clothes, including her pants and underwear, in their search for a missing iPod.[161] The court held that at the time of this unreasonable strip search, which lacked individualized suspicion or a possible dangerous threat to the school, the Eleventh Circuit had established precedent in line with the Supreme Court's later ruling in *Redding*.

Although the Supreme Court did not prohibit strip searches of students, enough caveats exist to alert school officials of the inherent risks of such intrusive personal searches. Before conducting such a search, school officials must have individualized suspicion that a student is involved in wrongdoing that poses a threat to the health and safety of the school. Furthermore, the scope must not be more intrusive than demanded in the circumstances; a more dangerous item would justify a more intrusive search.

SEIZURE OF STUDENTS. Courts have examined claims that detention of students by school officials constitutes an unlawful seizure. A seizure occurs when individuals feel they are not free to leave, such as students detained by school administrators for questioning. The Tenth Circuit, however, noted: "To qualify as a seizure in the school context, the limitation on the student's freedom of movement must significantly exceed that inherent in every-day, compulsory attendance."[162]

As in the cases involving searches, courts examine school officials' actions to determine if a seizure or detainment of a student is reasonable—that is, justified at its inception and not excessively intrusive in light of the student's age and sex and the specific infraction. The Third Circuit found the "seizure" of a student for approximately four hours

[159]Knisley v. Pike Cnty. Joint Vocational Sch. Dist., 604 F.3d 977 (6th Cir. 2010); *see also* Hearring v. Sliwowski, No. 3:10-cv-00746, 2012 U.S. Dist. LEXIS 9578 (M.D. Tenn. Jan. 26, 2012) (finding that a school nurse was not entitled to qualified immunity when she checked a six-year-old girl's vaginal area for a possible urinary infection without parental consent or a medical emergency).

[160]*See* Beard v. Whitmore Lake Sch. Dist., 402 F.3d 598 (6th Cir. 2005); *see also* Brannum v. Overton Cnty. Sch. Bd., 516 F.3d 489, 499 (6th Cir. 2008) (denying qualified immunity to school officials who installed security cameras in girls' and boys' locker rooms; the right to personal privacy was "clearly established").

[161]Foster v. Raspberry, 652 F. Supp. 2d 1342 (M.D. Ga. 2009). Not only did the school official not have individualized suspicion regarding the student, he knew from an informant that another student had taken the iPod; he had ordered the search of several students to protect his informant.

[162]Couture v. Bd. of Educ., 535 F.3d 1243, 1251 (10th Cir. 2008) (holding that repeated and lengthy time-outs were not unreasonable when related to the school's efforts to modify the student's behavior problems).

while school officials investigated a claim of sexual harassment to be reasonable in light of the serious nature of the accusation against the student.[163] A California district court concluded that the detention of an eighth-grade student in the principal's office for three hours was justified to prevent classroom disruptions, to discipline the student, and to prevent her from using drugs or giving them to others.[164]

Emphasizing that students cannot leave the school premises during the school day, the Ninth Circuit held that detaining a classroom of students for five to ten minutes in a snack bar area while school officials conducted an "unquestionably legitimate dog sniff" was not an impermissible seizure under the Fourth Amendment.[165] Similarly, a federal district court found that a New Hampshire school district's removal of students from their classrooms to the football field for ninety minutes while multiple police dogs sniffed the classrooms did not constitute a seizure.[166]

A teacher's momentary physical restraint of students has typically not been considered a "seizure" under the Fourth Amendment. Citing the special nature of the school environment, courts have ruled that physical restraint in disciplinary situations in the school environment does not involve the deprivation of liberty the Fourth Amendment prohibits.[167] Thus, a teacher who physically grasps a student by the shoulders and escorts him out of the classroom has not violated the student's Fourth Amendment right to be free from an unreasonable seizure.

Metal Detectors

With concern about the high rate of violence in schools, metal detectors have become more commonplace as school officials seek to maintain a safe educational environment. Moreover, the use of metal detectors is no longer limited to secondary schools. In 2000, the Chicago chief education officer approved metal detectors for all of the district's 489 elementary schools.[168] Although metal detectors have become standard equipment in airports and many public buildings, their use does constitute a search for Fourth Amendment purposes. Such public searches have been found to be reasonable in balancing the threat of violence against the minimally intrusive nature of the search. As challenges have been raised about the use of metal detectors in schools, similar reasoning has been applied.

The Pennsylvania high court upheld a general, uniform search of all students for weapons as they entered the high school building; each student's personal belongings

[163]Shuman v. Penn Manor Sch. Dist., 422 F.3d 141 (3d Cir. 2005); *see also* Wofford v. Evans, 390 F.3d 318 (4th Cir. 2004) (finding that school officials seized student but did not have to notify parents prior to detaining the student for questioning). *But see* Jones v. Hunt, 410 F.3d 1221 (10th Cir. 2005) (finding that a social worker's and police officer's three- to four-hour encounter with a student in the high school constituted a seizure and was not justified at its inception when the purpose of the seizure was to return the student to her father in contravention of a restraining order against the father); Doe *ex rel.* Doe v. Haw. Dep't. of Educ., 334 F.3d 906 (9th Cir. 2003) (ruling that the taping of a student to a tree for five minutes was a seizure); Pacheco v. Hopmeier, 770 F. Supp. 2d 1174 (D.N.M. 2011) (holding that an unreasonable seizure occurred when a school principal permitted police officers to take a student to the police station against his will; the student was a potential witness to a crime committed by someone else).

[164]Bravo *ex rel.* Ramirez v. Hsu, 404 F. Supp. 2d 1195 (C.D. Cal. 2005).

[165]B.C. v. Plumas Unified Sch. Dist., 192 F.3d 1260, 1269 (9th Cir. 1999).

[166]Doran v. Contoocook Valley Sch. Dist., 616 F. Supp. 2d 184 (D.N.H. 2009).

[167]*See, e.g.*, *Couture*, 535 F.3d 1243; Flores v. Sch. Bd. of DeSoto Parish, 116 F. App'x 504 (5th Cir. 2004).

[168]Jessica Portner, *Girl's Slaying Elicits Calls for Metal Detectors*, Educ. Wk., Mar. 15, 2000, at 3.

were searched, and then a security officer scanned each student with a metal detector.[169] Individualized suspicion was not required in light of the high rate of violence in the school district. The court concluded that the search involved a greater intrusion on students' privacy interests than the search of a locker, but still found it to be a minimal intrusion. Likewise, the Eighth Circuit found a search of all male students from grades six to twelve for dangerous weapons to be minimally intrusive based on reasonable suspicion that weapons had been brought to school that day.[170] Students were scanned with a metal detector after they removed their shoes and the contents of their pockets. If the metal detector sounded, a subsequent pat-down search was conducted.

An Illinois appellate court assessed the reasonableness of the use of metal detectors from the perspective of schools' "special needs."[171] In the first year of using the detectors, Chicago school officials confiscated over 300 weapons (including fifteen guns) from the high schools. With continued use of these devices, they showed a reduction of about 85 percent in weapons confiscated. The court, in concluding that individualized suspicion was not required to use metal detectors, noted that the purpose of the screening was to ensure a safe school environment for all students, not to secure evidence of a crime.

In each of the cases litigated, courts pointed to the violent context that led school officials to use metal detectors and the minimally intrusive nature of these devices. With increasing use, it can be expected that courts will continue to review the constitutional issues raised by metal detectors in school searches.

Drug-Detecting Canines

The use of drug-detecting dogs in searches raises a number of controversial questions regarding Fourth Amendment rights. Does a dog sniffing students constitute a search? Must reasonable suspicion exist to justify the use of dogs? Does the alert of a dog establish reasonable suspicion? A few courts have addressed these issues.

The Fifth Circuit confronted the question of whether sniffing by a dog is a search in terms of an individual's reasonable expectation of privacy.[172] The appellate court noted that most courts, including the United States Supreme Court, have held that a law enforcement agent's use of canines for sniffing objects does not constitute a search.[173] Specifically, the Fifth Circuit referenced cases involving checked luggage, shipped packages, public lockers, and cars on public streets. According to the court, a reasonable expectation of privacy does not extend to the airspace surrounding these objects. The court maintained that what has evolved is a doctrine of "public smell," equivalent to the "plain view" theory (that is, an object in plain view can be seized under certain circumstances).

[169]*In re* F.B., 726 A.2d 361 (Pa. 1999).

[170]Thompson v. Carthage Sch. Dist., 87 F.3d 979 (8th Cir. 1996).

[171]People v. Pruitt, 662 N.E.2d 540 (Ill. App. Ct. 1996); *see also In re* Latasha, 70 Cal. Rptr. 2d 886 (Ct. App. 1998) (holding that "special needs" administrative searches without individualized suspicion, such as use of metal detectors, involve minimal intrusion).

[172]Horton v. Goose Creek Indep. Sch. Dist., 690 F.2d 470 (5th Cir. 1982); *see also* Doran v. Contoocook Valley Sch. Dist., 616 F. Supp. 2d 184 (D.N.H. 2009).

[173]The Supreme Court concluded that the brief detention of a passenger's luggage at an airport for the purpose of subjecting it to a "sniff" test by a trained narcotics detection dog did not constitute a search under the Fourth Amendment. Use of canines was characterized as unique, involving a very limited investigation and minimal disclosure. United States v. Place, 462 U.S. 696 (1983); *see also Horton*, 690 F.2d at 477, for citations to other law enforcement cases.

This point was illustrated by the example of a police officer detecting the odor of marijuana from an object or property. No search is involved because the odor is considered to be in public view and thus unprotected.

From this line of reasoning, the Fifth Circuit noted that the use of canines has been seen as merely enhancing the ability to detect an odor, as the use of a flashlight improves vision. Accordingly, the court concluded that sniffing of student lockers and cars in public view was not a search, and therefore the Fourth Amendment did not apply. Although permitting the use of dogs to detect drugs, the court held that reasonable suspicion is required for a further search by school officials of a locker or car, and that such suspicion can be established only on showing that the dogs are reasonably reliable in detecting the actual presence of contraband.[174]

In most instances, judicial support for the use of dogs has been limited to the sniffing of objects. The Seventh Circuit, however, concluded that the presence of dogs in a classroom was not a search.[175] In this Indiana case, school officials, with the assistance of police officers, conducted a school-wide inspection for drugs in which trained dogs were brought into each classroom for approximately five minutes. When a dog alerted beside a student, school officials requested that the student remove the contents of his or her pockets or purse. A continued alert by the dog resulted in a strip search. The appellate court, in weighing the minimal intrusion of the dogs against the school's desire to eliminate a significant drug problem, concluded that sniffing of the students by the dogs did not constitute a search invoking Fourth Amendment protections. Search of pockets and purses, however, did involve an invasion of privacy but was justified because the dog's alert constituted reasonable cause to believe that the student possessed drugs. However, the court drew the line at conducting a strip search based on a dog's alert in the absence of other evidence to indicate the student was in possession of drugs.

In contrast to the reasoning of the Seventh Circuit, a Texas federal district court concluded that the use of dogs in a blanket "sniffing" (or inspection) of students did constitute a search. The court noted that drug-detecting dogs posed a greater intrusion on personal privacy than electronic surveillance devices, which have not required individualized suspicion. According to the court: "The dog's inspection was virtually equivalent to a physical entry into the students' pockets and personal possessions."[176] In finding the dog's sniffing to be a search, the court further held that for school authorities to use dogs in a search, they must have prior individualized suspicion that a student possesses contraband that will disrupt the educational process.[177] In essence, a dog alert cannot be used to establish such suspicion.

[174]Subsequently, in denying a rehearing, the court clarified the issue of the dogs' reliability. According to the court, a school district does not have to establish with "reasonable certainty that contraband is present . . . or even that there is probable cause to believe that contraband will be found." Rather, there must be some evidence to indicate that the dogs' performance is reliable enough to give rise to a reasonable suspicion. *Horton*, 693 F.2d at 525; *see also* Burlison v. Springfield Pub. Schs., No. 10-3395-CV-S-RED, 2012 U.S. Dist. LEXIS 8838 (W.D. Miss. Jan. 25, 2012) (ruling that using canines to sniff objects is not a search); Sims v. Bracken Cnty. Sch. Dist., No. 10-33DLB, 2010 U.S. Dist. LEXIS 110822 (E.D. Ky. Oct. 10, 2010) (noting in a motion to dismiss that an alert from a drug-sniffing dog establishes reasonable suspicion to search a student's car).

[175]Doe v. Renfrow, 631 F.2d 91 (7th Cir. 1980).

[176]Jones v. Latexo Indep. Sch. Dist., 499 F. Supp. 223, 233 (E.D. Tex. 1980).

[177]*Id.*; *see also* Kuehn v. Renton Sch. Dist. No. 403, 694 P.2d 1078, 1081 (Wash. 1985) (declaring that the "Fourth Amendment demands more than a generalized probability; it requires that the suspicion be particularized with respect to each individual searched").

Similarly, the Fifth Circuit held that sniffing of students by dogs significantly intrudes on an individual's privacy, thereby constituting a search.[178] Although recognizing that the sniffing of a person is a search, the court did not prohibit such searches but held that their intrusiveness must be weighed against the school's need to conduct the search. The court concluded that even with a significant need to search, individualized suspicion is required prior to the use of dogs because of the degree of intrusion on personal dignity and security. The Ninth Circuit concurred, noting that the significant intrusion on a student's expectation of privacy posed by dogs requires individualized suspicion.[179]

Given the scope of drug problems in public schools, it seems likely that school districts will continue to consider the use of drug-detecting canine units. Use of these canine units is unlikely to violate students' constitutional privacy rights so long as school officials focus on property or objects.[180]

Drug Testing

In an effort to control drug use among students,[181] some districts have considered schoolwide drug-testing programs. Such programs raise serious questions about students' privacy rights. In 1989, the Supreme Court held that urinalysis, the most frequently used means for drug testing, is a search under the Fourth Amendment.[182] Although the Court upheld the testing of government employees for drug use in two separate decisions, the holdings were narrowly drawn and based on a compelling governmental interest. In one case, the Court upheld the testing of railroad employees who are involved in certain types of accidents, emphasizing the highly regulated nature of the industry and the need to ensure the safety of the public.[183] In the second case, drug testing of customs employees seeking promotion to positions involving the interdiction of illegal drugs or requiring the use of firearms was justified based on safety and security concerns.[184] Individualized suspicion was not a precondition for conducting the urinalysis in these cases, but the narrow circumstances justifying the testing programs minimized the discretion of supervisors and the potential for arbitrariness.

The Supreme Court has rendered two decisions regarding the drug testing of students. In 1995, the Court in *Vernonia School District 47J v. Acton* upheld a school district's drug policy authorizing random urinalysis drug testing of students participating in athletic programs.[185] Emphasizing the district's "custodial and tutelary" responsibility for children,

[178]*Horton*, 690 F.2d 470.

[179]B.C. v. Plumas Unified Sch. Dist., 192 F.3d 1260 (9th Cir. 1999).

[180]*See* Todd A. DeMitchell, *Canine Drug Searches: A Law and Policy Discussion*, 269 Educ. Law Rep. 435 (2011).

[181]In 2012, the National Center on Addiction and Substance Abuse in its annual back-to-school survey of twelve- to seventeen-year-olds reported that more than 60 percent of teens continue to attend a high school that is drug-infested; one in four middle school students responded that drugs are used, kept, or sold at their schools. The data also showed that teens who spend time on social networking sites are more likely to smoke and to use alcohol and marijuana than teens who do not spend any time on the sites. National Center on Addiction and Substance Abuse, *National Survey of American Attitudes on Substance Abuse XVII: Teens and Parents* (NY: Columbia Univ., Aug. 2012), http://casacolumbia.org.

[182]Skinner v. Ry. Labor Executives' Ass'n, 489 U.S. 602 (1989); Nat'l Treasury Emps. Union v. Von Raab, 489 U.S. 656 (1989); *see also* Juran v. Independence, Or. Sch. Dist., 898 F. Supp. 728 (D. Or. 1995) (finding that breathalyzer tests also implicate Fourth Amendment protections).

[183]*Skinner*, 489 U.S. 602.

[184]*Nat'l Treasury Emps. Union*, 489 U.S. 656.

[185]515 U.S. 646 (1995).

the Court recognized that school personnel could exercise a degree of supervision and control over children that would not be permitted over adults. This relationship was held to be pivotal in assessing the reasonableness of the district's drug policy—a policy undertaken "in furtherance of the government's responsibilities, under a public school system, as guardian and tutor of children entrusted to its care."[186] Addressing students' legitimate privacy expectations, the Court noted that the lower privacy expectations within the school environment are reduced even further when a student elects to participate in sports. In concluding that students had a decreased expectation of privacy, the Court specifically identified the communal undress in locker rooms and showers and the highly regulated nature of athletics, involving physical examinations, conduct rules related to training and dress, and minimum grade point averages.

In examining the intrusiveness of the search, the Supreme Court found that the manner in which the urine samples were collected and monitored was not overly intrusive. Also, the Court stressed that the urinalysis report—which could reveal significant information about one's body, including not only drug use but other various medical conditions—was disclosed only to a limited number of individuals and was not reported to law enforcement authorities. Furthermore, the Court emphasized that the search was directed narrowly at athletes, a group in which drug use had been high and the risk for harm to themselves and others was significant.

In 2002, the Supreme Court in *Board of Education v. Earls* again reviewed a drug-testing policy, but one that applied to students in all extracurricular activities, including athletics.[187] The policy required students to take a drug test prior to participation, to submit to random drug testing while involved in the activity, and to agree to be tested at any time when reasonable suspicion existed. Acknowledging that athletes' lower expectation of privacy was noted in *Vernonia*, the Court emphasized that the critical element in upholding the earlier policy was the school context. In sustaining the drug-testing policy in *Earls*, the Court reasoned that the collection procedures, as in *Vernonia*, were minimally intrusive; information was kept in confidential files with limited access; and test results were not given to law enforcement authorities. Based on these factors, the Court concluded that the drug-testing policy was not a significant invasion of students' privacy rights. Although the students had argued that no pervasive drug problem existed to justify an intrusive measure like drug testing, the Court responded that it had never required such evidence before allowing the government to conduct suspicionless drug testing. Moreover, in light of the widespread use of drugs nationally and some evidence of increased use in this school, the Court found it entirely reasonable to enact this particular drug-testing policy.

Similar drug tests of students have been challenged under state constitutions. For example, the Supreme Court of Indiana, adhering to reasoning analogous to the Supreme Court's decision in *Earls*, found a school's policy of random drug testing of students participating in athletics, extracurricular, and cocurricular activities permissible under state law.[188] Moreover, the court indicated that the fact that the test was preventive and rehabilitative rather than punitive was an important factor under the Indiana Constitution. The Supreme Court of Wyoming followed the reasoning of the Indiana high

[186] *Id.* at 665.

[187] 536 U.S. 822 (2002).

[188] Linke v. Nw. Sch. Corp., 763 N.E.2d 972 (Ind. 2002).

court, concluding that drug testing of students involved in extracurricular activities did not violate the Wyoming Constitution; the school district was attempting to deter drug use, which was rampant among students according to statewide survey data.[189] However, both Pennsylvania and Washington high courts have held that suspicionless, random testing of students participating in extracurricular activities was unconstitutional under their state constitutions that provided stronger protection for individual privacy.[190] The Washington Constitution specifies that an individual's private affairs will not be disturbed "without authority of law"—that is, a warrant.[191] As such, the state high court has made few special needs exceptions and determined that random and suspicionless drug testing of athletes did not qualify for an exception to the warrant requirement. The Pennsylvania court noted that a special needs exception could not be made in the absence of a documented drug problem, and "individualized proof that the targeted students are at all likely to be part of whatever drug problem may (or may not) exist."[192]

Although it is clear that specific subgroups of students, such as athletes and participants in extracurricular activities, can be subjected to drug testing under the Fourth Amendment, courts have *not permitted blanket testing of all students.*[193] A Texas federal district court did not find exigent circumstances or other demonstrated compelling interests to justify a mandatory testing program of all students in grades six through twelve.[194] Accordingly, the federal court held the program unreasonable and unconstitutional under the Fourth Amendment. The Seventh Circuit rejected a school district's policy requiring drug and alcohol testing of all students suspended for three or more days for violating any school rule.[195] In this case, the student was suspended for fighting, and upon his return to school was informed that he was required to submit to a test for drug and alcohol use. When the student refused, school officials suspended him again; refusal to take the test was treated as admission of unlawful drug use. In ruling that the policy violated the Fourth Amendment, the court did not find a connection between fighting and use of drugs. Furthermore, the suspension procedures in Indiana require school officials to meet with students prior to suspension. At the initial suspension for fighting or any other infraction, it is possible to determine if individualized suspicion exists at that time to support testing a particular student for drugs or alcohol.

Although blanket or random drug testing of all students is not likely to withstand judicial challenge, many schools subject students to urinalysis based on individualized

[189]Hageman v. Goshen Cnty. Sch. Dist., 256 P.3d 487 (Wyo. 2011).

[190]York v. Wahkiakum Sch. Dist., 178 P.3d 995 (Wash. 2008); Theodore v. Delaware Valley Sch. Dist., 836 A.2d 76 (Pa. 2003); *see also* Brown v. Shasta Union High Sch. Dist., No. C061972, 2010 Cal. App. LEXIS 1660 (Cal. Ct. App. Sept. 17, 2010), *review denied*, No. S186839, 2010 Cal. LEXIS 12777 (Cal. Dec. 15, 2010) (affirming under the state constitution a preliminary injunction enjoining the use of a school district's expanded drug testing to all students participating in Competitive Representational Activities (CRAs); district did not establish a need to target the expanded CRAs).

[191]*York*, 178 P.3d at 1001.

[192]*Theodore*, 836 A.2d at 95; *see also* M.K. v. Del. Valley Sch. Dist., No. 434-2011 (Pa. Ct. Comm. Pl. July 21, 2011) (holding that the original school district in *Theodore* had not produced evidence to support its random drug-testing policy nor evidence that drug testing was an effective means to deter use).

[193]With the vast majority of students participating in extracurricular activities, school districts appear to be moving toward testing all students.

[194]Tannahill *ex rel.* Tannahill v. Lockney Indep. Sch. Dist., 133 F. Supp. 2d 919 (N.D. Tex. 2001).

[195]Willis v. Anderson Cmty. Sch., 158 F.3d 415 (7th Cir. 1998); *see also* Joy v. Penn-Harris-Madison Sch. Corp., 212 F.3d 1052 (7th Cir. 2000) (upholding random drug and alcohol testing of students involved in extracurricular activities and students driving to school; court rejected testing students for nicotine to determine tobacco use).

suspicion, and such practices have not been invalidated by courts. Any drug-testing program, however, must be carefully constructed to avoid impairing students' Fourth Amendment privacy rights. The policy must be clearly developed, specifically identifying reasons for testing. Data collection procedures must be precise and well defined.[196] Students and parents should be informed of the policy, and it is advisable to request students' consent prior to testing. However, neither student nor parental consent is required to conform to Fourth Amendment requirements. If the test indicates drug use, the student must be given an opportunity to explain the results. Providing for the rehabilitation of the student rather than punishment strengthens the policy.

Police Involvement

A "reasonable suspicion" or a "reasonable cause to believe" standard is invoked in assessing the legality of school searches, but a higher standard may be required when police officers are involved. The nature and extent of such involvement are important considerations in determining whether a search is reasonable. If the police role is one of finding evidence of a crime, probable cause would be required.[197] Whereas early decisions generally supported police participation in searches initiated and conducted by school officials, more recently courts have tended to draw a distinction between searches with and without police assistance.[198]

The more stringent judicial posture is represented in an Illinois case in which a school principal received a call that led him to suspect that three girls possessed illegal drugs.[199] On the superintendent's advice, the principal called the police to assist in the investigation. After the police arrived, the school nurse and the school psychologist searched each girl; however, no drugs were discovered. Subsequently, the students filed suit alleging that their civil rights had been violated. The court found that the police were not called merely to assist in maintaining school discipline but to search for evidence of a crime. Under the circumstances, the court concluded that the students had a constitutional right not to be searched unless the police had a warrant based on probable cause.

In contrast, the same Illinois court later held that a police officer's involvement in persuading a student to relinquish the contents of his pockets did not violate Fourth Amendment rights under the *T.L.O.* standard.[200] The police officer's role was quite limited in this case. He was in the school building on another matter, and his role in the

[196]An Indiana student, suspected of drug use, claimed that the manner in which the urinalysis test was administered violated his Fourth Amendment rights. The student was required to give the sample as he faced two male school administrators. The federal district court denied summary judgment to the school district in the case but did grant the administrators qualified immunity. Long v. Turner, 664 F. Supp. 2d 930 (S.D. Ind. 2009).

[197]*See, e.g.*, Pacheco v. Hopmeier, 770 F. Supp. 2d 1174 (D.N.M. 2011); Picha v. Wielgos, 410 F. Supp. 1214 (N.D. Ill. 1976); State v. K.L.M., 628 S.E.2d 651 (Ga. Ct. App. 2006).

[198]However, searches by trained police officers employed by or assigned to a school district generally are governed by the *T.L.O.* reasonable suspicion standard rather than the probable cause standard. *See, e.g.*, State v. Alaniz, 815 N.W.2d 234 (N.D. 2012); State v. J.M., 255 P.3d 828 (Wash. Ct. App. 2011); *In re* Angelia D.B., 564 N.W.2d 682 (Wis. 1997). *But see* Washington v. Meneese, 282 P.3d 83 (Wash. 2012) (finding that a school resource officer's (SRO) search of a student's backpack required a warrant because the SRO was seeking evidence of a crime, not enforcing school discipline).

[199]*Picha*, 410 F. Supp. 1214 (N.D. Ill. 1976).

[200]Martens v. Dist. No. 220, Bd. of Educ., 620 F. Supp. 29 (N.D. Ill. 1985).

search was restricted simply to asking the student to empty his pockets. There was no police involvement in the investigation that led to detaining the student, nor was the evidence used for criminal prosecution. Furthermore, the facts did not indicate that the school and the police officer were attempting to avoid the warrant and probable cause requirements.

Similarly, the Eighth Circuit held that the assistance of a police officer assigned as a liaison officer in a high school did not subject a search for stolen property to the Fourth Amendment's probable cause standard.[201] Relying on *T.L.O.*, the court found no evidence that the search activities were at the behest of a police official. Rather, the vice principal had initiated and conducted the investigation with limited assistance from the police officer. Although the police officer had participated in a pat-down search, it occurred only after the vice principal had discovered evidence of drug-related activity in a student's purse. The court found this search by a school official working in conjunction with a police officer to be permissible. Other courts have recognized the special role of school liaison or resource officers, noting that the "reasonable under the circumstances" standard applies when officers are working with school officials to maintain a safe school environment.[202] Some courts, however, have specifically noted or implied that the lower reasonable suspicion standard is not applicable if law enforcement officials are involved.[203]

In a Fifth Circuit case, students claimed violation of their constitutional rights when police officers called them out of class for questioning about a rumored after-school fight that was going to occur later that day.[204] Reviewing the case in the context of the special needs of the school environment, the court found the temporary "seizure" reasonable and constitutional. Recognizing that students can be detained and questioned about school discipline issues by school officials, the court concluded that the police officers did no more than the school officials could have done themselves to deter the fight. Similarly, the Fourth Circuit upheld the use of police when school officials received reliable information that a ten-year-old girl had brought a gun to school. Given police officers' expertise in locating hidden weapons, the court found school officials' action appropriate in requesting assistance to preserve the safety of students and staff.[205]

[201]Cason v. Cook, 810 F.2d 188 (8th Cir. 1987); *see also* Shade v. City of Farmington, 309 F.3d 1054 (8th Cir. 2002) (holding a police officer's search of a student at the request of school officials permissible even though it occurred en route to a body shop class away from school grounds).

[202]*See, e.g.*, Wilson *ex rel.* Adams v. Cahokia Sch. Dist., 470 F. Supp. 2d 897 (S.D. Ill. 2007); Ortiz v. State, 703 S.E. 2d 59 (Ga. Ct. App. 2010); *In re* Randy G., 28 P.3d 239 (Cal. 2001). *But see* Commonwealth v. Williams, 749 A.2d 957 (Pa. Super. Ct. 2000) (holding that school district police officers did not have authority to search a student's car parked off school property).

[203]*See, e.g.*, Rone v. Daviess Cnty. Bd. of Educ., 655 S.W.2d 28 (Ky. Ct. App. 1983); *see also* D.R.C. v. State, 646 P.2d 252 (Alaska Ct. App. 1982) (recognizing the implicit assumption that police involvement would require probable cause).

[204]Milligan v. City of Slidell, 226 F.3d 652 (5th Cir. 2000); *see also* Burreson v. Barneveld Sch. Dist., 434 F. Supp. 2d 588 (W.D. Wis. 2006) (concluding that the principal directing a student to his office to be interviewed by police for a nonschool matter did not violate the Fourth Amendment). *But see In re* R.H., 791 A.2d 331 (Pa. 2002) (holding that school officers were authorized to exercise the same powers as municipal police on school property and thus required to provide a student *Miranda* warnings prior to an interrogation that led to criminal charges).

[205]Wofford v. Evans, 390 F.3d 318 (4th Cir. 2004); *see also* Pace v. Talley, 206 F. App'x 388 (5th Cir. 2006) (finding that school officials' report to police of student's misconduct prior to talking with the student did not violate any established constitutional rights).

With the growing presence and involvement of school resource officers (SROs), students' right to be free from custodial police interrogation arises. Depending on a child's age and other circumstances related to custodial interrogation, the U.S. Supreme Court has held that when SROs or other police officers are involved, *Miranda* warnings may be required—informing the student of the right to remain silent, that any statements may be used as evidence, and that he or she has the right to an attorney.[206] The Court noted that "the custody analysis would be nonsensical absent some consideration of the suspect's age."[207] Recognizing the absurdity of evaluating the situation from the perspective of a reasonable person of average years rather than a child's age, the Court elaborated: "In other words, how would a reasonable adult understand his situation, after being removed from a seventh-grade social studies class by a uniformed school resource officer; being encouraged by his assistant principal to 'do the right thing'; and being warned by a police investigator of the prospect of juvenile detention and separation from his guardian and primary caretaker?"[208] According to the Court, the question then becomes whether a reasonable juvenile of the child's age under the circumstances understood that he or she did not have to answer the police officer's questions and was free to leave at any time. Custodial interrogation is an issue only when police officers are involved in the questioning of students; school officials remain free to meet with students and inquire into their actions.

Troubling questions, however, are raised when the fruits of warrantless searches result in the criminal prosecution of students. Classifying searches on the basis of who conducts the search and for what purpose is inadequate. As can be seen from the cases discussed, searches cannot be discreetly classified as either administrative (school related) or criminal. A search may be clearly criminal when the purpose is to find evidence of a crime, thereby necessitating probable cause prior to the search. But administrative searches undertaken strictly for disciplinary or safety purposes may result in prosecution of students if evidence of a crime is uncovered and reported to the police. In fact, school authorities have a duty to alert the police if evidence of a crime is discovered, even though the search was initiated for school purposes.

Although many legal issues involving search and seizure in schools still are controversial, school personnel can generally protect students' rights by adhering to a few basic guidelines. First, students and parents should be informed at the beginning of the school term of the procedures for conducting locker and personal searches. Second, any personal search conducted should be based on "reasonable suspicion" that a specific student possesses contraband that may be disruptive to the educational process. Third, the authorized person conducting a search should have another staff member present who can verify the procedures used in the search. Furthermore, school personnel should refrain from using mass searches of groups of students or conducting strip searches without individualized suspicion that the student possesses a dangerous item or substance that can be hidden on the body. And, finally, if police officials initiate a search in the school, either with or without the school's involvement, it is advisable for them to obtain a search warrant.

[206]J.D.B. v. North Carolina, 131 S. Ct. 2394 (2011); *see supra* text accompanying note 54.
[207]*Id.* at 2405.
[208]*Id.*

REMEDIES FOR UNLAWFUL DISCIPLINARY ACTIONS

Several remedies are available to students who are unlawfully disciplined by school authorities. When physical punishment is involved, students can seek damages through assault and battery suits against those who inflicted the harm. For unwarranted suspensions or expulsions, students are entitled to reinstatement without penalty to grades and to have their school records expunged of any reference to the illegal disciplinary action. Remedies for violation of procedural due process rights may include reversal of a school board's decision rather than remand for further proceedings. If academic penalties are unlawfully imposed, grades must be restored and transcripts altered accordingly. For unconstitutional searches, illegally seized evidence may be suppressed, school records may be expunged, and damages may be awarded if the unlawful search results in substantial injury to the student. Courts also may award court costs when students successfully challenge disciplinary actions.[209]

The Supreme Court has held that school officials can be sued for monetary damages in state courts as well as in federal courts under 42 U.S.C. § 1983 if they arbitrarily violate students' federally protected rights in disciplinary proceedings.[210] In *Wood v. Strickland*, the Court declared that ignorance of the law is not a valid defense to shield school officials from liability if they should have known that their actions would impair students' clearly established federal rights.[211] The Court recognized in *Wood* that educators are not charged with predicting the future direction of constitutional law. Other courts have reiterated school officials' potential liability in connection with student disciplinary proceedings, but to date, students have not been as successful as teachers in obtaining monetary awards for constitutional violations.

In 1978, the Supreme Court placed restrictions on the amount of damages that could be awarded to students in instances involving the impairment of procedural due process rights. In *Carey v. Piphus*, the Court declared that students who were suspended without a hearing, but were not otherwise injured, could recover only nominal damages (not to exceed one dollar).[212] This case involved two Chicago students who had been suspended without hearings for allegedly violating school regulations. They brought suit against the school district, claiming an abridgment of their constitutional rights. The Supreme Court ruled that substantial damages could be recovered only if the suspensions were unjustified. Accordingly, the case was remanded for the district court to determine whether the students would have been suspended if correct procedures had been followed.

[209]Also, under state law, school districts may be awarded restitution if a student's action resulted in costs. The Wisconsin appellate court assessed restitution in the amount of $18,026.01 for losses when a student was convicted of making a bomb threat. This included costs for salaries and benefits of employees during the evacuation. State v. Vanbeek, 765 N.W.2d 834 (Wis. Ct. App. 2009).

[210]Howlett v. Rose, 496 U.S. 356 (1990), *on remand*, 571 So. 2d 29 (Fla. Dist. Ct. App. 1990); Wood v. Strickland, 420 U.S. 308 (1975). 42 U.S.C. § 1983 provides a damages remedy for deprivations of federally protected rights under color of state law; *see also* Logiodice v. Trs., 296 F.3d 22 (1st Cir. 2002) (holding that a private school receiving tuition payments for high school students from several public school districts was not a state actor requiring it to provide a student procedural due process prior to suspension).

[211]420 U.S. 308 (1975).

[212]435 U.S. 247 (1978).

This decision may appear to have strengthened the position of school boards in exercising discretion in disciplinary proceedings, but the Supreme Court indicated that students might be entitled to substantial damages if suspensions are proven to be unwarranted. To illustrate, an Arkansas federal district court assessed punitive damages against a high school coach for intentionally impairing students' free speech rights in a disciplinary action.[213] Students also have received damages when subjected to unlawful searches. For example, the Seventh Circuit assessed damages against school officials for an intrusive body search,[214] and the court also affirmed damages in the amount of $25 when two students' free speech rights were violated.[215] The New Mexico Supreme Court affirmed substantial compensatory and punitive damages to two high school students subjected to an unconstitutional strip search.[216] In addition to damages, students also may be awarded attorneys' fees, however, a student who continues to pursue litigation when a claim is meritless may be responsible for the school district's attorneys' fees.[217]

Conclusion

In 1969, Justice Black noted, "school discipline, like parental discipline, is an integral and important part of training our children to be good citizens—to be better citizens."[218] Accordingly, school personnel have been empowered with the authority and duty to regulate pupil behavior in order to protect the interests of the student body and the school. Reasonable sanctions can be imposed if students do not adhere to legitimate conduct regulations. Courts, however, will intervene if disciplinary procedures are arbitrary or impair students' protected rights. Educators should take every precaution to afford fair and impartial treatment to students. School personnel would be wise to provide at least an informal hearing if in doubt as to whether a particular situation necessitates due process. Liability never results from the provision of too much due process, but damages can be assessed if violations of procedural rights result in unjustified suspensions, expulsions, or other disciplinary actions. Although constitutional and statutory due process requirements do not mandate that a specific procedure be followed in every situation, courts will carefully study the record to ensure that any procedural deficiencies do not impede the student's efforts to present a full defense.

Also, school authorities should ensure that constraints placed on student conduct are necessary for the proper functioning of the school. Educators have considerable latitude in controlling student behavior to maintain an appropriate educational environment and should not feel that the judiciary has curtailed their authority to discipline students. As noted in *Goss*, courts "have imposed requirements which are, if anything, less than a fair-minded principal would impose."[219]

Although the law pertaining to certain aspects of student discipline remains in a state of flux, judicial decisions support the following generalizations.

1. School authorities must be able to substantiate that any disciplinary regulation enacted is reasonable and necessary for the

[213]Boyd v. Bd. of Dirs., 612 F. Supp. 86 (E.D. Ark. 1985).
[214]Doe v. Renfrow, 631 F.2d 91 (7th Cir. 1980).
[215]Zamecnik v. Indian Prairie Sch. Dist., 636 F.3d 874 (7th Cir. 2011).
[216]Kennedy v. Dexter Consol. Schs., 10 P.3d 115 (N.M. 2000).
[217]Workman v. Dist. 13 Tanque Verde Unified Sch. Dist., 402 F. App'x 292 (9th Cir. 2010).
[218]Tinker v. Des Moines Indep. Sch. Dist., 393 U.S. 503, 524 (1969) (Black, J., dissenting).
[219]Goss v. Lopez, 419 U.S. 565, 583 (1975).

management of the school or for the welfare of pupils and school employees.

2. All regulations should be stated in precise terms and disseminated to students and parents.
3. Punishments for rule infractions should be appropriate for the offense and the characteristics of the offender (e.g., age, mental condition, and prior behavior).
4. Some type of procedural due process should be afforded to students prior to the imposition of punishments. For minor penalties, an informal hearing suffices; for serious punishments, more formal procedures are required (e.g., notification of parents, representation by counsel, opportunity to cross-examine witnesses).
5. Students can be punished for misbehavior occurring off school grounds if the conduct directly relates to the welfare of the school.
6. Suspensions and expulsions are legitimate punishments if accompanied by appropriate procedural safeguards and not arbitrarily imposed.
7. The transfer of students to different classes, programs, or schools for disciplinary reasons should be accompanied by procedural due process.
8. If not prohibited by state law or school board policy, reasonable corporal punishment can be used as a disciplinary technique.
9. Use of excessive force in administering corporal punishment that rises to the level of shocking the conscience may violate a student's substantive due process rights.
10. Academic sanctions for nonacademic reasons should be reasonable, related to absences from class, and serve a legitimate school purpose.
11. School personnel have broad latitude in searching school lockers, especially under school policies that inform students that lockers are subject to periodic inspections.
12. Educators can search students' personal effects on reasonable suspicion that the students possess contraband that is either illegal or in violation of school policy.
13. Strip searches should be avoided unless individualized reasonable suspicion exists that a student possesses something threatening to the safety and health of the school and the item can be hidden on the student's body.
14. General scanning of students with metal detectors is only minimally intrusive on students' Fourth Amendment rights when weighed against school officials' interest in providing a safe school environment.
15. The use of canines to sniff objects is generally not viewed as a search, but courts are not in agreement regarding whether their use with students is a search that would require individualized suspicion.
16. Students who voluntarily elect to participate in athletics and extracurricular activities may be subjected to random drug testing; others are required to submit to urinalysis based on individualized suspicion.
17. When law enforcement officials are involved in the search of a student to secure evidence of a crime, it is advisable for them to secure a search warrant.
18. If students are unlawfully punished, they are entitled to be restored (without penalty) to their status prior to the imposition of the punishment and to have their records expunged of any reference to the illegal punishment.
19. School officials can be held liable for compensatory damages if unlawful punishments result in substantial injury to students (e.g., unwarranted suspensions from school); however, only nominal damages, not to exceed one dollar, can be assessed against school officials for the abridgment of students' procedural rights (e.g., the denial of an adequate hearing).

MyEdLeadershipLab™

Go to Topic 6: *Student Discipline* on the MyEdLeadershipLab™ site (www.myedleadershiplab.com) for *Public School Law: Teachers' and Students' Rights*, Seventh Edition, where you can

- Find learning outcomes for *Student Discipline* along with the national standards that connect to these outcomes.
- Complete Assignments and Activities that can help you more deeply understand the chapter content.
- Apply and practice your understanding of the core skills identified in the chapter with the Building Leadership Skills unit.
- Prepare yourself for professional certification with a Practice for Certification quiz.

Terms and Conditions of Employment

MyEdLeadershipLab™

Visit the MyEdLeadershipLab™ site for *Public School Law: Teachers' and Students' Rights*, Seventh Edition, to enhance your understanding of chapter concepts. You'll have the opportunity to practice your skills through video- and case-based Assignments and Activities as well as Building Leadership Skills units, and to prepare for your certification exam with Practice for Certification quizzes.

Maintenance of a uniform system of public schools is one of the preeminent functions of the state, with the responsibility for the governance of education being vested with the legislature. The judiciary has clearly recognized the plenary power of the legislature in establishing, conducting, and regulating all public education functions. The legislature, through statutory law, establishes the boundaries within which educational systems operate; however, the actual administration of school systems is delegated to state boards of education, state departments of education, and local boards of education. These agencies enact rules and regulations pursuant to legislative policy for the operation of public schools.

While state statutes and regulations play a prominent role in defining school personnel's employment rights, they cannot be viewed independently of state and federal constitutional provisions, civil rights laws, and negotiated agreements between school boards and teachers' unions. These provisions may restrict or modify options available under the state school code. For example, the authority to transfer teachers may be vested in the school board, but the board cannot use this power to discipline a teacher for exercising protected constitutional rights. The board's discretion may be further limited if it has agreed in the master contract with the teachers' union to follow certain procedures prior to transferring an employee.

From Chapter 8 of *Public School Law: Teachers' and Students' Rights*, Seventh Edition. Martha M. McCarthy, Nelda H. Cambron-McCabe, Suzanne E. Eckes.

Terms and Conditions of Employment

Among the areas affected by state statutory and regulatory provisions are the terms and conditions of educators' employment. With the intense public pressure to improve students' academic performance to meet annual yearly progress (AYP) under the No Child Left Behind (NCLB) Act, most states have enacted education reform legislation demanding greater accountability from public schools.[1] Likewise, most states have adopted the Common Core Standards.[2] These efforts have had an impact not only on the curriculum and operation of schools but also on expectations for educators. NCLB demands that students be taught only by highly qualified educators in core subjects in each elementary and secondary school in all districts. At a minimum, highly qualified teachers hold a bachelor's degree, possess full state certification or licensure, and have demonstrated competence in their subject areas. Local school boards must ensure that these new demands are met, and courts have recognized the boards' expansive authority to fulfill these responsibilities. This chapter presents an overview of state requirements pertaining to licensure, employment, contracts, tenure, and related conditions of employment. Also, two topics of increasing interest to educators, using copyrighted materials and reporting child abuse, are addressed.

LICENSURE/CERTIFICATION

To qualify for a teaching position in public schools, prospective teachers must acquire a valid license or certificate. Licenses are issued according to each state's statutory provisions. States have not only the right but also the duty to establish minimum qualifications and to ensure that teachers meet these standards. Although the responsibility for licensing resides with legislatures, administration of the process has been delegated to state boards of education and departments of education. In addition to state licensure, many teachers seek National Board Certification, involving an intensive assessment of teaching knowledge and skills by the National Board for Professional Teaching Standards. States and local school districts often provide financial support for teachers seeking this designation and also may provide annual stipends for National Board Certified Teachers.[3]

Licenses are granted primarily on the basis of professional preparation. In most states, educational requirements include a college degree, with minimum credit hours or courses in various curricular areas. Other prerequisites to certification may include a minimum age, U.S. citizenship, signing of a loyalty oath, and passage of an academic examination. Additionally, an applicant for certification may be required to have "good moral character." The definition of what constitutes good character often is elusive, with a number of factors entering into the determination.[4] Courts generally will not rule on the

[1]20 U.S.C. § 6301 (2012).

[2]National Governor's Association, *Common Core Standards* (2012), http://www.corestandards.org/the-Standards.

[3]*See* National Board for Professional Teaching Standards, http://www.nbpts.org/resources/state_local_information, for state and local information regarding each state.

[4]*See* Wright v. Kan. State Bd. of Educ., 268 P.3d 1231 (Kan. Ct. App. 2012) (upholding the state board's denial of a disbarred attorney's application for a teaching license because of his prior conviction involving theft; even though his record was expunged, the court found that he violated the confidence that the public places on teachers); Landers v. Ark. Dep't of Educ., 2010 Ark. App. 312 (App. Ct. 2010) (upholding the denial of an applicant's teaching license because of her one-time felony theft conviction that had been expunged from her record).

wisdom of a certifying agency's assessment of character; they will intervene only if statutory or constitutional rights are abridged.[5]

Certification of teachers by examination was common prior to the expansion of teacher education programs in colleges and universities. With the emphasis on improving the quality of teachers and the strong movement toward standards-based licensure, most states now require some type of standardized test or performance-based assessment for teacher education programs, initial license, and license renewal.[6] If a state establishes a test or assessment process as an essential eligibility requirement, it can deny a license to individuals who do not pass.[7] Many states using standardized tests employ the National Teachers Examination. The United States Supreme Court has upheld its use even though the test has been shown to disproportionately disqualify minority applicants.[8]

Signing a loyalty oath may be a condition of obtaining a teaching certificate, but such oaths cannot be used to restrict association rights guaranteed under the United States Constitution. The Supreme Court has invalidated oaths that require teacher applicants to swear that they are not members of subversive organizations;[9] however, teachers can be required to sign an oath pledging faithful performance of duties and support for the Federal Constitution and an individual state's constitution.[10] According to the Supreme Court, these oaths must be narrowly limited to affirmation of support for the government.[11] Following the September 11, 2001, terrorist attacks, many states began enforcing the signing of existing loyalty oaths for public employment or enacted new laws. For example, Ohio's PATRIOT (Providing Appropriate Tools Required to Intercept and Obstruct Terrorism) Act allows the state to require applicants for some safety-sensitive positions to swear they are not terrorists and have no involvement with terrorist groups; refusal to sign the oath can result in exclusion from employment consideration.[12] A number of these new loyalty oaths may be challenged as too broad under the Supreme Court's earlier rulings.

[5]*Wright*, 268 P.3d at 1242 (holding that the State Board of Education will ultimately decide who is fit to teach in Kansas).

[6]Most states have set up professional standards boards to govern and regulate standards-based criteria and assessment for licenses. The principal purpose of these boards, whose membership is composed primarily of teachers, is to address issues of educator preparation, licensure, and renewal of license.

[7]*See* Ass'n of Mexican-Am. Educators v. California, 231 F.3d 572 (9th Cir. 2000); Dauer v. Dep't of Educ., 874 A.2d 159 (Pa. Commw. Ct. 2005); Feldman v. Bd. of Educ., 686 N.Y.S.2d 842 (App. Div. 1999); see also Nunez v. Simms, 341 F.3d 385 (5th Cir. 2003) (ruling that a teacher working under a temporary permit could not be continued after her third year of employment when she failed to pass the state examination); Mass. Fed'n of Teachers v. Bd. of Educ., 767 N.E.2d 549 (Mass. 2002) (finding the imposition of a math assessment test for recertification of teachers in certain schools to be within the state board's authority).

[8]United States v. South Carolina, 445 F. Supp. 1094 (D.S.C. 1977), *aff'd sub nom.* Nat'l Educ. Ass'n v. South Carolina, 434 U.S. 1026 (1978); *see also* Gulino v. N.Y. State Educ. Dep't, 460 F.3d 361 (2d Cir. 2006) (vacating and remanding for a determination of whether state's examination is job related). In challenges alleging discrimination, consent decrees between states and plaintiffs have contained agreements for the development of tests that reduce the discriminatory impact on minority candidates. *See, e.g.,* Allen v. Ala. State Bd. of Educ., 164 F.3d 1347 (11th Cir. 1999), *on remand*, 190 F.R.D. 602 (M.D. Ala. 2000).

[9]Keyishian v. Bd. of Regents, 385 U.S. 589 (1967).

[10]Ohlson v. Phillips, 397 U.S. 317 (1970), *aff'g* 304 F. Supp. 1152 (D. Col. 1969).

[11]Cole v. Richardson, 405 U.S. 676 (1972); Connell v. Higginbotham, 403 U.S. 207 (1971).

[12]OHIO REV. CODE § 2909.34 (2012).

As a condition of licensure, a teacher may be required to be a citizen of the United States. In 1979, the Supreme Court addressed whether such a New York statutory requirement violated the Equal Protection Clause of the Fourteenth Amendment.[13] Under the New York education laws, a teacher who is eligible for citizenship but refuses to apply for naturalization cannot be certified. Although the Supreme Court has placed restrictions on the states' ability to exclude aliens from governmental employment, it also has recognized that certain functions are "so bound up with the operation of the state as a governmental entity as to permit the exclusion from those functions of all persons who have not become part of the process of self-government."[14] Applying this principle, the Court held that teaching is an integral "governmental function"; thus, a state must show only a rational relationship between a citizenship requirement and a legitimate state interest. The Court concluded that New York's interest in furthering its educational goals justified the citizenship mandate for teachers. In another case, a Georgia federal district court, in issuing a permanent injunction against applying a citizenship requirement law, distinguished New York's citizenship licensure requirement from a Georgia statute banning aliens from all public employment. Because the law swept broadly across all government jobs rather than being narrowly drawn, the law failed to advance a compelling state interest.[15]

Some litigation has focused on legislative efforts to alter certification standards by imposing new or additional requirements as prerequisites to recertification. The Supreme Court of Texas held that teachers possessing life certificates could be required to pass an examination as a condition of continued employment.[16] Since the certificate was found to be a "license" rather than a "contract," the court held that new conditions for retention of the certificate could be imposed. The Supreme Court of Connecticut, even though recognizing teaching certificates as contracts, still upheld the state's authority to replace permanent certificates with five-year certificates renewable upon the completion of continuing education requirements.[17] Holding that this change was constitutionally acceptable, the court found only a minimal impairment of contractual rights, which could be justified by the state's significant interest in improving public education. Under statutory law, however, the Supreme Court of Rhode Island found that the State Board of Regents for Elementary and Secondary Education could not revoke valid five-year certificates for teachers' failure to meet new agency requirements.[18] Since state law provided that certificates were valid for a specified period of time and could be revoked only for cause, teachers could not be required to meet a state agency's new requirements until their certificates expired.

Licenses are issued for designated periods of time under various classifications such as emergency, temporary, provisional, professional, and permanent. Renewing or upgrading a license may require additional university coursework, other continuing education activities, or passage of an examination. Licenses also specify professional position (e.g., teacher, administrator, librarian), subject areas (e.g., history, English, math), and grade

[13]Ambach v. Norwick, 441 U.S. 68 (1979).

[14]*Id.* at 73–74.

[15]Chang v. Glynn Cnty. Sch. Dist., 457 F. Supp. 2d 1378 (S.D. Ga. 2006) (enjoining school district from discharging two resident alien teachers certified under Georgia law).

[16]State v. Project Principle, 724 S.W.2d 387 (Tex. 1987).

[17]Conn. Educ. Ass'n v. Tirozzi, 554 A.2d 1065 (Conn. 1989).

[18]Reback v. R.I. Bd. of Regents for Elementary & Secondary Educ., 560 A.2d 357 (R.I. 1989).

levels (e.g., elementary, high school). Where license subject areas have been established, a teacher must possess a valid license to teach a specific subject. A school district's failure to employ licensed teachers may result in the loss of state accreditation and financial support.

A certificate or license indicates only that a teacher has satisfied minimum state requirements; no absolute right exists to acquire a position. It does not entitle an individual to employment in a particular district or guarantee employment in the state, nor does it prevent a local school board from attaching additional prerequisites for employment. For example, an Iowa appellate court upheld a local school board's authority to require physical education teachers to complete training in cardiopulmonary resuscitation and water-safety instruction.[19] If a local board imposes additional standards, however, the requirements must be uniformly applied.

Teaching credentials must be in proper order to ensure full employment rights.[20] Under most state laws, teachers must file their certificates with the district of employment.[21] Failure to renew a certificate prior to expiration or to meet educational requirements necessary to maintain or acquire a higher grade certification can result in loss of employment. Without proper certification, a teaching contract is unenforceable.[22]

The state is empowered not only to certify teachers but also to suspend[23] or revoke certification. Although a local board may initiate charges against a teacher, only the state can alter the status of a teacher's certificate. Revocation is a harsh penalty, generally foreclosing future employment as a teacher. As such, it must be based on statutory cause with full procedural rights provided to the teacher.[24] The most frequently cited grounds for revoking certification are immorality, incompetency, contract violation, and neglect of duty. Examples of actions justifying revocation include misrepresenting experience and credentials in a job application and altering one's certificate (immorality),[25] theft of drugs and money (conduct unbecoming a teacher),[26] assault on a minor female (lack of good

[19]Pleasant Valley Educ. Ass'n v. Pleasant Valley Cmty. Sch. Dist., 449 N.W.2d 894 (Iowa Ct. App. 1989).

[20]*See* Keatley v. Mercer Cnty. Bd. of Educ., 490 S.E.2d 306 (W. Va. 1997) (ruling that an applicant who does not physically possess a certificate can be hired if all requirements will have been met for certification at the time of appointment).

[21]*See* Lucio v. Sch. Bd., 574 N.W.2d 737 (Minn. Ct. App. 1998) (ruling that the school district has a duty to determine the licensure status of teachers).

[22]*See* Condiff v. Hart Cnty. Sch. Dist., 770 F. Supp. 2d 876 (W.D. Ky. 2011) (holding that a teacher's contract was not renewed because her provisional certification had expired); Rettie v. Unified Sch. Dist., 167 P.3d 810 (Kan. Ct. App. 2007) (ruling that even though failure to maintain a valid certificate is grounds for termination, a teacher still has the right to a termination hearing under Kansas law); Giedra v. Mt. Adams Sch. Dist., 110 P.3d 232 (Wash. Ct. App. 2005) (ruling that teachers who failed to renew their certificates in a timely manner were entitled to a hearing prior to termination of their contracts; teachers had been denied an opportunity to explain the circumstances affecting their discharge).

[23]*See* Prof'l Standards Comm'n v. Denham, 556 S.E.2d 920 (Ga. Ct. App. 2001) (upholding suspension of license for six months for improperly coaching students for a standardized test).

[24]*See, e.g.*, Gee v. Prof'l Practices Comm'n, 491 S.E.2d 375 (Ga. 1997); Bowalick v. Commonwealth, 840 A.2d 519 (Pa. Commw. Ct. 2004).

[25]Nanko v. Dep't of Educ., 663 A.2d 312 (Pa. Commw. Ct. 1995); *see also* Patterson v. Superintendent of Pub. Instruction, 887 P.2d 411 (Wash. Ct. App. 1995) (supporting six-month suspension of certificate for falsifying and omitting information from application).

[26]Crumpler v. State Bd. of Educ., 594 N.E.2d 1071 (Ohio Ct. App. 1991).

moral character),[27] and harassment of other teachers, removal of confidential files, and inappropriate discussion of sex life (unprofessional conduct).[28]

When revocation or suspension of a certificate is being considered, assessment of a teacher's competency encompasses not only classroom performance but also actions outside the school setting that may impair the teacher's effectiveness.[29] A California appellate court upheld the State Commission on Teacher Credentialing's decision to suspend a teacher's license because she had three drunken driving convictions.[30] In a Texas case, an appellate court upheld the license revocation of a teacher who had exposed his penis and engaged in other indecent exposure incidents. The court found this conduct rendered him unworthy to instruct.[31] The Supreme Court of Kansas concluded that an act of burglary was sufficiently related to a teacher's fitness to teach to warrant suspension of the certificate for such a crime.[32] Courts will not overturn the judgment of state boards regarding an educator's fitness to teach unless evidence clearly establishes that the decision is unreasonable or unlawful.[33]

EMPLOYMENT BY LOCAL SCHOOL BOARDS

As noted, a certificate or license does not guarantee employment in a state; it attests only that educators have met minimum state requirements. The decision to employ a certified teacher or administrator is among the discretionary powers of local school boards.[34] While such powers are broad, school board actions may not be arbitrary, capricious,

[27]*In re* Appeal of Morrill, 765 A.2d 699 (N.H. 2001); *see also* Boguslawski v. Dep't of Educ., 837 A.2d 614 (Pa. Commw. Ct. 2003) (finding that a teacher's improper touching of fourth-grade male students supported revocation for immorality and intemperance).

[28]Bills v. Ariz. State Bd. of Educ., 819 P.2d 952 (Ariz. Ct. App. 1991); *see also* Knight v. Winn, 910 So. 2d 310 (Fla. Dist. Ct. App. 2005) (finding revocation of certificate appropriate for abusive comments to students and threats made in a letter of resignation); Prof'l Standards Comm'n v. Valentine, 603 S.E.2d 792 (Ga. Ct. App. 2004) (upholding a six-month suspension of teacher's license for verbal altercations on school grounds; teacher was being monitored by the commission because of an earlier DUI arrest).

[29]*See* Winters v. Ariz. Bd. of Educ., 83 P.3d 1114 (Ariz. Ct. App. 2004); *see also* Prof'l Standards Comm'n v. Peterson, 643 S.E.2d 899 (Ga. Ct. App. 2007) (determining that failure of two teachers to supervise underage drinking at a party in their home did not justify a short suspension of certificates; it did not affect their effectiveness in the classroom).

[30]Broney v. Cal. Comm'n on Teacher Credentialing, 184 Cal. App. 4th 462 (App. Ct. 2010).

[31]Gomez v. Tex. Educ. Agency, 354 S.W.3d 905 (Tex. Ct. App. 2011).

[32]Hainline v. Bond, 824 P.2d 959 (Kan. 1992).

[33]*See* Brehe v. Mo. Dep't of Elementary & Secondary Educ., 213 S.W.3d 720, 723 (Mo. Ct. App. 2007) (finding that pleading guilty to a second-degree child endangerment charge did not substantiate a "crime involving moral turpitude" under state law to justify suspension of license); Epstein v. Benson, 618 N.W.2d 224 (Wis. Ct. App. 2000) (concluding that carrying a concealed weapon is a crime but did not constitute immoral conduct to justify revocation of teaching certificate).

[34]*See* Carter Cnty. Bd. of Educ. v. Carter Cnty. Educ. Ass'n, 56 S.W.3d 1 (Tenn. Ct. App. 1996) (holding that selection of principals is a discretionary right of the school board; appointment is not subject to collective bargaining). In some instances, this discretionary power may be vested in local school-based councils. For example, under the Chicago School Reform Act, 105 ILL. COMP. STAT. § 5/34-2.2(c) (2012), the local school council is authorized to appoint a principal without school board approval. Under Kentucky's Education Reform Act, KY. REV. STAT. § 160.345(2)(h) (2012), superintendents must forward all principal applicants who meet statutory requirements to the site-based school council, not simply the ones the superintendent recommends and supports. *See* Young v. Hammond, 139 S.W.3d 895 (Ky. 2004). Massachusetts's Education Reform Act, MASS. GEN. LAWS ch. 71, § 59B (2012), lodges the responsibility for hiring and firing of teachers and other building personnel with school principals under the supervision of the superintendent.

or violate an individual's statutory or constitutional rights.[35] Furthermore, boards must comply with mandated statutory procedures as well as locally adopted procedures.[36] Employment decisions also must be neutral as to race, religion, national origin, and sex.[37] Unless protected individual rights are abridged, courts will not review the wisdom of a local school board's judgment in employment decisions made in good faith.

The responsibility for hiring teachers and administrators is generally vested in the school board as a collective body and is usually not delegated to the superintendent or board members individually.[38] In most states, binding employment agreements between a teacher or an administrator and the school board must be approved at legally scheduled board meetings. A number of state laws specify that the superintendent must make employment recommendations to the board; however, the board is not compelled to follow these recommendations unless mandated to do so by law.

School boards possess extensive authority in establishing job requirements and conditions of employment for school personnel. The following sections examine the school board's power to impose specific conditions on employment and to assign personnel.

Employment Requirements

State laws can impose various employment requirements for school personnel.[39] The state's establishment of minimum certification standards for educators does not preclude the local school board from requiring higher professional or academic standards so long as they are applied in a uniform and nondiscriminatory manner.[40] For example, school boards often establish continuing education requirements for teachers, and a board's right to dismiss teachers for failing to satisfy such requirements has been upheld by the Supreme Court.[41] The Court concluded that school officials merely had to establish that the requirement was rationally related to a legitimate state objective, which in this case was to provide competent, well-trained teachers.

School boards can adopt reasonable health and physical requirements for school personnel. Courts have recognized that such standards are necessary to safeguard the health and welfare of students and other employees. The First Circuit held that a school board could compel an administrator to submit to a psychiatric examination as a condition of continued employment because a reasonable basis existed for the board members to believe that the administrator might jeopardize the safety of students.[42] Similarly, the

[35]Intentionally left blank so that the remaining footnotes in the chapter can remain numbered as is.

[36]*See* Swanson v. Bd. of Educ., 600 S.E.2d 299 (W. Va. 2004).

[37]Under limited circumstances, sex may be a bona fide occupational qualification (e.g., supervision of the girls' locker room).

[38]*See* Watson v. N. Panola Sch. Dist., 188 F. App'x 291 (5th Cir. 2006). *But see* KY. REV. STAT. ANN. § 160.370 (2012) ("[The superintendent] shall be responsible for the hiring and dismissal of all personnel in the district").

[39]*See, e.g.*, Talley v. Brentwood Union Free Sch. Dist., 728 F. Supp. 2d 226 (E.D.N.Y. 2010) (finding that state law required a two-thirds majority vote by the school board in order to employ a teacher who is related by blood or marriage to a board member).

[40]*See, e.g.*, Dennery v. Bd. of Educ., 622 A.2d 858 (N.J. 1993); *see also* Bd. of Educ. v. Scott, 617 S.E.2d 478 (W. Va. 2005) (ruling that the school board could expand qualifications for an aide position to include licensure as a practical nurse).

[41]Harrah Indep. Sch. Dist. v. Martin, 440 U.S. 194 (1979) (upholding a policy requiring teachers to earn an additional five semester hours of college credit every three years while employed).

[42]Daury v. Smith, 842 F.2d 9 (1st Cir. 1988).

Sixth Circuit ruled that a school board could justifiably order a teacher to submit to mental and physical examinations when his aberrant behavior affected his job performance.[43]

Health and physical requirements imposed on school personnel, however, must not be applied in an arbitrary manner. The Second Circuit found a New York school board's actions arbitrary and unreasonable when it insisted that a female teacher on extended sick leave submit to an exam by the district's male physician rather than a female physician (to be selected by the board).[44] In another Second Circuit case, the court held that it was reasonable to request that a teacher undergo a psychiatric examination prior to returning to work after an extended sick leave, but the demand to release the teacher's medical records to the examining physician as well as the school board was arbitrary.[45] School officials were not competent to assess the records, thus the request served no legitimate purpose. School board standards for physical fitness also must be rationally related to the ability to perform teaching duties. Additionally, regulations must not contravene various state and federal laws designed to protect the rights of persons with disabilities.[46]

Under state laws, most school boards are required to conduct criminal records checks of all employees prior to employment. The screening process may require individuals to consent to fingerprinting. Concern for students' safety also has led some school districts to require teacher applicants to submit to drug testing. The Sixth Circuit upheld such testing, noting that teachers occupy safety-sensitive positions in a highly regulated environment with diminished privacy expectations.[47]

School boards may require school personnel to live within the school district as a condition of employment.[48] Typically, residency requirements have been imposed in urban communities and encompass all city employees, including educators. Proponents contend that the policy builds stronger community relationships and stabilizes the city tax base. Such requirements, however, have been challenged as impairing equal protection rights under the United States Constitution by interfering with interstate and intrastate travel on equal terms. The Supreme Court has upheld a municipal regulation requiring all employees hired after a specified date in Philadelphia to be residents of the city.[49] Those already employed were not required to alter their residence. A fire department employee who was terminated when he moved to New Jersey challenged the requirement as unconstitutionally interfering with interstate travel. In upholding the regulation, the Court distinguished a requirement of residency of a given duration prior to employment (which violates the right to interstate travel) from a continuing residency requirement applied after employment. The Court concluded that a continuing residency requirement,

[43]*See* Sullivan v. River Valley Sch. Dist., 197 F.3d 804 (6th Cir. 1999); *see also* Moore v. Bd. of Educ., 134 F.3d 781 (6th Cir. 1998) (upholding a finding of insubordination for refusing to submit to mental and physical examinations); Gardner v. Niskayuna Cent. Sch. Dist., 839 N.Y.S.2d 317 (App. Div. 2007) (finding that a school board is charged with determining that teachers are fit to teach; thereby, teachers may be required to submit to physical or mental exams).

[44]Gargiul v. Tompkins, 704 F.2d 661 (2d Cir. 1983), *vacated and remanded*, 465 U.S. 1016 (1984).

[45]O'Connor v. Pierson, 426 F.3d 187 (2d Cir. 2005).

[46]Intentionally left blank so that the remaining footnotes in the chapter can remain numbered as is.

[47]Knox Cnty. Educ. Ass'n v. Knox Cnty. Bd. of Educ., 158 F.3d 361 (6th Cir. 1998).

[48]*See, e.g.*, Matter of O'Connor v. Bd. of Educ., 852 N.Y.S.2d 537 (App. Div. 2008) (upholding refusal to reinstate teachers who had been dismissed for failing to comply with district's residency requirement).

[49]McCarthy v. Phila. Civil Serv. Comm'n, 424 U.S. 645 (1976).

if "appropriately defined and uniformly applied," does not violate an individual's constitutional rights.[50] Lower courts have applied similar reasoning in upholding residency requirements for public educators.[51] Although residency requirements after employment do not violate the Constitution, they may be impermissible under state law.[52]

Unlike residency requirements, school board policies requiring employees to send their children to public schools have been declared unconstitutional. Parents have a constitutionally protected right to direct the upbringing of their children that cannot be restricted without a compelling state interest. The Eleventh Circuit Appellate Court held that a school board policy requiring employees to enroll their children in public schools could not be justified to promote an integrated public school system and good relationships among teachers when weighed against the right of parents to direct the education of their children.[53]

Assignment of Personnel and Duties

The authority to assign teachers and administrators to schools within a district resides with the board of education.[54] As with employment in general, these decisions must not be arbitrary or made in bad faith or in retaliation for the exercise of protected rights. Within the limits of certification, a teacher can be assigned to teach in any school at any grade level.[55] Assignments designated in the teacher's contract, however, cannot be changed during a contractual period without the teacher's consent.[56] That is, a board cannot reassign a teacher to a first-grade class if the contract specifies a fifth-grade assignment. If the contract designates only a teaching assignment within the district, the assignment still must be in the teacher's area of certification. Also, objective, nondiscriminatory standards must be used in any employment or assignment decision. Assignments to achieve racial balance may be permitted in school districts under court order, because they have not eliminated the effects of school segregation. Any racial classification, however, must be temporary and necessary to eradicate the effects of prior discrimination.[57]

[50]*Id.* at 647. In several later cases, the Supreme Court reiterated that policies requiring residence prior to employment for conferring certain benefits or employment preference violate the Equal Protection Clause and the constitutional right to travel. *See, e.g.*, Attorney Gen. of N.Y. v. Soto-Lopez, 476 U.S. 898 (1986); Hooper v. Bernalillo Cnty. Assessor, 472 U.S. 612 (1985); Zobel v. Williams, 457 U.S. 55 (1982).

[51]*See, e.g.*, Wardwell v. Bd. of Educ., 529 F.2d 625 (6th Cir. 1976) (finding a rational basis for district's residency program); Providence Teachers' Union Local 958 v. City Council, 888 A.2d 948 (R.I. 2005) (determining district's residency program was lawful).

[52]*See, e.g.*, IND. CODE ANN. § 20-28-10-13 (2012); MASS. GEN. LAWS ch. 71 § 38 (2012).

[53]*See* Barrow v. Greenville Indep. Sch. Dist., 332 F.3d 844 (5th Cir. 2003); Barrett v. Steubenville City Schs, 388 F.3d 967 (6th Cir. 2004); Peterson v. Minidoka Cnty. Sch. Dist. No. 331, 118 F.3d 1351 (9th Cir. 1997); Curlee v. Fyfe, 902 F.2d 401 (5th Cir. 1990).

[54]*See, e.g.*, Lazuk v. Denver Sch. Dist. No. 1, 22 P.3d 548 (Colo. Ct. App. 2000) (ruling that state law permitted a school board to delegate the power to transfer a teacher; state statute limited the transfer to positions in which the teacher is qualified to teach). *But see* McCalister v. Sch. Bd. of Bay Cnty., 971 So. 2d 1020 (Fla. Dist. Ct. App. 2008) (finding school board did not have authority under state law to reject a superintendent's decision to transfer a principal from one position to another).

[55]*See, e.g.*, Gordon v. Nicoletti, 84 F. Supp. 2d 304 (D. Conn. 2000); Wells v. Del Norte Sch. Dist. C-7, 753 P.2d 770 (Colo. Ct. App. 1987); *see also* Hinckley v. Sch. Bd. of Indep. Sch. Dist. No. 2167, 678 N.W.2d 485 (Minn. Ct. App. 2004) (determining that school board is not required to change job duties to realign positions when individual does not hold valid license).

[56]The collective bargaining agreement also may limit a school board's discretion in transferring teachers. *See, e.g.*, Leary v. Daeschner, 228 F.3d 729 (6th Cir. 2000).

[57]*See* Wygant v. Jackson Bd. of Educ., 476 U.S. 267 (1986).

School boards retain the authority to assign or transfer teachers, but such decisions often are challenged as demotions requiring procedural due process. Depending on statutory law, factors considered in determining whether a reassignment is a demotion may include reduction in salary, responsibility, and stature of position.[58] The reassignment of an Ohio classroom teacher as a permanent substitute or floating teacher, however, was found to be a demotion in violation of the state tenure law.[59] The court recognized the pervasive authority of the superintendent and board to make teaching assignments but noted that other statutory provisions, such as the state tenure law, may limit this power. This reduction in status without notice and a hearing was found to deprive the teacher of due process guarantees. Likewise, administrative reassignments frequently are challenged as demotions because of reductions in salary, responsibility, and status of the position. Again, as in the assignment of teachers, statutory law defines an individual employee's rights. The South Carolina appellate court concluded that the reassignment of an assistant superintendent to a principal position was within the school board's discretion when it did not involve a reduction in salary or violate the district's regulations.[60] Similarly, the Seventh Circuit found that the reassignment of a principal to a central office position did not involve an economic loss requiring an opportunity for a hearing.[61] A reassignment from an administrative to a teaching position because of financial constraints or good faith reorganization is not a demotion requiring due process unless procedural protections are specified in state law.

A transfer may violate federal rights even if it is not considered a demotion under state law. The Eleventh Circuit noted that a transfer might establish an adverse employment action if it involves a reduction in pay, prestige, or responsibility. Under Georgia law, an individual must show a loss of all three to suffer a demotion. In remanding a case for trial under federal law, the appellate court noted that a female principal had presented sufficient evidence for a jury to conclude that she had suffered an adverse employment action when transferred to another administrative position.[62]

Statutory procedures and agency regulations established for transferring or demoting employees must be strictly followed. For example, under a West Virginia State Board of Education policy, school boards cannot initiate a disciplinary transfer unless there has been a prior evaluation informing the individual that specific conduct can result in a transfer.[63]

[58] *See* Manila Sch. Dist. No. 15 v. White, 992 S.W.2d 125 (Ark. 1999) (ruling that the elimination of a teacher's coaching duties and assigning him as a director/teacher of an alternative school was nonrenewal of contract, not reassignment); Hamilton v. Telfair Cnty. Sch. Dist., 455 S.E.2d 23 (Ga. 1995) (holding that one must show an adverse effect on salary, responsibility, and prestige); Ranta v. Eaton Rapids Sch. Bd., 721 N.W.2d 806 (Mich. Ct. App. 2006) (finding that board's cap on contribution to health insurance premiums did not constitute a demotion as defined by the Teacher Tenure Act; with salary increase, teachers did not receive less compensation).

[59] Mroczek v. Bd. of Educ., 400 N.E.2d 1362 (Ct. C.P. Cuyahoga Cnty. 1979). School boards can exercise significant discretion in the transfer of administrators so long as their decisions are not arbitrary or capricious or in violation of protected constitutional rights. *See* Finch v. Fort Bend Indep. Sch. Dist., 333 F.3d 555 (5th Cir. 2003).

[60] Barr v. Bd. of Trs., 462 S.E.2d 316 (S.C. Ct. App. 1995). *But see* Henry-Davenport v. Sch. Dist., No. 0:08-3258, 2011 U.S. Dist. LEXIS 59940 (D.S.C. June 2, 2011) (holding that a deputy superintendent of human resources who was moved to the position of director of food services had no right to retain his previous position and salary).

[61] Bordelon v. Chi. Sch. Reform Bd. of Trs., 233 F.3d 524 (7th Cir. 2000).

[62] Hinson v. Clinch Cnty., Ga. Bd. of Educ., 231 F.3d 821 (11th Cir. 2000); *see also* Kodl v. Bd. of Educ., 490 F.3d 558 (7th Cir. 2007) (finding that an older middle school teacher's transfer to an elementary school did not violate any federal rights).

[63] Hosaflook v. Nestor, 346 S.E.2d 798 (W. Va. 1986).

The assignment of noninstructional duties often is defined in a teacher's contract or the master contract negotiated between the school board and the teachers' union. In the absence of such specification, it is generally held that school officials can make reasonable and appropriate assignments. Courts usually restrict assignments to activities that are an integral part of the school program and, in some situations, to duties related to the employee's teaching responsibilities.[64] The reasonableness of an assignment is assessed in terms of the time required, the teacher's interests and skills, and the potential benefits for students.

CONTRACTS

The employment contract defines the rights and responsibilities of the teacher and the school board in the employment relationship. The general principles of contract law apply to this contractual relationship. Like all other legal contracts, it must contain the basic elements of (1) offer and acceptance, (2) competent parties, (3) consideration, (4) legal subject matter, and (5) proper form.[65] Beyond these basic elements, it also must meet the requirements specified in state law and administrative regulations.

The authority to contract with teachers is an exclusive right of the board. The school board's offer of a position to a teacher, including (1) designated salary, (2) specified period of time, and (3) identified duties and responsibilities, creates a binding contract when accepted by the teacher. In most states, only the board can make an offer, and this action must be approved by a majority of the board members in a properly called meeting. In a Washington case, the coordinator of special services extended a teacher an offer of employment at the beginning of the school year, pending a check of references from past employers. The recommendations were negative, and the teacher was not recommended to the board even though she had been teaching for several weeks. The state appellate court held that no enforceable contract existed; under state law, hiring authority resides with the board.[66]

School boards also can enforce the performance of a valid teacher's contract. Most state statutes specify a deadline for resignation of teaching positions for the next school year (e.g., July 1). Such provisions reduce disruptions in the opening of the school year. Resignation can occur after the statutory deadline if the school board agrees. If the board declines to accept a resignation, however, the contract is enforceable, and the teacher's license can be suspended for the year.[67]

Contracts can be invalidated because of lack of competent parties. To form a valid, binding contract, both parties must have the legal capacity to enter into an agreement.

[64]*See* Wolf v. Cuyahoga Falls City Sch. Dist., 556 N.E.2d 511 (Ohio 1990) (holding that supervision of the student newspaper was related to teaching journalism, but supplemental contract was required for the newspaper sponsor because other teachers who performed similar class-related duties were paid).

[65]For a discussion of contract elements, see KERN ALEXANDER & M. DAVID ALEXANDER, AMERICAN PUBLIC SCHOOL LAW, 8th ed. (Belmont, CA: West/Thomson Learning, 2012).

[66]McCormick v. Lake Wash. Sch. Dist., 992 P.2d 511 (Wash. Ct. App. 2000). *But see* Sch. Comm. of Newton v. Newton Sch. Custodians Ass'n, 784 N.E.2d 598 (Mass. 2003) (giving principals authority to hire certain school employees, such as a school cafeteria manager); Trahan v. Lafayette Parish Sch. Bd., 978 So. 2d 1105 (La. Ct. App. 2008) (upholding employment contract executed by superintendent on behalf of board). *But see* KY. REV. STAT. ANN. § 160.370 (2012) (stating that superintendent has the power regarding employment contract decisions).

[67]*See, e.g.*, Bd. of Educ. v. State Teachers Certification Bd., 842 N.E.2d 1230 (Ill. App. Ct. 2006); Bolyard v. Bd. of Educ., 589 S.E.2d 523 (W. Va. 2003).

The school board has been recognized as a legally competent party with the capacity to contract. A teacher who lacks certification or is under the statutorily required age for certification is not considered a competent party for contractual purposes. Consequently, a contract made with such an individual is not enforceable.[68]

Consideration is another essential element of a valid contract. Consideration is something of value that one party pays in return for the other party's performance. Teachers' monetary compensation is established in the salary schedule adopted by the school board or negotiated between the school board and teachers' association.[69] The contract also must involve a legal subject matter and follow the proper form required by law. Most states prescribe that a teacher's contract must be in writing to be enforceable,[70] but an implied contract based on an oral agreement may be permitted in certain contexts.[71]

In addition to employment rights derived from the teaching contract, other rights accrue from collective bargaining agreements in effect at the time of employment. Statutory provisions and school board rules and regulations also may be considered part of the terms and conditions of the contract.[72] If not included directly, the provisions existing at the time of the contract may be implied. Moreover, the contract cannot be used as a means of waiving teachers' statutory or constitutional rights.[73]

Term and Tenure Contracts

Two basic types of employment contracts are issued to teachers: term contracts and tenure contracts. Term contracts are valid for a fixed period of time (e.g., one or two years). At the end of the contract period, renewal is at the discretion of the school board; nonrenewal requires no explanation unless mandated by statute. Generally, a school board is required only to provide notice prior to the expiration of the contract that employment will not be renewed. Tenure contracts, created through state legislative action, ensure teachers that employment will be terminated only for adequate cause and that procedural due process will be provided.[74] After the award of tenure or during a term contract,

[68]*See, e.g.*, Nunez v. Simms, 341 F.3d 385 (5th Cir. 2003); Springer v. Bullitt Cnty. Bd. of Educ., 196 S.W.3d 528 (Ky. Ct. App. 2006).

[69]*See* Sherwood Nat'l Educ. Ass'n v. Sherwood-Cass R-VIII Sch. Dist., 168 S.W.3d 456 (Mo. Ct. App. 2005) (finding that an agreement to pay certain teachers "commitment fees," which were not part of the salary schedule, violated state law); Davis v. Greenwood Sch. Dist., 620 S.E.2d 65 (S.C. 2005) (holding that the reduction of a 10 percent annual incentive payment to teachers for acquiring national board certification to a $3,000 flat rate per year did not violate teachers' contracts and was within the board's discretion to manage the district's finances).

[70]*See* Jones v. Houston Indep. Sch. Dist., 805 F. Supp. 476 (S.D. Tex. 1991), *aff'd*, 979 F.2d 1004 (5th Cir. 1992); Bradley v. W. Sioux Cmty. Sch. Bd. of Educ., 510 N.W.2d 881 (Iowa 1994); Bd. of Educ. v. Jones, 823 S.W.2d 457 (Ky. 1992).

[71]Sexton v. KIPP Reach Acad. Charter Sch., 260 P.3d 435 (Okla. Civ. App. 2011) (finding an implied contract may have been created when teacher was given a faculty-only cell phone, provided a letter of intent, and enrolled in a teacher's conference).

[72]*See* Stone v. Mayflower Sch. Dist., 894 S.W.2d 881 (Ark. 1995); Mifflinburg Area Educ. Ass'n v. Mifflinburg Area Sch. Dist., 724 A.2d 339 (Pa. 1999).

[73]*See* Denuis v. Dunlap, 209 F.3d 944 (7th Cir. 2000) (holding that the teacher was not required to relinquish constitutional privacy rights regarding medical or financial records for an employment background check); Parker v. Indep. Sch. Dist. No. I-003 Okmulgee Cnty., Okla., 82 F.3d 952 (10th Cir. 1996) (ruling that a school board could not evade procedural protections of the Oklahoma Teacher Due Process Act by having a teacher sign a contract permitting summary removal as a teacher if her supplemental coaching position was terminated).

[74]*See* Scobey Sch. Dist. v. Radakovich, 135 P.3d 778 (Mont. 2006); Weston v. Indep. Sch. Dist. No. 35, 170 P.3d 539 (Okla. 2007).

school boards cannot unilaterally abrogate teachers' contracts. At a minimum, the teacher must be provided with notice of the dismissal charges and a hearing.[75]

Since tenure contracts involve statutory rights, specific procedures and protections vary among the states. Consequently, judicial interpretations in one state provide little guidance in understanding another state's law. Most tenure statutes specify requirements and procedures for obtaining tenure and identify causes and procedures for dismissing a tenured teacher. In interpreting tenure laws, courts have attempted to protect teachers' rights while simultaneously preserving school officials' flexibility in personnel management.

Prior to a school board's awarding a tenure contract to a teacher, most states require a probationary period of approximately three years to assess a teacher's ability and competence. During this probationary period, teachers receive term contracts, and there is no guarantee of employment beyond each contract. Tenure statutes generally require regular and continuous service to complete the probationary period. For example, the Supreme Court of Virginia held that the tenure law providing for a "probationary term of service of three years" required three consecutive years of employment immediately prior to the award of tenure. Interpreting this mandate, the court concluded that lapses in an appointment in which a teacher worked over a period of seven years did not qualify her for tenure.[76] Similarly, the Alaska Supreme Court found part-time employment totaling two years did not meet state statutory requirement of employment "continuously for two full school years."[77] Some state laws link teacher tenure to student performance. For example, in Indiana, a tenured or "professional" teacher may be returned to probationary status if the teacher is rated as ineffective based on student test scores.[78]

The authority to grant a tenure contract is a discretionary power of the local school board that cannot be delegated. Although the school board confers tenure, it cannot alter the tenure terms established by the legislature; the legislature determines the basis for tenure, eligibility requirements, and the procedures for acquiring tenure status.[79] Thus, if a statute requires a probationary period, this term of service must be completed prior to the school board awarding tenure. When teachers meet the statutory requirements, the school board cannot refuse to carry out its obligation to award tenure, nor can the board require new teachers to waive tenure rights as a precondition to employment. Moreover, a board may be compelled to award tenure if a teacher completes the statutory requirements and the school board does not take action to grant or deny tenure.[80]

[75]Tenure laws provide teachers employment security; they protect educators from political reprisal and prevent dismissals without cause. *See* Cimochowshi v. Hartford Pub. Schs., 802 A.2d 800 (Conn. 2002); Palmer v. La. State Bd. of Elementary & Secondary Educ., 842 So. 2d 363 (La. 2003); Wirt v. Parker Sch. Dist., 689 N.W.2d 901 (S.D. 2004); Hicks v. Gayville-Volin Sch. Dist., 668 N.W.2d 69 (S.D. 2003).

[76]Corns v. Russell Cnty. Va. Sch. Bd., 52 F.3d 56 (4th Cir. 1995), *certifying question to* 454 S.E.2d 728, 732 (Va. 1995).

[77]Fairbanks N. Star Borough Sch. Dist. v. NEA-Alaska, 817 P.2d 923, 925 (Alaska 1991).

[78]IND. CODE, § 20-28-6-7.5(d) (2012).

[79]*See* State *ex rel.* Cohn v. Shaker Heights City Sch. Dist., 678 N.E.2d 1385 (Ohio 1997); Scheer v. Indep. Sch. Dist. No. I-26, 948 P.2d 275 (Okla. 1997).

[80]*See, e.g.*, Speichler v. Bd. of Coop. Educ. Servs., 681 N.E.2d 366 (N.Y. 1997). *But see* Bowden v. Memphis Bd. of Educ., 29 S.W.3d 462 (Tenn. 2000) (ruling that a teacher did not acquire tenure upon reappointment after the probationary period when the superintendent failed to provide statutory notice to the school board that the teacher was eligible for tenure).

Unless specified in statute, however, tenure is not transferable from one school district to another.[81] This ensures that school officials are provided an opportunity to evaluate teachers before granting tenure.

A tenure contract provides a certain amount of job security, but it does not guarantee permanent employment, nor does it convey the right to teach in a particular school, grade, or subject area. Teachers may be reassigned to positions for which they are certified as well as dismissed for the causes specified in the tenure law.[82] In establishing tenure, a legislature may create a contractual relationship that cannot be altered without violating constitutional guarantees. If a tenure law is asserted to be contractual, the language of the act is critical in the judiciary's interpretation of legislative intent.

A number of states limit the award of tenure to teaching positions, thereby excluding administrative, supervisory, and staff positions. Where tenure is available for administrative positions, probationary service and other specified statutory terms must be met. Although tenure as a teacher usually does not imply tenure as an administrator, most courts have concluded that continued service as a certified professional employee, albeit as an administrator, does not alter tenure rights acquired as a teacher.[83] For example, under Florida law, a teacher who is promoted to an administrative position has the right to return to a teaching position if the administrator contract is terminated.[84] The Supreme Court of Wyoming noted: "It is desirable—and even important—to have people with extensive classroom teaching experience in administrative positions. It would be difficult to fill administrative positions with experienced teachers if the teachers would have to give up tenure upon accepting administrative roles."[85]

Supplemental Contracts

School boards can enter into supplement contracts with teachers for duties beyond the regular teaching assignments. For example, an appellate court in New York held that teachers who were under contract to attend three evening meetings per year could proceed with arbitration when the school district tried to impose a fourth meeting on them.[86] As with teaching contracts, authority to employ resides with the school board.[87] Generally, these are limited contracts specifying the additional duties, compensation, and time period and can be terminated at their completion without violating a teacher's due process rights.[88] Extra duties often relate to coaching, department chair duties, supervision of student activities or clubs, and extended school year assignments.

[81]*See, e.g.*, Washington v. Indep. Sch. Dist., 590 N.W.2d 655 (Minn. Ct. App. 1999); *see also* Nelson v. Bd. of Educ., 689 A.2d 1342 (N.J. 1997) (holding that tenure is earned in a specific position listed in state law only if the individual has served in that capacity; tenure as a supervisor did not extend to tenure as a principal or other administrative position).

[82]Intentionally left blank so that the remaining footnotes in the chapter can remain numbered as is.

[83]*See, e.g.*, Downing v. City of Lowell, 741 N.E.2d 469 (Mass. App. Ct. 2001); E. Canton Educ. Ass'n v. McIntosh, 709 N.W.2d 468 (Ohio 1999).

[84]School Bd. of Levy Cnty. v. Terrell, 967 So. 2d 394 (Fla. Dist. Ct. App. 2007).

[85]Spurlock v. Bd. of Trs., 699 P.2d 270, 272 (Wyo. 1985).

[86]*In re* Bd. of Educ. of Schenactady City Sch. Dist., 876 N.Y.S.2d 562 (App. Div. 2009).

[87]*See, e.g.*, Gilmore v. Bonner Cnty. Sch. Dist. No. 82, 971 P.2d 323 (Idaho 1999); *see also* Hanlon v. Logan Cnty. Bd. of Educ., 496 S.E.2d 447 (W. Va. 1997) (holding that a school board can enter into extracurricular assignment contracts with individuals who are not employed in the school system).

[88]*See, e.g.*, Norlin v. Bd. of Trs., 107 P.3d 445 (Kan. Ct. App. 2004).

Although supplemental service contracts are usually considered outside the scope of tenure protections, coaches, in particular, have asserted that supplemental contracts are an integral part of the teaching position and thereby must be afforded the procedural and substantive protections of state tenure laws. Several courts have noted that tenure rights apply only to employment in certified areas and that the lack of certification requirements for coaches in a state negates tenure claims for such positions.[89] The Supreme Court of Iowa held that even a requirement that coaches must be certified did not confer teachers' tenure rights on coaching positions.[90] In this case, the coaching assignment was found to be clearly an extra duty, requiring a separate contract and compensation based on an extra-duty pay scale.

Other courts also have distinguished coaching and various extra duties from teaching responsibilities based on the extracurricular nature of the assignment and supplemental compensation.[91] In denying the claim of a ten-year veteran baseball coach, the Ninth Circuit held that the coach did not have a protected interest in his coaching position since California law specified that extra-duty assignments could be terminated by the school board at any time.[92] When both classroom teaching and extra-duty assignments are covered in the same contract, however, protected property interests may be created. Accordingly, the teacher would be entitled to due process prior to the termination of the extra-duty assignment.[93]

Because coaching assignments generally require execution of a supplemental contract, a teacher can usually resign a coaching position and maintain the primary teaching position.[94] School boards having difficulty in filling coaching positions, however, may tender an offer to teach on the condition that an individual assume certain coaching responsibilities. If a single teaching and coaching contract is found to be indivisible, a teacher cannot unilaterally resign the coaching duties without relinquishing the teaching position.[95] Individual state laws must be consulted to determine the status of such

[89]*See, e.g.*, Coles v. Glenburn Pub. Sch. Dist. 26, 436 N.W.2d 262 (N.D. 1989); Lawrence Cnty. Educ. Ass'n v. Lawrence Cnty. Bd. of Educ., 244 S.W.3d 302 (Tenn. 2007).

[90]Slockett v. Iowa Valley Cmty. Sch. Dist., 359 N.W.2d 446 (Iowa 1984). *But see* Reid v. Huron Bd. of Educ., 449 N.W.2d 240 (S.D. 1989) (ruling that the position of head coach came under the continuing contract law since state administrative rules defined certification requirements for the job).

[91]*See, e.g.*, Ladner v. Hancock Cnty. Sch. Dist., 614 F. Supp. 2d 768 (S.D. Miss. 2008) (considering coach's contract separate from teaching contract, which allowed teaching contract to continue after coaching contract was not renewed). *But see* Smith v. Petal Sch. Dist., 956 So. 2d 273 (Miss. Ct. App. 2006) (upholding nonrenewal of teacher's contract that was for a single teacher/coach position because teacher, who was also a coach, did not effectively perform his coaching duties).

[92]Lagos v. Modesto City Schs. Dist., 843 F.2d 347 (9th Cir. 1988). *But see* Kingsford v. Salt Lake City Sch. Dist., 247 F.3d 1123 (10th Cir. 2001) (remanding to determine if school officials created an "implied-in-fact" promise that coaches would only be terminated for cause; case prompted state legislature to amend law to specify that extra-duty assignments are limited contracts).

[93]*See, e.g.*, Farner v. Idaho Falls Sch. Dist. No. 91, 17 P.3d 281 (Idaho 2000).

[94]*See, e.g.*, Lewis v. Bd. of Educ., 537 N.E.2d 435 (Ill. App. Ct. 1989), Hachiya v. Bd. of Educ., 750 P.2d 383 (Kan. 1988); *see also* Parker v. Indep. Sch. Dist. No. I-003, 82 F.3d 952 (10th Cir. 1996) (holding that the school board could not circumvent the teacher's entitlement to procedural due process with the termination of her teaching position by having the teacher sign a contract that specified she would not be reemployed as a teacher if her coaching contract was not renewed; court emphasized that the school board could not amend or repeal statutory rights).

[95]*See, e.g.*, Smith v. Petal Sch. Dist., 956 So. 2d 273 (Miss. Ct. App. 2006).

contracts. Where teaching and coaching positions are combined, a qualified teaching applicant who cannot assume the coaching duties may be rejected. This practice, however, may be vulnerable to legal challenge if certain classes of applicants, such as women, are excluded from consideration.[96]

Domestic Partner Benefits

Increasingly, legal challenges are being brought to secure health, retirement, and other benefits for domestic partners of gay, lesbian, bisexual, and transgendered employees. Same-sex marriage has not yet been recognized by the federal government, but rights may exist under state constitutional and statutory provisions or institutional policies. Vermont, Washington, Iowa, Massachusetts, New Hampshire, New York, Maryland, Connecticut, and the District of Columbia allow same-sex marriage. States that allow civil unions or domestic partnerships include Oregon, California, Nevada, Colorado, Illinois, Wisconsin, Hawaii, New Jersey, Rhode Island, Maine, and Delaware.[97] In reviewing claims for benefits, some courts have held that the denial of benefits discriminates on the basis of marital status or that unmarried partners have been treated differently by benefits policies, and denial is unrelated to any legitimate governmental interest.[98]

Yet other courts have firmly upheld the denial of benefits, finding no discrimination.[99] With the federal Defense of Marriage Act (DOMA) and subsequent adoption of mini-DOMAs in forty-two states, employees will continue to face significant challenges in achieving equality of benefits for their domestic partners.[100] For example, in 2007 the Michigan Court of Appeals interpreted the state's constitutional marriage amendment as precluding employers from providing same-sex domestic partner benefits. The court ruled that the law, which provides that "the union of one man and one woman in marriage shall be the only agreement recognized as a marriage or similar union for any purpose," blocks the recognition of domestic partnership agreements because it is a status *similar* to marriage.[101] Contrarily, the First and Second Circuits struck down portions of DOMA.[102]

[96] *See, e.g.*, Civil Rights Div. v. Amphitheater Unified Sch. Dist. No. 10, 706 P.2d 745 (Ariz. Ct. App. 1985).

[97] Lindsay Powers & Jerry Mosemak, *Where States Stand on Same-Sex Marriage*, USA TODAY (May 1, 2012), http://www.usatoday.com/news/nation/story/2012-03-01/maryland-gay-marriage-law/53319758/1.

[98] *See, e.g.*, Snetsinger v. Mont. Univ. Sys., 104 P.3d 445 (Mont. 2004); Tanner v. Or. Health Scis. Univ., 971 P.2d 435 (Or. Ct. App. 1998); Baker v. State, 744 A.2d 864 (Vt. 1999); *see also* Devlin v. City of Phila., 862 A.2d 1234 (Pa. 2004) (holding that city did not exceed its authority in extending benefits to life partners of its employees); Pritchard v. Madison Metro. Sch. Dist., 625 N.W.2d 613 (Wis. Ct. App. 2001) (denying plaintiffs' challenge that the school system was in violation of state law by providing insurance coverage for unmarried partners of a school district employee).

[99] *See* Rutgers Council of AAUP Chapters v. Rutgers State Univ., 689 A.2d 828 (N.J. Super. Ct. App. Div. 1997); Funderburke v. Uniondale Union Free Sch. Dist. No. 15, 660 N.Y.S.2d 659 (Sup. Ct. 1997); *see also* Donna Euben, *Domestic Partnership Benefits on Campus: A Litigation Update* (Washington, D.C.: American Association of University Professors, 2002).

[100] *See* Defense of Marriage Act, 1 U.S.C. § 7 (2012); 28 U.S.C. § 1738C (2012). Congress passed the DOMA in reaction to growing concern about states recognizing same-sex marriages. Under the federal law, marriage is defined as a union between a man and a woman. Furthermore, the Act states that individual states are not required to recognize same-sex marriages sanctioned by other states. However, in 2011, the Obama Administration stated it would no longer defend the constitutionality of § 3 (the definition of marriage) of the DOMA in court. *See* Dep't of Justice, *Statement of the Attorney General on Litigation Involving the Defense of Marriage Act* (Feb. 23, 2011), http://www.justice.gov/opa/pr/2011/February/11-ag-222.html.

[101] Nat'l Pride at Work v. Gov. of Mich., 732 N.W.2d 139, 143 (Mich. Ct. App. 2007), *aff'd*, 748 N.W.2d 524 (Mich. 2008).

[102] *See* Massachusetts v. U.S. Dep't of Health & Human Servs., 682 F.3d 1 (1st Cir. 2012); Windsor v. United States, no. 12-2334-cv(L), 2012 U.S. App. LEXIS 21785 (2d Cir. Sept. 27, 2012). The U.S. Supreme Court will address this issue in 2013.

Leaves of Absence

Contracts may specify various types of leaves of absence. Within the parameters of state law, school boards have discretion in establishing requirements for these leaves. A school board may place restrictions on when teachers can take personal leave, for example, such as mandating no leaves on the day before or after a holiday, or no more than two consecutive days of personal leave.[103] This topic often is the subject of collective bargaining, with leave provisions specified in bargained agreements. School boards, however, cannot negotiate leave policies that impair rights guaranteed by the United States Constitution and various federal and state anti-discrimination laws.[104] Likewise, where state law confers specific rights, local boards do not have the discretion to deny or alter these rights. Generally, statutes identify employees' rights related to various kinds of leaves, such as sick leave, personal leave, pregnancy or child-care leave, sabbatical leave, disability leave, and military leave. State laws pertaining to leaves of absence usually specify eligibility for benefits, minimum days that must be provided, whether leave must be granted with or without pay, and restrictions that may be imposed by local school boards. If a teacher meets all statutory and procedural requirements for a specific leave, a school board cannot deny the request.

PERSONNEL EVALUATIONS

As a result of the federal Race to the Top competition, more states are requiring annual teacher evaluations, and many are using evidence of student learning in these evaluations.[105] To be eligible for funding from the Race to the Top program, states needed to consider student test scores in teacher evaluation and allow charter schools to play a bigger role in turning around lower performing schools. Some states are considering paying teachers for performance as well.[106] Beyond the purposes of faculty improvement and remediation, results of evaluations may be used in a variety of employment decisions including retention, tenure, dismissal, promotion, salary, reassignment, and reduction in force. When adverse personnel decisions are based on evaluations, legal concerns of procedural fairness arise. Were established state and local procedures followed? Did school officials employ equitable standards? Was sufficient evidence collected to support the staffing decision? Were evaluations conducted in a uniform and consistent manner?

Historically, school systems have had broad discretionary powers to establish teacher performance criteria, but more state statutes are beginning to impose specific evaluation requirements. Between 2009 and 2011, thirty-three states made changes to their teacher evaluation policies.[107] Content and requirements vary substantially across states, with some states merely mandating the establishment of an appraisal system and

[103]*See, e.g.*, Amaral-Whittenberg v. Alanis, 123 S.W.3d 714 (Tex. App. 2003).

[104]Charges of discrimination in connection with leave policies pertaining to pregnancy-related absences and the observance of religious holidays are discussed in the chapter "Discrimination in Employment."

[105]Jennifer Dounay Zinth, *Teacher Evaluation: New Approaches for a New Decade*, Educ. Comm'n of the States (June 2012), http://www.ecs.org/html/Document.asp?chouseid=8621.

[106]Stephanie Rose, *Pay for Performance*, Educ. Comm'n of the States (July 2010), http://www.ecs.org/clearinghouse/87/06/8706.pdf. In the 2010 Race to the Top competition, each of the thirty-six states that applied for funding referenced pay for performance.

[107]Emily Douglas, *The State of Teacher Evaluation: Part I*, Educ. Wk. (Jan. 26, 2012), http://blogs.edweek.org/topschooljobs/k-12_talent_manager/2012/01/the_state_of_teacher_evaluation_part_1.html/.

others specifying procedures and criteria to be employed. For example, Indiana requires that the objective measure of student achievement inform the evaluation.[108] Maine enacted legislation that permits school districts to use student assessments as part of the teaching evaluation.[109] The proposed changes to the evaluation of teachers have led to litigation.[110]

Charter schools seemed to have avoided some of these conflicts, which could be due to the flexibility charters have in creating their own teacher evaluation systems. Specifically, many charter schools may not be constrained by state mandates or union rules; this leads to a wide variety of evaluation systems among charter schools. When evaluation procedures are identified in statutes, board policies, or employment contracts, courts generally require strict compliance with these provisions. A Washington appellate court required the reinstatement of a principal because the school board had not adopted evaluation criteria and procedures as required by law.[111] The court noted that in the absence of evaluation criteria, the principal would serve at the whim of the superintendent and would be deprived of guidelines to improve his performance. Under the Ohio statutory evaluation requirement for nontenured teachers, failure to comply with the twice-yearly evaluation mandate resulted in the reinstatement of a nontenured teacher.[112] The West Virginia Supreme Court held that a school system could not transfer an individual, because the decision was not based on performance evaluations as required by state board policy.[113]

Where school boards have been attentive to evaluation requirements, courts have upheld challenged employment decisions.[114] A California appellate court found that a teacher's dismissal comported with state evaluation requirements, because he received periodic appraisals noting specific instances of unsatisfactory performance.[115] The evaluation reports informed the teacher of the system's expectations, his specific teaching weaknesses, and actions needed to correct deficiencies. An Iowa court found a school district's policy requiring a formal evaluation every three years for nonprobationary teachers to be adequate under a statutory requirement that "the board shall establish evaluation criteria and shall implement evaluation procedures."[116] The court denied a teacher's claim that the law required an additional evaluation whenever termination of employment was contemplated. According to the Supreme Court of South Dakota, violation of an evaluation procedure per se does not

[108]IND. CODE ANN., §20-28-11.5-4(c)(2) (2012).

[109]ME P.L. 646, SP704(LD1799) (2012).

[110]*See* Stephen Frank, *Lawsuit Against LAUSD Could Shake Up How California Evaluates Teachers,* CAL. POLITICAL NEWS & VIEWS (Jan. 20, 2012).

[111]Hyde v. Wellpinit Sch. Dist. 49, 611 P.2d 1388 (Wash. Ct. App. 1980).

[112]Snyder v. Mendon-Union Local Sch. Dist. Bd. of Educ., 661 N.E.2d 717 (Ohio 1996); *see also* McComb v. Gahana-Jefferson City Sch. Dist. Bd. of Educ., 720 N.E.2d 984 (Ohio Ct. App. 1998) (concluding that prior to nonrenewal, the teacher was provided specific recommendations for improvement in evaluations as required by state law).

[113]Holland v. Bd. of Educ., 327 S.E.2d 155 (W. Va. 1985).

[114]*See, e.g.,* Tippecanoe Educ. Ass'n v. Tippecanoe Sch. Corp., 700 N.E.2d 241 (Ind. Ct. App. 1998); Thomas v. Bd. of Educ., 643 N.E.2d 132 (Ohio 1994).

[115]Perez v. Comm'n on Prof'l Competence, 197 Cal. Rptr. 390 (Ct. App. 1983); *see also* Hoffner v. Bismarck Pub. Sch. Dist., 589 N.W.2d 195 (N.D. 1999) (concluding that a principal's nonrenewal complied with the statute requiring that reasons be drawn from findings arising from written evaluations).

[116]Johnson v. Bd. of Educ., 353 N.W.2d 883, 887 (Iowa Ct. App. 1984).

require reinstatement of a teacher.[117] Reinstatement is justified only if the violation substantially interfered with a teacher's ability to improve deficiencies.

Courts are reluctant to interject their judgment into the teacher evaluation process. Judicial review generally is limited to the procedural issues of fairness and reasonableness. Several principles emerge from case law to guide educators in developing equitable systems. Standards for assessing teaching adequacy must be defined and communicated to teachers; criteria must be applied uniformly and consistently; an opportunity and direction for improvement must be provided; and procedures specified in state laws and school board policies must be followed.

PERSONNEL RECORDS

Because multiple statutes in each state (as well as employment contracts) govern school records, it is difficult to generalize as to the specific nature of teachers' privacy rights regarding personnel files. State privacy laws that place restrictions on maintenance and access to the records typically protect personnel information. Among other provisions, these laws usually require school boards to maintain only necessary and relevant information, provide individual employees access to their files,[118] inform employees of the various uses of the files, and establish a procedure for challenging the accuracy of information. Collective bargaining contracts may impose additional and more stringent requirements regarding access and dissemination of personnel information.[119]

A central issue in the confidentiality of personnel files is whether the information constitutes a public record that must be reasonably accessible to the general public. Public record, freedom of information, or right-to-know laws that grant broad access to school records may directly conflict with privacy laws, requiring courts to balance the interests of the teacher, the school officials, and the public. The specific provisions of state laws determine the level of confidentiality granted personnel records.[120] The federal Freedom of Information Act (FOIA),[121] which serves as a model for many state FOIAs, often is used

[117]Schaub v. Chamberlain Bd. of Educ., 339 N.W.2d 307 (S.D. 1983). It must be emphasized that failure to follow established evaluation procedures does not necessarily result in a denial of constitutional due process rights in termination actions if the minimum notice, specification of charges, and opportunity for a hearing are provided. *See, e.g.*, Goodrich v. Newport News Sch. Bd., 743 F.2d 225 (4th Cir. 1984); Farmer v. Kelleys Island Bd. of Educ., 638 N.E.2d 79 (Ohio 1994).

[118]*See* Cook v. Lisbon Sch. Comm., 682 A.2d 672 (Me. 1996) (holding that the school committee must produce documents requested by the employee within statutory time period of five working days; providing the material months after the request was made is inadequate); Boor v. McKenzie Cnty. Pub. Sch. Dist. No. 1, 560 N.W.2d 213 (N.D. 1997) (concluding that a principal's notations of complaints against a teacher in his desk journal did not violate state law prohibiting a secret personnel file when he had promptly brought the complaints to the teacher's attention).

[119]*But see* Bradley v. Bd. of Educ., 565 N.W.2d 650 (Mich. 1997) (holding that the board could not bargain away the requirements of the state Freedom of Information Act).

[120]*See* Wakefield Teachers Ass'n v. Sch. Comm., 731 N.E.2d 63 (Mass. 2000) (concluding that a disciplinary report is personal information that is exempt under the public records law); *see also* Gutman v. Bd. of Educ., 852 N.Y.S.2d 658 (App. Div. 2007) (holding that a disciplinary reprimand could not be placed in teachers' personnel files without due process, as mandated by state law); Bangor Area Educ. Ass'n, 720 A.2d 198 (Pa. Commw. Ct. 1998) (confirming that teachers' personnel files are not public records); Abbott v. N.E. Indep. Sch. Dist., 212 S.W.3d 364, 367 (Tex. App. 2006) (concluding that a principal's memorandum to a teacher about complaints and providing her directions for improvement was "a document evaluating the performance of a teacher" and thus exempt from release under the state's public information act).

[121]5 U.S.C. § 552 (2012).

by courts in interpreting state provisions. Unlike the federal law, however, many states do not exempt personnel records. In the absence of a specific exemption, most courts have concluded that any doubt as to the appropriateness of disclosure should be decided in favor of public disclosure.[122] The Supreme Court of Michigan held that teachers' personnel files are open to the public because they are not specifically exempt by law.[123] The Supreme Court of Washington noted that the Public Disclosure Act mandated disclosure of information that is of legitimate public concern.[124] As such, the state superintendent of public instruction was required to provide a newspaper publisher records specifying the reasons for teacher certificate revocations. The Supreme Court of Connecticut interpreted the state Freedom of Information Act exemption, prohibiting the release of information that would constitute an "invasion of personal privacy," to include employees' evaluations[125] but not their sick-leave records.[126] In the termination of a teacher for conducting pornographic Internet searches on his work computer, the Supreme Court of Wisconsin held that a memorandum and CD created from a forensic analysis of the teacher's computer were "records" subject to release under the state's Open Records Law after the school district completed its investigation.[127] Generally, information that must be maintained by law is a public record (i.e., personal directory information, salary, employment contracts, leave records, and teaching license) and must be released.

Educators have not been successful in asserting that privacy interests in personnel records are protected under either the Family Educational Rights and Privacy Act of 1974 (FERPA) or the United States Constitution. FERPA has been found to apply only to students and their educational records, not to employees' personnel records.[128] Similarly, employees' claims that their constitutional privacy rights bar disclosure of their personnel records have been unsuccessful. In a case in which a teacher's college transcript was sought by

[122]*See, e.g.*, Kirwan v. The Diamondback, 721 A.2d 196 (Md. 1998); Brouillet v. Cowles Pub. Co., 791 P.2d 526 (Wash. 1990); Wis. Newspress v. Sch. Dist., 546 N.W.2d 143 (Wis. 1996).

[123]Bradley v. Bd. of Educ., 565 N.W.2d 650 (Mich. 1997).

[124]*Brouillet*, 791 P.2d 526; *see also* S. Bend Tribune v. S. Bend Cmty. Sch. Corp., 740 N.E.2d 937 (Ind. Ct. App. 2000) (holding that a public agency must disclose designated personnel information for present or former employees but not information pertaining to applicants for positions); Cypress Media v. Hazleton Area Sch. Dist., 708 A.2d 866 (Pa. Commw. Ct. 1998) (finding that applications for employment are not public records).

[125]Chairman v. Freedom of Info. Comm'n, 585 A.2d 96 (Conn. 1991). *But see* DeMichele v. Greenburgh Cent. Sch. Dist. No. 7, 167 F.3d 784 (2d Cir. 1999) (noting that under New York law, the disposition of misconduct charges is not exempt private information); Carpenter v. Freedom of Info. Comm'n, 755 A.2d 364 (Conn. App. Ct. 2000) (ruling that a record of personal misconduct was not a record of teaching performance or evaluation exempt under state law); Linzmeyer v. Forcey, 646 N.W.2d 811 (Wis. 2002) (finding that the open records law applies to the report of a police investigation; the police had investigated a high school teacher for allegedly engaging in inappropriate conduct with female students).

[126]Perkins v. Freedom of Info. Comm'n, 635 A.2d 783 (Conn. 1993). *But see* Brogan v. Sch. Comm. of Westport, 516 N.E.2d 159 (Mass. 1987) (holding that individual absentee records noting dates and generic types of absences were not records of a "personal nature" exempt from disclosure under the Public Records Law); *see also* Scottsdale Unified Sch. Dist. No. 48 v. KPNX Broad. Co., 955 P.2d 534 (Ariz. 1998) (finding that the public availability of teachers' birth dates did not negate teachers' legitimate expectation of privacy).

[127]Zellner v. Cedarburg Sch. Dist., 731 N.W.2d 240 (Wis. 2007); *see also* Navarre v. S. Wash. Cnty. Schs., 652 N.W.2d 9 (Minn. 2002) (finding that the release of information about a disciplinary matter before final disposition violated the counselor's rights under state law protecting private personnel data); Williams v. Bd. of Educ., 747 A.2d 809 (N.J. Super. Ct. App. Div. 2000) (holding that tenure documents are a public record).

[128]*See, e.g.*, Klein Indep. Sch. Dist. v. Mattox, 830 F.2d 576 (5th Cir. 1987); Brouillet v. Cowles Publ'g Co., 791 P.2d 526 (Wash. 1990); *see also* Cypress Media v. Hazelton Area Sch. Dist., 708 A.2d 866 (Pa. Commw. Ct. 1998) (concluding that release of college transcripts of *applicants* for teaching positions would violate FERPA).

a third party under the Texas Open Records Act, the Fifth Circuit ruled that even if a teacher had a recognizable privacy interest in her transcript, that interest "is significantly outweighed by the public's interest in evaluating the competence of its school teachers."[129]

Access to personnel files also has been controversial in situations involving allegations of employment discrimination.[130] Personnel files must be relinquished if subpoenaed by a court. The Equal Employment Opportunity Commission (EEOC) also is authorized to subpoena relevant personnel files to enable the commission to investigate thoroughly allegations that a particular individual has been the victim of discriminatory treatment. Holding that confidential peer review materials used in university promotion and tenure decisions were not protected from disclosure to the EEOC, the Supreme Court ruled that under the provisions of Title VII of the Civil Rights Act of 1964, the Commission must only show relevance, not special reasons or justifications, in demanding specific records. Regarding access to peer review materials, the Court noted that "if there is a 'smoking gun' to be found that demonstrates discrimination in tenure decisions, it is likely to be tucked away in peer review files."[131]

With respect to the maintenance of records, information clearly cannot be placed in personnel files in retaliation for the exercise of constitutional rights. Courts have ordered letters of reprimand expunged from files when they have been predicated on protected speech and association activities. Reprimands, while not a direct prohibition on protected activities, may present a constitutional violation because of their potentially chilling effect on the exercise of constitutional rights.[132]

OTHER EMPLOYMENT ISSUES

In addition to the terms and conditions of employment already discussed, other reasonable requirements can be attached to public employment so long as civil rights laws are respected, and constitutional rights are not impaired without a compelling governmental justification. Public educators are expected to comply with such reasonable requirements as a condition of maintaining their jobs. Requirements pertaining to two topics have received substantial attention since the 1980s and warrant discussion here—using copyrighted materials and reporting child abuse/harassment.

[129]*Klein*, 830 F.2d at 580; *see also* Hovet v. Hebron Pub. Sch. Dist., 419 N.W.2d 189 (N.D. 1988).

[130]Federal Procedural Rules, approved by the Supreme Court in April 2006 and effective December 1, 2006, require employers to be more aware about the storage of electronic information. When school officials are involved in the discovery phase of litigation, they must be able to produce e-mail, instant messages, and other digital communications created in their system. The rules send a clear message that digital and electronic communications must be preserved as other documents are preserved.

[131]Univ. of Pa. v. EEOC, 493 U.S. 182, 193 (1990); *see also* Univ. of Pittsburgh v. Dep't of Labor & Indus., 896 A.2d 683 (Pa. Commw. Ct. 2006) (ruling under the state's Personnel Files Act that a faculty member did not have the right to inspect external letters written for his promotion file; letters were considered references rather than personnel evaluations that would have been open to inspection).

[132]*See* Aebisher v. Ryan, 622 F.2d 651 (2d Cir. 1980) (concluding that a letter of reprimand for speaking to the press about violence in the school implicated protected speech); Columbus Educ. Ass'n v. Columbus City Sch. Dist., 623 F.2d 1155 (6th Cir. 1980) (holding that a letter of reprimand issued to a union representative for zealous advocacy of a fellow teacher violated the First Amendment); Swilley v. Alexander, 629 F.2d 1018 (5th Cir. 1980) (ruling that a union president's press release was protected conduct, and letter of reprimand implicated liberty interests).

Using Copyrighted Materials

The U.S. Constitution provides Congress with the power "to promote the progress of science and useful arts, by securing for limited times to authors and inventors the exclusive right to their respective writings and discoveries."[133] This provision of the Constitution is known as the "copyright clause." Although copyright lawsuits involving school districts are not numerous, there has been litigation focused on whether the materials that teachers have created for class are copyrightable or whether teachers have violated copyright law by relying on others' materials.[134] Indeed, educators' extensive use of published materials and various other media in the classroom raises issues relating to federal copyright law. As a condition of employment, educators are expected to comply with restrictions on the use of copyrighted materials. As a general rule, teachers should assume material is copyrighted unless it is explicitly stated that it is in the public domain.[135]

Although the law grants the owner of a copyright exclusive control over the protected material, courts since the 1800s have recognized exceptions to this control under the doctrine of "fair use." The fair use doctrine cannot be precisely defined, but the judiciary frequently has described it as the "privilege on people other than the copyright owner to use the copyrighted material in a reasonable manner without his consent, notwithstanding the monopoly granted to the owner."[136]

Congress incorporated the judicially created fair use concept into the 1976 revisions of the Copyright Act.[137] In identifying the purposes of the fair use exception, Congress specifically noted teaching. The exception provides needed flexibility for teachers but by no interpretation grants them exemption from copyright infringement. The law stipulates four factors to assess whether the use of specific material constitutes fair use or an infringement:

> (1) the purpose and character of the use, including whether such use is of a commercial nature or is for non-profit educational purposes; (2) the nature of the copyrighted work; (3) the amount and substantiality of the portion used in relation to the copyrighted work as a whole; and (4) the effect of the use upon the potential market for or value of the copyrighted work.[138]

[133]U.S. CONST. art. I, § 8, cl. 8.

[134]Teachers' ideas might be excluded from copyright protection if the idea constitutes "works for hire." Works that are created as part of the employment relationship can be considered a work for hire, and the employer is considered the author unless the parties have expressly agreed to another arrangement,17 U.S.C. § 201(b) (2012); *see also* Clark v. Crues, 260 F. App'x 292 (Fed. Cir. 2008) (finding that a teacher who had developed a hall pass system had no copyrightable interest in that system); Brooks-Ngwenya v. Indianapolis Pub. Schs., 564 F.3d 804 (7th Cir. 2009) (affirming school district's motion for summary judgment because district personnel did not copy an educational award-system program developed by teacher). *But see* Pavlica v. Behr, 397 F. Supp. 2d 519 (S.D.N.Y. 2005) (dismissing school district's motion for summary judgment in a case involving a teacher who developed a manual for a new course).

[135]*See generally* Authors Guild v. Google, 770 F. Supp. 2d 666 (S.D.N.Y. 2011) (emphasizing that copyright is conferred the moment of creation and that the copyright symbol is no longer required); *see also* Kirtsaeng v. John Wiley & Sons, 132 S. Ct. 1905 (2012) (granting certiorari to determine the ability of U.S. owners to resell goods that were manufactured abroad and subject to copyright protection; the decision could have implications for the availability of some textbooks).

[136]Shepard v. Miler, No. 2:10-1863, 2010 U.S. Dist. LEXIS 136504, at *11 (E.D. Cal. Dec. 14, 2010).

[137]17 U.S.C. § 101 (2012). A Wisconsin teacher raised a novel "fair use" claim when he argued that his school district could not release to a newspaper a compact disc containing pornographic images he had downloaded from the Internet because the images were copyrighted works, thereby not a public record under the state's Open Records Law. The state high court ruled that the images were a public record because they could be accessed free of charge via the Internet, and the school district would not profit from distribution of the images. Zellner v. Cedarburg Sch. Dist., 731 N.W.2d 240 (Wis. 2007).

[138]17 U.S.C. § 107 (2012).

To clarify fair use pertaining to photocopying from books and periodicals, the House of Representatives and Senate conferees incorporated into their report a set of classroom guidelines developed by a group representing educators, authors, and publishers.[139] These guidelines are only part of the legislative history of the Act and do not have the force of law, but they have been widely used as persuasive authority in assessing the legality of reproducing printed materials in the educational environment. The guidelines permit making single copies of copyrighted material for teaching or research but are quite restrictive on the use of multiple copies. To use multiple copies of a work, the tests of brevity, spontaneity, and cumulative effect must be met. Brevity is precisely defined according to type of publication. For example, reproduction of a poem cannot exceed 250 words; copying from longer works cannot exceed 1,000 words or 10 percent of the work (whichever is less); only one chart or drawing can be reproduced from a book or an article. Spontaneity requires that the copying be initiated by the individual teacher (not an administrator or supervisor) and that it occur in such a manner that does not reasonably permit a timely request for permission. Cumulative effect restricts use of the copies to one course; limits material reproduced from the same author, book, and journal during the term; and sets a limit of nine instances of multiple copying for each course during one class term. Furthermore, the guidelines do not permit copying to substitute for anthologies or collective works or to replace consumable materials such as workbooks.

Publishers have taken legal action to ensure compliance with these guidelines. The Sixth Circuit held that Michigan Document Services, Inc., a commercial copy shop, violated the fair use doctrine in the reproduction of course packets for faculty at the University of Michigan. Three publishers (Macmillan, Princeton University Press, and St. Martin's Press) challenged the duplication of copyrighted material for commercial sale by a for-profit corporation. The copy shop owner argued that such reproduction of multiple copies for classroom use is a recognized statutory exemption. The appellate court disagreed, reasoning that the sale of multiple copies for commercial, rather than educational purposes, destroyed the publishers' potential licensing revenue from photocopying. Furthermore, course packets contained creative material and involved substantial portions of the copyrighted publications (as much as 30 percent for one work).[140] This ruling does not prevent faculty use of course packets or anthologies in the classroom, but it does require permission from publishers and the possible payment of fees prior to photocopying.

The fair use doctrine and congressional guidelines have been strictly construed in educational settings. Even though the materials reproduced meet the first factor in determining fair use—educational purpose—the remaining factors also must be met. The Ninth Circuit held that a teacher's use of a copyrighted booklet to make a learning activity packet abridged the copyright law.[141] The court concluded that fair use was not met in this case because the learning packet was used for the same purpose as the

[139]U.S. Copyright Office, *Circular 21: Reproduction of Copyrighted Works by Educators and Librarians* (2009), http://www.copyright.gov/circs/circ21.pdf.

[140]Princeton Univ. Press v. Mich. Document Servs., 99 F.3d 1381 (6th Cir. 1996); *see also* Basic Books v. Kinko's Graphics Corp., 758 F. Supp. 1522 (S.D.N.Y. 1991) (concluding that the photocopying of copyrighted works for course packets violated fair use; awarding eight publishers $510,000 in damages).

[141]Marcus v. Rowley, 695 F.2d 1171 (9th Cir. 1983).

protected booklet, the nature of the work reproduced was a "creative" effort rather than "information," and one-half of the packet was verbatim copy of the copyrighted material. Furthermore, the copying was found to violate the guideline of spontaneity in that it was reproduced several times over two school years. It is important to note that the appeals court did not find the absence of personal profit on the part of the teacher to lessen the violation.

Although not using the material for teaching purposes, a Chicago teacher and editor of a newspaper called *Substance* published copyrighted tests used to assess educational levels of Chicago public high school freshmen and sophomores. He published entire copies of a number of the subject area tests along with his criticism of the tests. The tests were clearly marked with the copyright notice and included a warning that the material could not be duplicated. The Chicago school board sued, claiming infringement of its copyright. An Illinois federal district court ruled that the teacher did not possess a First Amendment right to publish the copyrighted tests; the Copyright Act limits First Amendment freedoms.[142] Furthermore, the publication of the material did not fall within the "fair use" guidelines. In another case, however, a California federal district court observed that a parent had the right to see a copyrighted testing protocol before an IEP meeting because the materials fell under fair use.[143] Specifically, the copies were not to be used for commercial gain and were for educational purposes. Also, the court found that the amount to be copied was reasonable, and there was no evidence that the copying would create an adverse market effect.

Rapid developments in instructional technology pose a new set of legal questions regarding use of videotapes, DVDs, and computer software. Recognizing the need for guidance related to recording material, Congress issued guidelines for educational use in 1981.[144] These guidelines specify that recording must be made at the request of the teacher. The material recorded must be used for relevant classroom activities only once within the first ten days of recording. Additional use is limited to instructional reinforcement or evaluation purposes. After forty-five calendar days, the tape or DVD must be erased. A New York federal district court held that a school system violated the fair use standards by extensive off-the-air taping and replaying of entire television programs.[145] The recording interfered with the producers' ability to market the tapes and films. In a subsequent appeal, the school system sought permission for temporary taping; however, because of the availability of these programs for rental or lease, even temporary recording and use was held to violate fair use by interfering with the marketability of the films.[146]

[142]Chi. Sch. Reform Bd. v. Substance, Inc., 79 F. Supp. 2d 919 (N.D. Ill. 1999).

[143]Newport-Mesa Unified Sch. Dist. v. Cal. Dep't of Educ., 371 F. Supp. 2d 1170 (C.D. Cal. 2005). *But see* State *ex rel.* Perrea v. Pub. Schs., 916 N.E.2d 1049 (2009) (denying teacher access to semester exams that were developed by a school district because the exams were considered trade secrets).

[144]*Guidelines for Off-the-Air Recording of Broadcast Programming for Educational Purposes*, CONG. REC. § E4751 (daily ed. Oct.14, 1981).

[145]Encyclopedia Britannica Educ. Corp. v. Crooks, 542 F. Supp. 1156 (W.D.N.Y. 1982).

[146]Encyclopedia Britannica Educ. Corp. v. Crooks, 558 F. Supp. 1247 (W.D.N.Y. 1983); *see also* Sony Corp. v. Universal City Studios, 464 U.S. 417, 450 (1984) (finding that personal video recording for the purpose of "time shifting" for the viewer's convenience was permissible, but home recording for broader viewing by students in the classroom would necessitate careful adherence to the guidelines for limited use).

Publishers are often concerned about illegal copying of computer software in the school environment. Limited school budgets and high costs have led to abuse of copyrighted software. Even though the fair use defense likely protects consumers' rights in making a backup copy of a DVD for personal use, the law is sometimes ambiguous in other contexts.[147] In 1999, the Los Angeles Board of Education settled a significant case of software piracy discovered in public schools.[148] An investigation by a group of software companies discovered more than 1,400 copies of software, such as Microsoft Word and Adobe Photoshop, allegedly being used without authorization. The school district denied the violation but settled to avoid the costs of a trial.

A question not answered by the copyright law but plaguing schools is the legality of multiple use of a master program. That is, can a program be loaded onto a number of computers in a laboratory for simultaneous use, or can a program be modified for use in a network of microcomputers? Again, application of the fair use concept would indicate that multiple use is impermissible. The most significant factor is that the market for the educational software would be greatly diminished. A number of students using the master program one at a time (serial use), however, would appear not to violate the copyright law. To acquire broad use of particular software, school systems must either purchase multiple copies or negotiate site license agreements with the publishers.

As schools are developing their capacity to take advantage of the Internet, copyright law also is evolving. Congress amended the law in 1998, passing the Digital Millennium Copyright Act.[149] The White Paper produced by President Clinton's Working Group on Intellectual Property Issues identified numerous and complex issues that influenced the amended law.[150] Questions were raised about what constitutes distribution (traditionally interpreted as a hard copy being transferred to another individual as opposed to transmission over data lines) and publication (the current definition limits protection to physical copies). The amended law reinforces that an individual's copyright is secured when the work is created and "fixed in any tangible medium of expression."[151] Even though critics find many ambiguities in the law, they agree that it includes a clear commitment to extending "fair use" to digital technology for educators.

In 2002, greater clarity was provided for educators regarding the use of digital media in distance education with the enactment of the Technology, Education, and Copyright Harmonization (TEACH) Act (included in the 21st Century Department of Justice Appropriations Authorization Act, H.R. 2215).[152] The Act gives accredited nonprofit educational institutions more flexibility in using the Internet to distribute copyrighted materials in distance education programs. Basically, the TEACH Act allows copyrighted materials to be used in distance education courses in the same way they can be used in regular classrooms. Previously, the law did not permit two-way transmission of copyrighted materials and prevented sharing of materials through digital transmissions.

[147]*See* Realnetworks, Inc. v. DVD Copy Control Ass'n, 641 F. Supp. 2d 913 (N.D. Cal. 2009).

[148]*L.A. School Board Settles Software Copyright Suit*, 27 Sch. L. News 2 (Mar. 5, 1999). The case was settled for $300,000 plus an additional $1.5 million for a task force to monitor software usage over a three-year period.

[149]17 U.S.C. § 1201 (2012).

[150]Bruce A. Lehman, Chair, Information Infrastructure Task Force, Working Group on Intellectual Property Rights, *Report on Intellectual Property and the National Information Infrastructure* (Sept. 1995), http://www.uspto.gov/web/offices/com/doc/ipnii/front.pdf.

[151]17 U.S.C. § 102 (2012).

[152]17 U.S.C. §110 (2012); *see also* Constance Hawke, *The P2P File Sharing Controversy: Should Colleges Be Involved,* 184 Educ. L. Rep. 681 (2004).

Litigation clearly indicates that material published and distributed on the Internet will be fully protected by the basic principles of copyright law. For example, in 2001, the Ninth Circuit imposed an injunction against Napster Corporation and its distribution of a file-sharing program that allowed individuals to download music files.[153] In 2005, the Supreme Court found that two software companies, presenting themselves as "alternatives" to Napster, infringed the copyright of songwriters, music publishers, and motion picture studios who had brought suit to prevent unauthorized use of their protected property. Like Napster, the challenged software companies distributed free software products that allowed individuals to share electronic files through peer-to-peer networks. The Supreme Court specifically held that "one who distributes a device with the object of promoting its use to infringe copyright, as shown by clear expression or other affirmative steps taken to foster infringement, is liable for the resulting acts of infringement by third parties."[154] Although the file-sharing software had some lawful uses, its primary purpose and use was to share copyrighted files. That rendered the software companies culpable.

Extraordinary technological advances have given teachers and their school systems the means to access a wide range of instructional materials and products, but the federal copyright law that restricts unauthorized reproduction protects many of them. Because violation of the law can result in school district and educator liability, school boards should adopt policies or guidelines to prohibit infringement and to alert individuals of practices that violate protected materials.[155]

Reporting Suspected Child Abuse

Child abuse and neglect are recognized as national problems, with reported cases remaining at a high level.[156] Because the majority of these children are school age, educators are in a unique role to detect signs of potential abuse. States, recognizing the daily contact teachers have with students, have imposed certain *duties* for reporting suspected abuse.

All states have enacted laws identifying teachers among the professionals required to report signs of child abuse. Most state laws impose criminal liability for failure to report. Penalties may include fines ranging from $500 to $5,000, prison terms up to one year, or both. Civil suits also may be initiated against teachers for negligence in failing to make such reports.[157] However, some states have not found that a private cause of

[153] A&M Records v. Napster, 239 F.3d 1004 (9th Cir. 2001).

[154] Metro-Goldwyn-Mayer Studios Inc. v. Grokster, Ltd., 545 U.S. 913, 919 (2005). The lower courts had ruled that the software companies could not be held liable for unlawful use of the file-sharing programs, but the Supreme Court remanded the case to the district court for trial. The principal parties settled shortly after the Supreme Court decision.

[155] *See* 17 U.S.C. § 511(a) (2012). In response to several appellate court decisions holding that, under the Eleventh Amendment, states and their agents were not subject to suit in federal courts for the infringement of copyrights, Congress amended the copyright law (Copyright Remedy Clarification), specifically abrogating immunity. *See, e.g.*, BV Eng'g v. Univ. of Cal., L.A., 858 F.2d 1394 (9th Cir. 1988); Richard Anderson Photography v. Brown, 852 F.2d 114 (4th Cir. 1988).

[156] In 2011, 3.4 million referrals (involving approximately six million children) were made to child protection agencies. U.S. Department of Health & Human Services, Administration for Children & Families, *Child Maltreatment 2011* (Washington, D.C.: U.S. Government Printing Office, 2012). Over half of the reports were made by professionals, including educators, police, lawyers, and social services staff.

[157] Kraynak v. Youngstown City Sch. Dist. Bd. of Educ., 889 N.E.2d 528 (Ohio 2008).

action exists (e.g., right to sue) for violations of mandatory child abuse reporting laws.[158] Additionally, school systems may impose disciplinary measures against a teacher who does not follow the mandates of the law. The Seventh Circuit upheld the suspension and demotion of a teacher-psychologist for not promptly reporting suspected abuse.[159] The court rejected the teacher's claim to a federal right of confidentiality, noting the state's compelling interest to protect children from mistreatment.

Although specific aspects of the laws may vary from one state to another, definitions of abuse and neglect often are based on the federal Child Abuse Prevention and Treatment Act (CAPTA) of 1974, which provides funds to identify, treat, and prevent abuse. CAPTA identifies child abuse and neglect as

> the physical or mental injury, sexual abuse or exploitation, negligent treatment, or maltreatment of a child under the age of eighteen, or the age specified by the child protection law of the state in question, by a person who is responsible for the child's welfare under the circumstances which indicate that the child's health or welfare is harmed or threatened thereby.[160]

Several common elements are found in state child abuse statutes. The laws mandate that certain professionals such as doctors, nurses, and educators report suspected abuse. Statutes do not require that reporters have absolute knowledge, but rather "reasonable cause to believe" or "reason to believe" that a child has been abused or neglected.[161] Once abuse is suspected, the report must be made immediately to the designated child protection agency, department of welfare, or law enforcement unit as specified in state law. All states grant immunity from civil and criminal liability to individuals if reports are made in good faith.[162]

School districts often establish reporting procedures that require teachers to report suspected abuse to the school principal or school social worker. However, if statutory provisions specify that teachers must promptly report suspected abuse to another agency or law enforcement, teachers are not relieved of their individual obligation to report to state authorities. Furthermore, the Kentucky Supreme Court held that reporting to a supervisor then imposes a burden on the supervisor to make a separate report.[163] Some state laws do relieve teachers of the obligation to report if someone else has already reported or will be reporting the incident. But teachers should always follow up to ensure the report was made to the appropriate agency.

State laws are explicit on reporting requirements for suspected child abuse, but it is difficult to prove that a teacher had sufficient knowledge of abuse to trigger legal liability

[158]*See* Cuyler v. United States, 362 F.3d 949 (7th Cir. 2004); Collum v. Charlotte-Mecklenburg Bd. of Educ., 614 F. Supp. 2d 598 (W.D.N.C. 2008).

[159]Pesce v. J. Sterling Morton High Sch. Dist. 201, 830 F.2d 789 (7th Cir. 1987); *see also* State v. Grover, 437 N.W.2d 60 (Minn. 1989) (finding the principal criminally negligent for failure to report child abuse by a teacher).

[160]42 U.S.C. § 5101 (2012).

[161]*See, e.g.*, Kimberly S.M. v. Bradford Cent. Sch., 649 N.Y.S.2d 588 (App. Div. 1996); *see also* Hughes v. Stanley Cnty. Sch. Dist., 638 N.W.2d 50 (S.D. 2001) (finding that the school board lacked evidence to support its allegation that a teacher failed to report suspected abuse).

[162]*See, e.g.*, Landstrom v. Ill. Dep't of Children & Family Servs., 892 F.2d 670 (7th Cir. 1990); Liedtke v. Carrington, 763 N.E.2d 213 (Ohio Ct. App. 2001).

[163]Commonwealth v. Allen, 980 S.W.2d 278 (Ky. 1998); *see also* Barber v. State, 592 So. 2d 330 (Fla. Dist. Ct. App. 1992) (noting that requiring multiple reports of the same incident of abuse demonstrates the gravity of the situation).

for failure to report.[164] Therefore, it is desirable for school officials to establish policies and procedures to encourage effective reporting. The pervasiveness of the problem and concern about the lack of reporting by teachers also indicate a need for in-service programs to assist teachers in recognizing signs of abuse and neglect in children.

Recent litigation has not involved so much the failure of teachers to report but rather allegations that educators are the abusers.[165] These cases have received substantial publicity and raised questions regarding the duties of teachers, administrators, and school boards to report suspicion of abuse and to prevent such abuse by employees from occurring in the school setting.

Litigation has addressed whether a school district's failure to protect students from suspected abuse by school employees violates students' constitutional or statutory rights.[166] Damages can be sought under the Civil Rights Act of 1871, 42 U.S.C. § 1983, if a claimant has been deprived of a federally protected right by an individual acting under official state policy or custom.[167] Although the Supreme Court did not find a violation of a federal right in a case involving a social worker's failure to intervene when she knew a child was being severely beaten by his father (a private individual), abuse in the school setting involves actions by public employees.[168] The Third Circuit recognized a clearly established constitutional right to bodily security—to be free from sexual abuse—and found that school districts may violate this right by maintaining a policy, practice, or custom reflecting "deliberate indifference" to this right. The court concluded that the student's evidence showing that school officials' actions in discouraging and minimizing reports of sexual misconduct by teachers and failing to take action on complaints may have established a custom or practice in violation of § 1983.[169] If school officials do not have knowledge of abuse or act with indifference to complaints, liability will not be assessed.[170]

To impose liability on school districts under § 1983, students must show that the district maintained a "policy" or "custom" that deprived the students of their protected federal rights. The Eleventh Circuit did not find that a policy or custom existed when school officials consistently followed up on every complaint against a teacher. Evidence in the case did not show deliberate indifference, which could have been used to establish

[164]*See* Hargrove v. D.C., 5 A.3d 632 (D.C. 2010) (reversing criminal conviction for vice principal's and principal's failure to report suspected sexual abuse because the accusations were not considered credible).

[165]*See In re* Young, 995 A.2d 826 (N.J. 2010) (holding that even though allegations that a teacher sexually abused a student were unfounded by a state agency's independent evaluation, the teacher could still be terminated because evidence collected by school officials found proof of inappropriate sexual relations between the student and teacher); Ellis v. Maryland, 971 A.2d 379 (Md. App. 2009) (finding liability against teacher who had sexually abused student off-campus, because a teacher has responsibility for supervision of a child at school or when when away from school at a school-related activity); Frank v. Dep't of Children & Families, 37 A.3d 834 (Conn. App. Ct. 2012) (finding teacher was not on notice that his cheek-pinching and name-calling behavior toward a student amounted to child abuse under state law).

[166]*See* Doe v. Gooden, 214 F.3d 952 (8th Cir. 2000) (ruling that failure to report suspected abuse as required by state law does not establish unconstitutional misconduct); Abeyta v. Chama Valley Indep. Sch. Dist., 77 F.3d 1253 (10th Cir. 1996) (holding that sex-specific verbal abuse by a teacher does not give rise to a constitutional violation; calling a student a prostitute is a substantial abuse of authority but not a violation of substantive due process rights).

[167]Intentionally left blank so that the remaining footnotes in the chapter can remain numbered as is.

[168]DeShaney v. Winnebago Cnty. Dep't of Soc. Servs., 489 U.S. 189 (1989).

[169]Stoneking v. Bradford Area Sch. Dist., 882 F.2d 720 (3d Cir. 1989). For a definition of the "deliberate indifference" standard, see *City of Canton, Ohio v. Harris*, 489 U.S. 378 (1989).

[170]*See, e.g.*, P.H. v. Sch. Dist., 265 F.3d 653 (8th Cir. 2001); Canutillo Indep. Sch. Dist. v. Leija, 101 F.3d 393 (5th Cir. 1996); Gates v. Unified Sch. Dist. No. 449, 996 F.2d 1035 (10th Cir. 1993).

a "custom."[171] However, in denying summary judgment in a § 1983 suit, the Sixth Circuit concluded that a "custom" of inaction had been established when school officials repeatedly ignored and covered up a teacher's misconduct over a lengthy period of time.[172] Given the pattern of complaints and inappropriate behavior, the school district was on notice that the teacher posed a threat to the welfare of students; the unreasonable responses showed deliberate indifference.

With the judicial recognition that sexual abuse by school employees can result in school district liability, school boards are developing and implementing policies for handling child abuse complaints and protecting teachers and other school employees from becoming the targets of false child abuse charges.[173] Board policies protecting teachers from false reports are often the result of state laws that provide civil remedies for knowingly or recklessly making a false report of child abuse.[174] It is becoming increasingly common for school boards to prohibit physical contact between teachers and students in the absence of another adult and to place restrictions on private meetings between students and teachers before or after school. Some states have attempted to impose similar restrictions involving student and teacher communication over the Internet.[175] Employees can face disciplinary action for failing to comply with such directives,[176] even if they are not found guilty of actual child abuse.

Conclusion

Except for certain limitations imposed by constitutional provisions and federal civil rights laws, state statutes govern public educators' employment. The state prescribes general requirements for certification, contracts, tenure, and employment. Local school boards must follow state mandates and, in addition, may impose other requirements. In general, the following terms and conditions govern teacher employment.

1. The state establishes minimum qualifications for certification, which may include professional preparation, a minimum age, U.S. citizenship, good moral character, signing a loyalty oath, and passing an academic examination.
2. A teacher must acquire a valid certificate to teach in public schools.
3. Certification does not assure employment in a state.
4. Certification may be revoked for cause, generally identified in state law.
5. School boards are vested with the power to appoint teachers and to establish professional and academic employment standards above the state minimums.
6. Courts generally have upheld school board residency requirements, reasonable health and physical standards, and background checks prior to employment if formulated on a reasonable basis.

[171]*See* Sauls v. Pierce Cnty. Sch. Dist., 399 F.3d 1279 (11th Cir. 2005); Kline *ex rel.* Arndt v. Mansfield, 454 F. Supp. 2d 258 (E.D. Pa. 2006), *aff'd*, 255 F. App'x 624 (3d Cir. 2007).

[172]Doe v. Warren Consol. Schs., 93 F. App'x 812 (6th Cir. 2004).

[173]*See, e.g.*, Besett v. Wadena Cnty., No. 10-934, 2010 U.S. Dist. LEXIS 137112 (D. Minn. Dec. 7, 2010).

[174]*See* Minn. Stat. Ann. § 626.559(5) (2012).

[175]*See* Jennifer Preston, *Rules to Stop Pupil and Teacher from Getting Too Social Online*, N.Y. Times, Dec. 18, 2011, at A1.

[176]*See In re* Binghamton City Sch. Dist., 823 N.Y.S.2d 231 (App. Div. 2006).

7. A teacher may be assigned or transferred to any school or grade at the board's discretion, so long as the assignment is within the teacher's certification area and not circumscribed by contract terms.
8. School officials can make reasonable and appropriate extracurricular assignments.
9. Teacher contracts must satisfy the general principles of contract law as well as conform to any additional specifications contained in state law.
10. Tenure is a statutory right ensuring that dismissal is based on adequate cause and accompanied by procedural due process.
11. Tenure must be conferred in accordance with statutory provisions.
12. Supplemental contracts for extra-duty assignments are generally outside the scope of tenure laws.
13. A school board's extensive authority to determine teacher performance standards may be restricted by state-imposed evaluation requirements.
14. Maintenance, access, and dissemination of personnel information must conform to state law and contractual agreements.
15. Personnel records can be subpoenaed to assess discrimination charges.
16. Educators must comply with the federal copyright law; copyrighted materials may be used for instructional purposes without the publisher's permission if "fair use" guidelines are followed.
17. All states require teachers to report suspected child abuse and grant immunity from liability if reports are made in good faith.
18. School districts will be held liable for teacher harassment or abuse of students if someone in a position of authority to take corrective measures has actual knowledge of the abuse and responds with deliberate indifference.

MyEdLeadershipLab™

Go to Topic 9: *Terms and Conditions in Employment and Termination* on the MyEdLeadershipLab™ site (www.myedleadershiplab.com) for *Public School Law: Teachers' and Students' Rights*, Seventh Edition, where you can

- Find learning outcomes for *Terms and Conditions in Employment and Termination* along with the national standards that connect to these outcomes.
- Complete Assignments and Activities that can help you more deeply understand the chapter content.
- Apply and practice your understanding of the core skills identified in the chapter with the Building Leadership Skills unit.
- Prepare yourself for professional certification with a Practice for Certification quiz.

Teachers' Substantive Constitutional Rights

MyEdLeadershipLab™

Visit the MyEdLeadershipLab™ site for *Public School Law: Teachers' and Students' Rights*, Seventh Edition, to enhance your understanding of chapter concepts. You'll have the opportunity to practice your skills through video- and case-based Assignments and Activities as well as Building Leadership Skills units, and to prepare for your certification exam with Practice for Certification quizzes.

It is clear that teachers do not leave their constitutional rights at the schoolhouse gate. Yet, limitations may be placed on the exercise of these rights because of the special context of the school environment. For teachers, it becomes difficult to navigate through what is protected and what can be restricted. This chapter presents an overview of the scope of teachers' constitutional rights as defined by the judiciary in connection with free expression, academic freedom, freedom of association, freedom of choice in appearance, and privacy rights. Some of the cases do not involve school situations, but the legal principles apply to all public employees.

FREEDOM OF EXPRESSION

Until the mid-twentieth century, it was generally accepted that public school teachers could be dismissed or disciplined for expressing views considered objectionable by the school board. The private sector practice of firing such employees was assumed to apply to public employment as well. Although it is now clearly established that freedom of expression is not forfeited by accepting public school employment, courts have

From Chapter 9 of *Public School Law: Teachers' and Students' Rights*, Seventh Edition. Martha M. McCarthy, Nelda H. Cambron-McCabe, Suzanne E. Eckes.

acknowledged that this right must be weighed against the school district's interest in maintaining an effective and efficient school system. In this section, the evolution of legal principles and their application to specific school situations are reviewed.

Legal Principles

Similar to student free speech cases, an initial determination must be made regarding whether the public employee's claim involves expression *at all*. Expressive conduct is protected by the First Amendment, but the Supreme Court has emphasized that not all conduct is considered expression. An action constitutes expression for First Amendment purposes only if it attempts "to convey a particularized message" that will likely be understood by those receiving the message.[1]

In the landmark 1968 decision, *Pickering v. Board of Education*, the Supreme Court recognized that teachers have a First Amendment right to air their views on matters of public concern.[2] Pickering wrote a letter to a local newspaper, criticizing the school board's fiscal policies, especially the allocation of funds between the education and athletic programs. The school board dismissed Pickering because of the letter, which included false statements allegedly damaging the reputations of school board members and district administrators, and the Illinois courts upheld his dismissal.

Reversing the state courts, the U.S. Supreme Court first identified expression pertaining to matters of public concern as constitutionally protected and reasoned that the funding and allocation issues raised by Pickering were clearly questions of public interest requiring free and open debate. The Court then applied a balancing test, weighing the teacher's interest in expressing his views on public issues against the school board's interest in providing educational services. The Court recognized that the school board would prevail if Pickering's exercise of protected expression jeopardized his classroom performance, relationships with his immediate supervisor or coworkers, or school operations. Concluding that Pickering's letter did not have a detrimental effect in any of these areas, the Court found no justification for limiting his contribution to public debate. Indeed, the Court noted that a teacher's role provides a special vantage point from which to formulate "informed and definite opinions" on the allocation of school district funds, thus making it essential for teachers to be able to speak about public issues without fear of reprisal, unless the false statements are "knowingly or recklessly" made.[3]

Since *Pickering*, teachers have frequently challenged dismissals or other disciplinary actions on grounds that their exercise of protected expression elicited adverse employment

[1]Texas v. Johnson, 491 U.S. 397, 404 (1989). Conduct that does not possess sufficient communicative elements is not shielded by the First Amendment. *See, e.g.*, Montanye v. Wissahickon Sch. Dist., 218 F. App'x 126 (3d Cir. 2007) (finding a teacher's actions in scheduling a student's therapy sessions, transporting the student to those sessions, and attending some of the sessions did not involve intent to convey any message deserving First Amendment protection).

[2]391 U.S. 563 (1968); *see also* Givhan v. W. Line Consol. Sch. Dist., 439 U.S. 410 (1979) (concluding that so long as the expression pertains to matters of public concern, rather than personal grievances, statements made in private or through a public medium are constitutionally protected; the forum where the expression occurs does not determine whether it is of public or private interest).

[3]*Pickering*, 391 U.S. at 572, 574; *see also* Bd. of Cnty. Comm'rs v. Umbehr, 518 U.S. 668 (1996) (holding that independent contractors are considered the same as public employees in weighing the government's interests against the contractors' free speech interests under the *Pickering* balancing test).

consequences. In 1977, the Supreme Court in *Mt. Healthy City School District v. Doyle* established the principle that a public educator can be disciplined or dismissed if sufficient cause exists *independent* of the exercise of protected speech. In this case, a school board voted not to renew the contract of a nontenured teacher who had made a telephone call to a local radio station to comment on a proposed teacher grooming code. The teacher had been involved in several previous incidents, but in not renewing his contract, the board cited "lack of tact in handling professional matters" with reference only to the radio call and obscene gestures made to several female students.[4] The lower courts ruled in favor of the teacher, but the Supreme Court reversed and remanded the case. The Court held that on remand, the burden of proof is on the employee to show that the speech was constitutionally protected and was a substantial or motivating factor in the school board's adverse action. Once established, the burden then shifts to the school board to show by a preponderance of evidence that it would have reached the same decision in the absence of the teacher's exercise of protected speech. The Supreme Court reasoned that protected expression should not place a public employee in a better or worse position with regard to continued employment. On remand, the board established that there were sufficient grounds other than the radio station call to justify the teacher's nonrenewal.[5]

In a significant 1983 decision, *Connick v. Myers*, the Supreme Court's interpretation of the *Pickering* balancing test narrowed the circumstances under which public employees can prevail in free expression cases.[6] Of particular importance was the Court's conclusion that the *form* and *context* as well as the content of the expression should be considered in assessing whether it relates to matters of public concern or to personal grievances that are not protected by the First Amendment. Thus, the Court indicated that the factors applied under the *Pickering* balancing test to determine whether speech negatively affects governmental interests can be considered in the *initial* assessment of whether the expression informs public debate. If the expression is simply a personal grievance, the constitutional analysis ends.

In *Connick*, an assistant district attorney was dissatisfied with her proposed transfer and circulated to coworkers a questionnaire concerning office operations and morale, level of confidence in supervisors, and pressure to work in political campaigns. She was subsequently terminated and challenged the action as violating her First Amendment rights. Reversing the lower courts, the Supreme Court ruled that the questionnaire related primarily to a personal employment grievance rather than matters of public interest. Only one question (regarding pressure to participate in political campaigns) was found to involve a public issue. Weighing various factors—the importance of close working relationships to fulfill public responsibilities, the employee's attempt to solicit a vote of no confidence in the district attorney, distribution of the questionnaire during office hours, the district attorney's conclusion that his office operations were endangered, and the questionnaire's limited connection to a public concern—the Court concluded that the employee's dismissal did not offend the First Amendment.[7]

[4]429 U.S. 274, 282 (1977).

[5]Doyle v. Mt. Healthy City Sch. Dist., 670 F.2d 59 (6th Cir. 1982).

[6]461 U.S. 138 (1983).

[7]Courts often refer to the weighing of these factors as the "*Pickering/Connick* balancing test." *See, e.g.*, Eddy v. Corbett, 381 F. App'x 237, 238 (2010) (applying "*Pickering/Connick* balancing test" to public employee speech claim).

In 1994, the Supreme Court again addressed the scope of public employees' free speech rights in *Waters v. Churchill*.[8] Churchill, a nurse at a public hospital, was discharged for making critical comments about hospital operations to a coworker during a break. The comments were overheard by other coworkers, and although there was dispute about the exact nature of the comments, Churchill's supervisors maintained that the expression disrupted the work environment. Reversing the Seventh Circuit's decision, the Supreme Court plurality categorized Churchill's expression about the hospital's training policy and its impact on patient care as criticisms of her employer rather than comments on matters of public concern. The plurality further concluded that so long as the employer conducted an investigation and acted in good faith, it could discharge an employee for remarks it *believed* were made, regardless of what was actually said. In short, a government employer can reach its factual conclusions without being held to the evidentiary rules that courts must follow.

In 2006, the Supreme Court decided *Garcetti v. Ceballos*, adding another threshold question in assessing constitutional protection of public employees' expression and making it even more difficult for public employees to prevail in claims that their expression rights have been abridged (see Figure 1).[9] The Court established a bright-line rule that expression pursuant to official job responsibilities is not protected. Thus, whether the employee is speaking as a private citizen or as an employee is the first consideration, because if speaking as an employee, there is no further constitutional assessment.

In *Garcetti*, the Supreme Court ruled that the district attorney's office did not impair the free speech rights of Ceballos, an assistant district attorney, by allegedly retaliating against him for writing a memorandum indicating that the arresting deputy sheriff may have lied in the search warrant affidavit in a criminal case. Ceballos informed the defense counsel of his belief that the affidavit included false statements, and the defense subpoenaed Ceballos to testify at the hearing in which the warrant was unsuccessfully challenged. Ceballos alleged that he subsequently was mistreated by superiors, denied a promotion, given an undesirable transfer, and retaliated against in other ways.

The Ninth Circuit ruled in favor of Ceballos, but the Supreme Court reversed, reasoning that Ceballos was speaking about a task he was paid to perform and concluding that "when public employees make statements pursuant to their official duties, . . . the Constitution does not insulate their communications from employer discipline."[10] Whereas the Ninth Circuit placed its emphasis on whether the expression was of public or private concern, the Supreme Court majority placed its emphasis on whether the public employee was speaking as a citizen or in the context of job duties. The Court majority reiterated that the forum where the comments were made—inside the workplace—was not the central consideration, but rather the controlling factor was whether the expression occurred as part of official responsibilities.[11]

[8]511 U.S. 661 (1994); *see also* Rankin v. McPherson, 483 U.S. 378, 380 (1987) (assessing the content, form, and context of a public employee's pejorative statement to a coworker following the assassination attempt on President Reagan and finding no basis for the employee's dismissal in the absence of the expression interfering with job performance).

[9]547 U.S. 410 (2006).

[10]*Id.* at 421.

[11]*Id.* at 419–24. But the Court specifically left open whether its analysis would apply to speech related to instruction, *id.* at 425; *see infra* text accompanying note 80.

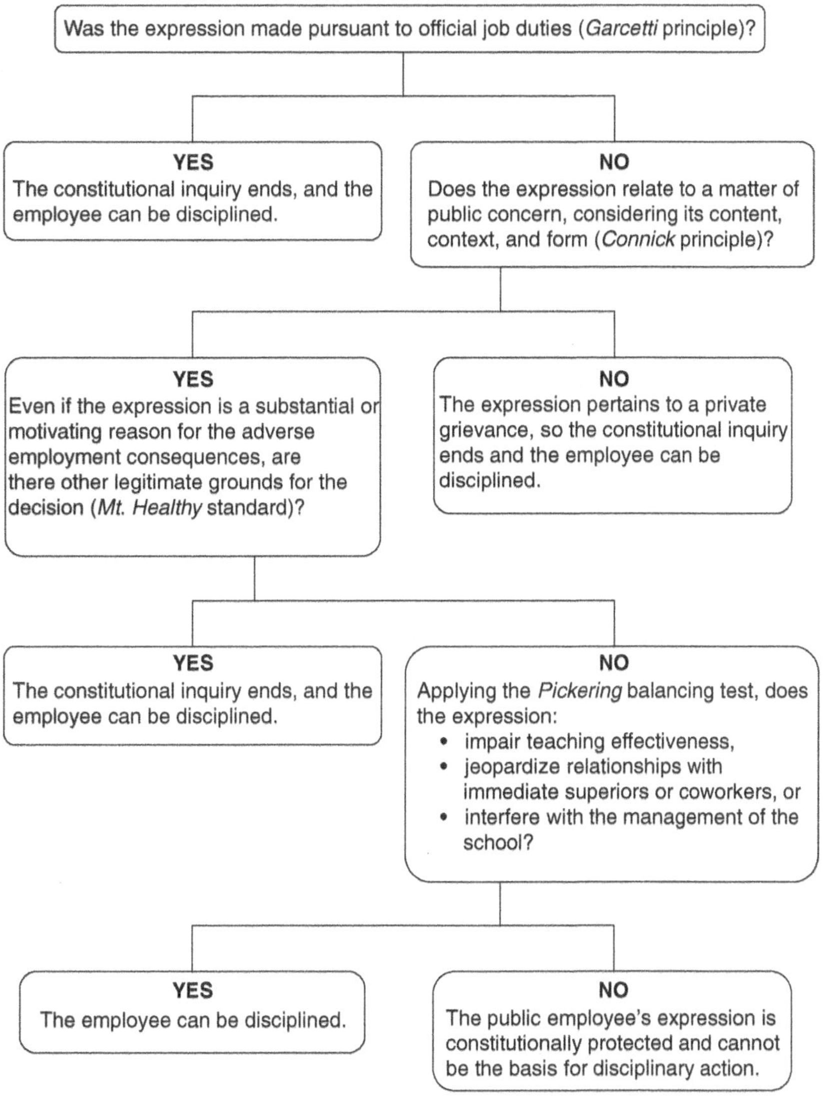

Was the expression made pursuant to official job duties (*Garcetti* principle)?

YES
The constitutional inquiry ends, and the employee can be disciplined.

NO
Does the expression relate to a matter of public concern, considering its content, context, and form (*Connick* principle)?

YES
Even if the expression is a substantial or motivating reason for the adverse employment consequences, are there other legitimate grounds for the decision (*Mt. Healthy* standard)?

NO
The expression pertains to a private grievance, so the constitutional inquiry ends and the employee can be disciplined.

YES
The constitutional inquiry ends, and the employee can be disciplined.

NO
Applying the *Pickering* balancing test, does the expression:

- impair teaching effectiveness,
- jeopardize relationships with immediate superiors or coworkers, or
- interfere with the management of the school?

YES
The employee can be disciplined.

NO
The public employee's expression is constitutionally protected and cannot be the basis for disciplinary action.

FIGURE 1 Analyzing Public Educators' Expression Rights

Application of the Legal Principles

For almost fifteen years following *Pickering*, lower courts broadly interpreted what constitutes expression relating to matters of public concern that is entitled to constitutional protection. During the 1970s and early 1980s, for example, courts relied on the *Pickering* balancing test in upholding public school teachers' rights to express their views on matters of public interest, such as wearing black arm bands as a symbolic protest against the

Vietnam War,[12] making public comments favoring a collective bargaining contract,[13] and criticizing the instructional program and other school policies.[14]

Since the early 1980s, however, courts have seemed increasingly inclined to view teachers' and other public employees' expression as relating to *private* employment disputes, rather than to matters of public concern. Many courts relied on *Connick*[15] in broadly interpreting what falls under the category of unprotected private grievances. To illustrate, courts considered the following types of expression to be unprotected: discussing salaries during a lunch break;[16] filing a grievance about being assigned a job-sharing teaching position;[17] accusing the superintendent of inciting student disturbances;[18] sending sarcastic, critical memoranda to school officials;[19] protesting unfavorable performance evaluations;[20] criticizing harassment and oppression at the high school in a faculty newsletter;[21] commenting about class size;[22] and complaining about the pace of an investigation into a school disciplinary matter.[23]

Some courts, however, applied the public/private distinction and found specific expression to pertain to matters of public concern and warrant constitutional protection.[24] Prior to the Supreme Court's 2006 *Garcetti* decision,[25] courts often afforded First Amendment protection to public educators who blew the whistle on unlawful or unethical school practices, even though such expression pertained to their job responsibilities. For example, federal appellate courts considered the following to be protected expression: a former assistant principal's complaints about a suspected cheating scheme involving student achievement tests;[26] a special education teacher's assertions that the adapted physical education program violated federal law;[27] and a school

[12]*See, e.g.*, James v. Bd. of Educ., 461 F.2d 566 (2d Cir. 1972).

[13]*See, e.g.*, McGill v. Bd. of Educ., 602 F.2d 774 (7th Cir. 1979).

[14]*See, e.g.*, Lemons v. Morgan, 629 F.2d 1389 (8th Cir. 1980); Bernasconi v. Tempe Elementary Sch. Dist. No. 3, 548 F.2d 857 (9th Cir. 1977).

[15]461 U.S. 138 (1983).

[16]Koehn v. Indian Hills Cmty. Coll., 371 F.3d 394 (8th Cir. 2004); *see also* Bouma v. Trent, No. 10-0267, 2010 U.S. Dist. LEXIS 37565 (D. Ariz. Apr. 14, 2010) (finding that a complaint about a salary schedule was not a matter of public concern).

[17]Renfroe v. Kirkpatrick, 722 F.2d 714 (11th Cir. 1984).

[18]Stevenson v. Lower Marion Cnty. Sch. Dist. No. 3, 327 S.E.2d 656 (S.C. 1985).

[19]Hesse v. Bd. of Educ., 848 F.2d 748 (7th Cir. 1988); *see also* Mitchell v. Hillsborough Cnty., 468 F.3d 1276 (11th Cir. 2006) (finding that a public employee's vulgar and tasteless comments about a female commissioner did not pertain to a public concern and could be the basis for dismissal).

[20]Day v. S. Park Indep. Sch. Dist., 768 F.2d 696 (5th Cir. 1985).

[21]Sanguigni v. Pittsburgh Bd. of Educ., 968 F.2d 393 (3d Cir. 1992).

[22]Cliff v. Bd. of Sch. Comm'rs of the City of Indianapolis, 42 F.3d 403 (7th Cir. 1995).

[23]Lucero v. Nettle Creek Sch. Corp., 566 F.3d 720 (7th Cir. 2009).

[24]The Sixth Circuit declared that "the key question is not whether a person is speaking in his role as an employee or a citizen, but whether the employee's speech in fact touches on matters of public concern." Cockrel v. Shelby Cnty. Sch. Dist., 270 F.3d 1036, 1052 (6th Cir. 2001) (citing Connick v. Myers, 461 U.S. 138, 148–49 (1983)); *see infra* text accompanying note 72; *see also* Nagle v. Marron, 663 F.3d 100 (2d Cir. 2011) (determining that teacher's complaint about abuse of students was protected under the First Amendment).

[25]547 U.S. 410 (2006); *see infra* text accompanying note 37.

[26]Canary v. Osborn, 211 F.3d 324 (6th Cir. 2000); *see also* Taylor v. Chief of Police, 338 F.3d 639 (6th Cir. 2003) (finding officers' report written in the course of their employment to be protected speech because it was intended to communicate potential wrongdoing of a fellow officer, which was a matter of public concern).

[27]Settlegoode v. Portland Pub. Schs., 371 F.3d 503 (9th Cir. 2004) (denying defendants' request for qualified immunity, entitling the teacher to the full jury award, including punitive damages, assessed against the school administrators for the violation of her constitutional rights).

nurse's criticisms of immunization practices, the heavy nursing caseload, and student safety.[28] These cases might have been decided differently if they had been rendered after *Garcetti.*

Specifically, *Garcetti* calls into question the public/private distinction as the guiding consideration and has added another initial consideration in deciding whether a public employee's expression will evoke the *Pickering* balancing test (see Figure 1). If the expression is made pursuant to official job responsibilities, it is not protected, and it is thus unnecessary to establish that the expression pertains to a private grievance or has a negative impact on agency operations. The content of the expression appeared to be the crucial consideration prior to the *Garcetti* ruling, but the role of the speaker now seems to trump the content.[29] The broad protection once given to public educators' expression under *Pickering* now is available only if the expression (1) does not occur pursuant to official duties, (2) relates to a public concern (considering its context and form as well as its content), and (3) is the motivating factor in the adverse employment action. *Pickering* has not been overturned, but far fewer circumstances trigger its balancing test.

In post-*Garcetti* decisions rejecting First Amendment claims, courts have tended to focus on whether the expression was made pursuant to job responsibilities. Whistleblowers have not been as successful in securing legal redress for retaliation as they were prior to *Garcetti.* For example, the Fifth Circuit held that an athletic director who wrote a letter to the school's office manager about appropriations for athletic activities was speaking pursuant to his official duties and could not claim retaliation for being removed from the athletic director position and for his contract not being renewed.[30] The Eleventh Circuit similarly found that a teacher's questions about the fairness of cheerleading tryouts pertained to her duties as a cheerleading sponsor and were not protected expression relating to educational quality issues, as she claimed.[31] The Tenth Circuit also ruled that a superintendent's comments about the Head Start program and possible violations of federal law were not protected as they were made in the course of her job duties.[32] A Delaware federal district court ruled that a school psychologist's complaints about the school's noncompliance with the Individuals with Disabilities Education Act

[28]Stever v. Indep. Sch. Dist. No. 625, 943 F.2d 845 (8th Cir. 1991); *see also* McGreevy v. Stroup, 413 F.3d 359 (3d Cir. 2005) (finding that a school nurse's low ratings were in retaliation for speaking out on behalf of two students with disabilities and objecting to pesticide spraying by an unlicensed person).

[29]Even prior to *Garcetti,* courts recognized that public employees in policy-making roles relinquished some free speech rights because of the impact of their expression on agency operations. *See, e.g.,* Sharp v. Lindsey, 285 F.3d 479 (6th Cir. 2002) (finding that a tension-free superintendent/principal relationship justified reassigning a principal to a teaching role after a public disagreement regarding the district's new dress code); Vargas-Harrison v. Racine Unified Sch. Dist., 272 F.3d 964 (7th Cir. 2001) (upholding demotion of a principal, who occupied a policy-making role, for expression critical of superiors' policies).

[30]Williams v. Dallas Indep. Sch. Dist., 480 F.3d 689 (5th Cir. 2007).

[31]Gilder-Lucas v. Elmore Cnty. Bd. of Educ., 186 F. App'x 885 (11th Cir. 2006); *see also* Cole v. Anne Arundel Cnty. Bd. of Educ., No. CCB-05-1579, 2006 U.S. Dist. LEXIS 89426 (D. Md. Nov. 30, 2006) (holding that a school bus driver who complained about bus safety was speaking pursuant to her official duties and could not claim retaliation for the expression).

[32]Casey v. W. Las Vegas Indep. Sch. Dist., 473 F.3d 1323 (10th Cir. 2007) (holding, however, that her comments about the New Mexico Open Meetings Act were outside the scope of her job, so her claim of retaliation for those comments may be legally viable).

pertained to his job assignment and were not protected by the First Amendment.[33] An office assistant's complaints to a supervisor about another school official who had encouraged her to misappropriate federal funds were not protected by the First Amendment. The federal district court found that she was speaking pursuant to her official job duties.[34]

Even where whistle-blowing is not at issue, public school personnel often have not prevailed in their free speech claims because courts have concluded that the expression at issue was pursuant to official job duties. To illustrate, the Eleventh Circuit rejected a terminated principal's claim that a Florida school board violated his First Amendment speech and association rights and his right to petition the government for redress of grievances.[35] He claimed that he was unconstitutionally terminated in retaliation for urging his teachers to support conversion of their school to a charter school. Noting that *Garcetti* shifted the threshold question from whether the employee is speaking on a matter of public concern to whether the employee is speaking as a private citizen, the Eleventh Circuit concluded that the principal was speaking in his professional role in seeking charter school status. Thus, his expression was not protected and could be the basis for dismissal. The court further found no evidence that the school board violated the principal's rights to association or to petition the government.

Likewise, the Sixth Circuit affirmed summary judgment in favor of the school district in a case involving a teacher who complained to her supervisors that her special education caseload violated the law. The court found that this complaint was not protected because the speech was made pursuant to her official job duties as a teacher.[36] The Second Circuit found that a teacher's complaint about an assistant principal forging her signature on a teaching evaluation form was not protected because the issue had no "practical significance to the general public."[37] In another Second Circuit case, a teacher's filing of a union grievance, after a school administrator failed to discipline a student who threw books at the teacher during class, was not protected speech because it was related to the teacher's "core duties" of "maintaining class discipline."[38]

Some employees, however, have succeeded in their expression claims in post-*Garcetti* cases. For example, the Sixth Circuit ruled in favor of a superintendent who claimed that he was not named Director of Schools when the superintendent position was abolished because he had expressed his view that associating with homosexuals is not immoral or improper, which the court considered a matter of public concern. The court reasoned that board members were not entitled to qualified immunity because the

[33]Houlihan v. Sussex Tech. Sch. Dist., 461 F. Supp. 2d 252 (D. Del. 2006) (holding, however, that the school psychologist stated a valid cause of action for retaliation under the federal Rehabilitation Act, so the school district's motion to dismiss her claim under this law was denied); *see also* Pagani v. Meriden Bd. of Educ., No. 3:05-CV-01115 (JCH), 2006 U.S. Dist. LEXIS 92267 (D. Conn. Dec. 19, 2006) (finding a teacher's report to the Department of Children and Families that a substitute teacher showed nude photos of himself with female students was made under the auspices of official responsibilities; the teacher could not claim retaliation for making the report after superiors advised him not to contact the agency).

[34]Williams v. Bd. of Educ., No. 07-cv-98c, 2012 U.S. Dist. LEXIS 36936 (W.D.N.Y. May 15, 2012).

[35]D'Angelo v. Sch. Bd., 497 F.3d 1203 (11th Cir. 2007).

[36]Fox v. Traverse City Area Pub. Schs., 605 F.3d 345 (6th Cir. 2010), *cert. denied*, 131 S. Ct. 643 (2010).

[37]Nagle v. Marron, 663 F.3d 100, 107 (2d Cir. 2011) (holding, however, that the teacher's complaints about the abuse of students was speech that pertained to a matter of public concern and was protected).

[38]Weintraub v. Bd. of Educ., 593 F.3d 196, 198 (2d Cir. 2010), *cert. denied*, 131 S. Ct. 444 (2010).

superintendent's expression rights were clearly established.[39] A North Carolina federal district court also found a principal's expressed concerns that a new school district policy would hurt overall student test scores of her elementary school to be a public issue, which could not be the basis for offering her a two-year instead of the promised four-year contract.[40] But the court noted that the record was not sufficiently developed regarding whether the expression was made pursuant to her official duties. The Tenth Circuit ruled in favor of a speech-language pathologist who alleged First Amendment retaliation when adverse action was taken against her for advocating for students with disabilities in the school. Reversing the district court's decision, the appellate court did not find that her advocacy was made pursuant to her official duties; her complaints went beyond her administrators and were made to the state board, which was not done pursuant to her official job duties.[41] The Tenth Circuit identified two factors to help determine if the employee is speaking as a private citizen, as opposed to speaking pursuant to an official job duty: (1) the employee's job duties do not relate to the reporting of any wrongdoing, and (2) the employee went outside the chain of command. The court found that the speech pathologist's complaint satisfied both factors.

Even if protected speech is involved, courts have relied on *Mt. Healthy* to uphold terminations or transfers where other legitimate reasons justify the personnel actions. In an illustrative case, a principal who gave a speech at a public hearing expressing opposition to closing a school was demoted to a teaching position. He claimed retaliation for his protected expression, but a Kentucky federal court found no evidence that the speech was the motivating factor in the demotion.[42] The Seventh Circuit also rejected a teacher's challenge to disciplinary action for her critical comments pertaining to the need for additional textbooks at her school. The court ruled that the teacher failed to prove that her speech was a substantial or motivating factor in the disciplinary action, given the well-documented incidents of the teacher's misconduct or insubordination.[43] The Tenth Circuit similarly found that a director of bilingual education could not establish that speaking about the program's noncompliance with state guidelines and writing a letter to the editor of the local newspaper were the motivating factors in her termination and held instead that poor job performance justified the action.[44]

School authorities cannot rely on *Mt. Healthy* to justify termination or other disciplinary action if the school officials' stated reasons for personnel decisions are merely a pretext to restrict protected expression. For example, a federal district court denied a

[39]Scarbrough v. Morgan Cnty. Bd. of Educ., 470 F.3d 250 (6th Cir. 2006); *see also* Posey v. Lake Pend Oreille Sch. Dist. No. 84, 546 F.3d 1121 (9th Cir. 2008) (reversing lower court's grant of summary judgment in favor of the school district because issues of fact remained about whether a school district parking lot attendant's complaints about safety issues were related to his job duties).

[40]Locklear v. Person Cnty. of Educ., No. 1:05CV00255, 2006 U.S. Dist. LEXIS 42203 (M.D.N.C. June 22, 2006).

[41]Reinhardt v. Albuquerque Pub. Schs., 595 F.3d 1126 (10th Cir. 2010).

[42]Painter v. Campbell Cnty. Bd. of Educ., 417 F. Supp. 2d 854 (E.D. Ky. 2006); *see also* Phelps v. Fullenwider, 126 F. App'x 381 (9th Cir. 2005) (rejecting claim that protected speech was the motivating reason for a school employee's dismissal; finding that parental complaints of inappropriate behavior with students justified the personnel decision).

[43]Smith v. Dunn, 368 F.3d 705 (7th Cir. 2004); *see also* Love v. Chi. Bd. of Educ., 241 F.3d 564 (7th Cir. 2001) (finding teachers' dismissal was based on poor performance rather than criticism of a specific academic program and of the principal's interactions with teachers).

[44]Deschenie v. Bd. of Educ., 473 F.3d 1271 (10th Cir. 2007) (holding that the time between the expression and termination was too attenuated to show a causal connection).

school district's motion for summary judgment because an administrator, who was allegedly fired for not complying with the district's school improvement plan, may have actually been fired in retaliation for complaining to the superintendent that many of the elementary school classrooms were racially segregated.[45]

Once determined that expression is protected, the employee then has the burden of demonstrating that it was a key factor in the dismissal or disciplinary decision. Even if the employee can establish that expression on matters of public concern was the sole basis for the adverse action, the public employer still may prevail under the *Pickering* balancing test by showing that its interests in protecting the public agency outweigh the individual's free speech rights.[46]

Prior Restraint and Channel Rules

Although *reprisals* for expression have been the focus of most litigation, courts also have addressed *prior restraints* on public employees' expression and restrictions on the channels through which views may be aired. The judiciary has been more reluctant to condone such prior restraints on expression, which chill "potential speech before it happens,"[47] than it has to uphold disciplinary action after the expression has occurred. A central consideration is whether the prior restraint is content based, triggering strict judicial scrutiny, or whether it is content neutral, thus receiving a "less rigorous examination."[48]

For example, the Tenth Circuit struck down a portion of an Oklahoma law authorizing the termination of teachers for "advocating . . . public or private homosexual activity in a manner that creates a substantial risk that such conduct will come to the attention of school children or school employees."[49] The appellate court held that such restrictions on teachers' expression could not be imposed unless shown to be necessary to prevent a disruption of school activities. The Supreme Court divided evenly in this case, thereby affirming the appellate court's ruling without setting a national precedent. In another Tenth Circuit case, a group of teachers alleged prior restraints on speech when their principal prohibited them from meeting together to discuss school-related issues and then retaliated against them when they met. The Tenth Circuit found that the teachers had standing to challenge the principal because their speech and association were chilled by the fear of the principal's directives.[50]

Whether the school has created a forum for expression is important in controversies pertaining to the use of internal communication channels. In a significant 1983 decision, *Perry Education Association v. Perry Local Educators' Association*, the Supreme Court ruled that a school district is not constitutionally obligated to allow a rival teachers' union

[45]Howell v. Marion Sch. Dist. 1, No. 4:07:cv-1811, 2009 U.S. Dist. LEXIS 22723 (D.S.C. Mar. 19, 2009).

[46]*See* Fales v. Garst, 235 F.3d 1122 (8th Cir. 2001) (finding teachers' interests in speaking about incidents with special education students was outweighed by school district's interest in efficiently administering the middle school, given the upheaval caused by the expression); Mataraza v. Newburgh Enlarged City Sch. Dist., 294 F. Supp. 2d 483 (S.D.N.Y. 2003) (applying the *Pickering* balancing test and upholding denial of promotion to an assistant principal whose criticisms of the district's curriculum alignment efforts would disrupt implementation of the initiative).

[47]Arndt v. Koby, 309 F.3d 1247, 1251 (10th Cir. 2002).

[48]Eclipse Enter. v. Gulotta, 134 F.3d 63, 66 (2d Cir. 1997).

[49]Nat'l Gay Task Force v. Bd. of Educ., 729 F.2d 1270, 1274 (10th Cir. 1984), *aff'd by an equally divided Court*, 470 U.S. 903 (1985).

[50]Brammer-Hoelfer v. Twin Peaks Charter Acad., 602 F.3d 1175 (10th Cir. 2010).

access to school mailboxes although the exclusive bargaining agent is granted such access. Holding that a public school's internal mail system is not a public forum for expression, the Court declared that "the state may reserve the forum for its intended purposes, communicative or otherwise, as long as the regulation on speech is reasonable and not an effort to suppress expression merely because public officials oppose the speaker's view."[51] The Court determined that alternative communication channels were available to the rival union.

Subsequently, the Supreme Court affirmed the Fifth Circuit's conclusion that a Texas school district had not created a public forum in either its schools or school mail facilities; therefore, the district could deny school access during school hours to representatives of teachers' organizations and could bar their use of the school mail system.[52] However, the Fifth Circuit found a First Amendment violation in school policies that denied teachers the right to discuss employee organizations during nonclass time or to use school mail facilities for communications including *any* mention of such organizations.

In a later case, the same court reiterated that a state university's internal mail system is not a public forum and thus declined to interfere with an institution's decision to use e-mail spam guards and to cancel e-mail accounts of adjuncts during semesters they are not teaching.[53] In addition, the Fourth Circuit upheld restrictions on state employees' use of computers owned or leased by the state to access to sexually explicit materials over the Internet.[54] Also, the Seventh Circuit concluded that a part-time university employee could be required to remove a quotation she affixed to work-related e-mail messages, because the employer considered a word in the quotation to be vulgar. The court found a minimal burden on the employee's expression rights and an overriding interest in restricting inappropriate language in the workplace.[55]

Under certain circumstances, a school's mail system might be considered a public forum if school officials have designated it as such. Applying the principle articulated in *Perry*, the Fifth Circuit reasoned that a school was not obligated to open its internal mail system to the general public, but since the school had designated its mail system as a forum for all employee organizations, it could not selectively deny access to some groups.[56] The court also found the school district's guidelines, requiring prior clearance of material distributed through the mail system, to be unconstitutionally vague.

[51]460 U.S. 37, 46 (1983).

[52]Tex. State Teachers Ass'n v. Garland Indep. Sch. Dist., 777 F.2d 1046 (5th Cir. 1985), *aff'd mem.*, 479 U.S. 801 (1986) (holding that the school's selective visitation policy, under which certain groups of educators and representatives of textbook companies and civic and charitable groups were allowed to meet with teachers during school hours, did not create a public forum). *See also* Fla. Family Ass'n v. Sch. Bd., 494 F. Supp. 2d 1311 (M.D. Fla. 2007) (holding that the school board did not deprive family organization of its First Amendment rights by blocking its mass e-mail campaign criticizing the board's removal of religious holidays from the school calendar).

[53]Faculty Rights Coal. v. Shahrokhi, 204 F. App'x 416 (5th Cir. 2006); *see also* Educ. Minn. Lakeville v. Indep. Sch. Dist. No. 194, 341 F. Supp. 2d 1070 (D. Minn. 2004) (rejecting unions' argument that the school district's policy prohibiting the use of internal communication channels to distribute literature endorsing political candidates violated the First Amendment).

[54]Urofsky v. Gilmore, 216 F.3d 401 (4th Cir. 2000); *see also* Herbert v. Wash. St. Pub. Disclosure Comm'n, 148 P.3d 1102 (Wash. Ct. App. 2006) (finding that teachers violated state law by using school mail and e-mail, nonpublic forums, to collect signatures on petitions for ballot measures).

[55]Pichelmann v. Madsen, 31 F. App'x 322 (7th Cir. 2002).

[56]Ysleta Fed'n of Teachers v. Ysleta Indep. Sch. Dist., 720 F.2d 1429 (5th Cir. 1983) (holding further that the school board had not yet produced evidence of a compelling interest for limiting employee organizations to one distribution of recruitment literature per year through the school mail system).

Policies limiting teachers' access to the school board also have generated legal disputes, and several courts have struck down policies prohibiting individual teachers from communicating directly with the board. In 1976, the Supreme Court held that a nonunion teacher has a free speech right to comment on a bargaining issue at a public school board meeting.[57] Subsequently, the Ninth Circuit awarded a teacher-coach damages for his suspension as a coach, which occurred because he did not advise the superintendent before writing a letter to school board members about an issue of public concern.[58] Similarly, the Seventh Circuit struck down a policy requiring that all communication to the school board be directed through the superintendent and ordered a reprimand for violating the policy to be removed from a teacher's personnel file.[59]

Although prior restraints on teachers' free speech rights are vulnerable to legal attack, courts have upheld reasonable time, place, and manner regulations. Such restrictions must not be based on the content of the speech, and they must serve significant governmental interests and leave alternative communication channels open.[60] In general, time, place, and manner restrictions will be upheld if justified to prevent a disruption of the educational environment and if other avenues are available for employees to express their views.

Internet Speech

Educators' speech on social networking sites has been the subject of litigation as well. In some of these cases, courts have relied on *Garcetti* if the teacher wrote something on the Internet that was pursuant to his or her job responsibilities. For speech outside the scope of one's job duties, *Pickering* and *Connick* have also been used. For example, when a teacher made disparaging and unsubstantiated remarks about coworkers on his website, the West Virginia Supreme Court held that the teacher had no First Amendment right at stake because his statements both on and off the website would not be considered matters of public concern. The court further noted that the teacher's comments could have destroyed feelings of loyalty and confidence among his colleagues.[61]

The Ninth Circuit Court of Appeals also found that a curriculum specialist's postings on her personal blog, which included inappropriate comments about colleagues, were not protected speech. The court observed that although some of the comments on her blog may have related to a matter of public concern, the comments interfered with her relationships at school.[62] In another case, a teacher alleged that school officials violated his First Amendment rights when his contract was not renewed as a result of comments he had posted on his MySpace page. Holding in favor of the school district, the federal district court found no First Amendment violation because there was no connection between the teacher's postings and his dismissal. The court reasoned that even if there had

[57]City of Madison, Joint Sch. Dist. No. 8 v. Wis. Emp't Relations Comm'n, 429 U.S. 167 (1976).

[58]Anderson v. Cent. Point Sch. Dist. No. 6, 746 F.2d 505 (9th Cir. 1984).

[59]Knapp v. Whitaker, 757 F.2d 827 (7th Cir. 1985), *appeal dismissed*, 474 U.S. 803 (1985).

[60]*See, e.g.*, Godwin v. E. Baton Rouge Parish Sch. Bd., 408 So. 2d 1214 (La. 1981), *appeal dismissed*, 459 U.S. 807 (1982) (finding a ban on handheld signs in the school board offices to serve the legitimate governmental interest of ensuring that school board meetings were conducted in an orderly fashion); *see also* Partee v. Metro. Sch. Dist., 954 F.2d 454 (7th Cir. 1992).

[61]Alderman v. Pocahontas Cnty. Bd. of Educ., 675 S.E.2d 907 (W.Va. 2009).

[62]Richerson v. Beckon, 337 F. App'x 637 (9th Cir. 2009).

been such a connection, the school district could have taken the same adverse actions because the teacher's speech was likely to disrupt school activities.[63]

Student teachers should also be cautious when using social networking sites. In a Pennsylvania case, a federal district court denied a student teacher injunctive relief in a case involving postings on her MySpace page. The student teacher was not awarded teacher certification after she received unsatisfactory ratings during student teaching as a result of her unprofessionalism involving her MySpace page that her students had viewed. The court determined that her postings related to only personal matters and did not touch upon matters of public concern.[64]

Problems with teachers posting inappropriate commentary on their Facebook pages has led some states to consider laws to regulate employees' Internet speech. Of course, such laws have created a backlash with employees arguing that the laws abridge First Amendment rights. Missouri had passed a law prohibiting teachers and students from being friends on Facebook, but the law was later repealed as a result of First Amendment concerns.[65]

Expressing Personal Views in the Classroom

Traditionally, it has been assumed that restrictions can be placed on teachers expressing their personal views in the classroom. Because of the captive student audience, teachers cannot use their classrooms—nonpublic forums—to proselytize children. Since 1988, many courts have applied *Hazelwood v. Kuhlmeier* to assess the constitutionality of teachers' classroom expression of personal opinions,[66] holding that such expression could be curtailed for legitimate pedagogical reasons, an easy standard for school districts to satisfy. For example, the First Circuit held that a teacher's discussion of aborting fetuses with Down syndrome could be censored, noting that the school board may limit a teacher's classroom expression in the interest of promoting educational goals.[67] The Tenth Circuit relied on *Kuhlmeier* in upholding disciplinary action against a teacher who made comments during class about rumors that two students had engaged in sexual intercourse on the school tennis court during lunch hour, reasoning that the ninth-grade government class was not a public forum.[68] Also, a Missouri federal district court upheld termination of a teacher for making disparaging classroom comments about interracial relationships, finding no protected expression and noting that the teacher was aware of the district's anti-harassment policy.[69]

[63]Spanierman v. Hughes, 576 F. Supp. 2d 292 (D. Conn. 2008).

[64]Snyder v. Millersville Univ., No. 07-1660, 2008 U.S. Dist. LEXIS 97943 (E.D. Pa. Dec. 3, 2008).

[65]David A. Lieb, *Missouri Repeals Law Restricting Teacher-Student Internet and Facebook Interaction*, HUFFINGTON POST (Oct. 21, 2011), http://www.huffingtonpost.com/2011/10/21/missouri-repeals-law-rest_n_1025761.html.

[66]484 U.S. 260 (1988).

[67]Ward v. Hickey, 996 F.2d 448 (1st Cir. 1993).

[68]Miles v. Denver Pub. Schs., 944 F.2d 773 (10th Cir. 1991); *see also* Abeyta v. Chama Valley Indep. Sch. Dist. No. 19, 77 F.3d 1253 (10th Cir. 1996) (recognizing that while a teacher calling a student a prostitute in class would be an abuse of authority under state law, such action would not give rise to a federal claim for damages for violating substantive due process rights).

[69]Loeffelman v. Bd. of Educ., 134 S.W.3d 637 (Mo. Ct. App. 2004). *But see* Scruggs v. Keen, 900 F. Supp. 821 (W.D. Va. 1995) (holding that a teacher's comments on interracial dating made in response to students' questions during study hall pertained to a public concern; the school district's request for summary judgment was denied because of questions regarding whether the teacher's contract was not renewed to sweep the incident under the rug or if it was based on evidence that her comments included racial slurs).

In several cases, public school teachers have not prevailed in their efforts to express their views via materials posted in their classrooms or on the adjacent hall walls. To illustrate, the decision of school authorities was upheld in censoring material a teacher had posted outside his classroom that denounced homosexuality and extolled traditional family values to offset the school district's materials recognizing Gay and Lesbian Awareness Month.[70] Reasoning that the teacher was speaking for the school, the Ninth Circuit concluded that teachers are not entitled to express views in the classroom that are counter to the adopted curriculum. The Ninth Circuit held also that a math teacher had no First Amendment right to display religious banners in his classroom.[71] The court observed that a public school math teacher may not present his personal views of the role of God in class.

The Sixth Circuit seemed to depart from the prevailing trend when it upheld a teacher's right to invite a guest speaker (actor Woody Harrelson) and present information to her fifth-grade class on the industrial and environmental benefits of hemp. Even though the teacher was speaking as an employee, the court concluded that the content of her speech involved political and social concerns in the community.[72] Thus, the court found genuine issues of material fact regarding whether the school district's proffered grounds for terminating the teacher based on insubordination, conduct unbecoming a teacher, and other grounds were a pretext for the dismissal based on protected expression. The court recognized that the school district's interest in efficient and harmonious school operations did not outweigh the teacher's interests in speaking to her students about an issue of substantial concern in the state.

It is unclear how the *Garcetti* ruling will affect litigation pertaining to classroom expression. Indeed, the *Garcetti* majority emphasized that "we need not, and for that reason do not, decide whether the analysis we conduct today would apply in the same manner to a case involving speech related to scholarship or teaching."[73] Thus, some ambiguity remains regarding whether courts will continue to apply *Hazelwood* or will rely on *Garcetti* in assessing teachers' expression pursuant to their instructional duties.[74]

Some federal appellate courts have relied on *Garcetti* in this regard. The Seventh Circuit ruled that classroom expression clearly is part of public educators' official duties and can be censored to protect the captive student audience.[75] Accordingly, the court

[70]Downs v. L.A. Unified Sch. Dist., 228 F.3d 1003 (9th Cir. 2000); *see also* Newton v. Slye, 116 F. Supp. 2d 677 (W.D. Va. 2000) (finding no First Amendment right for a teacher to post outside his classroom door the American Library Association's pamphlet listing banned books, which the principal and superintendent felt potentially compromised the school's family life education program and other initiatives).

[71]Johnson v. Poway Unified Sch. Dist., 658 F.3d 954 (9th Cir. 2011), *cert. denied*, 132 S. Ct. 1807 (2012); *see also* Lee v. York Cnty. Sch. Div., 484 F.3d 687 (4th Cir. 2007) (finding a school district did not violate a teacher's rights when it ordered him to remove religious material from classroom bulletin board).

[72]Cockrel v. Shelby Cnty. Sch. Dist., 270 F.3d 1036 (6th Cir. 2001). *But see* Debro v. San Leandro Unified Sch. Dist., No. C-99-0676 VRW, 2001 U.S. Dist. LEXIS 17388 (N.D. Cal. Oct. 11, 2001) (holding that a teacher had no First Amendment right to depart from classroom instruction to discuss tolerance toward homosexuals, even though it is an issue of public interest).

[73]Garcetti v. Ceballos, 547 U.S. 410, 425 (2006).

[74]*See, e.g.*, Sheldon v. Dhillon, No. C-08-03438, 2009 U.S. Dist. LEXIS 110275, at *14 (N.D. Cal. Nov. 25, 2009) (applying *Hazelwood*, the court noted that the Ninth Circuit has not yet determined if *Garcetti* applies to classroom speech). *But see* Evans-Marshall v. Bd. of Educ., 624 F.3d 332 (6th Cir. 2010), *cert. denied*, 131 S. Ct. 3068 (2011) (finding that *Garcetti* does extend to teacher's classroom speech).

[75]Mayer v. Monroe Cnty. Cmty. Sch. Corp., 474 F.3d 477 (7th Cir. 2007).

ruled that the teacher's expression of negative views about the war in Iraq during a current events session was not constitutionally protected. The court reasoned that *Garcetti* directly applied in this case because the teacher's current event lesson was an assigned classroom task.

Also, a few lower courts have addressed classroom expression issues. For example, a teacher in Michigan alleged that he was retaliated against after he wore a T-shirt to school that contained a printed message about the teachers' union not being under contract. The federal district court held that the T-shirt worn in his classes caused or had the potential to cause disharmony in the workplace. Although recognizing that the issue of labor negotiations touches on a matter of public concern, the court found the school district's interest in ensuring a professional workplace outweighed the teacher's rights in this instance. The court noted that under *Garcetti*, "government employers, like private employers, need a significant degree of control over their employees' words and actions; without it, there would be little chance for the efficient provision of public services."[76]

In a New York case, a teacher claimed that she was forced to resign after she refused to take down a picture of George Bush. The teacher displayed the picture during an election year and discussed her support for the incumbent. The school district argued that it had no knowledge of the teacher's political activities and requested that she either remove the picture or display one of John Kerry to appear balanced. The federal district court denied the district's summary judgment motion because issues of fact existed including the applicability of *Garcetti* in this instance.[77] Whether courts apply *Garcetti* or *Hazelwood* may have little practical significance, because teachers' classroom expression has always been subject to restrictions to protect students from proselytization.

ACADEMIC FREEDOM

The concept of academic freedom historically was applied to postsecondary education and embodied the principle that faculty members should be free from governmental controls in conducting research and imparting knowledge to students. University faculty members have further claimed a First Amendment right to academic freedom applies to activities away from the classroom as well.

Public school teachers have asserted a similar right to academic freedom, but courts have not extended the broad protections found in higher education to public elementary and secondary schools.[78] Teachers possess judicially recognized academic interests, but courts have refrained from establishing precise legal principles in this domain. Rather, controversies have been resolved on a case-by-case basis, involving a delicate balancing of teachers' interests in academic freedom against school boards' interests in assuring an appropriate instructional program and efficient school operations.

This section concentrates specifically on public educators' rights to academic freedom within the classroom setting. Can a teacher determine the most appropriate materials

[76]Montle v. Westwood Heights Sch. Dist., 437 F. Supp. 2d 652, 654 (E.D. Mich. 2006).

[77]Caruso v. Massapequa Union Free Sch. Dist., 478 F. Supp. 2d 377 (E.D.N.Y. 2007).

[78]Although generally agreed that professors in higher education have more academic freedom than public school teachers, limits can be placed on classroom activities in postsecondary institutions. *See, e.g.*, Nichols v. Univ. S. Miss., 669 F. Supp. 2d 684 (S.D. Miss. 2009) (determining nonrenewal of interim professor's contract was appropriate after he made derogatory comments about homosexuality to a gay student).

for classroom use? Is a teacher free to determine teaching methodologies? What topics or issues can a teacher discuss in a course?

Course Content

Public school teachers in elementary and secondary schools have never possessed the legal authority to determine the content of the instructional program. State legislatures have plenary power to set the public school curriculum, and they usually grant local school boards considerable authority to establish programs of study and prescribe course content, including the scope and sequence of materials. Several courts have declared that school boards are not legally obligated to accept teachers' curricular recommendations in the absence of a board policy to that effect. In an early case, the Tenth Circuit recognized the school board's authority to determine the curriculum and rejected the notion that teachers "have an unlimited liberty as to structure and content of the courses."[79] Subsequently, the Fifth Circuit recognized that teachers cannot assert a First Amendment right to substitute their own supplemental reading list for the officially adopted list without securing administrative approval.[80]

The Fourth Circuit held that a high school teacher did not have complete discretion to select the plays performed by her students at state competitions.[81] Because of parental complaints, the principal ordered certain material to be deleted from a play pertaining to a dysfunctional, single-parent family. Finding production of the play to be part of the curriculum, the court recognized that school officials have legitimate pedagogical interests in regulating the content of the curriculum. Also, a federal district court upheld a school district's decision to not renew a probationary teacher's contract after she used an icebreaker exercise in connection with a human reproduction lesson where she asked the students to sketch the male reproductive system. The court held that this exercise was unnecessary and that the teacher could have explained the reproductive system in a more appropriate way.[82]

Teachers are not permitted to ignore or omit prescribed course content under the guise of academic freedom. To illustrate, the Seventh Circuit upheld a school board's dismissal of a kindergarten teacher who refused to teach patriotic topics for religious reasons.[83] Similarly, other courts have upheld school board requirements for conformity in content and pedagogy. The Third Circuit held that a teacher could not assert a First Amendment right to disregard school board instructions and continue using a classroom management technique, Learnball, which gave students responsibility for establishing class rules and grading procedures.[84] The Colorado Supreme Court also upheld a policy requiring administrative review of "controversial learning resources," noting the district's

[79]Adams v. Campbell Cnty. Sch. Dist., 511 F.2d 1242, 1247 (10th Cir. 1975).

[80]Kirkland v. Northside Indep. Sch. Dist., 890 F.2d 794 (5th Cir. 1989).

[81]Boring v. Buncombe Cnty. Bd. of Educ., 136 F.3d 364 (4th Cir. 1998) (rejecting the teacher's challenge to her transfer based on personal conflicts precipitated by her failure to follow the school system's policy regarding controversial materials).

[82]Kirby v. Yonkers Sch. Dist., 767 F. Supp. 2d 452 (S.D.N.Y. 2011).

[83]Palmer v. Bd. of Educ., 603 F.2d 1271 (7th Cir. 1979).

[84]Murray v. Pittsburgh Bd. of Educ., 919 F. Supp. 838 (W.D. Pa. 1996), *aff'd mem.*, 141 F.3d 1154 (3d Cir. 1998).

legitimate pedagogical interest in shaping its secondary school curriculum.[85] Likewise recognizing that states control the curriculum, the Ninth Circuit rejected a vagueness challenge to California legislation holding teachers personally liable for damages if they willfully refuse to teach predominantly in English.[86]

But educators are not legally vulnerable when they are teaching the prescribed curriculum, even though it might be criticized by school patrons.[87] For example, the Sixth Circuit ruled in favor of a teacher who was teaching a life science course in conformance with the school board's directives, finding that community protests did not justify school authorities placing restrictions on his course content. After declining to alter his course, the teacher was suspended and told that he would be terminated for refusing to accept a letter of reprimand. Noting that the films and text used by the teacher had been approved by the school board and used for several years, the court found the teacher's classroom behavior appropriate and consistent with the course objectives.[88] In another case, after a Maine teacher received several complaints about his curriculum from members of a Christian church, the school board ordered the teacher to refrain from teaching certain social science subjects pertaining to prehistoric times and Greek, Roman, and Asian history. The teacher challenged the board's action, and the district court denied the board's request for summary judgment, reasoning that the teacher was threatened with termination for teaching "non-Christian" ancient history. The federal district court emphasized that classrooms cannot be used to promote Christian ideology.[89]

Teaching Strategies

State laws and school board policies establish the basic contours of the curriculum, but teachers retain some discretion in choosing *strategies* to convey prescribed content. However, if the school board has required or prohibited a particular strategy, a teacher cannot assert a right to disregard such directives.[90] In reviewing school board restrictions on teachers' classroom activities, the judiciary considers a number of factors, such as whether teachers have been provided adequate notice that use of specific teaching methodologies or materials will result in disciplinary action, the relevance of the method to the course of study, the threat of disruption posed by the method, and the impact of the strategy on community norms.

[85]Bd. of Educ. v. Wilder, 960 P.2d 695, 702 (Colo. 1998) (upholding termination of a teacher for showing his high school class portions of a movie that included nudity, profanity, and graphic violence; also rejecting the teacher's due process claim since sufficient notice of the policy had been provided); *see infra* text accompanying note 91.

[86]Cal. Teachers Ass'n v. State Bd. of Educ., 271 F.3d 1141 (9th Cir. 2001) (noting that it would almost always be clear to teachers when they were dispensing the *instructional curriculum*, which triggers the English language restriction).

[87]It should also be noted that school counselors may discuss controversial issues in confidence with counselees and provide information as well as referrals. For example, counselors can provide factual information on the legal status of abortions, but they cannot urge or coerce students to have an abortion. *See* Arnold v. Bd. of Educ., 880 F.2d 305 (11th Cir. 1989), *on remand*, 754 F. Supp. 853 (S.D. Ala. 1990).

[88]Stachura v. Truszkowski, 763 F.2d 211 (6th Cir. 1985), *rev'd and remanded* (regarding award of compensatory damages) *sub nom.* Stachura v. Memphis Cmty. Sch. Dist., 477 U.S. 299 (1986).

[89]Cole v. Me. Sch. Admin. Dist. No. 1, 350 F. Supp. 2d 143 (D. Me. 2004).

[90]*See, e.g.*, Greenshields v. Indep. Sch. Dist. I-1016, 174 F. App'x 426 (10th Cir. 2006) (holding that a teacher did not argue a First Amendment right to refuse to use an inquiry-based approach employing learning modules to teach science, so the court could not assess the alleged retaliation against her for critical letters she wrote to school administrators about this instructional approach).

ADEQUATE NOTICE. Courts in general have recognized teachers' discretion to select appropriate teaching methods that serve a demonstrated educational purpose. If a particular method is supported by professional educators, the teacher has no reason to anticipate that its use might result in disciplinary action unless there is a regulation forbidding the method. This procedural right of notice that specific methods are prohibited often is the decisive factor in academic freedom cases.

Failure to provide notice was questioned in an early case in which a teacher was dismissed for using a slang term for sexual intercourse in a high school discussion of taboo words. The First Circuit ordered the teacher's reinstatement because there was no regulation prohibiting this teaching method.[91] In contrast, the First Circuit found no First Amendment violation in a teacher's suspension for handing a document to a student that contained indecent content. The court noted that the Massachusetts law permitting termination for "conduct unbecoming a teacher" furnishes sufficient notice that indecent speech directed toward students is impermissible.[92] Courts addressing the procedural due process issue have indicated that while teachers enjoy some measure of discretion, the school board can restrict use of specific methods if proper notice is given.

RELEVANCY. A primary consideration in reviewing the legitimacy of classroom activities is whether instructional strategies are related to course objectives. In the absence of such a relationship, the teacher's behavior is not constitutionally protected. Relevancy applies not only to objectives but also to the age and maturity of the students; a controversial topic appropriate for high school students would not necessarily be suitable for elementary and middle school pupils. Even though a certain method may be considered relevant, if it lacks the general support of the teaching profession, a school board still may prevail in barring its use.

In an early case, the Seventh Circuit upheld dismissal of teachers for distributing without explanation a brochure on the pleasures of drug use and sex to an eighth-grade class; the brochure was unrelated to class activities and lacked a legitimate educational purpose.[93] Relevance to course objectives also has been found lacking in several cases in which teachers have shown R-rated movies to public school students.[94] Similarly, the Eighth Circuit upheld the termination of a teacher who willfully violated board policy by permitting her students to use profanity in their creative writing assignments.[95]

A teacher in New York was unsuccessful in her First Amendment claim against the district involving a lesson in a health course. During a lesson on HIV transmission, the teacher had students identify slang words for body parts or bodily fluid. She wrote

[91]Mailloux v. Kiley, 448 F.2d 1242 (1st Cir. 1971) (acknowledging, however, that such language lacks professional support and could be the basis for dismissal if proper notice had been given).

[92]Conward v. Cambridge Sch. Comm., 171 F.3d 12 (1st Cir. 1999).

[93]Brubaker v. Bd. of Educ., 502 F.2d 973 (7th Cir. 1974).

[94]*See, e.g.*, Fowler v. Bd. of Educ., 819 F.2d 657 (6th Cir. 1987); Roberts v. Rapides Parish Sch. Bd., 617 So. 2d 187 (La. Ct. App. 1993); *see also* Silano v. Sag Harbor Union Free Sch. Dist., 42 F.3d 719 (2d Cir. 1994) (upholding censure of guest lecturer for showing film clips of bare-chested women during a lecture on the scientific phenomenon of persistence of vision). *But see* West v. Tangipahoa Parish Sch. Bd., 615 So. 2d 979 (La. Ct. App. 1993) (overturning dismissal of a teacher with an excellent record for showing two R-rated movies to students).

[95]Lacks v. Ferguson Reorganized Sch. Dist. R-2, 147 F.3d 718 (8th Cir. 1998); *see also* Oleske v. Hilliard City Sch. Dist., 764 N.E.2d 1110 (Ohio Ct. App. 2001) (upholding dismissal of a teacher who told dirty jokes to middle school students and referred to another teacher by a derogatory name).

the terms on the blackboard and then identified acceptable equivalents. As a result of this lesson, she was reassigned to nonclassroom duties, and she asserted that school officials violated her First Amendment rights. The federal district court granted the school district's motion for summary judgment, holding that her classroom speech did not relate to a matter of public concern and that school officials may regulate vulgar terms in the classroom.[96] The Sixth Circuit also recognized that a high school English teacher's curricular and pedagogical choices are not free from school district oversight. This case arose when the teacher's contract was not renewed after a dispute involving an assignment where students were asked to examine the American Library Association's list of banned books. The appellate court held that under *Garcetti*, the teacher's right to free speech does not extend to in-class curricular speech.[97] The court reasoned that when a teacher speaks as a government employee, the school board can regulate the content of that speech.

However, teachers cannot be forced to discontinue instructionally relevant activities solely because of parental displeasure. To illustrate, the Fifth Circuit ruled that a teacher's use of a simulation to teach about post–Civil War U.S. history was related to legitimate educational objectives and therefore could not be the basis for dismissal.[98]

THREAT OF DISRUPTION. Among the factors that courts examine in assessing restrictions on classroom instruction is whether the activities pose a threat of disruption to the operation of the school. An Oregon federal district court found a school board's policy of banning all political speakers from the high school unreasonable on several grounds, including the fact that no disruptions had occurred or could be anticipated from political discussions.[99] The ban was imposed after some community residents protested a civics teacher's decision to invite a Communist speaker to address her class as part of a series of presentations representing different political viewpoints. In a case discussed previously, the Fifth Circuit concluded that numerous complaints from parents and students about the use of a simulation to teach history did not constitute a sufficient disruption to destroy the teacher's effectiveness in the classroom. The court stated that the "test is not whether substantial disruption occurs but whether such disruption overbalances the teacher's usefulness as an instructor."[100] However, an Illinois federal district court recognized that a school board does not necessarily have to show that instructional materials actually caused a disruption to justify nonrenewal of a teacher's contract. Materials may be considered inappropriate for classroom use, such as films with vulgarity and sexually explicit scenes, even though students "quietly acquiesce" to their use.[101]

COMMUNITY STANDARDS. Courts have been protective of school boards' authority to design the curriculum to reflect community values. The Seventh Circuit recognized that

[96]Kramer v. N.Y. City Bd. of Educ., 715 F. Supp. 2d 335 (E.D.N.Y. 2010).

[97]Evans-Marshall v. Bd. of Educ., 624 F.3d 332 (6th Cir. 2010), *cert. denied*, 131 S. Ct. 3068 (2011); *see supra* text accompanying note 74.

[98]Kingsville Indep. Sch. Dist. v. Cooper, 611 F.2d 1109 (5th Cir. 1980); *see also* Hosford v. Sch. Comm. of Sandwich, 659 N.E.2d 1178 (Mass. 1996) (overturning suspension of a teacher for her brief, pedagogically valid discussion of vulgar words).

[99]Wilson v. Chancellor, 418 F. Supp. 1358 (D. Or. 1976).

[100]*Kingsville Indep. Sch. Dist.*, 611 F.2d at 1113.

[101]Krizek v. Bd. of Educ., 713 F. Supp. 1131, 1140–41 (N.D. Ill. 1989) (noting further that the severity of the action against the teacher also must be considered in assessing the legitimacy of the board's sanctions).

school board members represent the community, which "has a legitimate, even a vital and compelling interest in the 'choice of and adherence to a suitable curriculum for the benefit of our young citizens.'"[102] Other courts similarly have acknowledged that community standards can be considered in determining the appropriateness of teaching materials and methods; school boards are empowered to establish the curriculum to transmit community values and to dismiss teachers who repeatedly offend community mores. For example, a New York appeals court held that a teacher who defied warnings that use of certain materials and sexual words in classroom discussions offended community mores had no First Amendment grounds to challenge his reprimand.[103]

FREEDOM OF ASSOCIATION

Although freedom of association is not specifically addressed in the First Amendment, the Supreme Court has recognized that associational rights are "implicit in the freedoms of speech, assembly, and petition."[104] The Court has consistently declared that infringements on the right to associate for expressive purposes can be justified only by a compelling governmental interest, unrelated to suppressing ideas, which cannot be achieved through less-restrictive means.[105] Accordingly, public educators cannot be disciplined for forming or joining political, labor, religious, or social organizations.[106] Limitations, however, may be placed on associational activities that disrupt school operations or interfere with teachers' professional duties.[107] This section presents an overview of teachers' associational rights in connection with political affiliations and activities.

Political Affiliations

States have made frequent attempts to prohibit or limit teachers' affiliations with subversive political organizations. These restrictions have been imposed to protect public schools from treasonable and seditious acts. In early cases, the Supreme Court held that associational rights could be restricted when a public employee was fully knowledgeable of an organization's subversive purpose,[108] but in the mid-1960s this stance was rejected. Although teachers can be required to affirm their support of the federal and state constitutions,[109] the Supreme Court has invalidated loyalty oaths requiring individuals to deny membership in subversive organizations, such as the Communist Party, as unduly vague or

[102]Zykan v. Warsaw Cmty. Sch. Corp., 631 F.2d 1300, 1304 (7th Cir. 1980) (quoting Palmer v. Bd. of Educ., 603 F.2d 1271, 1274 (7th Cir. 1979)).

[103]*In re* Arbitration Between Bernstein & Norwich City Sch. Dist., 726 N.Y.S.2d 474 (App. Div. 2001).

[104]Healy v. James, 408 U.S. 169, 181 (1972).

[105]*See, e.g.*, NAACP v. Button, 371 U.S. 415 (1963).

[106]Brammer-Hoelfer v. Twin Peak Charter Acad., 602 F.3d 1175 (10th Cir. 2010).

[107]*See* Klug v. Chi. Sch. Reform Bd. of Trs., 197 F.3d 853 (7th Cir. 1999) (finding no violation of associational rights in an employee's transfer from a high school dean of students to an elementary school teaching position to neutralize bickering factions at the high school).

[108]*See* Adler v. Bd. of Educ., 342 U.S. 485 (1952).

[109]*See* Cole v. Richardson, 405 U.S. 676 (1972); Connell v. Higginbotham, 403 U.S. 207 (1971). Employees also can be required to pledge that they will oppose the overthrow of the government and that they will fulfill their job responsibilities.

imposing sanctions for guilt by association.[110] The Supreme Court has firmly established that mere membership in such an organization, without the specific intent to further its unlawful aims, cannot disqualify an individual for public school employment.[111] Thus, state statutes barring members of subversive or controversial organizations from public employment are clearly unconstitutional.[112] Neither can a school system impose restrictions, directly or indirectly, on teachers' memberships or their lawful activities in certain organizations. As with protected speech, dismissal of a teacher will not be supported if the motivating factor behind the decision is the teacher's exercise of associational rights.

Governmental action need not proscribe organizational membership to impair freedom of association. Courts will invalidate challenged laws that *inhibit* the free exercise of constitutional guarantees unless the state can show that such measures are substantially related to a compelling governmental interest. The Supreme Court overturned an Arkansas law that required all teachers to submit annually a list of every organization they had joined or regularly supported during the prior five years as constituting "comprehensive interference with associational freedom."[113] Similarly, the Fifth Circuit struck down a Texas statute that allowed county judges to compel certain organizations engaged in activities designed to disrupt public schools to disclose their membership lists.[114] As in the Arkansas case, this law also swept too broadly by exposing to public recrimination those members who did not participate in disruptive activities.

The First Amendment, however, does not preclude school administrators from questioning teachers about associational activities that may adversely affect teaching. In *Beilan v. Board of Public Education*, the Supreme Court held that questions regarding a teacher's activities in the Communist Party were relevant to an assessment of his fitness to serve as a classroom teacher, and that refusal to answer the superintendent's inquiries could result in dismissal.[115] Although organizational membership per se is protected, a teacher must respond to queries about associational activities that are related to competence to teach.

Conditioning public employment on partisan political affiliation also has been controversial. The Supreme Court struck down patronage dismissals beyond policy-making roles in 1976 when it ruled that the patronage system in an Illinois sheriff's office placed a severe restriction on political association and belief[116] and in 1980 when it reiterated that the democratic process would be preserved by limiting patronage dismissals to policy-making positions.[117] A decade later, the Court extended the principle established in the political firing cases to all aspects of public employment, ruling that party affiliation cannot influence promotion, transfer, recall, and other decisions pertaining to employees who do not establish policies.[118]

[110]*See, e.g.*, Keyishian v. Bd. of Regents, 385 U.S. 589, 606–07 (1967); Elfbrandt v. Russell, 384 U.S. 11, 19 (1966).

[111]*Keyishian*, 385 U.S. at 606–07.

[112]*See, e.g.*, NAACP v. Alabama *ex rel.* Patterson, 357 U.S. 449 (1958); *see also In re* Bay Area Citizens Against Lawsuit Abuse, 982 S.W.2d 371, 376 (Tex. 1998) (recognizing that "curtailing the freedom of association is subject to the closest scrutiny," regardless of the beliefs sought to be advanced by the association (quoting *NAACP*, 357 U.S. at 460–61)).

[113]Shelton v. Tucker, 364 U.S. 479, 490 (1960).

[114]Familias Unidas v. Briscoe, 619 F.2d 391 (5th Cir. 1980).

[115]357 U.S. 399 (1958).

[116]Elrod v. Burns, 427 U.S. 347 (1976).

[117]Branti v. Finkel, 445 U.S. 507 (1980).

[118]Rutan v. Republican Party, 497 U.S. 62 (1990).

Despite being insulated from partisan politics by state law, in some instances, public educators have asserted that employment decisions have been based on party affiliation. In such cases, the burden has been placed on the school employee to demonstrate that protected political affiliation was the motivating factor in the board's employment decision. If an employee satisfies this burden, then the board must demonstrate by a preponderance of evidence that it would have reached the same decision in the absence of the political association. In an illustrative case, the First Circuit ordered reinstatement of a school superintendent because evidence supported that her political party affiliation was the motivating factor in the decision to demote her.[119] Also, the Sixth Circuit denied summary judgment to a Kentucky school board that had demoted an administrator who supported the superintendent's opponents. The court noted that the role of grants department director was not a policy-making position and did not involve sensitive or confidential duties or control lines of communication between the superintendent and the public, so the board could not substantiate a policy-making need for her demotion to a classroom teacher.[120]

Political Activity

Teachers, like all citizens, are guaranteed the right to participate in the political process. Often, however, active participation has prompted school officials to place limitations on the exercise of this right, raising difficult legal questions. Can teachers run for political offices? What types of political activities are permitted in the school setting? Can certain political activities outside the school be restricted?

CAMPAIGNING AND OTHER ACTIVITIES. First Amendment association and free speech rights have been invoked to protect public educators in expressing political views and campaigning for candidates.[121] Even though such political activity is constitutionally protected, restrictions can be placed on educators' activities in the school setting. Making campaign speeches in the classroom is clearly prohibited; teachers cannot take advantage of their position of authority with an impressionable captive audience to impose their

[119]Estrada-Izquierdo v. Aponte-Roque, 850 F.2d 10 (1st Cir. 1988); *see also* Piazza v. Aponte-Roque, 909 F.2d 35 (1st Cir. 1990) (finding that nonrenewal of contracts of teachers' aides because of their political party affiliation impaired associational rights); Burris v. Willis Indep. Sch. Dist., 713 F.2d 1087 (5th Cir. 1983) (holding that nonrenewal of an administrator's contract was predicated on his association with previous "old line" board members and thereby violated his associational rights).

[120]Justice v. Pike Cnty. Bd. of Educ., 348 F.3d 554 (6th Cir. 2003). *But see* Rivera-Torres v. Rey-Hernandez, 352 F. Supp. 2d 152 (D.P.R. 2004) (rejecting claim by former employees of the Department of Education that their one-year contracts were not renewed because they were politcally affiliated with the prior administration; they lacked a property interest in their contracts beyond the current year).

[121]Expression and association rights were at issue in two Supreme Court decisions addressing federal campaign reforms that place limitations on corporations using general treasury funds to pay for "electioneering communication" within thirty days of a federal primary election or sixty days of a federal general election. Bipartisan Campaign Reform Act of 2002, 2 U.S.C. § 441b(b)(2)(2012). *See* Fed. Election Comm'n v. Wis. Right to Life, 551 U.S. 449 (2007) (holding that corporate or union ads, which are not explicit advocacy or its functional equivalent, cannot be curtailed without a compelling interest to justify the burden on expression, such as the ads explicitly urging a vote for or against a specific candidate). *Federal Election Commission* largely negates the Court's holding four years earlier in *McConnell v. Federal Election Commission*, 540 U.S. 93 (2003) (upholding the federal restrictions on express advocacy as encompassing ads that purport to educate voters about issues but are really aimed at candidates).

political views.[122] However, if campaign issues are related to the class topic, a teacher can present election issues and candidates in a nonpartisan manner.

In general, political activity that would cause divisiveness within the school district also can be restricted. A federal district court upheld a regulation that prohibits political campaign buttons in school buildings because of legitimate pedagogical concerns related to entanglement of public education with partisan politics.[123] The court observed that the board's regulation of the campaign buttons was based on good faith professional judgment. The Kentucky Supreme Court addressed a statutory prohibition on school employees taking part in the management or activities of any school board campaign. Although finding the word *activities* too vague to describe the prohibited involvement, the court upheld the constitutionality of the prohibition on school employees taking part in the *management* of school board campaigns as reasonable to advance the state's compelling interest in running school districts efficiently.[124]

Courts have tended to reject restrictions affecting teachers' political activities *outside* the school. Public employees are constitutionally protected from retaliation for participation in political affairs at the local, state, and federal levels. For example, the Sixth Circuit held that the coordinator of gifted education, which was not a policy-making position, could not be reassigned for the exercise of constitutionally protected political expression and association in connection with actively supporting an unsuccessful candidate for school superintendent.[125] The appeals court rejected the contention that political loyalty was essential in carrying out the coordinator's role. Other courts have overturned dismissals, transfers, or demotions predicated on the support or nonsupport of particular candidates in school board elections where protected political activity was a motivating or substantial factor in the adverse employment action against nonpolicy-making employees, and the political activities did not interfere with school operations.[126]

The Federal Constitution protects the right of political party members to champion candidates for government office, but public employees who occupy policy-making positions may be vulnerable to dismissal or other disciplinary action for their political

[122]*See* Mayer v. Monroe Cnty. Cmty. Sch. Corp., 474 F.3d 477 (7th Cir. 2007); *supra* text accompanying note 75.

[123]Weingarten v. Bd. of Educ., 680 F. Supp. 2d 595 (S.D.N.Y. 2010); *see also* Turlock Joint Elementary Sch. Dist. v. Pub. Emp't Relations Bd., 5 Cal. Rptr. 3d 308 (Ct. App. 2003) (concluding that teachers could be prohibited from wearing union buttons while delivering instruction); Green Twp. Educ. Ass'n v. Rowe, 746 A.2d 499 (N.J. Super. Ct. App. Div. 2000) (upholding restriction on political activity in front of students, including wearing buttons, but finding overbroad a restriction on employees campaigning outside the presence of students on school property).

[124]State Bd. for Elementary & Secondary Educ. v. Howard, 834 S.W.2d 657 (Ky. 1992); *see also* Castle v. Colonial Sch. Dist., 933 F. Supp. 458 (E.D. Pa. 1996) (finding that a prohibition on school employees engaging in political activities on school district property violated First Amendment rights of off-duty employees to solicit votes at official polling places on school grounds).

[125]Hager v. Pike Cnty. Bd. of Educ., 286 F.3d 366 (6th Cir. 2002).

[126]*See, e.g.*, Kercado-Melendez v. Aponte-Roque, 829 F.2d 255 (1st Cir. 1987) (holding that dismissal of school superintendent and revocation of her teaching license when new political party took office violated First Amendment rights; awarding injunctive relief, back pay, and damages for the unconstitutional dismissal based on political affiliation); Banks v. Burkich, 788 F.2d 1161 (6th Cir. 1986) (ordering reinstatement of a school truant officer who had been demoted for lack of funding but was not rehired for political reasons when funds became available). *But see* Simmons v. Chi. Bd. of Educ., 289 F.3d 488 (7th Cir. 2002) (ruling that a school district employee was demoted for disobeying his supervisor's instructions and micromanaging his office rather than for his unsuccessful campaign for an alderman seat prior to being hired as treasurer of the Chicago Board of Education); Beattie v. Madison Cnty. Sch. Dist., 254 F.3d 595 (5th Cir. 2001) (finding insufficient causal link between employee's termination and her support for the incumbent superintendent candidate).

activities. The Fifth Circuit held that a Texas superintendent's free speech and political association rights were not violated when he was relieved of his duties by school board members against whom he had actively campaigned.[127] The court reasoned that the superintendent's political activities precluded an effective working relationship with the new school board. Also, the Fourth Circuit found no First Amendment impairment in demoting a community/schools coordinator with policy-making and public relations responsibilities after she campaigned for an unsuccessful school board candidate and openly criticized board members and school policies.[128]

States have also attempted to curtail political activities of teachers' unions. In an Eleventh Circuit case, the Alabama teachers' union sought a preliminary injunction to stop enforcement of a state law that would not allow state and local public employees to use payroll deductions to contribute to organizations involved in "political activity." The union argued that this law violated its First Amendment rights.[129] The district court granted the injunction, finding that the law impinged on the union's First Amendment rights. The appellate court narrowed the injunction and certified the question to the Alabama Supreme Court to interpret the law, particularly to provide more clarity on the "or otherwise" and "political activity" language, which would seem to prevent public employees from donating to a very broad range of organizations. In another case involving payroll deductions, the Michigan Supreme Court upheld a decision to stop deductions from school district employees to collect political contributions for the union.[130] The court found that the Michigan Campaign Finance law prohibits schools and other public bodies from using public resources to make political contributions. Right-to-work laws also will certainly impact teachers' political activities.[131]

HOLDING PUBLIC OFFICE. Certain categories of public employees have been prevented from running for political office. In 1973, the Supreme Court upheld a federal law (the Hatch Act) that prevents *federal* employees from holding formal positions in political parties, playing substantial roles in partisan campaigns, and running for partisan office.[132] The Court recognized that legitimate reasons exist for restricting political activities of public employees, such as the need to ensure impartial and effective government, to remove employees from political pressure, and to prevent employee selection based on political factors. In a companion case, the Court upheld an Oklahoma law forbidding classified civil servants from running for paid political offices.[133] Lower courts similarly have endorsed certain restrictions on state and municipal employees running for elective office,

[127]Kinsey v. Salado Indep. Sch. Dist., 950 F.2d 988 (5th Cir. 1992).

[128]Dabbs v. Amos, 70 F.3d 1261 (4th Cir. 1995) (unpublished).

[129]Ala. Educ. Assoc. v. State Superintendent of Educ., 665 F.3d 1234 (11th Cir. 2011). *But see* Ysursa v. Pocatello Educ. Ass'n, 555 U.S. 353 (2009) (finding no First Amendment violation of state law that banned public employee payroll deductions for political activities).

[130]Mich. Educ. Ass'n v. Sec'y of State, 801 N.W.2d 35 (Mich. 2011).

[131]*See Ala. Educ. Assoc.*, 665 F.3d at 1235.

[132]U.S. Civil Serv. Comm'n v. Nat'l Ass'n of Letter Carriers, 413 U.S. 548 (1973). *See* 5 U.S.C. § 7324 (2012).

[133]Broadrick v. Oklahoma, 413 U.S. 601 (1973).

[134]*See, e.g.*, Fletcher v. Marino, 882 F.2d 605 (2d Cir. 1989); Cranston Teachers Alliance v. Miele, 495 A.2d 233 (R.I. 1985); Acevedo v. City of N. Pole, 672 P.2d 130 (Alaska 1983).

[133]Broadrick v. Oklahoma, 413 U.S. 601 (1973).

such as forbidding municipal employees from holding elective office in the city or town where they are employed.[134]

Laws or policies prohibiting *all* public employees from running for *any* political office have been struck down as overly broad.[135] Additionally, several courts have held that public educators, unlike public employees who are directly involved in the operation of governmental agencies, have the right to run for and hold public office. The Utah Supreme Court, for example, ruled that public school teachers and administrators were not disqualified from serving in the state legislature.[136] A New Mexico appeals court also found that service in the legislature by a teacher and administrator would not violate the constitutional separation of powers provision,[137] and the Ohio Supreme Court upheld a public school principal's right to serve as a county commissioner.[138]

Of course, restrictions can be imposed that are necessary to protect the integrity of the educational system. Courts have recognized that certain offices are incompatible with public school employment, especially if they involve an employer/employee relationship. Common law has established that such incompatibility exists when a teacher seeks a position on the school board where employed,[139] but a teacher would not be prevented from serving on the school board of another school district.[140]

The Supreme Court affirmed a lower court's decision striking down a Georgia school board's policy requiring any school employee who became a candidate for public office to take a leave of absence without pay for the duration of the candidacy. Finding this policy to be a violation of the federal Voting Rights Act, the Court recognized that it created a substantial economic deterrent to seeking elective public office and was potentially discriminatory since it was adopted after an African American employee announced his candidacy for the state legislature.[141] However, the Supreme Court subsequently upheld the school board's revised policy, which denied special leaves of absence for political purpose.[142] The modified policy was considered a legitimate reaffirmation of the board's authority to require employees to fulfill their contracts.

Although school boards must respect employees' associational rights, they are obligated to ensure that the political activities of public school personnel do not adversely affect the school. Disciplinary actions can be imposed if educators neglect instructional duties to campaign for issues or candidates, use the classroom as a political forum, or disrupt school operations because of their political activities. But school boards must be certain that constraints imposed on employees' freedom of association are not based on mere disagreement with the political orientation of the activities. Personnel actions must be justified as necessary to protect the interests of students and the school.

[134]*See, e.g.*, Fletcher v. Marino, 882 F.2d 605 (2d Cir. 1989); Cranston Teachers Alliance v. Miele, 495 A.2d 233 (R.I. 1985); Acevedo v. City of N. Pole, 672 P.2d 130 (Alaska 1983).

[135]*See, e.g.*, *Cranston Teachers Alliance*, 495 A.2d 233; Minielly v. State, 411 P.2d 69 (Or. 1966).

[136]Jenkins v. Bishop, 589 P.2d 770 (Utah 1978) (*per curiam*).

[137]Stratton v. Roswell Indep. Schs., 806 P.2d 1085 (N.M. Ct. App. 1991).

[138]State *ex rel.* Gretick v. Jeffrey, 465 N.E.2d 412 (Ohio 1984).

[139]*See, e.g.*, Unified Sch. Dist. No. 501 v. Baker, 6 P.3d 848 (Kan. 2000) (invalidating election of teacher to school board where state legislature had not negated the common law doctrine of job incompatibility by authorizing the holding of dual offices).

[140]*See* La Bosco v. Dunn, 502 N.Y.S.2d 200 (App. Div. 1986).

[141]Dougherty Cnty. Bd. of Educ. v. White, 439 U.S. 32 (1978).

[142]White v. Dougherty Cnty. Bd. of Educ., 579 F. Supp. 1480 (M.D. Ga. 1984), *aff'd mem.*, 470 U.S. 1067 (1985).

PERSONAL APPEARANCE

Historically, school boards often imposed rigid grooming restrictions on teachers. In the 1970s, such attempts to regulate teachers' appearance generated considerable litigation, as did grooming standards for students.[143] Controversies have subsided for the most part, but a few constraints on school employees' appearance continue to be challenged.[144] School boards have defended their efforts to regulate teacher appearance on the perceived need to provide appropriate role models, set a proper tone in the classroom, and enforce similar appearance and dress codes for students. Teachers have contested these requirements as abridgments of their constitutionally protected privacy, liberty, and free expression rights.

Most courts since the mid-1970s have supported school officials in imposing reasonable grooming and dress restrictions on teachers.[145] The Supreme Court provided some clarification of public employers' authority regarding regulation of employee appearance in a 1976 decision upholding a hair-grooming regulation for police officers. The Court placed the burden on the individual to demonstrate the lack of a rational connection between the regulation and a legitimate public purpose.[146]

The Supreme Court's justification for upholding the grooming regulation for police officers has been followed by lower courts assessing dress and appearance restrictions for teachers. For example, the Second Circuit upheld a Connecticut school board's requirement that all male teachers wear ties as a rational means to promote respect for authority, traditional values, and classroom discipline.[147] Because of the uniquely influential role of teachers, the court noted that they may be subjected to restrictions in their professional lives that otherwise would not be acceptable. Applying similar reasoning, the First Circuit upheld a school board's dismissal of a teacher for wearing short skirts,[148] and a Connecticut federal court ruled that a school board did not violate a teacher's rights by instructing her to cover the message on her T-shirt, "Jesus 2000-J2K," or change into another top.[149]

Restrictions will not be upheld, however, if found to be arbitrary, discriminatory, or unrelated to a legitimate governmental concern. To illustrate, the Seventh Circuit overturned a school bus driver's suspension after he violated a regulation prohibiting school bus drivers from wearing mustaches.[150] Finding no valid purpose for the policy, the court

[143]Intentionally left blank so that the remaining footnotes in the chapter can remain numbered as is.

[144]*See* Polk Cnty. Bd. of Educ. v. Polk Cnty. Educ. Ass'n, 139 S.W.3d 304 (Tenn. Ct. App. 2004) (holding that the adoption of an employee dress code may be a management prerogative, but its enforcement must be bargained with the teachers' association).

[145]*See, e.g.*, Domico v. Rapides Parish Sch. Bd., 675 F.2d 100 (5th Cir. 1982) (finding prohibitions on teachers' wearing beards to be a minor deprivation of protected rights and to advance legitimate school board interests in instilling discipline and compelling uniformity).

[146]Kelley v. Johnson, 425 U.S. 238 (1976).

[147]E. Hartford Educ. Ass'n v. Bd. of Educ., 562 F.2d 838 (2d Cir. 1977).

[148]Tardif v. Quinn, 545 F.2d 761 (1st Cir. 1976); *see also* Zalewska v. Cnty. of Sullivan, 180 F. Supp. 2d 486 (S.D.N.Y. 2002) (upholding uniform policy for school district's van drivers to project a professional appearance and ensure safety of vans with chair lifts; the policy's incidental restrictions on expression were minimal).

[149]Downing v. W. Haven Bd. of Educ., 162 F. Supp. 2d 19 (D. Conn. 2001).

[150]Pence v. Rosenquist, 573 F.2d 395 (7th Cir. 1978); *see also* Nichol v. Arin Intermediate Unit 28, 268 F. Supp. 2d 536 (W.D. Pa. 2003) (upholding an instructional assistant's right to wear a small cross and reasoning that the state's religious garb statute was overtly adverse to religion because it singled out and punished only religious, and not secular, symbolic expression).

noted that its irrationality was exemplified by the fact that the bus driver also was a full-time teacher but was not suspended from his teaching position.

CONSTITUTIONAL PRIVACY RIGHTS

Public employees have asserted the right to be free from unwarranted governmental intrusions in their personal activities.[151] Although the Federal Constitution does not explicitly enumerate personal privacy rights, the Supreme Court has recognized that certain *implied* fundamental rights warrant constitutional protection because of their close relationship to explicit constitutional guarantees. Protected privacy rights have been interpreted as encompassing personal choices in matters such as marriage, contraception, sexual relations, procreation, family relationships, and child rearing.[152] Employment decisions cannot be based on relinquishing such rights without a compelling justification. Litigation covered in this section focuses on constitutional privacy claims initiated under the Fourth Amendment (protection against unreasonable searches and seizures), the Ninth Amendment (personal privacy as an unenumerated right reserved to the people), and the Fourteenth Amendment (equal protection rights and protection against state action impairing personal liberties without due process of law).

In some instances, public employees have asserted that governmental action has impaired their privacy right to intimate association related to creating and maintaining a family. To assess such claims, courts must weigh the employee's rights against the government's interests in promoting efficient public services. For example, public educators cannot be deprived of their jobs because of the politics or other activities of their partners or spouses. Recognizing a classified employee's First Amendment right to associate with her husband, who disagreed with policies of the school system, the Sixth Circuit found an inference that the superintendent's nonrenewal recommendation was impermissibly based on the employee's marital relationship.[153] Also, a federal court held that a nontenured teacher, who received excellent ratings until subpoenaed at school to testify against her live-in fiancé in a child abuse case, could claim that her contract nonrenewal violated intimate associational rights.[154]

However, public educators cannot assert an association or privacy right to disregard anti-nepotism policies that prohibit teachers from reporting to their spouses or working in the same building as their spouses. The Sixth Circuit reasoned that such an anti-nepotism

[151]Most states have laws giving employees access to their personnel files and safeguarding the confidentiality of the records.

[152]*See* Lawrence v. Texas, 539 U.S. 558 (2003); Loving v. Virginia, 388 U.S. 1 (1967); Griswold v. Conneticut, 381 U.S. 479 (1965); Skinner v. Oklahoma, 316 U.S. 535 (1942); Pierce v. Soc'y of Sisters, 268 U.S. 510 (1925). The Supreme Court in 1973 ruled that the decision to have an abortion also was among these protected privacy rights, Roe v. Wade, 410 U.S. 113 (1973), but the Court has allowed states to place some restrictions (e.g., twenty-four-hour waiting period, informed consent, parental consent) on the individual's discretion to have an abortion.

[153]Adkins v. Bd. of Educ., 982 F.2d 952 (6th Cir. 1993).

[154]LaSota v. Town of Topsfield, 979 F. Supp. 45 (D. Mass. 1997); *see also* Trujillo v. Bd. of Educ., 212 F. App'x 760 (10th Cir. 2007) (remanding a high school instructor's retaliation claim for supporting his wife's discrimination complaint that resulted from her failure to be hired in a supervisory role; further fact finding was needed to determine whether the instructor spoke pursuant to his official duties). *But see* Finnegan v. Bd. of Educ., 30 F.3d 273 (2d Cir. 1994) (finding inadequate evidence that a probationary teacher was removed from a coaching position and denied tenure because he had married a former member of his volleyball team shortly after she graduated).

policy did not interfere with the fundamental right to marry, because the policy affected working conditions, not the marriage itself.[155] The fact that such policies do not apply to employees who are cohabiting or dating has not nullified anti-nepotism provisions.

The Fifth Circuit recognized that a teacher's interest in breast-feeding her child at school during noninstructional time was sufficiently close to fundamental rights regarding family relationships and child rearing to trigger constitutional protection.[156] The court acknowledged, however, that trial courts must determine whether school boards' interests in avoiding disruption of the educational process, ensuring that teachers perform their duties without distraction, and avoiding liability for potential injuries are sufficiently compelling to justify restrictions imposed on teachers' fundamental privacy interests. The Second Circuit also upheld a teacher's privacy claim in her refusal to submit to a physical examination by the school district's male physician and found support for the unreasonableness of the board's action because the teacher offered to go at her own expense to any female physician the board selected.[157]

Courts in some cases have concluded that governmental interests in ensuring the welfare of students override teachers' privacy interests. For example, teachers cannot claim privacy rights to have sexual relationships with students or perhaps even former students who have recently graduated.[158] Also, the Second Circuit ruled that a school board did not violate a tenured teacher's privacy rights by not allowing her to return from an extended medical absence unless she provided medical records from the physician and submitted to a physical examination by the school board doctor.[159] Likewise, the First Circuit held that a principal's constitutional privacy rights were not impaired when he was required to undergo a psychiatric examination before returning to work, as there was reason to believe that the welfare of students might be jeopardized.[160]

Search and Seizure

Public educators, like all citizens, are shielded by the Fourth Amendment against unreasonable governmental invasions of their person and property. This amendment requires police officers and other state agents to secure a search warrant (based on probable cause that evidence of a crime will be found) before conducting personal searches. The

[155]Montgomery v. Carr, 101 F.3d 1117 (6th Cir. 1996); *see also* Williams v. Augusta Cnty. Sch. Bd., 445 S.E.2d 118 (Va. 1994) (finding that a teacher was ineligible to be rehired by a school board that her brother-in-law chaired).

[156]Dike v. Sch. Bd., 650 F.2d 783 (5th Cir. 1981).

[157]Gargiul v. Tompkins, 704 F.2d 661 (2d Cir. 1983), *vacated and remanded*, 465 U.S. 1016 (1984); *see also* Appel v. Spiridon, 463 F. Supp. 2d 255 (D. Conn. 2006) (awarding preliminary injunction to restrain a university from requiring a professor to undergo a mental health evaluation; no other faculty members had been subjected to such involuntary psychiatric examinations as a condition of maintaining their positions when questions were raised about their professional conduct).

[158]*See* Flaskamp v. Dearborn Pub. Schs., 385 F.3d 935 (6th Cir. 2004) (upholding suspension and denial of tenure to a teacher who had an intimate relationship with a former student; the school board could prohibit such activity within a year or two of graduation, given the importance of deterring student/teacher sexual relationships); Berkovsky v. State, 209 S.W. 3d 252 (Tex. Ct. App. 2006) (finding that the statute prohibiting improper sexual relationships between educators and students did not implicate a fundamental constitutional right and was not facially overbroad; the statute did not interfere with privacy rights of an educator who had a consensual sexual relationship with an eighteen-year-old student in violation of the law).

[159]Strong v. Bd. of Educ., 902 F.2d 208 (2d Cir. 1990).

[160]Daury v. Smith, 842 F.2d 9 (1st Cir. 1988). *But see Appel*, 463 F. Supp. 2d 255; *supra* text accompanying note 157.

Supreme Court has not addressed teachers' rights in connection with searches initiated by public school authorities, but it has upheld warrantless personal searches of students based on reasonable suspicion that contraband detrimental to the educational process is concealed.[161]

While technology has eased communication in the workplace, it has also presented privacy issues for public employees. In 2010, the Supreme Court held that a police department's search of an officer's employer-provided pager was reasonable under the Fourth Amendment. The police department searched the pager because the officer went over his allotted monthly text characters on the pager plan, and the employer was interested in learning whether the texting plan needed to be increased. During the search of the officer's pager, the police department found personal and sexually explicit text messages. The officer had signed a policy stating that pager users have no expectation of privacy.[162]

The judiciary has recognized that the reasonableness of a job-related search or seizure by a supervisor in public schools rests on whether educational interests outweigh the individual employee's expectation of privacy.[163] For example, a federal district court held that a teacher had a reasonable expectation of privacy with her password protected e-mail account even though school officials had warned that e-mails may be discoverable.[164] The court reasoned that the district's acceptable use policy stated that teachers had a reasonable expectation of privacy, and it was not common practice to monitor the e-mail accounts of employees. It is important to note that when school districts have policies that clearly indicate employees' Internet activities may be monitored, the expectation of privacy will be much lower.

In some cases, employers have attempted to gain access to employees' Facebook pages. It is not surprising that employers' attempts to acquire Facebook passwords from job applicants have been criticized. California lawmakers are trying to make the practice of employers asking applicants for Facebook passwords illegal,[165] and Maryland has already made it illegal for employers and potential employers to do so.[166]

The Fourth Amendment prohibits *arbitrary* invasions of teachers' personal effects by school officials, but in some situations, the school's interests are overriding.[167] To illustrate, the Second Circuit upheld the search of a teacher's classroom after he had been suspended for alleged sexual harassment of a student and was provided two opportunities to

[161]New Jersey v. T.L.O., 469 U.S. 325 (1985).

[162]City of Ontario v. Quon, 130 S. Ct. 2619 (2010); *see also* O'Connor v. Ortega, 480 U.S. 709 (1987) (finding that public employees have a reasonable expectation of privacy in their desks and files, but that a warrant was not required for work-related searches that are necessary to carry out the business of the public agency).

[163]*See, e.g.*, Gillard v. Schmidt, 579 F.2d 825 (3d Cir. 1978) (invalidating search of school counselor's desk by a school board member, because the search was politically motivated and lacked sufficient work-related justification).

[164]Brown-Criscuolo v. Wolfe, 601 F. Supp. 2d 441 (D. Conn. 2009).

[165]Jessica Guynn, *Assembly Votes to Keep Facebook Passwords Private from Employers*, L.A. TIMES (May 10, 2012), http://articles.latimes.com/2012/may/10/business/la-fi-tn-assembly-votes-to-keep-facebook-passwords-private-from-employers-20120510.

[166]Joanna Stern, *Maryland Bill Bans Employers from Facebook Passwords*, ABC NEWS (Apr. 11, 2012), http://abcnews.go.com/blogs/technology/2012/04/maryland-bill-bans-employers-from-facebook-passwords/.

[167]*See, e.g.*, Alinovi v. Worcester Sch. Comm., 777 F.2d 776 (1st Cir. 1985) (finding that a teacher had no expectation of privacy in withholding from the school administration a paper she had written for a graduate course—and shared with others—about a child with disabilities in her class).

remove personal items from the classroom.[168] The court further held that the teacher had no valid claim to materials he had prepared in the course of his employment.

Public school employees' Fourth Amendment rights also have been asserted in connection with drug-screening programs. School boards can require employees to have physical examinations as a condition of employment, but mandatory screening for drugs has been challenged as impairing privacy rights. Teachers in a Tennessee school district secured an injunction prohibiting the school board from requiring all teachers to submit to random suspicionless drug testing.[169] The court declared that the school district's policy as written and implemented was unconstitutional. Likewise, a North Carolina appellate court found a school board's policy requiring all employees to submit to random, suspicionless drug and alcohol testing violated the guarantee against unreasonable searches.[170] The court observed that there was no reason for the employees to have a reduced expectation of privacy because they worked in a public school and that there was no evidence of any drug problems among the school employees. A Georgia federal district court in an earlier case also struck down a statewide drug-testing law that would have required all new state employees and veteran employees transferring to another school district or state agency to submit to urinalysis screening.[171] The court reasoned that the general interest in maintaining a drug-free workplace was not a compelling governmental interest to justify testing *all* job applicants.

In contrast to *blanket* testing, support for *limited* drug-testing of public employees can be found in two Supreme Court decisions outside the school domain that upheld mandatory drug testing of railroad employees involved in accidents[172] and customs employees who carry firearms or are involved in the interdiction of illegal drugs.[173] The Court found that the safety and security interests served by the programs outweighed employees' privacy concerns. In several rulings, the District of Columbia Circuit subsequently upheld random urinalysis testing of federal employees in safety-sensitive or security-sensitive roles, including Department of Education employees.[174] The same court upheld the District of Columbia Public Schools' policy requiring all employees whose duties affect child safety, such as bus attendants, to submit to a drug test as part of routine medical examinations.[175] The Fifth Circuit also upheld drug testing of school employees

[168]Shaul v. Cherry Valley-Springfield Cent. Sch. Dist., 363 F.3d 177 (2d Cir. 2004); *see also* Soderstrand v. Okla. *ex rel.* Bd. of Regents, 463 F. Supp. 2d 1308 (W.D. Okla. 2006) (upholding university authorities in seizing a laptop computer from an employee's desk during an investigation of workplace misconduct involving child pornography).

[169]Smith Cnty. Educ. Assoc. v. Smith Cnty. Bd. of Educ., No. 2:08-0076, 2012 U.S. Dist. LEXIS 3020 (M.D. Tenn. Jan. 10, 2012) (distinguishing this case from the Sixth Circuit decision upholding a drug-testing policy that specifically targeted only those applying for teaching positions or those seeking promotion within the district); *infra* text accompanying note 177; *see also* Am. Fed'n of Teachers-W. Va. v. Kanawha Cnty. Bd. of Educ., 592 F. Supp. 2d 883 (S.D. W. Va. 2009) (prohibiting school district from suspicionless drug testing of employees).

[170]Jones v. Graham Cnty. Bd. of Educ., 677 S.E.2d 171 (N.C. Ct. App. 2009).

[171]Ga. Ass'n of Educators v. Harris, 749 F. Supp. 1110 (N.D. Ga. 1990); *see also* Chandler v. Miller, 520 U.S. 305 (1997) (striking down a Georgia law requiring candidates for state office to pass a drug test; finding no special need based on public safety to override the individual's privacy interests).

[172]Skinner v. Ry. Labor Executives' Ass'n, 489 U.S. 602 (1989). In this case, the Court also upheld alcohol testing of employees.

[173]Nat'l Treasury Emps. Union v. Von Raab, 489 U.S. 656 (1989).

[174]*See, e.g.*, Stigile v. Clinton, 110 F.3d 801 (D.C. Cir. 1997); Am. Fed'n of Gov't Emps., AFL-CIO v. Sanders, 926 F.2d 1215 (D.C. Cir. 1991) (unpublished); Nat'l Treasury Emps. Union v. Yeutter, 918 F.2d 968 (D.C. Cir. 1990).

[175]Jones v. McKenzie, 833 F.2d 335 (D.C. Cir. 1987), *vacated and remanded sub nom.* Jenkins v. Jones, 490 U.S. 1001 (1989), *on remand*, 878 F.2d 1476 (D.C. Cir. 1989).

in safety-sensitive positions, including the school custodian, whose performance of maintenance duties affects almost 900 students.[176]

What constitutes safety-sensitive roles in the school context, however, remains unclear. Some courts now seem more inclined than they were in the past to interpret expansively the positions in this category. The Sixth Circuit upheld a school district's policy requiring suspicionless drug testing for all individuals who apply for, transfer to, or are promoted to safety-sensitive positions, including teachers who are entrusted with the care of children and are on the "frontline" of school security.[177] Furthermore, the court upheld drug testing of any individual for whom there was reasonable suspicion of drug possession or use, but it remanded the case for additional factual inquiry regarding the provision calling for alcohol testing of all employees.[178] A Kentucky federal district court subsequently upheld random, suspicionless drug testing of a school district's employees in safety-sensitive roles, including teachers, as justified to comply with the Drug-Free Workplace Act of 1988, designed to ensure that recipients of federal grant funds maintain a drug-free work environment.[179] But the Fifth Circuit struck down policies in two Louisiana school districts that required employees injured in the course of employment to submit to urinalysis, finding an insufficient nexus between such injuries and drug use.[180]

Of course, employees, like students, can be subjected to alcohol and drug testing where there is reasonable suspicion that the individual is under the influence of those substances. For example, a Texas federal district court found that because two witnesses raised concerns about a teacher being under the influence of some substance, there was sufficient reason to justify drug testing the teacher.[181] Employees can be dismissed for refusing to submit to such a test,[182] but in some instances, such dismissals have been overturned when reasonable suspicion was not established to justify targeting particular individuals.[183] The law is still evolving regarding what constitutes individualized suspicion of drug use and the circumstances under which certain public employees can be subjected to urinalysis without such suspicion.

[176]Aubrey v. Sch. Bd., 148 F.3d 559 (5th Cir. 1998); *see also* English v. Talladega Cnty. Bd. of Educ., 938 F. Supp. 775 (N.D. Ala. 1996) (upholding random drug testing of school bus mechanics).

[177]Knox Cnty. Educ. Ass'n v. Knox Cnty Bd. of Educ., 158 F.3d 361, 375 (6th Cir. 1998).

[178]*Id.* at 386 (remanding this issue for the district court to determine whether the low level of alcohol impairment identified, .02, was reasonably related to the purpose of the testing program).

[179]Crager v. Bd. of Educ., 313 F. Supp. 2d 690 (E.D. Ky. 2004) (citing 41 U.S.C. § 702 (2012)). This law stipulates that federal grant and contract recipients cannot receive federal funds unless they implement policies to ensure that workplaces are free from the illegal use, possession, or distribution of controlled substances and establish drug-free awareness programs to inform employees about the policies, the dangers of drug abuse, penalties for drug use violations, and employee assistance available.

[180]United Teachers v. Orleans Parish Sch. Bd., 142 F.3d 853 (5th Cir. 1998).

[181]Catlett v. Duncanville Indep. Sch. Dist., No. 3:09-cv-1245-k, 2010 U.S. Dist. LEXIS 91931 (N.D. Tex. Sept. 2, 2010).

[182]*See, e.g.*, Hearn v. Bd. of Pub. Educ., 191 F.3d 1329 (11th Cir. 1999) (upholding termination of a teacher who refused to undergo urinalysis after a drug-detecting dog identified marijuana in her car).

[183]*See, e.g.*, Warren v. Bd. of Educ., 200 F. Supp. 2d 1053 (E.D. Mo. 2001) (finding genuine issues as to whether the teacher's behavior suggested drug use and whether she consented to the drug test); Best v. Dep't of Health & Human Servs., 563 S.E.2d 573 (N.C. Ct. App. 2002) (overturning public employees' dismissals for refusal to submit to a drug test in the absence of reasonable cause for a public employer to believe they were using a controlled substance).

Out-of-School Conduct

Although regulations are far less restrictive today than in the early 1900s, when some school districts prohibited female teachers from marrying or even dating, school boards still attempt to proscribe aspects of teachers' personal lives that are inimical to community values. School officials have defended some behavior constraints on the grounds that teachers serve as exemplars for students and therefore should conform to community norms to ensure an appropriate educational environment. The Supreme Court has acknowledged that a "teacher serves as a role model for . . . students, exerting a subtle but important influence over their perceptions and values."[184] Recognizing that teachers are held to a higher standard of conduct than general citizens, the judiciary has upheld dismissals for behavior that jeopardizes student welfare, even if it takes place during the summer break.[185]

In recent years, teachers frequently have challenged school officials' authority to place restrictions on their personal lifestyles or out-of-school conduct. Although the right to such personal freedom is not an enumerated constitutional guarantee, it is a right implied in the concept of personal liberty embodied in the Fourteenth Amendment. Constitutional protection afforded to teachers' privacy rights is determined not only by the *location* of the conduct, but also by the *nature* of the activity. The judiciary has attempted to balance teachers' privacy rights against the school board's legitimate interests in safeguarding the welfare of students and the effective management of the school. Sanctions cannot be imposed solely because school officials disapprove of teachers' personal and private conduct, but restrictions can be placed on unconventional behavior that is detrimental to job performance or harmful to students. Educators can be terminated based on evidence that would not be sufficient to support criminal charges,[186] but they cannot be dismissed for unsubstantiated rumors about their activities.[187] Some courts have based termination decisions on whether teachers' out-of-school conduct had a negative impact on their teaching effectiveness.[188]

The precise contours of public educators' constitutional privacy rights have not been clearly delineated; constitutional claims involving pregnancies out of wedlock, unconventional living arrangements, homosexuality, and other alleged sexual

[184]Ambach v. Norwick, 441 U.S. 68, 78–79 (1979).

[185]*See, e.g.*, Bd. of Educ. v. Wood, 717 S.W.2d 837 (Ky. 1986).

[186]*See, e.g.*, Montefusco v. Nassau Cnty., 39 F. Supp. 2d 231 (E.D.N.Y. 1999) (holding that although the criminal investigation did not result in criminal charges, the school board could suspend the teacher with pay and remove extracurricular assignments for his possession of candid pictures of teenagers taken at the teacher's home).

[187]*See, e.g.*, Peaster Indep. Sch. Dist. v. Glodfelty, 63 S.W.3d 1 (Tex. App. 2001) (holding that widespread gossip triggered by unproven allegations of sexual misconduct could not be the basis for not renewing teachers' contracts).

[188]*See, e.g.*, Teacher Standards & Practices Comm'n v. Bergerson, 153 P.3d 84 (Or. 2007) (reinstating teacher who took large quantities of prescription drugs and ran her car into her estranged husband's truck, because there was no clear nexus between her misconduct and her professional duties); Land v. L'Anse Creuse Pub. Sch. Bd. of Educ., No. 288612, 2010 Mich. App. LEXIS 999 (Ct. App. May 27, 2010) (reinstating teacher who was terminated after pictures were posted on the Internet of her simulating the act of fellatio on a male mannequin at a bachelorette party, because her ability to teach effectively was not adversely impacted enough to justify the dismissal).

improprieties usually have been decided on a case-by-case basis. The following discussion is confined to an overview of the constitutional issues.

Recognizing that decisions pertaining to marriage and parenthood involve constitutionally protected privacy rights, courts have been reluctant to support dismissal actions based on teachers' unwed, pregnant status in the absence of evidence that the condition impairs fitness to teach. In a typical case, the Fifth Circuit invalidated a Mississippi school district's rule prohibiting the employment of unwed parents in order to promote a "properly moral scholastic environment," reasoning that the policy violated equal protection and due process rights by equating birth of an illegitimate child with immoral conduct.[189] Compelled leaves of absence for pregnant, unmarried employees similarly have been invalidated as violating constitutional privacy rights.[190]

Most courts have reasoned that public employees, including educators, have a protected privacy right to engage in consenting sexual relationships out of wedlock and that such relationships cannot be the basis for dismissal unless teaching effectiveness is impaired. For example, the Sixth Circuit ruled that a school board's nonrenewal of a nontenured teacher because of her involvement in a divorce abridged constitutional privacy rights,[191] and a Florida appeals court overturned a school board's termination of an unmarried teacher for lacking good moral character because at times she spent the night with an unmarried man.[192]

Some courts, however, have upheld dismissals or other disciplinary actions based on public employees' lifestyles that involve adulterous or other unconventional sexual relationships or activities that allegedly impaired job performance. To illustrate, the U.S. Supreme Court upheld the dismissal of a police officer for selling videotapes of himself stripping off a police uniform and masturbating.[193] The Court rejected the officer's assertion that his off-duty conduct was constitutionally protected expression unrelated to his employment. A New York federal court also upheld the termination of a teacher for actively participating in a group supporting consensual sexual activity between men and boys, reasoning that his activities in this organization were likely to impair teaching effectiveness and disrupt the school.[194]

In a case involving privacy issues and the Internet, an English teacher in Georgia was forced to resign over two pictures that were posted on Facebook that showed her drinking while on vacation in Ireland. The teacher had activated privacy settings and had not communicated with her students via Facebook. School officials, however, learned

[189]*See, e.g.*, Andrews v. Drew Mun. Separate Sch. Dist., 507 F.2d 611, 614 (5th Cir. 1975) (equating birth of an illegitimate child with immoral conduct impairs equal protection and due process rights).

[190]*See* Ponton v. Newport News Sch. Bd., 632 F. Supp. 1056 (E.D. Va. 1986).

[191]Littlejohn v. Rose, 768 F.2d 765 (6th Cir. 1985); *see also* Bertolini v. Whitehall City Sch. Dist., 744 N.E.2d 1245 (Ohio Ct. App. 2000).

[192]Sherburne v. Sch, Bd., 455 So. 2d 1057 (Fla. Dist. Ct. App. 1984).

[193]City of San Diego v. Roe, 543 U.S. 77 (2004) (finding no protected expression involved); *see also* City of Sherman v. Henry, 928 S.W.2d 464 (Tex. 1996) (finding no fundamental right to engage in adultery, so a patrolman's constitutional privacy rights were not violated when he was denied a promotion based on his affair with a fellow officer's wife).

[194]Melzer v. Bd. of Educ., 196 F. Supp. 2d 229 (E.D.N.Y. 2002), *aff'd mem.*, 336 F.3d 185 (2d Cir. 2003).

about the pictures from a concerned parent. The teacher claimed that she was bullied into resigning and then sued the district when it refused to reinstate her. A state court judge ruled that she could not force school officials to give her a hearing, because it was within the school district's legal rights to deny the request.[195] Had the teacher been dismissed as a result of the Facebook pictures, it seems unlikely that school officials would have prevailed in this case.

Whether employment decisions can be based on a teacher's sexual orientation has been controversial, and the scope of constitutional protections afforded to lesbian, gay, bisexual, and transgendered (LGBT) educators continues to evolve. Among factors courts consider are the nature of the conduct (public or private), the notoriety it generates, and its impact on teaching effectiveness.

In 2003, the Supreme Court delivered a significant decision, *Lawrence v. Texas*, in which it recognized a privacy right for consenting adults of the same sex to have sexual relations in the privacy of their homes by striking down a Texas law imposing criminal penalties for such conduct.[196] This ruling overturned a 1986 Supreme Court decision in which the Court upheld a Georgia law attaching criminal penalties to public *or private* consensual sodomy.[197] The Court in *Lawrence* emphasized that private, consensual sexual behavior in one's home is constitutionally protected and cannot be the basis for criminal action.

In addition to asserting protected privacy rights, some LGBT employees have claimed discrimination under the Equal Protection Clause of the Fourteenth Amendment. Equal protection claims pertaining to LGBT educators are reviewed only briefly here. To substantiate an Equal Protection Clause violation, a teacher must prove that sexual orientation was the motivating factor in the adverse employment action and that there was no rational basis for the differential treatment.[198]

Dismissals of public educators based solely on sexual orientation, in the absence of criminal charges, have generated a range of judicial interpretations. During the 1970s and 1980s, a few courts permitted school districts to dismiss LGBT teachers or reassign them to nonteaching roles, even when there was no link to teaching effectiveness.[199] The Sixth Circuit upheld a school district in not renewing a guidance counselor's contract after she revealed her sexual orientation and that of two students to other school employees. Rejecting the claim that the nonrenewal impaired free speech rights, the court held that her statements regarding her sexual orientation were not matters of

[195]Merritt Melancon, *Barrow Teacher Presses Forward with Facebook Lawsuit*, ATHENS BANNER-HERALD (Oct. 11, 2011), http://onlineathens.com/local-news/2011-10-11/barrow-teacher-denied-her-old-job-presses-forward-lawsuit.

[196]539 U.S. 558 (2003).

[197]Bowers v. Hardwick, 478 U.S. 186 (1986).

[198]*See* Romer v. Evans, 517 U.S. 620 (1996) (invalidating an amendment to the Colorado Constitution that prohibited all legislative, executive, or judicial action designed to protect gay individuals).

[199]*See, e.g.*, Burton v. Cascade Sch. Dist., 512 F.2d 850 (9th Cir. 1975); Acanfora v. Bd. of Educ., 491 F.2d 498 (4th Cir. 1974); Gaylord v. Tacoma Sch. Dist. No. 10, 559 P.2d 1340 (Wash. 1977). *But see* Bd. of Educ. v. Jack M., 566 P.2d 602 (Cal. 1977); Morrison v. State Bd. of Educ., 461 P.2d 375 (Cal. 1969) (requiring evidence of impaired teaching effectiveness to discharge teachers for private homosexuality).

public concern.[200] Subsequently, the Tenth Circuit, even though recognizing that refusal to hire a teacher on the basis of perceived homosexual tendencies was arbitrary and capricious, nonetheless held that the law was not clearly established in this regard in 1988 and thus granted the principal immunity for his role in the personnel decision based on sexual orientation.[201]

Litigation since the 1990s requires school districts to provide evidence that one's sexual orientation has a negative impact on teaching effectiveness before disciplinary action can be imposed. To illustrate, a Utah federal court overturned the school district's removal of a girls' volleyball coach, finding no job-related basis for the coach's removal based solely on the community's negative response to her sexual orientation. The court also noted that the school district could not instruct the coach to avoid mentioning her sexual orientation and ordered the coach to be reinstated and paid damages.[202] An Ohio federal district court similarly awarded a teacher reinstatement, back pay, and damages after finding that his contract was not renewed because of his sexual orientation rather than for his teaching deficiencies as the school board had asserted.[203]

A New Jersey teacher prevailed in his claim that he was harassed by teachers and students because he was gay and that his resulting anxiety attacks forced him to take a leave of absence, after which his contract was not renewed.[204] A New York federal district court also held that a teacher had stated a valid claim, precluding summary judgment, that a school district violated her Fourteenth Amendment equal protection rights when it failed to discipline students who harassed the teacher because she was a lesbian and treated her differently from other similarly situated non-LGBT teachers.[205] However, the Seventh Circuit held that a school had not violated a teacher's equal protection rights in connection with parental and student harassment of the teacher based on sexual orientation, because school officials took some action to respond to the teacher's complaints of harassment and treated the allegations as they would treat harassment complaints filed by other teachers.[206]

The case law suggests that there has been a shift from condoning dismissals for merely being LGBT to requiring evidence that an individual's sexual orientation has an adverse impact on job performance. Teachers do not become poor role models simply because of their sexual orientation, and it would be difficult to produce a rational basis for terminating or treating LGBT teachers differently from other educators.

[200]Rowland v. Mad River Local Sch. Dist., 730 F.2d 444 (6th Cir. 1984) (rejecting also the Fourteenth Amendment equal protection claim because the counselor was not treated differently from other similarly situated employees facing nonrenewal of their contracts).

[201]Jantz v. Muci, 976 F.2d 623, 629 (10th Cir. 1992) (recognizing also that under Kansas law the authority to hire rests with school boards, not with principals, and finding no evidence of a delegation of such discretionary authority); *see also* Snyder v. Jefferson Cnty. Sch. Dist. R-1, 842 P.2d 624 (Colo. 1992) (upholding termination of a teacher who let his teaching certificate expire while on leave to have gender reassignment surgery).

[202]Weaver v. Nebo Sch. Dist., 29 F. Supp. 2d 1279 (D. Utah 1998).

[203]Glover v. Williamsburg Local Sch. Dist., 20 F. Supp. 2d 1160 (S.D. Ohio 1998).

[204]Curcio v. Collingswood Bd. of Educ., No. 04-5100 (JBS), 2006 U.S. Dist. LEXIS 46648 (D.N.J. June 28, 2006); *see also* Murray v. Oceanside Unified Sch. Dist., 95 Cal. Rptr. 2d 28 (Ct. App. 2000) (ruling in favor of an award-winning biology teacher who used the California nondiscrimination law to challenge years of harassment by colleagues based on her sexual orientation).

[205]Lovell v. Comsewogue Sch. Dist., 214 F. Supp. 2d 319 (E.D.N.Y. 2002).

[206]Schroeder v. Hamilton Sch. Dist., 282 F.3d 946 (7th Cir. 2002).

Conclusion

Although public educators do not shed their constitutional rights as a condition of public employment, under certain circumstances, restrictions on these freedoms are justified by overriding governmental interests. Constitutional protections afforded to educators continue to be delineated by the judiciary; the following generalizations reflect the status of the law in the substantive areas discussed in this chapter.

1. When speaking as citizens, public educators have a First Amendment right to express their views on issues of public concern; dismissal or other retaliatory personnel action, such as transfers, demotions, or written reprimands, cannot be predicated solely on protected speech.
2. Public employees' expression pursuant to official job responsibilities is not constitutionally protected.
3. Expression pertaining to personal employment disputes, attacks on supervisors, or speech intended to disrupt the school is not constitutionally protected.
4. If a public employer acts in good faith, conducts a reasonable investigation, and concludes from the evidence that the employee's offensive comments are unprotected, the employee can be dismissed for the expression.
5. The exercise of protected speech will not invalidate a dismissal action if the school board can show by a preponderance of evidence that it would have reached the same decision had the protected speech not occurred.
6. Even if expression made as a citizen on public issues is the sole basis for an adverse employment action, the school board still might prevail under the *Pickering* balancing test if it can establish that its interests in providing effective and efficient educational services outweigh the individual's free expression rights.
7. A school's internal mail system is not a traditional open forum for expression, and unless designated as such, access to the mail system can be restricted to business relating to the school's educational function so long as restrictions are not viewpoint based.
8. Reasonable time, place, and manner restrictions can be imposed on educators' expression, including Internet expression, but arbitrary prior restraints on the content and channel of communication violate the First Amendment.
9. Public school teachers do not have the right to determine the content of the instructional program, but they do have some latitude in selecting appropriate strategies to convey the prescribed content.
10. In evaluating the appropriateness of teaching materials and strategies, courts consider relevance to course objectives, threat of disruption, age and maturity of students, and community standards.
11. Public employees cannot be retaliated against because of their membership in labor unions, political groups, or organizations with unlawful purposes.
12. A public educator's participation in political activities outside the classroom cannot be the basis for adverse employment decisions, unless the employee has policy-making responsibilities and such participation would jeopardize relationships at work.
13. State laws can impose restrictions on the types of elected offices that public educators can hold (e.g., two incompatible positions cannot be held).
14. Public employees can be required to take temporary leave from their positions to campaign for political office if it can be established that campaign demands would interfere with professional responsibilities.
15. School officials can impose reasonable restrictions on educators' personal appearance if there is a rational basis for such regulations.
16. Public educators' desks and files at school can be searched based on reasonable

suspicion that the search is necessary for educational reasons.

17. Public educators can be subjected to urinalysis with reasonable suspicion of drug use; employees in safety-sensitive roles can be subjected to blanket or random drug testing.

18. Public educators enjoy protected privacy rights in their out-of-school conduct; however, adverse employment consequences may be justified if their private lives have a detrimental effect on job performance.

19. In general, school districts cannot disadvantage employees based on their sexual orientation unless an employee's conduct has a negative impact on teaching effectiveness or other job duties.

MyEdLeadershipLab™

Go to Topic 10: *Employees' Rights* on the MyEdLeadershipLab™ site (www.myedleadershiplab.com) for *Public School Law: Teachers' and Students' Rights*, Seventh Edition, where you can

- Find learning outcomes for *Employees' Rights* along with the national standards that connect to these outcomes.
- Complete Assignments and Activities that can help you more deeply understand the chapter content.
- Apply and practice your understanding of the core skills identified in the chapter with the Building Leadership Skills unit.
- Prepare yourself for professional certification with a Practice for Certification quiz.

Discrimination in Employment

From Chapter 10 of *Public School Law: Teachers' and Students' Rights*, Seventh Edition. Martha M. McCarthy, Nelda H. Cambron-McCabe, Suzanne E. Eckes.

Discrimination in Employment

MyEdLeadershipLab™

Visit the MyEdLeadershipLab™ site for *Public School Law: Teachers' and Students' Rights*, Seventh Edition, to enhance your understanding of chapter concepts. You'll have the opportunity to practice your skills through video- and case-based Assignments and Activities as well as Building Leadership Skills units, and to prepare for your certification exam with Practice for Certification quizzes.

All persons and groups are potential victims of discrimination in employment. People of color and women claim discrimination in traditionally segregated job categories, whereas Caucasians and males claim that affirmative action has denied them the right to compete on equal grounds. The young argue that the old already hold the good jobs and that entry is nearly impossible, and the old contend that they often are let go when "downsizing" occurs and that reemployment at the same level and salary is unlikely. Religious minorities might not be allowed to dress the way they please or may be denied leave for religious observances, and religious majorities (particularly in private schools) have concerns about governmental intrusion into their homogeneous work environments. Likewise, persons with disabilities often complain that they are not given the opportunity to show what they can do, whereas employers may contend that the costs of accommodating those with disabilities can be significant and never ending. Given these diverse factors, it is not surprising that literally thousands of employment discrimination suits are filed each year.

LEGAL CONTEXT

Most, but not all, forms of employment discrimination violate either federal or state law. Foremost among these legal protections are the Fourteenth Amendment to the United States Constitution and Title VII of the Civil Rights Act of 1964; both are discussed here, given their broad application. Other more narrowly tailored statutes are reviewed in the respective sections addressing discrimination based on race and national origin, sex, sexual orientation, religion, age, and disability.

Fourteenth Amendment

The Fourteenth Amendment to the United States Constitution mandates that no state shall deny any person within its jurisdiction equal protection of the laws. This applies to subdivisions of the state, including public school districts. Under the Equal Protection Clause, if a government policy or law facially discriminates in employment, one of three forms of scrutiny will be used to determine its constitutionality: *strict*, *intermediate*, or *rational basis*.

Facial discrimination occurs when a school district's intent to discriminate is apparent "on the face" of a job description, policy, or other action. For example, the posting of an elementary school principal's position stipulating that it has been reserved for a female applicant would be facially discriminatory. Where facial discrimination exists, the government employer bears the burden of justifying its policies, practices, or acts. The degree of difficulty in carrying that burden is in part determined by the level of scrutiny applied by courts. A policy or practice that discriminates based on race, national origin, or alienage is *strictly scrutinized* and can be justified only if narrowly tailored and supported by a compelling state interest.[1] When a plaintiff claims discrimination based on sex or illegitimacy (i.e., being born to parents who are not married), *intermediate scrutiny* is used, requiring the classification to serve important governmental objectives and the discriminatory acts to be substantially related to the achievement of those objectives.[2] And, finally, *rational basis scrutiny* is applied when any other plaintiff class is involved (e.g., classes based on religion, age, sexual orientation, disability).[3] This level of scrutiny requires only that the justification not be arbitrary, capricious, or without foundation.

Whereas intent to discriminate is apparent with facial discrimination, some policies or practices are facially neutral but result in a disproportionate impact on a protected group, such as use of a standardized test in hiring that results in disparate impact based on race. Unlike Title VII (discussed below), to establish a constitutional violation when the discriminatory intent is not facially apparent, the employee must prove that the employer intended to discriminate. To substantiate discriminatory *intent*, the court will examine criteria such as the pattern of discriminatory impact; the historical background of

[1]*See, e.g.*, Graham v. Richardson, 403 U.S. 365 (1971) (alienage); Hunter v. Erickson, 393 U.S. 385 (1969) (race); Korematsu v. United States, 323 U.S. 214 (1944) (nationality).

[2]Clark v. Jeter, 486 U.S. 456 (1988) (illegitimacy); Miss. Univ. for Women v. Hogan, 458 U.S. 718 (1982) (sex).

[3]*See* Johnson v. Univ. of Iowa, 431 F.3d 325 (8th Cir. 2005) (concluding that rational basis scrutiny is all that is required where adoptive parents were permitted leave time but natural fathers were not; the court noted that rational basis was met, as adoptive parents do not have insurance to offset costs associated with adoption and may be required to take time off work to perform necessary paperwork).

the act, policy, or practice that supports a discriminatory motive; the specific sequence of events leading up to the allegedly unconstitutional behavior; and departures from normal procedures.[4] Although disproportionate impact is relevant in these cases, it is not "the sole touchstone of invidious discrimination forbidden by the Constitution,"[5] and without more does not violate the Fourteenth Amendment.

Title VII

Title VII is enforced by the Equal Employment Opportunity Commission (EEOC) and prohibits employers with fifteen or more employees from discriminating on the basis of race, color, religion, sex, or national origin and covers hiring, promotion, and compensation practices as well as fringe benefits and other terms and conditions of employment.[6] However, protection against discriminatory employment practices is not absolute for individuals within these classifications since both Congress and the courts have identified exceptions (e.g., employers might not accommodate a Jewish basketball coach's request to be excused from every Friday and Saturday night basketball games so that he may observe the Jewish Sabbath from sundown on Friday until sundown on Saturday if the accommodation creates an undue hardship on the school district). Also, in creating and amending Title VII over the years, Congress has expressly permitted employers to facially discriminate based on religion, sex, or national origin (but not on race or color) if they can show the existence of a bona fide occupational qualification (BFOQ) that is reasonably necessary to the normal operation of their particular enterprise (e.g., a parochial school could require that members of the teaching staff be of the same denomination). Additionally, courts have specified that employers may use facially neutral employment practices that result in a disparate impact on a protected class, but only if a *business necessity* is identified in the use of that practice and there are no less discriminatory ways of meeting that need.

In a significant case, *Hosanna-Tabor Evangelical Lutheran Church v. EEOC*, the U.S. Supreme Court recognized a "ministerial exception" to Title VII and other employment discrimination laws.[7] A teacher who developed narcolepsy and was terminated from her parochial school position, filed a complaint with the EEOC, claiming that her firing violated the Americans with Disabilities Act (ADA). The EEOC eventually sued the religious institution, and the Supreme Court recognized the ministerial exception, which bars lawsuits filed on behalf of ministers by their churches. The teacher's role in the school was considered ministerial because she completed religious training and taught religious courses at the school. This decision's broad interpretation of the ministerial exception affects religious school employees in Title VII and other discrimination claims.

QUALIFYING AS AN EMPLOYER. Title VII applies to employers with fifteen or more employees, each of whom works twenty or more weeks during the calendar year. Although

[4]Vill. of Arlington Heights v. Metro. Hous. Dev. Corp., 429 U.S. 252, 265–68 (1977).
[5]Washington v. Davis, 426 U.S. 229, 242 (1976).
[6]42 U.S.C. § 2000e (2012).
[7]132 S. Ct. 694 (2012).

this requirement is seemingly simple, its application has been complex. The Supreme Court resolved some of the issues in *Walters v. Metropolitan Educational Enterprises*,[8] in which it adopted the "payroll method" to assess employment status. All that is necessary under this approach is to determine when the employee began employment and when he or she left (if at all).[9]

DISPARATE TREATMENT AND IMPACT. When evaluating Title VII claims, courts have developed two legal theories: disparate treatment and disparate impact. *Disparate treatment* is applied when an individual claims less favorable treatment when compared to other applicants or employees. *Disparate impact* is used when an employer's ostensibly neutral practice has a discriminatory impact on the class to which the claimant belongs. In proving disparate treatment, plaintiffs may use direct or circumstantial evidence to prove their employer's discriminatory intent.[10] *Direct evidence* has been defined as evidence, which if believed, proves existence of fact without any inference or assumption.[11] Examples of what has constituted direct evidence in recent cases include an employer making the statement, "You're fired, too. You're too religious,"[12] and a senior employee saying that African American employees are "lazy and malingerers."[13]

Notwithstanding the above, plaintiffs usually do not have direct evidence of discrimination so they often rely on circumstantial evidence[14] to substantiate that they received less favorable treatment and that such conduct, if otherwise unexplained, is "more likely than not based on the consideration of impermissible factors."[15] To support a circumstantial claim, the plaintiff must show that he or she:

- was a member of a protected class;
- applied for and was qualified for the job; and
- was denied the position, while the employer continued to seek applicants with the plaintiff's qualifications.

These criteria were articulated by the Supreme Court in 1973 in *McDonnell Douglas Corporation v. Green*[16] and, with some modification, are applied beyond claims of hiring discrimination to alleged disparate treatment in areas such as promotion, termination, and tenure.

[8]519 U.S. 202 (1997).

[9]Although *Walters* is a Title VII retaliation case, the definition established by the Supreme Court has been applied to cases under the Americans with Disabilities Act (ADA), given the similarity of the two statutes. *See, e.g.*, Owens v. S. Devel. Council, 59 F. Supp. 2d 1210 (M.D. Ala. 1999).

[10]*See, e.g.*, Cole v. Del. Tech. & Cmty. Coll., 459 F. Supp. 2d 296 (D. Del. 2006).

[11]Lex K. Larson on Employment Discrimination § 8.07 (Matthew Bender, a member of the Lexis/Nexis Group, 2012).

[12]Dixon v. Hallmark Cos., 627 F.3d 849, 853 (11th Cir. 2010).

[13]Metoyer v. Chassman, 504 F.3d 919, 925 (9th Cir. 2007).

[14]*See, e.g.*, Walker v. Bd. of Regents of Univ. of Wis. Sys., 410 F.3d 387 (7th Cir. 2005).

[15]Furnco Constr. Corp. v. Waters, 438 U.S. 567, 577 (1978); *see also* Glover v. Bd. of Educ. of Rockford Pub. Schs., 187 F. App'x 614 (7th Cir. 2006) (finding no evidence that supported the use of a discriminatory motive on the part of the employer).

[16]411 U.S. 792, 802 (1973).

If the claim is supported, the burden shifts to the employer to state a "legitimate nondiscriminatory" reason for its action that does not violate Title VII. Such a reason may be either objective (e.g., a higher level academic degree), subjective (e.g., stronger interpersonal skills), or a combination. If the employer is unable to produce a nondiscriminatory reason for the action, a directed verdict for the employee should be granted.[17]

But given the ease of presenting a nondiscriminatory reason, employers in nearly every instance provide a response. After the employer provides a rebuttal, the employee then has the additional burden of proving by a preponderance of the evidence not only that the proffered reason was false but also that it served as a pretext for prohibited intentional discrimination.[18] In most instances of alleged discrimination, the plaintiff is unable to show that the employer's purported nondiscriminatory basis was pretextual.

In contrast to disparate treatment claims, to prove disparate impact, the plaintiff is not initially required to show discriminatory intent but must establish that an employer's facially neutral practice had a disproportionate impact on the plaintiff's protected class. This generally is accomplished through the use of statistics. Once this type of prima facie case is established, the employer then must show that the challenged policies or practices (or its employment practices in the aggregate) are job related and justified by a business necessity. Accordingly, an employer's nondiscriminatory reason for the act is insufficient to rebut a prima facie case of discriminatory impact. Moreover, although difficult to do, even if a business necessity is identified, an employee still may prevail by showing that the employer's facially neutral practice had a discriminatory purpose.

The Supreme Court has recognized, however, that mere awareness of a policy's adverse impact on a protected class does not constitute proof of unlawful motive; a discriminatory purpose "implies that the decisionmaker . . . selected or reaffirmed a particular course of action at least in part 'because of,' not merely 'in spite of,' its adverse effects upon an identifiable group."[19] Nonetheless, foreseeably discriminatory consequences can be considered by courts in assessing intent, although more will be needed to substantiate unlawful motive. Furthermore, the employee may prevail if it is shown that the employer refused to adopt an alternative policy identified by the employee that realistically would have met the employer's business needs without resulting in disparate impact.

[17]*See* note 50 in the chapter "Legal Framework of Public Education" for a discussion of directed verdict.

[18]*See, e.g.*, St. Mary's Honor Ctr. v. Hicks, 509 U.S. 502, 514–15 (1993); *see also* Riley v. Birmingham Bd. of Educ., 154 F. App'x 114 (11th Cir. 2005) (determining that a Caucasian employee failed to show that race was a factor in his demotion and his failure to be selected for the head coaching position; testimony that the African American principal, who had hired African Americans for several positions, had stated "we have to take care of our own," was found insufficient to show pretext); Sarmiento v. Queens Coll., 153 F. App'x 21 (2d Cir. 2005) (finding that a rejected applicant for a teaching position failed to support either race discrimination or retaliation; noting that although at least one of the defendants confirmed animosity toward the plaintiff, there was no proof that such animosity was due to race).

[19]Personnel Adm'r of Mass. v. Feeney, 442 U.S. 256, 279 (1979).

RETALIATION. By the time a complaint is filed with the EEOC or a state or federal court, the working relationship between the employer and the employee is strained, sometimes beyond repair. In response to filing, an employee may not be terminated, demoted, or harassed, but less extreme acts such as rudeness or "the cold shoulder" will not typically violate Title VII.[20] Where actionable behavior occurs, the employee may file a second claim alleging retaliation.[21] To support this type of case, the employee is required to show that he or she participated in statutorily protected activity (i.e., the filing of a complaint or suit), an adverse employment action was taken by the employer, and a causal connection existed between the protected activity and the adverse action.[22] If the employee can show that filing the complaint was the basis for the adverse employment decision, even if the original complaint of discrimination fails, the court will provide appropriate relief.[23] It also is critical to show that the retaliatory action followed soon after engagement in the protected activity. Furthermore, showing that the administrator responsible for the adverse action knew of the filing of the original complaint is essential to establishing that he or she retaliated in response to that filing.[24]

RELIEF. If it is proven that the employee was a victim of prohibited discrimination, courts have the authority to require a *make-whole remedy* where the person is placed in the same position he or she otherwise would have been, absent discriminatory activity. In meeting this objective, courts may provide injunctive and declaratory relief; require that a person be reinstated, hired, tenured, or promoted; direct the payment of back pay, interest on back pay, or front pay;[25] assign retroactive seniority; and provide attorneys' fees and court costs. Requiring the employer to apologize for the discrimination appears to go beyond the court's authority, however.[26] In cases where intentional discrimination is proven, a court also may provide compensatory and punitive damages. But an employer may not be held liable for the discriminatory acts of its managerial staff when their decisions are contrary to the employer's good faith efforts to comply with Title VII.[27]

[20]David J. Walsh, Employment Law for Human Resource Practice, 3d ed. (Mason, OH: Thomson Southwestern, 2010).

[21]*See* Thompson v. N. Am. Stainless, 131 S. Ct. 863 (2011) (finding that Title VII protected a worker who was fired in retaliation for a complaint made by his fiancé who was also an employee).

[22]*See, e.g.*, Valdes v. Union City Bd. of Educ., 186 F. App'x 319 (3d Cir. 2006).

[23]*See* Nye v. Roberts, 145 F. App'x 1 (4th Cir. 2005) (concluding that a letter of reprimand chastising the plaintiff for filing a complaint of sexual harassment may allow a jury to find that the school district retaliated against the plaintiff); *see also* Jackson v. Birmingham Bd. of Educ., 544 U.S. 167 (2005) (holding that retaliation against a girls' basketball coach who had complained of discrimination could support a sex discrimination suit under Title IX, even though the coach's initial complaints of sex discrimination were unfounded).

[24]*See, e.g.*, Boynton v. W. Wyo. Cmty. Coll., 157 F. App'x 33 (10th Cir. 2005).

[25]For example, if a teacher were denied a principalship due to race, the court may direct the district to hire the teacher for the next available position. If the principalship line provided greater compensation than did the teacher line, the court could require that the difference in salary be awarded to the teacher up to the time of promotion. That portion of the salary paid in the future is termed "front pay," while that portion paid for the period between the failure to hire and the court's ruling is termed "back pay."

[26]Woodruff v. Ohman, 29 F. App'x 337 (6th Cir. 2002).

[27]Kolstad v. Am. Dental Ass'n, 527 U.S. 526 (1999).

RACE AND NATIONAL ORIGIN DISCRIMINATION

Race and national origin discrimination in employment continue in spite of nearly 140 years of protective statutes and constitutional amendments.[28] For most of that period, however, the relief received by plaintiffs was typically limited to a make-whole remedy and seldom penalized the employer sufficiently to discourage future discrimination. Due to changes in statutes and case law, it now is possible for successful plaintiffs to receive substantial monetary awards well beyond a make-whole remedy. Race and national origin lawsuits are filed under the Fourteenth Amendment,[29] Title VII, and 42 U.S.C. § 1981.

Section 1981 originally was § 1 of the Civil Rights Act of 1866. At one time, this statute prohibited only race discrimination in making and enforcing contracts, but now § 1981 applies when either race or ethnicity discrimination is alleged in making, performing, modifying, and terminating contracts, as well as in the enjoyment of all benefits, privileges, terms, and conditions of the contractual relationship.[30]

Hiring and Promotion Practices

Unless a school district is under a narrowly tailored court order to correct prior proven acts of race discrimination, it may not advantage or disadvantage an applicant or employee because of that individual's race. When unsuccessful candidates believe that race played a role in the decision-making process, they will generally allege disparate treatment, requiring the heightened proof of discriminatory intent. In attempting to support such a claim, many plaintiffs have difficulty overcoming employers' purported nondiscriminatory reasons for their decisions.[31] For example, in a Fifth Circuit case, a substitute teacher alleged race discrimination and other claims under Title VII against a school district when she was not hired for three full-time history teaching positions. Instead of choosing the substitute teacher, the district hired one black male, one white female, and one white male for the three different positions. Finding in favor of the school district, the court held that the teacher failed to demonstrate pretext for discrimination or that her qualifications were more impressive than those of the three candidates who were hired.[32]

[28]*See* King v. Hardesty, 517 F.3d 1049 (8th Cir. 2008) (ruling that a statement made to an African American teacher about white teachers being able to teach African American students better than African American teachers was evidence that may be viewed as discriminatory); Waite v. Bd. of Trs. of Ill. Cmty. Coll. Dist. No. 508, 408 F.3d 339 (7th Cir. 2005) (finding one statement by one employee that the Jamaican plaintiff had a "plantation mentality" sufficient for a jury to find discriminatory intent, even though the person uttering the phrase was not a decision maker in the plaintiff's suspension).

[29]The Fourteenth Amendment requires the application of strict scrutiny in cases in which race or national origin discrimination is facial and proof of intent where the alleged discrimination is facially neutral.

[30]*See, e.g.*, Amini v. Oberlin Coll., 440 F.3d 350 (6th Cir. 2006).

[31]*See, e.g.*, Barber v. Univ. of Med. & Dentistry of N.J., 118 F. App'x 588 (3d Cir. 2004); Mosby v. Norwalk Bd. of Educ., 4 F. App'x 15 (2d Cir. 2001); Spady v. Wesley Coll., No. 09-834, 2010 U.S. Dist. LEXIS 103967 (D. Del. Sept. 29, 2010).

[32]Godfrey v. Katy Indep. Sch. Dist., 395 F. App'x 88 (5th Cir. 2012); *see also* Brown v. Unified Sch. Dist. No. 501, No. 11-3170, 2012 U.S. App. LEXIS 1815 (10th Cir. 2012) (finding no showing of pretext in teacher's race discrimination claim when teacher was not rehired for three positions).

At other times, plaintiffs are able to show that no legitimate bases supported the employer's decision and that the selection was based on impermissible factors.[33] A Fourth Circuit case focused on national origin discrimination; the teacher was of Russian descent and was not hired for a teaching position. Even though she had superior teaching credentials, the school district deviated from its hiring procedures and hired someone else. After the teacher complained that the district had not followed hiring protocol by not interviewing the most qualified applicant, she was told that the district would not hire a Russian. Reversing the district court's dismissal of the complaint, the appellate court remanded the case because the applicant sufficiently stated a claim that she was the most qualified for the position.[34]

TESTING. Among the more controversial objective measures used in hiring and promotion (e.g., academic degree level, a specified number of years' experience) is the use of standardized test scores. The EEOC requires employers to conduct validity studies for tests used in making employment decisions if they result in adverse impact on a protected class. *Adverse impact* exists when:

- one group succeeds at a rate that is less than four-fifths, or 80 percent, of that achieved by the group with the highest passing rate (e.g., adverse impact results if 90 percent of Caucasians pass a test, but fewer than 72 percent of African Americans do so); *or*
- for small populations, the difference in scores between the two groups is statistically significant.

For tests with a disparate impact to be used, they must be reliable and valid, and they must qualify as a business necessity.[35] Also, tests may be administered to applicants for positions other than those for which the tests have been validated, but only if there are no significant differences in the skills, knowledge, and abilities required by the jobs.[36] Tests may not be discriminatorily administered, nor may their results be discriminatorily used. Moreover, employers may not use different cut-off scores for different racial groups or discard scores based on race.[37]

Notwithstanding the restrictions posed above, many employers (both small and large) feel that the use of tests is so important to the accomplishment of organizational goals that they are compelled to use them. For example, a state has the right to require its current and future teachers to demonstrate their general literacy as well as their content knowledge. In *United States v. South Carolina*, the Supreme Court affirmed a lower court's conclusion that South Carolina's use of the National Teachers Examination (NTE)

[33]*See, e.g.*, Stern v. Trs. of Columbia Univ., 131 F.3d 305 (2d Cir. 1997).

[34]Dolgaleva v. Va. Beach City Pub. Sch., No. 08-1515, 2010 U.S. App. LEXIS 2048 (4th Cir. Jan. 29, 2010).

[35]Griggs v. Duke Power Co., 401 U.S. 424, 432 (1971). In *Griggs*, the Court held that a private company's use of both a high school diploma requirement and a test of general intelligence as prerequisites to initial employment and a condition of transfer violated Title VII; neither requirement was shown to be related to successful job performance, and both operated to disqualify minority applicants at a higher rate than those who were Caucasian.

[36]Albemarle Paper Co. v. Moody, 422 U.S. 405, 432 (1975).

[37]Ricci v. DeStefano, 557 U.S. 557 (2009) (holding that city fire department's choice to ignore test results for promotions because no black fire fighter scored high enough to be considered for promotion violated Title VII).

for teacher certification and salary purposes satisfied the Equal Protection Clause.[38] The federal district court had held that the test was valid, since it measured knowledge of course content in teacher preparation courses, and that it was not administered with an intent to discriminate against minority applicants for teacher certification. The court also found sufficient evidence to establish a relationship between the use of the test scores in determining the placement of teachers on the salary scale and legitimate employment objectives, such as encouraging teachers to upgrade their skills. The option proposed by the plaintiffs (i.e., graduation from an approved teacher preparation program) was rejected by the court as incapable of assuring minimally competent teachers because of the wide range in university admission requirements, academic standards, and grading practices.

It is likely that states, districts, and teacher-training institutions will continue to use tests as a requirement for admission to teacher education training programs; a prerequisite to licensure; and a basis for graduation, hiring, and promotion. To avoid discriminatory actions, test performance should not be the sole criterion for making personnel decisions. Also, even when multiple criteria are used, each criterion must be validated if it results in disproportionate impact or if it is part of a process that in the aggregate results in disproportionate impact.[39]

Adverse Decisions

Employers cannot dismiss, decline to renew, or demote employees on the basis of race or national origin.[40] In an illustrative case, a teacher established a Title VII claim for discrimination by submitting evidence that the principal made derogatory remarks about her Polish national origin, which could be linked to the teacher's contract not being renewed at the end of the year.[41] Reversing the district court's decision, the Seventh Circuit remanded the national origin claim because it was a question for the jury to decide regarding whether there was a connection between the principal's discriminatory statements and the nonrenewal of the teacher's contract. In an Ohio case, an administrator's contract was only renewed for one year, and she alleged race discrimination under Title VII. The Sixth Circuit granted the school board's motion for summary judgment because the administrator failed to establish any evidence of disparate treatment. Specifically, the administrator did not have direct evidence of discrimination, and she unsuccessfully attempted to use statistics to show that the district favored hiring white principals.[42] Further, the court held that her qualifications were

[38]445 F. Supp. 1094 (D.S.C. 1977), *aff'd sub nom.* Nat'l Educ. Ass'n v. South Carolina, 434 U.S. 1026 (1978).

[39]Connecticut v. Teal, 457 U.S. 440 (1982).

[40]*See, e.g.*, Seagrave v. Dean, 908 So. 2d 41 (La. Ct. App. 2005). Title VII also prohibits race-motivated harassment in the workplace. *But see* Sallis v. Univ. of Minn., 408 F.3d 470 (8th Cir. 2005) (concluding that rude and insensitive racial remarks that were infrequently used did not create a hostile work environment).

[41]Darchak v. City of Chi. Bd. of Educ., 580 F.3d 622 (7th Cir. 2009).

[42]Hopkins v. Canton City Bd. of Educ., 477 F. App'x 349 (6th Cir. 2012); *see also* St. Mary's v. Honor Center v. Hicks, 509 U.S. 502 (1993) (finding employee at a halfway house failed to demonstrate that race was a factor in his termination); Good v. Univ. of Chi. Med. Ctr., 673 F.3d 670 (7th Cir. 2012) (finding no "reverse discrimination" under Title VII when minority employees with deficient performance reviews were given demotions and white employee was terminated).

not any better than other successful candidates—some of whom were also African American. Likewise, in a case involving a race discrimination claim under state law, a Massachusetts state court granted summary judgment to a school district, finding the district had demonstrated that the reason for the teacher's termination was related to poor performance. Finding no evidence that the district's conduct was motivated by race, the court observed that the teacher and principal were of the same race (Caucasian).[43]

In some cases, plaintiffs even have difficulty in showing that the conduct of their employers qualified as adverse actions (e.g., change of school, grade level, teaching assignment).[44] The Eleventh Circuit, for example, upheld summary judgment in favor of the school district in a race discrimination case.[45] Although the African American teacher had been given poor performance evaluations by a relatively new principal as well as an independent observer, her nonrenewal notice was not delivered in a timely manner. As a result, she was offered a contract, but elected to decline it. The court reasoned that because a new contract had been proffered, the plaintiff failed to show that she was subjected to an adverse employment act. The threat of nonrenewal and close supervision of her performance were insufficient to qualify as adverse acts. Likewise, an Indian teacher failed to show that her dismissal was based on national origin discrimination.[46] The teacher taught third grade in the district and was reassigned to seventh grade as a result of budget cuts. She was later terminated because of her poor teaching evaluations. Her national origin discrimination claim failed when the Seventh Circuit ruled that being moved from third to seventh grade should not be considered an adverse employment action. Also, the principal's alleged statement that the teacher should try to find a job on "the North side where most of the Indians go" was not related to her discharge.[47]

Affirmative Action

Affirmative action within the context of employment has been defined as "steps taken to remedy the grossly disparate staffing and recruitment patterns that are the present consequences of past discrimination and to prevent the occurrence of employment discrimination in the future."[48] Correcting such imbalances requires the employer to engage in activities such as expanding its training programs, becoming actively involved in recruitment, eliminating invalid selection criteria that result in disparate impact, and modifying collective bargaining agreements that impermissibly restrict the promotion and retention of minorities. Courts will uphold most strategies that the EEOC identifies as affirmative action under both Title VII (for which the EEOC has regulatory authority) and the Fourteenth Amendment (for which the EEOC does not have regulatory authority). However, courts

[43]Pierson v. Stembridge, 957 N.E.2d 254 (Mass. App. Ct. 2011); *see also* Brown v. Sch. Bd., 459 F. App'x 817 (11th Cir. 2012) (finding no discrimination of teacher whose contract was not renewed because he failed to identify other similarly situated individuals who were treated differently).

[44]*See, e.g.*, Pipkin v. Bridgeport Bd. of Educ., 159 F. App'x 259 (2d Cir. 2005).

[45]Christian v. Cartersville City Schs., 167 F. App'x 89 (11th Cir. 2006).

[46]Dass v. Chi. Bd. of Educ., 675 F.3d 1060 (7th Cir. 2012).

[47]*Id.* at 1071.

[48]U.S. Comm'n on Civil Rights, *Statement of Affirmative Action for Equal Employment Opportunities* (1973).

will prohibit the use of affirmative action plans that provide a discriminatory "preference" rather than an "equal opportunity."

In 1989, the Supreme Court began to question a variety of public sector practices that provided racial preferences.[49] In the aggregate, these cases applied strict scrutiny to race-based affirmative action programs operated by federal, state, and local levels of government; discredited societal discrimination as a justification for such programs; required showing specific discriminatory action to impose a race-based remedy; and allowed only narrowly tailored plans that would further a compelling interest. Given these precedents, existing public sector affirmative action plans that provide racial preferences without a proven history of discrimination or are based only on underrepresentation are likely to be found unconstitutional. To illustrate, the Eighth Circuit held that a white teacher presented sufficient evidence of unlawful discrimination and demonstrated that genuine issues of material fact remained about whether the school district's affirmative action policy was valid. The teacher claimed that she was not promoted to an assistant principal position because the district's affirmative action policy unlawfully required that at least one assistant principal at each school be a different race than the school's principal.[50]

In addition to affirmative action in hiring and promotion, efforts have been made to protect the diversity gained through court order and voluntary affirmative action by providing a preference in organization downsizing. When a reduction in school staff is necessary due to financial exigency, declining enrollment, or a change in education priorities, it generally is based, at least in part, on tenure and seniority within teaching areas. Accordingly, it is important for all employees to be in their rightful place on the seniority list. To obtain their rightful place, employees have been awarded varying levels of retroactive seniority (i.e., time between rejection of the application due to impermissible discrimination and court-ordered initial employment), in addition to those years they have accrued while actually on the job.[51]

In some cases, employers have proposed the modification of seniority systems to give an overall preference to all minorities regarding eligibility for promotion and other job benefits or protection from a reduction-in-force (RIF). Such affirmative action plans are similar to awards of retroactive seniority, but in contrast to seniority adjustments for *individual* discrimination victims, *class remedies* benefit class members who may not have been the victim of prior acts of discrimination. Courts will prohibit such practices, even if the employer is found guilty of a pattern or practice of racial discrimination.[52] The appropriate form of relief is to award competitive seniority to individual victims to

[49] *See, e.g.*, Adarand Constructors v. Pena, 515 U.S. 200 (1995); Ne. Fla. Chapter of the Associated Gen. Contractors of Am. v. City of Jacksonville, 508 U.S. 656 (1993); Martin v. Wilks, 490 U.S. 755 (1989).

[50] Humphries v. Pulaski Cnty. Special Sch. Dist., 580 F.3d 688 (8th Cir. 2009); *see also* Taxman v. Bd. of Educ., 91 F.3d 1547 (3d Cir. 1996) (concluding that an affirmative action plan preferring minority teachers over equally qualified nonminority teachers violated Title VII; and finding that the plan had been adopted to promote racial diversity rather than to remedy prior race discrimination by the district, provided preference of "unlimited duration," imposed job loss on tenured nonminority employees, and unnecessarily trammeled the interests of nonminority employees).

[51] *See, e.g.*, Franks v. Bowman Trans. Co., 424 U.S. 747 (1976).

[52] *See, e.g.*, Firefighters Local Union No. 1784 v. Stotts, 467 U.S. 561 (1984).

restore them to their rightful place. Moreover, courts may not disregard a seniority system in fashioning a class remedy.

In 1986, the Supreme Court reviewed a school case involving a voluntary affirmative action plan that included a layoff quota, *Wygant v. Jackson Board of Education.*[53] In that case, the Court struck down a school district's collective bargaining agreement that protected minority teachers from layoffs to preserve the percentage of minority personnel employed prior to the RIF. The Court reasoned that the quota system, which resulted in the release of some Caucasian teachers with greater seniority than some of the minority teachers who were retained, violated the Equal Protection Clause. Societal discrimination alone was not sufficient to justify the class preference. Recognizing that racial classifications in employment must be justified by a compelling governmental interest and that means must be narrowly tailored to accomplish that purpose, the Court concluded that the layoff provision did not satisfy either of these conditions. The Court further rejected the lower courts' reliance on the "role model" theory tying the percentage of minority teachers to the percentage of minority students, noting that the proper comparison for determining employment discrimination is between the racial composition of the teaching staff and the qualified relevant labor market.[54]

Case law involving affirmative action and racial preference may increase given the Supreme Court's decision in *Grutter v. University of Michigan*[55] and the desire of many educational entities to increase the diversity of their instructional and administrative staffs. At this time, however, it is questionable whether the compelling interest identified in *Grutter* (i.e., the benefits derived from a diverse student body) will expand to include employees and whether the Justices' five-to-four decision will effectively negate years of Supreme Court precedent prohibiting the explicit use of race without showing prior institutional discrimination. Even then, the district's affirmative action plan would have to be narrowly tailored.

SEX DISCRIMINATION

Prior to 1963, there were no federal statutes prohibiting discrimination based on sex. Women were commonly denied employment when a qualified male applicant was in the pool, were offered less money for the same or similar job, or were expected to do work that would not have been asked of a man. Today, most forms of sex discrimination are prohibited, including those associated with hiring, promotion, and virtually all terms and conditions of employment. The Fourteenth Amendment,[56] Title VII of the Civil Rights Act of 1964, and other federal and state laws have played significant roles in allowing victims of sex discrimination to attempt to vindicate their rights in court. For example, in a Fifth Circuit case, the plaintiff claimed that although he was better qualified, he was not selected for a technology position, in large part due to the successful female candidate

[53]476 U.S. 267 (1986).
[54]*Wygant*, 476 U.S. at 275–76.
[55]539 U.S. 306 (2003).
[56]The Fourteenth Amendment requires the application of intermediate scrutiny in cases in which sex discrimination is facial and proof of intent in cases in which the alleged discrimination is facially neutral.

having an affair with a high-ranking university administrator.[57] In finding no Title VII violation, the Fifth Circuit noted that the law prohibited sex discrimination (i.e., due to being male or female), not paramour favoritism. Such a basis, although perhaps unfair, results in discrimination against both males and females who were not paramours and, accordingly, is not centered on plaintiff's sex.

Hiring and Promotion Practices

Sex discrimination is facial when an employer openly seeks a person of a particular sex (e.g., the posting of a position for a female guidance counselor). It becomes illegal discrimination when being male or female is unrelated to meeting job requirements (e.g., hiring only males as basketball coaches).[58] At other times, employment practices are facially neutral (e.g., requiring head coaching experience in football in order to qualify as athletic director), but nevertheless result in nearly the same level of exclusion as when the discrimination is facial. If this occurs, an action will be upheld only if found to qualify as a business necessity, and other less discriminatory options do not meet the needs of the organization.

Where applicants or employees have been treated unfairly solely because of their sex, plaintiffs typically file a Title VII suit alleging disparate treatment. The standards for a sex-based prima facie case are similar to those used for race. Also, assuming that a claim is supported, the employer then must identify a basis other than sex for its decision, such as showing that the successful applicant was equally or better qualified or that the plaintiff was unqualified.[59] Where a nondiscriminatory basis has been identified, applicants still may obtain relief if the reasons are shown to be pretextual.[60] For example, rejected applicants could likely prevail where employers base their decisions on stereotypic attitudes about the capabilities of the applicant's sex; job advertisements include phrases, "prefer male" or "prefer female"; or job descriptions are specifically drafted to exclude qualified applicants of a particular sex.

One of the most significant cases involving sex-based discrimination in promotion was a 1981 Supreme Court decision, *Texas Department of Community Affairs v. Burdine*.[61] In this case, a female accounting clerk was denied promotion and later was terminated along with two other employees, although two males were retained. In response to the female's prima facie case, the public employer claimed that the three terminated employees did not work well together and that the male who was promoted to the position sought by the female employee was subjectively better qualified, although he had been her subordinate prior to the promotion. In rendering its decision, the Court emphasized that Title VII does not require the hiring or promotion of equally qualified women or the restructuring of employment practices to maximize the number of underrepresented employees. Instead, the employer has the discretion to choose among

[57]Wilson v. Delta State Univ., 143 F. App'x 611 (5th Cir. 2005).

[58]*See, e.g.*, Fuhr v. Sch. Dist. of City of Hazel Park, 364 F.3d 753 (6th Cir. 2004) (upholding jury award because school board failed to appoint female to coach boys' basketball team, and evidence suggested the decision not to appoint her was motivated by sex).

[59]*See, e.g.*, Straughter v. Vicksburg Warren Sch. Dist., 152 F. App'x 407 (5th Cir. 2005).

[60]*See, e.g.*, Goodwin v. Bd. of Trs. Univ. of Ill., 442 F.3d 611 (7th Cir. 2006).

[61]450 U.S. 248 (1981).

equally qualified candidates so long as the decision is not based on unlawful criteria. In this case, the female employee failed to show pretext, resulting in a decision for the employer.

In subsequent cases, employees have struggled to establish a pretext for discrimination as well. In an illustrative case, a teacher alleged that she was not hired for a transportation supervisor position because she was female. The teacher contended that she was more qualified because she had twenty years' experience as a teacher and four years' experience as a substitute licensed bus driver. The district posited that the male who was hired had more bus driving experience, among other skills. The teacher then argued that driving experience was a pretext for discrimination because this qualification was never listed in the job description. Even though bus driving experience was not listed in the job description, the court held that it did not support a claim of pretext. A second job applicant in this case was also unsuccessful when she claimed sex discrimination after a male was selected for a principal position she had applied for in the district. The court reasoned that considering leadership styles and other subjective criteria when hiring were not pretext for discrimination.[62]

Not all sex-based distinctions are prohibited as Title VII explicitly allows for a bona fide occupational qualification (BFOQ) exception. For a BFOQ to be upheld, it needs to be narrowly defined and applied only when necessary to achieve the employer's objectives. There have been few school-based BFOQ cases, since the vast majority of jobs in education can be performed by either males or females. The only readily identifiable BFOQ in education would be the hiring of a female to supervise the girls' locker room and the hiring of a male to supervise the boys' locker room.

Moreover, where sex does not qualify as a BFOQ, a position may not be left vacant when qualified persons of the nonpreferred sex are available in the labor pool. In such a case, the Seventh Circuit concluded that a reasonable jury had sufficient data to conclude that the plaintiff, a male, was discriminated against solely because of sex when the dean refused to accept his nomination for a position that the dean hoped would be filled by a female.[63] The dean based his decision on the need to meet the affirmative action target for his college. The target was established to create a diversified staff, not to eradicate the consequences of prior discrimination.

Compensation Practices

Claims of sex-based compensation discrimination involving comparative entry salaries, raises, supplemental or overtime opportunities, or other perquisites and benefits are not uncommon within business and industry, and even occur at times in higher education. The U.S. Supreme Court case, *Ledbetter v. Goodyear Tire and Rubber Co.*, brought national attention to compensation discrimination in 2007. The Court held that the statute of limitations for alleging an equal pay lawsuit begins when the employer makes the initial discriminatory wage decision.[64] As a result of the public outcry related to this decision, Congress passed the Lilly Ledbetter Fair Pay Act of 2009, which addresses the time for

[62]Pate v. Chilton Cnty. Bd. of Educ., 853 F. Supp. 2d 1117 (M.D. Ala. 2012).
[63]Hill v. Ross, 183 F.3d 586 (7th Cir. 1999).
[64]550 U.S. 618 (2007).

filing a claim under Title VII for sex discrimination in employment.[65] The amendments to the Civil Rights Act of 1964 changed the 180-day statute of limitations for filing an equal pay lawsuit. Under the amended law, notice of pay discrimination resets with the issuance of each new discriminatory paycheck. This act allows plaintiffs who allege compensation discrimination a much longer window to file their claims. Although the Act would apply to the public school context, most PK–12 salary decisions are based on objective criteria such as seniority and degree level. Teachers, staff, and administrators have challenged the use of facially neutral salary adjustments, such as "head of household" or "principal wage earner" allowances. These practices have been invalidated if not shown to be job related.[66]

The Fourteenth Amendment, Title VII, and the Equal Pay Act (EPA) of 1963 may be used where plaintiffs claim that their salaries are based in whole or in part on their sex. The EPA applies only when the dispute involves sex-based wage discrimination claims of unequal pay for equal work.[67] As a result, the Act does not apply when race-based or age-based salary differences are challenged or when the work is unequal.[68] The plaintiff need not prove that the employer intended to discriminate, as with Title VII disputes; proof that the compensation is different and not based on factors other than sex will suffice. Furthermore, the law prohibits the lowering of the salaries for the higher paid group and therefore requires the salaries for the lower paid group to be raised. It is important to note that relief under the EPA is not barred by Eleventh Amendment immunity.[69] In one case, a principal argued that the district discriminated against her by paying male principals more in violation of the EPA. The female principal argued that five male principals at other similarly situated high schools had higher salaries, bonuses, and other financial incentives. Holding in favor of the district, the federal district court ruled that the female principal had failed to produce any evidence that the male principals had comparable job duties.[70]

Because the EPA is limited to controversies dealing with equal work, its application is restricted to those circumstances where there are male and female employees performing substantially the same work but for different pay. Accordingly, if there are no male secretaries for a salary comparison, there can be no EPA violation, regardless of how abysmal the salaries of female secretaries may be. In determining whether the jobs in question are equal, courts look at more than position titles and will examine the comparative skills, effort, responsibilities, and working conditions associated with each

[65]42 U.S.C. § 2000e-5(e) (2012).

[66]*See, e.g.*, EEOC v. Fremont Christian Sch., 781 F.2d 1362 (9th Cir. 1986).

[67]29 U.S.C. § 206(d) (2012); *see also* Ghirardo v. Univ. of S. Cal., 156 F. App'x 914 (9th Cir. 2005) (finding no EPA violation when plaintiff failed to show that her total compensation or annual raises were due to her sex; rather, her total salary was comparable to males, and recent raises were minor due to her undisputed failure to attend retreats, refusal to meet with the dean, and other instances of recalcitrance).

[68]*See, e.g.*, Vasquez v. El Paso Cnty. Cmty. Coll., 177 F. App'x 422 (5th Cir. 2006). In the 1980s, the comparable worth doctrine was used as an attempt to remedy pay inequity that resulted from a history of sex-segregation in employment. For example, if working in childcare (historically a profession dominated by females) is as important and difficult as working as a butcher (historically a profession dominated by males), then childcare workers and butchers should receive similar pay. Although courts have been skeptical of this doctrine, its merits continue to be debated.

[69]*See, e.g.*, Siler-Khodr v. Univ. of Tex. Health Sci. Ctr., 261 F.3d 542 (5th Cir. 2001).

[70]Musgrove v. Dist. of Columbia, 775 F. Supp. 2d 158 (D.D.C. 2011).

job and the nature of the required tasks. If the jobs are found substantially equal but with unequal pay, the employer then must show that the different salaries were based on seniority, merit, quantity or quality of production, or any factor other than sex.[71] Where the employer purports to be using a merit system, it should be uniformly applied and based on established criteria.[72]

Termination, Nonrenewal, and Denial of Tenure

Title VII prohibits arbitrary removal of employees and the denial of tenure if based on sex or other prohibited factors.[73] In disparate treatment cases, the employee is required to prove that the employer elected to terminate or not renew the employee's contract due to sex rather than job performance, inappropriate conduct, interpersonal relationships, financial exigency, or other just cause. As in most cases where proof of intent is required, employees alleging sex discrimination often have difficulty supporting their claims, even if true. Occasionally, however, corroborating evidence will be inadvertently provided by officials responsible for making personnel decisions.

In a Tenth Circuit case, a female former principal was "bumped" by an associate superintendent who assumed her position as well as his own. The district initially proposed that the RIF was necessary due to financial exigency but later claimed that the female principal had continuing difficulty with her faculty, which allegedly was the basis for her contract not being renewed. The appeals court found the evidence to be contradictory, including the superintendent's annual evaluation of the principal in which she received high marks for establishing and maintaining staff cooperation and creating an environment conducive to learning. Given such discrepancies, the appeals court reversed the lower court's grant of summary judgment for the school district.[74]

Where facial discrimination does not exist, most plaintiffs will attempt to show that persons of the opposite sex were treated differently (e.g., required to meet different standards, assessed differently in meeting the same standards). With this approach, however, it often is difficult to identify a comparable party or to challenge subjective judgments regarding performance or potential.

Sexual Harassment

Sexual harassment generally refers to repeated and unwelcome sexual advances, sexually suggestive comments, or sexually demeaning gestures or acts. Both men and women

[71] *See, e.g.*, Wollenburg v. Comtech Mfg. Co., 201 F.3d 973 (7th Cir. 2000); Mullins v. Bd. of Regents of Univ. of Wis. Sys., No. 05-C-581-S, 2006 U.S. Dist. LEXIS 11497 (W.D. Wis. Mar. 10, 2006).

[72] *See, e.g.*, Port Auth. v. Ryduchowski, 530 U.S. 1276 (2000).

[73] Weinstock v. Columbia Univ., 224 F.3d 33 (2d Cir. 2000). Moreover, Title VII also prohibits behaviors that would result in the constructive discharge of employees. *See, e.g.*, Palomo v. Trs. of Columbia Univ., 170 F. App'x 194 (2d Cir. 2006).

[74] Cole v. Ruidoso Mun. Sch., 43 F.3d 1373 (10th Cir. 1994). *But see* Atkinson v. LaFayette Coll., 460 F.3d 447 (3d Cir. 2006) (determining that the university administration provided sufficient documentation showing that the plaintiff had alienated others in her leadership role and that her ineffective interpersonal skills created poor relations and low morale within her unit).

have been victims of sexual harassment from persons of the opposite or same sex.[75] The harasser may be a supervisor, an agent of the employer, a coworker, a nonemployee, or even a student. Critical to a successful claim is proof that the harassment is indeed based on sex, rather than sexual orientation, being transsexual, transvestism, or another factor. For example, in an Eleventh Circuit case, a male teacher and female teacher had a consensual relationship that the male eventually ended. The female then began making threatening overtures toward the wife and son of her former lover, resulting in the wife acquiring a restraining order. As the teachers taught at the same school, the female also sought to embarrass her male colleague in front of other staff and students whenever possible. After unsuccessful administrative claims, the male teacher filed suit, claiming hostile work environment harassment. The Eleventh Circuit disagreed and determined that the female teacher had targeted the male teacher because he ended their relationship and not because he was male.[76]

There are two types of harassment cognizable under Title VII:[77] quid pro quo and hostile work environment. Each is reviewed briefly here.

QUID PRO QUO. Quid pro quo literally means "this for that," or, in this context, giving something for something. To establish a prima facie case of quid pro quo harassment against an employer, the employee must show that he or she was subjected to unwelcome sexual harassment in the form of sexual advances and requests for sexual favors, that the harassment was based on the person's sex (i.e., being male or female), and that submission to the unwelcome advances was an express or implied condition for either favorable actions or avoidance of adverse actions by the employer. Although only a preponderance of evidence is required in such cases, acquiring the necessary 51 percent can be difficult, particularly given that the violator is unlikely to provide corroborating testimony. Also, the alleged behavior usually takes place behind closed doors, limiting the opportunity for others to observe the conduct. If the employee succeeds, however, the law imposes strict liability on the employer, because of the harasser's authority to alter the terms and conditions of employment.

HOSTILE WORK ENVIRONMENT. In *Meritor Savings Bank v. Vinson*, the Supreme Court recognized for the first time that a Title VII violation can be predicated on harassment that creates a hostile or offensive work environment in addition to harassment that involves conditioning employment benefits on sexual favors.[78] To prevail under this theory, the plaintiff must show that the environment in fact is hostile and that it is severe or pervasive.[79] Conduct unreasonably interfering with an individual's work performance or creating an

[75]*See, e.g.*, Oncale v. Sundowner Offshore Servs., 523 U.S. 75 (1998).

[76]Succar v. Dade Cnty. Sch. Bd., 229 F.3d 1343 (11th Cir. 2000).

[77]In addition to filing a Title VII claim, plaintiffs may file charges under state employment law or state tort law. Tort claims may include intentional infliction of emotional distress, assault and battery, invasion of privacy, and defamation.

[78]477 U.S. 57 (1986).

[79]*See, e.g.*, Cosby v. Purdue Univ., No. 4:08-CV-88-RRC, 2010 U.S. Dist. LEXIS 72625 (N.D. Ind. July 16, 2010). *But see* Whittaker v. N. Ill. Univ., 424 F.3d 640 (7th Cir. 2005) (concluding that offensive comments that were not made in plaintiff's presence and were unknown to her until after her employment did not contribute to the creation of a hostile environment).

intimidating, hostile, or offensive work environment is actionable. Courts generally consider whether the victim:

- solicited or initiated the conduct;
- considered the conduct undesirable and offensive;
- contributed to creating the environment; and
- informed the harasser that the unwelcome conduct was offensive.

Although the Supreme Court provided significant guidance in the *Meritor* case, it left unanswered questions regarding the need to prove psychological injury, particularly in the absence of tangible job losses. The Supreme Court addressed this issue later in *Harris v. Forklift Systems.*[80] In *Harris*, a female executive was regularly exposed to hostile and abusive conduct by the company's president. Among the president's controversial behaviors was his request of female staff to get coins from his front pants pocket or for them to retrieve coins that he had tossed on the floor. Following the president's comment that the plaintiff must have promised sex to a customer to have acquired a lucrative contract, she quit her job and eventually sued. The lower court held that a reasonable victim would have found the president's conduct offensive but that it was not so egregious as to interfere with her work performance or to cause injury; this opinion was affirmed by the Sixth Circuit.

In a rare unanimous decision, the Supreme Court reversed and identified what it perceived to be a middle path between finding conduct that is merely offensive to violate Title VII and requiring the conduct to cause a diagnosed psychological injury. The Court held that Title VII is violated if the environment would reasonably be perceived as hostile and abusive and that psychological injury need not be proven. The Court suggested the following criteria in assessing whether an environment is in fact hostile:

- the frequency and severity of the discriminatory conduct;
- whether the behavior is physically threatening or humiliating, or merely an offensive utterance; and
- whether the conduct unreasonably interferes with an employee's work performance.

Employer liability in hostile environment claims is more difficult to establish than in quid pro quo claims, but it may be easier to substantiate in light of *Burlington Industries v. Ellerth*[81] and *Faragher v. City of Boca Raton.*[82] In these cases, the Supreme Court proclaimed that an employer is subject to vicarious liability for the acts of its supervisors with immediate authority over an alleged victim. However, the employer may raise an affirmative defense to liability if the employee suffered no tangible employment loss. Such a defense requires that the employer exercise reasonable care to prevent or promptly correct harassing behavior *and* that the employee failed to take advantage of preventive and corrective opportunities provided by the employer.[83] Accordingly, to guard against liability, school districts should:

- Prepare and disseminate sexual harassment policies.
- Provide appropriate in-service training.

[80]510 U.S. 17 (1993).
[81]524 U.S. 742 (1998).
[82]524 U.S. 775 (1998).
[83]*See* Penn. State Police v. Suders, 542 U.S. 129 (2004) (holding that although the employee did not avail herself of her employer's anti-harassment procedures, a question of triable fact remained regarding the adequacy of those procedures).

- Establish appropriate grievance procedures, including at least two avenues for reporting in case one avenue is blocked by the harasser or a supportive colleague of the harasser.
- Select both male and female disinterested investigators.
- Take claims seriously and investigate promptly.
- Take corrective action in a timely manner.
- Maintain thorough records of all claims and activities.

While most of this discussion has focused on employers harassing employees, there have been some cases where teachers have alleged under Title VII that they were harassed by students.[84]

Pregnancy Discrimination

Under the Pregnancy Discrimination Act (PDA),[85] an amendment to Title VII enacted in 1978, employers may not discriminate based on pregnancy, childbirth, or related medical conditions.[86] As such, pregnancy may not be used as a basis for refusing to hire an otherwise qualified applicant; denying disability, medical, or other benefits; or terminating or nonrenewal of employment. To succeed, the employee must show that the employer knew she was pregnant prior to the adverse action and that the pregnancy, rather than some other factor, was the basis of an adverse decision.[87]

If an employer requires a doctor's statement for other conditions, it also may require one for pregnancy prior to granting leave or paying benefits.[88] And, if employees are unable to perform their jobs due to pregnancy, the employer is required to treat them the same as any other temporarily disabled person.[89] Possible forms of accommodation may be to modify tasks, alternate assignments, or provide disability leave (with or without pay). If a pregnant employee takes a leave of absence, her position must be held open the same length of time that it would be if she were sick or disabled. Moreover, maternity leave cannot be considered an interruption in employment for the purposes of accumulating credit toward tenure or seniority if employees retain seniority rights when on leave for other disabilities.[90]

[84]*See* Lucero v. Nettle Creek Sch. Corp., 566 F.3d 720 (7th Cir. 2009) (rejecting teacher's claim that she had been harassed by students because students had been disciplined by school officials); Mongelli v. Clay Consol. Sch. Dist., 491 F. Supp. 2d 467 (D. Del. 2007) (finding harassment of teacher by special education student was actionable under Title VII); Plaza-Torres v. Rey, 376 F. Supp. 2d 171 (D.P.R. 2005) (reasoning that student-on-teacher harassment is actionable under Title VII).

[85]42 U.S.C. § 2000e(k) (2012).

[86]The PDA was passed in response to two Supreme Court decisions in which the denial of benefits for pregnancy-related conditions was found not to violate either Title VII or the Fourteenth Amendment. *See* Gen. Elec. Co. v. Gilbert, 429 U.S. 125 (1976); Geduldig v. Aiello, 417 U.S. 484 (1974).

[87]*See, e.g.*, Silverman v. Bd. of Educ. of City of Chic., 637 F.3d 729 (7th Cir. 2012) (holding that a principal's decision not to renew a teacher's contract was not pregnancy discrimination because the principal's decision was based on the need to eliminate a teaching position).

[88]EEOC v. Elgin Teachers Ass'n, 27 F.3d 292 (N.D. Ill. 1994) (validating the association's maternity leave procedures, which conditioned the teacher's pay on a showing of "actual inability to work" during the six-week period).

[89]29 C.F.R. pt. 1604, Appendix (2012).

[90]Nashville Gas Co. v. Satty, 434 U.S. 136 (1977).

Mandatory pregnancy leave policies requiring teachers to take a leave of absence prior to the birth of their children and specifying a return date also violate the Due Process Clause by creating an *irrebuttable presumption* that all pregnant teachers are physically incompetent as of a specified date.[91] School boards, however, may establish maternity leave policies that are justified by a business necessity, such as the requirement that the employee notify the administration of her intended departure and return dates, assuming this is required for other forms of extended personal leave. The business necessity of such a policy is to allow for planning and staffing in the employee's absence.

Although employers may not treat pregnant employees less favorably, they may grant special leave and other benefits that are unavailable to nonpregnant persons. As indicated by the Ninth Circuit, the PDA was intended "to construct a floor beneath which pregnancy disability benefits may not drop" rather than "a ceiling above which they may not rise."[92] However, supplemental benefits that go beyond those made available to other employees may have additional restrictions and limitations. For example, the Seventh Circuit determined that a school district's maternity leave procedures may be more restrictive than the procedures for other forms of leave and still not violate the PDA.[93] The appeals court concluded that the school board treated pregnant and nonpregnant teachers the same with regard to other forms of leave, plus gave pregnant teachers a further option of using maternity leave, albeit with some restrictions.

Notwithstanding the fact that special benefits may be available only to pregnant employees, the Third Circuit invalidated a leave policy that permitted female employees, but not male employees, to use up to one year of combined sick leave and unpaid leave for child rearing.[94] Noting that the leave was not tied to any continuing disability related to pregnancy or childbirth, the court held that denial of a year of unpaid leave for child rearing to a male teacher constituted sex discrimination under Title VII.[95]

Retirement Benefits

Although the longevity figures for men and women have narrowed over the past thirty-five years, it remains true that women on average live longer than men. In fact, in 2007, women had a projected life expectancy five years longer than that for men, although that number had been on the decline since 1970, when it peaked at 7.6 years.[96] Recognition of female longevity historically resulted in differential treatment of women with respect to retirement benefits, since employers either required women to make a higher contribution or awarded them lower annual benefits upon retirement. But in 1978, the Supreme Court rejected the use of sex-segregated actuarial tables in retirement benefits programs.

[91]Cleveland Bd. of Educ. v. LaFleur, 414 U.S. 632 (1974).

[92]Cal. Fed. Savings & Loan Ass'n v. Guerra, 758 F.2d 390, 396 (9th Cir. 1985), *aff'd*, 479 U.S. 272 (1987).

[93]United States v. Bd. of Educ., 983 F.2d 790 (7th Cir. 1993).

[94]Schafer v. Bd. of Pub. Educ., 903 F.2d 243 (3d Cir. 1990).

[95]*See* Family Medical Leave Act, 29 U.S.C. § 2612 (2012) (permitting eligible employees to take up to twelve work weeks of leave in a twelve-month period to care for a newborn or adopted child, as well as a spouse, parent, or child with health issues).

[96]Elizabeth Arias, *United States Life Tables, 2007*, NATIONAL VITAL STATISTICS REPORTS (Sept. 28, 2011), http://www.cdc.gov/nchs/data/nvsr/nvsr59/nvsr59_09.pdf.

The Court invalidated a retirement program requiring women to make a higher contribution to receive equal benefits on retirement, noting that sex was the only factor considered in predicting life expectancy.[97] This case established that women cannot receive lower benefits for equal contributions either.

SEXUAL ORIENTATION DISCRIMINATION

When public employees are discriminated against due to sexual orientation in hiring, promotion, termination, or any other term or condition of employment, they may file suit under the Fourteenth Amendment.[98] Both public sector and private sector employees also may base related complaints on state statutes and local ordinances, where they exist. Although Title VII does not specifically prohibit discrimination based on sexual orientation, the EEOC ruled recently that Title VII protections extend to transgendered employees.[99]

Access to Benefits and Other Rights

Some states, locales, and employers—through their constitutions, statutes, ordinances, policies, or common law—have elected to permit same-sex partners to receive benefits. But unless restricted by state law or local ordinance, school districts may limit the availability of family benefits to legal spouses and dependents. Likewise, in those states that recognize only heterosexual marriages, benefits such as retirement, death, health care, eye care, and dental are not generally available to same-sex partners or the children of same-sex partners, unless the children have been legally adopted by the employee.[100] This position was fortified in 1996 by the passage of the Defense of Marriage Act (DOMA).[101] That statute gives states the option of refusing to extend marriage benefits to same-sex partners who were legally married in another state, territory, or country, but this statute has been under scrutiny. In 2011, the Obama Administration stated it would no longer defend the constitutionality of the DOMA in court.[102] Also, in 2012, the First and Second Circuits declared part of DOMA to be unconstitutional because it discriminates against married same-sex couples by denying them the same benefits afforded to heterosexual couples.[103] The Supreme Court will address many of these unsettled issues in 2013.

[97]City of L.A. Dep't of Water & Power v. Manhart, 435 U.S. 702 (1978).

[98]Under the Fourteenth Amendment, rational-basis scrutiny is applied in sexual orientation cases when facial discrimination is supported, whereas discriminatory intent must be proven when the discrimination is facially neutral.

[99]Macy v. Holder, Appeal No. 0120120821 (EEOC, Apr. 20, 2012) The EEOC observed that "intentional discrimination against a transgender individual because that person is transgender is, by definition, discrimination based on . . . sex, and such discrimination therefore violates Title VII."

[100]Rutgers Council of AAUP Chapters v. Rutgers, 689 A.2d 828 (N.J. Superior Ct. App. Div. 1997).

[101]28 U.S.C. § 1738C (2012).

[102]*See* Dep't of Justice, *Statement of the Attorney General on Litigation Involving the Defense of Marriage Act* (Feb. 23, 2011), http://www.justice.gov/opa/pr/2011/February/11-ag-222.html.

[103]*See* Massachusetts v. U.S. Dep't of Health & Human Servs., 682 F.3d 1 (1st Cir. 2012); Windsor v. United States, No. 12-2334-cv(L), 2012 U.S. App. LEXIS 21785 (2d Cir. Sept. 27, 2012), *cert. granted*, 2012 U.S. LEXIS 9413 (U.S. Dec. 7, 2012) (No. 12-307).

Harassment

The harassment of employees based on sexual orientation also may violate state and local laws as well as the Fourteenth Amendment. Meeting the required intent standard may be difficult, however, in situations where school district employees are not directly responsible for the harassment. The Seventh Circuit was confronted with a case where a former teacher claimed that the school district failed to take reasonable measures to prevent students, parents, and colleagues from harassing him due to his sexual orientation.[104] The teacher demanded that the district engage in system-wide sensitivity training to condemn discrimination against homosexuals, given that a related memorandum and the disciplining of a few violating students had proved ineffectual. The principal suggested that the teacher try to ignore students' behavior, as getting them to stop would be difficult, if not impossible. The teacher sued under the Fourteenth Amendment but was unable to prove either that the district demonstrated the intent to discriminate or was deliberately indifferent to his treatment by students. District personnel were found to have made legitimate efforts to reduce or eliminate the harassment.

Adverse Employment Decisions

Terminating or not renewing employment of a public employee solely due to sexual orientation is unlikely to meet even rational basis scrutiny. In an illustrative case, a teacher's contract was not renewed after she showed her civics classes a PowerPoint presentation on the National Day of Silence—a day on which individuals remain silent to bring attention to the animus and discrimination faced by gay students. The teacher, known by school administrators and students to be a lesbian, had refused to speak as the PowerPoint presentation played. The school board contended that its decision was based on reduced student enrollment and the limited nature of the teacher's certificate. The court found, however, that a genuine issue of fact existed as to whether those reasons were pretextual, given that a heterosexual teacher who had also discussed gay issues with his students was retained. The dismissed teacher was able to offer evidence that student enrollment was sufficient to justify retaining her and that she was fully qualified to teach her government classes. Moreover, she offered evidence that her controversial presentation had been discussed by administrators and school board members prior to their decision not to renew her contract. Accordingly, the court found that the teacher had established a prima facie case of discrimination based on sexual orientation and allowed her equal protection claim to proceed to trial.[105]

In another case, although a New York district court held that Title VII substantive anti-discrimination provisions do not cover claims based on sexual orientation, it did find that the law's anti-retaliation provisions extend to claims based on sexual orientation. While employed by the school district, a former gay guidance counselor was told by his principal to limit his contact with fifth graders after several teachers complained that they did not want their students counseled by a gay man. When he told the principal that he

[104]Schroeder v. Hamilton Sch. Dist., 282 F.3d 946 (7th Cir. 2002).

[105]Beall v. London City Sch. Dist. Bd. of Ed., 98 Fair Empl. Prac. Cas. (BNA) 1425 (S.D. Ohio 2006).

planned to file a grievance, she allegedly retaliated against him by eliminating his position. The court ruled that the former counselor had stated a valid claim for Title VII retaliation based on sexual orientation.[106]

As noted, a private sector employee must seek protection under either state law or local ordinance and must show that sexual orientation was in fact the basis of the adverse action to substantiate a valid discrimination claim. Such state and local provisions may not violate federal constitutional rights in their application, however. In *Boy Scouts of America v. Dale*, the Supreme Court found that the New Jersey public accommodation law, previously interpreted to require the Boy Scouts to admit a homosexual assistant scoutmaster to its ranks, violated the private nonprofit organization's expressive association rights.[107] The Court observed that the plaintiff's openness about his own sexual orientation and advocacy of related rights operated against those expressed by the Scouts, and that to require the Scouts to retain him would significantly burden the organization in its effort to oppose homosexual conduct.[108]

DISCRIMINATION BASED ON RELIGION

The United States is now more culturally and religiously diverse than at any time in its history. When discrimination occurs, or an employer fails to provide reasonable accommodations, First and Fourteenth Amendment[109] claims have been filed as well as claims under Title VII.

The first issue in such cases is whether the discrimination is based on sincerely held religious beliefs. A person's religion does not have to be organized, recognized, or well known. Curiously, even opposition to abortion, the draft, and nuclear power have qualified as "religious" beliefs,[110] although a belief in veganism has not.[111] Nonetheless, employers generally should accept an employee's representation of a sincerely held belief, at least for accommodation purposes.[112] Where the employee suffers an adverse employment outcome due to religion, the employer then must show either that an accommodation

[106]Birkholz v. City of N.Y., No. 10-cv-479, 2012 U.S. Dist. LEXIS 22445 (E.D.N.Y. Feb. 22, 2012).

[107]530 U.S. 640 (2000).

[108]*See also* Hall v. Baptist Mem. Health Care Corp., 215 F.3d 618 (6th Cir. 2000) (finding no religious discrimination when a religious employer terminated a student services specialist because of her expressed views and sexual orientation; the decision was based on the religious discrimination exception under Title VII).

[109]If an employee claims an Equal Protection Clause violation due to religious-based facial discrimination by government, either strict scrutiny or rational-basis scrutiny could apply, depending on the form of the discrimination. When the government infringes upon the employee's First Amendment right to exercise religious beliefs (a fundamental right), strict scrutiny is applied. On the other hand, if the employee is a victim of discrimination based on religion, rational-basis scrutiny is applied. Intent must be proven in cases involving facially neutral discrimination.

[110]*See, e.g.*, Wilson v. U.S. W. Communications, 58 F.3d 1337 (8th Cir. 1995); Am. Postal Workers Union v. Postmaster Gen., 781 F.2d 772 (9th Cir. 1986); Best v. Cal. Apprenticeship Council, 207 Cal. Rptr. 863 (Ct. App. 1984).

[111]Friedman v. S. Cal. Permanente Med. Group, 125 Cal. Rptr. 2d 663 (Ct. App. 2002).

[112]*But see* Bushhouse v. Local Union 2209, 164 F. Supp. 2d 1066 (N.D. Ind. 2001) (concluding that there was no Title VII violation when a union sought to verify the religious beliefs of an employee who did not want to pay dues based on those beliefs).

was offered, but not taken, or that no reasonable accommodation existed that would not result in hardship for the employer.

Hiring and Promotion Practices

Private religious organizations are exempt from First and Fourteenth Amendment claims and in large part from the religious restrictions imposed by Title VII.[113] As a result, they are not generally prohibited from establishing religion as a bona fide occupational qualification (BFOQ) (e.g., when a Methodist theological seminary requires that its instructors be Methodists) or from making employment decisions that are consistent with the tenets of their particular faith.[114]

In contrast, religion will never qualify as a BFOQ in public education, and public employers may not inquire as to an applicant's religious beliefs, use the interview process as an opportunity to indoctrinate, or require prospective employees to profess a belief in a particular faith or in God.[115] A person's religious affiliation or practice, if any, should not be considered in making an employment decision.

Accommodation

Recommended forms of religious accommodation include activities such as accepting voluntary substitutions and assignment exchanges, using a flexible schedule, and modifying job assignments. Tests, interviews, and other selection procedures should not be scheduled at times when an applicant cannot attend for religious reasons. However, if requested accommodations would compromise the constitutional, statutory, or contractual rights of others (e.g., interfere with a bona fide seniority system) or result in undue hardship, Title VII does not require the employer to make the accommodation.[116] Undue hardship results when extensive changes are required in business practices or when the costs of religious accommodations are more than minimal. The burden is on school personnel to inform the district if certain activities would offend their religious beliefs.[117] Some of the more often litigated controversies regarding religious accommodation in public education involve dress codes, personal leave, and job assignments.

ATTIRE RESTRICTIONS. As a general rule, public school district restrictions on the wearing of religious apparel, even if also purportedly cultural, will be upheld where young and impressionable students would perceive the garment as religious. In an illustrative case, the Third Circuit held that a district's refusal to accommodate a Muslim substitute teacher who sought to wear religious attire in the public school classroom did not

[113]42 U.S.C. § 2000e-1(a) (2012).
[114]See *supra* text accompanying note 7 for a discussion of the ministerial exception.
[115]Torcaso v. Watkins, 367 U.S. 488 (1961).
[116]Harrell v. Donahue, 638 F.3d 975 (8th Cir. 2011) (determining that it would be an undue hardship and a violation of the collective bargaining agreement to accommodate a postal employee who is a Seventh Day Adventist by not scheduling him to work on Saturdays).
[117]Wilkerson v. New Media Tech. Charter Sch., 522 F.3d 315 (3d Cir. 2008) (dismissing teacher's Title VII claim involving a failure to accommodate her Christian beliefs because school officials were not informed that a "libations ceremony" at the school banquet would offend her religious beliefs).

violate Title VII.[118] The district's action was pursuant to a state statute that regarded the wearing of religious clothing as a significant threat to the maintenance of a religiously neutral public school system. Similar decisions have been reached by a federal court in Mississippi when it upheld the termination of a teacher aide who refused to comply with the school's dress code proscribing religious attire,[119] and by the Oregon Supreme Court when it upheld a statutory prohibition on religious attire in public schools as applied to a female Sikh who dressed in white clothes and turban.[120]

PERSONAL LEAVE. Although most public school calendars allow time off for Christmas and Easter to coincide with semester and spring breaks, holy days of religions other than Christianity are not so routinely accommodated. But when a school district serves a significant number of students or employs a large number of teachers or staff of another religion, it is not uncommon for schools to be closed on several of the more significant days of worship for that religion as well. The "secular purpose" of such an act is the need to operate the school efficiently. If schools were to remain open when many people were absent, administrators would be required to hire numerous substitutes, and teachers would have to prepare a burdensome level of make-up work. When districts elect to remain open in spite of the absence of a large number of students or teachers, substitute teachers often are instructed not to present new material to reduce the need for repetitive lessons.

Although the aforementioned approach may provide satisfactory results when attempting to accommodate one or two faiths, it is unrealistic to assume that public schools will be closed for the holy days of every religion. Alternatively, school districts often provide a variety of accommodations to avoid unduly burdening the religious beliefs of their employees (e.g., use of personal leave days, flexible schedules), depending upon the nature of their employment.

Modest requests for religious absences are typically met, but others may result in hardship both for the district as well as for students.[121] Where leave has been provided, some employees have been satisfied when allowed to have the day off without adverse impact; others have requested that leave be accompanied with full or partial pay. In *Ansonia Board of Education v. Philbrook*, a teacher asserted that the negotiated agreement violated Title VII by permitting employees to use only three days of paid leave for religious purposes, whereas three additional days of paid personal business leave could be used for specified secular activities.[122] The teacher proposed either permitting the use of the paid personal business leave days for religious observances or allowing employees to receive full pay and cover the costs of substitute teachers for each additional day missed for religious reasons. The Supreme Court, in upholding the agreement, held that

[118]United States v. Bd. of Educ., 911 F.2d 882 (3d Cir. 1990). *But see* Brown v. F.L. Roberts & Co., 896 N.E.2d 1279 (Mass. 2008) (overturning summary judgment for the employer and holding that a Rastafarian service technician may have had a legitimate religious discrimination claim under state law after the employer required him to have short hair and to shave).

[119]McGlothin v. Jackson Mun. Separate Sch. Dist., 829 F. Supp. 853 (S.D. Miss. 1992).

[120]Cooper v. Eugene Sch. Dist. No. 4J, 723 P.2d 298 (Or. 1986).

[121]*See* Trans World Airlines v. Hardison, 432 U.S. 63 (1977) (finding no Title VII violation involving an employee who, for religious reasons, could not work on Saturdays; the employer was not required to bear more than minimal costs in making religious accommodations).

[122]479 U.S. 60 (1986).

the employer was not required to show that each of the plaintiff's proposed alternatives would result in undue hardship, and noted that the employer could satisfy Title VII by offering a reasonable accommodation, which may or may not be the one the employee preferred.

It is important to note that religious leave need not be paid unless compensation is provided for other forms of leave.[123] In a Tenth Circuit case, the court rejected a teacher's claim that the school district's leave policy violated Title VII and burdened his free exercise of religion because he occasionally had to take unpaid leave to observe Jewish holidays.[124] The policy allowed teachers two days of paid leave that could be used for religious purposes. The court concluded that the availability of unpaid leave for additional religious observances constituted a reasonable accommodation under Title VII and did not place a substantial burden on free exercise rights. In another case, a Muslim teacher sued the school district for religious discrimination when she was denied an unpaid three-week leave of absence so she could make a pilgrimage to Mecca, Saudi Arabia. The once-in-a-lifetime pilgrimage, or Hajj, is considered one of the most important religious requirements for the Muslim faith. The U.S. Department of Justice reached a settlement with the school district, which accommodated the teacher with unpaid leave.[125]

JOB ASSIGNMENTS AND RESPONSIBILITIES. If an employee is hired to perform a certain job, he or she must be willing and able to perform all of the essential functions of the job. In a somewhat unusual case, an interpreter for the hearing impaired refused to translate or sign any cursing or bad language and used her religious beliefs as a basis for the refusal.[126] Given her willing violation of district policy and administrative directives, her contract was terminated. The Missouri appeals court upheld her termination under state law and concluded that the teacher could not have been accommodated without compromising the educational entitlements of her students and that requiring a literal translation of classroom dialogue was not unreasonable.

Likewise, the Third Circuit found that a university hospital had reasonably accommodated a nurse who had refused to participate in abortions, given her Pentecostal religious beliefs.[127] She had been permitted to trade assignments with other nurses, unless an emergency existed. When she failed to treat pregnant patients when they were experiencing life-threatening situations, the hospital gave her the option of transferring to a comparable job where her beliefs would not conflict with essential job requirements, but the nurse refused. The court upheld her subsequent termination and indicated that the public trust requires public health care practitioners to provide treatment in the time of emergency.

[123]*Id.* at 71.

[124]Pinsker v. Joint Dist. No. 28J, 735 F.2d 388 (10th Cir. 1984).

[125]Manya A. Brachear, *Settlement Reached in Muslim's Suit over Denial of Time Off for Hajj*, CHI. TRIB. (Oct. 19, 2011), http://articles.chicagotribune.com/2011-10-19/news/ct-met-hajj-time-off-20111019_1_safoorah-khan-hajj-pilgrimage.

[126]Sedalia # 200 Sch. Dist. v. Mo. Comm'n on Human Rights, 843 S.W.2d 928 (Mo. Ct. App. 1992).

[127]Shelton v. Univ. of Med. & Dentistry, 223 F.3d 220 (3d Cir. 2000); *see also* Bruff v. N. Miss. Health Servs., 244 F.3d 495 (5th Cir. 2001) (upholding termination of a Christian counselor who refused to work with homosexuals or persons living together outside of marriage); Keeton v. Anderson-Wiley, 664 F.3d 865 (11th Cir. 2011) (upholding decision to discipline counseling student who made a religiously based negative statement in class about gays and lesbians). *But see* Ward v. Polite, 667 F.3d 727 (6th Cir. 2012) (granting summary judgment in favor of counseling student who had been disciplined for refusing to counsel LGBT clients for religious reasons).

Adverse Employment Decisions

Employees at times have claimed religious discrimination when they have been transferred, demoted, nonrenewed, terminated, or denied tenure. As with other claims of employment discrimination, the burden is on the employee to prove that the adverse action was motivated by an impermissible reason—specifically, the employee's religious beliefs, practices, or affiliation. Employees experience difficulty in winning such cases as employers typically can identify one or more legitimate bases for the adverse action (e.g., lack of commitment,[128] excessive absenteeism[129]). In a private sector employment case reviewed by the Ninth Circuit, a former employee claimed religious discrimination when terminated.[130] To support its slogan that "diversity is our strength," the employer displayed diversity posters, including those regarding gays. The employee believed that homosexual activity violated the Bible and began posting within his cubicle large-typeface passages from the Bible that could be interpreted to condemn homosexuality. After he refused to remove the postings unless his employer removed its diversity displays regarding gays, he was terminated for insubordination. The court reasoned that the employee failed to support his claim of discrimination and that to permit him to maintain his postings, as a religious accommodation, would result in undue hardship on the employer as the material was demeaning and degrading to members of the workforce.[131]

AGE DISCRIMINATION

Unlike other characteristics that generate charges of discrimination, age is unique in that everyone is subject to the aging process and eventually will fall within the age-protected category. The mean age of the U.S. population has climbed steadily in recent years, and this phenomenon has been accompanied by an increase in judicial activity pertaining to age discrimination by persons over age forty. In fact, the median age advanced 4.3 years between 1990 (32.9) and 2010 (37.2).[132] There is no reason to believe that the median age will not continue to grow, given continued advancements in health care. Over time, this trend will result in a significant portion of the population that will be age protected in employment and eligible for a range of public services, Medicare, and eventually retirement. Age discrimination employment claims may be filed under the Equal Protection Clause (any age),[133] the Age Discrimination in Employment Act (ADEA) (over age forty),[134] and state statutes. The EEOC is responsible for the enforcement of the ADEA.

The purpose of the ADEA is to promote the employment of older persons based on their ability, to prohibit arbitrary age discrimination in employment, and to find ways of addressing problems arising from the impact of age on employment. The ADEA

[128] *See, e.g.*, Lee v. Wise Cnty. Sch. Bd., No. 97-1471, 1998 U.S. App. LEXIS 367 (4th Cir. Jan. 12, 1998).

[129] *See, e.g.*, Rosenbaum v. Bd. of Trs. of Montgomery Cmty. Coll., No. 98-1773, 1999 U.S. App. LEXIS 4744 (4th Cir. Mar. 19, 1999).

[130] Peterson v. Hewlett-Packard Co., 358 F.3d 599 (9th Cir. 2004).

[131] *See supra* text accompanying note 7.

[132] U.S. Census Bureau, *2010 Census Briefs: Age and Sex Composition: 2010* (May 2011), http://www.census.gov/prod/cen2010/briefs/c2010br-03.pdf.

[133] Facially discriminatory procedures and practices that classify individuals on the basis of age can satisfy the Equal Protection Clause if they are rationally related to a legitimate governmental objective, whereas facially neutral criteria may be successfully challenged only with proof of discriminatory intent.

[134] 29 U.S.C. § 621 (2012).

specifically stipulates that "it shall be unlawful for an employer . . . to fail or refuse to hire or to discharge any individual or otherwise discriminate . . . with respect to his compensation, terms, conditions, or privileges of employment, because of such individual's age."[135] However, if the employment decision is based on any reasonable factor other than age (e.g., merit, seniority, vesting in a retirement plan), even though correlated with or associated with age, there is no violation of the ADEA. This standard requires less than is mandated under Title VII (i.e., intent in treatment cases; proof that the practice, policy, or requirement was job related and consistent with business necessity in impact cases). Moreover, if a reasonable factor is identified, the employer avoids liability even if other factors with less discriminatory impact are available and not used. Also, for a violation to be substantiated, age must play a role in the decision-making process *and* have a determinative influence on the outcome.[136]

Where violations of the ADEA are found, courts may provide injunctive relief; compel employment, reinstatement, or promotion; and provide back pay (including interest), liquidated damages, and attorneys' fees. Punitive damages, however, are not available.[137] As with other types of discrimination complaints, an ADEA claim must be brought to the EEOC before the lawsuit can be filed in federal court.[138]

The Supreme Court in *Kimel v. Florida Board of Regents* held that Eleventh Amendment immunity may be claimed as a defense where money damages to be paid out of the state treasury are sought in federal court.[139] Accordingly, immunity may be claimed where state laws consider school districts to be "arms of the state" rather than political subdivisions. But even where the Eleventh Amendment is used as a defense, plaintiffs can sue under comparable state statutes to vindicate their rights.[140] Since the vast majority of school districts are not "arms of the state," the *Kimel* decision has not deterred teachers from arguing discrimination under the ADEA. For example, an Iowa teacher alleged that she was not hired as a counselor because of her age. The Eighth Circuit affirmed the district court's decision granting the school district's motion for summary judgment because the teacher did not provide evidence that she was discriminated against based on age. The school district had demonstrated that she was not chosen for the counseling position because she did not hold a counseling license.[141]

Hiring and Promotion Practices

As indicated, under the ADEA, except in those circumstances where age qualifies as a bona fide occupational qualification, selection among applicants for hiring or promotion may be based on any factor other than age. Although a BFOQ defense in an educational setting is unlikely in cases involving staff, teachers, or administrators, claims could conceivably be made for school bus drivers and pilots. Where a BFOQ is applied, the employer carries the burden of persuasion to demonstrate that there is reasonable cause to

[135]29 U.S.C. § 623(a)(1) (2012).
[136]*See, e.g.*, Hazen Paper Co. v. Biggins, 507 U.S. 604, 617 (1993).
[137]29 U.S.C. §§ 216, 626(b) (2012).
[138]29 U.S.C. § 626(d) (2012).
[139]528 U.S. 62 (2000).
[140]Intentionally left blank so that the remaining footnotes in the chapter can remain numbered as is.
[141]Tusing v. Des Moines Indep. Cmty. Sch. Dist., 639 F.3d 507 (8th Cir. 2011).

believe that all, or substantially all, applicants beyond a certain age would be unable to perform a job safely and efficiently.

As with Title VII cases, courts will permit employees in ADEA cases to provide either direct evidence of discrimination or meet *McDonnell Douglas* criteria.[142] In a Sixth Circuit case, a part-time substitute teacher was denied several full-time positions.[143] At trial, the teacher met the requirements for a prima facie case, while the board proffered the archetypical response (i.e., better-qualified candidates were hired[144]). It then became the teacher's responsibility to show that the board's purported reasons were unworthy of credence and a pretext to age discrimination.[145] This proved difficult, as there were over 2,000 applicants, and 41 percent of those hired were over age forty. Under such circumstances, it would be exceedingly difficult to show that if not for the consideration of age, the teacher would have been among those selected. Accordingly, when the teacher was unable to fulfill his entire burden, the board's motion for summary judgment was granted.

In the effort to show pretext, an employee need not discredit each and every proffered reason for the rejection, but must cast substantial doubt on many, if not most, of the purported bases so that a fact finder then could rationally disbelieve the remaining reasons given the employer's loss of credibility. In an illustrative Second Circuit case, a less-experienced, unqualified, younger teacher was selected over the plaintiff.[146] The district purported that the selected applicant performed better during the interview and was chosen largely on that basis. In ruling that pretext had been shown, the court noted that the successful candidate did not possess the specified degree and had submitted an incomplete file; that the employer had made misleading statements and destroyed relevant evidence; and that the plaintiff possessed superior credentials, except perhaps as to the interview. The fact that the previously selected applicant also was over the age of forty was irrelevant; what mattered was that she was substantially younger (i.e., age forty-two) than the plaintiff (age sixty-four).[147]

Compensation and Benefits

Few public school employees have alleged age-based salary discrimination. In large part, this is due to the fact that teachers and staff primarily are paid on salary schedules based on seniority and degree level. As employees become older, they concomitantly gain seniority and receive a higher scheduled salary. Consequently, claims of age-based salary discrimination are less likely to occur within public schools, except possibly for

[142]*See supra* text accompanying note 16.

[143]Wooden v. Bd. of Educ., 931 F.2d 376 (6th Cir. 1991).

[144]*But see* Patrick v. Ridge, 394 F.3d 311, 316 (5th Cir. 2004) (noting that when an allegedly better-qualified candidate is selected, it is important that such person actually be in the pool of candidates when the plaintiff is rejected).

[145]*See* Stone v. Bd. of Educ. of Saranac Cent. Sch. Dist., 153 F. App'x 44 (2d Cir. 2005) (determining that age was not the basis of plaintiff's denial of employment and concluding that she did not interview well and was unfamiliar with newer teaching methods); Herbick v. Salem City Sch. Dist., 151 F. App'x 463 (6th Cir. 2005) (concluding that teacher failed to show pretext in her age discrimination claim—the district had elected to combine two part-time teaching positions to create one full-time position rather than continue to rehire plaintiff on one-year contracts following her retirement).

[146]Byrnie v. Town of Cromwell, Bd. of Educ., 243 F.3d 93 (2d Cir. 2001).

[147]*See also* Brennan v. Metro. Opera Ass'n, 192 F.3d 310 (2d Cir. 1999) (noting that the fact that the replacement is substantially younger than the plaintiff is a more valuable indicator of age discrimination than whether the replacement was over age forty).

administrators and noncertified staff. Where age discrimination is alleged, the burden of proof remains with the employee to prove that age—rather than performance, longevity, or other factors—was used to determine the level of compensation. Claims of both disparate treatment and disparate impact may be filed.

In a seminal case in 2005, *Smith v. City of Jackson*, the Supreme Court examined a claim by police and public safety officers that raises were less generous to officers over age forty than to those who were younger.[148] The city had elected to increase the salaries of beginning and lower echelon employees in order to bring their salary levels in line with comparable positions available in the area. Officials asserted that this was necessary to attract new employees and to retain those who were recently hired. Individuals with greater than five years tenure and working in higher-level positions received smaller raises than did the targeted employees. The Court found the city's decision to base the level of raise on position qualified as a "reasonable factor other than age" and thus did not identify an ADEA violation.[149]

In addition to the prohibition on age-based compensation discrimination, school districts may not spend less on the benefits package of older employees than on those who are younger. The cost of the benefits package must be the same, even though the benefits derived from an equal expenditure may represent a lower level of benefits for an older worker (e.g., health and life insurance benefits for older workers at times are less, unless a higher premium is paid).[150]

Adverse Employment Actions

Courts often are asked to determine whether an employee's age was used as a basis to terminate, nonrenew, downsize, fail to rehire following a layoff, demote, or transfer an employee. However, as in most other discrimination cases, every action by an employer that the employee perceives as "adverse" might not qualify as such under law. For example, in a Sixth Circuit case, a university professor had his laboratory space reduced, was required to submit grant proposals for internal review, and had his graduate research assistant removed during one summer.[151] Nonetheless, he failed to show that any of these actions qualified as "adverse," as the employer was able to show that the professor failed to generate sufficient revenue to support the space and graduate assistant and that this failure was due to his poor grant preparation. The court made clear that mere inconvenience or an alteration of job responsibilities will not be enough to constitute adverse action. In contrast, where a challenged act qualifies as adverse, an employee must show that the reason submitted by the employer is false *and* that age was used as the basis for the adverse action.

The termination of at-will employees[152] is comparatively simple as are the removal of nontenured teachers and the elimination of unnecessary teaching and administrative positions, assuming strict adherence to approved policy. In contrast, to terminate tenured

[148] 544 U.S. 228 (2005).

[149] *Id.* at 242. Interestingly, the business necessity test was not used. Among other inquiries, this test asks whether there are other ways for the employer to achieve a goal that does not result in disparate impact on a protected class. In this case, the chosen method of determining salary level did not have to be the best method or even one that resulted in less disparate impact. It simply had to qualify as reasonable.

[150] 29 C.F.R. § 1625.10(a)(1) (2012).

[151] Mitchell v. Vanderbilt Univ., 389 F.3d 177 (6th Cir. 2004).

[152] At-will employees have no contract or job expectation and may leave or be terminated at any time. In many states, charter school employees are "at-will" even though they are considered public school employees.

employees, as well as those working within a long-term contract, a "for cause" hearing will be required to permit the school district to show why the removal of the employee is necessary.[153] Although many factors may be considered in making such decisions (e.g., morality, efficiency), the employee's age may not be used, unless age qualifies as a BFOQ. In a 2000 Supreme Court case, *Reeves v. Sanderson Plumbing Products*, a fifty-seven-year-old employee was terminated and replaced with a person in his thirties.[154] In remanding and ruling that the company was not entitled to summary judgment, the Court noted that the plaintiff was able to establish a prima facie case, create a jury issue concerning the falsity of the employer's basis for the action, and introduce additional evidence showing that the director was motivated by age-related animus.

In comparison, summary judgment was awarded in an Eleventh Circuit case in which a teacher failed to support her claim of age discrimination, among other claims, when she was not offered a fifth one-year contract or tenure.[155] The teacher failed to provide documentation regarding the age of those selected, other than her general claim that they were younger, and stated in her own deposition that she had no personal knowledge that hiring decisions were made on the basis of age.[156] As a result, the lower court ruling on behalf of the school district was affirmed.

To establish an ADEA claim, when an employee is subjected to an involuntary transfer, he or she will be required to show that such reassignment was based on age and that the new position was materially less prestigious, less suited to current skills and expertise, or less conducive to career advancement. The fact that the employee preferred one position over another does not establish an ADEA violation. Most courts have ruled for school districts when transfers have been challenged, as they seldom view a change of school or a change of grade level to represent a materially significant disadvantage or to be tantamount to a demotion.

Retaliation

Additionally, as with cases filed under Title VII, employers may not retaliate against employees when they file ADEA complaints or suits. A plaintiff need not establish the validity of the original complaint in order to succeed in a case claiming retaliation, but it would be helpful to show that the person responsible for the adverse decisions at least knew of the prior charges of discrimination. Furthermore, the plaintiff shoulders the burden to show that the adverse action was an act of retaliation, and not otherwise justified due to incompetence, insubordination, immorality, or the like.

Retirement

Given that the mandatory retirement of school employees has been eliminated, districts have attempted to entice older employees to retire through attractive retirement benefits

[153]Intentionally left blank so that the remaining footnotes in the chapter can remain numbered as is.

[154]530 U.S. 133 (2000).

[155]Bartes v. Sch. Bd. of Alachua Cnty., No. 04-15459, 2005 U.S. App. LEXIS 23386 (11th Cir. Oct. 26, 2005).

[156]In addition to termination and nonrenewal cases, at times, employees allege that they were constructively discharged due to their age. To succeed, the employee must show that the conditions created by the employer were such that a reasonable person similarly situated would find the work intolerable and that the employer acted with the intent of forcing the employee to quit. *See, e.g.*, Dirusso v. Aspen Sch. Dist. No. 1, 123 F. App'x 826 (10th Cir. 2004).

packages. Under the ADEA, employers can follow the terms of a bona fide retirement plan so long as the plan is not a subterfuge to evade the purposes of the Act.[157] Also, employers may not reduce annual benefits or cease the accrual of benefits after employees attain a certain age as an inducement for them to retire.[158] In a Seventh Circuit case, a school district had offered early retirement to teachers age fifty-eight to sixty-one. The longer teachers waited to retire after their fifty-eighth birthday, the less they received in total dollars as a retirement incentive. The court found the practice to facially discriminate based on age in violation of the ADEA.[159] Likewise, an Arizona school district was required to pay a large settlement in an age discrimination suit related to retirement benefits. The district was paying employees retirement based on their age. For example, employees over age sixty received 43 percent of what they were owed, while younger employees received 52 percent. The EEOC found that the plan was trying to encourage personnel to retire early and that the retirement plan was facially discriminatory.[160]

There also can be legal problems when an employee is terminated prior to becoming eligible for full retirement benefits (i.e., prior to becoming vested). In a 1993 Supreme Court decision, *Hazen Paper Co. v. Biggins*, the plaintiff was fired at age sixty-two, only a few weeks before completing ten years of service and being vested in his pension plan.[161] Two issues before the Supreme Court were whether the employer's interference with the vesting of pension benefits violated the ADEA *and* whether the standard for liquidated damages[162] applied to informal age-based decisions by employers in addition to those that were based on formal policies that facially discriminate based on age.

In a unanimous opinion, the Court vacated and remanded the lower court decision for a determination of whether the jury had sufficient evidence to find an ADEA violation. The Court made it clear, however, that disparate treatment is not supported when the factor motivating the employer is something other than the employee's age, even if it is correlated with age (e.g., vesting or pension status).[163] Because age and years of service are distinctly different factors, an employer may take one into account, yet ignore the other. Where violations are found and liquidated damages are sought, the Supreme Court opined that the employee bears the burden of showing that the act was willful in that the employer knew or showed reckless disregard for whether its conduct would violate the ADEA.[164]

Although it is difficult to prevail in an age discrimination claim, expect the number of cases to remain high as the "baby boomers" become sexagenarians over the next decade. Some will be denied employment, promotion, or vesting, whereas others may be

[157] *See, e.g.*, United Air Lines v. McMann, 434 U.S. 192 (1977).

[158] 29 U.S.C. § 623(i)(1) (2012).

[159] Solon v. Gary Cmty. Sch. Corp., 180 F.3d 844 (7th Cir. 1999).

[160] Kerry Fehr-Snyder, *Tempe District Settles Age-Bias Suit for Nearly $150,000*, THE REPUBLIC (May 24, 2012), http://www.azcentral.com/12news/news/articles/2012/05/24/20120524tempe-district-must-pay-settle-age-discrimination-suit.html.

[161] 507 U.S. 604 (1993).

[162] For a discussion of liquidated damages, see *Trans World Airlines v. Thurston*, 469 U.S. 111, 126 (1985).

[163] In dicta, the Court observed that an employer could be in violation of § 510 of the Employee Retirement Income Security Act, 29 U.S.C. §§ 1001–1461 (2012), if it were to fire employees in order to prevent them from vesting in the retirement program.

[164] In so stating, the Court was critical of lower courts for developing alternative standards for liquidated damages (i.e., that the conduct of the employer must be outrageous, that the evidence be direct rather than circumstantial, and that age must be the predominant factor rather than simply a determinative one).

disappointed in their retirement packages. Plaintiffs will allege age discrimination, but in most instances, those claims will be successfully rebutted by employers.

DISABILITY DISCRIMINATION

Prior to 1973, federal claims regarding disability discrimination in employment were filed under the Equal Protection Clause.[165] The Fourteenth Amendment is now less often used due to the applicability of two federal statutes: the Rehabilitation Act of 1973 (particularly § 504[166]), which applies to recipients of federal financial assistance, and Title I of the Americans with Disabilities Act of 1990 (ADA),[167] which applies to most employers with fifteen or more employees. These statutes require nondiscrimination against employees with disabilities involving any term, condition, or privilege of employment. Section 504 complaints are submitted to the Office for Civil Rights within the Department of Education.[168] In comparison, the Equal Employment Opportunity Commission, the Department of Justice, and private litigants have enforcement rights under the ADA.

The issue of whether Eleventh Amendment immunity may be claimed specifically in Title I, ADA suits was addressed by the Supreme Court in 2001 in *Board of Trustees of the University of Alabama v. Garrett.*[169] In that case, two state employees (a nurse and a prison guard) with disabilities sued the state for monetary damages when their respective employers allegedly discriminated against them. After undergoing a lumpectomy, radiation treatment, and chemotherapy, the nurse returned to work but was forced to resign from her director position; she then applied for and received a lower-paying position as a manager. In contrast, the guard claimed that he had been denied necessary work accommodations (i.e., transfer to a daytime shift and reduced exposure to carbon monoxide and cigarette smoke), given his chronic asthma and sleep apnea.

The primary issue on appeal to the Supreme Court was whether, under Title I of the ADA, a federal court could award monetary damages to be paid by a state employer or, in the alternative, whether the Eleventh Amendment prohibited such relief. The Court found that the award violated the Constitution and that there was no proven history or pattern of employment discrimination by the state against employees with disabilities. As with other federal claims discussed in this chapter, a few school districts that are viewed as arms of the state may be immune from liability under the ADA.[170]

Notwithstanding the fact that the Eleventh Amendment may prohibit awards of monetary damages within a few jurisdictions, do not assume that persons who have been subjected to disability discrimination in employment are powerless to vindicate their rights.

[165]The Fourteenth Amendment requires the application of rational-basis scrutiny in cases where disability discrimination is facial and proof of intent where the alleged discrimination is facially neutral.

[166]29 U.S.C. § 794 (2012).

[167]42 U.S.C. § 12101 (2012).

[168]Complaint forms must be filed in a timely manner and signed by the employee. *See* Fry v. Muscogee Cnty. Sch. Dist., 150 F. App'x 980 (11th Cir. 2005) (concluding that an employee with morbid obesity failed to sign and thereby verify her ADA complaint—her attorney had signed it for her, but later failed to acquire her signature or properly amend the claim).

[169]531 U.S. 356 (2001).

[170]*See* Mt. Healthy City Sch. Dist. v. Doyle, 429 U.S. 274 (1977) (concluding in a First Amendment suit that the school district was not entitled to assert Eleventh Amendment immunity since under state law, the board was more like a county or a city, rather than an arm of the state).

The ADA, Title I, still prescribes standards that are applicable to state employers. Also, many state disability laws provide identical or at least similar coverage to that mandated by the ADA and permit monetary damages under certain circumstances. Furthermore, because all (or nearly all) public schools are recipients of federal financial assistance, they must meet substantially similar obligations under the Rehabilitation Act—a law that at times permits the awarding of money damages.

Qualifying as Disabled

When cases are filed, courts often are asked to resolve questions regarding whether the plaintiff is in fact disabled and, if so, what accommodations are required. A person qualifies as disabled under § 504 and the ADA if he or she:

- has a physical or mental impairment that substantially limits one or more major life activities;
- has a record of impairment;[171] or
- is regarded as having an impairment.[172]

However, more is required than simple knowledge of a condition that is physically or mentally limiting for the employee to establish that the employer regarded the employee as having an impairment.[173] To illustrate, recently the Eighth Circuit granted the school district's motion for summary judgment because a teacher with multiple sclerosis did not demonstrate that she had an impairment that substantially limited a major life activity, had a record of impairment, or was regarded as having an impairment. The court reasoned that the school district's knowledge of the teacher's physical impairments did not establish that school officials regarded her as disabled nor did the accommodations that were provided establish such.[174]

Although federal regulations define physical or mental impairment broadly,[175] persons who currently are involved in the use of illegal drugs,[176] are unable to perform the duties of the job due to alcohol, have a contagious disease,[177] or otherwise represent a direct threat to the safety or health of themselves or others do not qualify as disabled. If the individual is disqualified due to health issues, the decision needs to be based on current medical evidence and not on stereotypes or fears. Likewise, persons claiming discrimination due to transvestism, transsexualism, pedophilia, exhibitionism, voyeurism,

[171]For example, when a person is discriminatorily treated because of having a history of hospitalization due to tuberculosis, alcoholism, or drug addiction, the person would qualify for protection as he is viewed as "having a record of impairment." *See* ADA, 42 U.S.C. § 12102(1)(B) (2012) (disability means an individual who has "a record of such an impairment").

[172]For example, when a person is discriminatorily treated because of being HIV positive, but does not have AIDS or any type of current physical impairment limiting a major life activity, the person would qualify for protection as he is "regarded as having an impairment." *See* ADA, 42 U.S.C. § 12102(1)(C) (2012).

[173]*See, e.g.*, Amadio v. Ford Motor Co., 238 F.3d 919 (7th Cir. 2001).

[174]Nyprov v. Indep. Sch. Dist., 616 F.3d 728 (8th Cir. 2010).

[175]34 C.F.R. § 104.3(j)(2)(i) (2012).

[176]*See, e.g.*, McKissick v. Cnty. of N.Y., No. 1:09-cv-1840, 2011 U.S. Dist. LEXIS 123158 (M.D. Pa. Oct. 25, 2011) (noting that drug addiction can constitute a physical or mental impairment under the ADA, but the term "qualified individual with a disability" does not include individuals currently using illegal drugs).

[177]*But see* P.R. v. Metro. Sch. Dist. of Wash. Twp., No. 1:08-cv-1562, 2010 U.S. Dist. LEXIS 116223 (S.D. Ind. Nov. 1, 2010) (finding HIV infection is a physical impairment which substantially limits a major life activity).

gender identity disorders not resulting from physical impairments, other sexual behavior disorders, compulsive gambling, kleptomania, pyromania, and psychoactive substance use disorders resulting from current illegal drug use are not protected by either the ADA or § 504.

Qualifying as disabled requires a two-step process: identifying a physical or mental impairment *and* determining whether the impairment substantially limits a major life activity. The EEOC identifies several major life activities (i.e., walking, seeing, hearing, speaking, breathing, learning, and working) in its guidelines for the ADA[178] and others in related manuals (i.e., caring for oneself, sitting, standing, lifting, concentrating, thinking, and interacting with others),[179] while the Supreme Court has expanded the list also to include both reproduction and performing manual tasks.[180] It is important to note that in 2008, the ADA was amended to clarify that mitigating measures should not be considered when determining whether someone has a disability under the ADA. In other words, even individuals who are able to control their disability with medication would still be considered disabled.[181]

Performance is substantially limited when an employee is unable to perform, or is significantly restricted in performing, a major life activity that can be accomplished by the average person in the general population. The nature, severity, duration, and long-term impact of the impairment are considered when determining whether a condition is substantially limiting.[182] Also, an impairment that is substantially limiting for one person may not be for another. To qualify, it must prevent or restrict an individual from performing tasks that are of central importance to most people's daily lives. If the life activity claimed is working, impairments are not substantially limiting unless they restrict the ability to perform a broad range of jobs and not just a single or specialized job.[183] In such cases, courts will consider the geographic area to which the plaintiff has reasonable access and the nature of the job from which the individual was disqualified, as well as other jobs that require similar training, knowledge, ability, or skill.[184] When contagious disease is involved, the employer should consider how the disease is transmitted, how long the employee is infectious, the potential harm to others, and the probability of transmission.[185]

In 2002, the Supreme Court reviewed a claim by an assembly line worker in *Toyota Motor Manufacturing v. Williams*. She asserted that her employer failed to accommodate her bilateral carpal tunnel syndrome, which seemed to be exacerbated by the use of pneumatic tools, repetitive motion, and lifting any significant weight.[186] The Court

[178]29 C.F.R. § 1630.2(i) (2012).

[179]Equal Employment Opportunity Commission, *Technical Assistance Manual on the Employment Provisions (Title I) of the Americans with Disabilities Act* II-3 (Jan. 1992), http://archive.org/details/technicalassista00unse; Equal Employment Opportunity Commission, *Enforcement Guidance on the Americans with Disabilities Act and Psychiatric Disabilities*, No. 915.002, 6-7 (Mar. 25, 1997), http://www.eeoc.gov/policy/docs/psych.html.

[180]Bragdon v. Abbott, 524 U.S. 624 (1998) (reproduction); Toyota Motor Mfg. v. Williams, 534 U.S. 184 (2002) (manual tasks).

[181]The Americans with Disabilities Amendments Act of 2008, 42 U.S.C. § 12101 (2012).

[182]29 C.F.R. § 1630.2(j)(1), (2) (2012).

[183]*See, e.g.*, Samuels v. Kansas City Mo. Sch. Dist., 437 F.3d 797 (8th Cir. 2006).

[184]29 C.F.R. § 1630.2(j)(2)(3) (2012).

[185]Sch. Bd. of Nassau Cnty. v. Arline, 480 U.S. 273 (1987).

[186]534 U.S. 184 (2002).

reasoned that to be substantially limiting, a permanent or long-term impairment must prevent or severely restrict the individual from doing activities that are of central importance to most people's daily lives. This will require a case-by-case analysis, as symptoms vary widely for most impairments. Accordingly, the Court ruled that in qualifying the plaintiff as disabled, the lower court should not have relied on her inability to perform the difficult manual tasks in her specialized assembly line job, but rather should have considered whether she could brush her teeth, bathe, and perform household chores, as these were the activities that were necessary to daily living.

Otherwise Qualified

If a person qualifies as disabled, it then must be determined whether he or she is "otherwise qualified." To be an otherwise qualified individual with a disability, the applicant or employee must be able to perform the essential functions of the job in spite of the disability, although reasonable accommodation at times may be necessary. Generally, employers should not impose a blanket exclusion of persons with particular disabilities, but rather should provide individual review of each person. Only in rare instances will a particular disability disqualify an applicant (e.g., where federal or state law establishes health or ability requirements for particular types of employment).

In identifying the essential functions of the job, courts will give consideration to what the employer perceives to be essential. As long as each identified requirement for employment is either training related (for initial employment) or job related, the employer should not have difficulty in substantiating its claim of business necessity. For example, being on time to work and being at work on a regular daily basis can qualify as a business necessity for most positions in education as well as elsewhere. Employees often have claimed that their respective disabilities were the basis for their lateness or nonarrival. Although this may have been true, courts generally have not found such employees to be otherwise qualified.[187] In 1994, an instructor with an autoimmune system disorder claimed disability discrimination when she was fired for not meeting the attendance requirements of the job. In ruling for the employer, the Fourth Circuit held that the employer was not required to restructure the entire work schedule to accommodate the employee in her efforts to deal with her own needs as well as those of her son, who also had a disability.[188]

Nevertheless, the burden will be on the district to show that the absences are excessive, that the requested accommodations are unreasonable, or that undue hardship would result if the employee were reinstated. In *School Board of Nassau County, Florida v. Arline*, a teacher had three relapses of tuberculosis over a two-year period for which leave was given, and she was terminated prior to returning to work following the third leave.[189] The Supreme Court held that the teacher qualified as disabled under § 504 due to her record of physical impairment and hospitalization, but remanded the case for the district court to determine whether risks of infection to others precluded her from being otherwise qualified and whether her condition could be reasonably accommodated without an undue burden on the district. Following remand, the teacher was found to

[187]*See, e.g.*, Carr v. Reno, 23 F.3d 525 (D.C. Cir. 1994); Walders v. Garrett, 956 F.2d 1163 (4th Cir. 1992).
[188]Tyndall v. Nat'l Educ. Ctrs., 31 F.3d 209 (4th Cir. 1994).
[189]480 U.S. 273 (1987), *on remand*, 692 F. Supp. 1286 (M.D. Fla. 1988).

be otherwise qualified, since she posed little risk of infecting others, and was ordered reinstated with back pay.

Reasonable Accommodation

Persons with disabilities must be able to perform all of the essential functions of the position, either with accommodation or without. Employers are responsible for providing reasonable accommodations, such as making necessary facilities accessible and usable, restructuring work schedules, acquiring or modifying equipment, and providing readers or interpreters.[190] Also, when not restricted by bargaining rights or other entitlements, transfer within the organization may qualify as a reasonable accommodation.[191] However, federal law does not require the employer to bump a current employee to allow a person with a disability to fill the position, to fill a vacant position it did not intend to fill, to violate seniority rights, to refrain from disciplining an employee for misconduct, to eliminate essential functions of the job, or to create a new unnecessary position. Moreover, an employer need not transfer the employee to a better position, or select a less-qualified or unqualified applicant solely because of disability.[192] Such forms of accommodation may be theoretically possible but would result in undue hardship to the employer and discriminate against other employees.

Courts determine whether undue hardship results after a review of the size of the program and its budget, the number of employees, the type of facilities and operation, and the nature and cost of accommodation. Because there is no fixed formula for calculations, courts have differed markedly in identifying what they consider reasonable.

In selecting reasonable accommodations, the employer should engage in an ongoing *interactive process* with the employee with a disability and consult state and federal agencies when needed. Employees often are a good source for identifying accommodations that will assist them in meeting the essential functions of the job. Note, however, that the employee does not select the accommodations. The employer has the right to select among effective reasonable accommodations. To facilitate the process, it is helpful for the employer to have policies identifying the steps taken in (1) establishing an interactive process with the employee with a disability; (2) requesting reasonable accommodations; and (3) determining those accommodations to be provided.

If the employee remains dissatisfied, the employer should have an internal procedure for appeal. Following this appeal, if the employee is still dissatisfied, a formal complaint may be filed with the appropriate federal or state agency given the nature of the claim. Critical to a successful claim would be proving that the employer was aware of the employee's disability[193] and that a reasonable accommodation exists that would enable the employee to fulfill job requirements.[194]

[190]*See* Lowe v. Indep. Sch. Dist. No. 1, 363 F. App'x 548 (10th Cir. 2010) (finding school district failed to identify an appropriate accommodation for a teacher with a post-polio condition who resigned after being reassigned to a small and crowded classroom); Ekstrand v. Sch. Dist. of Somerset, 583 F.3d 972 (7th Cir. 2009) (finding that a jury could determine that the school district was required under the ADA to provide a classroom with natural light for a teacher who suffered from seasonal affective disorder).

[191]*See, e.g.*, Smith v. Midland Brake, 180 F.3d 1154 (10th Cir. 1999) (en banc).

[192]*See, e.g.*, Lors v. Dean, 595 F.3d 831 (8th Cir. 2010) (finding that the ADA is not an affirmative action statute).

[193]*See, e.g.*, Whitney v. Bd. of Educ., 292 F.3d 1280 (10th Cir. 2002).

[194]*But see* Merrell v. ICEE-USA Corp., No. 99-4173, 2000 U.S. App. LEXIS 33327 (10th Cir. Dec. 19, 2000) (finding no reasonable accommodation that would allow a man with a back injury who stocked carbonated beverage machines to meet essential job functions).

Termination and Nonrenewal

There are more individuals with disabilities in the workplace today than ever before, with many achieving leadership positions. Not all persons with disabilities have fared well, however, as some have not been selected for initial employment, granted tenure, promoted, or paid fairly, while others have been arbitrarily discharged or forced to resign or retire.[195] At times, such adverse decisions were due to inadequate qualifications or skills, better-qualified applicants, poor job performance, posing a risk, or criminal wrongdoing.[196] At other times, the employee's disability was found to be the basis for the adverse decision, or the environment had become so hostile that the employee's decision to quit qualified as being constructively discharged.[197]

To support a disparate treatment adverse action claim, employees must show that (1) they have a disability that substantially limits a major life activity as compared to the average person in the population; (2) they were the target of an action that qualified as adverse; and (3) the adverse action was taken due to their being disabled. A Second Circuit case illustrates how one employee had difficulty substantiating this type of claim. In this case, a teacher was terminated for chronic tardiness and ineffective teaching, which she argued was a pretext for discrimination. The Second Circuit found that the teacher's back injury and her severe fatigue and insomnia, which were linked to her thyroid cancer, were not disabilities under the ADA. The teacher failed to demonstrate that she could not stand for moderate periods of time because of the back injury and failed to establish that she was limited by her inability to sleep.[198]

Similarly, a former Kentucky teacher claimed that her termination allegedly due to conduct unbecoming was actually based on disability. In her defense, she argued that the alleged questionable behaviors were symptomatic of a head injury she had suffered thirteen years earlier in a bicycle accident and that she had not committed most of the violations claimed by the board—threatening students and making inappropriate comments about students and their families. In support of her termination, the court noted that she already had been found guilty in criminal court for nine counts of "terroristic threatening" against students. Her conduct, even if disability related, rendered her unqualified to continue as an educator.[199] There should continue to be ample case law dealing with termination and other claims filed by employees with disabilities. Such claims are likely to focus on the ADA rather than § 504, given its broader application. Expect school officials to continue to struggle in their efforts to provide effective, cost-efficient accommodations, but also expect generally good faith efforts as educators attempt to comply with federal and state disability laws.

[195] *See, e.g.*, Cigan v. Chippewa Falls Sch. Dist., 388 F.3d 331 (7th Cir. 2004).

[196] *See, e.g.*, Haulbrook v. Michelin N. Am., 252 F.3d 696 (4th Cir. 2001) (unable to perform job duties); Borgialli v. Thunder Basin Coal Co., 235 F.3d 1284 (10th Cir. 2000) (not qualified for position).

[197] *See, e.g.*, Spells v. Cuyahoga Cmty. Coll., 889 F. Supp. 1023 (N.D. Ohio 1994), *aff'd mem.* 51 F.3d 273 (6th Cir. 1995).

[198] Farina v. Branford Bd. of Educ., 458 F. App'x 13 (2d Cir. 2011); *see also* Cardo v. Arlington Sch. Dist., No. 11-580-cv, 2012 U.S. App. LEXIS 6263 (2d Cir. Mar. 28, 2012) (ruling that assistant wrestling coach's ADA claim failed because even though the head coach suggested that the assistant coach lacked the agility to safely demonstrate wrestling techniques, this did not establish that the assistant coach was considered substantially limited in a major life activity).

[199] Macy v. Hopkins Cnty. Sch. Bd. of Educ., 484 F.3d 357 (6th Cir. 2007).

Conclusion

Federal law requires that employment decisions be based on qualifications, performance, merit, seniority, and the like, rather than factors such as race, national origin, sex, sexual orientation, religion, age, or disability. Statutes vary considerably, however, as to what they require. Moreover, federal regulations are extensive, complex, and at times confounding. As a result, courts differ in applying the law. Even though many questions remain, the following generalizations reflect the current status of the law.

1. The United States Constitution and various civil rights laws protect employees from discrimination in employment based on race, national origin, sex, sexual orientation, religion, age, and disability.
2. For Fourteenth Amendment facial discrimination cases, race, and national origin discrimination claims, courts apply strict scrutiny; sex and illegitimacy discrimination receive intermediate scrutiny; and all other employment classifications need to be justified by any rational basis.
3. For Fourteenth Amendment facially neutral cases, regardless of the type of classification involved, the employee is required to show that the employer intended to discriminate.
4. Race may never qualify as a bona fide occupational qualification, although sex, religion, national origin, and age may be used under narrowly tailored conditions.
5. Adverse impact of a facially neutral employment practice on a protected group does not establish a constitutional violation, but such impact can violate Title VII if the employer is unable to show that the challenged practice serves a business necessity.
6. A reliable and valid standardized test can be used to screen job applicants, even though it has a disproportionate impact on a protected class, so long as the test is used to advance legitimate job objectives.
7. In Title VII disparate treatment cases, after plaintiffs establish a prima facie case of discrimination, the employer can rebut the inference of discrimination by articulating a legitimate nondiscriminatory basis for the practice; to prevail, the plaintiff then must prove that the proffered reasons are not to be believed and are a pretext for discrimination.
8. Public employers may not engage in affirmative action plans involving preferences in hiring and promotion unless a court has determined that the institution has been involved in specific prior acts of discrimination and the affirmative action plan is narrowly tailored to attain a workforce reflecting the qualified relevant labor market.
9. Under narrowly tailored circumstances, courts may order hiring and promotion preferences to remedy prior acts of intentional employment discrimination but may not impose layoff quotas.
10. Pregnancy-related conditions cannot be treated less favorably than other temporary disabilities in medical and disability insurance plans or leave policies.
11. Employees cannot be required to take maternity leave at a specified date during the pregnancy unless the policy is justified as a business necessity.
12. Employers cannot make a distinction between men and women in retirement contributions and benefits.
13. Employees can gain relief under Title VII for sexual harassment that results in the loss of tangible benefits or creates a hostile working environment.
14. Title VII provides remedies for sex discrimination in compensation that extends beyond the Equal Pay Act guarantee of equal pay for equal work.
15. Persons who are victims of sexual orientation discrimination may file suit under the Fourteenth Amendment (public sector) or under applicable state laws or local ordinances, where they exist (public and private sectors).

16. School boards can establish bona fide retirement benefits programs, but the Age Discrimination in Employment Act (ADEA) precludes mandatory retirement based on age.
17. For a violation to be substantiated under the ADEA, age must play a role in the decision-making process *and* have a determinative influence on the outcome.
18. Employers must make reasonable accommodations to enable employees to practice their religious beliefs; however, Title VII does not require accommodations that result in undue hardship to the employer.
19. An otherwise qualified individual cannot be excluded from employment solely on the basis of a disability, and employers are required to provide reasonable accommodations for employees with disabilities.

MyEdLeadershipLab™

Go to Topic 11: *Discrimination in Employment* on the MyEdLeadershipLab™ site (www.myedleadershiplab.com) for *Public School Law: Teachers' and Students' Rights*, Seventh Edition, where you can

- Find learning outcomes for *Discrimination in Employment* along with the national standards that connect to these outcomes.
- Complete Assignments and Activities that can help you more deeply understand the chapter content.
- Apply and practice your understanding of the core skills identified in the chapter with the Building Leadership Skills unit.
- Prepare yourself for professional certification with a Practice for Certification quiz.

Termination of Employment

Termination of Employment

MyEdLeadershipLab™

Visit the **MyEdLeadershipLab™** site for *Public School Law: Teachers' and Students' Rights*, Seventh Edition, to enhance your understanding of chapter concepts. You'll have the opportunity to practice your skills through video- and case-based Assignments and Activities as well as Building Leadership Skills units, and to prepare for your certification exam with Practice for Certification quizzes.

State laws delineate the authority of school boards in terminating school personnel. Generally, these laws specify the causes for which a teacher may be terminated and the procedures that must be followed. The school board's right to determine the fitness of teachers is well established; in fact, courts have declared that school boards have a duty as well as a right to make such determinations. In an early case, the United States Supreme Court stated:

> A teacher works in a sensitive area in a schoolroom. There he shapes the attitude of young minds towards the society in which they live. In this, the state has a vital concern. It must preserve the integrity of the schools. That the school authorities have *the right and the duty to screen* the officials, teachers, and employees as to their fitness to maintain the integrity of the schools as a part of ordered society, cannot be doubted.[1]

This chapter addresses the procedures that must be followed in the termination of a teacher's employment and the grounds for dismissal. The first section provides an overview of due process in connection with nonrenewal and dismissal. Since due process is required only if a teacher is able to establish that a constitutionally protected property or liberty

[1]Adler v. Bd. of Educ., 342 U.S. 485, 493 (1952) (emphasis added).

interest is at stake, the dimensions of teachers' property and liberty rights are explored in the context of employment termination. In the next section, specific procedural requirements are identified and discussed. A survey of judicial interpretations of state laws regarding causes for dismissal is presented in the third section. The concluding section provides an overview of remedies available to teachers for violation of their protected rights.

PROCEDURAL DUE PROCESS IN GENERAL

Basic due process rights are embodied in the Fourteenth Amendment, which guarantees that no state shall "deprive any person of life, liberty, or property without due process of law."[2] Due process safeguards apply not only in judicial proceedings but also to acts of governmental agencies such as school boards. Constitutional due process entails *substantive* protections against arbitrary governmental action and *procedural* protections when the government threatens an individual's life, liberty, or property interests. Most teacher termination cases have focused on procedural due process requirements.

The individual and governmental interests at stake and applicable state laws influence the nature of procedural due process required. Courts have established that a teacher's interest in public employment may entail significant "property" and "liberty" rights, necessitating due process prior to employment termination. A *property interest* is a "legitimate claim of entitlement" to continued employment that is created by state law.[3] The granting of tenure conveys such a property right to a teacher. Also, a contract establishes a property right to employment within its stated terms.[4] A property interest in continued employment, however, does not mean that an individual cannot be terminated; it simply means that an employer must follow the requirements of due process and substantiate cause.

The judiciary has recognized that Fourteenth Amendment *liberty rights* encompass fundamental constitutional guarantees, such as freedom of speech. Procedural due process always is required when a termination implicates such fundamental liberties. A liberty interest also is involved when termination creates a stigma or damages an individual's reputation in a manner that forecloses future employment opportunities. If protected liberty or property interests are implicated, the Fourteenth Amendment entitles the teacher to at least notice of the reasons for the school board's action and an opportunity for a hearing.

Employment terminations are classified as either dismissals or nonrenewals. The distinction between the two has significant implications for teachers' procedural rights. In this section, the procedural safeguards that must be provided to the tenured teacher and the nontenured teacher are distinguished. Specific attention is given to the conditions that may give rise to a nontenured teacher acquiring a protected liberty or property interest in employment, thereby establishing a claim to procedural due process.

[2]The Fourteenth Amendment restricts state, in contrast to private, action.

[3]*See* Bd. of Regents v. Roth, 408 U.S. 564 (1972).

[4]*See, e.g.*, Coggin v. Longview Indep. Sch. Dist., 337 F.3d 459 (5th Cir. 2003); *see also* Watson v. N. Panola Sch. Dist., 188 F. App'x 291 (5th Cir. 2006) (ruling that principal's oral job offer to teacher did not constitute a contract without school board approval; the teacher could not allege deprivation of a property right). *But see* Sexton v. KIPP Reach Acad. Charter Sch., 260 P.3d 435 (Okla. Ct. App. 2011) (finding an implied contract may have been created when a teacher was given a faculty-only cell phone, provided a letter of intent, and enrolled in a teacher's conference).

Dismissal

Dismissal refers to the termination for cause of any tenured teacher or a probationary teacher within the contract period. Both tenure statutes[5] and employment contracts[6] establish a property interest entitling teachers to full procedural protection. Beyond the basic constitutional requirements of appropriate notice and an opportunity to be heard, state laws and school board policies often contain detailed procedures that must be followed. Failure to provide these additional procedures, however, results in a violation of state law, rather than constitutional law. Statutory procedures vary as to specificity, with some states enumerating detailed steps and others identifying only broad parameters. In addition to complying with state law, a school district must abide by its own procedures, even if they exceed state law. For example, if school board policy provides for a preliminary notice of teaching inadequacies and an opportunity to correct remediable deficiencies prior to dismissal, the board must follow these steps.

A critical element in dismissal actions is a showing of justifiable cause for termination of employment. If causes are identified in state law, a school board must base dismissal on those grounds. Failure to relate the charges to statutory grounds can invalidate the termination decision. Because statutes typically list broad causes—such as incompetency, insubordination, immorality, unprofessional conduct, and neglect of duty—notice of discharge must indicate specific conduct substantiating the legal charges. Procedural safeguards ensure not only that a teacher is informed of the specific reasons and grounds for dismissal, but also that the school board bases its decision on evidence substantiating those grounds. Detailed aspects of procedural due process requirements and dismissal for cause are addressed in subsequent sections of this chapter.

Nonrenewal

Unless specified in state law, procedural protections are not accorded the probationary teacher when the employment contract is not renewed.[7] At the end of the contract period, employment can be terminated for any or no reason, so long as the reason is not constitutionally impermissible (e.g., denial of protected speech) and satisfies state law.[8]

[5]If a statute conferring specific property rights (e.g., tenure) is rescinded or amended to eliminate those rights, individuals are not entitled to procedural due process related to that deprivation; statutory benefits can be revoked without due process unless the change impairs contractual rights. *See, e.g.*, Indiana *ex rel.* Anderson v. Brand, 303 U.S. 95 (1938); Pittman v. Chi. Bd. of Educ., 64 F.3d 1098 (7th Cir. 1995). However, school boards generally cannot amend, repeal, or circumvent statutory rights (e.g., entitlement to procedural due process) through the employment contract. *See, e.g.*, Parker v. Indep. Sch. Dist. No. I-003 Okmulgee Cnty., Okla., 82 F.3d 952 (10th Cir. 1996).

[6]*See, e.g.*, Gibson v. Caruthersville Sch. Dist. No. 8, 336 F.3d 768 (8th Cir. 2003); Achene v. Pierce Joint Unified Sch. Dist., 97 Cal. Rptr. 3d 899 (Ct. App. 2009).

[7]*See, e.g.*, Lighton v. Univ. of Utah, 209 F.3d 1213 (10th Cir. 2000); Tucker v. Bd. of Educ., 624 N.E.2d 643 (N.Y. 1993).

[8]*See* Grossman v. S. Shore Pub. Sch. Dist., 507 F.3d 1097 (7th Cir. 2007) (ruling that a school district's decision to not renew a guidance counselor's contract because of conduct in praying with students, promoting abstinence, and condemning contraception did not violate her First Amendment rights); Back v. Hastings on Hudson Union Free Sch. Dist., 365 F.3d 107 (2d Cir. 2004) (denying summary judgment to defendants when evidence proffered indicated that school psychologist's denial of tenure was based on gender stereotyping); Flaskamp v. Dearborn Pub. Schs., 385 F.3d 935 (6th Cir. 2004) (ruling that nonrenewal resulting in denial of tenure did not abridge privacy rights of teacher who was not candid in answering principal's questions about a relationship with a former student that appeared to have begun prior to graduation).

The most common statutory requirement is notification of nonrenewal on or before a specified date prior to the expiration of the contract. Courts strictly construe the timeliness of nonrenewal notices. When a statute designates a deadline for nonrenewal, a school board must notify a teacher on or before the established date. The fact that the school board has set in motion notification (e.g., mailed the notice) generally does not satisfy the statutory requirement; the teacher's actual receipt of the notice is required. A teacher, however, cannot avoid or deliberately thwart delivery of notice and then claim insufficiency of notice.[9] Failure of school officials to observe the notice deadline may result in a teacher's reinstatement for an additional year[10] but generally does not result in an award of tenure if the teacher has not met probationary requirements.[11]

In the nonrenewal of teachers' contracts, some states require a written statement of reasons and may even provide an opportunity for a hearing at the teacher's request.[12] Unlike evidentiary hearings for dismissal of a teacher, the school board is not required to show cause for nonrenewal;[13] a teacher is simply provided the reasons underlying the nonrenewal and an opportunity to address the school board. When a school board is required to provide reasons, broad general statements such as "the school district's interest would be best served," "the district can find a better teacher," or "the term contract has expired" will not suffice; the teacher must be given specific information about deficiencies, such as lack of classroom control or ineffective classroom instruction. The Arkansas high court noted that state law requires boards to give "simple but complete reasons."[14] The Mississippi high court emphasized that although a school board must show that "demonstrable reason" exists for a nonrenewal decision, the burden of proof remains with the teacher to prove that the board had no basis for the decision not to renew.[15] Where state law establishes specific requirements and procedures for nonrenewal, failure to abide by these provisions may invalidate a school board's decision. Failure to follow the prescribed statutory procedures for evaluating nontenured teachers in Ohio can result in reversal of a nonrenewal decision with reinstatement for an additional year.[16] Furthermore, a school board must not only follow state law but also must comply *substantially* with its own nonrenewal procedures.[17]

[9]*See, e.g.*, Sullivan v. Centinela Valley Union High Sch. Dist., 122 Cal. Rptr. 3d 871 (Ct. App. 2011).

[10]*See, e.g.*, Kiel v. Green Local Sch. Dist. Bd. of Educ., 630 N.E.2d 716 (Ohio 1994).

[11]Andrews v. Bd. of Educ., N.Y.C., 938 N.Y.S.2d 67 (App. Div. 2012); *see also* Brenes v. Bd. of Educ., N.Y.C., No. 07-5549-cv, 2009 U.S. App. LEXIS 6270, at *8 (2d Cir. Mar. 23, 2009) (noting that tenure by estoppel is obtained "when a school board accepts the continued services of a teacher or administrator, but fails to take the action required by law to either grant or deny tenure prior to the expiration of the teacher's probationary term").

[12]*See* Kolmel v. Bd. of Educ., N.Y.C., 930 N.Y.S.2d 573 (App. Div. 2011) (holding that a teacher denied tenure at the end of the probationary period based on two unsatisfactory ratings that were done without observing the teacher showed bad faith, thereby, resulting in the annulment of the decision); Naylor v. Cardinal Local Sch. Dist. Bd. of Educ., 630 N.E.2d 725 (Ohio 1994) (holding that a "hearing" under Ohio law is more than an informal session with the school board; it includes the right to present evidence, confront and examine witnesses, and review both parties' arguments).

[13]*See, e.g.*, Flath v. Garrison Pub. Sch. Dist. No. 51, 82 F.3d 244 (8th Cir. 1996); Brown v. Reg'l Sch. Dist. 13, 328 F. Supp. 2d 289 (D. Conn. 2004).

[14]Hamilton v. Pulaski Cnty. Special Sch. Dist., 900 S.W.2d 205 (Ark. 1995). Although statements must inform the teacher of specific deficiencies, school officials should be careful to avoid communicating stigmatizing reasons that would require a name-clearing hearing.

[15]Buck v. Lowndes Cnty. Sch. Dist., 761 So. 2d 144 (Miss. 2000).

[16]Snyder v. Mendon-Union Dist. Bd. of Educ., 661 N.E.2d 717 (Ohio 1996).

[17]*See, e.g.*, Ventroy v. Lafayette Parish Sch. Bd., 6 So. 3d 1039 (La. Ct. App. 2009).

Although state laws may not provide the probationary teacher with specific procedural protections, a teacher's interest in continued public employment may be constitutionally protected if a liberty or property right guaranteed by the Fourteenth Amendment has been abridged. Infringement of these interests entitles a probationary teacher to due process rights similar to the rights of tenured teachers. These rights are delineated next.

Establishing Protected Property and Liberty Interests

The United States Supreme Court addressed the scope of protected interests encompassed by the Fourteenth Amendment in 1972 in two significant decisions: *Board of Regents v. Roth*[18] and *Perry v. Sindermann*.[19] These decisions addressed whether the infringement of a liberty or property interest entitles a probationary teacher to due process rights similar to the rights of tenured teachers. The cases involved faculty members at the postsecondary level, but the rulings are equally applicable to public elementary and secondary school teachers.

In *Roth*, the question presented to the Court was whether a nontenured teacher had a constitutional right to a statement of reasons and a hearing prior to nonreappointment. Roth was hired on a one-year contract, and the university elected not to rehire him for a second year. Since Roth did not have tenure, there was no entitlement under Wisconsin law to an explanation of charges or a hearing; the university simply did not reemploy him for the succeeding year. Roth challenged the nonrenewal, alleging that failure to provide notice of reasons and an opportunity for a hearing impaired his due process rights.

The Supreme Court held that nonrenewal did not require procedural protection unless impairment of a protected liberty or property interest could be shown. To establish infringement of a liberty interest, the Court held that the teacher must show that the employer's action (1) resulted in damage to his or her reputation and standing in the community or (2) imposed a stigma that foreclosed other employment opportunities. The evidence presented by Roth indicated that there was no such damage to his reputation or future employment. Accordingly, the Court concluded: "It stretches the concept too far to suggest that a person is deprived of 'liberty' when he simply is not rehired in one job but remains as free as before to seek another."[20]

The Court also rejected Roth's claim that he had a protected property interest to continued employment. In order to establish a valid property right, the Court held that an individual must have more than an "abstract need or desire" for a position; there must be a "legitimate claim of entitlement."[21] The federal Constitution does not define property interests; rather, state laws or employment contracts secure specific benefits. An abstract desire or unilateral expectation of continued employment alone does not constitute a property right. The terms of Roth's one-year appointment and the state law precluded any claim of entitlement.

On the same day it rendered the *Roth* decision, the Supreme Court in the *Sindermann* case explained the circumstances that might create a legitimate expectation of reemployment for a nontenured teacher.[22] Sindermann was a nontenured faculty member in his fourth

[18] 408 U.S. 564 (1972).
[19] 408 U.S. 593 (1972).
[20] *Roth*, 408 U.S. at 575.
[21] *Id.* at 577.
[22] 408 U.S. 593 (1972).

year of teaching when he was notified, without a statement of reasons or an opportunity for a hearing, that his contract would not be renewed. He challenged the lack of procedural due process, alleging that nonrenewal deprived him of a property interest protected by the Fourteenth Amendment and violated his First Amendment right to freedom of speech.

In advancing a protected property right, Sindermann claimed that the college, which lacked a formal tenure system, had created an informal, or de facto, tenure system through various practices and policies. Specifically, Sindermann cited a provision in the faculty guide: "The College wishes the faculty member to feel that he has permanent tenure as long as his teaching services are satisfactory."[23] The Supreme Court found that Sindermann's claim, unlike Roth's, might have been based on a legitimate expectation of reemployment promulgated by the college. According to the Court, the lack of a formal tenure system did not foreclose the possibility of an institution fostering entitlement to a position through its personnel policies.

In assessing Sindermann's free speech claim, the Supreme Court confirmed that a teacher's lack of tenure does not void a claim that nonrenewal was based on the exercise of constitutionally protected conduct. Procedural due process must be afforded when a substantive constitutional right is violated. In a later case, however, the Supreme Court held that if a constitutional right is implicated in a nonrenewal, the teacher bears the burden of showing that the protected conduct was a substantial or motivating factor in the school board's decision.[24] The establishment of this inference of a constitutional violation then shifts the burden to the school board to show by a preponderance of evidence that it would have reached the same decision in the absence of the protected activity.

The *Roth* and *Sindermann* cases are the legal precedents for assessing the procedural rights of nontenured teachers. To summarize, the Supreme Court held that a nontenured teacher does not have a constitutionally protected property right to employment requiring procedural due process before denial of reappointment. Certain actions of the school board, however, may create conditions entitling the teacher to notice and a hearing similar to the tenured teacher. Such actions would include:

- nonrenewal decisions damaging an individual's reputation and integrity;
- nonrenewal decisions foreclosing other employment opportunities;
- policies and practices creating a valid claim to reemployment; and
- nonrenewal decisions violating fundamental constitutional guarantees.

Since the Supreme Court has held that impairment of a teacher's property or liberty interests triggers procedural protections, the question arises as to what constitutes a violation of these interests. Courts have purposely avoided precisely defining the concepts of liberty and property, preferring to allow experience and time to shape their meanings.[25] Since 1972, the Supreme Court and federal appellate courts have rendered a number of decisions that provide some guidance in understanding these concepts.

PROPERTY INTEREST. In general, a nontenured employee does not have a property claim to reappointment unless state or local governmental action has clearly established such

[23]*Id.* at 600.
[24]Mt. Healthy City Sch. Dist. Bd. of Educ. v. Doyle, 429 U.S. 274 (1977).
[25]*See Roth*, 408 U.S. at 572.

a right.[26] For example, the Seventh Circuit concluded that a nontenured teacher could not assert a property interest in continued employment based on a principal's positive midyear evaluation indicating that the teacher's contract would be renewed.[27] Following the positive evaluation, the teacher demonstrated a lack of professionalism in handling several incidents with students. In contrast, the Seventh Circuit found that a promise of two years of employment to a coach/athletic director established a legitimate expectation of continued employment.[28] To persuade the athletic director to accept the position, the board had assured him that his one-year contract would be extended for a second year. Based on such an implied contract, the court found that unilateral termination of the contract after one year violated his due process rights.

Protected property interests are not created by mere longevity in employment. Both the Fourth and Tenth Circuits found that issuing an employee a series of annual contracts did not constitute a valid claim to continued employment in the absence of a guarantee in state law, local policy, or an employment contract.[29] Similarly, a statute or collective bargaining agreement providing a teacher, upon request, a hearing and statement of reasons for nonrenewal does not confer a property interest in employment requiring legally sufficient cause for termination.[30] Such a provision simply gives the teacher an opportunity to present reasons the contract should be renewed.[31] Also, a state's tenure law may not confer tenure on all positions in a school. For example, the Minnesota Supreme Court interpreted its state law as encompassing only positions that require a license from the department of education.[32] Thus, a teacher who had held the position of activities director did not acquire a property interest in his job since no license was required.

Although a contract establishes a property interest within the contract terms, due process generally is not required in transferring or reassigning a teacher or administrator unless an identifiable economic impact can be shown. For example, a Chicago principal who was reassigned to the central office was not entitled to a hearing since he continued to receive his regular salary and benefits; deprivations related to professional satisfaction and reputation did not constitute actionable injuries.[33] In contrast, the Sixth Circuit

[26] *See, e.g.*, Coreia v. Schuylkill Cnty. Area Vocational-Tech. Sch. Auth., 241 F. App'x 47 (3d Cir. 2007); Kyle v. Morton High Sch., 144 F.3d 448 (7th Cir. 1998); Spanierman v. Hughes, 576 F. Supp. 2d 292 (D. Conn. 2008); *see also* Nunez v. Simms, 341 F.3d 385 (5th Cir. 2003) (holding that when a teacher working under a three-year temporary permit failed to acquire standard certification, her employment contract was void; no right to due process existed).

[27] Halfhill v. Ne. Sch. Corp., 472 F.3d 496 (7th Cir. 2006).

[28] Vail v. Bd. of Educ., 706 F.2d 1435 (7th Cir. 1983), *aff'd by an equally divided court*, 466 U.S. 377 (1984).

[29] Martin v. Unified Sch. Dist. No. 434, 728 F.2d 453 (10th Cir. 1984); Robertson v. Rogers, 679 F.2d 1090 (4th Cir. 1982); *see also* Ray v. Nash, 438 F. App'x 332 (5th Cir. 2011) (holding that a teacher's expectancy of reemployment because she had been successful in her teaching did not create a protected property interest).

[30] *See, e.g.*, Perkins v. Bd. of Dirs., 686 F.2d 49 (1st Cir. 1982); Schaub v. Chamberlain Bd. of Educ., 339 N.W.2d 307 (S.D. 1983).

[31] *See Schaub*, 339 N.W.2d 307 (holding that a hearing may be available to a nontenured teacher, but the board is not required to speak, produce evidence, or even answer questions at the hearing); *see also* Angstadt v. Red Clay Consol. Sch. Dist., 4 A.3d 382 (Del. 2009) (holding that state law prevented a school district from considering letters that were not properly placed in a teacher's personnel file in the nonrenewal of the teacher; however, other documented materials such as performance appraisals sufficed to nonrenew the teacher in this case).

[32] Emerson v. Sch. Bd., 809 N.W.2d 679 (Minn. 2012).

[33] Bordelon v. Chi. Sch. Reform Bd. of Trs., 233 F.3d 524 (7th Cir. 2000); *see also* Howard v. Columbia Pub. Sch. Dist., 363 F.3d 797 (8th Cir. 2004) (holding that principal's contract did not specify employment in a particular school); Ulichny v. Merton Cmty. Sch. Dist., 249 F.3d 686 (7th Cir. 2001) (finding that the reduction of a principal's duties and responsibilities did not impair property rights).

reasoned that a collective bargaining agreement specifying that teachers may not be transferred except for "good cause" and "extenuating circumstances" established a property interest in a particular position in a specific school.[34]

As noted, property rights are created by state laws or contracts but also may emanate from policies, regulations, or ordinances made by a governmental employer pursuant to statutory rule-making authority. Such policies or regulations must create an expectation of employment and impose a binding obligation on the employer in order to create a property interest in continued employment. The sufficiency of the claim, however, must be interpreted in light of state law, irrespective of the claim's origin. In some instances, reference to state law can narrowly restrict or limit alleged property interests. For example, the United States Supreme Court, in construing a North Carolina employee's property rights, relied on the state supreme court's opinion that "an enforceable expectation of continued public employment in that state can exist only if the employer by *statute* or *contract* has actually granted some form of guarantee."[35] In that case, a city ordinance gave rise to an expectancy of reemployment after the successful completion of a six-month probationary period, but the Court reasoned that, in the absence of a statutory or contractual obligation, the employee worked at the will and pleasure of the city. To establish a property right, then, it is necessary to prove not only that the employer's actions create an expectation of employment but also that state law does not limit the claim.

LIBERTY INTEREST. As noted previously, liberty interests encompass fundamental constitutional guarantees such as freedom of expression and privacy rights. If governmental action in the nonrenewal of employment threatens the exercise of these fundamental liberties, procedural due process must be afforded. Most nonrenewals, however, do not overtly implicate fundamental rights, and thus the burden is on the aggrieved employee to prove that the proffered reason is pretextual to mask impermissible grounds.

A liberty interest also may be implicated if the nonrenewal of employment damages an individual's reputation. The Supreme Court established in *Roth* that damage to a teacher's reputation and future employability could infringe Fourteenth Amendment liberty rights. In subsequent decisions, the Court identified prerequisite conditions for establishing that a constitutionally impermissible stigma has been imposed. According to the Court, procedural protections must be afforded only if stigma or damaging statements are related to loss of employment, publicly disclosed, alleged to be false, and virtually foreclose opportunities for future employment.[36]

Under this "stigma-plus" test, governmental action damaging a teacher's reputation, standing alone, is insufficient to invoke the Fourteenth Amendment's procedural safeguards.[37] As such, an educator who has been reassigned, transferred, suspended, or denied a promotion cannot claim violation of a liberty interest.[38] The Fifth Circuit noted that

[34]Leary v. Daeschner, 228 F.3d 729 (6th Cir. 2000).

[35]Bishop v. Wood, 426 U.S. 341, 345 (1976) (emphasis added).

[36]*See* Codd v. Velger, 429 U.S. 624 (1977); Bishop v. Wood, 426 U.S. 341 (1976); Paul v. Davis, 424 U.S. 693 (1976).

[37]State constitutions, however, may provide greater protection of due process rights encompassing damage to reputation alone. *See, e.g.*, Kadetsky v. Egg Harbor Twp. Bd. of Educ., 82 F. Supp. 2d 327 (D.N.J. 2000).

[38]*See, e.g.*, Brown v. Simmons, 478 F.3d 922 (8th Cir. 2007); Ulichny v. Merton Cmty. Sch. Dist., 249 F.3d 686 (7th Cir. 2001).

the internal transfer of an employee, unless it is regarded essentially as a loss of employment, does not provide the loss of a tangible interest necessary to give rise to a liberty interest.[39] The Vermont Supreme Court found such a loss when a principal was placed on paid administrative leave, which the court characterized as "tantamount to dismissal," fulfilling the "plus" requirement of a loss.[40] However, this action did not violate his liberty interests since no evidence supported that the action stigmatized him. Furthermore, to sustain a stigmatization claim, an individual must show that a request was made for a name-clearing hearing and that the request was denied.[41]

The primary issue in these terminations is determining what charges stigmatize an individual. Nonrenewal alone is insufficient. As the Ninth Circuit noted: "Nearly any reason assigned for dismissal is likely to be to some extent a negative reflection on an individual's ability, temperament, or character," but circumstances giving rise to a liberty interest are narrow.[42] Not every comment or accusation by school officials that affects one's reputation is actionable under the Fourteenth Amendment.[43] Charges must be serious implications against character, such as immorality and dishonesty, to create a stigma of constitutional magnitude that virtually forecloses other employment. According to the Fifth Circuit, a charge must give rise to "a 'badge of infamy,' public scorn, or the like."[44] Such a liberty violation was clearly illustrated by the termination of a life-science teacher after public attacks on his teaching of human reproduction.[45] In this case, the court found that the teacher was subjected to extensive, embarrassing publicity in the local, national, and even international media (e.g., being referred to as a sex maniac); incurred substantial personal harassment; and suffered permanent damage to his professional career. Termination of a New York probationary teacher implicated a liberty interest when her professional integrity and reputation were impugned by allegations that she helped students cheat on standardized tests, urged other teachers to cheat, and tried to assault another teacher who refused to participate in the scheme.[46] Allegations such as these represent serious accusations that damage an educator's standing and pose significant threats to future employability, thereby, requiring a opportunity for a name-clearing hearing.

Among other accusations that courts have found to necessitate a hearing are a serious drinking problem, emotional instability, mental illness, immoral conduct, accusation

[39]Moore v. Otero, 557 F.2d 435, 438 (5th Cir. 1977). *But see* Winegar v. Des Moines Indep. Cmty. Sch. Dist., 20 F.3d 895 (8th Cir. 1994) (holding that disciplinary transfer to another school because of the physical abuse of a student involved a significant liberty interest necessitating an opportunity to be heard).

[40]Herrera v. Union No. 39 Sch. Dist., 975 A.2d 619, 624 (Vt. 2009).

[41]*See, e.g.*, Puchalski v. Sch. Dist., 161 F. Supp. 2d 395 (E.D. Pa. 2001); *see also* Segal v. Bd. of Educ., N.Y.C., 459 F.3d 207 (2d Cir. 2006) (ruling that the availability of adequate process, even if not used by teacher, defeats claim).

[42]Gray v. Union Cnty. Intermediate Educ. Dist., 520 F.2d 803, 806 (9th Cir. 1975); *see, e.g.*, Beischel v. Stone Bank Sch. Dist., 362 F.3d 430 (7th Cir. 2004); Howard v. Columbia Pub. Sch. Dist., 363 F.3d 797 (8th Cir. 2004).

[43]*See, e.g.*, Ulichny v. Merton Cmty. Sch. Dist., 249 F.3d 686 (7th Cir. 2001); *see also* Kohn v. Sch. Dist., 817 F. Supp 2d 487, 499 (M.D. Pa. 2011) (finding that mayor's comments accusing superintendent of criminal conduct in his job performance were "rhetorical hyperbole" and thus not considered stigmatizing).

[44]Ball v. Bd. of Trs., 584 F.2d 684, 685 (5th Cir. 1978).

[45]Stachura v. Memphis Cmty. Sch. Dist., 763 F.2d 211 (6th Cir. 1985), *rev'd on damages issue*, 477 U.S. 299 (1986).

[46]Rivera v. Cmty. Sch. Dist. Nine, 145 F. Supp. 2d 302 (S.D.N.Y. 2001); *see also* Knox v. N.Y.C. Dep't of Educ., 924 N.Y.S.2d 389 (App. Div. 2011) (holding that a widely disseminated report detailing alleged dishonesty and placement on the department of education's Ineligible/Inquiry List of a school psychologist substantiated "stigma-plus," necessitating a name-clearing hearing). *But see* McPherson v. N.Y.C. Dep't of Educ., 457 F.3d 211 (2d Cir. 2006) (finding that placement of a teacher's name alone on the school board's Ineligible/Inquiry List, which indicates removal for cause, did not specify reasons to justify a due process claim).

of child molestation, and extensive professional inadequacies.[47] Reasons held to pose no threat to a liberty interest include job-related comments such as personality differences and difficulty in working with others, hostility toward authority, aggressive behavior, ineffective leadership, and nonperformance.[48] Charges relating to job performance may have an impact on future employment but do not create a stigma of constitutional magnitude.

Liberty interests are not implicated unless damaging reasons are publicly communicated in the process of denying employment.[49] The primary purpose of a hearing is to enable individuals to clear their names. Without public knowledge of the reasons for nonreappointment, such a hearing is not required. Furthermore, a protected liberty interest generally is affected only if the *school board publicizes* the stigmatizing reasons, rather than an individual, media, or another source. Accordingly, statements that are disclosed in a public meeting requested by the teacher or made by the teacher to the media or others do not require a name-clearing hearing. Likewise, rumors or hearsay remarks surfacing as a result of nonrenewal do not impair liberty interests. The First Circuit noted: "In terms of likely stigmatizing effect, there is a world of difference between official charges (such as excessive drinking) made publicly and a campus rumor based upon hearsay."[50] Even when a school board publicly announces stigmatizing reasons for its action, there must be a factual dispute regarding the truth of the allegations for a hearing to be required. If a teacher does not challenge the truth of the statements, a name-clearing hearing serves no purpose.[51] A teacher, however, is not required to establish that the statements are false to be entitled to a hearing; that is the purpose of the hearing.[52]

PROCEDURAL REQUIREMENTS IN DISCHARGE PROCEEDINGS

Since termination of a tenured teacher or a nontenured teacher during the contract period requires procedural due process, the central question becomes, *what process is due?* Courts have noted that no fixed set of procedures applies under all circumstances. Rather, due process entails a balancing of the individual and governmental interests affected in each situation. According to the Supreme Court, a determination of the specific aspects of due process requires the following considerations:

> first, the private interest that will be affected by the official action; second, the risk of an erroneous deprivation of such interest through the procedures used, and the probable value, if any, of additional or substitute procedural safeguards; and finally, the government's interest, including the function involved and the fiscal and administrative burdens that the additional or substitute procedural requirement would entail.[53]

[47]*See, e.g.*, Donato v. Plainview-Old Bethpage Cent. Sch. Dist., 96 F.3d 623 (2d Cir. 1996); Vanelli v. Reynolds Sch. Dist. No. 7, 667 F.2d 773 (9th Cir. 1982); Carroll v. Robinson, 874 P.2d 1010 (Ariz. Ct. App. 1994).

[48]*See, e.g.*, Gilder-Lucas v. Elmore Cnty. Bd. of Educ., 186 F. App'x 885 (11th Cir. 2006); Lybrook v. Members of Farmington Mun. Schs. Bd., 232 F.3d 1334 (10th Cir. 2000); Hayes v. Phoenix-Talent Sch. Dist. No. 4, 893 F.2d 235 (9th Cir. 1990).

[49]*See, e.g.*, Vega v. Miller, 273 F.3d 460 (2d Cir. 2001); *see also* Segal v. City of New York, 459 F.3d 207 (2d Cir. 2006) (holding that placement of damaging statements in a teacher's personnel file can meet the public disclosure aspect of a stigma-plus claim; future employers may have access to the file); Vandine v. Greece Cent. Sch. Dist., 905 N.Y.S.2d 428 (App. Div. 2010). *But see* Burton v. Town of Littleton, 426 F.3d 9 (1st Cir. 2005) (declaring that a superintendent sending a letter of employee's termination to state commissioner of education did not constitute public dissemination).

[50]Beitzell v. Jeffrey, 643 F.2d 870, 879 (1st Cir. 1981).

[51]*See, e.g.*, Codd v. Velger, 429 U.S. 624 (1977); Coleman v. Reed, 147 F.3d 751 (8th Cir. 1998).

[52]*See, e.g.*, O'Neill v. City of Auburn, 23 F.3d 685 (2d Cir. 1994).

[53]Mathews v. Eldridge, 424 U.S. 319, 335 (1976).

Application of these standards would require only minimum procedures in suspending a student but a more extensive, formal process in dismissing a teacher.

The Fourteenth Amendment requires at least that dismissal proceedings be based on established rules or standards. Specific procedures will depend on state law, school board regulations, and collective bargaining agreements,[54] but they cannot drop below constitutional minimums. For example, a statute requiring tenured teachers to pay half the cost of a hearing that constitutionally must be provided by the school board violates federal rights.[55] In assessing the adequacy of procedural safeguards, the judiciary looks for the provision of certain basic elements to meet constitutional guarantees. At the same time, courts will not find a deprivation of procedural due process rights if educators do not avail themselves of the existing safeguards.[56]

Courts generally have held that a teacher facing a severe loss such as termination must be afforded procedures encompassing the following elements:[57]

- notification of charges;
- opportunity for a hearing;
- adequate time to prepare a rebuttal to the charges;
- access to evidence and names of witnesses;
- hearing before an impartial tribunal;
- representation by legal counsel;
- opportunity to present evidence and witnesses;
- opportunity to cross-examine adverse witnesses;
- decision based on evidence and findings of the hearing;
- transcript or record of the hearing; and
- opportunity to appeal an adverse decision.

Beyond these constitutional considerations, courts also strictly enforce any additional procedural protections conferred by state laws and local policies. Examples of such requirements might be providing detailed performance evaluations prior to termination, notifying teachers of weaknesses, and allowing an opportunity for improvement before dismissal. Although failure to comply with these stipulations may invalidate the school board's action under state law, federal due process rights per se are not violated if minimal constitutional procedures are provided.

Except in limited circumstances, individuals are required to exhaust administrative procedures, or the grievance procedures specified in the collective bargaining agreement,

[54]*See, e.g.*, Hanover Sch. Dist. No 28 v. Barbour, 171 P.3d 223 (Colo. 2007); *see also* Kohn v. Sch. Dist., 817 F. Supp. 2d 487 (M.D. Pa. 2011) (holding that superintendent's employment contract provided for termination only for cause; he was not an "at-will" employee who could be terminated by the new school board without full procedural due process); State *ex rel.* Carna v. Teays Valley Local Sch. Dist., 967 N.E.2d 193 (Ohio 2012) (finding that when a principal requested to meet with the school board prior to nonrenewal of her contract, state law required the board to meet); *In re* Sch. Admin. Unit #44, 27 A.3d 819, 829 (N.H. 2011) (concluding that due process did not require notice and an opportunity to remedy the situation prior to the termination of a superintendent who misused federal grant money).

[55]*See* Rankin v. Indep. Sch. Dist. No. I-3, Noble Cnty., Okla., 876 F.2d 838 (10th Cir. 1989); *see also* Cal. Teachers Ass'n v. State, 975 P.2d 622, 643 (Cal. 1999) (concluding that imposing half the cost of an administrative law judge "chills the exercise of the right to a hearing and vigorous advocacy on behalf of the teacher").

[56]*See, e.g.*, Segal v. City of New York, 459 F.3d 207 (2d Cir. 2006).

[57]This chapter focuses on procedural protections required in teacher terminations. It should be noted, however, that other school board decisions (e.g., transfers, demotions, or mandatory leaves) may impose similar constraints on decision making.

prior to seeking judicial review. Pursuing an administrative hearing promotes resolution of a controversy at the agency level. Furthermore, if the issue is ultimately submitted for judicial review, the court has the benefit of the agency's findings and conclusions. Exhaustion is not required, however, if administrative review would be futile or inadequate. For example, the Connecticut Supreme Court reasoned that seeking an administrative remedy would have been futile for a principal who had been constructively discharged (forced to resign by the superintendent). Since the principal had not been discharged on statutory grounds, an administrative hearing could not grant the relief sought by the principal.[58]

Various elements of due process proceedings may be contested as inadequate. Questions arise regarding the sufficiency of notice, impartiality of the board members, and placement of the burden of proof. The aspects of procedural due process that courts frequently scrutinize in assessing the fundamental fairness of school board actions are examined next.

Notice

In general, a constitutionally adequate notice is timely, informs the teacher of specific charges, and allows the teacher sufficient time to prepare a response. Beyond the constitutional guarantees, state laws and regulations as well as school board policies usually impose very specific requirements relating to form, timeliness, and content of notice.[59] In legal challenges, the adequacy of a notice is assessed in terms of whether it meets constitutional as well as other requirements. Failure to comply substantially with mandated requisites will void school board action.

The form or substance of notice is usually stipulated in statutes. In determining appropriateness of notice, courts generally have held that substantial compliance with form requirements (as opposed to strict compliance required for notice deadlines) is sufficient. Under this standard, the decisive factor is whether the notice adequately informs the teacher of the pending action rather than the actual form of the notice. For example, if a statute requires notification by certified mail and the notice is mailed by registered mail or is personally delivered, it substantially complies with the state requirement. However, oral notification will not suffice if the law requires written notification. If the form of the notice is not specified by statute, any timely notice that informs a teacher is adequate.

For a notice to comply with constitutional due process guarantees, the teacher must receive the notice. In a New York case, the Board of Education mailed the notice of intent to terminate a teacher's employment by certified and regular mail to an outdated address.[60] The regular mail copy was not returned, but the certified copy was returned

[58]Mendillo v. Bd. of Educ., 717 A.2d 1177 (Conn. 1998).

[59]*See* Sajko v. Jefferson Cnty. Bd. of Educ., 314 S.W.3d 290 (Ky. 2010) (interpreting state law that requires a teacher challenging a dismissal to notify school officials within ten days of the receipt of termination notice to mean *actual receipt—not postmarked within ten days*); Hoschler v. Sacramento City Unified Sch. Dist., 57 Cal. Rptr. 3d 115 (Ct. App. 2007) (concluding that a statute silent on the method of delivery required personal delivery rather than certified mail); Clark Cnty. Sch. Dist. v. Riley, 14 P.3d 22 (Nev. 2000) (finding that only four days' notice with no mention of the right to a hearing violated a statute requiring fifteen days' notice and the right to a hearing).

[60]Norgrove v. Bd. of Educ., N.Y.C., 881 N.Y.S.2d 802 (Sup. Ct. 2009) (quoting Jones v. Flowers, 547 U.S. 220, 239 (2006) (finding that multiple means of contact were possible where a notice letter of intent to sell an individual's property for unpaid taxes was returned as unclaimed; the Court noted: "We are confident that additional reasonable steps were available").

as unclaimed. Consequently, the teacher claimed he did not receive the notice and could not request a hearing. The court held that the notice did not meet statutory requirements because the Board of Education was aware that the notice was returned as unclaimed and did not make additional efforts, such as hand delivery of the notice to the teacher in his classroom.

Although form and timeliness are important concerns in issuing a notice, the primary consideration is the statement of reasons for an action. With termination of a teacher's contract, school boards must bring specific charges against the teacher, including not only the factual basis for the charges but also the names of accusers.[61] State laws may impose further specifications, such as North Dakota's requirement that reasons for termination in the notice must be based on issues raised in prior written evaluations.[62] If the state law identifies grounds for dismissal, charges also must be based on the statutory causes. But a teacher cannot be forced to defend against vague and indefinite charges that simply restate the statutory categories, such as incompetency or neglect of duty. Notice must include specific accusations to allow the teacher to prepare a proper defense. The Arkansas Supreme Court interpreted its state Teacher Fair Dismissal Act as requiring sufficient notice "such that *a reasonable teacher* could defend against the reasons given."[63] Furthermore, only charges identified in the notice can form the basis for dismissal.

Hearing

In addition to notice, some type of hearing is required before an employer makes the initial termination decision; post-termination hearings do not satisfy federal constitutional due process requirements. In a 1985 decision, *Cleveland Board of Education v. Loudermill*, the United States Supreme Court recognized the necessity for some kind of a pre-termination hearing. Although the Court emphasized that a full evidentiary hearing to resolve the propriety of the discharge is not required, an initial hearing must be provided to serve as a check against wrong decisions.[64] This would entail determining if there are reasonable grounds to believe that the charges are true and that they support the dismissal. Essentially, in such a pre-termination hearing, an employee is entitled to notice of the charges and evidence as well as an opportunity to respond, orally or in writing, as to why the proposed action should not be taken. If only the minimal pre-termination procedures outlined by the Supreme Court are provided, a full evidentiary post-termination hearing is required.[65] Even extenuating circumstances involving severe disruption to the educational process cannot justify the omission of a preliminary determination.[66] Under

[61]*See, e.g.*, Martin v. Sch. Dist. No. 394, 393 F. Supp. 2d 1028 (D. Idaho 2005).

[62]Hoffner v. Bismarck Pub. Sch. Dist., 589 N.W.2d 195 (N.D. 1999).

[63]Russell v. Watson Chapel Sch. Dist., 313 S.W.3d 1 (Ark. 2009).

[64]470 U.S. 532 (1985).

[65]*See* Curtis v. Montgomery Cnty. Pub. Schs., 242 F. App'x 109 (4th Cir. 2007) (concluding that the predismissal process provided to a teacher, including notice that he was being investigated regarding serious allegations and placed on suspension, satisfied pre-termination rights); Rodriguez v. Ysleta Indep. Sch. Dist., 217 F. App'x 294 (5th Cir. 2007) (finding adequate due process when a teacher was provided a pre-termination hearing and an opportunity for three additional post-termination hearings under Texas law).

[66]*But see* Gilbert v. Homar, 520 U.S. 924 (1997) (ruling that a temporary suspension without pay of an employee charged with a felony does not require a pre-termination hearing when an employee occupies a position of great public trust); Jerrytone v. Musto, 167 F. App'x 295 (3d Cir. 2006) (ruling that a pre-termination hearing was not required prior to a teacher's suspension without pay when criminal charges were filed against him).

emergency conditions, however, teachers can be suspended with pay pending a termination hearing.

Courts have not prescribed in detail the procedures to be followed in administrative hearings. Basically, the fundamental constitutional requirement is fair play—that is, an opportunity to be heard at a meaningful time and in a meaningful manner. Beyond this general requirement, the specific aspects of a hearing are influenced by the circumstances of the case, with the potential for grievous losses necessitating more extensive safeguards. According to the Missouri Supreme Court, a hearing generally should include a meaningful opportunity to be heard, to state one's position, to present witnesses, and to cross-examine witnesses; the accused also has the right to counsel and access to written reports in advance of the hearing.[67] Implicit in these rudimentary requirements are the assumptions that the hearing will be conducted by an impartial decision maker and will result in a decision based on the evidence presented. This section examines issues that may arise in adversarial hearings before the school board.

ADEQUATE NOTICE OF HEARING. As noted, due process rights afford an individual the opportunity to be heard at a meaningful time. This implies sufficient time between notice of the hearing and the scheduled meeting. Unless state law designates a time period, the school board can establish a reasonable date for the hearing, taking into consideration the specific facts and circumstances. In a termination action, the school board would be expected to provide ample time for the teacher to prepare a defense; however, the teacher bears the burden of requesting additional time if the length of notice is insufficient to prepare an adequate response. A notice as short as two days was upheld as satisfying due process requirements where the teacher participated in the hearing and did not object to the time or request a postponement.[68] Similarly, a one-day notice was found constitutionally sufficient when the teacher did not attend the meeting to raise objections.[69] A teacher who participates fully in the hearing process or waives the right to a hearing by failure to attend cannot later assert "lack of adequate time" to invalidate the due process proceedings.

WAIVER OF HEARING. Although a hearing is an essential element of due process, a teacher can waive this right by failing to request a hearing, refusing to attend it, or walking out of the hearing.[70] Voluntary resignation of a position also waives an individual's entitlement to a hearing.[71] In some states, a hearing before the school board may be waived by an employee's election of an alternative hearing procedure, such as

[67]Valter v. Orchard Farm Sch. Dist., 541 S.W.2d 550 (Mo. 1976); *see also* McClure v. Indep. Sch. Dist. No. 16, 228 F.3d 1205 (10th Cir. 2000) (holding that a teacher was deprived of due process rights when she was not allowed to cross-examine witnesses who provided testimony by affidavit at a termination hearing).

[68]Ahern v. Bd. of Educ., 456 F.2d 399 (8th Cir. 1972).

[69]Birdwell v. Hazelwood Sch. Dist., 491 F.2d 490 (8th Cir. 1974).

[70]*See, e.g.*, Jefferson v. Sch. Bd., 452 F. App'x 356 (4th Cir. 2011); Miller v. Clark Cnty. Sch. Dist., 378 F. App'x. 623 (9th Cir. 2010); Schimenti v. Sch. Bd., 73 So. 3d 831 (Fla. Dist. Ct. App. 2011); Smith v. Caddo Parish Sch. Bd., 69 So. 3d 543 (La. Ct. App. 2011); *see also* McKnight v. Sch. Dist., 171 F. Supp. 2d 446 (E.D. Pa. 2001), *aff'd*, 64 F. App'x 851 (3d Cir. 2003) (holding that a teacher's right to hearing was not violated when he attended but refused to participate; the school board needed only to provide an opportunity for a hearing). *But see* Baird v. Bd. of Educ. Warren Cmty. Unit Sch. Dist. No. 205, 389 F.3d 685 (7th Cir. 2004) (finding that a superintendent did not waive his rights when he attended his pre-termination hearing only to request his right to full procedural due process).

[71]*See, e.g.*, Kirkland v. St. Vrain Valley Sch. Dist. No. RE1J, 464 F.3d 1182 (10th Cir. 2006).

a grievance mechanism or an impartial referee. For example, the Third Circuit held that an employee's choice of either a hearing before the school board or arbitration under the collective bargaining agreement met the constitutional requirements of due process; the school board was not required to provide the individual a hearing in addition to the arbitration proceeding.[72] Similarly, an Ohio federal district court ruled that a teacher who selected a hearing before an impartial referee was not entitled to be heard by the school board prior to its decision on the referee's report.[73]

IMPARTIAL HEARING. A central question raised regarding hearings is the school board's impartiality as a hearing body. This issue arises because school boards often perform multiple functions in a hearing; they may investigate the allegations against a teacher, initiate the proceedings, and render the final judgment. Teachers have contended that such expansive involvement violates their right to an unbiased decision maker. Rejecting the idea that combining the adjudicative and investigative functions violates due process rights, courts generally have determined that prior knowledge of the facts does not disqualify school board members.[74] In addition, the fact that the board makes the initial decision to terminate employment does not render subsequent review impermissibly biased. Neither is a hearing prejudiced by a limited, preliminary inquiry to determine if there is a basis for terminating a teacher. Since hearings are costly and time consuming, such a preliminary investigation may save time as well as potential embarrassment.

In *Hortonville Joint School District No. 1 v. Hortonville Education Association*, the United States Supreme Court firmly established that the school board is a proper review body to conduct dismissal hearings.[75] The Court held that a school board's involvement in collective negotiations did not disqualify it as an impartial hearing board in the subsequent dismissal of striking teachers. The Court noted that "a showing that the Board was 'involved' in the events preceding this decision, in light of the important interest in leaving with the board the power given by the state legislature, is not enough to overcome the presumption of honesty and integrity in policymakers with decision-making power."[76]

Although the school board is the proper hearing body, bias on the part of the board or its members is constitutionally unacceptable. A teacher challenging the impartiality of the board has the burden of proving actual, not merely potential, bias. This requires the teacher to show more than board members' predecision involvement or prior knowledge of the issues.[77] A high probability of bias, however, can be shown if a board member has a

[72]Pederson v. S. Williamsport Area Sch. Dist., 677 F.2d 312 (3d Cir. 1982).

[73]Jones v. Morris, 541 F. Supp. 11 (S.D. Ohio 1981), *aff'd*, 455 U.S. 1009 (1982).

[74]*See, e.g.*, Withrow v. Larkin, 421 U.S. 35 (1975); *see also* Yukadinovich v. Bd. of Sch. Trs., 278 F.3d 693 (7th Cir. 2002) (concluding that a teacher did not establish bias in a termination hearing held in front of the school board that he had publicly criticized); Moore v. Bd. of Educ., 134 F.3d 781 (6th Cir. 1998) (finding that a superintendent's dual roles as presiding officer at the hearing and investigator did not deprive a teacher of due process).

[75]426 U.S. 482 (1976).

[76]*Id.* at 496–97; *see also* James v. Indep. Sch. Dist. No. I-050, 448 F. App'x 792 (10th Cir. 2011) (ruling that board members' previous criticisms of administrators' performance did not render them biased when they eliminated positions due to urgent financial conditions); Batagiannis v. W. Lafayette Cmty. Sch. Corp., 454 F.3d 738 (7th Cir. 2006) (finding that school board members did not exhibit bias that would disqualify them from conducting the superintendent's termination hearing, even though board members disagreed with the superintendent about how the schools should be run).

[77]*See, e.g.*, Say v. Umatilla Sch. Dist. 6, 364 F. App'x 385 (9th Cir. 2010); Beischel v. Stone Bank Sch. Dist., 362 F.3d 430 (7th Cir. 2004).

personal interest in the outcome of the hearing or has suffered personal abuse or criticism from a teacher.

Several cases illustrate instances of unacceptable bias. For example, the Alabama Supreme Court invalidated a teacher termination hearing for intolerably high bias created by a school board member's son testifying against the teacher; the son had been the target of alleged personal abuse by the teacher.[78] The Tenth Circuit also ruled that bias was shown in the termination of a superintendent because one of the board members had campaigned to remove the superintendent from his position, and two other board members had made unfavorable statements to the effect that the superintendent "had to go."[79] The Iowa Supreme Court concluded that a school board's role of "investigation, instigation, prosecution, and verdict rendering" denied a teacher an impartial hearing since the board used no witnesses and relied solely on its personal knowledge of the case in reaching a decision.[80] A lack of impartiality or inferences of partiality may include board members testifying as witnesses, prior announcements by board members of views and positions showing closed minds, and board members assuming adversarial or prosecutorial roles.[81]

EVIDENCE. Under teacher tenure laws, the burden of proof is on the school board to show cause for dismissal. The standard of proof generally applied to administrative bodies is to produce a *preponderance of evidence*.[82] Administrative hearings are not held to the more stringent standards applied in criminal proceedings (i.e., clear and convincing evidence beyond a reasonable doubt). Proof by a preponderance of evidence simply indicates that the majority of the evidence supports the board's decision or, as the New York high court stated, "such relevant proof as a reasonable mind may accept as adequate to support a conclusion."[83] If the board fails to meet this burden of proof, the judiciary will not uphold the termination decision. For example, the Nebraska Supreme Court, in overturning a school board's dismissal decision, concluded that dissatisfaction of parents and school board members was not sufficient evidence to substantiate incompetency charges against a teacher who had received above-average performance evaluations during her entire term of employment.[84]

[78]*Ex parte* Greenberg v. Ala. State Tenure Comm'n, 395 So. 2d 1000 (Ala. 1981); *see also* Katruska v. Dep't of Educ., 767 A.2d 1051 (Pa. 2001) (concluding that the testimony of a board member's wife against the principal created the appearance of bias in a hearing, but the Secretary of Education's de nova review met due process).

[79]Staton v. Mayes, 552 F.2d 908, 914 (10th Cir. 1977). *But see* Welch v. Barham, 635 F.2d 1322 (8th Cir. 1980) (finding that statements by two board members at trial that they could not think of any evidence that would have changed their minds about terminating the individual did not show the degree of bias necessary to disqualify a decision maker).

[80]Keith v. Cmty. Sch. Dist., 262 N.W.2d 249, 260 (Iowa 1978).

[81]*See, e.g.*, McClure v. Indep. Sch. Dist. No. 16, 228 F.3d 1205 (10th Cir. 2000); Baker v. Poughkeepsie City Sch. Dist., 945 N.Y.S.2d 589 (N.Y. 2012).

[82]*See, e.g.*, Sias v. Iberia Parish Sch. Bd., 74 So. 3d 800 (La. Ct. App. 2011), *review denied*, 78 So. 3d 143 (La. 2012); Chattooga Cnty. Bd. of Educ. v. Searels, 691 S.E.2d 629 (Ga. Ct. App. 2010); Martinek v. Belmond-Klemme Cmty. Sch. Dist., 772 N.W.2d 758 (Iowa 2009).

[83]Altsheler v. Bd. of Educ., 464 N.E.2d 979, 979–80 (N.Y. 1984).

[84]Schulz v. Bd. of Educ., 315 N.W.2d 633 (Neb. 1982); *see also* Weston v. Indep. Sch. Dist. No. 35, 170 P.3d 539 (Okla. 2007) (ordering a school district to reinstate a teacher because officials did not prove by a preponderance of evidence that dismissal was warranted).

The objective of school board hearings is to ascertain the relevant facts of the situation; the board hears evidence from both the teacher and the district officials recommending termination. These hearings are not encumbered by technical judicial rules of evidence, even if charges also carry criminal liability. Termination proceedings are separate from the criminal proceedings, and, as such, dismissal might be warranted based on the evidence presented, even though such evidence would not satisfy the more stringent requirements to sustain a criminal conviction. For example, a teacher could be dismissed on evidence of drug use, even though criminal charges are dropped due to a defective search warrant.

Only relevant, well-documented evidence presented at the hearing can be the basis for the board's decision.[85] Unlike formal judicial proceedings, hearsay evidence may be admissible in administrative hearings.[86] Courts have held that such evidence provides the background necessary for understanding the situation. Comments and complaints of parents have been considered relevant, but hearsay statements of students generally have been given little weight.[87]

FINDINGS OF FACT. At the conclusion of the hearing, the board must make specific findings of fact. A written report of the findings on which the board based its decision is essential. Without a report of the findings of fact, appropriate administrative or judicial review would be impeded. The Minnesota Supreme Court noted that "if the trial court were to review the merits of the case without findings of fact, there would be no safeguard against judicial encroachment on the school board's function since the trial court might affirm on a charge rejected by the school board."[88] Similarly, the Oklahoma Supreme Court held that a probationary teacher's statutory entitlement to a hearing includes the right to know the rationale for the board's decision. The court admonished that "an absence of required findings is fatal to the validity of administrative decisions even if the record discloses evidence to support proper findings."[89] The findings of fact need not be issued in technical language but simply in a form that explains the reasons for the action.

If an independent panel or hearing officer conducts the hearing, the school board is bound by the panel's findings of fact but can accept or reject the panel's conclusions and recommendations.[90] Accordingly, the board can decide to terminate an individual who has been supported by the panel so long as the board bases its decision on the evidence included in the panel's factual findings.

[85]*See, e.g.*, Goldberg v. Kelly, 397 U.S. 254, 271 (1970).

[86]*See, e.g.*, Colon v. N.Y.C. Dep't of Educ., 941 N.Y.S.2d 628 (App. Div. 2012); Drummond v. Todd Cnty. Bd. of Educ., 349 S.W.3d 316 (Ky. Ct. App. 2011); *see also* Waisanen v. Clatskanie Sch. Dist. #6J, 215 P.3d 882 (Or. Ct. App. 2009) (holding that student's polygraph exam results were admissible, particularly since the student was subject to cross-examination).

[87]*See, e.g.*, Daily v. Bd. of Educ., 588 N.W.2d 813 (Neb. 1999).

[88]Morey v. Sch. Bd., 128 N.W.2d 302, 307 (Minn. 1964).

[89]Jackson v. Indep. Sch. Dist. No. 16, 648 P.2d 26, 31 (Okla. 1982).

[90]*See, e.g.*, Raitzik v. Bd. of Educ., 826 N.E.2d 568 (Ill. App. Ct. 2005); Rogers v. Bd. of Educ., 749 A.2d 1173 (Conn. 2000). *But see* City Sch. Dist. v. Campbell, 798 N.Y.S.2d 54 (App. Div. 2005) (noting that an arbitrator's award may not be vacated unless it is clearly irrational or against public policy; court found hearing officer's reinstatement of a teacher, who pled guilty to drug charges, as coordinator of a program to deter student drug use defied common sense).

DISMISSAL FOR CAUSE

Tenure laws are designed to assure competent teachers continued employment as long as their performance is satisfactory. With the protection of tenure, a teacher can be dismissed only for cause and only in accordance with the procedures specified by law.[91] Tenure rights accrue under state laws and therefore must be interpreted in light of each state's requirements.

Where grounds for dismissal of a permanent teacher are identified by statute, a school board cannot base dismissal on reasons other than those specified. To cover unexpected matters, statutes often include a catchall phrase such as "other good and just cause." Grounds included in statutes vary considerably among states and range from an extensive listing of individual grounds to a simple statement that dismissal must be based on cause. The most frequently cited statutory causes are incompetency, immorality, insubordination, and neglect of duty.

Since grounds for dismissal are determined by statute, it is difficult to provide generalizations for all teachers. The causes are broad in scope and application; in fact, individual causes often have been attacked for impermissible vagueness. It is not unusual to find dismissal cases with similar factual situations based on different grounds across states. In addition, a number of grounds often are introduced and supported in a single termination case. Illustrative case law is examined here in relation to the more frequently cited grounds for dismissal. Educators should consult state laws and judicial rulings in their states to gain an understanding of their specific employment rights.[92]

Incompetency

Courts have broadly defined incompetency. Although it usually refers to classroom performance, it has been extended in some instances to a teacher's private life. The term is legally defined as "lack of ability, legal qualifications, or fitness to discharge the required duty."[93] Incompetency has been challenged as unconstitutionally vague, but courts have found the term sufficiently precise to give fair warning of prohibited conduct. Incompetency cases often involve issues relating to teaching methods, grading procedures, classroom management, and professional relationships. In general, dismissals for incompetency are based on a number of factors or a pattern of behavior rather than isolated incidents. In a Minnesota case, indicators of incompetency included poor rapport with students, inappropriate use of class time, irrational grading of students, and lack of student progress.[94] A Pennsylvania court interpreted incompetency as deficiencies in personality, composure, judgment, and attitude that have a detrimental effect on a teacher's performance.[95] Incompetency in this case was supported by evidence that the teacher was a disruptive influence in the school; could not maintain control of students; and failed to maintain her composure in dealing with students, other professionals, and parents.

[91]*See* Michael Long, *Studying the "Dismissal Gap": Research on Teacher Incompetence and Dismissals*, ORC Macro International (Washington, D.C., Mar. 2007). Long synthesized research on teacher dismissals and analyzed the National Center for Education Statistics' Schools and Staffing Survey, finding that both showed less than 1 percent of teachers are terminated each year.

[92]Claims that dismissals impair constitutional rights are discussed in the chapter "Teachers' Substantive Constitutional Rights".

[93]BLACK'S LAW DICTIONARY (9th ed.) (Eagen, MN: Thomas Reuter, 2009).

[94]Whaley v. Anoka-Hennepin Indep. Sch. Dist. No. 11, 325 N.W.2d 128 (Minn. 1982).

[95]Hamburg v. N. Penn Sch. Dist., 484 A.2d 867 (Pa. Commw. Ct. 1984).

Dismissals for incompetency have included a wide range of charges and occasionally have involved only a single incident. To illustrate, dismissals have been upheld for incompetency where a teacher brandished a starter pistol in an attempt to gain control of a group of students,[96] and an assistant principal permitted teachers to conduct a strip search of a fifth- and sixth-grade physical education class against explicit board policy.[97] A Louisiana court of appeals, however, held that a social studies teacher could not be dismissed for showing two R-rated movies; the court viewed the penalty as too harsh for a teacher with a fourteen-year unblemished teaching record.[98] Similarly, the South Dakota high court did not find a teacher's indiscreet answer to a fourth-grader's question about homosexual activity following a sex education video to be the type of "habitual and ongoing action" needed to support a charge of incompetency.[99]

Frequently, school boards have based charges of incompetency on teachers' lack of proper classroom management and control. Such dismissals have been contested on the grounds that the penalty of discharge was too severe for the offense. Courts have generally held that school boards have latitude in determining penalties, and their decisions will be overturned only if disproportionate to the offense. So long as evidence is presented to substantiate the board's charge, poor classroom management can result in termination.[100]

Termination for incompetency usually requires school officials systematically to document a teacher's performance. Providing opportunities and support for a teacher to achieve expected performance standards can be an important component in substantiating that a teacher had adequate notice of deficiencies.

Immorality

Immorality, one of the most frequently cited causes for dismissal, is generally not defined in state laws. In defining the term, the judiciary has tended to interpret immorality broadly as unacceptable conduct that affects a teacher's fitness to teach. Traditionally, the teacher has been viewed as an exemplar whose conduct is influential in shaping the lives of young students.

Sexually related conduct per se between a teacher and student has consistently been held to constitute immoral conduct justifying termination of employment. The Supreme Court of Colorado stated that when a teacher engages in sexually provocative or exploitative conduct with students, "a strong presumption of unfitness arises against the teacher."[101] Similarly, a Washington appellate court found that a male teacher's sexual relationship with a minor student justified dismissal.[102] The court declined to hold that

[96]Myres v. Orleans Parish Sch. Bd., 423 So. 2d 1303 (La. Ct. App. 1983).

[97]Rogers v. Bd. of Educ., 749 A.2d 1173 (Conn. 2000).

[98]West v. Tangipahoa Parish Sch. Bd., 615 So. 2d 979 (La. Ct. App. 1993).

[99]Collins v. Faith Sch. Dist. No. 46-2, 574 N.W.2d 889, 893 (S.D. 1998); *see also In re* Termination of Kibbe, 996 P.2d 419 (N.M. 1999) (ruling that a school board did not provide substantial evidence to show that a teacher's arrest for driving under the influence of alcohol was rationally related to his competence to teach).

[100]*See, e.g.*, Jones v. Jefferson Parish Sch. Bd., 688 F.2d 837 (5th Cir. 1982); Linstad v. Sitka Sch. Dist., 963 P.2d 246 (Alaska 1998); *see also* Ketchersid v. Rhea Cnty. Bd. of Educ., 174 S.W.3d 163 (Tenn. Ct. App. 2005) (finding that a teacher exhibited incompetence, defined as evident unfitness for service, by grabbing the faces of students and hitting them over the head with books to gain their attention).

[101]Weissman v. Bd. of Educ., 547 P.2d 1267, 1273 (Colo. 1976).

[102]Denton v. S. Kitsap Sch. Dist. No. 402, 516 P.2d 1080 (Wash. Ct. App. 1973); *see also* DeMichele v. Greenburgh Cent. Sch. Dist. No. 7, 167 F.3d 784 (2d Cir. 1999) (ruling that termination of a teacher for sexual misconduct with students occurring twenty-four years earlier did not violate his due process rights); Gongora v. N.Y.C. Dep't of Educ., 951 N.Y.S.2d 137 (App. Div. 2012) (finding that calling a student's home, asking the student out on a date, and urging the student not to report the call constituted sexual misconduct justifiying the termination of a teacher).

an adverse effect on fitness to teach must be shown. Rather, the court concluded that when a teacher and a minor student are involved, the board might reasonably decide that such conduct is harmful to the school district. In upholding the termination of a teacher involved in a sexual relationship with a minor, the Supreme Court of Delaware declared that such sexual contact directly relates to a teacher's fitness to teach and affects the community.[103]

Teachers discharged for sexually related conduct have challenged the statutory grounds of "immorality" or "immoral conduct" as impermissibly vague. An Alabama teacher, dismissed for sexual advances toward female students, asserted that the term "immorality" did not adequately warn a teacher as to what behavior would constitute an offense. The court acknowledged the lack of clarity but rejected the teacher's contention, reasoning that his behavior fell "squarely within the hard core of the statute's proscriptions."[104] The court noted that the teacher should have been aware that his conduct was improper, and the claim of vagueness or over breadth could not invalidate his dismissal. A Missouri federal district court conceded that the term immoral conduct is abstract, but, when construed in the overall statutory scheme, can be precisely defined as any conduct rendering a teacher unfit to teach.[105]

A New York case highlights the delicate balance between a teacher's First Amendment expressive rights and the need to protect students from a self-described pedophile.[106] In this instance, a thirty-year, successful teacher was terminated for advocating sexual activity between men and young boys. He was a long-term member of the North American Man/Boy Love Association (NAMBLA) and was closely involved with editing and writing the group's publication. With public notoriety, the school board found that the teacher could no longer be effective in the classroom. Even though no evidence existed that he had been illegally involved with young boys, the Second Circuit upheld the dismissal, noting that the school board did not base its decision on membership in NAMBLA but on the disruption his activities caused.

Sexual harassment involving inappropriate comments, touching, and teasing may result in termination for immorality.[107] The West Virginia high court upheld the termination of a teacher for repeated comments of a sexual nature to students; the comments had continued in spite of warnings to desist.[108]

In addition to sexual improprieties with students, which clearly are grounds for dismissal, other conduct that sets a bad example for students may be considered immoral under the "role model" standard. Courts, however, generally have required

[103]Lehto v. Bd. of Educ., 962 A.2d 222 (Del. 2008); *see also* State of Kansas v. Edwards, No. 106,435, slip op. at 3 (Kan. App. Ct. Nov. 2, 2012) (upholding the constitutionality of a statute that makes a sexual relationship between a teacher and a student a crime; with the disparity in power between a teacher and student, the court concluded that "the right of privacy does not encompass the right of a high school teacher to have sex with students enrolled in the same school system").

[104]Kilpatrick v. Wright, 437 F. Supp. 397, 399 (M.D. Ala. 1977).

[105]Thompson v. Sw. Sch. Dist., 483 F. Supp. 1170 (W.D. Mo. 1980).

[106]Melzer v. Bd. of Educ., N.Y.C., 336 F.3d 185 (2d Cir. 2003).

[107]Intentionally left blank so that the remaining footnotes in the chapter can remain numbered as is.

[108]Harry v. Marion Cnty. Bd. of Educ., 506 S.E.2d 319 (W. Va. 1998); *see also* Forte v. Mills, 672 N.Y.S.2d 497 (App. Div. 1998) (ruling that a teacher's inappropriate touching of fourth- and fifth-grade girls was sexually harassing conduct justifying termination for insubordination and conduct unbecoming to a teacher; he had received repeated warnings to desist).

school officials to show that misconduct or a particular lifestyle has an adverse impact on fitness to teach. They have recognized that allowing dismissal merely upon a showing of immoral behavior without consideration of the nexus between the conduct and fitness to teach would be an unwarranted intrusion on a teacher's right to privacy. For example, an Ohio appellate court found that school officials had not produced evidence to show that a teacher's adulterous affair with another school employee constituted immorality when it did not have a hostile impact on the school community.[109]

A California appellate court examined whether a teacher's immoral conduct rendered him unfit to teach.[110] In this case, the teacher, a dean of students in a middle school, posted a sexually explicit ad with pornographic images of himself on Craigslist in the "men seeking men" category. An anonymous report to the local police led to the police notifying local school officials and the subsequent termination of the teacher. Although the teacher argued that no connection existed between his behavior and his teaching effectiveness, the appellate court disagreed, noting that at least one parent and several school officials had seen the ad. The principal, specifically, said she had lost confidence in the teacher's ability to serve as a role model in light of his behavior. In upholding the termination, the court noted: "There are certain professions which impose upon persons attracted to them, responsibilities and limitations on freedom of action which do not exist in regard to other callings."[111] The court also noted that judges, police officers, and teachers are in this category.[112]

Teachers' sexual orientation has been an issue in several controversial dismissal cases. Although these cases often have raised constitutional issues related to freedom of expression and privacy, courts also have confronted the question of whether sexual orientation per se is evidence of unfitness to teach or whether it must be shown that this lifestyle impairs teaching effectiveness.[113] Courts have rendered diverse opinions regarding lesbian, gay, bisexual, and transgendered (LGBT) educators. According to the Supreme Court of California, immoral or unprofessional conduct or moral turpitude must be related to unfitness to teach to justify termination.[114] Yet the Supreme Court of Washington upheld the dismissal of a teacher based simply on the knowledge of his homosexuality.[115] The court feared that public controversy could interfere with the teacher's classroom effectiveness.

In recent years, however, courts have been reluctant to support the dismissal of LGBT educators simply because the school board does not approve of a particular

[109]Bertolini v. Whitehall City Sch. Dist. Bd. of Educ., 744 N.E.2d 1245 (Ohio Ct. App. 2000).

[110]San Diego Unified Sch. Dist. v. Comm'n on Prof'l Competence, 124 Cal. Rptr. 3d 320 (Ct. App. 2011).

[111]*Id.* at 327.

[112]The California court cited a U.S. Supreme Court decision holding a police officer could be terminated for selling sexually explicit videos of himself on eBay, establishing that termination for public distribution or posting of such material does not violate constitutional rights of public employees. *See* City of San Diego v. Roe, 543 U.S. 77 (2004).

[113]Intentionally left blank so that the remaining footnotes in the chapter can remain numbered as is.

[114]Morrison v. State Bd. of Educ., 461 P.2d 375 (Cal. 1969). *But see* Rowland v. Mad River Local Sch. Dist., 730 F.2d 444 (6th Cir. 1984) (upholding the nonrenewal of a guidance counselor who revealed her homosexuality).

[115]Gaylord v. Tacoma Sch. Dist. No. 10, 559 P.2d 1340 (Wash. 1977).

private lifestyle. For example, an Ohio federal court concluded that the nonrenewal of a teacher because of his homosexuality did not bear a rational relationship to a legitimate government purpose, thereby violating the Equal Protection Clause.[116] The court ordered reinstatement with a two-year contract and assessed damages against the school board.

Whereas many dismissals for immorality involve sexual conduct, immorality is much broader in meaning and scope. As one court noted, it covers conduct that "is hostile to the welfare of the school community."[117] Such hostile conduct has included, among other things, dishonest acts, criminal conduct, and drug-related conduct. Frequently, criminal conduct has resulted in dismissals for immoral behavior. For example, Alaska statutes define immorality as "an act which, under the laws of the state, constitutes a crime involving moral turpitude," and the state high court held that a conviction for unlawfully diverting electricity was such a crime.[118] Under Georgia law, conviction for submitting false tax documents was sufficient grounds to dismiss a principal for moral turpitude.[119] Other acts found to substantiate charges of immorality include being involved in the sale of illegal drugs,[120] possessing cocaine,[121] pleading guilty to grand larceny,[122] reporting to school under the influence of marijuana,[123] and pressuring a young incarcerated woman to give up her eleven-month-old child for adoption.[124]

In the absence of a statutory specification, however, the West Virginia Supreme Court found that a school board could not conclude that a conviction for a misdemeanor was per se immoral conduct.[125] A Pennsylvania court held that a conviction for threatening an individual did not substantiate immoral conduct; the court cautioned that not all unprofessional conduct is automatically immoral conduct.[126] Similarly, the Supreme Court of Oklahoma concluded that a teacher's verbal threats on school grounds against a school superintendent and another teacher may have been unprofessional and inappropriate, but the comments did not rise to the level of moral turpitude under state law to justify dismissal.[127]

[116]Glover v. Williamsburg Local Sch. Dist., 20 F. Supp. 2d 1160 (S.D. Ohio 1998).

[117]Jarvella v. Willoughby-Eastlake City Sch. Dist., 233 N.E.2d 143, 145 (Ohio 1967).

[118]Kenai Peninsula Borough Bd. of Educ. v. Brown, 691 P.2d 1034, 1036 (Alaska 1984); *see also* Toney v. Fairbanks N. Star Borough Sch. Dist., 881 P.2d 1112 (Alaska 1994) (finding that a teacher's sexual relationship with a fifteen-year-old student occurring prior to his employment by the school district was a crime of moral turpitude supporting termination; the court commented that it is questionable whether such a crime could ever be too remote to be considered in determining a teacher's fitness to teach).

[119]Logan v. Warren Cnty. Bd. of Educ., 549 F. Supp. 145 (S.D. Ga. 1982).

[120]Woo v. Putnam Cnty. Bd. of Educ., 504 S.E.2d 644 (W. Va. 1998).

[121]Gedney v. Bd. of Educ., 703 A.2d 804 (Conn. App. Ct. 1997).

[122]Green v. N.Y. City Dep't of Educ., 793 N.Y.S.2d 405 (App. Div. 2005); *see also* Patterson v. City of N.Y., 946 N.Y.S.2d 472 (App. Div. 2012) (finding misconduct justifying dismissal when a teacher provided an Albany address to avoid paying New York City income taxes).

[123]Younge v. Bd. of Educ., 788 N.E.2d 1153 (Ill. App. Ct. 2003).

[124]Homa v. Carthage R-IX Sch. Dist., 345 S.W.3d 266 (Mo. Ct. App. 2011).

[125]Golden v. Bd. of Educ., 285 S.E.2d 665 (W. Va. 1981) *But see* Zelno v. Lincoln Intermediate Unit No. 12 Bd. of Dirs, 786 A.2d 1022 (Pa. Commw. Ct. 2001) (finding that a teacher could be terminated for immoral conduct based on three drunken driving convictions and two convictions for driving without a license).

[126]Horton v. Jefferson Cnty.-Dubois Area Vocational Tech. Sch., 630 A.2d 481 (Pa. Commw. Ct. 1993).

[127]Ballard v. Indep. Sch. Dist. No. 4, 77 P.3d 1084 (Okla. 2003).

Although immorality is an abstract term that can encompass broad-ranging behavior, it is understood to refer to actions that violate moral standards and render a teacher unfit to teach. Courts consistently hold that school officials must link the challenged conduct to impairment of the teacher's effectiveness in the classroom to justify termination for immorality.

Insubordination

Insubordination, another frequently cited cause for dismissal, is generally defined as the willful disregard of or refusal to obey school regulations and official orders. Teachers can be dismissed for violation of administrative regulations and policies even though classroom performance is satisfactory; school officials are not required to establish a relationship between the conduct and fitness to teach.

With the plethora of regulations enacted by school districts, wide diversity is found in the types of behavior adjudicated as insubordination. Dismissals based on insubordination have been upheld in cases involving refusal to abide by specific school directives, unwillingness to cooperate with superiors, unauthorized absences, and numerous other actions. Because conduct is measured against the existence of a rule or policy, a school board may more readily document insubordination than most other legal causes for dismissal.

Many state laws and court decisions require that acts be "willful and persistent" to be considered insubordinate. A Florida teacher's continuous refusal to provide lesson plans during school absences resulted in termination for insubordination. A Florida appellate court, upholding the dismissal, noted insubordination under state law as "constant or continuing intentional refusal to obey a direct order, reasonable in nature, and given by and with proper authority."[128] A California appellate court upheld the termination of a tenured teacher for "persistent violation or refusal to obey a district regulation."[129] To meet a state mandate, the school board required all teachers to be become certified to teach English language learners (ELLs) and provided financial support for the training. A teacher, who held a life credential, was terminated after she repeatedly refused to pursue the certification. The court ruled that it was within the school board's authority to impose this additional requirement.

Insubordination charges often are the result of conflicts arising from the administrator/teacher relationship. For example, a North Carolina teacher's refusal to discontinue a classroom project that the principal and curriculum specialist determined to be lacking in any educational value and her subsequent refusal to develop and implement a professional growth plan supported dismissal.[130] The South Dakota

[128]Dolega v. Sch. Bd., 840 So. 2d 445, 446 (Fla. Dist. Ct. App. 2003); *see also* Miller v. Clark Cnty. Sch. Dist., 378 F. App'x 623 (9th Cir. 2010) (holding that evidence showing prior warnings, admonitions, and suspensions established grounds to dismiss a teacher for insubordination); Chattooga Cnty. Bd. of Educ. v. Searels, 691 S.E.2d 629 (Ga. Ct. App. 2010) (finding termination justified when a teacher continued to make inappropriate statements about students after repeated warnings from her principal).

[129]Governing Bd. v. Comm'n on Prof'l Conduct, 99 Cal. Rptr. 3d 903, 913 (Ct. App. 2009); *see also* Overton v. Bd. of Educ., 900 N.Y.S.2d 338, 339 (App. Div. 2010) (ruling that both misconduct and insubordination were established by the teacher's "pattern of poor work performance and disruptive behavior").

[130]Hope v. Charlotte-Mecklenburg Bd. of Educ., 430 S.E.2d 472 (N.C. Ct. App. 1993).

Supreme Court upheld the dismissal of a teacher who refused to submit to the principal's authority; the teacher's repeated refusals to respond to reasonable requests and orders were characterized as disobedient, confrontational, adversarial, insolent, and defensive.[131]

Teachers cannot ignore reasonable directives and policies of administrators or school boards. If the school board has prohibited corporal punishment or prescribed procedures for its administration, teachers must strictly adhere to board requirements. In upholding the termination of a Colorado teacher, the state supreme court ruled that tapping a student on the head with a three-foot pointer supported termination because the teacher had been warned and disciplined previously for using physical force in violation of school district policy.[132] Repeatedly failing to follow official directives in administering corporal punishment also resulted in the termination of a Texas teacher.[133] The Eleventh Circuit found that insubordination was established when a teacher refused to undergo urinalysis within two hours of the discovery of marijuana in her car in the school parking lot, as required by school board policy.[134] The Eighth Circuit upheld the dismissal of a teacher for violating a school board policy that prohibited students' use of profanity in the classroom; students had used profanity in various creative writing assignments such as plays and poems.[135] Other instances of failure to follow administrative directives justifying dismissal for insubordination include viewing pornographic images on a school computer in violation of policy and continuing to emphasize sexual aspects of literature after administrative warnings.[136]

Generally, the key factor in dismissal for insubordination is whether a teacher has persisted in disobeying a reasonable and valid school policy or directive. That is, school officials must show that specific requests have been made related to the teacher's classroom performance or other professional matters, and the teacher failed to comply. In a few instances, a severe or substantial single incident may be adequate for dismissal action.[137]

Neglect of Duty

Neglect of duty arises when an educator fails to carry out assigned duties. This may involve an intentional omission or may result from ineffectual performance. In a Colorado case, neglect of duty was found when a teacher failed to discipline students consistent

[131]Barnes v. Spearfish Sch. Dist. No. 40-2, 725 N.W.2d 226 (S.D. 2006).

[132]Bd. of Educ. v. Flaming, 938 P.2d 151 (Colo. 1997). *But see In re* Principe v. N.Y.C. Dep't of Educ., 941 N.Y.S.2d 574 (App. Div. 2012) (finding the termination of a middle school dean of students for violating the policy against corporal punishment excessive when he physically restrained students in two separate incidents; the action was found not to be premeditated and was taken in his role of disciplinarian), *review denied*, 976 N.E.2d 238 (N.Y. 2012).

[133]Burton v. Kirby, 775 S.W.2d 834 (Tex. Ct. App. 1989).

[134]Hearn v. Bd. of Pub. Educ., 191 F.3d 1329 (11th Cir. 1999).

[135]Lacks v. Ferguson Reorganized Sch. Dist. R-2, 147 F.3d 718 (8th Cir. 1998).

[136]Zellner v. Herrick, 639 F.3d 371 (7th Cir. 2011) (viewing pornographic images); *In re* Bernstein and Norwich City Sch. Dist., 726 N.Y.S.2d 474 (App. Div. 2001) (emphasizing sexual aspects of literature).

[137]*See* Ware v. Morgan Cnty. Sch. Dist., 748 P.2d 1295 (Colo. 1988) (finding one-time use of profanity, after being ordered not to use profanity with students, supported termination). *But see* Trimble v. W. Va. Bd. of Dirs., 549 S.E.2d 294 (W. Va. 2001) (concluding that termination for a minor incident of insubordination denied individual constitutional due process).

with school policy.[138] Similarly, the Louisiana high court ruled that a teacher repeatedly sending unescorted students to the principal's office in violation of school policy substantiated willful neglect of duty.[139] The Oregon appellate court concluded that a teacher's failure to maintain a professional working relationship with students, parents, staff, and other teachers constituted neglect of duty.[140]

The United States Supreme Court upheld the dismissal of an Oklahoma teacher for "willful neglect of duty" in failing to comply with the school board's continuing education requirement.[141] For a period of time, lack of compliance was dealt with through denial of salary increases. Upon enactment of a state law requiring salary increases for all teachers, the board notified teachers that noncompliance with the requirement would result in termination. Affirming the board's action, the Supreme Court found the sanction of dismissal to be rationally related to the board's objective of improving its teaching force through continuing education requirements.

The Supreme Court of Nebraska addressed what constitutes neglect of duty when a teacher allegedly had failed on several occasions to perform certain duties and at other times had not performed duties competently.[142] Evidence revealed that the teacher had not violated any administrative orders or school laws, had received good evaluations, and had been recommended for retention by the administrators. The court concluded that the facts did not support just cause for dismissal. In addition, the court cautioned that in evaluating a teacher's performance, neglect of duty is not measured "against a standard of perfection, but, instead, must be measured against the standard required of others performing the same or similar duties."[143] It was not demonstrated that the teacher's performance was below expectations for other teachers in similar positions.

In a later case, the Nebraska high court ruled that a superintendent's failure to file a funding form did not constitute neglect of duty to support the termination of his contract.[144] Similarly, a Louisiana appellate court held that a teacher's showing of an R-rated film did not warrant dismissal for neglect of duty and incompetence.[145] Also, the Louisiana high court concluded that a teacher bringing a loaded gun to school in his car did not substantiate willful neglect of duty to support termination.[146] The court

[138]Bd. of Educ. v. Flaming, 938 P.2d 151 (Colo. 1997); *see also* Flickinger v. Lebanon Sch. Dist., 898 A.2d 62 (Pa. Commw. Ct. 2006) (concluding that principal's failure to immediately respond to a report of a gun in the middle school established willful neglect of duty; school procedures specified that such a crisis situation must be handled without delay).

[139]Wise v. Bossier Parish Sch. Bd., 851 So. 2d 1090 (La. 2003).

[140]Bellairs v. Beaverton Sch. Dist., 136 P.3d 93 (Or. Ct. App. 2006).

[141]Harrah Indep. Sch. Dist. v. Martin, 440 U.S. 194 (1979).

[142]Sanders v. Bd. of Educ., 263 N.W.2d 461 (Neb. 1978).

[143]*Sanders*, 263 N.W.2d at 465; *see also* Eshom v. Bd. of Educ., 364 N.W.2d 7 (Neb. 1985) (ruling that dismissal was supported by detailed evaluations comparing a terminated teacher with other teachers).

[144]Boss v. Fillmore Sch. Dist. No. 19, 559 N.W.2d 448 (Neb. 1997). *But see* Smith v. Bullock Cnty. Bd. of Educ., 906 So. 2d 938 (Ala. Civ. App. 2004) (ruling that principal's failure to establish procedures to prevent the theft of about $25,000 of athletic funds was neglect of duty).

[145]Jones v. Rapides Parish Sch. Bd., 634 So. 2d 1197 (La. Ct. App. 1993).

[146]Howard v. W. Baton Rouge Parish Sch. Bd., 793 So. 2d 153 (La. 2001). *But see* Sias v. Iberia Parish Sch. Bd., 74 So. 3d 800 (La. Ct. App. 2011) (ruling that the school board had sufficient evidence to substantiate willful neglect of duties when a principal was arrested for possession of various drugs, weapons, and counterfeit money in his house), *review denied*, 78 So. 3d 143 (La. 2012); Spurlock v. E. Feliciana Parish Sch., 885 So. 2d 1225 (La. Ct. App. 2004) (ruling that a teacher could be terminated for willful neglect of duty for making misbehaving second-grade students simulate a sex act in front of the class; the teacher did not violate a specific policy or fail to follow orders, however, the court opined that she should have known that her egregious behavior was improper).

commented that his action was certainly a mistake and possibly endangered students, but it did not involve a failure to follow orders or an identifiable school policy required for dismissal under state law.

Teachers can be discharged for neglect of duty when their performance does not measure up to expected professional standards in the school system. Often, charges relate to a failure to perform but also can be brought for ineffective performance. Again, as with other efforts to terminate employment, documentation must substantiate that performance is unacceptable.

Unprofessional Conduct

A number of states identify either unprofessional conduct or conduct unbecoming a teacher as cause for dismissal. A teacher's activities both inside and outside of school can be used to substantiate this charge when they interfere with teaching effectiveness. Dismissals for unprofessional conduct, neglect of duty, and unfitness to teach often are based on quite similar facts. Facts that establish unprofessional conduct in one state may be deemed neglect of duty in another state. Although causes for dismissal are identified in state statutes, they are defined through case law and administrative rulings in individual states.

Most courts have defined unprofessional conduct as actions directly related to the fitness of educators to perform in their professional capacity.[147] The working definition adopted by the Supreme Court of Nebraska specified unprofessional conduct as breaching the rules or ethical code of a profession or "unbecoming a member in good standing of a profession." Under this definition, the court reasoned that a teacher had engaged in unprofessional conduct when he "smacked" a student on the head hard enough to make the student cry, thereby violating the state prohibition against corporal punishment.[148]

Courts have upheld dismissal for unprofessional conduct based on a number of grounds, such as permitting students to kick or hit each other for violations of classroom rules,[149] engaging in sexual harassment of female students,[150] engaging in an inappropriate relationship with a female student,[151] losing complete control of the classroom,[152] engaging in inappropriate touching of students,[153] taking photos of a female student nude above the waist,[154] and showing a sexually explicit film to a classroom of adolescents without previewing it.[155] As with dismissals based on incompetency, courts often require prior warning that the behavior may result in dismissal.

[147]*See, e.g.*, Sweetwater Union High Sch. Dist. v. Comm'n on Prof'l Competence, No. D058832, 2012 Cal. App. LEXIS 1663 (Cal. Ct. App. Mar. 2, 2012) (unpublished); Federal Way Sch. Dist. v. Vinson, 261 P.3d 145 (Wash. 2011).

[148]Daily v. Bd. of Educ., 588 N.W.2d 813, 824 (Neb. 1999). Following a hearing to consider termination of employment, the school board instead imposed a thirty-day suspension on the teacher.

[149]Roberts v. Santa Cruz Valley Unified Sch. Dist. No. 35, 778 P.2d 1294 (Ariz. Ct. App. 1989).

[150]Conward v. Cambridge Sch. Comm., 171 F.3d 12 (1st Cir. 1999).

[151]Crosby v. Holt, 320 S.W.3d 805 (Tenn. Ct. App. 2009).

[152]Walker v. Highlands Cnty. Sch. Bd., 752 So. 2d 127 (Fla. Dist. Ct. App. 2000).

[153]*In re* Watt, 925 N.Y.S.2d 681 (App. Div. 2011).

[154]Dixon v. Clem, 492 F.3d 665 (6th Cir. 2007).

[155]Fowler v. Bd. of Educ., 819 F.2d 657 (6th Cir. 1987).

Other Good and Just Cause

Not unexpectedly, "other good and just cause" as grounds for dismissal often has been challenged as vague and overbroad. Courts have been faced with the task of determining whether the phrase's meaning is limited to the specific grounds enumerated in the statute or whether it is a separate, expanded cause. An Indiana appellate court interpreted it as permitting termination for reasons other than those specified in the tenure law, if evidence indicated that the board's decision was based on "good cause."[156] As such, dismissal of a teacher convicted of a misdemeanor was upheld, even though the teacher had no prior indication that such conduct was sufficient cause. A Connecticut court found "good cause" to be any ground that is put forward in good faith that is not "arbitrary, irrational, unreasonable, or irrelevant to the board's task of building up and maintaining an efficient school system."[157] Terminating a teacher for altering students' responses on state mandatory proficiency tests was held to be relevant to that task.

The Second Circuit found "other due and sufficient cause" as a ground for dismissal to be "appropriate in an area such as discipline of teachers, where a myriad of uncontemplated situations may arise and it is not reasonable to require a legislature to elucidate in advance every act that requires sanction."[158] The court declined to rule on the vagueness of the term, but rather noted that courts generally assess the teacher's conduct in relation to the statutory grounds for dismissal. That is, if the specific behavior is sufficiently related to the causes specified in state law, it is assumed that the teacher should have reasonably known that the conduct was improper. In this case, where a teacher repeatedly humiliated and harassed students (and school administrators had discussed the problem with him), the court concluded that the teacher was aware of the impropriety of his conduct.

The Supreme Court of Iowa supported the termination of a teacher for shoplifting under a statute permitting teachers to be terminated during the contract year for "just cause."[159] Although the teacher claimed that her compulsion to shoplift was related to a mental illness, the court found the weighing of the teacher's position as a role model, the character of the illness, and the school board's needs provided substantial evidence to terminate the teacher's employment. In a subsequent case, the Iowa high court ruled

[156]Gary Teachers Union, Local No. 4, AFT v. Sch. City of Gary, 332 N.E.2d 256, 263 (Ind. Ct. App. 1975); *see also* Hierlmeier v. N. Judson-San Pierre Bd., 730 N.E.2d 821 (Ind. Ct. App. 2000) (ruling that sexual harassment of female students and other inappropriate conduct toward students substantiated good and just cause for termination); Sheldon Cmty. Sch. Dist. Bd. of Dirs. v. Lundblad, 528 N.W.2d 593 (Iowa 1995) (finding frequent sarcastic remarks to adolescents to establish "just cause" under Iowa law). *But see* Trs. Lincoln Cnty. Sch. Dist. No. 13 v. Holden, 754 P.2d 506 (Mont. 1988) (concluding that two instances of calling students crude names did not support good cause for dismissal).

[157]Hanes v. Bd. of Educ., 783 A.2d 1, 6 (Conn. App. Ct. 2001); *see also* Cooledge v. Riverdale Local Sch. Dist., 797 N.E.2d 61 (Ohio 2003) (ruling that a teacher receiving temporary total disability compensation under state law could not be discharged for absenteeism; termination of the teacher for "other good and just cause" violated public policy).

[158]diLeo v. Greenfield, 541 F.2d 949, 954 (2d Cir. 1976).

[159]Bd. of Dirs. v. Davies, 489 N.W.2d 19 (Iowa 1992); *see also* Snyder v. Jefferson Cnty. Sch. Dist. R-1, 842 P.2d 624 (Colo. 1992) (holding that expiration of a teacher's certificate constituted other good and just cause for termination).

"just cause" existed to terminate a teacher who had knowledge of her son and his high school friends drinking at a campsite on her property. She failed to monitor their activities, and four students who left to buy more beer died in a car crash. The court agreed with the school board that the teacher's effectiveness as a role model was significantly diminished.[160]

Reductions in Force

In addition to dismissal for causes related to teacher performance and fitness, legislation generally permits the release of teachers for reasons related to declining enrollment, financial exigency, and school district consolidation. Whereas most state statutes provide for such terminations, a number of states also have adopted legislation that specifies the basis for selection of released teachers, procedures to be followed, and provisions for reinstatement. These terminations, characterized as reductions in force (RIF), also may be governed by board policies and negotiated bargaining agreements.

Unlike other termination cases, the employee challenging a RIF decision shoulders the burden of proof. There is a presumption that the board has acted in good faith with permissible motives. Legal controversies in this area usually involve questions related to the necessity for the reductions, board compliance with mandated procedures, and possible subterfuge for impermissible termination (such as denial of constitutional rights, subversion of tenure rights, or discrimination).[161]

If statutory or contractual restrictions exist for teacher layoffs, there must be substantial compliance with the provisions. One of the provisions most frequently included is a method for selecting teachers for release. In general, reductions are based on seniority, and a tenured teacher, rather than a nontenured teacher, must be retained if both are qualified to fill the same position. Some state statutes require that both licensure and seniority be considered; a teacher lacking a license in the area would not be permitted to teach while a permanent teacher with proper credentials, but less seniority, would be dismissed.[162] Along with seniority, merit-rating systems may be included in the determination of reductions. School districts in Pennsylvania use a combination of ratings and seniority; ratings are the primary determinant unless no substantial difference exists in ratings, and then seniority becomes the basis for the layoff.[163] Both the Montana and Nebraska high courts concluded that school boards have broad discretion in deciding what factors to use in their RIF policies and how to weigh those factors.[164] Guidelines and criteria established by state law or state and

[160]Walthart v. Bd. of Dirs., 694 N.W.2d 740 (Iowa 2005).

[161]*See* Impey v. Bd. of Educ., 662 A.2d 960 (N.J. 1995) (holding that a school board did not need to eliminate programs or services to eliminate teaching positions; all services were provided less expensively through a contract with an external agency).

[162]*See, e.g.*, DeGeorgeo v. Indep. Sch. Dist. No. 833, 563 N.W.2d 755 (Minn. Ct. App. 1997); Summers Cnty. Bd. of Educ. v. Allen, 450 S.E.2d 658 (W. Va. 1994).

[163]24 PA. STAT. ANN. § 11-1124 (2012).

[164]Scobey Sch. Dist. v. Radakovich, 135 P.3d 778 (Mont. 2006); Nickel v. Saline Cnty. Sch. Dist. No. 163, 559 N.W.2d 480 (Neb. 1997).

local education agencies, however, must be applied in a uniform and nondiscriminatory manner. For example, under New Mexico law, the school board must determine that no other positions exist for teachers targeted for release.[165]

The Fourteenth Amendment requires minimal procedural protections in dismissals for cause, but courts have not clearly defined the due process requirements for RIFs. The Eighth Circuit noted that tenured teachers possess a property interest in continued employment and thereby must be provided notice and an opportunity to be heard.[166] Specific procedural protections for employees, however, vary according to interpretations of state law, bargaining agreements, and board policy. The District of Columbia Circuit held that due process did not require pre-termination hearings when post-termination proceedings were available.[167] A Michigan court found no need for a hearing over staff reductions, because there were no charges to refute.[168] The court emphasized that the law protected the released teacher, who, subject to qualifications, was entitled to the next vacancy. In contrast, a Pennsylvania commonwealth court held that a hearing must be provided to assure the teacher (1) that termination was for reasons specified by law and (2) that the board followed the correct statutory procedures in selecting the teacher for discharge.[169]

State law or other policies may give employment preference to teachers who are released due to a reduction in force. Typically, under such requirements, a school board cannot hire a nonemployee until each qualified teacher on the preferred recall list is reemployed.[170] Although statutes often require that a teacher be appointed to the first vacancy for which he or she is licensed and qualified, courts have held that reappointment is still at the board's discretion. A Michigan appeals court recognized that a teacher could be licensed in an area, but in the opinion of the board, not necessarily qualified.[171] Additionally, a board is generally not obligated to realign or rearrange teaching assignments to create a position for a released teacher.[172]

[165]Aguilera v. Bd. of Educ., 132 P.3d 587 (N.M. 2006).

[166]Boner v. Eminence R-1 Sch. Dist., 55 F.3d 1339 (8th Cir. 1995); *see also* Chandler v. Bd. of Educ., 92 F. Supp. 2d 760 (N.D. Ill. 2000) (ruling that a teacher must be provided a notice describing the reasons for termination of employment); Westport Sch. Comm. v. Coelho, 692 N.E.2d 540 (Mass. App. Ct. 1998) (interpreting state-level arbitration to apply to performance-based dismissals, not budget-induced layoffs).

[167]Wash. Teachers' Union v. Bd. of Educ., 109 F.3d 774 (D.C. Cir. 1997).

[168]Steeby v. Sch. Dist. of Highland Park, 224 N.W.2d 97 (Mich. Ct. App. 1974).

[169]Fatscher v. Bd. of Sch. Dirs., 367 A.2d 1130 (Pa. Commw. Ct. 1977).

[170]*See, e.g.*, Bd. of Educ. v. Owensby, 526 S.E.2d 831 (W. Va. 1999); *see also* Davis v. Chester Upland Sch. Dist., 786 A.2d 186 (Pa. 2001) (ruling that teachers who challenged the district's failure to recall them must exhaust collective bargaining grievance procedures before filing for judicial review). *But see* Chi. Teachers Union v. Bd. of Educ., 476 F. App'x 83 (7th Cir. 2012) (vacating an injunction after the Illinois Supreme Court (963 N.E.2d 918 (Ill. 2012)) ruled that teachers had no recall rights under state law; thus, such rights would exist only if specified in the negotiated agreement).

[171]Chester v. Harper Woods Sch. Dist., 273 N.W.2d 916 (Mich. Ct. App. 1978).

[172]*See, e.g.*, Hanson v. Vermillion Sch. Dist., 727 N.W.2d 459 (S.D. 2007); Hinckley v. Sch. Bd., 678 N.W.2d 485 (Minn. Ct. App. 2004). *But see* Pennell v. Bd. of Educ., 484 N.E.2d 445 (Ill. App. Ct. 1985) (ruling that restructuring positions is not required, but bad faith realignment of positions to avoid existence of a position for a tenured teacher is prohibited).

REMEDIES FOR VIOLATIONS OF PROTECTED RIGHTS

When it can be established that school districts or officials have violated an employee's rights that are protected by federal or state law, several remedies are available to the aggrieved individual. In some situations, the employee may seek a court injunction ordering the unlawful action to cease. This remedy might be sought if a school board has unconstitutionally imposed restraints on teachers' expression. Where terminations, transfers, or other adverse employment consequences have been unconstitutionally imposed, courts will order school districts to return the affected employees to their original status with back pay.

In addition to these remedies, educators are increasingly bringing suits to recover damages for actions that violate their federally protected rights. Claims are usually based on 42 U.S.C. § 1983, which provides that any person who acts under color of state law to deprive another individual of rights secured by the Federal Constitution or federal laws is subject to personal liability. This law, originally enacted in 1871 to prevent discrimination against African American citizens, has been broadly interpreted as conferring liability on school personnel and school districts, not only for racial discrimination but also for actions that may result in the impairment of other federally protected rights.[173]

Suits seeking damages under § 1983 for violations of federal rights can be initiated in federal or state courts,[174] and exhaustion of state administrative remedies is not required before initiating a federal suit.[175] When a federal law authorizes an exclusive nondamages remedy, however, a § 1983 suit is precluded.[176] This section focuses on the liability of school officials and districts for the violation of protected rights and on the types of damages available to aggrieved employees and others.

Liability of School Officials

In § 1983 claims, public school employees acting under color of state law can be held personally liable for actions abridging students' or teachers' federal rights. The Supreme Court, however, has recognized that government officials cannot be held liable for damages under § 1983 for the actions of their subordinates, thus rejecting the doctrine of respondeat superior, even where school officials have general supervisory authority over the activities of the wrongdoers. In order to be held liable, the officials must have personally participated in, or had personal knowledge of, the unlawful acts or promulgated official policy under which the acts were taken.[177]

[173]Maine v. Thiboutot, 448 U.S. 1 (1980).

[174]The Supreme Court has rejected the assertion that school officials are immune from a § 1983 suit initiated in a state court. Howlett v. Rose, 496 U.S. 356 (1990).

[175]Patsy v. Bd. of Regents, 457 U.S. 496 (1982).

[176]*See, e.g.*, Gonzaga Univ. v. Doe, 536 U.S. 273 (2002); Blessing v. Freestone, 520 U.S. 329 (1997). The Supreme Court, however, has ruled that a federal statute lacking an expressed private remedy leaves open the door to pursue damages under § 1983 for Fourteenth Amendment equal protection violations. Specifically, the Court held that Title IX of the Education Amendments of 1972 (20 U.S.C. § 1681) does not preclude individuals also pursuing a § 1983 damages claim for unconstitutional sex discrimination under the Equal Protection Clause. Fitzgerald v. Barnstable Sch. Comm., 555 U.S. 246 (2009).

[177]*See* Ashcroft v. Iqbal, 556 U.S. 662 (2009); Am. Mfrs. Mut. Ins. Co. v. Sullivan, 526 U.S. 40 (1999); Rizzo v. Goode, 423 U.S. 362 (1976).

Furthermore, the Supreme Court has ruled that public officials are absolutely immune from suit under § 1983 for their legislative activities.[178] These actions involve discretionary policy-making decisions and enactment of regulations, often with budgetary implications. Subsequently, courts clarified that employment decisions related to individual employees (such as hiring, dismissal, or demotions) are administrative, not legislative, in nature.[179]

The Supreme Court has recognized that in some circumstances, school officials can claim qualified immunity to protect themselves from personal liability. In *Harlow v. Fitzgerald*, the Court ruled that "government officials performing discretionary functions generally are shielded from liability for civil damages insofar as their conduct does not violate clearly established statutory or constitutional rights of which a reasonable person would have known."[180] In 2002, the Supreme Court emphasized that the overriding issue regarding qualified immunity was whether the law at the time an individual acted gave "clear and fair warning" that rights were established.[181] The "clear and fair warning" standard, however, has resulted in a range of interpretations by lower courts. More recently, the Supreme Court provided further clarification of this standard when it examined the reasonableness of school officials' strip search of a thirteen-year-old student. The Court in *Safford Unified School District #1 v. Redding*[182] held the actions violated the basic legal framework established in *New Jersey v. T.L.O.*[183] However, the Court ruled that school officials were entitled to qualified immunity based on lower courts' "divergent conclusions regarding how the *T.L.O.* standard applied to school searches."[184] In this case, the lower courts' decisions were so substantially different that the Court found immunity was warranted. The Court did caution that divergent views among other courts regarding a right "does not automatically render the law unclear" if the Supreme Court has been clear.[185]

Following the Supreme Court's *Redding* decision, some courts have denied qualified immunity to school officials because of legal precedents within their circuits. While the illustrative cases here involve strip searches of students, they have implications for legal controversies related to educators and students where a federal circuit court has rendered an opinion. In denying qualified immunity to school officials on remand, the Sixth Circuit pointed to an earlier case in which it had denied immunity to school officials where an entire class of students had been strip searched to find cash and credit

[178]Bogan v. Scott-Harris, 523 U.S. 44 (1998).

[179]*See, e.g.*, Canary v. Osborn, 211 F.3d 324 (6th Cir. 2000); Harhay v. Town of Ellington Bd. of Educ., 323 F.3d 206 (2d Cir. 2003).

[180]457 U.S. 800, 818 (1982); *see also* Filarsky v. Delia, 132 S. Ct. 1657 (2012) (unanimously ruling that a private individual employed by the government to perform a job can claim qualified immunity from suit under 42 U.S.C. § 1983).

[181]Hope v. Pelzer, 536 U.S. 730 (2002). *See also* Ashcroft v. al-Kidd, 131 S. Ct. 2074, 2085 (2011) (holding that qualified immunity gives officials "breathing room to make reasonable but mistaken judgments about open legal questions;" if properly applied, "it protects 'all but the plainly incompetent or those who knowingly violate the law'").

[182]557 U.S. 364 (2009).

[183]469 U.S. 325 (1985).

[184]*Safford*, 557 U.S. at 378.

[185]*Id.* Reconsidering an earlier high court decision that mandated lower courts initially to assess whether the facts of a case establish a constitutional violation prior to determining immunity, the Supreme Court more recently granted lower courts discretion to consider whether immunity exists prior to considering the alleged constitutional violation. Pearson v. Callahan, 555 U.S. 223 (2009).

cards.[186] In that decision, the appellate court had clearly concluded that the students had a legitimate expectation of privacy; the scope was not reasonable; the searches were highly intrusive; the target of the search was monetary, not threatening; and no individualized suspicion existed. Accordingly, the appellate court ruled that school officials in the Sixth Circuit had "fair warning" that such a search was unconstitutional.[187] Likewise, a Georgia federal district court concluded that the controlling law in the Eleventh Circuit had clearly placed school officials on notice that a strip search for a missing iPod did not pose an extreme threat justifying an intrusive search without individualized suspicion.[188]

School officials have been denied qualified immunity when they disregard well-established legal principles in areas such as due process, protected expression, and privacy. For example, school board members violated a superintendent's procedural due process by failing to provide him a fair hearing.[189] Similarly, a superintendent was not protected by qualified immunity for refusing to recommend a teacher's reemployment based on constitutionally impermissible reasons pertaining to her involvement in a divorce.[190] The Third Circuit, in remanding a case for further proceedings, noted that a superintendent who appeared to have maliciously prosecuted a teacher for theft in retaliation for the exercise of her First Amendment activities was not entitled to qualified immunity.[191] The Fifth Circuit likewise found school board members were not entitled to qualified immunity when they failed to extend an employee's contract because he had reported illegal activities of others to the Federal Bureau of Investigation, which constituted retaliation in violation of the employee's clearly recognized First Amendment rights.[192] Public officials are not expected to predict the future course of constitutional law, but they are expected to adhere to principles of law that were *clearly established* at the time of the violation.

Liability of School Districts

In 1978, the Supreme Court departed from precedent and ruled that local governments are considered "persons" under § 1983.[193] In essence, school districts can be assessed damages when action taken pursuant to official policy or custom violates federally protected rights.[194] To prevail against a school district, an individual must present evidence

[186]Knisley v. Pike Cnty. Joint Vocational Sch. Dist., 604 F.3d 977 (6th Cir. 2010); *see* Beard v. Whitmore Lake Sch. Dist., 402 F.3d 598 (6th Cir. 2005) (establishing precedent in this circuit that a strip search of a student in a non-threatening situation without individualized suspicion was unconstitutional).

[187]*Knisley*, 604 F.3d at 982.

[188]Foster v. Raspberry, 652 F. Supp. 2d 1342 (M.D. Ga. 2009).

[189]Baird v. Bd. of Educ., 389 F.3d 685 (7th Cir. 2004).

[190]Littlejohn v. Rose, 768 F.2d 765 (6th Cir. 1985); *see also* Heyne v. Metro. Nashville Pub. Schs, 655 F.3d 556 (6th Cir. 2011) (denying a motion to dismiss because evidence showed that a student's race may have motivated school officials' disciplinary action in violation of the Equal Protection Clause; the student's right was clearly established, thus negating qualified immunity for officials).

[191]Merkle v. Upper Dublin Sch. Dist., 211 F.3d 782 (3d Cir. 2000). The court also noted that injury to reputation alone does not violate the Fourteenth Amendment; however, if the teacher is able to show damage to her reputation during the deprivation of a constitutional right, she can establish a claim under § 1983 for a Fourteenth Amendment violation. *See* Evans-Marshall v. Bd. of Educ., Tipp City Sch. Dist., 428 F.3d 223 (6th Cir. 2005).

[192]Juarez v. Aguilar, 666 F.3d 35 (5th Cir. 2011).

[193]Monell v. Dep't of Soc. Servs., 436 U.S. 658 (1978).

[194]*See* L.A. Cnty., Cal. v. Humphries, 131 S. Ct. 447 (2010) (reaffirming that local government liability occurs when it is the agency's own policy, practice, or custom that violates protected federal rights; the case involved a state law that did not provide procedures for individuals to challenge their placement in the child abuse database).

that the district acted with deliberate indifference in establishing and maintaining a policy, practice, or custom that directly deprived an individual of constitutionally protected rights.[195]

The governmental unit (like the individual official), however, cannot be held liable under the respondeat superior doctrine for the wrongful acts committed solely by its employees. Liability under § 1983 against the agency can be imposed only when execution of official policy by an individual with final authority impairs a federally protected right.[196] The Supreme Court has held that a single egregious act of a low-level employee does not imply an official policy of inadequate training and supervision,[197] but an agency can be liable for "deliberate indifference" in failing to adequately train employees.[198]

The Supreme Court has ruled that school districts and other governmental subdivisions cannot claim qualified immunity based on good faith actions of their officials. The Court acknowledged that under certain circumstances, sovereign immunity can shield municipal corporations from state tort suits, but concluded that § 1983 abrogated governmental immunity in situations involving the impairment of federally protected rights.[199]

To avoid liability for constitutional violations, school districts have introduced claims of Eleventh Amendment immunity.[200] The Eleventh Amendment, explicitly prohibiting citizens of one state from bringing suit against another state without its consent, also has been interpreted by the Supreme Court to preclude federal lawsuits against a state by its own citizens.[201] A state can waive this immunity by specifically consenting to be sued, and Congress can abrogate state immunity through legislation enacted to enforce the Fourteenth Amendment. Such congressional intent, however, must be explicit in the federal legislation.[202]

[195]*See* Thomas v. Bd. of Educ., 467 F. Supp. 2d 483 (W.D. Pa. 2006) (rejecting claim that school district was aware of teacher's previous abuse of corporal punishment but had taken no action, thereby establishing an unconstitutional custom).

[196]*See, e.g.*, Collins v. City of Harker Heights, 503 U.S. 115 (1992); St. Louis v. Praprotnik, 485 U.S. 112 (1988); Pembaur v. City of Cincinnati, 475 U.S. 469 (1986); Seamons v. Snow, 206 F.3d 1021 (10th Cir. 2000).

[197]Okla. City v. Tuttle, 471 U.S. 808 (1985).

[198]City of Canton, Ohio v. Harris, 489 U.S. 378 (1989).

[199]Owen v. City of Independence, Mo., 445 U.S. 622 (1980).

[200]Under certain circumstances, school districts may be able to use other defenses to preclude liability in a § 1983 suit. Claims that have already been decided in a state case (res judicata) or could have been litigated between the same parties in a prior state action (collateral estoppel) may be barred in a federal suit under § 1983. *See* Migra v. Warren City Sch. Dist., 465 U.S. 75 (1984); Allen v. McCurry, 449 U.S. 90 (1980).

[201]*See* Hans v. Louisiana, 134 U.S. 1 (1890); *see also* Will v. Mich. Dep't of State Police, 491 U.S. 58 (1989) (holding that § 1983 does not permit a suit against a state; Congress did not intend the word "person" to include states).

[202]The Supreme Court held that the Family Educational Rights and Privacy Act of 1974 does not explicitly confer individually enforceable rights. Gonzaga Univ. v. Doe, 536 U.S. 273 (2002). Also, in deciding whether an individual can sue a state for money damages in federal court under the Americans with Disabilities Act (ADA) of 1990, the Supreme Court ruled that Congress did not act within its constitutional authority when it abrogated Eleventh Amendment immunity. Bd. of Trs. v. Garrett, 531 U.S. 356 (2000). *But see* Lee-Thomas v. Prince George's Cnty. Pub. Schs, 666 F.3d 244 (4th Cir. 2012) (holding that Eleventh Amendment immunity under the ADA had been waived by a Maryland statute for claims that do not exceed $100,000; the federal court relied on the state high court's interpretation of the state statute).

School districts have asserted Eleventh Amendment protection based on the fact that they perform a state function. Admittedly, education is a state function, but it does not necessarily follow that school districts gain Eleventh Amendment immunity against claims of constitutional abridgments. For the Eleventh Amendment to be invoked in a suit against a school district, the state must be the real party in interest. The Third Circuit identified the following factors in determining if a governmental agency, such as a school district, is entitled to Eleventh Amendment protection: (1) whether payment of the judgment will be from the state treasury, (2) whether a governmental or proprietary function is being performed,[203] (3) whether the agency has autonomy over its operation, (4) whether it has the power to sue and be sued, (5) whether it can enter into contracts, and (6) whether the agency's property is immune from state taxation.[204] The most significant of these factors in determining if a district is shielded by Eleventh Amendment immunity has been whether the judgment will be recovered from state funds. If funds are to be paid from the state treasury, courts have declared the state to be the real party in interest.[205]

For many states, the Eleventh Amendment question with respect to school district immunity was resolved in the *Mt. Healthy* case.[206] The Supreme Court concluded that the issue in that case hinged on whether, under Ohio law, a school district is considered an arm of the state as opposed to a municipality or other political subdivision. Considering the taxing power and autonomy of school district operations, the Supreme Court found school districts to be more like counties or cities than extensions of the state. Thus, the Court ruled that school districts could not claim Eleventh Amendment immunity.

Remedies

Depending on employment status, judicial remedies for the violation of protected rights may include compensatory and punitive damages, reinstatement with back pay, and attorneys' fees. The specific nature of the award depends on federal and state statutory provisions and the discretion of courts. Federal and state laws often identify damages that may be recovered or place limitations on types of awards. Unless these provisions restrict specific remedies, courts have broad discretionary power to formulate equitable settlements.

DAMAGES. When a school official or school district is found liable for violating an individual's protected rights, an award of damages is assessed to compensate the claimant

[203]Governmental functions are those performed in discharging the agency's official duties; proprietary functions are often for profit and could be performed by private corporations.

[204]Urbano v. Bd. of Managers, 415 F.2d 247, 250–51 (3d Cir. 1969).

[205]Eleventh Amendment immunity covers only federal suits; it does not have any bearing on immunity in state actions.

[206]Mt. Healthy City Sch. Dist. v. Doyle, 429 U.S. 274 (1977); *see* Adams v. Recovery Sch. Dist., 463 F. App'x 297 (5th Cir. 2012); Woods v. Rondout Valley Cent. Sch. Dist. Bd. of Educ., 466 F.3d 232 (2d Cir. 2006); Febres v. Camden Bd. of Educ., 445 F.3d 227 (3d Cir. 2006). *But see* Belanger v. Madera Unified Sch. Dist., 963 F.2d 248 (9th Cir. 1992) (holding that California school boards are indivisible agencies of the state and thus are entitled to Eleventh Amendment immunity).

for the injury.[207] Actual injury must be shown for the aggrieved party to recover damages; without evidence of monetary or mental injury, the plaintiff is entitled only to nominal damages (not to exceed one dollar), even though an impairment of protected rights is established.[208] Significant monetary damages, however, may be awarded for a wrongful termination if a teacher is able to demonstrate substantial losses. At the same time, individuals' efforts to mitigate damages by other appropriate employment are considered in determining actual loss.[209]

The Supreme Court held in 1986 that compensatory damages could not be based on a jury's perception of the value or importance of constitutional rights.[210] In this case, involving the award of compensatory damages to a teacher for his unconstitutional dismissal, the Supreme Court declared that although individuals are entitled to full compensation for the injury suffered, they are not entitled to supplementary damages based on the perceived value of the constitutional rights that have been abridged. The Court remanded the case for a determination of the amount of damages necessary to compensate the teacher for the *actual* injury suffered.

In some instances, aggrieved individuals have sought punitive as well as compensatory damages. The judiciary has ruled that school officials can be liable for punitive damages (to punish the wrongdoer) if a jury concludes that the individual's conduct is willful or in reckless and callous disregard of federally protected rights.[211] Punitive as well as compensatory damages were assessed against a principal and superintendent who, without authority, discharged a teacher in retaliation for the exercise of protected speech.[212]

In 1981, the Supreme Court ruled that § 1983 does not authorize the award of punitive damages against a municipality.[213] Recognizing that compensation for injuries is an obligation of a municipality, the Court held that punitive damages were appropriate only for the *individual* wrongdoers and not for the municipality itself. The Court also noted that punitive damages constitute punishment against individuals to deter similar conduct in the future, but they are not intended to punish innocent taxpayers. This ruling does not bar claims for punitive damages for violations of federal rights in

[207] *See* McGee v. S. Pemiscot Sch. Dist. R-V, 712 F.2d 339 (8th Cir. 1983) (concluding that even though a teacher-coach, who was dismissed for exercising protected speech, found a higher-paying job, he was entitled to $10,000 in damages for mental anguish, loss of professional reputation, and expenses incurred in obtaining new employment).

[208] *See* Farrar v. Hobby, 506 U.S. 103 (1992) (concluding that an award of nominal damages is mandatory when a procedural due process violation is established but no actual injury is shown); Carey v. Piphus, 435 U.S. 247 (1978) (holding that pupils who were denied procedural due process in a disciplinary proceeding would be entitled only to nominal damages unless it was established that lack of proper procedures resulted in actual injury to the students).

[209] *See, e.g.*, McDaniel v. Princeton City Sch. Dist., 45 F. App'x 354 (6th Cir. 2002); McClure v. Indep. Sch. Dist. No. 16, 228 F.3d 1205 (10th Cir. 2000); Kanawha Cnty. Bd. of Educ. v. Fulmer, 719 S.E.2d 375 (W.Va. 2011).

[210] Memphis Cmty. Sch. Dist. v. Stachura, 477 U.S. 299 (1986).

[211] *See* Smith v. Wade, 461 U.S. 30 (1983). In 1991, the Supreme Court refused to place a limit on the amount of punitive damages that properly instructed juries might award in common law suits, but it did note that extremely high awards might be viewed as unacceptable under the Due Process Clause of the Fourteenth Amendment. Pac. Mut. Life Ins. Co. v. Haslip, 499 U.S. 1 (1991); *see also* Standley v. Chilhowee R-IV Sch. Dist., 5 F.3d 319 (8th Cir. 1993) (holding that evidence did not support evil motive or reckless or callous indifference).

[212] Fishman v. Clancy, 763 F.2d 485 (1st Cir. 1985).

[213] City of Newport v. Fact Concerts, 453 U.S. 247 (1981).

school cases, but such claims must be brought against *individuals* rather than against the school district itself.

The following cases illustrate the diverse circumstances that have resulted in awards of damages. An Illinois school board was required to pay a teacher $750,000 in compensatory damages for wrongfully terminating her for an out-of-wedlock pregnancy.[214] A principal's failure to respond adequately to a student's complaints of sexual abuse by a teacher resulted in an award of $350,000 against the principal.[215] An Ohio teacher's wrongful termination resulted in reinstatement, back wages (including retirement contributions and health insurance costs), and attorneys' fees for a total award of $172,675.[216] A North Carolina teacher received $78,000 in damages based on mental distress evidenced by depression and insomnia following procedural violations in his termination.[217]

Given the success teachers have had in securing damages to compensate for the violation of constitutional rights, school officials should ensure that dismissals or other disciplinary actions are based on legitimate reasons and accompanied by appropriate procedural safeguards. Courts, however, have not awarded damages unless the evidence shows that a teacher has suffered actual injury. As the Supreme Court has noted, compensatory damages are intended to provide full compensation for the loss or injury suffered but are not to be based simply on a jury's perception of the value of the constitutional rights impaired.[218]

REINSTATEMENT. Whether a court orders reinstatement as a remedy for school board action depends on the protected interests involved and the discretion of the court, unless a specific provision for reinstatement is specified in state law. If a tenured teacher is unjustly dismissed, the property interest gives rise to an expectation of reemployment; reinstatement in such instances is usually the appropriate remedy. A nontenured teacher wrongfully dismissed during the contract period, however, is normally entitled only to damages, not reinstatement.

A valid property or liberty claim entitles a teacher to procedural due process, but the teacher can still be dismissed for cause after proper procedures have been followed. If a teacher is terminated without proper procedures and can establish that the action is not justified, reinstatement will be ordered.[219] If it is proven that the actual reason for the

[214]Eckmann v. Bd. of Educ., 636 F. Supp. 1214 (N.D. Ill. 1986); *see also* Welton v. Osborn, 124 F. Supp. 2d 1114 (S.D. Ohio 2000) (awarding $177,000 in compensatory damages, $65,625 in punitive damages, and $77,747 in attorneys' fees and costs against the superintendent for retaliation toward the principal for exercising constitutionally protected speech).

[215]Baynard v. Malone, 268 F.3d 228 (4th Cir. 2001).

[216]McDaniel v. Princeton City Sch. Dist. Bd. of Educ., 45 F. App'x 354 (6th Cir. 2002); *see also* Glover v. Williamsburg Local Sch. Dist. Bd. of Educ., 20 F. Supp. 2d 1160 (S.D. Ohio. 1998) (awarding compensatory damages of $71,494 and reinstatement for two years for impermissible nonrenewal based on sexual orientation).

[217]Crump v. Bd. of Educ., 392 S.E.2d 579 (N.C. 1990) (awarding damages for procedural violation even though discharge was upheld); *see also* Dishnow v. Sch. Dist., 77 F.3d 194 (7th Cir. 1996) (upholding a damages award for humiliation and injury to reputation in the firing of a teacher based on the exercise of his free speech rights).

[218]Memphis Cmty. Sch. Dist. v. Stachura, 477 U.S. 299 (1986).

[219]*See, e.g., McDaniel*, 45 F. App'x 354; Brewer v. Chauvin, 938 F.2d 860 (8th Cir. 1991). *But see* Hanover Sch. Dist. No. 28 v. Barbour, 171 P.3d 223 (Colo. 2007) (awarding back pay but not reinstatement).

nonrenewal of a teacher's contract is retaliation for the exercise of constitutional rights (e.g., protected speech), reinstatement would be warranted, although substantiation of such a claim is difficult.

The failure to comply with statutory requirements in nonrenewals and dismissals may result in reinstatement. When statutory dates are specified for notice of nonrenewal, failure to comply strictly with the deadline provides grounds for reinstatement of the teacher. Courts may interpret this as continued employment for an additional year.[220] In contrast to the remedy for lack of proper notice, the remedy for failure to provide an appropriate hearing is generally a remand for a hearing, not reinstatement.[221]

ATTORNEYS' FEES. Attorneys' fees are not automatically granted to the teacher who prevails in a lawsuit but are generally dependent on statutory authorization. At the federal level, the Civil Rights Attorneys' Fees Award Act gives federal courts discretion to award fees in civil rights suits.[222] In congressional debate concerning attorneys' fees, it was stated that "private citizens must be given not only the right to go to court, but also the legal resources. If the citizen does not have the resources, his day in court is denied him."[223]

To receive attorneys' fees, the teacher must be the prevailing party; that is, damages or some form of equitable relief must be granted to the teacher. The Supreme Court has held that a prevailing party is one who is successful in achieving some benefit on any significant issue in the case, but not necessarily the primary issue. At a minimum, the Court ruled, "the plaintiff must be able to point to a resolution of the dispute which changes the legal relationship between itself and the defendant."[224] If a plaintiff achieves only partial success, the fees requested may be reduced.

Because § 1983 does not require exhaustion of state administrative proceedings before initiating litigation, the Supreme Court has denied the award of attorneys' fees for school board administrative proceedings conducted prior to filing a federal suit. Unlike Title VII's explicit requirement that individuals must first pursue administrative remedies, plaintiffs can bring a § 1983 claim directly to a federal court. In a wrongful termination case, a Tennessee teacher was awarded attorneys' fees as a prevailing litigant for the time spent on the judicial proceedings, but was unsuccessful in persuading the Supreme Court that the local administrative proceedings were part of the preparation for court action.[225]

Although it has been established that the plaintiff who prevails in a civil rights suit may, at the court's discretion, be entitled to attorneys' fees, the same standard is not applied to defendants.[226] When a prevailing educator is awarded attorneys' fees,

[220]*See, e.g.*, Kiel v. Green Local Sch. Dist. Bd. of Educ., 630 N.E.2d 716 (Ohio 1994).

[221]*See* Snowden v. Adams, 814 F. Supp. 2d 854 (C.D. Ill. 2011) (noting that an inadequate name-clearing hearing may entitle an individual to compensatory damages when remand for another hearing would be too late to remedy the damage to reputation).

[222]42 U.S.C. § 1988 (2012).

[223]122 CONG. REC. 33,313 (1976).

[224]Tex. State Teachers Ass'n v. Garland Indep. Sch. Dist., 489 U.S. 782, 792 (1989).

[225]Webb v. Bd. of Educ., 471 U.S. 234 (1985); *see also* N.C. Dep't of Transp. v. Crest St. Cmty. Council, 479 U.S. 6 (1986) (ruling that attorneys' fees could not be recovered in administrative proceedings independent of enforcement of Title VI of the Civil Rights Act of 1964).

[226]*But see* Daddow v. Carlsbad Mun. Sch. Dist., 898 P.2d 1235 (N.M. 1995) (applying state law that entitles the prevailing party to an award of costs unless the court rules otherwise).

the assessment is against a party who has violated a federal law. Different criteria are applied when a prevailing defendant seeks attorneys' fees. The Supreme Court has held that such fees cannot be imposed on a plaintiff unless the claim was "frivolous, unreasonable, or groundless."[227] Although awards of damages to prevailing defendants have not been common, in some situations, such awards have been made to deter groundless lawsuits.

Conclusion

Through state laws and the Federal Constitution, extensive safeguards protect educators' employment security. Most states have adopted tenure laws that precisely delineate teachers' employment rights in termination and disciplinary proceedings. Additionally, in the absence of specific state guarantees, the Fourteenth Amendment ensures that teachers will be afforded procedural due process when property or liberty interests are implicated. Legal decisions interpreting both state and federal rights in dismissal actions have established broad guidelines as to when due process is required, the types of procedures that must be provided, and the legitimate causes required to substantiate dismissal action. Generalizations applicable to teacher employment termination are enumerated here.

1. A teacher is entitled to procedural due process if dismissal impairs a property or liberty interest.
2. Tenure status, defined by state law, confers upon teachers a property interest in continued employment; tenured teachers can be dismissed only for cause specified in state law.
3. Courts generally have held that probationary employment does not involve a property interest, except within the contract period.
4. A probationary teacher may establish a liberty interest, and thus entitlement to a hearing, if nonrenewal implicates a constitutional right, imposes a stigma, or forecloses opportunities for future employment.
5. When a liberty or property interest is implicated, the Fourteenth Amendment requires that a teacher be notified of charges and provided with an opportunity for a hearing that includes representation by counsel, examination and cross-examination of witnesses, and a record of the proceedings; however, formal trial procedures are not required.
6. An adequate notice of dismissal must adhere to statutory deadlines, follow designated form, allow the teacher time to prepare for a hearing, and specify charges.
7. The school board is considered an impartial hearing tribunal unless bias of its members can be clearly established.
8. The school board bears the burden of proof to introduce sufficient evidence to support a teacher's dismissal.
9. Causes for dismissal vary widely among the states, but usually include such grounds as incompetency, neglect of duty, immorality, insubordination, unprofessional conduct, and other good and just cause.
10. Incompetency is generally defined in relation to classroom performance—classroom management, teaching methods, grading, pupil/teacher relationships, and general attitude.

[227]Christiansburg Garment Co. v. EEOC, 434 U.S. 412, 422 (1978); *see* Jefferson v. Jefferson Cnty. Pub. Sch. Sys., 360 F.3d 583 (6th Cir. 2004); Potlatch Educ. Ass'n v. Potlatch Sch. Dist., 226 P.3d 1277 (Idaho 2010).

11. Immoral conduct, as the basis for dismissal, includes dishonest acts, improper sexual conduct, criminal acts, drug-related conduct, and other improprieties that have a negative impact on the teacher's effectiveness.
12. Dismissal for insubordination is based on a teacher's refusal to follow school regulations and policies.
13. Declining enrollment and financial exigencies constitute adequate causes for dismissing tenured teachers.
14. Wrongfully terminated employees may be entitled to reinstatement with back pay, compensatory and punitive damages, and attorneys' fees for the violation of protected rights.
15. An individual can recover only nominal damages for the impairment of constitutional rights unless monetary, emotional, or mental injury can be proven.
16. School officials can plead immunity to protect themselves from liability if their actions do not violate clearly established principles of law.
17. School districts cannot plead good faith as a defense against § 1983 liability for compensatory damages in connection with the impairment of federally protected civil rights.
18. Punitive damages to punish the wrongdoer can be assessed against individual school officials, but not against school districts.
19. Most courts have not considered school districts an arm of the state for purposes of Eleventh Amendment immunity from federal suits initiated by the state's citizens.

MyEdLeadershipLab™

Go to Topic 9: *Terms and Conditions in Employment and Termination* on the MyEdLeadershipLab™ site (www.myedleadershiplab.com) for *Public School Law: Teachers' and Students' Rights*, Seventh Edition, where you can

- Find learning outcomes for *Terms and Conditions in Employment and Termination* along with the national standards that connect to these outcomes.
- Complete Assignments and Activities that can help you more deeply understand the chapter content.
- Apply and practice your understanding of the core skills identified in the chapter with the Building Leadership Skills unit.
- Prepare yourself for professional certification with a Practice for Certification quiz.

Labor Relations

MyEdLeadershipLab™

Visit the MyEdLeadershipLab™ site for *Public School Law: Teachers' and Students' Rights*, Seventh Edition, to enhance your understanding of chapter concepts. You'll have the opportunity to practice your skills through video- and case-based Assignments and Activities as well as Building Leadership Skills units, and to prepare for your certification exam with Practice for Certification quizzes.

Historically, boards of education had unilateral control over the management and operation of public schools. Teachers, as employees of the school board, were only minimally involved in decision making. To achieve a balance of power and a voice in school affairs, teachers turned to collective action during the 1960s and acquired significant labor rights. Labor laws and judicial rulings governing this shift in power were modeled after private sector bargaining, resulting in labor relations in schools taking on an adversarial character.[1]

At the most fundamental level, collective bargaining pits teachers' demands for improved wages, hours, and conditions of employment against school boards' efforts to retain authority over educational policies and school operations. However, since the emergence of formalized collective bargaining in the early 1960s, negotiated contracts have evolved from a few pages addressing salaries to lengthy agreements that frequently are complex and impenetrable. Moreover, labor relations also are controlled by numerous other documents interpreting or amending the contract, such as state labor relations board

[1]Pressures to reform schools have focused attention on creating collaborative negotiation processes that reduce the adversarial nature of conventional bargaining. While some innovations have been implemented in the bargaining process, the basic legal structure explored in this chapter remains unchanged and shapes labor relations in school districts.

From Chapter 12 of *Public School Law: Teachers' and Students' Rights*, Seventh Edition. Martha M. McCarthy, Nelda H. Cambron-McCabe, Suzanne E. Eckes.

decisions, arbitration rulings, and memoranda of understanding related to the operation of the contract, that often lead to limited flexibility for teachers and administrators.[2]

Diversity in labor laws and bargaining practices among the states makes it difficult to generalize about collective bargaining and teachers' labor rights. State labor laws, state employment relations board rulings, and court decisions must be consulted to determine specific rights, because there is no federal labor law covering public school employees.[3] Over two-thirds of the states have enacted bargaining laws, varying widely in coverage from very comprehensive laws controlling most aspects of negotiations to laws granting the minimal right to meet and confer. Still other states, in the absence of legislation, rely on judicial rulings to define the basic rights of public employees in the labor relations arena.

Most recently, we have seen unprecedented attacks on public employees' bargaining rights, resulting in radical changes to the public employee bargaining laws in some states. Governors across these states have used their financial crises to argue that public employers must have greater flexibility in controlling their budgets. The most publicized of the state changes occurred in Wisconsin, which, in 1959 was the first state to recognize public employees' right to bargain. Under the new Wisconsin law for general public employees (not safety employees), the scope of bargaining is restricted as follows: base pay rates cannot exceed the rate of inflation unless submitted to a referendum for approval; dues checkoff enabling union dues to be paid through payroll deduction is prohibited; and fair share agreements where nonmembers pay a fee are impermissible. In addition, unions must be certified each year by a majority of the union members (not a majority of members voting).[4] The Ohio governor also signed into law similar radical changes to the state's public employee bargaining but included safety and all other public employees. Through a public referendum, the new Ohio law was rejected in 2011 by 62 percent of the voters. Other states have introduced anti-union laws that attempt to limit the scope of bargaining, eliminate payroll deductions, prohibit arbitration over contract grievances, and increase pension contributions. Many of these proposed laws are still being debated, and others have been placed on hold by courts while appeals are pending.

In this chapter, the legal structure in which bargaining occurs and public school teachers' employment rights under state labor laws are examined. Specific topics include bargaining subjects, dues and service fees, grievances, negotiation impasse, and strikes.[5]

[2]For an analysis of this "contract behind the contract," see Howard Fuller, George Mitchell & Michael Hartmann, The Milwaukee Public Schools' Teacher Union Contract: Its History, Content, and Impact on Education (Milwaukee, WI: Institute for Transformation of Learning, Marquette University, 1997).

[3]*See infra* text accompanying note 21.

[4]2011 Wis. Act 10; *see also* Wis. Educ. Ass'n Council v. Walker, 824 F. Supp. 2d 856, 876 (W.D. 2012) (issuing an injunction requiring school districts to continue to deduct dues and enjoining the recertification of unions based on the more favorable treatment of safety employees in the new Wisconsin law; according to the court, it could not "uphold the State of Wisconsin's apparent, if not, actual, favoritism and entanglement in partisan politics by discriminating in favor of fundraising efforts on behalf of public safety unions over general employee unions"); Madison Teachers Inc. v. Walker, No. 11CV3774 (Dane Cnty. Cir. Ct. Sept. 14, 2012) (holding that the Wisconsin bargaining law violated union members' speech and association rights under both the federal and state constitutions); Joseph Slater, *The Assault on Public Sector Collective Bargaining: Real Harms and Imaginary Benefits* (Washington: American Constitution Society for Law and Policy, June, 7 2011), https://www.acslaw.org/sites/default/files/Slater_Collective_Bargaining.pdf.

[5]As collective bargaining has matured in the public sector, state labor relations board decisions have become a substantial source of legal precedent for each state, with courts rendering fewer decisions in the labor arena. In fact, courts defer to the boards' rulings unless they are clearly contrary to law. While specific rulings of labor boards are not included in this chapter, educators are encouraged to examine that extensive body of law if a board governs negotiations in their state.

EMPLOYEES' BARGAINING RIGHTS IN THE PRIVATE AND PUBLIC SECTORS

Although there are basic differences in employment between the public and private sectors, collective bargaining legislation in the private sector has been significant in shaping statutory and judicial regulation of negotiations in the public sector. Similarities between the two sectors can be noted in a number of areas, such as unfair labor practices, union representation, and impasse procedures. Because of the influence of private sector legislation on the public sector, a brief overview of its major legislative acts is warranted.

Prior to the 1930s, labor relations in the private sector were dominated by the judiciary, which strongly favored management. The extensive use of judicial injunctions against strikes and boycotts effectively countered employee efforts to obtain recognition for purposes of bargaining.[6] Consequently, courts reinforced the powers of management and substantially curtailed the development and influence of unions. To bolster the position of the worker, Congress enacted the Norris-LaGuardia Act in 1932.[7] The purpose of this federal law was to circumscribe the role of courts in labor disputes by preventing the use of the injunction, except where union activities were unlawful or jeopardized public safety and health. In essence, the legislation did not confer any new rights on employees or unions but simply restricted judicial authority that had impeded the development of unions.

Following the Norris-LaGuardia Act, in 1935 Congress passed the National Labor Relations Act (NLRA), commonly known as the Wagner Act.[8] This Act created substantial rights for private sector employees, but one of the most important outcomes was that it granted legitimacy to the collective bargaining process. In addition to defining employees' rights to organize and bargain collectively, the Act established a mechanism to safeguard these rights—the National Labor Relations Board (NLRB). The NLRB was created specifically to monitor claims of unfair labor practices, such as interference with employees' rights to organize, discrimination against employees in hiring or discharge because of union membership, and failure to bargain in good faith.[9]

Congress amended the NLRA in 1947 with the enactment of the Labor Management Relations Act (commonly known as the Taft-Hartley Act).[10] While the Wagner Act

[6]For a historical discussion of the use and control of labor injunctions, see FRED WITNEY & BENJAMIN TAYLOR, LABOR RELATIONS LAW, 7th ed. (Englewood Cliffs, NJ: Prentice Hall, 1995).

[7]29 U.S.C. § 101 (2012). This Act also rendered "yellow dog" contracts—which required employees to promise not to join a union—unenforceable by courts.

[8]The Wagner Act states that "employees shall have the right to self-organization, to form, join or assist labor organizations, to bargain collectively through representatives of their own choosing, and to engage in concerted activities, for the purpose of collective bargaining or other mutual aid or protection." 29 U.S.C. § 157 (2012).

[9]The application of private sector labor laws to private schools, most of which are church related, has been controversial. Only private schools with a gross annual revenue of $1 million or more come under the jurisdiction of the NLRB; however, the majority of private schools do not reach this income level. Furthermore, the United States Supreme Court has held that the NLRB does not have jurisdiction over lay faculty in parochial schools in the absence of a clear expression of congressional intent to cover teachers in church-related schools under the NLRA. Nat'l Labor Relations Bd. v. Catholic Bishop of Chi., 440 U.S. 490 (1979). The Second Circuit, however, concluded that Catholic schools in New York come under the jurisdiction of the state labor relations board. Since the ruling involved bargaining activities of lay teachers regarding only secular employment practices, no infringement of the Establishment Clause or Free Exercise Clause of the First Amendment was found. Catholic High Sch. Ass'n v. Culvert, 753 F.2d 1161 (2d Cir. 1985). *But see* Mich. Educ. Ass'n v. Christian Bros. Inst., 706 N.W.2d 423 (Mich. Ct. App. 2005) (holding that the legislature did not grant the Michigan Employment Relations Commission jurisdiction over lay teachers in parochial schools).

[10]29 U.S.C. § 141 (2012).

regulated employers' activities, the Taft-Hartley Act was an attempt to balance the scales in collective bargaining by regulating abusive union practices, such as interfering with employees' organizational rights, failing to provide fair representation for all employees in the bargaining unit, and refusing to bargain in good faith. Since 1947, other amendments to the Taft-Hartley Act have further limited union abuses. Federal legislation has restricted interference from both the employer and the union, thereby ensuring the individual employee greater freedom of choice in collective bargaining.

Although the NLRA specifically exempted bargaining by governmental employees, a number of state public employee statutes have been modeled after this law, and judicial decisions interpreting the NLRA have been used to define certain provisions in public sector laws. The recognition of the sovereign power of public employers, however, is clearly present in public labor laws. For example, many public laws require employers to bargain over wages, hours, and other terms and conditions of employment as in the NLRA, but this requirement then is restricted by management rights clauses limiting the scope of bargaining.

Several fundamental differences exist in bargaining between the public and private sectors. First, the removal of decision-making authority from public officials through bargaining has been viewed as an infringement on the government's sovereign power, which has resulted in the enactment of labor laws strongly favoring public employers. Public employees' rights have been further weakened by prohibitions of work stoppages. Whereas employees' ability to strike is considered essential to the effective operation of collective decision making in the private sector, this view has been rejected in the public sector because of the nature and structure of governmental services.

Bargaining rights developed slowly for public employees, who historically had been deprived of the right to organize and bargain collectively. President Kennedy's Executive Order 10988 in 1962, which gave federal employees the right to form, join, and assist employee organizations, was a significant milestone for all public employees. The granting of organizational rights to federal employees provided the impetus for similar gains at the state and local levels.

Until the late 1960s, however, public employees' constitutional right to join a union had not been fully established. A large number of public employees actively participated in collective bargaining, but statutes and regulations in some states prohibited union membership. These restrictions against union membership were challenged as impairing association freedoms protected by the First Amendment. Although not addressing union membership, the Supreme Court held in 1967 that public employment could not be conditioned on the relinquishment of free association rights.[11] In a later decision, the Seventh Circuit clearly announced that "an individual's right to form and join a union is protected by the First Amendment."[12] Other courts followed this precedent by invalidating state statutory provisions that blocked union membership.[13]

As it did with other public employees, the judiciary acknowledged teachers' constitutional rights to participate fully in union activities. School officials have been prohibited

[11]Keyishian v. Bd. of Regents, 385 U.S. 589 (1967).

[12]McLaughlin v. Tilendis, 398 F.2d 287, 289 (7th Cir. 1968); *see also* St. Clair Cnty. Intermediate Sch. Dist. v. St. Clair Cnty. Educ. Ass'n, 630 N.W.2d 909 (Mich. Ct. App. 2001) (ruling that a school district violated a school nurse's rights when a supervisor told her either not to join the union or face losing her job).

[13]*See, e.g.*, Atkins v. City of Charlotte, 296 F. Supp. 1068 (W.D.N.C. 1969); Dade Cnty. Classroom Teachers' Ass'n v. Ryan, 225 So. 2d 903 (Fla. 1969).

from imposing sanctions or denying benefits to discourage protected association rights. For example, the Sixth Circuit overturned a school board's dismissal of a teacher because of union activities.[14] The Eighth Circuit held that a teacher's allegation that the superintendent placed her on probation to punish her for union activities was sufficient to establish a claim against the superintendent.[15] Similarly, the Connecticut Federal District Court found that the transfer of a teacher to another school in retaliation for using the negotiated grievance procedure was constitutionally prohibited.[16] The Seventh Circuit, however, held that a teacher, who had been union president and engaged in contentious and combative battles with school officials, did not establish that he was terminated for his union activities.[17] The school board was able to show a legitimate, nondiscriminatory reason for its decision; in direct violation of known school district policy, the teacher had conducted computer searches at school that produced pornographic images.

The United States Constitution has been interpreted as protecting public employees' rights to organize, but the right to form and join a union does not ensure the right to bargain collectively with a public employer; individual state statutes and constitutions govern such bargaining rights. Whether identified as professional negotiations, collective negotiations, or collective bargaining, the process entails bilateral decision making in which the teachers' representative and the school board attempt to reach mutual agreement on matters affecting teacher employment. This process is governed in over thirty states by legislation granting specific bargaining rights to teachers and their professional associations. Courts, viewing collective bargaining as within the scope of legislative authority, have restricted their role primarily to interpreting statutory and constitutional provisions. The judiciary has been reluctant to interfere with legislative authority to define the collective bargaining relationship between public employers and employees unless protected rights have been compromised.

Because of the variations in labor laws, as well as the lack of such laws in some states, substantial differences exist in bargaining rights and practices. A few states, such as New York, have a detailed, comprehensive collective bargaining statute that delineates specific bargaining rights. In contrast, negotiated contracts between teachers' organizations and school boards are prohibited in North Carolina. Under North Carolina law, all contracts between public employers and employee associations are invalid.[18] Similarly, the Virginia Supreme Court declared that a negotiated contract between a teachers' organization and a school board is null and void in the absence of express enabling legislation.[19] The board maintained that its power to enter into contracts allowed it also to bargain collectively with employee organizations, but the court concluded that such implied power was contrary to legislative intent.

[14]Hickman v. Valley Local Sch. Dist. Bd. of Educ., 619 F.2d 606 (6th Cir. 1980); *see also* Cent. Sch. Dist. 13J v. Cent. Educ. Ass'n, 962 P.2d 763 (Or. Ct. App. 1998) (ruling that teacher could not be discharged for exercising association rights protected under state law).

[15]Springdale Educ. Ass'n v. Springdale Sch. Dist., 133 F.3d 649 (8th Cir. 1998).

[16]Stellmaker v. DePetrillo, 710 F. Supp. 891 (D. Conn. 1989); *see also* Speed Dist. 802 v. Warning, 950 N.E.2d 1069 (Ill. 2011) (concluding that nonrenewed teacher was not engaging in a protected union activity when she demanded union representation at remediation meetings with principal; agreement did not provide for representation, and the record showed nonrenewal was substantiated due to teaching deficiencies).

[17]Zellner v. Herrick, 639 F.3d 371 (7th Cir. 2011).

[18]N.C. GEN. STAT. §§ 95–98 (2012).

[19]Commonwealth v. Cnty. Bd. of Arlington Cnty., 232 S.E.2d 30 (Va. 1977).

In contrast to North Carolina and Virginia, other states without legislation have permitted negotiated agreements. The Kentucky Supreme Court ruled that a public employer may recognize an employee organization for the purpose of collective bargaining, even though state law is silent regarding public employee bargaining rights.[20] The decision does not impose a duty on local school boards to bargain but merely allows a board the discretion to negotiate. This ruling is consistent with a number of other decisions permitting negotiated contracts in the absence of specific legislation. The board's power and authority to enter into contracts for the operation and maintenance of the school system have been construed to include the ability to enter into negotiated agreements with employee organizations.

Unless bargaining is mandated by statute, courts have not compelled school boards to negotiate. Whether to negotiate is thus at the school board's discretion. Once a school board extends recognition to a bargaining agent and commences bargaining, however, the board's actions in the negotiation process are governed by established judicial principles. Although the employer maintains certain prerogatives, such as recognition of the bargaining unit and determination of bargainable items, specific judicially recognized rights also are conferred on the employee organization. For example, there is a legal duty for the board to bargain in good faith. Furthermore, if the negotiation process reaches an impasse, the board may not unilaterally terminate bargaining. Also, after signing a contract, the board is bound by the provisions and cannot abrogate the agreement on the basis that no duty existed to bargain. Hence, the school board is subject to a number of legal constraints after it enters into the negotiation process.

The diversity across states in protected bargaining rights for public employees has led many individuals and groups to advocate a federal bargaining law for all state and local employees. Several national organizations have supported such a proposal, including the National Education Association; the American Federation of Teachers; and the American Federation of State, County, and Municipal Employees. Although it appears that a federal law would be within congressional authority under the Commerce Clause,[21] for the immediate future, bargaining rights seem destined to be controlled either by individual state legislation or, in the absence of such legislation, by court rulings. As noted previously, governors and legislators are considering significant reform of the existing public employee bargaining laws.[22]

TEACHERS' STATUTORY BARGAINING RIGHTS

In the states that have enacted statutes governing teachers' bargaining rights, school boards must negotiate with teachers in accordance with the statutorily prescribed process. Generally, public employee bargaining laws address employer and employee rights, bargaining units, scope of bargaining, impasse resolution, grievance procedures, unfair labor practices, and penalties for prohibited practices. Many states have established labor

[20]Bd. of Trs. of Univ. of Ky. v. Pub. Emps. Council No. 51, 571 S.W.2d 616 (Ky. 1978); *see also* Independence-Nat'l Educ. Ass'n v. Independence Sch. Dist., 223 S.W.3d 131 (Mo. 2007), *overruling* City of Springfield v. Clouse, 206 S.W.2d 539, 542 (Mo. 1947) (holding that state constitutional provision guaranteeing "employees" the right to organize and bargain collectively includes both public and private employees).

[21]*See* Garcia v. San Antonio Metro. Transit Auth., 469 U.S. 528 (1985).

[22]*See supra* text accompanying note 4.

relations boards to monitor bargaining under their statutes. Although the specific functions of these boards vary widely, their general purpose is to resolve questions arising from the implementation of state law. Functions assigned to such boards include determination of membership in bargaining units, resolution of union recognition claims, investigation of unfair labor practices, and interpretation of the general intent of statutory bargaining clauses. Usually, judicial review cannot be pursued until administrative review before labor boards is exhausted. Thus, decisions of labor boards are an important source of labor law, since many of the issues addressed by boards are never appealed to courts. When the boards' decisions are challenged in court, substantial deference is given to their findings and determinations.[23]

State laws generally provide that the school board will negotiate with an exclusive representative selected by the teachers. Procedures are specified for certification of the bargaining representative, election of the representative by employees, and recognition by the employer. Once the state labor relations board recognizes an exclusive representative, the employer must bargain with that representative. In addition to certification, state laws address cause and process for decertification of the exclusive representative.

Like the NLRA, state statutes require bargaining "in good faith." Good faith bargaining has been interpreted as requiring parties to meet at reasonable times and attempt to reach mutual agreement without compulsion on either side to agree. A number of states have followed the federal law in stipulating that this "does not compel either party to agree to a proposal or to require the making of a concession."[24] However, it does mean that an employer cannot make unilateral changes in a term or condition in the contract to circumvent its obligation to bargain collectively.[25] Good faith bargaining has been open to a range of interpretations, and judicial decisions in the public sector have relied extensively on private sector rulings that have clarified the phrase.

Statutes impose certain restrictions or obligations on both the school board and the employee organization. Violation of the law by either party can result in an unfair labor practice claim with the imposition of penalties. Allegations of unfair labor practices are brought before the state public employee relations board for a hearing and judgment. Specific unfair labor practices, often modeled after those in the NLRA, are included in state statutes. The most common prohibited labor practice in both public and private employment is that an employer or union will not interfere with, restrain, or coerce public employees in exercising their rights under the labor law.[26] Among other prohibited *employer* practices are interference with union operations, discrimination against employees because of union membership, refusal to bargain collectively with the exclusive representative, and failure to bargain in good faith. *Unions* are prevented from causing an employer to discriminate against employees on the basis of union membership, refusing

[23]*See, e.g., In re* Kennedy, 27 A.3d 844 (N.H. 2011); Dodgeland Educ. Ass'n v. Wis. Emp't Relations Comm'n, 639 N.W. 2d 733 (Wis. 2002).

[24]29 U.S.C. § 158(d) (2012); *see also* Bd. of Educ. v. Sered, 850 N.E.2d 821 (Ill. App. Ct. 2006) (finding that a tentative oral agreement made by the board's representatives was valid; the board could not disregard or modify the terms of the agreement).

[25]Educ. Minn.-Greenway v. Indep. Sch. Dist., 673 N.W.2d 843 (Minn. Ct. App. 2004).

[26]*See* Cal. Teachers Ass'n v. Pub. Emp't Relations Bd., 87 Cal. Rptr. 3d 530 (App. Ct. 2009) (holding that the act of organizing teachers through signing a letter was a protected act); Ft. Frye Teachers Ass'n v. SERB, 809 N.E.2d 1130 (Ohio 2004) (ruling the nonrenewal of a teacher's contract for union activities constitutes an unfair labor practice; the state labor board was directed to act upon the court's finding).

to bargain or failing to bargain in good faith, failing to represent all employees in the bargaining unit,[27] and engaging in unlawful activities such as strikes or boycotts identified in the bargaining law.

Upon completion of the negotiation process, the members of the bargaining unit and the school board must ratify the written agreement (usually referred to as the master contract). These agreements often contain similar standard contract language and clauses, beginning with recognition of the exclusive bargaining representative and union security issues (i.e., fair share fees). Management rights and association rights also are detailed. Management clauses emphasize the board's control over the establishment of educational policies, and union clauses may include the right to use school facilities or communication systems. The remaining provisions relate to the scope of bargaining, which is defined by the state's labor law or common law. These items not only include salary and fringe benefits but also may address grievance procedures, employee evaluations, preparation time, length of workday, class size, procedural process for employee discipline, transfers, layoff and recall procedures, assignment of duties, and procedures for filling vacancies. The range in the negotiability of these issues can be seen in the next section.

SCOPE OF NEGOTIATIONS

Should the teachers' organization have input into class size? Who will determine the length of the school day? How will extra-duty assignments be determined? Will reductions in force necessitated by declining enrollment be based on seniority or merit? These questions and others are raised in determining the scope of negotiations. "Scope" refers to the range of issues or subjects that are negotiable, and determining scope is one of the most difficult tasks in public sector bargaining. Public employers argue that issues must be narrowly defined to protect the government's policy-making role, whereas employee unions counter that bargaining subjects must be defined broadly for negotiations to be meaningful.

Restrictions on scope of bargaining vary considerably among states. Consequently, to determine a particular state's negotiable items, the state's collective bargaining law, other statutes, and litigation interpreting these laws must be examined. The specification of negotiable items in labor laws may include broad guidelines or detailed enumeration. Many states have modeled their bargaining statutes after the National Labor Relations Act, which stipulates that representatives of the employer and employees must meet and confer "with respect to wages, hours, and other terms and conditions of employment."[28] A few states have elected to deal directly with the scope of bargaining by identifying each item that must be negotiated.[29] Some states specify prohibited subjects of bargaining. For example, Michigan's prohibited subjects include decisions

[27]*See* United Teachers v. Sch. Dist. of Miami-Dade Cnty., 68 So. 3d 1003 (Fla. Dist. Ct. App. 2011) (finding that bargained agreement denied nonunion teachers the right of representation at performance review proceedings; the union committed an unfair labor practice when it entered into the agreement); S. Sioux City Educ. Ass'n v. Dakota Cnty. Sch. Dist., 772 N.W.2d 564 (Neb. 2009) (ruling that school board committed a prohibited labor practice when it classified a certificated teacher as a long-term substitute rather than a probationary teacher, resulting in compensation less than the bargained contract amount).

[28]29 U.S.C. § 158(d) (2012).

[29]*See, e.g.*, Iowa Code § 20.9 (2012); Nev. Rev. Stat. § 288.150 (2012); *see also* Blount Cnty. Educ. Ass'n v. Blount Cnty. Bd. of Educ., 78 S.W.3d 307 (Tenn. Ct. App. 2002) (ruling that the state legislature did not intend to give "working conditions" a broad interpretation when it specifically listed eight mandatory bargaining topics).

related to the establishment of the starting date for the school year, composition of site-based decision-making bodies, interdistrict and intradistrict open enrollment opportunities, authorization of public school academies, use of volunteers in providing services at schools, and establishment and staffing of experimental programs.[30] Generally, statutory mandates cannot be preempted by collective bargaining agreements;[31] however, in some states, the negotiated agreement prevails over conflicting state laws, unless the laws are specifically exempted.[32] Furthermore, the school board cannot agree to a specific term in the contract and then assert that it is illegal. A Pennsylvania court held that a school board could not deny a female teacher's request to return to work early after a pregnancy under a policy in the negotiated agreement permitting the return.[33] The board had argued that the agreement violated public policy against sex discrimination because no provision was made for males to request an early return from leave.

All proposed subjects for negotiation can be classified as mandatory, permissive, or prohibited. Mandatory items must be negotiated.[34] Failure of the school board to meet and confer on such items is evidence of lack of good faith bargaining. Permissive items can be negotiated if both parties agree; however, there is no legal duty to consider the items. Furthermore, in most states permissive items cannot be pursued to the point of negotiation impasse, and an employer can make unilateral changes with respect to these items if a negotiated agreement is not reached. Prohibited items are beyond the power of the board to negotiate; an illegal delegation of power results if the board agrees to negotiate regarding these items. Since most statutory scope provisions are general in nature, courts or labor relations boards often have been asked to differentiate between negotiable and nonnegotiable items.[35] The following sections highlight issues related to governmental policy and specific bargaining topics.

Governmental Policy

Defining managerial rights is one of the key elements in establishing limitations on negotiable subjects at the bargaining table. State laws specify that public employers cannot be required to negotiate governmental policy matters, and courts have held that it is impermissible for a school board to bargain away certain rights and responsibilities in the

[30]MICH. COMP. LAWS § 423.215(3)(4) (2012).

[31]*See, e.g.*, Mifflinburg Area Educ. Ass'n v. Mifflinburg Area Sch. Dist., 724 A.2d 339 (Pa. 1999); Bd. of Educ. v. Ill. Educ. Labor Relations Bd., 649 N.E.2d 369 (Ill. 1995). Furthermore, collective bargaining agreements cannot deprive individuals of rights guaranteed by federal laws. Abrahamson v. Bd. of Educ., 374 F.3d 66 (2d Cir. 2004).

[32]*See, e.g.*, Hickey v. N.Y.C. Dep't of Educ., 952 N.E.2d 993 (N.Y. 2011); Streetsboro Educ. Ass'n v. Streetsboro City Sch. Dist., 626 N.E.2d 110 (Ohio 1994); *see also* State Dep't of Admin. v. Pub. Emps. Relations Bd., 894 P.2d 777 (Kan. 1995) (holding that a collective bargaining agreement takes precedence over conflicting civil service regulations).

[33]W. Allegheny Sch. Dist. v. W. Allegheny Educ. Ass'n, 997 A.2d 411 (Pa. Commw. Ct. 2010).

[34]Wages definitely fall within the mandatory category. A wage-related area that has received recent attention is the payment of "signing bonuses" to attract teachers for difficult-to-fill positions. Failure to bargain these payments may constitute an unfair labor practice. *See, e.g.*, Ekalaka Unified Bd. of Trs. v. Ekalaka Teachers' Ass'n, 149 P.3d 902 (Mont. 2006); Crete Educ. Ass'n v. Salie Cnty. Sch. Dist., 654 N.W.2d 166 (Neb. 2002).

[35]*See* Junction City Educ. Ass'n v. Bd. of Educ., 955 P.2d 1266 (Kan. 1998) (ruling that issues of negotiability should be determined initially by the state administrative agency rather than through a declaratory judgment action in a district court).

public policy area.[36] Generally, educational policy matters are defined through provisions in collective bargaining statutes, such as "management rights" and "scope of bargaining" clauses. Policy issues (e.g., class size and decisions related to the granting of tenure) are totally excluded as negotiable items in a few states; however, most states stipulate only that employers will not be *required* to bargain policy rights.

Public employee labor laws requiring the negotiation of "conditions of employment" can include far-reaching policy matters since most decisions made by a school board either directly or indirectly affect the teacher at the classroom level. The difficulty in distinguishing between educational policy and matters relating to teachers' employment was noted by the Maryland high court: "Virtually every managerial decision in some way relates to 'salaries, wages, hours, and other working conditions,' and is therefore arguably negotiable. At the same time, virtually every such decision also involves educational policy considerations and is therefore arguably nonnegotiable."[37] In many states, the interpretation of what is negotiable resides with the labor relations board. Often, these boards, as well as courts, employ a balancing test, beginning with an inquiry into whether a particular matter involves wages, hours, and terms and conditions of employment. If it does, then the labor board or court must determine if the matter also is one of inherent managerial policy. If the response is "no" to this second question, the matter is a mandatory subject of bargaining. However, if the response is "yes," then the benefits of bargaining on the decision-making process must be balanced against the burden on the employer's authority.[38] Accordingly, this process entails a fact-specific analysis.

Judicial decisions interpreting negotiability illustrate the range in bargainable matters. The Supreme Court of New Jersey narrowly interpreted "conditions of employment" to mean wages, benefits, and work schedules, thereby removing governmental policy items such as teacher transfers, course offerings, and evaluations.[39] A number of courts, however, have construed conditions of employment in broader terms. As such, the Nevada Supreme Court ruled that items *significantly* related to wages, hours, and working conditions are negotiable.[40] Similarly, the Pennsylvania Supreme Court concluded that an issue's *impact* on conditions of employment must be weighed in determining whether it should be considered outside the educational policy area.[41]

[36]*See, e.g.*, Bd. of Educ. v. N.Y. State Pub. Emp't Relations Bd., 554 N.E.2d 1247, 1251 (N.Y. 1990); Raines v. Indep. Sch. Dist. No. 6, 796 P.2d 303 (Okla. 1990); Montgomery Cnty. Educ. Ass'n v. Bd. of Educ., 534 A.2d 980 (Md. 1987); *see also* City Univ. of N.Y. v. Prof'l Staff Cong., 837 N.Y.S.2d 121 (App. Div. 2007) (holding that employer could not bargain away its right to inspect teacher personnel files; agreement was against public policy to investigate discrimination complaints).

[37]*Montgomery Cnty. Educ. Ass'n*, 534 A.2d at 986.

[38]*See, e.g.*, Dodgeland Educ. Ass'n v. Wis. Emp't Relations Comm'n, 639 N.W. 2d 733 (Wis. 2002); Cent. City Educ. Ass'n v. Ill. Educ. Labor Relations Bd., 599 N.E.2d 892 (Ill. 1992); City of Beloit v. Wis. Emp't Relations Bd., 242 N.W.2d 231 (Wis. 1976); *see also* Sherrard Cmty. Unit Sch. v. Ill. Educ. Labor Relations Bd., 696 N.E.2d 833 (Ill. App. Ct. 1998) (finding that the reassignment of teachers involves the exercise of managerial discretion that generally is not a mandatory bargaining subject; actions of the school board in directly negotiating with a teacher made it a mandatory bargaining subject).

[39]Ridgefield Park Educ. Ass'n v. Ridgefield Park Bd. of Educ., 393 A.2d 278 (N.J. 1978); *see also* Polk Cnty. Bd. of Educ. v. Polk Cnty. Educ. Ass'n, 139 S.W.3d 304 (Tenn. Ct. App. 2004) (ruling that a dress code policy constituted a "working condition," not a managerial prerogative).

[40]Clark Cnty. Sch. Dist. v. Local Gov't Emp.-Mgmt. Relations Bd., 530 P.2d 114 (Nev. 1974); *see also* Governing Bd. v. Comm'n on Prof'l Conduct, 99 Cal. Rptr. 3d 903 (App. Ct. 2009) (finding that the negotiated agreement requiring all teachers to acquire English learner certification was "reasonably related" to hours, wages, and conditions of employment).

[41]Pa. Labor Relations Bd. v. State Coll. Area Sch. Dist., 337 A.2d 262 (Pa. 1975).

Even though courts are in agreement that school boards cannot be *required* to negotiate inherent managerial rights pertaining to policy matters, these rights are viewed as *permissive* subjects of bargaining in some states. That is, the board may agree to negotiate a particular "right" in the absence of statutory or judicial prohibitions.[42] If the board does negotiate a policy item, it is bound by the agreement in the same manner as if the issue were a mandatory item.[43]

Selected Bargaining Subjects

Beyond wages, hours, and fringe benefits, there is a lack of agreement among states as to what is negotiable. Similar enabling legislation has been interpreted quite differently among states, as illustrated by the subjects discussed below.

CLASS SIZE. This has been one of the most controversial policy subjects, and one that courts and state legislatures have been reluctant to designate as negotiable. Only a few states specifically identify class size as a mandatory bargaining item,[44] and the majority of courts reviewing the issue have found it to be a nonmandatory item.[45] The Nevada Supreme Court interpreted the state collective bargaining statute as including class size among mandatory subjects by implication,[46] but the legislature responded by revising the state law to exclude class size from a detailed list of bargainable items.[47] An Illinois appellate court, however, held that class size is a mandatory issue for bargaining,[48] and several other courts have found it to be a *permissive* subject of bargaining.[49] Although the Wisconsin Supreme Court found class size to be such a permissive subject, the court held that negotiations on the *impact* of class size (e.g., more projects to supervise, potential for more disciplinary problems, and so forth) on teachers' conditions of employment would be mandatory.[50] Similarly, a Florida appellate court concluded that class size and staffing

[42]*See, e.g.*, Blount Cnty. Educ. Ass'n v. Blount Cnty. Bd. of Educ., 78 S.W.3d 307 (Tenn. Ct. App. 2002). *But see* Colonial Sch. Bd. v. Colonial Affiliate, 449 A.2d 243 (Del. 1982) (holding that the state law does not recognize bargaining of permissive subjects); *Montgomery Cnty. Educ. Ass'n*, 534 A.2d 980 (finding no provision for permissive subjects to be bargained).

[43]*See, e.g., In re* White Mountain Reg'l Sch. Dist., 908 A.2d 790 (N.H. 2006); DiPiazza v. Bd. of Educ., 625 N.Y.S.2d 298 (App. Div. 1995); *see also* Univ. of Haw. Prof'l Assembly v. Cayetano, 183 F.3d 1096 (9th Cir. 1999) (noting that past practices are important in interpreting the requirements of a negotiated agreement; holding that the employer changing the timing of the payroll schedule contradicted past practice); Malahoff v. Saito, 140 P.3d 401 (Haw. 2006) (ruling that no constitutional violation regarding collective bargaining occurred with the state shifting pay dates by one to four days a month since employees did not experience any loss of wages; however, implementation of change was impermissible because the statute providing for such a shift had expired); Bd. of Educ. v. Ward, 974 P.2d 824 (Utah 1999) (finding that school boards have substantial discretion to interpret their policies, but do not have that discretion if the policy is part of a negotiated collective bargaining contract).

[44]*See, e.g.*, MASS. GEN. LAWS ch. 150E, § 6 (2012).

[45]*See* Cent. State Univ. v. Am. Ass'n of Univ. Professors, 526 U.S. 124 (1999), *on remand* 717 N.E.2d 286 (Ohio 1999) (upholding an Ohio statute excluding faculty workload in public universities from collective bargaining).

[46]Clark Cnty. Sch. Dist. v. Local Gov't Emp. Mgmt. Relations Bd., 530 P.2d 114 (Nev. 1974).

[47]NEV. REV. STAT. 288 § 150.3 (2012).

[48]Decatur Bd. of Educ., Dist. No. 61 v. Ill. Educ. Labor Relations Bd., 536 N.E.2d 743 (Ill. App. Ct. 1989).

[49]*See, e.g.*, Nat'l Educ. Ass'n-Kan. City v. Unified Sch. Dist., Wyandotte Cnty., 608 P.2d 415 (Kan. 1980); Fargo Educ. Ass'n v. Fargo Pub. Sch. Dist., 291 N.W.2d 267 (N.D. 1980); City of Beloit v. Wis. Emp't Relations Comm'n, 242 N.W.2d 231 (Wis. 1976).

[50]*City of Beloit*, 242 N.W.2d 231; *see also* Tualatin Valley Bargaining Council v. Tigard Sch. Dist., 840 P.2d 657 (Or. 1992) (holding that class size was not automatically a mandatory subject under "other conditions of employment" because it related to a teacher's workload; an assessment must be made relative to its effect on working conditions).

levels were not mandatorily bargainable, but noted that bargaining on the impact or effect of the implementation of these decisions would be mandatory.[51]

SCHOOL CALENDAR. Establishment of the school calendar generally has been held to be a managerial prerogative.[52] Reflecting the judicial trend that it is a nonnegotiable managerial decision, the Maine high court stated: "The commencement and termination of the school year and the scheduling and length of intermediate vacations during the school year, at least insofar as students and teachers are congruently involved, must be held matters of 'educational policies' bearing too substantially upon too many and important non-teacher interests to be settled by collective bargaining."[53] An Indiana appellate court agreed, noting that the impact of the school calendar on students and other public interests outweighed teachers' interests.[54] Notwithstanding that the establishment of the school calendar is a managerial prerogative, the Supreme Court of New Jersey ruled that decisions impacting the days worked and compensation for those days implicates a term and condition of employment.[55] Departing from the prevailing view, the Wisconsin Supreme Court upheld a ruling of the Wisconsin Employment Relations Commission declaring the school calendar mandatorily bargainable; calendar issues are more closely related to terms of employment than to policy matters.[56]

TEACHER EVALUATION. Employee unions have made significant gains in securing the right to negotiate various aspects of teacher performance evaluations. Most states have not specified evaluation as a mandatory bargaining item, but a number of courts have found it to be significantly related to conditions of employment and thus negotiable. Although courts have been receptive to union proposals to negotiate the technical and procedural elements of evaluation, they have been reluctant to mandate the negotiation of evaluation criteria. In ruling that teacher evaluation was not a prohibited bargaining subject, the Supreme Court of New Hampshire noted that the contested evaluation plan provided only the procedures for evaluations, not the standards by which the teachers would be reviewed.[57] Similarly, the Supreme Court of Kansas distinguished between managerial policies and the mechanics of such policies; the mechanics of developing the evaluation procedures were found to be mandatorily negotiable, but not the evaluation

[51]Hillsborough Classroom Teachers Ass'n v. Sch. Bd., 423 So. 2d 969 (Fla. Dist. Ct. App. 1982).

[52]*See, e.g.*, W. Cent. Educ. Ass'n v. W. Cent. Sch. Dist., 655 N.W.2d 916 (S.D. 2002); Piscataway Twp. Educ. Ass'n v. Piscataway Twp. Bd. of Educ., 704 A.2d 981 (N.J. 1998); Pub. Emp. Relations Bd. v. Wash. Teachers' Union Local 6, 556 A.2d 206 (D.C. Cir. 1989).

[53]City of Biddeford v. Biddeford Teachers Ass'n, 304 A.2d 387, 421 (Me. 1973).

[54]Eastbrook Cmty. Sch. Corp. v. Ind. Educ. Emp't Relations Bd., 446 N.E.2d 1007 (Ind. Ct. App. 1983).

[55]Troy v. Rutgers, 774 A.2d 476 (N.J. 2001).

[56]City of Beloit v. Emp't Relations Comm'n, 242 N.W.2d 231 (Wis. 1976); *see also* Lincoln Cnty. Educ. Ass'n v. Lincoln Cnty. Sch. Dist., 67 P.3d 951 (Or. Ct. App. 2003) (finding that the amount of student contact time each day for teachers was a mandatory subject of bargaining and could not be changed without negotiation). *But see* Racine Educ. Ass'n v. Wis. Emp't Relations Comm'n, 571 N.W.2d 887 (Wis. Ct. App. 1997) (upholding the Wisconsin Employment Relations Commission's (WERC) determination that the implementation of a pilot year-round school calendar was not subject to mandatory bargaining; in balancing the employer and employee interests in this specific situation, WERC found the year-round program primarily related to educational policy).

[57]*In re* Pittsfield Sch. Dist., 744 A.2d 594 (N.H. 1999). In a later case, the New Hampshire court held that a school district breached the collective bargaining contract when it implemented new procedures under a change in state law; the previously negotiated procedures were to remain in effect until the expiration of the contract. *In re* White Mountain Reg'l Sch. Dist., 908 A.2d 790 (N.H. 2006).

criteria, which were designated as a managerial prerogative.[58] The Supreme Court of Iowa, however, found a statutory requirement to negotiate *evaluation procedures* to encompass substantive criteria for evaluation because the term *procedures* had been interpreted broadly in previous judicial rulings.[59]

REDUCTIONS IN FORCE. With declining student enrollments and financial exigency faced by many school districts, staff reductions in force (RIFs) have become a threat to tenured as well as nontenured teachers. The threat has resulted in employee unions demanding input into decisions to reduce staff, criteria for reductions, and procedures for selecting teachers for release. Courts generally have held that the decision to reduce staff and the criteria used to make that decision are educational policy matters and thus are not negotiable.[60] State laws also may specifically prohibit collective bargaining of reduction in force decisions. The *impact* of RIFs on employee rights, however, may necessitate negotiation of procedures for the reduction. The Supreme Court of South Dakota held that the decision to reduce teaching positions was a nonnegotiable managerial decision, but concluded that the mechanics of staff reductions, such as how staff would be selected and procedures for recall, were mandatorily negotiable.[61] The Supreme Court of Wisconsin found that notice and timing of layoffs had to be bargained as they were primarily related to employees' interest and had "a direct impact on wages and job security."[62] In a case involving the recall rights of Chicago Public School teachers, the Seventh Circuit appellate court[63] asked the Supreme Court of Illinois to interpret the Illinois laws regarding tenure and recall rights for Chicago teachers.[64] According to the Illinois high court, teachers are considered "permanent" employees after acquiring tenure, but they can be removed for cause, which includes layoffs. Although the state law does identify criteria for school boards to consider *if* they negotiate recall procedures, the Illinois court stated that permanent status did not confer any residual property rights to be considered for reemployment. The Seventh Circuit thus concluded that the Chicago teachers could not assert any state law rights because recall procedures were not negotiated in the bargaining agreement.

[58]Bd. of Educ. v. NEA-Goodland, 785 P.2d 993 (Kan. 1990).

[59]Aplington Cmty. Sch. Dist. v. Iowa Pub. Emp't Relations Bd., 392 N.W.2d 495 (Iowa 1986); *see also* Snyder v. Mendon-Union Local Sch. Dist. Bd. of Educ., 661 N.E.2d 717 (Ohio 1996) (ruling that, in the absence of a collective bargaining agreement specifying otherwise, state law governs the evaluation of a nontenured teacher); Atl. Educ. Ass'n v. Atl. Cmty. Sch. Dist., 469 N.W.2d 689 (Iowa 1991) (concluding that the collective bargaining contract did not provide for arbitration of performance evaluation in the absence of negotiated performance criteria; the negotiated agreement addressed only procedural aspects, which were not contested by the teacher).

[60]*See, e.g.*, Thompson v. Unified Sch. Dist. No. 259, 819 P.2d 1236 (Kan. Ct. App. 1991); N. Star Sch. Dist. v. N. Star Educ. Ass'n, 625 A.2d 159 (Pa. Commw. Ct. 1993); Blount Cnty. Educ. Ass'n v. Blount Cnty. Bd. of Educ., 78 S.W.3d 307 (Tenn. Ct. App. 2002). *But see In re* Hillsboro-Deering Sch. Dist., 737 A.2d 1098 (N.H. 1999) (ruling that a school district's decision to release all employees in a bargaining unit in order to enter into a contract with a private company did not constitute a true layoff involving managerial rights, and therefore it was subject to bargaining).

[61]Webster Educ. Ass'n v. Webster Sch. Dist., 631 N.W.2d 202 (S.D. 2001). *See* Hanson v. Vermillion Sch. Dist., 727 N.W.2d 459 (S.D. 2007); Davis v. Chester Upland Sch. Dist., 786 A.2d 186 (Pa. 2001).

[62]W. Bend Educ. Ass'n v. Wis. Emp't Relations Comm'n, 357 N.W.2d 534, 543 (Wis. 1984). The court developed a balancing test for weighing employees' interests in wages, hours, and conditions of employment against the employer's right to make managerial policy decisions. If an item is "primarily related" to wages, hours, and conditions of employment, it is a mandatory subject of bargaining; if not, there is no duty to bargain.

[63]Chi. Teachers Union v. Bd. of Educ., 662 F.3d 761 (7th Cir. 2011).

[64]Chi. Teachers Union v. Bd. of Educ., 963 N.E.2d 918 (Ill. 2012).

If procedures are agreed to in the collective bargaining contract, they must be followed. An Idaho school district argued that its contract agreement specifying notification by May 15 conflicted with a statutory requirement that districts provide notice by June 15. The state supreme court ruled that the Idaho Code gives school trustees broad authority to negotiate "matters specified in any such negotiation agreement," which expressly enabled the district to bind itself to the earlier date.[65] Teachers, however, may possess independent statutory rights that cannot be subordinated to collective bargaining agreements. A Massachusetts appellate court held that a teacher possessed "bumping" rights across the school system under statutory law, not merely within her bargaining unit as specified in the collective bargaining agreement.[66] The school district argued that she could not bump a less senior teacher in another high school that involved a different bargaining unit. Ruling that state law prevailed, the appellate court noted that the legislature did not list the statute protecting seniority rights as subordinate to negotiated agreements.

Procedures negotiated by the employer and the teachers' union for staff reductions must not violate the constitutional rights of any employees. The Supreme Court overturned a collective bargaining agreement that was designed to protect members of certain minority groups from layoffs.[67] The agreement ensured that the percentage of minority teachers would not fall below the percentage employed before any reductions in force. Without evidence that there had been prior employment discrimination, the Court held that the plan violated the equal protection rights of nonminority teachers.

NONRENEWAL AND TENURE DECISIONS. Decisions to retain a teacher or grant tenure clearly are managerial rights and are not mandatorily bargainable.[68] If a school board negotiates procedural aspects of these decisions, however, the provisions generally are binding. For example, collective bargaining agreements may entitle nontenured teachers to procedural protections that ordinarily would not be required under state laws or the Fourteenth Amendment.[69] The Supreme Court of New Hampshire held that state law did not prevent a school board from agreeing to provide probationary teachers with a statement of reasons for nonrenewal; the board retained its managerial prerogative not to renew the teacher's contract.[70] An Illinois federal district court ruled that under Illinois law, a teacher's failure to exhaust his contractual remedies under the collective bargaining agreement prevented him from challenging his nonrenewal in court.[71]

[65]Hunting v. Clark Cnty. Sch. Dist. No. 161, 931 P.2d 628, 633 (Idaho 1997).

[66]Ballotte v. City of Worcester, 748 N.E.2d 987 (Mass. App. Ct. 2001); *see* Marino v. Bd. of Educ, 691 N.Y.S.2d 537 (App. Div. 1999).

[67]Wygant v. Jackson Bd. of Educ., 476 U.S. 267 (1986); *see* Milwaukee Bd. of Sch. Dirs. v. Wis. Emp't Relations Comm'n, 472 N.W.2d 553 (Wis. Ct. App. 1991).

[68]Under most state laws, reemployment of probationary teachers and tenure decisions have been found to be prohibited subjects of bargaining. *See, e.g.*, Chi. Sch. Reform Bd. v. Ill. Educ. Labor Relations Bd., 721 N.E.2d 676 (Ill. App. Ct. 1999); Mindemann v. Indep. Sch. Dist. No. 6, 771 P.2d 996 (Okla. 1989); Honeoye Falls-Lima Cent. Sch. Dist. v. Honeoye Falls-Lima Educ. Ass'n, 402 N.E.2d 1165 (N.Y. 1980). *But see* State *ex rel.* Rollins v. Bd. of Educ., 532 N.E.2d 1289 (Ohio 1988) (holding that under the collective bargaining law, a negotiated agreement prevails over another conflicting law).

[69]Kentwood Pub. Sch. v. Kent Cnty. Educ. Ass'n, 520 N.W.2d 682 (Mich. Ct. App. 1994). *But see* Bd. of Educ. v. Round Valley Teachers' Ass'n, 914 P.2d 193 (Cal. 1996) (ruling that negotiated procedures beyond statutory minimum for not rehiring probationary employees were preempted by the Education Code; when exclusive discretion is vested in the board to determine scope of procedures, the subject matter may not be subjected to mandatory or permissive bargaining).

[70]*In re* Watson, 448 A.2d 417 (N.H. 1982).

[71]Lombardi v. Bd. of Trs. Hinson Sch. Dist., 463 F. Supp. 2d 867 (N.D. Ill. 2006).

Failure of school boards to follow negotiated procedures has resulted in arbitrators' ordering reinstatement of discharged teachers. Permissibility of such awards, however, depends on how a school board's authority is interpreted under state law. The Supreme Court of Alaska rejected an arbitrator's reinstatement of a teacher, reasoning that school boards "possess the exclusive power, not subject to *any* appeal, to decide whether to 'nonrenew' a provisional employee."[72] The court noted that a range of other remedies was available for the board's violation of the negotiated nonretention procedures. In contrast, the Supreme Court of Montana concluded that reinstatement of teachers by an arbitrator did not usurp school board authority but simply provided appropriate relief for the board's failure to abide by the negotiated due process procedures.[73]

Under Maine law, school boards can enter into negotiated agreements containing binding grievance arbitration for employee dismissal. The state high court ruled that a school board voluntarily negotiating such an arbitration process could not then seek to overturn an arbitrator's reinstatement decision by arguing that the decision causes the board to violate its duty to provide a safe learning environment. By agreeing to submit the dismissal to an arbitrator, the board agreed to abide by the arbitrator's interpretation of the law.[74]

UNION SECURITY PROVISIONS

To ensure their strength and viability, unions attempt to obtain various security provisions in the collective bargaining contract. The nature and extent of these provisions will depend on state laws and constitutional limitations. In this section, provisions related to union revenue and exclusive privileges are addressed.

Dues and Service Fees

In bargaining with employees, unions seek to gain provisions that require all employees either to join the association or pay fees for its services. Since a union must represent all individuals in the bargaining unit, it is argued that such provisions are necessary to eliminate "free riders"—the individuals who receive the benefits of the union's work without paying the dues for membership. Union security provisions take several forms. The *closed shop*, requiring an employer to hire only union members, does not exist in the public sector and is unlawful in the private sector under the National Labor Relations Act and the Taft-Hartley amendments. The *union shop* agreement requires an employee to join the union within a designated period of time after employment to retain a position. Even though union shop agreements are prevalent in the private sector, they are not authorized

[72]Jones v. Wrangell Sch. Dist., 696 P.2d 677, 680 (Alaska 1985). *See* Sch. Comm. v. Johnston Fed'n of Teachers, 652 A.2d 976 (R.I. 1995) (finding that the collective bargaining contract did not provide for arbitration of nonrenewal decisions and further that under state law, the school board did not have the power to negotiate this decision).

[73]Savage Educ. Ass'n v. Trs., 692 P.2d 1237 (Mont. 1984).

[74]Union River Valley Teachers Ass'n v. Lamoine Sch. Comm., 748 A.2d 990 (Me. 2000); *see also* Clark Cnty. Sch. Dist. v. Riley, 14 P.3d 22 (Nev. 2000) (finding that teacher's termination was subject to statutory law and thus could be reviewed by the court; there was no agreement to submit postprobationary actions to arbitration); Juniata-Mifflin Cntys. Area Vocational-Tech. Sch. v. Corbin, 691 A.2d 924 (Pa. 1997) (upholding arbitrator's determination that the language of the negotiated agreement evidenced intent to incorporate the statutory code, thus rendering teacher dismissal subject to grievance arbitration).

by most public sector laws and are limited or proscribed in a number of states under "right-to-work" laws.[75] The security provisions most frequently found in the public sector are *agency shop* and *fair share* agreements—terms that often are used interchangeably. An agency shop provision requires an employee to pay union dues but does not mandate membership, while a fair share arrangement requires a nonmember simply to pay a service fee to cover the cost of bargaining activities.

Nonunion teachers have challenged mandatory fees as a violation of their First Amendment speech and association rights. The Supreme Court, however, has held that the payment of fair share fees by public employees is constitutional. In *Abood v. Detroit Board of Education*, the Court rejected the nonunion members' First Amendment claims, noting the importance of ensuring labor peace and eliminating "free riders."[76] Nonetheless, the Court concluded that employees could not be compelled to contribute to the support of ideological causes they may oppose as a condition of maintaining their employment as public school teachers. Accordingly, the fee for nonmember teachers who object to forced contributions to a union's political activities must be adjusted to eliminate costs not related to unions' collective bargaining functions.[77]

Under the *Abood* ruling, the nonunion employee bears the burden to object to the union's use of the agency fee,[78] and the union then must establish the proportionate service fee share related to employee representation. The Supreme Court noted the difficulty in drawing the line between collective bargaining activities and ideological activities unrelated to collective bargaining. In subsequent cases, the Supreme Court and other courts have attempted to define this dividing line as well as the procedural protections necessary to respond to nonmembers' objections.

In *Ellis v. Brotherhood of Railway, Airline, and Steamship Clerks*, a private sector case, the Supreme Court advanced a standard for determining which union expenditures can be assessed against objecting employees:

> The test must be whether the challenged expenditures are necessarily or reasonably incurred for the purpose of performing the duties of an exclusive representative of the employees in dealing with the employer on labor-management issues. Under this standard, objecting employees may be compelled to pay their fair share of not only the direct costs of negotiating and administering a collective-bargaining contract and of settling grievances and disputes, but also the expenses of activities or undertakings normally or reasonably employed to implement or effectuate the duties of the union as exclusive representative of the employees in the bargaining unit.[79]

In applying this test, the Court upheld the assessment of costs related to union conventions, social activities, and publications, but disallowed expenditures related to

[75]In 2012, Indiana and Michigan passed "right to work" laws that specifically declare that an individual's employment cannot be conditioned on joining a union or paying fees to a union. A strong movement fueled by anti-union sentiment can be seen across states with right to work legislation being pursued in Missouri; Maine, Minnesota, and New Hampshire have tabled bills at this point.

[76]431 U.S. 209 (1977).

[77]Under Title VII of the Civil Rights Act of 1964, an employee who objects to payment of a service fee on religious grounds must be allowed to substitute a contribution to a charitable organization.

[78]*Abood*, 431 U.S. 209. The Supreme Court ruled in 2007 that a state law requiring unions to obtain affirmative authorization from nonmembers prior to spending agency fees for election-related purposes is not unconstitutional. The state gave the unions the right to collect the fees and could also place limitations on the use. Davenport v. Wash. Educ. Ass'n, 551 U.S. 177 (2007).

[79]466 U.S. 435, 448 (1984).

organizing activities and litigation unrelated to negotiations, contract administration, and fair representation.

Later, in *Lehnert v. Ferris Faculty Association*, a Michigan public sector case,[80] the Supreme Court ruled that unions may not assess nonmembers for lobbying and other political activities that are unrelated to contract ratification or implementation, for litigation that does not involve the local bargaining unit, and for public relations efforts to enhance the image of the teaching profession. Significant for unions, however, was the recognition that contributions to the state and national affiliates are chargeable expenditures even in the absence of a "direct and tangible impact" on the local bargaining unit.

The constitutionality of union procedures adopted to respond to nonmembers who object to the fair share fee continues to create debate. Generally, after a nonmember raises an objection, unions have provided a rebate of the portion of the fee unrelated to bargaining activities. In the *Ellis* decision, however, the Supreme Court found a *pure rebate* procedure inadequate. Characterizing this approach as an "involuntary loan," the Court stated that "by exacting and using full dues, then refunding months later the portion that it was not allowed to exact in the first place, the union effectively charges the employees for activities that are outside the scope of the statutory authorization."[81] Because other alternatives such as advance reduction of dues and escrow accounts exist, the Court found even temporary use of dissenters' funds impermissible.

In *Chicago Teachers' Union, Local No. 1 v. Hudson*, the Supreme Court provided further guidance in determining the adequacy of union procedural safeguards to protect nonmember employees' constitutional rights in the apportionment and assessment of representation fees. According to the Court, constitutional requirements for the collection of an agency fee include "an adequate explanation of the basis for the fee, a reasonably prompt opportunity to challenge the amount of the fee before an impartial decision maker, and an escrow for the amounts reasonably in dispute while such challenges are pending."[82] The contested Chicago union's plan included an advance reduction of dues, but it was found to be flawed because nonmembers were required to file an objection in order to receive any information about the calculation of the proportionate share, and they were not provided sufficient information to judge the appropriateness of the fee. The Court held that adequate disclosure required more than identification of expenditures that did not benefit objecting employees; reasons had to be provided for assessment of the fair share. The Court went further than the *Ellis* prohibition on a pure rebate procedure and held that, even if an advance reduction is made, any additional amounts in dispute must be placed in escrow. Subsequently, most federal appellate courts have found that escrow schemes adequately protect an individual's constitutional rights.[83]

The adequacy of unions' financial reporting practices, as required in *Hudson*, has been contested. According to the Supreme Court, financial disclosure must be adequate or sufficient, not an exhaustive and detailed list of all expenditures. The Court specifically

[80]500 U.S. 507 (1991).

[81]*Ellis*, 466 U.S. at 444.

[82]475 U.S. 292, 310 (1986).

[83]*See, e.g.*, Grunwald v. San Bernardino City Unified Sch. Dist., 994 F.2d 1370 (9th Cir. 1993); Gibson v. Fla. Bar, 906 F.2d 624 (11th Cir. 1990). *But see* Tavernor v. Ill. Fed'n of Teachers, 226 F.3d 842 (7th Cir. 2000) (ruling that collecting 100 percent of the union dues from nonmembers and placing the funds in an escrow account was impermissible when the association's calculation showed that fair share generally was about 85 percent of full dues).

stated in *Hudson* that the union must provide enough detail to enable nonmembers to make an informed decision about the "propriety of the union's fee."[84] The Sixth Circuit held that this does not require unions to provide financial information audited at the "highest" available level of audit services.[85] In that case, the court concluded that the union's financial disclosure, including budgets, audited financial statements, and audited supplemental schedules of the state and national associations, was constitutionally adequate. Other courts have emphasized that although a formal audit may not be required, unions, regardless of size, must provide independent verification of expenses incurred.[86]

In recent years, questions have arisen about limitations on unions' expenditures to influence electoral outcomes with nonunion members' fees. The state of Washington authorized public sector unions to negotiate agency shop arrangements, but specified that any expenditure of nonunion members' fees for election purposes or for the operation of a political committee required the affirmative authorization of the nonmember. The union challenged the state's restriction as a violation of the First Amendment. In finding no constitutional violation, the Supreme Court noted that the state had given the union "this extraordinary power" to compel employees to pay fees and had placed a reasonable condition related to nonmembers' payments.[87] The union was still free to spend its funds for election-related purposes. Similarly, Idaho's Right to Work Act, which prohibits payroll deductions for political activities, was challenged as impermissible because it singled out political speech based on its content.[88] Disagreeing, the Supreme Court stated that the government must accommodate speech in some contexts but certainly is not required to assist in subsidizing particular views.[89] The Court further commented: "Idaho does not suppress political speech but simply declines to promote it through public employer checkoffs for political activities."[90]

Although the Supreme Court has upheld fair share arrangements, they may not be permitted under some state laws. The Maine high court held that forced payment of dues was "tantamount to coercion toward membership."[91] The Maine statute ensures employees the right to join a union *voluntarily*, and the court interpreted this provision as including the right to *refrain* from joining. Similarly, the Vermont Supreme Court held that fees were prohibited under the Vermont Labor Relations for Teachers Act, which specified that teachers have the right to join or not to join, assist, or participate in a labor organization.[92]

[84]*Hudson*, 475 U.S. at 306; *see also* Knox v. Serv. Emps. Int'l Union, 132 S. Ct. 2277 (2012) (finding that the union infringed on nonmembers' First Amendment rights by imposing an additional mandatory special fee for political purposes; such an assessment requires a fresh *Hudson* notice and affirmative consent from nonmembers).

[85]Gwirtz v. Ohio Educ. Ass'n, 887 F.2d 678 (6th Cir. 1989).

[86]*See, e.g.*, Otto v. Penn. State Educ. Ass'n-NEA, 330 F.3d 125 (3d Cir. 2003); Harik v. Cal. Teachers Ass'n, 326 F.2d 1042 (9th Cir. 2003).

[87]Davenport v. Wash. Educ. Ass'n, 551 U.S. 177, 184 (2007).

[88]Idaho Code §§ 44-2601–44-2605, § 44-2004 (2012). Political activities are defined as "electoral activities, independent expenditures, or expenditures made to any candidate, political party, political action committee, or political issues committee or in support of or against any ballot initiative." *Id.* § 44-2602(1)(e).

[89]Ysursa v. Pocatello Educ. Ass'n, 555 U.S. 353 (2009).

[90]*Id.* at 361.

[91]Churchill v. Sch. Adm'r Dist. No. 49 Teachers Ass'n, 380 A.2d 186 (Me. 1977).

[92]Weissenstein v. Burlington Bd. of Sch. Comm'rs, 543 A.2d 691 (Vt. 1988). *But see* Nashua Teachers Union v. Nashua Sch. Dist., 707 A.2d 448 (N.H. 1998) (interpreting state law that permits negotiation of *other terms and conditions of employment* as authorizing agency fees to promote labor peace; rejecting the argument that the fees were an unfair labor practice encouraging union membership).

Representation fees do not violate the Federal Constitution and have been upheld in most states, but legal controversy surrounds enforcement of the provisions. Some collective bargaining agreements require employers to discharge teachers who refuse to pay the fees. In Pennsylvania, an appellate court overturned the dismissal of two teachers, stating that refusal to pay dues did not constitute persistent and willful violation of the school laws to justify dismissal.[93] Several courts have attempted to reconcile labor laws that authorize the negotiation of fair share fees as a condition of employment with tenure laws that permit dismissal only for specified causes. The Supreme Court of Michigan ruled that the state labor law prevails when it conflicts with another statute.[94] Accordingly, a tenured teacher who fails to pay the agency service fee can be discharged without resort to procedural requirements of the teacher tenure law.

Exclusive Privileges

The designated employee bargaining representative gains security through negotiating exclusive rights or privileges such as dues checkoff, the use of the school mail systems, and access to school facilities. Although exclusive arrangements strengthen the majority union and may make it difficult for minority unions to survive, courts often support these provisions as a means of promoting labor peace and ensuring efficient operation of the school system.

DUES CHECKOFF. The exclusive privilege most often found in collective bargaining contracts is dues checkoff, a provision that authorizes employers to deduct union dues and other fees when authorized by employees. Over half of the states with public employee bargaining laws specify dues checkoff as a mandatory subject for bargaining. The Supreme Court, however, has held that employee unions do not have a constitutional right to payroll deductions.[95] The Fourth Circuit ruled that state legislation permitting payroll deductions for charitable organizations but not labor unions was not an infringement of the First Amendment; the law did not deny the union members the right to associate, speak, publish, recruit members, or express their views.[96] Unless prohibited by state law, most courts have upheld negotiated agreements between the designated bargaining representative and the employer that deny rival unions checkoff rights.

State laws also may place other restrictions on unions' request for the use of the school district's payroll deduction system. The Michigan Education Association (MEA) entered into agreements with school districts across the state that required the districts to administrator a payroll deduction plan for members to contribute to its political action committee (MEA-PAC). The deductions were challenged as a violation of the Michigan Campaign Finance Act, which prohibits public entities from using any public funds to make a contribution or expenditure for political purposes.[97] The Michigan Supreme Court declared that the payroll deductions to MEA-PAC were prohibited because they

[93]Langley v. Uniontown Area Sch. Dist., 367 A.2d 736 (Pa. Commw. Ct. 1977). *But see* Belhumeur v. Labor Relations Comm'n, 589 N.E.2d 352 (Mass. App. Ct. 1992) (affirming the five-day suspension of three teachers who refused to remit an agency service fee; teachers did not follow procedures for protesting the fee).
[94]Bd. of Educ. v. Parks, 335 N.W.2d 641 (Mich. 1983).
[95]City of Charlotte v. Local 660, Int'l Ass'n of Firefighters, 426 U.S. 283 (1976).
[96]S.C. Educ. Ass'n v. Campbell, 883 F.2d 1251 (4th Cir. 1989).
[97]Mich. Educ. Ass'n v. Sec'y of State, 801 N.W.2d 35 (Mich. 2011); *see also* Mich. Comp. Laws § 169.257(1) (2012).

constituted a *contribution* as well as an *expenditure* in support of the MEA-PAC's partisan political activities related to elections and legislative and policy initiatives.

USE OF SCHOOL MAIL FACILITIES. Often, unions negotiate *exclusive* access to the internal school mail system, which denies rival unions the right to use teachers' mailboxes. The Supreme Court clarified the constitutionality of exclusive use in an Indiana case where the negotiated agreement between the exclusive bargaining representative and an Indiana school board denied all rival unions access to the interschool mail system and teacher mailboxes.[98] One of the rival unions challenged the agreement as a violation of First and Fourteenth Amendment rights. The Supreme Court upheld the arrangement, reasoning that the First Amendment does not require "equivalent access to all parts of a school building in which some form of communicative activity occurs."[99] The Court concluded that the school mail facility was not a public forum for communication, and thereby its use could be restricted to official school business. The fact that several community groups (e.g., Scouts, civic organizations) used the school mail system did not create a public forum. The Court noted that, even if such access by community groups created a limited public forum, access would be extended only to similar groups—not to labor organizations. The Court's emphasis on the availability of alternative channels of communication (e.g., bulletin boards and meeting facilities), however, indicates that total exclusion of rival unions would not be permitted.

The Fifth Circuit subsequently ruled, and the Supreme Court affirmed, that denial of access to the school mail system to all teacher organizations did not violate the First Amendment when other channels of communication were available.[100] The Court, however, found unconstitutional a policy prohibiting individual teachers from discussing employee organizations during nonclass time or using the internal mail system or bulletin boards to mention employee organizations. Such limitations on an individual employee's expression would be permissible only if a threat of material and substantial disruption were shown.

Although a school board may provide access to mailboxes and school facilities, a school board cannot deliver a union's mail through its interschool mail delivery system. Under the federal Private Express Statutes,[101] an employer is permitted to deliver only mail related to its business through the "letters of the carrier" exception to the federal law. In 1988, the United States Supreme Court held that this exception did not permit a union attempting to organize faculty in a university to use the university's internal mail system; the activity did not relate to the university's "current business."[102] Subsequently, the Seventh Circuit ruled that the delivery of mail of the exclusive bargaining representative

[98]Perry Educ. Ass'n v. Perry Local Educators' Ass'n, 460 U.S. 37 (1983); *see also* San Leandro Teachers Ass'n v. Governing Bd., 209 P.3d 73 (Cal. 2009) (ruling that state law prohibits unions from using school mailboxes to distribute political endorsement information; the contested law does not violate the state and federal constitutions); Unified Sch. Dist. No. 233 v. Kan. Ass'n of Am. Educators, 64 P.3d 372 (Kan. 2003) (finding that a school district could not permit a rival professional association to distribute its membership materials through the district's internal mail system when the collective bargaining representative had negotiated exclusive use of the mail system).

[99]*Perry Educ. Ass'n*, 460 U.S. at 44.

[100]Tex. State Teachers Ass'n v. Garland Indep. Sch. Dist., 777 F.2d 1046 (5th Cir. 1985), *aff'd*, 470 U.S. 801 (1986).

[101]18 U.S.C. § 1693 (2012); 39 U.S.C. § 601 (2012). These laws establish a postal monopoly and, in general, prohibit the private delivery of letters without payment to the United States Postal Service.

[102]Univ. of Cal. v. Pub. Emp't Relations Bd., 485 U.S. 589 (1988).

did not relate to the school's current business, but rather to the union's business.[103] The case was remanded for further review to determine if some correspondence related to joint school/union committees could be characterized as the school's business.

EXCLUSIVE RECOGNITION. In most states, school boards negotiate only with the designated bargaining representative. Under this exclusive recognition provision, other unions and teacher groups can be denied the right to engage in official exchanges with an employer. The Supreme Court has held that nonmembers of a bargaining unit or members who disagree with the views of the representative do not have a constitutional right "to force the government to listen to their views."[104] The Court concluded that a Minnesota statute requiring employers to "meet and confer" only with the designated bargaining representative did not violate other employees' speech or associational rights as public employees or as citizens since these sessions were not a public forum. According to the Court, "the Constitution does not grant to members of the public generally a right to be heard by public bodies making decisions of policy."[105]

Nonetheless, if a public forum, such as a school board meeting, is involved, a nonunion teacher has a constitutional right to address the public employer, even on a subject of negotiation. The Supreme Court concluded in a Wisconsin case that a nonunion teacher had the right to express concerns to the school board.[106] In this case, negotiation between the board and union had reached a deadlock on the issue of an agency shop provision. A nonunion teacher, representing a minority group of teachers, addressed the board at a regular public meeting and requested postponement of a decision until further study of the issue. The Court reasoned that the teacher was not attempting to negotiate, but merely to speak on an important issue before the board—a right any citizen possesses.

While union security provisions such as fair share arrangements and exclusive use of specific school facilities can be negotiated, nonunion teachers' constitutional rights cannot be infringed. Teachers must be ensured an effective mechanism for challenging financial contributions that might be used to support ideological causes or political activities to which they object. If specific communication channels for nonmembers are restricted through the negotiation process, alternative options must remain open.

GRIEVANCES

Disputes concerning employee rights under the terms of a collective bargaining agreement are resolved through the negotiated grievance procedures, which generally must be exhausted before pursuing review by state labor relations boards or courts.[107] The exhaustion requirement sustains the integrity of the collective bargaining process, encouraging

[103]Ft. Wayne Cmty. Schs. v. Ft. Wayne Educ. Ass'n, 977 F.2d 358 (7th Cir. 1992).

[104]Minn. State Bd. for Cmty. Colls. v. Knight, 465 U.S. 271, 283 (1984); *see also* Sherrard Cmty. Unit Sch. Dist. v. Ill. Educ. Labor Relations Bd., 696 N.E.2d 833 (Ill. App. Ct. 1998) (ruling that a school board's direct negotiation with a nonunion teacher regarding her proposed involuntary reassignment was an unfair labor practice).

[105]*Knight*, 465 U.S. at 283.

[106]City of Madison v. Wis. Emp't Relations Comm'n, 429 U.S. 167 (1976).

[107]*See, e.g.*, Reynolds v. Sch. Dist. No. 1, 69 F.3d 1523 (10th Cir. 1995); Milton Educ. Ass'n v. Milton Bd. of Sch. Trs., 759 A.2d 479 (Vt. 2000); Hokama v. Univ. of Haw., 990 P.2d 1150 (Haw. 1999).

the orderly and efficient settlement of disputes at the local level. Grievance procedures usually provide for a neutral third party, an arbitrator, to conduct a hearing and render a decision. *Grievance* arbitration, which addresses enforcement of rights under the contract, is distinct from *interest* arbitration, which may take place in resolving an impasse in the bargaining process.[108]

Depending on state law and the negotiated contract, the decision in grievance arbitration may be advisory or binding. Public employers, adhering to the doctrine of the sovereign power of government, have been reluctant to agree to procedures that might result in a loss of public authority. Allowing grievance procedures to include final decision making by a third party significantly lessens a school board's power, effectively equating the positions of the teachers' organization and the school board. Nevertheless, as bargaining has expanded, legislative bodies have favored binding arbitration as a means of settling labor disputes. About half of the states have enacted laws permitting school boards to negotiate grievance procedures with binding arbitration, and several states require binding arbitration as the final step in the grievance procedure.[109] With the widespread use of grievance arbitration, it is one of the most contested areas in collective bargaining. Suits have challenged the arbitrator's authority to render decisions in specific disputes as well as the authority to provide certain remedies.

One of the primary issues in establishing a grievance procedure is the definition of a grievance—that is, what can be grieved. In the private sector, a grievance is usually defined as any dispute between the employer and the employee. Teachers' grievances, on the other hand, are generally limited to controversies arising from the interpretation or application of the negotiated contract. Arbitrability of a dispute then depends on whether the school board and union agreed to settle the issue by arbitration, or whether the agreement shows such intent.[110] Arbitrators generally make decisions as to arbitrability, and courts presume that the decisions are valid when derived from the construction of the negotiated agreement, thus making contractual language central to any determination of arbitrability.[111] The Supreme Court of Iowa noted that because the law favors arbitration, the court's duty is to construe the agreement broadly, recognizing arbitrability "unless it may be said with positive assurance that the arbitration clause is not susceptible to an interpretation that covers the asserted dispute. Doubts should be resolved in favor of coverage."[112]

[108]As noted in the next section, binding interest arbitration has met resistance in the public sector as a method to resolve negotiation impasses. If it were permitted regarding monetary issues, school boards would relinquish control of the power to determine the budget.

[109]Among the few states requiring binding grievance arbitration are Alaska, Florida, Illinois, Minnesota, and Pennsylvania. *See In re* Silverstein, 37 A.3d 382 (N.H. 2012) (finding that the state labor board had no authority to review a grievance under a bargaining contract that contained a final and binding grievance process within the district).

[110]*See, e.g.*, Classified Emps. Ass'n v. Matanuska-Susitna Borough Sch. Dist., 204 P.3d 347 (Alaska 2009); Bd. of Educ. v. Wallingford Educ. Ass'n, 858 A.2d 762 (Conn. 2004); Mount Adams Sch. Dist. v. Cook, 81 P.3d 111 (Wash. 2003).

[111]*See* Linden Bd. of Educ. v Linden Educ. Ass'n, 997 A.2d 185, 192 (N.J. 2010) (noting that New Jersey courts "repeatedly consult" federal jurisprudence for guidance in arbitration matters).

[112]Postville Cmty. Sch. Dist. v. Billmeyer, 548 N.W.2d 558, 560 (Iowa 1996) (quoting Sergeant Bluff-Luton Educ. Ass'n v. Sergeant Bluff-Luton Cmty. Sch. Dist., 282 N.W.2d 144, 147–48 (Iowa 1979)); *see also* E. Associated Coal Corp. v. United Mine Workers, 531 U.S. 57 (2000) (reaffirming the strong federal policy of judicial deference to arbitration in labor disputes).

A recent Supreme Court case adds another dimension to what can be arbitrated. In *14 Penn Plaza LLC v. Pyett*, a group of employees filed an age discrimination claim against their employer in federal court under the Age Discrimination in Employment Act (ADEA) while the union pursued the claim through the arbitration process in the collective bargaining contract.[113] The employer argued that the negotiated contract specified that all age discrimination claims must be resolved through arbitration, thereby, preventing employees from seeking judicial redress. Both the federal district court and Second Circuit found the arbitration clause to be unenforceable, emphasizing that employees cannot be deprived of federal rights created by Congress.[114] Reversing the courts below, the Supreme Court, however, held that "a collective-bargaining agreement that clearly and unmistakably requires union members to arbitrate ADEA claims is enforceable as a matter of federal law."[115] The Court found no indication in the legislative history of the ADEA that precludes such an agreement.

Disputes that have been held to be arbitrable based on specific negotiated contracts include unsatisfactory teacher performance, assignment of an additional class load, validity of a teacher's contract, contribution to health insurance premiums, involuntary transfer of a teacher, and just cause for teacher termination.[116] Although a range of issues has been found to be arbitrable, courts have ruled that issues related to nondelegable policy matters under state law are outside the scope of arbitration. For example, impermissible issues have involved tenure decisions, employee dismissal, reappointment of nontenured teachers, evaluation of teacher qualifications, transfer of teachers, reinstatement of an employee, approval or denial of a charter school petition, curriculum content, teacher discipline, and provision of health services to special education students.[117] Also, issues that are specifically excluded in the contract cannot be submitted to arbitration.

Moreover, arbitration awards or remedies have been challenged. Again, as with arbitrability, courts have adopted a narrow scope of review, with many courts presuming the validity of awards. The deference afforded an arbitrator's award is evident from the Supreme Court's statement that "unless the arbitral decision does not 'draw its essence from the collective bargaining agreement,' a court is bound to enforce the award and is not entitled to review the merits of the contract dispute."[118] So long as an

[113]556 U.S. 247 (2009). Since this challenge related to a federal law, Congress can amend the law if it disagrees with the Court's interpretation.

[114]Pyett v. Pa. Bldg. Co., No. 04 Civ. 7536 (NRB), 2006 U.S. Dist. LEXIS 35952 (S.D.N.Y. May 31, 2006), *aff'd*, 498 F.3d 88 (2d Cir. 2007).

[115]*14 Penn Plaza*, 556 U.S. at 274.

[116]*See, e.g.*, Kalispell Educ. Ass'n v. Bd. of Trustees, 255 P.3d 199 (Mont. 2011) (teacher contract); *In re* Haessig and Oswego City Sch. Dist., 936 N.Y.S.2d 442 (App. Div. 2011) (teacher class loads); *Linden Bd. of Educ.*, 997 A.2d 185 (just cause for termination); *In re* Bd. of Educ. & Schenectady Fed'n of Teachers, 876 N.Y.S.2d 562 (App. Div. 2009) (compensation for attending additional evening meeting); Sch. Comm. v. United Educators of Pittsfield, 784 N.E.2d 11 (Mass. 2003) (involuntary transfer of teacher); *In re* Bd. of Educ., 710 N.E.2d 1064 (N.Y. 1999) (health insurance).

[117]*See, e.g.*, United Teachers of L.A. v. L.A. Unified Sch. Dist., 278 P.3d 1204 (Cal. 2012) (charter school petition); Westmoreland Intermediate Unit #7 v. Westmoreland Intermediate Unit #7 Classroom Assistants Ass'n, 977 A.2d 1205 (Pa. Commw. Ct. 2009) (reinstatement of drug user); Woonsocket Teachers' Guild v. Woonsocket Sch. Comm., 770 A.2d 834 (R.I. 2001) (health services for special education students); Sch. Comm. v. Peabody Fed'n of Teachers, 748 N.E.2d 992 (Mass. App. Ct. 2001) (teacher transfers); Chi. Sch. Reform Bd. of Trs. v. Ill. Educ. Labor Relations Bd., 721 N.E.2d 676 (Ill. App. Ct. 1999) (dismissal of teachers); Sch. Admin. Dist. No. 58 v. Mount Abram Teachers Ass'n, 704 A.2d 349 (Me. 1997) (curriculum content); Raines v. Indep. Sch. Dist. No. 6, 796 P.2d 303 (Okla. 1990) (teacher discipline).

[118]W. R. Grace & Co. v. Local 759, United Rubber Workers of Am., 461 U.S. 757, 764 (1983).

arbitrator's award can be interpreted as rationally derived from the language and context of the agreement, courts have found that it "draws its essence" from the agreement.[119] According to the Wisconsin Supreme Court, an arbitrator's award will not be vacated unless it "perversely misconstrues" the negotiated agreement.[120] Furthermore, courts do not interfere with arbitration awards simply because they would have provided a different remedy.[121]

NEGOTIATION IMPASSE

An impasse occurs in bargaining when an agreement cannot be reached and neither party will compromise. When negotiations reach such a stalemate, several options are available for resolution: mediation, fact finding, and arbitration. As discussed in the final section of this chapter, the most effective means for resolving negotiation impasse—the strike—is not legally available to the majority of public employees. Most comprehensive state statutes address impasse procedures, with provisions ranging from allowing impasse procedures to be negotiated to mandating detailed steps that must be followed. Alternatives most frequently employed to resolve impasse are identified below.

Mediation is often the first step to reopening negotiations. A neutral third party assists both sides in finding a basis for agreement. The mediator serves as a facilitator rather than a decision maker, thus enabling the school board's representative and the teachers' association jointly to reach an agreement. Mediation may be optional or required by law; the mediator is selected by the negotiation teams or, upon request, appointed by a public employee relations board.

Failure to reach agreement through mediation frequently results in fact finding (often called advisory arbitration). The process may be mandated by law or may be entered into by mutual agreement of both parties. Fact finding involves a third party investigating the causes for the dispute, collecting facts and testimony to clarify the dispute, and formulating a judgment. Because of the advisory nature of the process, proposed solutions are not binding on either party. However, since fact-finding reports are made available to the public, they provide an impetus to settle a contract that is not present in mediation.

In a number of states, the final step in impasse procedures is fact finding, which may leave both parties without a satisfactory solution. A few states permit a third alternative—binding interest arbitration. This process is similar to fact finding except that the decision of the arbitrator, related to the terms of the negotiated agreement, is binding on

[119]*See, e.g.*, Sch. Comm. v. Hull Teachers Ass'n, 872 N.E.2d 767 (Mass. App. Ct. 2007); Danville Area Sch. Dist. v. Danville Area Educ. Ass'n, 754 A.2d 1255 (Pa. 2000); *see also* Merrick Union Free Sch. Dist. v. Merrick Faculty Ass'n, 928 N.Y.S.2d 60 (App. Div. 2011) (holding under the contract agreement the arbitrator could only direct the parties to negotiate an issue, not prescribe relief); *In re* Liberty Cent. Sch. Dist., 808 N.Y.S.2d 445 (App. Div. 2006) (finding arbitrator's award of back pay and health insurance costs in nonrenewal of teacher to be irrational); Sch. Comm. v. Hanover Teachers Ass'n, 761 N.E.2d 918 (Mass. 2002) (finding that arbitrator exceeded his authority when he did not follow the plain language of the agreement); Rochester Sch. Dist. v. Rochester Educ. Ass'n, 747 A.2d 971 (Pa. Commw. Ct. 2000) (finding arbitrator's decision that school board must work with association in developing all policies, such as standards for student honor roll in this case, did not draw its essence from the agreement; the board had preserved the right to develop inherent managerial policies when it signed the negotiated agreement).

[120]Baldwin-Woodville Area Sch. Dist. v. W. Cent. Educ. Ass'n, 766 N.W.2d 591, 597 (Wis. 2009).

[121]*See, e.g.*, Kalispell Educ. Ass'n v. Bd. of Trustees, 255 P.3d 199 (Mont. 2011); Union River Valley Teacher Ass'n v. Lamoine Sch. Comm., 748 A.2d 990 (Me. 2000).

both parties. States that permit binding arbitration often place restrictions on its use.[122] For example, Ohio, Oregon, and Rhode Island permit binding arbitration on matters of mutual consent;[123] Maine allows binding arbitration on all items except salaries, pensions, and insurance.[124]

It is generally agreed that mediation and fact finding, because of their advisory nature, do not provide the most effective means for resolving negotiation disputes. Since strikes are prohibited among public employees in most states, conditional binding arbitration has been considered a viable alternative in resolving deadlocks. Although a greater balance of power is achieved between the school board and the teachers' association with binding arbitration, public sector employers, who often view it as an illegal delegation of power, have not readily embraced it. As a result, interest arbitration generally has occurred in the educational setting only on a voluntary or conditional basis.

If a collective bargaining agreement expires while the employer and the union are attempting to reach an agreement, the status quo must be maintained. Adhering to this principle means that all terms and conditions of employment remain in effect during the continuing bargaining process.[125] Unless restricted by state law, the majority of courts have held that this means the continuance of annual salary increments for teachers.[126] After the exhaustion of all required impasse resolution procedures, generally an employer can implement its best and last offer,[127] or state law may allow employees to strike in a few instances.

STRIKES

While it is argued that there can be no true collective bargaining without the right to withhold services, which characterizes the bargaining process in the private sector, most teachers are prohibited from striking by either state statute or common law. In those

[122]To avoid strikes among certain groups of public employees, interest arbitration may be mandatory. *See, e.g.*, Ohio Rev. Code § 4117.14 (D)(l) (2012).

[123]Ohio Rev. Code § 4117.14 (C) (2012); Or. Rev. Stat. 243 § 712 (2)(e) (2012); R.I. Gen. Laws 28 § 9.3-9 (2012).

[124]Me. Rev. Stat. 26 § 979.D(4)(D) (2012).

[125]*See* NLRB v. Katz, 369 U.S. 736 (1962) (establishing in the private sector that unilateral changes in terms and conditions of employment are unlawful; this principle has been applied broadly in the public sector); Cent. City Educ. Ass'n v. Merrick Cnty. Sch. Dist., 783 N.W.2d 600 (Neb. 2010) (finding the payment for unused sick leave and personal time to be part of the contract continuance clause); Coatesville Area Sch. Dist. v. Coatesville Area Teachers' Ass'n, 978 A.2d 413 (Pa. Commw. Ct. 2009) (ruling that school district could not unilaterally change provisions related to extracurricular activities at contract expiration; they were subject to negotiation in the contract). *But see* Providence Teachers Union v. Providence Sch. Bd., 689 A.2d 388 (R.I. 1997) (deciding that the grievance arbitration provisions in the expired contract were not applicable to disputes arising after expiration of the agreement and unrelated to vested rights in the expired contract).

[126]*See, e.g.*, Jackson Cnty. Coll. Classified & Tech. Ass'n v. Jackson Cnty. Coll., 468 N.W.2d 61 (Mich. Ct. App. 1991); *In re* Cobleskill Cent. Sch. Dist., 481 N.Y.S.2d 795 (App. Div. 1984). *But see* Neshaminy Fed'n of Teachers Local Union v. Pa. Labor Relations Bd., 986 A.2d 908 (Pa. Commw. Ct. 2009) (holding that maintaining the status quo freezes wage increases for longevity and academic credits); Bd. of Trs. v. Assoc. Colt Staff, 659 A.2d 842 (Me. 1995) (finding that maintenance of the status quo is freezing salaries at the level existing at the expiration of the contract); *In re* Alton Sch. Dist., 666 A.2d 937 (N.H. 1995) (ruling that under state law, teachers receive the annual salary increment for experience at the expiration of the negotiated contract only if the contract contains an automatic renewal clause; however, salary increases for additional training must be recognized and health benefits must be continued to maintain the status quo).

[127]*See, e.g.*, Kenmare Educ. Ass'n v. Kenmare Pub. Sch. Dist., 717 N.W.2d 603 (N.D. 2006); Ranta v. Eaton Rapids Pub. Schs., 721 N.W.2d 806 (Mich. Ct. App. 2006); *see also* Spearfish Educ. Ass'n v. Spearfish Sch. Dist., 780 N.W.2d 481 (S.D. 2010) (ruling that the last offer must be applied uniformly across all members; board's decision to apply the offer to selected members was a grievable offense).

states that have legislation granting public employees a limited right to strike,[128] certain conditions, specified by statute, must be met prior to the initiation of a work stoppage. Designated conditions vary but usually include: (1) the exhaustion of statutory mediation and fact-finding steps, (2) expiration of the contract, (3) elapse of a certain time period prior to commencing the strike, (4) written notice of the union's intent to strike, and (5) evidence that the strike will not constitute a danger to public health or safety. In contrast to the few states permitting strikes, most states with public employee collective bargaining statutes have specific "no-strike" provisions.[129]

Courts consistently have upheld "no-strike" laws and generally have denied the right to strike unless it has been affirmatively granted by the state.[130] Several early cases are still representative of the dominant judicial posture on public teachers' strikes. In a Connecticut case, the state high court stated that permitting teachers to strike could be equated with asserting that "they can deny the authority of government."[131] The court in this case denied teachers the right to strike, emphasizing that a teacher is an agent of the government, possessing a portion of the state's sovereignty. The Supreme Court of Indiana issued a restraining order against striking teachers, affirming the same public welfare rationale.[132] Addressing the legality of strikes, a New Jersey appellate court declared that legislative authorization for bargaining did not reflect the intent to depart from the common law rule prohibiting strikes by public employees.[133] In contrast to the prevailing common law position, the Louisiana high court declared strikes permissible for some public employees, including teachers. The court found under state law "an intent to afford public employees a system of organizational rights that parallels that afforded to employees in the private sector."[134]

A strike is more than simply a work stoppage; states define the term broadly to include a range of concerted activities such as work slowdowns, massive absences for "sick" days, and refusal to perform certain duties. For example, the Massachusetts high court found that refusal to perform customary activities, such as grading papers and preparing lesson plans after the end of the school day, constituted a strike.[135] A Missouri appellate

[128]A limited right to strike exists under state law for public employees in Alaska, Colorado, Hawaii, Illinois, Minnesota, Montana, Ohio, Oregon, Pennsylvania, and Vermont. Alaska law has been interpreted as prohibiting teachers from striking even though most other public employees are permitted to strike. Anchorage Educ. Ass'n v. Anchorage Sch. Dist., 648 P.2d 993 (Alaska 1982); *see also* Reichley v. N. Penn Sch. Dist., 626 A.2d 123 (Pa. 1993) (upholding constitutionality of the statute allowing strikes by public educators; the court noted that this is a policy consideration for the legislature rather than an issue for the judicial system); Martin v. Montezuma-Cortez Sch. Dist., 841 P.2d 237 (Colo. 1992) (interpreting Colorado's Industrial Relations Act to include a limited right to strike).

[129]*See* Mich. State AFL-CIO v. Emp't Relations Comm'n, 551 N.W.2d 165 (Mich. 1996) (upholding statutory prohibition on strikes protesting unfair labor practices; provision does not violate First Amendment free speech guarantee regardless of the employees' motivation for the strike).

[130]*See, e.g.*, Jefferson Cnty. Bd. of Educ. v. Jefferson Cnty. Educ. Ass'n, 393 S.E.2d 653 (W. Va.1990); Passaic Twp. Bd. of Educ. v. Passaic Twp. Educ. Ass'n, 536 A.2d 1276 (N.J. Super. Ct. App. Div. 1987).

[131]Norwalk Teachers Ass'n v. Bd. of Educ., 83 A.2d 482, 485 (Conn. 1951).

[132]Anderson Fed'n of Teachers v. Sch. City of Anderson, 251 N.E.2d 15 (Ind. 1969).

[133]Passaic Twp. Bd. of Educ. v. Passaic Twp. Educ. Ass'n, 536 A.2d 1276 (N.J. Super Ct. App. Div. 1987).

[134]Davis v. Henry, 555 So. 2d 457, 464–65 (La. 1990).

[135]Lenox Educ. Ass'n v. Labor Relations Comm'n, 471 N.E.2d 81 (Mass. 1984). Concerted activity may extend beyond activities related to the negotiation of the contract. *See* Cent. Sch. Dist. 13J v. Cent. Educ. Ass'n, 962 P.2d 763 (Or. Ct. App. 1998) (ruling that concerted activity to enforce the rights in a union contract is protected under state law; a teacher bringing a representative of his choice to a meeting that could have disciplinary consequences was such a protected activity).

court upheld the right of the St. Louis school superintendent to request documentation from 1,190 teachers that a "sick" day was not related to a labor dispute surrounding the negotiation of a new contract.[136] In the absence of documentation from the teachers, the school district could deny payment for the day.

State laws, in addition to prohibiting work stoppages, usually identify penalties for involvement in strikes. Such penalties can include withholding compensation for strike days, prohibiting salary increases for designated periods of time (e.g., one year), and dismissal. Penalties for illegal strikes also are imposed on unions. Sanctions may include fines, decertification of the union, and loss of certain privileges such as dues checkoff.[137]

Despite statutory prohibitions against strikes, many teachers, as well as other public employees, participate in work stoppages each year. Public employers can request a court injunction against teachers who threaten to strike or initiate such action. Most courts have granted injunctions, concluding, as did the Supreme Court of Alaska, that the "illegality of the strike is a sufficient harm to justify injunctive relief."[138] Failure of teachers and unions to comply with such a restraining order can result in charges of contempt of court, with resulting fines and/or imprisonment. For example, teachers in a Maryland school district who refused to obey an injunction were found guilty of criminal contempt.[139] In issuing an injunction, a New Jersey court ordered incarceration rather than monetary penalties for teachers who failed to return to work; the court noted that monetary fines had not been effective in the state in forcing teachers to return to work.[140] In South Bend, Indiana, refusal to comply with an injunction resulted in a contempt-of-court charge and fines totaling $200,000 against two unions.[141] Establishing the level of fines involves a consideration of factors such as the magnitude of the threatened harm and the association's financial condition. A Massachusetts appellate court remanded a case in which the trial court judge failed to consider relevant factors in imposing a $20,000 fine for each day the union refused to return to work.[142]

Even though the injunction has been the most effective response to strikes, courts have been reluctant to impose this sanction automatically. Other factors have been considered, such as whether the board bargained in good faith, whether the strike constituted a clear and present danger to public safety, and whether irreparable harm would result

[136]Franklin v. St. Louis Bd. of Educ., 904 S.W.2d 433 (Mo. Ct. App. 1995).

[137]*See, e.g.*, Buffalo Teachers Fed'n v. Helsby, 676 F.2d 28 (2d Cir. 1982); Nat'l Educ. Ass'n-S. Bend v. S. Bend Cmty. Sch. Corp., 655 N.E.2d 516 (Ind. Ct. App. 1995); E. Brunswick Bd. of Educ. v. E. Brunswick Educ. Ass'n, 563 A.2d 55 (N.J. Super. Ct. App. Div. 1989).

[138]Anchorage Educ. Ass'n v. Anchorage Sch. Dist., 648 P.2d 993, 998 (Alaska 1982); *see also* Carroll v. Ringgold Educ. Ass'n, 680 A.2d 1137 (Pa. 1996) (holding that an injunction could include provisions for court-monitored bargaining between the parties). *But see* Wilson v. Pulaski Ass'n of Classroom Teachers, 954 S.W.2d 221 (Ark. 1997) (requiring proof of irreparable harm to issue a preliminary injunction). In an Arkansas case, the Eighth Circuit also declined to issue an injunction requested by the school board to enforce a desegregation consent decree. The court did not find that its power to enforce the consent decree gave it authority to resolve other disputes arising in the district. Knight v. Pulaski Cnty. Special Sch. Dist., 112 F.3d 953 (8th Cir. 1997).

[139]Harford Cnty. Educ. Ass'n v. Bd. of Educ., 380 A.2d 1041 (Md. 1977).

[140]Bd. of Educ. v. Middletown Twp. Educ. Ass'n, 800 A.2d 286 (N.J. Super. Ct. App. Div. 2001).

[141]Nat'l Educ. Ass'n-S. Bend v. S. Bend Cmty. Sch. Corp., 655 N.E.2d 516 (Ind. Ct. App. 1995); *see also* Franklin Twp. Bd. of Educ. v. Quakertown Educ. Ass'n, 643 A.2d 34 (N.J. Super. Ct. App. Div. 1994) (holding that the school board could be awarded attorneys' fees and damages associated with a strike and that the trial court could impose additional monetary sanctions to pressure compliance with a court order to return to work).

[142]Labor Relations Comm'n v. Salem Teachers Union, 706 N.E.2d 1146 (Mass. App. Ct. 1999).

from the strike.[143] The Supreme Court of Arkansas ruled that the party requesting an injunction must "establish irreparable harm."[144] The court found this to be true regardless of whether the strike is illegal per se. Evidence required by school boards to demonstrate sufficient cause for an injunction has varied according to the legal jurisdiction and the interpretation of applicable state statutes.

The procedures required for dismissal of striking teachers have received judicial attention. Courts have held that due process procedures must be provided, but questions arise as to the nature and type of hearing that must be afforded. Reversing the Wisconsin Supreme Court, the U.S. Supreme Court ruled that a school board can serve as an impartial hearing panel. The Court maintained that the board's involvement did not overcome "the presumption of honesty and integrity in policymakers with decision-making power."[145] The Court further held that "permitting the board to make the decision at issue here preserves its control over school district affairs, leaves the balance of power in labor relations where the state legislature struck it, and assures that the decision whether to dismiss the teachers will be made by the body responsible for that decision under state law."[146] While noting that the Fourteenth Amendment guarantees each teacher procedural due process, the Supreme Court concluded that a hearing before the school board satisfies this requirement.

State legislatures and courts generally have refused to grant public school teachers the right to strike. Even in the few states where a limited right to strike has been gained, extensive restrictions have been placed on its use.[147] Teachers participating in an illegal strike are subject to court-imposed penalties and, in most states, to statutory penalties. Refusal of teachers to return to the classroom can result in dismissal.[148]

Conclusion

Because of the diversity in collective bargaining laws among states, legal principles with universal application are necessarily broad. Despite the uncertainty discussed earlier regarding public sector bargaining laws in the present political context, the following generalizations currently are applicable to most teachers.

1. Teachers have a constitutionally protected right to form and join a union.
2. Specific bargaining rights are conferred through state statutes or judicial interpretations of state constitutions, thus creating wide divergence in teachers' bargaining rights across states.
3. School boards are not required to bargain with employee organizations unless mandated to do so by state law.
4. Collective bargaining must be conducted "in good faith," which means that the school board and teachers' organization attempt to reach agreement without compulsion on either side to agree.

[143]*See, e.g.*, Jefferson Cnty. Bd. of Educ. v. Jefferson Cnty. Educ. Ass'n, 393 S.E.2d 653 (W. Va. 1990); Jersey Shore Area Sch. Dist. v. Jersey Shore Educ. Ass'n, 548 A.2d 1202 (Pa. 1988); Joint Sch. Dist. No. 1 v. Wis. Rapids Educ. Ass'n, 234 N.W.2d 289 (Wis. 1975).

[144]Wilson v. Pulaski Ass'n of Classroom Teachers, 954 S.W.2d 221, 224 (Ark. 1997).

[145]Hortonville Educ. Ass'n v. Hortonville Joint Sch. Dist., 426 U.S. 482, 497 (1976), *rev'g* 225 N.W.2d 658 (Wis. 1975).

[146]426 U.S. at 496.

[147]*See supra* text accompanying note 129.

[148]The National Labor Relations Act, in the private sector, preserves the employer's right to permanently replace economic strikers; this right offsets employees' right to strike. 29 U.S.C. § 151 (2012).

5. The scope of negotiations is generally defined as including wages, hours, and other terms and conditions of employment, such as teaching load, planning time, and lunch periods.
6. Governmental policy matters are not mandatorily bargainable but may be permissive subjects unless prohibited by law.
7. State legislation permitting the negotiation of a service fee (fair share) provision for nonunion members is constitutional; however, if a public employee objects to supporting specific ideological or political causes, the fee must be adjusted to reflect chargeable bargaining costs.
8. To collect a fair share fee from a nonunion teacher who raises First Amendment objections, the union must provide adequate information regarding the basis of the fee, independent verification of union expenses, procedural safeguards to ensure a prompt response to employees who may object, and an escrow account for challenged amounts.
9. Unions may constitutionally negotiate exclusive privileges such as the use of the school mail and dues checkoff; other communication options, however, must be available to rival unions.
10. State laws that prohibit payroll deductions for politically related activities do not violate the unions' protected speech rights.
11. Nonunion teachers have the right to express a viewpoint before the school board on an issue under negotiation between the board and union.
12. Negotiated agreements generally include a grievance procedure for resolving conflicts that arise under the terms of the contract; the procedures may provide for either advisory or binding arbitration, depending on state law.
13. Impasse procedures for public sector bargaining are generally limited to mediation and fact finding, with the public employer retaining final decision-making authority.
14. Teacher strikes, except in limited situations in a few states, are illegal and punishable by dismissal, fines, and imprisonment.

MyEdLeadershipLab™

Go to Topic 9: *Terms and Conditions in Employment and Termination* on the MyEdLeadershipLab™ site (www.myedleadershiplab.com) for *Public School Law: Teachers' and Students' Rights*, Seventh Edition, where you can

- Find learning outcomes for *Terms and Conditions in Employment and Termination* along with the national standards that connect to these outcomes.
- Complete Assignments and Activities that can help you more deeply understand the chapter content.
- Apply and practice your understanding of the core skills identified in the chapter with the Building Leadership Skills unit.
- Prepare yourself for professional certification with a Practice for Certification quiz.

Tort Liability

From Chapter 13 of *Public School Law: Teachers' and Students' Rights*, Seventh Edition. Martha M. McCarthy, Nelda H. Cambron-McCabe, Suzanne E. Eckes.

Tort Liability

MyEdLeadershipLab™

Visit the MyEdLeadershipLab™ site for *Public School Law: Teachers' and Students' Rights*, Seventh Edition, to enhance your understanding of chapter concepts. You'll have the opportunity to practice your skills through video- and case-based Assignments and Activities as well as Building Leadership Skills units, and to prepare for your certification exam with Practice for Certification quizzes.

Tort law offers civil rather than criminal remedies to individuals for harm caused by the unreasonable conduct of others. A tort is described as a civil wrong, independent of breach of contract, for which a court will provide relief in the form of damages. Tort cases primarily involve state law and are grounded in the fundamental premise that individuals are liable for the consequences of their conduct that result in injury to others.[1] Most school tort actions can be grouped into three primary categories: negligence, intentional torts, and defamation.

[1]Similar claims also have been brought under 42 U.S.C. § 1983 (2012), which entitles individuals to sue persons acting under color of state law for damages in connection with the impairment of federally protected rights. In such controversies, there is generally no respondeat superior liability, and state action is required. *Compare* Preschooler II v. Clark Cnty. Sch. Bd. of Trs., 479 F.3d 1175 (9th Cir. 2007) (denying qualified immunity when public school educators were directly responsible for the physical abuse of a four-year-old child with disabilities) *with* Harry A. v. Duncan, No. 05-35206, 2007 U.S. App. LEXIS 7474 (9th Cir. Mar. 27, 2007) (finding no state action where three boys videotaped activity in the girls' locker room and then circulated the tape among their peers).

NEGLIGENCE

Negligence is a breach of one's legal duty to protect others from unreasonable risks of harm. The failure to act or the commission of an improper act, which results in injury or loss to another person, can constitute negligence. To establish negligence, an injury must be avoidable by the exercise of reasonable care. Additionally, each of the following four elements must be present to support a successful claim:

- The defendant has a *duty* to protect the plaintiff.
- The *duty is breached* by the failure to exercise an appropriate standard of care.
- The negligent conduct is the *proximate or legal cause* of the injury.
- An actual *injury* occurs.

Duty

School officials have a common law duty to anticipate foreseeable dangers and to take necessary precautions to protect students entrusted in their care.[2] Among the specific duties school personnel owe students are to:

- provide adequate supervision;
- give proper instruction;
- maintain equipment, facilities, and grounds; and
- warn of known dangers.

SUPERVISION. Although state statutes require educators to provide proper supervision, school personnel are not expected to have every child under surveillance at all times during the school day or to anticipate every possible accident or incident that might occur. Moreover, there is no set level of supervision required under common law (e.g., there is no predetermined student-teacher ratio mandated by courts) for each activity or population. The level of supervision required in any given situation is determined by the aggregate of circumstances, including the age, maturity, and prior experience of the students; the specific activity in progress; and the presence of external threats. Accordingly, there may be situations in which no direct temporary supervision is needed, for example, when a nondisruptive student is permitted to leave the classroom to use adjacent restroom facilities in a building with no known dangers,[3] where close supervision is prudent (e.g., when students with a history of inappropriate behavior are assigned to the same activity), and even in situations where one-to-one supervision is required (e.g., an aquatic exercise class involving students with significant physical disabilities).

In assessing if adequate supervision has been provided, courts will determine whether the events leading up to the injury foreseeably placed the student at risk and whether the injury could have been prevented with proper supervision. Two student cases involving injuries in school bathrooms illustrate this point. In one instance, the

[2]*See, e.g.*, A.W. v. Lancaster Cnty. Sch. Dist. 0001, 784 N.W.2d 907 (Neb. 2010).

[3]*See, e.g.*, Patel v. Kent Sch. Dist., 648 F.3d 965 (9th Cir. 2011) (finding no teacher liability after unsupervised student was injured while using a bathroom immediately adjacent to the classroom). *But see* Miami-Dade Cnty. Sch. Bd. v. A.N., 905 So. 2d 203 (Fla. Dist. Ct. App. 2005) (affirming jury verdict when the board failed to warn a substitute teacher of the sexually aggressive history of a student; the student was permitted to go to the restroom unsupervised and while in the restroom attacked another student).

court found the school district liable for negligence because the evidence suggested that the teacher had been on notice about previous problematic behavior in the bathroom involving the same students. Students had been playing in the bathroom for four minutes, and during that time, a student was injured after being picked up and dropped on the floor.[4] The injured student had reported to the teacher a similar bathroom incident on a previous occasion. In another case, after a student was assaulted in the bathroom, the court found that school officials were not on notice about similar prior assaults. Thus, no liability was assessed for failing to provide adequate supervision.[5]

Proper supervision is particularly important in settings that pose significant risks to students, such as vocational shops, gymnasiums, science laboratories, and school grounds where known dangers exist. In these settings, it is critical that school personnel provide both proper instruction and adequate supervision to reduce the likelihood of injury to children and staff. Even when such care is provided, courts acknowledge that accidents will occur. In a New York case, a high school student injured his leg while playing floor hockey in gym class.[6] In ruling for the school district, the court observed that no level of supervision could have prevented the injury.

The school district's duty to supervise also includes the responsibility to protect pupils and employees from foreseeable risks posed by other students or school personnel, as well as persons not associated with the district. Depending on the circumstances of a particular case, districts can meet this duty by warning potential victims, increasing the number of supervisory personnel, or providing increased security where assaults, batteries, or other violent acts are reasonably foreseeable. Courts do not expect schools to ensure the safety of students in the event of unforeseeable risks, but do require that officials respond promptly and professionally when confronted with potentially dangerous circumstances.[7]

In New York, a student was punched and kicked by another student during a class. Reversing summary judgment in favor of the school district, the court held that issues of fact remained about the school district's knowledge of the student's propensity toward assaultive behavior.[8] Specifically, it may have been foreseeable that a student with an extensive disciplinary record, including ten reported prior charges, may have a tendency toward this type of behavior. When the alleged violator is a school employee, a school district may be held liable under the doctrine of respondeat superior if the school employee committed a tort while performing a job duty.[9] Some

[4]Johnson v. Ken-Ton Union Free Sch. Dist. 850 N.Y.S.2d 813 (App. Div. 2008).

[5]Shannea M. v. City of N.Y., 886 N.Y.S.2d 483 (App. Div. 2009).

[6]Odekirk v. Bellmore-Merrick Cent. Sch. Dist., 895 N.Y.S.2d 184 (App. Div. 2010); *see also* Tanenbaum v. Minnesauke Elem. Sch., 901 N.Y.S.2d 102 (App. Div. 2010) (determining that an accident involving a second-grade student who was injured after being pushed in the lunch line could not have been prevented and that school districts should not be found liable when intense supervision could not have prevented the accident).

[7]*Compare* Coleman v. St. Tammany Parish Sch. Bd., 13 So. 3d 644 (La. Ct. App. 2009) (denying school board's motion for summary judgment because it may have been foreseeable that a student would be attacked on the playground at lunchtime) *with* Brandy B. v. Eden Cent. Sch. Dist. 907 N.Y.S.2d 735 (App. Div. 2010) (finding that a school district had no notice that a student would attack another student and that school personnel did not have specific knowledge to guard against the attack).

[8]Wood v. Watervliet City Sch. Dist., 815 N.Y.S.2d 360 (App. Div. 2006). *But see* Peretin v. Caddo Parish Sch. Bd., 889 So. 2d 1190 (La. Ct. App. 2004) (finding no foreseeability where one student injured another student by placing her pencil in his chair as he was sitting down; the act was considered unexpected and spontaneous).

[9]Schafer v. Hicksville Union Free Sch. Dist., 06-cv-2531, 2011 U.S. Dist. LEXIS 35435 (E.D.N.Y. Mar. 31, 2011).

courts have rejected claims of school district liability, finding conduct such as battery and sexual assault to represent independent acts outside an individual's scope of employment.[10] Generally, the conduct of the individual violator and not the negligent supervision of the district is the proximate cause of injury. For example, in an Indiana case, the Seventh Circuit found no school district liability for negligent hiring, supervision, or retention because the parents failed to demonstrate that school officials knew that a teacher who had a sexual relationship with their daughter had a demonstrated habit of such conduct.[11] In contrast, the California Supreme Court held that a school district was liable for the negligence of supervisory personnel who knew or should have known about a counselor's propensity toward sexual harassment and nonetheless hired and inadequately supervised her. The court reasoned that the school district has a special relationship with pupils that imposes a duty to use reasonable measures to protect them from foreseeable injury, including harassment and abuse by school employees.[12]

Notwithstanding the general requirement to provide supervision, there may be times when students pass out of the "orbit of school authority," even though they may remain on school property. This often occurs today, given the wide range of uses of school buildings and the variety of activities. In such a case, an Indiana appeals court found that a district had no duty to supervise male students who secretly videotaped female lifeguards in their locker room in various stages of undress.[13] The tape later was circulated at the school, and the victims claimed that the school district's negligence caused their emotional distress. The lifeguard class, although held in school facilities, was not part of the public school curriculum (i.e., it was sponsored by the Red Cross after school hours), and school employees neither taught nor supervised the course. When school officials learned what had transpired, they investigated the incident, identified and suspended those responsible, and confiscated the one remaining tape. The taping was found to be unforeseeable, and no special duty was established for the district either to provide security or to supervise the class.

Supervision of students en route to and from school also has generated considerable litigation. Over the years, parents have argued that school officials are responsible for their children from the time they leave home until the time they return.[14] The Louisiana Supreme Court found that a school district provided reasonable supervision after a twelve-year-old student was raped on her two and a half-mile walk home from school. State law required the district to provide transportation to students who lived more than one mile from the school. The student in this case was kept after school for a behavior clinic. The district offered to arrange transportation for her, but the student chose to walk home.[15] There is no bright-line test to assist courts in rendering uniform decisions in cases involving students en route to and from school because such a test would place an unrealistic

[10] *See, e.g.*, Acosta-Rodriguez v. City of N.Y., 909 N.Y.S.2d 712 (App. Div. 2010).

[11] Hansen v. Bd. of Tr. of Hamilton Se. Sch. Corp. 551 F.3d 599 (7th Cir. 2008).

[12] C.A. v. William S. Hart Union High Sch. Dist., 270 P.3d 699 (Cal. 2012).

[13] Roe v. N. Adams Cmty. Sch. Corp., 647 N.E.2d 655 (Ind. Ct. App. 1995).

[14] Also, some parents have unsuccessfully asserted that their respective school districts should provide supervision when private individuals transport students to school functions. *See, e.g.*, Gylten v. Swalboski, 246 F.3d 1139 (8th Cir. 2001).

[15] S.J. v. LaFayette Parish Sch. Bd., 41 So. 3d 1119 (La. 2010).

demand on school resources and an unfair burden on personnel. Thus, courts instead focus on whether:

- the events that caused the injury were foreseeable;
- the district had an express or implied duty to provide supervision on and off school grounds both before and after school hours; and
- the child was injured due to a breach of that duty.

Where the district is responsible for providing transportation, officials should ensure that involved staff are properly trained and district procedures are communicated and practiced. Personnel should strictly adhere to transportation requirements, including those related to special licensure; background checks of drivers; vehicle maintenance; driving, loading, and unloading practices; conduct during transport; and criteria for when an aide is to be assigned.[16]

In addition, school officials have a duty to provide supervision during school-sponsored off-campus activities. As with other supervisory roles, school officials accompanying the students need to assess foreseeable risks associated with each activity and be aware of the abilities of participating students.[17] However, when the activity is neither curricular nor school sponsored, liability is less likely, given the difficulty of identifying a continuing duty on the part of school officials to provide supervision. To illustrate, no school district liability was found when a student died in a car accident after attending an off-campus event where alcohol was consumed.[18] The court reasoned that the party was not school related, as the group organizing it was not endorsed by the school; the partygoers had not asked the school's permission to host the event; and the school year had ended prior to the party. In those instances in which districts are not responsible for transporting children to and from school, proper supervision still should be provided at the pick-up and drop-off area; crossing guards should be stationed at nearby intersections for "walkers"; and assistance should be provided to parents and children to help identify safe routes to and from school.

Moreover, parents need to be informed about the earliest time supervision will be provided before school so that students will not arrive prior to school personnel. Parents also should be aware of when supervision ends after the school day. Where a student was assaulted by other youths while walking from school, no school district liability was found because the assault occurred thirty minutes after the student left school grounds. The court held that the student was no longer in the custody or control of the school.[19] As a general rule, school districts are not expected to protect truant and nonattending students, or students who are injured in their homes.[20] This is true for those who never arrive at school as well as for those who exit school grounds during the school day without permission, notwithstanding an appropriate level of surveillance of the school building

[16]*See, e.g.*, Miloscia v. N.Y.C. Bd. of Educ. 896 N.Y.S.2d 109 (App. Div. 2010) (finding bus driver did not create a dangerous situation when he stopped quickly to avoid an accident, and a student on the bus was injured).

[17]*See* Hansen v. Bath & Tennis Marina Corp., 900 N.Y.S.2d 365 (App. Div. 2010) (determining that it was not foreseeable or preventable when a student burned herself at a school-sponsored event).

[18]Archbishop Coleman F. Carroll High Sch. v. Maynoldi, 30 So. 3d 533 (Fla. Dist. Ct. App. 2010).

[19]Pistolese v. William Floyd Union Free Sch. Dist., 895 N.Y.S.2d 125 (App. Div. 2010). *But see* Nash v. Port Wash. Union Free Sch. Dist., 922 N.Y.S.2d 408 (App. Div. 2011) (affirming summary judgment in favor of student who was severely burned while working on science experiment after school).

[20]*See, e.g.*, Maldonado v. Tuckahoe, 817 N.Y.S.2d 376 (App. Div. 2006).

and grounds as determined by the age and ability of the students. For example, no duty to supervise existed where a high school student was hit by a car after she left school property before the school day to smoke. The student failed to use the traffic signal, crosswalk, or the crossing guard near the school. The court reasoned that the school district did not owe a duty to the student to provide supervision after she left school grounds.[21]

Moreover, extreme measures to keep students at school may themselves result in liability. A Kentucky teacher chained a student by the ankle and later, when the student "escaped," chained him by the neck to a tree to prevent him from leaving school grounds again. The student had arrived late or skipped class on numerous occasions. The appeals court determined that the lower court erred in granting a directed verdict to the teacher and that proof of emotional damages should be submitted to the jury on remand.[22]

INSTRUCTION. Teachers have a duty to provide students with adequate and appropriate instruction prior to commencing an activity that may pose a risk of harm—the greater the risk, the greater the need for proper instruction.[23] Following such instruction, effort should be made to determine whether the material was heard and understood. This can be accomplished through assessments such as paper and pencil tests, oral tests, or observations, as appropriate for the activity. Proper instruction was not given when a Nebraska freshman was severely burned in a welding course when his flannel shirt ignited.[24] The school failed to make protective leather aprons available to the students, as was recommended for such activities, and the instructor had informed the students simply to wear old shirts. Perhaps most damaging to the district's case was the testimony of the instructor, who stated on four separate occasions that it was not his responsibility to ensure that students wore protective clothing. "Safety garments" as a topic was briefly mentioned in one of many handouts distributed in class, but no effort was made to determine whether students read or understood the material, and on no occasion did the instructor prevent a student from participating based on the type of clothing worn.

MAINTENANCE OF BUILDINGS, GROUNDS, AND EQUIPMENT. Some states by law protect frequenters of public buildings from danger to life, health, safety, or welfare. These *safe place statutes* may be used by individuals to obtain damages from school districts for injuries resulting from defective conditions of school buildings and grounds. Moreover, school officials have a common law duty to maintain facilities and equipment in a reasonably safe condition. Districts can be held liable when they are aware of, or should be aware of, hazardous conditions and do not take the necessary steps to repair or correct the conditions. For example, school districts are responsible for the removal or encasement of asbestos materials;[25] failure to do so can result in injury and accompanying tort suits when injuries are shown to be related to exposure. The fear of future disease, however, appears to be insufficient grounds upon which to base a claim.[26] Because state and federal support for asbestos removal has been limited, numerous districts have sued

[21]Dalton v. Memminger, 889 N.Y.S.2d 785 (App. Div. 2009).

[22]Banks v. Fritsch, 39 S.W.3d 474 (Ky. Ct. App. 2001).

[23]*See, e.g.*, Traficenti v. Moore Catholic High Sch., 724 N.Y.S.2d 24 (App. Div. 2001).

[24]Norman v. Ogallala Pub. Sch. Dist., 609 N.W.2d 338 (Neb. 2000).

[25]Asbestos School Hazard Detection & Control Act, 20 U.S.C. § 3601 (2012); Asbestos Hazard Emergency Response Act of 1986, 15 U.S.C. § 2641 (2012).

[26]Brooks v. Stone Architecture, 934 So. 2d 350 (Miss. Ct. App. 2006).

asbestos manufacturers and suppliers to recover extraction costs because such providers failed to test the materials to determine whether they were hazardous or to warn consumers of potential dangers.[27]

The duty to provide reasonable maintenance of facilities does not place an obligation on school personnel to anticipate every possible danger or to be aware of and correct every minor defect as soon as the condition occurs. For example, a Louisiana student was unsuccessful in establishing a breach of duty in connection with an injury sustained when she slipped and fell in a puddle of liquid on the hallway floor.[28] The state appeals court explained that the presence of liquid on the hallway floor did not automatically create liability; the plaintiff, in failing to demonstrate how long the liquid had been on the floor, had not shown that the school had knowledge of any hazardous condition. Accordingly, the court affirmed the trial court's judgment for the school board. Similarly, a school district in New York was not found negligent for an injury that occurred when a student slipped on a puddle of water in the cafeteria that school personnel had no knowledge was there.[29]

If dangers are known, damages may be awarded when injuries result from unsafe conditions of buildings or grounds. A Michigan student was successful in obtaining damages for the loss of sight in one eye; the injury was sustained while playing in a pile of dirt and sand on the playground after school hours.[30] The area was not fenced, and prior to the incident, parents had complained to school officials about "dirt fights" among children. The state appeals court concluded that the school district breached its duty to maintain the school grounds in a safe condition. In contrast, when a student was injured after her thigh hit the net winder on the school district's tennis courts, the court did not find the district negligent in the maintenance of the courts and found no creation of any specific safety hazard.[31]

In addition to maintaining buildings and grounds, school personnel are required to maintain equipment and to use it safely, such as in woodshop, science labs, athletics, or transportation.[32] A Texas appeals court determined that immunity would be waived in part where a five-year-old child fell asleep on her way to school and was locked in the bus for the remainder of the school day. The court reasoned that although the district was immune for its alleged failure to supervise the unloading of the children, the district could be sued for the negligent locking of the door, given that such an act did not qualify as the "operation or use of a motor vehicle" for which immunity is granted.[33]

WARN OF KNOWN DANGERS. Courts in nearly all states today have recognized either a statutory or common law duty to warn students, parents, and at times educators and staff of known risks they may encounter. This duty has been identified in areas such as physical education and interscholastic sports, vocational education, laboratory science,

[27]*See, e.g., In re* Asbestos Sch. Litig., Pfizer, 46 F.3d 1284 (3d Cir. 1994); Adam Pub. Sch. Dist. v. Asbestos Corp., 7 F.3d 717 (8th Cir. 1993).

[28]DeGruy v. Orleans Parish Sch. Bd., 573 So. 2d 1188 (La. Ct. App. 1991).

[29]Musachio v. Smithtown Cent. Sch. Dist., 892 N.Y.S.2d 123 (App. Div. 2009).

[30]Monfils v. City of Sterling Heights, 269 N.W.2d 588 (Mich. Ct. App. 1978).

[31]Bendig v. Bethpage Union Free Sch. Dist., 904 N.Y.S.2d 731 (App. Div. 2010).

[32]*See, e.g.,* Arteman v. Clinton Cmty. Unit Sch. Dist. No. 15, 740 N.E.2d 47 (Ill. App. Ct. 2000).

[33]Elgin Indep. Sch. Dist. v. R.N., 191 S.W.3d 263, 267 (Tex. App. 2006).

and other occasions when a student uses potentially dangerous machinery or equipment.[34] Informing, if not warning, those involved of known dangers is necessary so that they then may appreciate the risk and be in a better position to decide whether to assume it.

In addition to the somewhat traditional warnings connected with sports or the use of equipment, educators, school psychologists, and counselors have a duty to warn when they learn through advising, counseling, or therapy that students intend to harm themselves or others. Those in receipt of such information are required to inform potential victims or to notify parents if the student threatens to self-injure. This requirement supersedes claims of professional ethics, discretion, therapist/client privilege, or confidentiality. Typically, however, school officials will not be found liable when the harmful act is unforeseeable (i.e., the threat of suicide was neither explicitly stated nor apparent), even if they knew that a particular student was under stress or seemed depressed or preoccupied. The Ninth Circuit found no school district liability when a student committed suicide at home.[35] While at school, the student had walked out of the building to attend a civil rights rally. When he returned, the vice principal called him dumb and threatened to notify the police. The student was especially worried about being found truant because he was already on probation for bringing a knife to school. After the meeting with the vice principal, he returned to class. Later that night at home, he shot himself. The court observed that the student had the opportunity to appreciate the nature of his actions after he returned to class and that school officials could not be found liable for his decision to take his own life.[36]

School officials also have a duty to warn employees of known dangers, whether structural, environmental, or human. Accordingly, a Florida court reversed a lower court's grant of summary judgment in a case in which district officials failed to warn a teacher about a student's propensity for violence.[37] On remand, to overcome the general rule of workers' compensation[38] immunity, the battered teacher will have to show that the employer engaged in conduct that was substantially certain to result in injury.[39] To aid the lower court in reaching its decision, the appeals court noted that the student had (1) been classified as severely emotionally disabled with a multiple personality disorder, (2) been involved in numerous acts of violence, (3) previously threatened teachers, and (4) been ordered by a court to undergo inpatient treatment for slamming his mother's head against the floor. Moreover, the district had either concealed or misrepresented these facts in its effort to place the student in his current school.

[34]*See, e.g.*, Mangold v. Ind. Dep't of Natural Res., 756 N.E.2d 970 (Ind. 2001).

[35]Corales v. Bennett, 567 F.3d 554 (9th Cir. 2009).

[36]*Id.* at 572. *See also* Mikell v. Sch. Admin. Unit No. 33, 972 A.2d 1050 (N.H. 2009) (finding no school district liability when student suicide is considered a deliberate, intentional, and intervening act).

[37]Patrick v. Palm Beach Cnty. Sch. Bd., 927 So. 2d 973 (Fla. Dist. Ct. App. 2006), *aff'd mem.*, 50 So. 3d 1161 (Fla. Dist. Ct. App. 2010).

[38]*See, e.g.*, Wyble v. Acadiana Preparatory Sch., 956 So. 2d 722 (La. Ct. App. 2007) (determining that a school employee was eligible for workers' compensation when injured at work while moving a desk; it did not matter that the task was routine rather than an accident).

[39]Workers' compensation immunity protects employers from liability when employees are injured on the job while involved in performing job-related responsibilities. To avoid the application of this form of immunity, the employee is required to show that the employer intended to injure the employee or, in the alternative, required the employee to engage in conduct that was substantially likely to result in injury.

In contrast, school officials had no duty to warn an independent contractor who was injured after attaching his cable to an unstable section of the school building. The court found that the defective condition was created by the contractor, and no duty could be imposed on the school district.[40]

Breach of Duty/Standard of Care

Once a duty has been established, the injured individual must show that the duty was breached by the failure of another to exercise an appropriate standard of care.[41] The degree of care teachers owe students is determined by:

- the age, experience, and maturity level of the students;
- the environment within which the incident occurs; and
- the type of instructional or recreational activity.

For example, primary grade students will generally require closer supervision and more detailed and repetitive instructions than will high school students, and a class in woodwork will require closer supervision than will a class in English literature. Variability in the level of care deemed reasonable is illustrated in a Louisiana case in which a mentally retarded student was fatally injured when he darted into a busy thoroughfare while being escorted with nine other classmates to a park three blocks from the school.[42] The state appellate court noted that the general level of care required for all students becomes greater when children with disabilities are involved, particularly when they are taken away from the school campus. The court found the supervision to be inadequate and the selected route to be less safe than alternate routes. The reasonableness of any given action will be pivotal in determining whether there is liability.

REASONABLE PERSON. In assessing whether appropriate care has been taken, courts consider if the defendant acted as a "reasonable person" would have acted under the circumstances. The reasonable person is a hypothetical individual who has:

- the physical attributes of the defendant;
- normal intelligence, problem-solving ability, and temperament;
- normal perception and memory with a minimum level of information and experience common to the community; and
- such superior skill and knowledge as the defendant has or purports to have.

Courts will not assume that a defendant possesses any predetermined physical attributes (e.g., size, strength, agility), but rather will consider each defendant's actual physical abilities and disabilities in determining whether the defendant was responsible in whole or in part for an individual's injury. Accordingly, if a child requires physical assistance

[40]Wombacher v. Greater Johnstown Sch. Dist. 20 A.3d 1240 (Pa. Commw. Ct. 2011).
[41]*See, e.g.*, S.J. v. LaFayette Parish Sch. Bd., 41 So. 3d 1119 (La. 2010).
[42]Foster v. Houston Gen. Ins. Co., 407 So. 2d 759, 763 (La. Ct. App. 1981).

to avoid being attacked by another student, a different expectation will exist for a large, physically fit teacher as compared to a small, frail teacher.

Although a defendant's actual physical characteristics and capabilities are used in determining whether his or her conduct was reasonable, that is not the case when considering mental capacity. Courts will assume all adult individuals have normal intelligence, problem-solving ability, and temperament, even when the evidence indicates that they do not possess such attributes.[43] This may initially appear unfair, but any other approach is likely to result in defense claims that are judicially unmanageable. For example, if defendants' own intellect were used, they could argue that consideration should be given to factors such as their inability to make good or quick decisions, lack of perception or concentration, poor attention to detail, confrontational personality, or inability to deal with stress. Trying to determine each person's mental abilities and capabilities would be impractical, if not impossible, given the dearth of valid and reliable assessment instruments or techniques and the ease of those being assessed to misrepresent their abilities. The current approach of assuming normal intelligence provides a more objective procedure and requires defendants to be responsible for injuries they cause others.

Courts also expect a defendant to have a normal perception of the environment (e.g., to be aware that the rear of the school yard is bordered by a small river) and an accurate memory of what has occurred previously within that environment (e.g., recalling that the playground floods following a heavy rain).[44] This requirement does not assume that the defendant will know all facts, foresee all risks, or be aware of all things. Instead, it is based on the position that a reasonable adult, with normal intellect, should know certain facts.

In an effort to determine whether the defendant acted as a reasonable person, courts also consider whether the defendant had or claimed to have had any superior knowledge or skill. Teachers, who are college graduates and state licensed, are expected to act like reasonable persons with similar education. In addition, any special training an individual has received may affect whether a given act is considered reasonable. To illustrate, a physical education instructor who is a certified lifeguard or a teacher with an advanced degree in chemistry may be held to higher standards of care than others with lesser skills and knowledge when, respectively, a student is drowning or chemicals in a school laboratory are mixed improperly and ignite.

INVITEE, LICENSEE, AND TRESPASSER. In reaching a decision on whether an appropriate standard of care has been provided, courts also determine whether an injured individual was an invitee, licensee, or trespasser, with invitees receiving the greatest level of care and trespassers receiving the least. In a school setting, an invitee is one who enters the school premises on the expressed or implied invitation of the school district or one of its agents. The district then has an affirmative duty to exercise reasonable care for the safety of invitees commensurate with the risks and circumstances involved. Furthermore, invitees must be protected against known dangers as well as those that might be discovered with reasonable care. Under most circumstances, students, teachers, and administrators

[43]Dan B. Dobbs, The Law of Torts 284–85 (St. Paul, MN: West, 2000).
[44]*Id.* at 288.

are invitees of the district. Students who break into a school after hours, however, have exceeded the "period of invitation" and become trespassers.[45]

Where permission to be on school premises is requested and granted, the person is usually considered a licensee (e.g., requests by unsolicited visitors, salespersons, parents, newspersons).[46] Even schoolchildren may qualify as licensees under certain circumstances (e.g., while engaged in activities of a local nonschool organization that has been permitted evening or weekend use of a school classroom). Such persons enter the building or grounds facing the same conditions and threats as the occupier. Nevertheless, districts still need to warn licensees of known dangers and not allow intentional injuries or injuries by willful, wanton, or reckless conduct.

When the individual has neither been invited nor received consent, the person is guilty of trespass upon accessing school property. Although state laws often blur the distinction between licensee and trespasser, less care is required for the safety of trespassers. Adult trespassers in particular have no right to a safe place and must assume the risk of what they may encounter. Generally, the owner owes no duty to trespassers other than to refrain from willfully or wantonly injuring them (e.g., by setting traps). In selected jurisdictions, however, if the owner knows that trespassers are on the premises (e.g., vagrants living in an abandoned school building), the owner must use reasonable care not to expose the trespasser to an environment that is known to be dangerous. When the trespasser is a child, as often is the case on school property, it is prudent to take additional steps to restrict access or to remove known dangers. In such narrow instances, there is little legal distinction between a trespasser and a licensee in regard to the standard of care required.

Proximate Cause

The plaintiff must demonstrate a causal link between the negligent act and the harm before the defendant can be found liable for negligence.[47] In order to prevail, the plaintiff must show that the defendant's conduct that constituted a breach of duty caused the harm.[48]

There are two types of causation: cause-in-fact and proximate cause. In determining whether a school official's conduct was the cause-in-fact of the student's injury, sometimes courts employ the "but for" test. Under this test, the plaintiff would need to show that "but for" the defendant's act or failure to act, there would not have been an injury. With proximate cause, courts decide whether the teacher's action is close enough to the chain of events that caused the harm. For example, there must be a causal connection between the alleged misconduct and the resulting injury. The courts might ask

[45]*See, e.g.*, Howard Cnty. Bd. of Educ. v. Cheyne, 636 A.2d 22 (Md. Ct. App. 1994) (holding that a four-year-old was an invitee when she initially entered a gymnasium to attend a sports function, but that a question remained for the jury to determine whether she had exceeded the "scope of her invitation" at the time of the injury—following a school basketball game, the child was injured while retrieving basketballs her mother had shot); *see also* Tincani v. Inland Empire Zoological Soc'y, 875 P.2d 621, 631 (Wash. 1994) (remanding a case in which a student sued a zoo after falling off a cliff during a field trip; the court questioned whether he became a licensee when he strayed beyond the "area of his invitation").

[46]*See, e.g.*, Yates v. Johnson Cnty. Bd., 888 N.E.2d 842 (Ind. Ct. App. 2008) (reversing grant of summary judgment in favor of school district because issues of fact remained about whether the plaintiff, who was injured while attending a town fundraiser on school property, was an invitee).

[47]David G. Owen, *The Five Elements of Negligence*, 35 Hofstra L. Rev. 1680–82 (2007).

[48]*Id.*

whether the incident was foreseeable when making a determination regarding proximate cause.[49]

To illustrate, while playing tag in gym class, a fourth-grade student was unintentionally knocked down by a classmate. He lost two front teeth when a different student tripped over him and caused his face to hit the floor. The injured student alleged that the teacher's aide and the gym teacher were negligent because they failed to observe the initial collision and intervene, which could have prevented the tripping incident.[50] Affirming the lower court's decision to grant summary judgment in favor of the school district, the appellate court found that the student failed to establish that lack of supervision was the proximate cause of the injury. Similarly, a New York court held that a school district's lack of supervision was not the proximate cause of a student's injuries where a fight, in which the student was injured, occurred in such a short period of time that not even the most intense supervision could have prevented it.[51]

Injury

Legal negligence does not exist unless actual injury is incurred either directly by the individual or by the individual's property. Most often, an individual will know of the injury as soon as it occurs; in some instances, however, the individual may not be aware of the injury for many months or even years (e.g., development of asbestosis due to exposure to asbestos twenty years previously). In most states, there is a statute of limitations of one to three years on tort claims, although the actual time can be greater if the limitations period does not begin until the plaintiff reaches the age of majority or becomes aware of the injury.

When students are injured in the school setting, school personnel have a duty to provide reasonable assistance commensurate with their training and experience. Where reasonable treatment is provided, no liability will generally be assessed, even if the treatment later is proven to be inappropriate or inadequate.

Defenses against Negligence

Although tort law is generally addressed in state courts, teachers might find protection against claims of negligence under a federal law. The Paul D. Coverdell Teacher Protection Act, which is included in the No Child Left Behind Act, provides protection to teachers who are "acting within the scope of the teacher's employment or responsibilities to a school" or when the teacher is attempting "to control, discipline, expel, or suspend a student or maintain order or control in the classroom or school."[52]

In addition, there are several defenses available to school districts when employees have been charged with negligence. At times, in an effort to thwart liability claims, districts have identified procedural defects (e.g., the failure to adhere to statutory requirements regarding notice of claim), or have proposed that an individual's injury was caused by uncontrollable events of nature (i.e., an act of God). More commonly, defenses such as

[49]*Id.*
[50]Doyle v. Binghamton City Sch. Dist., 874 N.Y.S.2d 607 (App. Div. 2009).
[51]Keaveny v. Mahopac Cent. Sch. Dist., 897 N.Y.S.2d 222 (App. Div. 2010).
[52]20 U.S.C. § 6736(a) (2012).

immunity, contributory negligence, comparative negligence, and assumption of risk have been asserted.

GOVERNMENTAL IMMUNITY. In rare cases in which governmental immunity is comprehensively applied, governmental entities including school districts cannot be sued for any reason. But, this defense is available to employees only when state law specifically confers such immunity for acts within the scope of employment, or courts interpret the law to do so.[53] Immunity is seldom comprehensively applied today, as nearly all states have limited its use by considering factors such as whether (1) the claim was related to the maintenance of the school building or property, (2) acts were governmental or proprietary, (3) decisions qualified as discretionary or ministerial, (4) school property was being used for recreational purposes, or (5) the injury was compensable under the state's workers' compensation laws (employees only).

In most jurisdictions, school districts can be held liable for injuries arising from a dangerous realty condition if authorities have knowledge of a defect and do not take corrective action or if they maintain an attractive nuisance.[54] An *attractive nuisance* is a facility, structure, or piece of equipment that entices the public to engage in activity that is potentially dangerous. Swimming pools and ponds on school property often are classified as attractive nuisances. Because of the potential for serious injury, school districts may claim immunity only if proper precautions are taken to prevent public access to such areas.

In some states, a distinction has been made between governmental and proprietary functions in determining whether a school district is immune. Governmental functions are those that are performed in discharging the agency's official duties (e.g., hiring faculty) that are generally considered immune from liability. On the other hand, proprietary functions are those that are only tangentially related to the curriculum, can as easily be performed by the private sector, and often require the payment of a fee (e.g., community use of school pool); these activities have been permissible targets for tort actions. Except in the most extreme cases, however, it may be difficult to identify activities that are proprietary because most school endeavors in some way can be linked to the mission of the district.

In other states, the distinction between discretionary and ministerial functions is used to determine whether liability exists. As with governmental and propriety functions, differentiation between those that qualify as discretionary and ministerial will be obvious only when assessing extreme examples.[55] By definition, *discretionary functions* are those that require consideration of alternatives, deliberation, judgment, and the making of a decision (e.g., the discretion used in the selection of a new teacher). In contrast, *ministerial functions* are those that are performed in a prescribed manner, in obedience to legal authority, and without discretion (e.g., procedures used for stopping

[53]*See, e.g.*, Brown v. Fountain Hill Sch. Dist., 1 S.W.3d 27 (Ark. Ct. App. 1999); Coonse v. Boise Sch. Dist., 979 P.2d 1161 (Idaho 1999).

[54]*See supra* text accompanying note 30.

[55]*See, e.g.*, Univ. of Tex. at San Antonio v. Trevino, 153 S.W.3d 58 (Tex. App. 2002) (distinguishing discretionary and ministerial functions where a three-year-old died when she fell between the railings of the bleachers by applying the design/maintenance test for structures and equipment—i.e., immunity is granted for the design of the bleachers but not for their maintenance or operation).

a school bus at a railroad crossing).[56] As a rule, districts will be liable for negligence involving ministerial duties but immune from liability for negligence associated with duties that are discretionary.[57] Some states also differentiate between policy-level discretionary acts (for which immunity is granted) and operational-level discretionary acts that deal with policy implementation (for which immunity is not granted).[58] A grant of discretionary-function immunity was provided in an Ohio case.[59] A coach elected to have the girls' basketball team practice with older boys, given his belief that the boys used sound skills and would help take the girls' team to the next level athletically. During practice, one of the girls incurred a broken arm when a boy attempted to slap the ball from her hands. There was no personal contact, and had the slap of the ball occurred during a game, no foul would have been called. The court determined that the coach had exercised discretionary authority with the intent to improve his team's skills and competitive ability.

Another type of immunity defense exists for *recreational use*. Such statutes have been passed to encourage property and landowners (including public sector entities) to open their lands and waters for public recreational use. School gymnasiums, playgrounds, and athletic fields at times have been labeled as recreational facilities or areas, although state laws vary considerably.[60] Immunity for injuries incurred while on the property is provided unless the entrant was charged a fee for admission or was injured because of the owner's willful or wanton misconduct. In Kansas, a football player collapsed at the end of his first mandatory practice and died the following day; plaintiffs claimed that his death was caused by the failure to provide proper supervision. The court applied recreational-use immunity in regard to the ordinary negligence claim, but remanded the case for a determination of whether the defendant's conduct amounted to gross or wanton negligence.[61] If the defendant's conduct were found gross or wanton, neither recreational use nor discretionary function immunity would protect the district from liability.

Immunity also may be used as a defense when an injury is compensable under the state's workers' compensation statute. Workers' compensation laws are intended to reduce or eliminate negligence litigation (i.e., they do not protect employers or employees who engage in intentional torts), encourage employer interest in safety and rehabilitation, and promote the study of the causes of accidents rather than concealment of fault, thereby

[56]*See, e.g.*, Harrison v. Hardin Cnty. Cmty. Unit Sch. Dist. No. 1, 758 N.E.2d 848 (Ill. 2001).

[57]*See, e.g.*, Pauley v. Anchorage Sch. Dist., 31 P.3d 1284 (Alaska 2001); Trotter v. Sch. Dist. 218, 733 N.E.2d 363 (Ill. App. Ct. 2000).

[58]Norman v. Ogallala Pub. Sch. Dist., 609 N.W.2d 338 (Neb. 2000).

[59]Schnarrs v. Girard Bd. of Educ., 858 N.E.2d 1258 (Ohio Ct. App. 2006); *see also* Worthington v. Elmore Cnty. Bd. of Educ., 160 F. App'x 877 (11th Cir. 2005) (granting immunity when a student claimed to have been sexually abused by another student while being transported on a bus for special needs children, and reasoning that the supervision of students was a discretionary, rather than ministerial, function and that even if it were not, there was insufficient evidence to find the driver negligent; his alleged failure to properly supervise the students was found not to be the "moving force" behind the assault).

[60]*See, e.g.*, Fear v. Indep. Sch. Dist. 911, 634 N.W.2d 204 (Minn. Ct. App. 2001) (holding that a district was not necessarily entitled to immunity when an elementary school child fell from piled snow and was injured; whether recreational immunity applied was a question to be answered at trial by applying the child trespasser standard); M.M. v. Fargo Public Sch. Dist., 783 N.W.2d 806 (N.D. 2010) (concluding that the recreational immunity statute did not shield the district from liability for injuries to a student occurring shortly after school was dismissed), *aff'd mem.*, 815 N.W.2d 273 (N.D. 2012).

[61]Barrett v. Unified Sch. Dist. No. 259, 32 P.3d 1156 (Kan. 2001).

reducing the occurrence of preventable accidents.[62] Under workers' compensation, liability exists regardless of negligence or fault on the part of the employer or employee, provided that the injury was accidental *and* arose out of and in the course of employment. However, not all injuries that occur at work are necessarily "work related." A Kentucky court upheld the denial of a teacher's worker's compensation benefits on the ground that the teacher's injuries resulted from a personal rather than work-related dispute; the teacher was injured when a student and parent confronted the teacher at a department store. Although the teacher had disciplined the student a few days before the confrontation, the trial judge concluded that the parties' animosity was long-standing and unrelated to the teacher's work duties.[63]

A corollary issue in some states has been whether the purchase of liability insurance has impliedly waived immunity, notwithstanding explicit state statutes granting it. Courts have been divided on the matter with some maintaining immunity (in whole or in part) and others abrogating it.[64] In some states, it is clear that public school districts may be sued, but often only to the extent of insurance coverage.[65]

CONTRIBUTORY NEGLIGENCE. Under the contributory model, only the injured party bears financial responsibility if ultimately found responsible for the act leading to an injury; it makes no difference that the defendant was also negligent and partially at fault. Over the years, the contributory defense has been modified and weakened by courts due to a number of factors, including its harshness to injured plaintiffs, the ease of negligent defendants to avoid liability, and a change in social viewpoint (i.e., from the need to protect new industries early in the twentieth century to the desire to compensate injured persons).[66] As a result, in most jurisdictions today, a slight degree of fault will not prevent a plaintiff from prevailing.

In assessing whether contributory negligence exists, children are not necessarily held to the same standard of care as adults. Rather, their actions must be reasonable for persons of similar age, maturity, intelligence, and experience. Many courts make individualized determinations as to whether a minor plaintiff appreciated the risks involved and acted as a reasonable person of like characteristics and abilities. Other courts have established age ranges in an effort to more objectively and uniformly determine whether children have the capacity to contribute to or cause their own injuries.[67]

[62]For a related discussion, see STEPHEN B. THOMAS, STUDENTS, COLLEGES, AND DISABILITY LAW 270–72 (Dayton: Education Law Association, 2002).

[63]Taylor v. Wayne Cnty. Bd. of Educ., No. 2009-CA-001392-WC, 2010 Ky. App. Unpub. LEXIS 332 (Ct. App. Apr. 16, 2010).

[64]*Compare* Brock v. Sumter Cnty. Sch. Bd., 542 S.E.2d 547 (Ga. Ct. App. 2000) (holding that the district had not waived sovereign immunity through the purchase of motor vehicle liability insurance) *with* Crowell v. Sch. Dist. No. 7, Gallatin Cnty., 805 P.2d 522 (Mont. 1991) (holding that the purchase of insurance constituted a waiver of immunity).

[65]*See, e.g.*, Helena-W. Helena Sch. Dist. v. Monday, 204 S.W.3d 514 (Ark. 2005).

[66]DOBBS, *supra* note 43, at 494–503

[67]*See, e.g.*, Berman v. Phila. Bd. of Educ., 456 A.2d 545 (Pa. 1983) (finding that an eleven-year-old student who was injured by a hockey stick after the school failed to provide gear could not be found contributorily negligent); *see also* Winkinson v. Hartford, 411 So. 2d 22 (La. 1982) (finding that the age of the student who was injured in a school gymnasium must be considered in determining contributory negligence).

Although courts vary greatly and designated ages may seem arbitrary, the most commonly used ranges are:

- children below the age of seven are considered incapable of negligence;
- children between the ages of seven and fourteen are considered incapable of negligence, but this presumption can be rebutted;[68] and
- students age fourteen and over are generally presumed capable of negligence, although this presumption too can be rebutted.

When adults are injured on school grounds or at school functions, courts will assess the nature of the risk involved and whether such a risk was known to the injured party or reasonably should have been known. An Indiana court upheld a grant of summary judgment where a father fell from backless bleachers while watching his son participate in a basketball game. The court found the plaintiff to be contributorily negligent in that he failed to exercise the degree of care that an ordinary, reasonable, and prudent person in a similar situation would exercise.[69] Similarly, a California appeals court concluded that a district was not liable for the death of a student on school grounds after regular school hours.[70] Although the playground was accessible to the public, unsupervised, and in disrepair, the court concluded that the student's death resulted from his own conduct in attempting to perform a hazardous skateboard activity, not from defective playground conditions.

COMPARATIVE NEGLIGENCE. With the comparative model, the plaintiff and/or one or more defendants bear responsibility in proportion to fault. For example, a school district in Wisconsin was found 80 percent liable for an injury sustained by an eighth-grade student while dissecting a plant with a scalpel. The court observed that the teacher was aware that others had been injured in the past and that she could have done more to avoid this injury.[71] Similarly, an Arizona appeals court upheld a jury verdict where a student was hit by a car when he ran into the street trying to flee another student after he safely exited a school bus on his way home. Liability was apportioned to the injured boy (45 percent), his parents (40 percent), and the district (15 percent) in a $6 million award. Although the school district was not responsible for escorting the child home, school officials were aware of the conduct of the students at the bus stop, a nearby busy street with fast-moving traffic, and the availability of an alternative and safer bus stop.[72]

ASSUMPTION OF RISK. This defense can be either express or implied. *Express assumption* occurs when the plaintiff consents in advance to take his or her chances of injury, given a known danger. On the other hand, *implied assumption* occurs without an express written or oral agreement, yet is logically assumed, given the plaintiff's conduct. For example, implied assumption would exist where spectators at a baseball game elect to sit

[68]*See, e.g.*, Clay City Consol. Sch. Corp. v. Timberman, 918 N.E.2d 292 (Ind. 2009) (observing that children between ages seven and fourteen are incapable of negligence in a case involving a thirteen-year-old student who died at basketball practice and was not found to be contributorily negligent).

[69]Funston v. Sch. Town of Munster, 849 N.E.2d 595 (Ind. 2006).

[70]Bartell v. Palos Verdes Peninsula Sch. Dist., 147 Cal. Rptr. 898 (Ct. App. 1978).

[71]Heuser v. Cmty. Ins. Corp., 774 N.W.2d 653 (Wis. Ct. App. 2009).

[72]Warrington v. Tempe Elementary Sch. Dist. No. 3, 3 P.3d 988 (Ariz. Ct. App. 1999).

in unscreened seats; such persons assume the risk of possible injury even if they failed to sign an agreement.

Inherent risks are associated with athletics or recreation, but it cannot be assumed that all participants, regardless of age, maturity, and experience, understand those risks. For example, a student was found not to have assumed the risk involved in an obstacle course he participated in on a school-sponsored field trip. The court observed that the assumed risk of the activity does not relieve the school district of its obligation to use reasonable care.[73] As a result, school personnel must exercise reasonable care to protect students from unassumed, concealed, or unreasonably high risks. This duty can be met when participation is voluntary and the student is knowledgeable of and assumes the risks associated with the activity. For instance, in Indiana, a football player died following extensive conditioning in hot and humid weather. His mother had signed a release form providing permission for him to participate in organized athletics and acknowledging that injuries and even death may result.[74] The appeals court concluded that the lower court was correct in permitting the admission of the form as part of the district's defense. The athlete had several years of general football experience and in prior years had participated in the conditioning program of the current coach.[75]

In regard to sports, however, student athletes assume only those risks that occur during normal participation. For example, in New York, the court found that the student assumed the risk of injury when he landed on a metal cross bar attached to a portable basketball hoop. The court observed that the bar did not create a dangerous condition above the usual dangers of basketball.[76] But students do not assume unknown risks associated with a coach's negligence. Moreover, they are not assuming that they will be exposed to intentional torts or conduct that represents a reckless disregard for the safety of others. Likewise, students do not assume a risk when they are compelled to participate in athletic events. In an illustrative case, a school board was denied its motion for summary judgment after a student allegedly was compelled to participate in a race. The fifth-grade student fell and sustained injuries in a backward relay race during the school's field day.[77] The court reasoned that as the plaintiff had raised a triable issue of fact as to whether participation was compulsory, summary judgment on the basis of assumption of risk was inappropriate.

INTENTIONAL TORTS

Among the more common types of intentional torts are assault, battery, false imprisonment, and intentional infliction of mental distress. Each of these torts is discussed briefly below.

[73]Garman v. E. Rochester Sch. Dist., 850 N.Y.S.2d 306 (App. Div. 2007).

[74]Stowers v. Clinton Cent. Sch. Corp., 855 N.E.2d 739 (Ind. Ct. App. 2006); *see also* Ribaudo v. La Salle Inst., 846 N.Y.S.2d 209 (App. Div. 2007) (determining that the student had assumed the risks associated with playing basketball when she was injured after running into the wall).

[75]Given the national attention to concussion-related injuries, many school districts and some states are requiring schools to adopt concussion management plans to educate students, parents, and school personnel about concussion prevention and responses. *See, e.g.*, Nat'l Sch. Bds. Ass'n, *Youth Football Organization Adopts New Rules Aimed at Reducing Player Concussions*, Legal Clips (June 21, 2012), http://legalclips.nsba.org/?p=14941.

[76]Milea v. Our Lady of Miracles Roman Catholic Church, 736 N.Y.S.2d 84 (App. Div. 2002).

[77]Smith v. J.H. West Elem. Sch., 861 N.Y.S.2d 690 (App. Div. 2008). Other negligence defenses, of course, can still be used in situations where student participation is compelled.

Assault and Battery

Assault consists of an overt attempt to place another in fear of bodily harm; no actual physical contact need take place. Examples include threatening with words, pointing a gun, waving a knife, or shaking a fist. For there to be an assault, the plaintiff needs to be aware of the threat, and the person committing the assault needs to be perceived as having the ability to carry out the threat. In contrast, a battery is committed when an assault is consummated. Examples include being shot, stabbed, beaten, or struck. Actual injury need not result for a battery claim to succeed (e.g., the person could have been punched but not injured due to a comparatively weak blow). For the plaintiff to prevail in either an assault or a battery case, the act must be *intentional*; there is no such thing as a negligent assault or battery.

Some school-based assault and battery cases have involved students fighting at school. For example, in Ohio, a student struck another student in the face with a cell phone causing injury.[78] Other assault and battery cases have included the administration of corporal punishment and other forms of discipline that require physical touching. Generally, courts have been reluctant to interfere with a teacher's authority to discipline students and have sanctioned the use of reasonable force to control pupil behavior. The Oregon appeals court ruled that a teacher was not guilty of assault and battery for using force to remove a student from the classroom. After the pupil defiantly refused to leave, the teacher held his arms and led him toward the door. The student extricated himself, swung at the teacher, and broke a window, thereby cutting his arm. The court concluded that the teacher used reasonable force with the student and dismissed the assault and battery charges.[79] In contrast, a Louisiana student was successful in obtaining damages.[80] The pupil sustained a broken arm when a teacher shook him, lifted him against the bleachers in the gymnasium, and then let him fall to the floor. The court reasoned that the teacher's action was unnecessary either to discipline the student or to protect himself.

Although comparatively uncommon, school personnel may initiate battery suits against students who injure them.[81] Suits are not barred simply because the person committing the tort is a minor. A Wisconsin appeals court awarded damages to a teacher when he was physically attacked outside the school building while attempting to escort a student to the office for violating a smoking ban.[82] The court held that the student, who had five previous fighting violations, acted with malicious intent in repeatedly striking the teacher and in pushing the teacher's face into the corner of a building. Both actual and punitive damages were awarded, notwithstanding the fact that the student was a minor at the time of the battery and that the student's psychiatrist had

[78]Watkins v. New Albany Plain Local Schs., 711 F. Supp. 2d 817 (S.D. Ohio 2010).

[79]Simms v. Sch. Dist. No. 1, 508 P.2d 236 (Or. Ct. App. 1973); *see also* Frame v. Comeaux, 735 So. 2d 753 (La. Ct. App. 1999) (finding no battery when a substitute teacher grabbed a confrontational eighth-grade student by the arm and escorted him out of the room—the student had been talking during a test).

[80]Frank v. Orleans Parish Sch. Bd., 195 So. 2d 451 (La. Ct. App. 1967).

[81]In addition, some negligence suits are filed by school personnel against their districts when they have been battered at work. In most cases, however, courts have found that the incidents were unforeseen and that no special duty existed on the part of the district to prevent the battery. *See, e.g.*, Genao v. Bd. of Educ., 888 F. Supp. 501 (S.D.N.Y. 1995) (finding the school district had not established a special duty to protect the teacher in several incidents involving battery).

[82]Anello v. Savignac, 342 N.W.2d 440 (Wis. Ct. App. 1983).

testified during trial that a punitive award would not be a deterrent for his impulsive conduct. The trial court also was not persuaded by the argument that the student's violence and anger were due to his poor self-control or that he had a learning disability. In conclusion, the court noted that if the student expected to continue to live freely in society, he would have to learn to control his assaultive behavior, or "appreciate" the consequences.

Self-defense often has been used to shield an individual from liability for alleged battery. An individual need not wait to be struck to engage in defensive acts, although reasonable grounds must exist to substantiate that harm is imminent. The "test" in such cases is to determine whether a reasonable person may have engaged in conduct such as the defendant's, given the circumstances. Consideration should be given to the magnitude of the existing threat, possible alternatives to physical contact, and the time frame available to make a decision (i.e., whether the defendant acted instantaneously or had time for contemplation and deliberation).[83] Even where contact is justified, the defendant must use only force that is reasonably necessary for self-protection. Furthermore, if the alleged aggressor is disarmed, rendered helpless, or no longer capable of aggressive behavior, the defendant may not take the opportunity to punish or engage in revenge. In addition to self-defense, individuals accused of battery also may claim that they were acting in the defense of others. This type of tort defense is of particular importance in a school setting where educators often are called on to separate students who are fighting or to come to the aid of someone being attacked. Most jurisdictions not only permit such action on behalf of others but also consider it to be a responsibility or duty of educators, assuming good faith and the use of reasonable and necessary force.

False Imprisonment

False imprisonment results when physical action, verbal command, or intimidation is used to restrain or detain persons against their will. All restrictions on the freedom of movement or the effort to enter or exit will not qualify as false imprisonment. For example, the court found no false imprisonment where a student was placed for seven minutes in a holding cell in a county detention facility for continually disrupting a tour of the building—the student's behavior jeopardized the safety of the children and disrupted an otherwise orderly environment.[84] Also, a student who was taken out of class to be questioned by the principal and a magistrate judge regarding sexual activities on the Internet could not claim false imprisonment.[85] To be falsely imprisoned, one need not be incarcerated; walls, locks, or physical force are not required. Rather, imprisonment can result from being placed in a closet, room, corner, automobile, or even a circle in the middle of a football field; it can occur when confined to an entire building or when forced to accompany another person on a walk or a trip. The taking of a purse, car keys, or other property with the intent to detain the person also may qualify as imprisonment. Tone of voice, body language, and what was reasonably understood or even implied from the defendant's conduct will be considered.

[83]Kenneth S. Abraham, A Concise Restatement of Torts 19 (St. Paul, MN: American Law Institute, 2000).
[84]Harris *ex rel.* Tucker v. Cnty. of Forsyth, 921 F. Supp. 325 (M.D.N.C. 1996).
[85]Howard v. Yakovac, No. CV04-202-S-EJL, 2006 U.S. Dist. LEXIS 27253 (D. Idaho May 2, 2006).

In false imprisonment cases, the plaintiff need not demonstrate that physical force was used; it will suffice that the plaintiff submitted given the apprehension of force. The plaintiff must be aware of the restraint, but does not have to show damages beyond the confinement itself to prevail at trial. Accordingly, any time children are unjustifiably restrained against their will, tied or taped to chairs, or bound and gagged, the tort of false imprisonment (as well as other possible violations[86]) may be claimed. For example, a school district's motion for summary judgment was denied when a student with special needs was confined to a very small time-out room. In examining his false imprisonment claim against the district, the record reflected that the student's confinement violated New York law.[87] The plaintiff successfully demonstrated that school personnel intended to confine him, the student was aware of the confinement, and the confinement was not otherwise privileged.

Although there are times when the use of physical restraints may be necessary, educators need to document the circumstances requiring such actions and provide a narrative explaining why restraint is an appropriate and reasoned response to the behavior. Where explanations are insufficient, liability will be possible, if not probable.

Intentional Infliction of Mental or Emotional Distress

This area of tort law is relatively new because of the historic resistance to awarding damages for a mental injury when it was not accompanied by a physical injury (e.g., pain and suffering associated with a broken leg). This reluctance purportedly was due to the difficulty of generating proof of both injury and proximate cause and then determining the appropriate amount of damages to be awarded. Nevertheless, a tort claim of intentional infliction of mental or emotional distress now is available to individuals who have experienced severe mental anguish. This claim, however, does not provide a remedy for every trivial indignity, insult, bad manners, annoyance, or sexist or racist comment, even if disturbing to the plaintiff.

Some forms of communication can result in an assault claim (e.g., a threat to strike another) or defamation suit (e.g., an unfounded claim that a teacher has been sexually involved with students).[88] Other communications might provide a basis for discrimination suits under federal laws (e.g., sexual or racial harassment). For the conduct to result in intentional infliction of mental or emotional distress under tort law, it must be flagrant, extreme, or outrageous; it must go beyond all possible bounds of decency and be regarded as atrocious and utterly intolerable in civilized society.[89] No reasonable person should be expected to endure such conduct (e.g., severe and extreme acts of stalking, harassment, and assault). Moreover, in most instances, the conduct needs to be prolonged and recurring, since single acts seldom meet the necessary threshold.

[86]For example, plaintiffs also may claim a Fourth Amendment "seizure" violation that could be accompanied by 42 U.S.C. § 1983 (2012).

[87]Schafer v. Hicksville Free Sch. Dist., No. 06-cv-2531, 2011 U.S. Dist. LEXIS 35435 (E.D.N.Y. Mar. 31, 2011).

[88]*See infra* text accompanying note 96.

[89]Dobbs, *supra* note 43, at 81; *see also* Ott v. Edinburgh Cmty. Sch. Corp., 189 F. App'x 507 (7th Cir. 2006) (concluding that a former coach was not defamed, nor did statements made about him rise to the level of outrageousness that would cause mental or emotional distress, when a school board member disclosed to the superintendent that the coach had a criminal record).

Given the difficulty of meeting this stringent standard, it is not surprising that few school-based intentional infliction of emotional distress claims succeed. Numerous claims have involved injured feelings or reputations, appearing trivial at best. In one such claim that bordered on disingenuous, a sixth-grade Oregon student claimed intentional infliction of mental distress when two of her teachers refused to use her nickname, Boo. "Boo" also is the street name for marijuana and was recognized as such by other students. Neither teacher had ever stated that the student used or condoned the use of drugs. In granting summary judgment for the teachers, the court concluded that no juror could reasonably find that the conduct of the teachers was an "extraordinary transgression of the bounds of socially tolerable conduct."[90] Other unsuccessful claims include a school supervisor who was callous and offensive when he ridiculed a subordinate's speech impediment;[91] a teacher making a false report against a student for misconduct;[92] and a school administrator who sent a letter to parents and students indicating that a teacher who had made racially offensive remarks that perpetuated negative stereotypes was returning to work following a ten-day suspension.[93] None of these cases were found to have met the necessary threshold to qualify as outrageous or extreme.

In contrast, an Illinois federal district court supported parents' claim of intentional infliction of mental distress against a teacher who had sexually abused their first-grade children.[94] The court noted that the teacher's conduct toward the students was extreme and outrageous. Parents may also file such claims against the district if they suffered mental anguish as a result of their child's injury. For example, a parent was successful in an intentional infliction of emotional distress claim when the school released the student to an unauthorized person, and the student was kidnapped.[95]

DEFAMATION

Most tort actions have involved claims for damages that were due to physical or mental injuries, but plaintiffs also have claimed injury to their reputations in the form of defamation.[96] School districts may be liable for the defamatory acts of their employees, but only when they are engaged in school district work and their conduct is within the scope of their authority.[97] Otherwise, claims may be filed only against the individual responsible for the alleged defamation. *Slander* is the term generally associated with spoken

[90]Phillips v. Lincoln Cnty. Sch. Dist., 984 P.2d 947, 951 (Or. Ct. App. 1999); *see also* Green v. San Diego Unified Sch. Dist., 226 F. App'x 677 (9th Cir. 2007) (determining that defendant's conduct was neither extreme nor outrageous, and plaintiff failed to meet the standard for emotional distress).

[91]Shipman v. Glenn, 443 S.E.2d 921 (S.C. Ct. App. 1994).

[92]Mikell v. Sch. Admin. Unit No. 22, 972 A.2d 1050 (N.H. 2009).

[93]Elstrom v. Indep. Sch. Dist. No. 270, 533 N.W.2d 51 (Minn. Ct. App. 1995).

[94]Doe v. White, 627 F. Supp. 2d 905 (C.D. Ill. 2009); *see also* M.S. v. Seminole Cnty. Sch. Bd., 636 F. Supp. 2d 1317 (M.D. Fla. 2009) (denying defendant's motion for summary judgment, the court found that a teacher who physically abused a student with autism could be held liable for her outrageous behavior).

[95]Ramirez v. Escondido Unified Sch. Dist., No. 11cv1823, 2012 U.S. Dist. LEXIS 26138 (S.D. Cal. Feb. 29, 2012).

[96]*See, e.g.*, Draker v. Schreiber, 271 S.W.3d 318 (Tex. App. 2008) (dismissing vice principal's causes of action against two students who had created mock MySpace profiles that included personal information and sexual references about her).

[97]*See, e.g.*, Henderson v. Walled Lake Consol. Schs., 469 F.3d 479 (6th Cir. 2006) (finding that a coach's slanderous comments were not made within the scope of his authority as a soccer coach).

defamation (but also includes sign language), whereas *libel* often is used to refer to written defamation (but also includes pictures, statues, motion pictures, and conduct carrying a defamatory imputation—e.g., hanging a person in effigy).[98] In determining whether defamation has occurred, courts will consider whether:

- the targeted individual was a private or public person;
- the communication was false;
- the expression qualified as opinion or fact; and
- the comment was privileged.

Private and Public Persons

To prevail in a defamation case, private individuals need prove only that a false publication by the defendant was received and understood by a third party and that injury resulted.[99] Receipt of potentially defamatory information that is not understood (e.g., receiving an unintelligible encrypted message on a computer, hearing Morse code over a radio, receiving a phone call in an unknown language) cannot adversely affect the plaintiff's reputation, dignity, or community standing and does not qualify as defamation. Individuals considered public figures or officials additionally must show that the publication was made with either malice or a reckless disregard for the truth. Definitions vary considerably by state, but public figures generally are those who are known or recognized by the public (e.g., professional athletes, actors), whereas public officials are those who have substantial control over governmental affairs (e.g., politicians, school board members).

Although the trend in recent years has been to broaden the class of public officials and figures, it is fortunate for teachers that the vast majority of courts have not found them to be "public," in large part because their authority typically is limited to students.[100] Some courts, however, have found school administrators and coaches to be either public officials or figures.[101] This does not mean that all administrators and coaches, even within the same jurisdiction, will qualify as public persons; such a determination is made on an individual basis and is dependent on the role, responsibility, degree of notoriety, and authority of the specific individual.

Veracity of Statements

In assessing defamation claims, courts also consider whether a statement is true or false. If the statement is found to be true, or at least substantially true, judgment will

[98]DOBBS, *supra* note 43.

[99]*See, e.g.*, Harris v. Pontotoc Cnty. Sch. Dist., 635 F.3d 685 (6th Cir. 2011) (finding no defamation because the teacher who accused a student of being a computer hacker did not communicate the information to a third party).

[100]McCutcheon v. Moran, 425 N.E.2d 1130 (Ill. App. Ct. 1981). *But see* Elstrom v. Indep. Sch. Dist. No. 270, 533 N.W.2d 51 (Minn. Ct. App. 1995) (concluding that a teacher was a public official).

[101]*See, e.g.*, Jordan v. World Publ'g Co., 872 P.2d 946 (Okla. Ct. App. 1994) (principal); Johnson v. Sw. Newspapers Corp., 855 S.W. 2d 182 (Tex. App. 1993) (football coach). *But see* O'Connor v. Burningham, 165 P.3d 1214 (Utah 2007) (determining that a coach was not a public official as school athletics did not affect in any material way the civic affairs of a community).

generally be for the defendant, assuming that critical facts have not been omitted, taken out of context, or otherwise artificially juxtaposed to misrepresent.[102] Educators must be particularly careful, however, when discussing students and must avoid making comments in bad faith that will result in liability. For example, if a teacher were to comment in class that a particular female student was a "slut," the comments would qualify as defamation per se.[103] In such cases, no proof of actual harm to reputation is required.

In addition to proving a communication to be false, the individual must show that he or she was the subject addressed. Interestingly, the individual's identity need not be clear to all third parties (i.e., readers, viewers, or hearers of the defamation); so long as at least one third party can identify the individual, the claim is actionable even though the individual is not mentioned by name.[104] Furthermore, the defamatory content need not be explicit; it may be implied or may be understood only by third parties with additional information.

Fact versus Opinion

Most opinions receive constitutional protection, particularly when public figures or officials are involved or the issue is one of public concern. To qualify as opinion, the communication must not lend itself to being realistically proven as true or false and must be communicated in such a way as to be considered a personal perspective on the matter.[105] For example, when a teacher made professional recommendations that were included in a special education student's Individual Education Program (IEP), the court did not find it to be defamation. The statements were opinions and not facts or false statements.[106] Parents may express critical opinions about a teacher (verbally or in writing) and may submit such opinions to a principal or school board.[107] Moreover, parents may even express negative views directly to the teacher, assuming that the expression does not amount to "fighting words"[108] or qualify as an assault.

Notwithstanding these examples, allegations that "the teacher sold drugs to a student" or that "the superintendent stole school funds" are factual statements capable of being substantiated and therefore may qualify as defamation unless proven true. The

[102]Determining whether something is true can be difficult, as perspectives and standards will vary. *See, e.g.*, Woodruff v. Ohman, 166 F. App'x 212 (6th Cir. 2006) (concluding that plaintiff's former boss defamed her in letters stating that she had not been a productive scholar; finding the defendant's statements to be false, defamatory, and malicious since the plaintiff had accumulated the necessary data for a paper and presented her research in the form of an abstract, even if she had no actual product).

[103]*See, e.g.*, Smith v. Atkins, 622 So. 2d 795 (La. Ct. App. 1993).

[104]*See, e.g.*, McCormack v. Port Wash. Union Free Sch. Dist., 638 N.Y.S.2d 488 (App. Div. 1996).

[105]*Compare* Milkovich v. Lorain Journal Co., 497 U.S. 1 (1990) (observing that statements made by a newspaper about a high school wrestling coach implied that the coach committed perjury in a judicial proceeding; because the statements could be proven true or false, they did not qualify as opinion) *with* Maynard v. Daily Gazette Co., 447 S.E.2d 293 (W. Va. 1994) (holding that a former athletic director was not defamed by an editorial identifying him as one of several parties responsible for the poor graduation rates of athletes; statements expressed in the newspaper were constitutionally protected opinions regarding topics of public interest).

[106]Luo v. Baldwin Free Sch. Dist., No. 10-cv-1985, 2011 U.S. Dist. LEXIS 26836 (E.D.N.Y. Mar. 15, 2011).

[107]Ansorian v. Zimmerman, 627 N.Y.S.2d 706 (App. Div. 1995).

[108]"Fighting words" are, by their nature, likely to result in an immediate breach of the peace and do not qualify as First Amendment protected speech.

appeals court in Ohio reversed a lower court dismissal where letters and a news article stated that a football coach had his entire team batter one of the players on the team. On remand, in reexamining the facts of the case, the lower court was directed to assess the totality of circumstances, including the specific language used in the statement, whether the statement was verifiable, and the general context of the statement.[109]

Privilege

Whether a communication qualifies as "privileged" also may affect whether defamation is supported. Statements that are considered *absolutely privileged* cannot serve as a basis for defamation under any circumstance, even if they are false and result in injury.[110] An absolute privilege defense has been selectively applied in cases involving superintendents and school board members, although it is less common in education than qualified privilege. For example, the North Dakota Supreme Court held that a board member's statements at a school board meeting about a superintendent were absolutely privileged.[111] Similarly, a New York court ruled that a superintendent's written reprimand to a coach for failure to follow regulations in the operation of the interscholastic athletic program was protected by absolute privilege.[112]

Communication between parties with qualified or conditional privilege also may be immune from liability if made in good faith, "upon a proper occasion, from a proper motive, in a proper manner, and based upon reasonable or probable cause."[113] But, conditional privilege may be lost if actual malice exists (i.e., a person made a defamatory statement that was known to be false, acted with a high degree of awareness of probable falsity, or entertained serious doubts as to whether the statement was true). Qualified privilege has been supported in administrators' rating of school personnel,[114] a board member commenting on the suspension of a student for marijuana possession,[115] and a teacher informing school officials about the inappropriate conduct of another teacher during a school trip.[116]

Qualified privilege was not supported where an Iowa superintendent stated during an open session board meeting that a former employee, with whom he had numerous disagreements, was dangerous and had created an unsafe workplace.[117] Only a single incident substantiated the superintendent's position—a staff member had received a minor bruise when she came into contact with the plaintiff as they both rushed to a file cabinet

[109]Rich v. Thompson Newspapers, Inc., 842 N.E.2d 1081 (Ohio Ct. App. 2005).

[110]*See, e.g.*, Gallegos v. Escalon, 993 S.W.2d 422 (Tex. App. 1999).

[111]Rykowsky v. Dickinson Pub. Sch. Dist. No. 1, 508 N.W.2d 348 (N.D. 1993). *But see* Overall v. Univ. of Pa., 412 F.3d 492 (3d Cir. 2005) (determining that statements made in a private internal university grievance proceeding were not quasi-judicial and not, therefore, entitled to absolute privilege).

[112]Santavicca v. City of Yonkers, 518 N.Y.S.2d 29 (App. Div. 1987).

[113]Baskett v. Crossfield, 228 S.W. 673, 675 (Ky. 1920); *see also* Phillips v. Winston-Salem/Forsyth Cnty. Bd. of Educ., 450 S.E.2d 753 (N.C. Ct. App. 1994) (holding that a board did not defame a discharged assistant superintendent since the board's communications with the superintendent were protected by qualified privilege).

[114]*See, e.g.*, Malia v. Monchak, 543 A.2d 184 (Pa. Commw. Ct. 1988).

[115]Morrison v. Mobile Cnty. Bd. of Educ., 495 So. 2d 1086 (Ala. 1986).

[116]Rocci v. Ecole Secondaire MacDonald-Cartier, 755 A.2d 583 (N.J. 2000).

[117]Smith v. Des Moines Pub. Schs., 259 F.3d 942 (8th Cir. 2001).

that contained "secret" records about the plaintiff. The jury found that this accidental injury did not support the superintendent's claim and held that the plaintiff had been defamed; that opinion and a $250,000 award were upheld on appeal.

DAMAGES

Damages in tort suits can be either compensatory or punitive, and many include attorneys' fees that are typically calculated as a percent of the total award (often one-third if the case settles prior to trial and 40 percent if the case is tried). Compensatory damages include past and future economic loss, medical expenses, and pain and suffering. These awards are intended to make the plaintiff whole, at least to the degree that money is capable of doing so. If a plaintiff's previous injury has been aggravated, the defendant is generally liable only for the additional loss.

Although damages vary by state, it is common to cap awards for intangibles (e.g., pain, suffering, loss of consortium, mental anguish) but not to cap damages for actual loss. When plaintiffs prevail, it is important to note that school district assets are not subject to execution, sale, garnishment, or attachment to satisfy the judgment. Instead, judgments are paid from funds appropriated specifically for that purpose, acquired through revenue bonds, or available because of insurance. If sufficient funds are not forthcoming, it is common for states to require fiscal officers to certify the amount of unpaid judgment to the taxing authority for inclusion in the next budget. When the amounts are significant, many states permit districts to pay installments (at times up to ten years) for payment of damages that do not represent actual loss.[118]

Furthermore, in most states, educators can be sued individually unless they are "save harmlessed" by their school district. Under save harmless provisions, the school district agrees to provide legal representation and pay any resulting liability. When educators are not "save harmlessed" and do not have personal insurance coverage, their personal assets (e.g., cars, boats, bank accounts) may be attached, their wages may be garnished, and a lien may be placed on their property. Where a lien is filed, the property may not be sold until the debt is satisfied. Moreover, debtors are not permitted to transfer ownership to avoid attachment (i.e., this would represent *fraudulent conveyance*). It is common for persons in law enforcement (e.g., a county sheriff) to be authorized to seize the property and hold it for sale at public auction. Because the debtor's financial worth is not a factor in calculating actual damages, the award may exceed the debtor's ability to pay. If the debtor is eventually successful in filing for bankruptcy, the plaintiff/creditor is typically paid in the same manner as other creditors.

Punitive damages are awarded to punish particularly wanton or reckless acts and are in addition to actual damages. The amount is discretionary with the jury and is based on the circumstances, behaviors, and acts. Unlike the calculation of actual damages, the debtor's financial worth may be a factor in determining punitive amounts. When jury verdicts are seemingly out of line, the court may reduce (remittitur) or increase (additur) the amount where either passion or prejudice is a factor.

[118]Jonathan E. Buchter, Susan C. Hastings, Timothy J. Sheeran & Gregory W. Stype, Ohio School Law 862 (Cleveland: West, 2001).

Conclusion

All individuals, including educators, are responsible for their actions and can be liable for damages if they intentionally or negligently cause injury to others. Educators have a responsibility to act reasonably, but some negligent conduct is likely to occur. Consequently, educators should be knowledgeable about their potential liability under applicable state laws and should ensure that they are either protected by their school districts or have adequate insurance coverage for any damages that might be assessed against them. To guard against liability, teachers and administrators should be cognizant of the following principles of tort law.

1. The propriety of an educator's conduct in a given situation is gauged by whether a reasonably prudent educator (with the special skills and training associated with that role) would have acted in a similar fashion under like conditions.
2. Educators owe students a duty to provide proper instruction and adequate supervision; to maintain equipment, buildings, and grounds in proper condition; and to provide warnings regarding any known dangers.
3. Educators are expected to exercise a standard of care commensurate with the duty owed.
4. Foreseeability of harm is a crucial element in determining whether an educator's actions are negligent.
5. If an educator has information that a student poses a danger to self or others, parents and identifiable victims must be notified.
6. An intervening act can relieve a teacher of liability for negligence if the act caused the injury and the teacher had no reason to anticipate that it would occur.
7. The common law doctrine of governmental immunity has been abrogated or qualified in most states (e.g., "safe place" statutes).
8. Where recognized, contributory negligence can be used to relieve school personnel of liability if it is established that the injured party's own actions were significant in producing the injury.
9. Under comparative negligence statutes, damages may be apportioned among negligent defendants and plaintiffs.
10. If an individual knowingly and voluntarily assumes a risk of harm, recovery for an injury may be barred.
11. School personnel can be held liable for battery if it is determined that they used excessive force with students.
12. Unnecessary restraint and excessive detainment of students can result in false imprisonment allegations.
13. In severe cases in which conduct qualifies as "extreme" or "outrageous," educators or students can be found liable for the intentional infliction of mental distress.
14. Public officials can recover damages for defamation from the media for statements pertaining to public issues only if malice or an intentional disregard for the truth is shown.
15. Educators generally are protected from defamation charges by "qualified privilege" when their statements about students are made to appropriate persons and are motivated by proper intentions.

Summary of Legal Generalizations

From Chapter 14 of *Public School Law: Teachers' and Students' Rights*, Seventh Edition. Martha M. McCarthy, Nelda H. Cambron-McCabe, Suzanne E. Eckes.

Summary of Legal Generalizations

MyEdLeadershipLab™

Visit the MyEdLeadershipLab™ site for *Public School Law: Teachers' and Students' Rights*, Seventh Edition, to enhance your understanding of chapter concepts. You'll have the opportunity to practice your skills through video- and case-based Assignments and Activities as well as Building Leadership Skills units, and to prepare for your certification exam with Practice for Certification quizzes.

Today, the most difficult situations confronting school personnel are those without specific legislative or judicial guidance. In such circumstances, educators must make judgments based on their professional training and general knowledge of the law as it applies to education. The following broad generalizations are presented to assist educators in making such determinations.

GENERALIZATIONS

THE LEGAL CONTROL OF PUBLIC EDUCATION RESIDES WITH THE STATE AS ONE OF ITS SOVEREIGN POWERS. In attempting to comply with the law, school personnel must keep in mind the scope of the state's authority to regulate educational activities. Courts consistently have held that state legislatures possess plenary power in establishing and operating public schools; this power is restricted only by federal and state constitutions and civil rights laws. Where the federal judiciary has interpreted the United States Constitution as prohibiting a given practice in public education, such as racial discrimination, the state or its agents cannot enact laws or policies that conflict with the constitutional mandate. In contrast, if the Federal Constitution and civil rights laws have been interpreted as permitting a certain activity, such as use of corporal punishment in public schools, states retain discretion in either restricting or expanding the practice. Under such circumstances, standards vary across states, and legislation becomes more important in specifying the scope of protected rights. For example, the U.S. Supreme Court has rejected the claim that probationary teachers have an inherent federal right to due process prior to contract nonrenewal, but state legislatures have the authority to create such a right under state law. Similarly, the Supreme Court has found no Fourth Amendment violation in blanket or random drug testing of public school students who participate in extracurricular activities; however, state law may place restrictions on school authorities in conducting such searches. Also, the Supreme Court has found no Establishment Clause violation in tax relief measures for private school tuition and the participation of sectarian schools in state-supported voucher programs to fund education, but these programs might run afoul of state constitutional provisions prohibiting the use of public funds for religious purposes.

Unless constitutional rights are at stake, courts defer to the will of legislative bodies in determining educational matters. State legislatures have the authority to create and redesign school districts; to collect and distribute educational funds; and to determine teacher qualifications, curricular offerings, and minimum student performance standards. With the pervasive control vested in the states, a thorough understanding of the operation of a specific educational system can be acquired only by examining an individual state's statutes, administrative regulations, and judicial decisions that interpret these provisions.

Certain prerequisites to public school employment are defined through statutes and state board of education regulations. For example, all states stipulate that a public school teacher must possess a valid teaching license based on satisfying specified requirements. State laws also delineate the permanency of the employment relationship, dismissal procedures for tenured and nontenured teachers, and the extent to which teachers can engage in collective bargaining.

State laws similarly govern conditions of school attendance. Every state has enacted a compulsory attendance statute to ensure an educated citizenry. These laws are applicable to all children, with only a few legally recognized exceptions. In addition to mandating school attendance, states have the authority to prescribe courses of study and instructional materials. Courts will not invalidate these decisions unless constitutional rights are abridged.

Courts also apply comparable reasoning in upholding the state's power to establish academic standards and graduation requirements. To determine whether students and school districts are progressing in a manner consistent with state standards and federal expectations, students are being subjected to more testing than ever before. Assessments determine the level and type of instruction provided; whether the child should be promoted from grade to grade or is eligible for graduation; and if the local school district has achieved required outcomes. Increasingly, states and local districts are enacting policies that base the evaluation of school personnel in part on student performance on standardized tests.

It is a widely held perception that local school boards control public education, but local boards hold only those discretionary powers conferred by the state. Depending on the state, a local board's discretionary authority may be quite broad, narrowly defined by statutory guidelines, or somewhere in between. School board regulations enacted pursuant to statutory authority are legally binding on employees and students. For example, school boards can place conditions on employment (e.g., continuing education requirements, residency requirements) beyond state minimums, if not prohibited by law.

Courts will not overturn decisions made by school boards or school-based councils unless clearly arbitrary, discriminatory, or beyond their scope of authority. School board discretion, however, may be limited by negotiated contracts with teachers' associations. These bargained agreements may affect terms and conditions of employment in areas such as teacher evaluation, work calendar, teaching loads, extra-duty assignments, and grievance procedures. Negotiated agreements in some states can take precedence over state laws under certain circumstances so long as protected rights are not impaired.

In many states, charter schools are exempt from specific state regulations applied to other public schools in order to foster innovative practices. Also, state tenure laws and collective bargaining agreements do not govern charter school employees in some states. Where charter school personnel are considered at-will employees, they are not entitled to the procedural protections prior to dismissal that are afforded to other public school employees. It is imperative for educators to become familiar with all of these sources of legal rights and responsibilities and how they vary depending on the state and the nature of their assignment.

ALL SCHOOL POLICIES AND PRACTICES THAT IMPINGE ON PROTECTED PERSONAL FREEDOMS MUST BE SUBSTANTIATED AS NECESSARY TO ADVANCE THE SCHOOL'S EDUCATIONAL MISSION. The state and its agents have broad authority to regulate public schools, but policies that impair federal constitutional rights must be justified by an overriding public interest. Although courts do not enact laws as legislative bodies do, they significantly influence educational policies and practices by interpreting constitutional and statutory provisions. Both school attendance and public employment traditionally were considered privileges bestowed at the will of the state, but the Supreme Court has recognized that teachers and students do not lose their constitutional rights when they enter public schools. The state controls education, but this power must be exercised in conformance with the Federal Constitution.

It is important to keep in mind that the Bill of Rights places restrictions on governmental, not private, action that interferes with personal freedoms. To illustrate, public schools may have to tolerate private student expression under certain circumstances, but expression representing the school can be censored for educational reasons. Similarly, the Establishment Clause prohibits public school employees from directing or condoning devotional activities in public education, whereas student-initiated religious groups in secondary schools must be treated like other student groups in terms of school access during noninstructional time. Furthermore, community religious groups, even those involved in religious instruction targeting elementary school children, must be treated like other community groups in terms of access during nonschool hours.

In balancing public and individual interests, courts weigh the importance of the protected personal right against the governmental need to restrict its exercise. For example, courts have reasoned that there is no overriding public interest to justify compelling students to salute the American flag if such an observance conflicts with religious or philosophical beliefs. In contrast, mandatory vaccination against communicable diseases has been upheld as a prerequisite to school attendance, even if opposition to immunization is based on religious grounds. Courts have reasoned that the overriding public interest in safeguarding the health of all students justifies such a requirement.

Restrictions can be placed on students' activities if necessary to advance legitimate school objectives. The judiciary has recognized that students' constitutional rights must be assessed in light of the special circumstances of the school. Consequently, school authorities can impose dress codes, and even student uniforms, if shown to advance legitimate educational objectives, such as reducing disciplinary problems and gang influences, and the requirement is not intended to stifle expression. Although school authorities are considered state officials, they can conduct warrantless searches of students based on reasonable suspicion that contraband posing a threat to the school environment is concealed. Similarly, vulgar speech or expression promoting illegal activity that might be protected by the First Amendment for adults can be curtailed among public school students to further the school's legitimate interest in maintaining standards of decency. As noted, student expression that gives the appearance of representing the school also can be censored to ensure its consistency with educational objectives. And even private student expression of ideological views, including electronic expression initiated off school grounds, can be restricted if linked to a disruption of the educational process.

Similarly, constraints can be placed on school employees if justified by valid school objectives. Prerequisites to employment, such as examinations and residency requirements, can be imposed if necessary to advance legitimate governmental interests. Furthermore, restrictions on teachers' rights to govern their appearance and out-of-school conduct can be justified when their behavior impinges on their effectiveness in the classroom. Although teachers enjoy a First Amendment right to express views on matters of public concern, expression pursuant to job responsibilities is not protected by the First Amendment. Even if educators are speaking as private citizens, expression relating to private employment grievances, rather than a public concern, can be the basis for disciplinary action. And teachers' expression on public issues can be curtailed if it impedes the management of the school, work relationships, or teaching effectiveness. Also, educators' expression on school-owned computers, pagers, and other equipment can be monitored for educational reasons.

Every regulation that impairs individual rights must be based on valid educational considerations and be necessary to carry out the school's mission. Such regulations also should be clearly stated and well publicized so that all individuals understand the basis for the rules and the penalties for infractions.

SCHOOL POLICIES AND PRACTICES MUST NOT DISADVANTAGE SPECIFIC INDIVIDUALS OR GROUPS. The inherent personal right to remain free from governmental discrimination has been emphasized throughout this text. Strict judicial scrutiny has been applied in evaluating state action that creates a suspect classification, such as race. In school desegregation cases, courts have charged school officials with an affirmative duty to take necessary steps to overcome the lingering effects of past discrimination. Similarly, intentional racial discrimination associated with testing methods, suspension procedures, employee hiring, and promotion practices has been disallowed. Whether voluntary race-based school or program assignments that further the goal of diversity will be upheld in de facto segregated school districts will depend on the ability of school officials to devise sufficiently narrowly tailored means to achieve their desired objective.

In contrast, neutral policies, uniformly applied, are not necessarily unconstitutional, even though they may have a disparate impact on minorities. For example, prerequisites to employment, such as tests that disqualify a disproportionate number of minority applicants, have been upheld so long as their use is justified by legitimate employment objectives and not accompanied by discriminatory intent. Also, the placement of a disproportionate number of minority students in lower instructional tracks is permissible if such assignments are based on legitimate educational criteria that are applied in the best interests of students. Likewise, school segregation that is not the result of intentional state action does not implicate constitutional rights.

In addition to racial classifications, other bases for distinguishing among employees and students have been invalidated if they disadvantage individuals. Federal civil rights laws, in conjunction with state statutes, have reinforced constitutional protections afforded to various segments of society that traditionally have suffered discrimination. Indeed, the judiciary has recognized that legislative bodies are empowered to go beyond constitutional minimums in protecting citizens from discriminatory practices. Accordingly, laws have been enacted that place specific responsibilities on employers to ensure that employees are not disadvantaged on the basis of race, sex, age, religion, national origin, or disabilities. If an inference of discrimination is established, employers must produce legitimate nondiscriminatory reasons to justify their actions. School officials can be held liable for damages if it is substantiated that benefits have been withheld from certain individuals because of their inherent characteristics.

Federal and state mandates also stipulate that students cannot be denied school attendance or be otherwise disadvantaged based on characteristics such as race, sex, disability, national origin, marriage, or pregnancy. In addition, disciplinary procedures that disproportionately disadvantage identified groups of students are vulnerable to legal challenge. Educators should ensure that all school policies are applied in a nondiscriminatory manner.

Courts will scrutinize grouping practices to ensure that they do not impede students' rights to equal educational opportunities. Nondiscrimination, however, does not require identical treatment. Students can be classified according to their unique needs, but any differential treatment must be justified in terms of providing more appropriate services. Indeed, judicial rulings and federal and state laws have placed an obligation on school districts to provide appropriate programs and services to meet the needs of children with disabilities and to eliminate the language barriers of those with English-language deficiencies.

DUE PROCESS IS A BASIC TENET OF THE UNITED STATES SYSTEM OF JUSTICE—THE FOUNDATION OF FUNDAMENTAL FAIRNESS. The notion of due process, embodied in the Fifth and Fourteenth Amendments, has been an underlying theme throughout the discussion of teachers' and students' rights. The judiciary has recognized that due process guarantees protect individuals against arbitrary governmental action impairing life, liberty, or property interests and ensure that procedural safeguards accompany any governmental interference with these interests.

In the absence of greater statutory specificity, courts have held that the United States Constitution requires, at a minimum, notice of the charges and a hearing before an impartial decision maker when personnel actions impair public educators' property or liberty rights. A property claim to due process can be established by tenure status, contractual agreement, or school board action that creates a valid expectation of reemployment. A liberty claim to due process can be asserted if the employer's action implicates constitutionally protected rights or damages the teacher's reputation by imposing such a stigma that the opportunity to obtain other employment is foreclosed.

Many state legislatures have specified procedures beyond constitutional minimums that also must be followed before a tenured teacher is dismissed. The provision of federal and state due process procedures does not imply that a teacher will not be dismissed or that sanctions will not be imposed. But it does mean that the teacher must be given the opportunity to refute the charges and that the decision shall be made fairly and be supported by evidence.

Students, as well as teachers, have due process rights. Students have a state-created property right to attend school that cannot be denied without procedural requisites. The nature of the proceedings depends on the deprivation involved, with more serious impairments necessitating more formal proceedings. If punishments are arbitrary or excessive, students' substantive due process rights may be implicated. Children with disabilities have due process rights in placement decisions as well as in disciplinary matters. Since school authorities are never faulted for providing too much due process, at least minimum procedural safeguards are advisable when making any nonroutine change in a student's status.

Inherent in the notion of due process is the assumption that all individuals have a right to a hearing if state action impinges on protected rights. Such a hearing need not be elaborate in every situation; an informal conversation can suffice under some circumstances, such as brief student suspensions from school. Moreover, such an informal hearing can serve to clarify issues and facilitate agreement, thus eliminating the need for more formal proceedings. The crucial element is for all affected parties to have an opportunity to air their views and present evidence that might alter the decision.

EDUCATORS ARE EXPECTED TO FOLLOW THE LAW, TO ACT REASONABLY, AND TO ANTICIPATE POTENTIALLY ADVERSE CONSEQUENCES OF THEIR ACTIONS. Public school personnel are presumed to be knowledgeable of federal and state constitutional and statutory provisions as well as school board policies affecting their roles. The Supreme Court has emphasized that ignorance of the law is no defense for violating clearly established legal principles. For example, being unaware of the Supreme Court's interpretation of Title IX restrictions under the Education Amendments of 1972 would not shield a school district from liability for school authorities' failure to respond to student complaints of sexual harassment.

Educators hold themselves out as having certain knowledge and skills by the nature of their special training and certification. Accordingly, they are expected to exercise sound professional judgment in the performance of their duties. To illustrate, in administering pupil punishments, teachers are expected to consider the student's age, mental condition, and past behavior as well as the specific circumstances surrounding the rule infraction. Failure to exercise reasonable judgment can result in dismissal or possibly financial liability for impairing students' rights.

Moreover, teachers are expected to make reasonable decisions pertaining to academic programs. Materials and methodology should be appropriate for the students' age and educational objectives. If students are grouped for instructional purposes, teachers are expected to base such decisions on legitimate educational considerations. In addition, educators are accountable for acting reasonably in supervising students, providing appropriate instructions, maintaining equipment in proper repair, and warning students of any known dangers. Teachers must exercise a standard of care commensurate with their duty to protect students from unreasonable risks of harm. Personal liability can be assessed for negligence if a school employee should have foreseen that an event could result in injury to a student.

Educators also are expected to exercise sound judgment in personal activities that affect their professional roles. Teachers do not relinquish their privacy rights as a condition of public employment, but private behavior that impairs teaching effectiveness or disrupts the school can be the basis for adverse personnel action. As role models for students, teachers and other school personnel are held to a higher level of discretion in their private lives than expected of the general public.

Conclusion

One objective of this text has been to alleviate educators' fears that the scales of justice have been tipped against them. It is hoped that this objective has been achieved. In most instances, courts and legislatures have not imposed on school personnel any requirements that fair-minded educators would not impose on themselves. Courts have consistently upheld reasonable policies and practices based on legitimate educational objectives. If anything, legislative and judicial mandates have clarified and supported the authority as well as the duty of school personnel to make and enforce regulations that are necessary to maintain an effective and efficient educational environment.

The federal judiciary in the late 1960s and early 1970s expanded constitutional protection of individual liberties against governmental interference. Since the 1980s, however, federal courts have exhibited more restraint and reinforced the authority of state and local education agencies to make decisions necessary to advance the school's educational mission, even if such decisions impinge on protected personal freedoms. Of course, courts will continue to invalidate school practices and policies if they are arbitrary, unrelated to educational objectives, or impair protected individual rights without an overriding justification.

Because reform is usually easier to implement when designed from within than when externally imposed, educators should become more assertive in identifying and altering those practices that have the potential to generate legal intervention. Internet censorship, peer sexual harassment, bullying, hazing, and other intimidating behaviors are a few issues now requiring educators' attention. Furthermore, school personnel should stay abreast of legal developments since new laws are enacted each year, and courts are continually interpreting constitutional and statutory provisions.

In addition to understanding basic legal rights and responsibilities, educators are expected to transmit this knowledge to students. Pupils also need to understand their constitutional and statutory rights, the balancing of interests that takes place in legislative and judicial forums, and the rationale for legal enactments, including school regulations. Only with increased awareness of fundamental legal principles can all individuals involved in the educational process develop a greater respect for the law and for the responsibilities that accompany legal rights.

GLOSSARY

absolute privilege protection from liability for communication made in the performance of public service or the administration of justice.

administrative law judge a hearing officer who presides over hearings that involve government agencies.

appeal a petition to a higher court to alter the decision of a lower court.

appellant an individual who appeals a court decision because he or she lost in the lower court. The appellant may be called the petitioner in some jurisdictions.

appellate court a tribunal having jurisdiction to review decisions on appeal from lower courts.

appellee an individual who won in the lower court but now must defend that decision because the lower court case has been appealed. The appellee may be called the respondent in some jurisdictions.

arbitration (binding) a process whereby an impartial third party, chosen by both parties in a dispute, makes a final determination regarding a contested issue.

assault the placing of another in fear of bodily harm.

battery the unlawful touching of another with intent to harm.

certiorari a writ of review whereby an action is removed from a lower court to an appellate court for additional proceedings.

civil action a judicial proceeding to redress an infringement of individual civil rights, in contrast to a criminal action brought by the state to redress public wrongs.

civil right a personal right that accompanies citizenship and is protected by the Constitution (e.g., freedom of speech, freedom from discrimination).

class action suit a judicial proceeding brought on behalf of a number of persons similarly situated.

common law a body of rules and principles derived from usage or from judicial decisions enforcing such usage.

compensatory damages monetary award to compensate an individual for injury sustained (e.g., financial losses, emotional pain, inconvenience) and restore the injured party to the position held prior to the injury.

concurring opinion a statement by a judge or judges, separate from the majority opinion, that endorses the result of the majority decision but offers its own reasons for reaching that decision.

consent decree an agreement, sanctioned by a court, that is binding on the consenting parties.

consideration something of value given or promised for the purpose of forming a contract.

contract an agreement between two or more competent parties that creates, alters, or dissolves a legal relationship.

criminal action a judicial proceeding brought by the state against a person charged with a public offense.

damages an award made to an individual because of a legal wrong.

declaratory relief a judicial declaration of the rights of the plaintiff without an assessment of damages against the defendant.

de facto segregation separation of the races that exists but does not result from action of the state or its agents.

de jure segregation separation of the races by law or by action of the state or its agents.

de minimis something that is insignificant, not worthy of judicial review.

de novo a new review.

defamation false and intentional communication that injures a person's character or reputation; slander is spoken, and libel is written communication.

defendant the party against whom a court action is brought.

dictum a statement made by a judge in delivering an opinion that does not relate directly to the issue being decided and does not embody the sentiment of the court.

directed verdict the verdict provided when a plaintiff fails to support a prima facie case for jury consideration or the defendant fails to produce a necessary defense.

discretionary power/authority authority that involves the exercise of judgment.

dissenting opinion a statement by a judge or judges who disagree with the decision of the majority of the justices in a case.

en banc the full bench; refers to a session where the court's full membership participates in the decision rather than the usual quorum of the court.

fact finding a process whereby a third party investigates an impasse in the negotiation process to determine the facts, identify the issues, and make a recommendation for settlement.

friend-of-the-court briefs briefs provided by nonparties to inform or perhaps persuade the court (also termed amicus curiae briefs).

governmental function activity performed in discharging official duties of a federal, state, or municipal agency.

governmental immunity the common law doctrine that governmental agencies cannot be held liable for the negligent acts of their officers, agents, or employees.

impasse a deadlock in the negotiation process in which parties are unable to resolve an issue without assistance of a third party.

injunction a writ issued by a court prohibiting a defendant from acting in a prescribed manner.

in loco parentis in place of parent; charged with rights and duties of a parent.

liquidated damages contractual amounts representing a reasonable estimation of the damages owed to one of the parties for a breach of the agreement by the other.

mediation the process by which a neutral third party serving as an intermediary attempts to persuade disagreeing parties to settle their dispute.

ministerial duty an act that does not involve discretion and must be carried out in a manner specified by legal authority.

negligence the failure to exercise the degree of care that a reasonably prudent person would exercise under similar conditions; conduct that falls below the standard established by law for the protection of others against unreasonable risk of harm.

per curiam a court's brief disposition of a case that is not accompanied by a written opinion.

plaintiff the party initiating a judicial action.

plenary power full, complete, absolute power.

plurality opinion an opinion agreed to by less than a majority of the court; the concurring judges agree as to which party prevails, but disagree as to reasoning; plurality opinions carry less weight under stare decisis than do majority opinions.

precedent a judicial decision serving as authority for subsequent cases involving similar questions of law.

preponderance of evidence a standard that requires more evidence to support than refute a claim; it also is termed the 51 percent rule.

prima facie on its face presumed to be true unless disproven by contrary evidence.

probable cause reasonable grounds, supported by sufficient evidence, to warrant a cautious person to believe that the individual is guilty of the offense charged.

procedural due process the fundamental right to notice of charges and an opportunity to rebut the charges before a fair tribunal if life, liberty, or property rights are at stake.

proprietary function an activity (often for profit) performed by a state or municipal agency that could as easily be performed by a private corporation.

punitive damages a monetary punishment where the defendant is found to have acted with either malice or reckless indifference.

qualified immunity an affirmative defense that shields public officials performing discretionary functions from civil damages if their conduct does not violate clearly established statutory or constitutional rights.

qualified privilege protection from liability for communication made in good faith, for proper reasons, and to appropriate parties.

reasonable suspicion specific and articulable facts, which, taken together with rational inferences from the facts, justify a warrantless search.

remand to send a case back to the original court for additional proceedings.

res judicata a rule that requires a final judgment on the merits of the case to be conclusive, which prevents an unsatisfied party from relitigating the issue.

respondeat superior a legal doctrine whereby the master is responsible for acts of the servant; a governmental unit is liable for acts of its employees.

save harmless clause an agreement whereby one party agrees to indemnify and hold harmless another party for suits that may be brought against that party.

stare decisis to abide by decided cases; to adhere to precedent.

statute an act by the legislative branch of government expressing its will and constituting the law within the jurisdiction.

sua sponte when the court takes up the action on its own initiative.

substantive due process requirements embodied in the Fifth and Fourteenth Amendments that legislation must be fair and reasonable in content as well as application; protection against arbitrary, capricious, or unreasonable governmental action.

summary judgment disposition of a controversy without a trial when there is no genuine dispute over factual issues.

tenure a statutory right that confers permanent employment on teachers, protecting them from dismissal except for adequate cause.

tort a civil wrong, independent of contract, for which a remedy in damages is sought.

ultra vires beyond the scope of authority to act on the subject.

vacate to set aside; to render a judgment void.

verdict a decision of a jury on questions submitted for trial.

Index

Page references followed by "f" indicate illustrated figures or photographs; followed by "t" indicates a table.

D

E

F